THE MUSIC
of
ARTHUR HONEGGER

THE MUSIC of ARTHUR HONEGGER

by
Geoffrey K. Spratt

Cork University Press

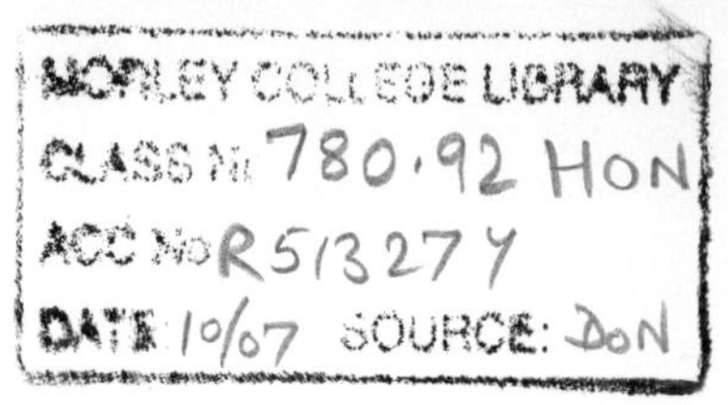

First published in September 1987 by
Cork University Press, University College Cork, Ireland.

British Library Cataloguing in Publication Data

The Music of Arthur Honegger.
1. Honegger, Arthur — Criticism and interpretation
780′. 92′ 4 ML410. H79

ISBN 0-902561-34-0

Printed by Cahill Printers Ltd, East Wall Road, Dublin 3, Ireland.

To

Vivien Spratt and Pascale Honegger

Contents

List of illustrations

(i) List of analytical diagrams

Pages

(ii) List of tables

See (i) on page ix

Author's Preface

Synopsis:– After an initial survey of Honegger's early works (1910-21) in order to establish the framework of his musical language and experience, the bulk of this study is devoted to a chronological discussion of the nine major dramatic works — *Le roi David*, *Judith*, *Antigone*, *Amphion*, *Cris du monde*, *Jeanne d'Arc au bûcher*, *La danse des morts*, *Nicolas de Flue* and *Une cantate de Noël*. The book culminates in a chapter dealing with the final 'drama' — the last four symphonies. All the various intermediary works are discussed briefly to maintain perspective.

The results of detailed analysis are employed continuously to illustrate the development of his musical language, to reveal the dramatic and musical viability of the large-scale works and to highlight the evolution of his creative personality. An attempt is made throughout to assess his role in twentieth-century music — in particular that of France.

An important element of this study is contained in the three bibliographic supplements — the Catalogue of Works, the Discography and the Bibliography — which represent the most complete and accurate detailings available.

An essentially non-biographical approach has been adopted because the books on Honegger available in French or German provide adequate information (see Part II of the Bibliography). Such that is present is regarded as having a direct bearing on the work in question.

A decision was made to make no detailed reference to any of his Incidental Music, Ballet or Film Scores as it would be fundamentally meaningless to talk of the music divorced from the equally important visual and textual aspects over which he had neither absolute control nor significant influence. Furthermore, the majority of the Incidental Music and Film Scores consist of a myriad of tiny fragments, all obviously programmatic in nature. Finally, the impracticalities of any sort of meaningful consideration are exacerbated by the fact that most of them were not published and many of the manuscripts have disappeared. In the case of *Le roi David* and *Judith* this decision naturally precluded a discussion of the original version of the work and those interested in such are therefore referred to Pierre Meylan's book *René Morax et Arthur Honegger au Théâtre du Jorat* (Editions du Cervin, Lausanne/Libraire Ploix, Paris, 1966.)

This study is offered as a musicological tribute to one of the finest and most significant composers of this century who is at present suffering most unfairly and unjustly from the period of neglect that follows many a creative artist's death, in the sincere hope that it may contribute in some small way to a reappraisal and to a reawakening of interest in his honourable achievement.

Acknowledgements

I would like to express the debt of gratitude which I owe to the following people who all gave me advice, assistance and encouragement at various stages of my research: Derek Ashley and the late Joan Ashley (Bristol), James Barry (Cork), Monsieur M. Barthèlemy (Liège), Dr Adrian Beaumont (University of Bristol), Donal Counihan (Executive Secretary, Cork University Press), Jean-Christophe Curtet (Geneva), Professor Dr Kurt von Fischer (Erlenbach), Emeritus Professor Aloys Fleischmann (University College Cork), Pascale Honegger (Geneva), Anne Lee (Cork University Press), Fedelmia O'Herlihy (Cork), Joseph Roy (Dijon), Frank Squire and the late Antoinette Squire (Worcester Park), the late Andrée Vaurabourg-Honegger (Paris), Professor Raymond Warren (University of Bristol) and Katherine Weldon (Cork). The staff of the following libraries where I worked deserve my thanks for their assistance: Bibliothèque Nationale, Paris, British Library, London, University College Cork Library and the University of Bristol Library. I am particularly grateful to Mr. E. Hughes of the British Institute of Recorded Sound because, without his generous placing of personal catalogues at my disposal, the Discography would not be nearly so exhaustive. The following publishers willingly lent me scores and granted permission for the reproduction of examples: J. and W. Chester/Edition Wilhelm Hansen London Ltd., Edition Max Eschig, Paris, Editions Salabert, Paris, and Hug Musique SA (Edition Fœtisch), Lausanne. All the music examples which are not reproduced from published scores were prepared by Elaine and Andrew Shiels of Bantry, Co. Cork, Ireland, whom I thank for their professionalism and courtesy. I am also grateful to the Arts Faculty of University College Cork for the award of two grants from the Faculty Fund which enabled me to undertake research trips to France and Switzerland. It would not have been possible for the Cork University Press to publish this book but for the financial support of Monsieur Paul Sacher (Pratteln), Dr et Madame J. J. Oeri (Basle) and Monsieur et Madame Jean Henneberger (Lausanne) — their generosity is remarkable. Finally, but by no means least, I offer my sincerest thanks to my wife Vivien who, in addition to giving me every help with the French language and sharing very many hours of proof-reading, supported me spiritually throughout the long gestation of this book.

Notes

(i) In footnotes and translations Arthur Honegger's name has been abbreviated to A.H.

(ii) With respect to both the text and the diagrams, the following will act as an explanation of the method of abbreviation adopted when making reference to specific bars in the printed editions:

(Reproduit avec l'autorisation des Editions Salabert, Paris, propriétaires de l'œuvre.)

(iii) With respect to the diagrams in this book:

(a) lower-case letters represent the minor mode, and capital letters the major mode according to the usual convention regarding tonality;

(b) letters representing formal structures have been placed in parentheses to avoid confusion with tonalities when the two are represented in the same diagram;

(c) when representing formal structures, the use of the same letters in relation to separate sections does *not* imply any cross-reference unless specifically indicated;

(d) there is no representation of the duration of any one tonality in relation to any other or to the length of the movement or section;

(e) it is not intended that these diagrams should be regarded as purporting to represent an all-embracing analytical picture of the work or movement in question. The use of terminology including 'a summary of principal tonalities' and 'subsidiary formal design features' is deliberate because, taking full account of the variety of methods and the subjective elements involved in musical analysis, it would be wrong to claim to have represented everything to everyone's satisfaction. Therefore, only the integrity of the specified aims and contextual relevance of such diagrams can stand as defence against any charges that features have been omitted either through neglect or wilful suppression.

(iv) Where a theme or motif has been given a descriptive label relative to its function in the section, movement or work concerned, these annotations are my own unless otherwise acknowledged.

(v) A deliberate effort has been made in the translations which appear immediately after a quotation in a foreign language to parallel the stylistic characteristics of the original writer and the vocabulary of the period. Where quotations are made from published English translations no attempt has been made to alter any archaisms except by the provision of footnoted clarifications where confusion might otherwise arise.

"Nothing worthwhile can be accomplished in art without enthusiasm."

"Only when the form is quite clear to you will the spirit become clear too."
[Robert Schumann, *Aphorisms*]

Arthur Honegger

Born Le Havre, 10 March 1892

Died Paris, 27 November 1955

CHAPTER I

The works prior to *Le roi David* : the foundations

Part I : Before *Les Six*

Honegger's first published work was the *Trois pièces* for piano distributed by Desforges of Le Havre in 1910. Whilst it is easy to point to Mendelssohn, Grieg and Beethoven as the influences on the respective movements — *Scherzo, Humoresque, Adagio espressivo* — it is perhaps more significant to reflect on the potential of his talent and to bear in mind that, as something of a child prodigy, he had already composed a couple of operas — *Philippa* and *Sigismond* (a third, *Esmeralda,* after Victor Hugo, was left unfinished), and an oratorio *Le Calvaire* (1908).

He was a violin pupil of Santreuil and amongst the voluminous amount of chamber music are many pieces for two violins and piano that were intended for performance by himself, a fellow pupil, Georges Tobler, and his mother. Le Havre was little more than a cultural backwater, so Honegger learnt what he could from his mother through her record collection and copies of the Beethoven *Piano Sonatas,* attended all the performances given by visiting opera and concert artists and eventually went to study harmony with the organist at the Church of St Michel, Robert Charles Martin, to whom he dedicated both his *Trois pièces* (1910) and the *Fugue* (1917) for organ.

Fortunately his father was the rich owner of a coffee importing house with many friends of rank both in Le Havre and his native Switzerland. The turning point in Honegger's career came in 1909 whilst on holiday in Switzerland with the family. He was introduced to Dr Friedrich Hegar, a personal friend of Brahms and Director of the Conservatory in Zürich, who was sufficiently impressed by his talent to recommend two years of compositional studies under his personal supervision. During this period he also continued studying the violin with Wilhelm de Boer and went to Lothar Kemptar for theory. The influence of this period, heavily biased towards a study of composition involving analysis of music by the Classical masters and the works of Wagner, R. Strauss and Reger, cannot be overstressed when the elements of Honegger's personal musical language are examined — at the very least they represent a framework that always distinguishes Honegger from the purely French school of composers.

Following his return from Zürich in the summer of 1911, he enrolled at the Paris Conservatoire. He commuted twice weekly until 1913 when, because his father had retired and the family had returned to their native Switzerland, he settled in Montmartre where he was to live for the rest of his life. Despite a short period near the beginning of the First World War as a frontier guard in Switzerland (made necessary by his holding of dual French-Swiss nationality and passport), he remained a student there until 1918. He studied the violin with Capet, counterpoint and fugue with Gédalge, composition and orchestration with Widor, conducting with d'Indy and history with Emmanuel.

The most important influence on Honegger when he arrived in Paris proved to be Darius Milhaud. Already an extremely accomplished and well-known musician, Milhaud was the temperamental opposite of Honegger, but, as classmates, they were to become the closest of friends. Milhaud introduced Honegger not only to the music of Debussy, Ravel, Roussel, Satie, Schönberg and Stravinsky, but also to the artistic world of Paul Valéry, Larbaud, Cocteau, Max Jacob, Paul Claudel and Francis Jammes, of which he and Auric were already such a part.

The largest piece of music he composed whilst studying in Zürich was apparently a symphonic poem entitled *In den Alpen,* of a similar nature to *Pastorale d'été* (1920). There was also an *Adagio* for violin and piano which particularly impressed Hegar[1]. However, none of the music he wrote whilst in Zürich survives and it is the first movement of the *String Quartet (No. 1)* (1916 -17) which contains the earliest music that remains from the first two years of his studies in Paris. This movement is based on a 'Study' that was dated by Honegger 'September 1913', and in it can be clearly seen the polarity which exists in the style between the elements of his earlier German training — notably the Reger-like chromaticism and the Beethovenian tonal structure and overall mood — and those to which he was being subjected at the time — the Franckian harmonic idiom via Widor, d'Indy's passion for severe Classical form and symmetry and the vigorous counterpoint of Gédalge. Superimposed on this seething mass of diverse elements are moments of tonal liberation that reveal the influence of Schönbergian atonalism to such an extent that d'Indy was typically prompted to warn Honegger against the dangers of 'de trop grande liberté tonale'[2] [excessive tonal freedom].

Despite the variety of textures there is a tendency towards an almost oppressive density of sound, encouraged by the polyphonic complexity and predominance of writing *à 4*, that seems a result of some compromise with orchestral sound qualities (and brings to mind the *String Quintet* of its dedicatee, Florent Schmitt, where similar problems exist in an even more marked way). Similarly destructive is the way in which the chromaticism is confined almost exclusively to the accompaniment: the basically very simple melodic lines lose much of their effectiveness by virtue of the extreme relief into which they are thrown and the framework itself sounds divorced and contrived. The worst fault, however, is much more fundamental, even if obscure: there is a conflict between the linear aspect of the counterpoint, which permeates the whole, and the harmonic idiom, which is essentially Classical in concept, that remains unresolved. Neither is the force of such antagonism harnessed to the aid of the dramatic construction of the piece: Honegger had still to come to terms with his penchant for contrapuntal polyphony in the light of his apparent determination not to negate the responsibilities of a viable vertical harmonic argument.

Nevertheless, there are some features of this movement which justify Honegger's professed liking of this work as a whole[3]: the long controlled span of the melodic line [1] - [2], the satisfying architectural symmetry and the strength of the music (almost histrionic at times), are three of the most important qualities of all his greatest music (see Music Example 1 below).

Music Example 1 : *String Quartet* [*No. 1*], first movement, bars 1-18

1
sempre crescendo
crescendo
crescendo
2

> I arrived in Paris at the age of nineteen, nourished on the classics and romantics, enamoured of Richard Strauss and Max Reger, the latter completely unknown in Paris. In contrast I found, not that school, but the Debussyites in full bloom; I was introduced to d'Indy and to Fauré. I gave much time to fathoming the character of Fauré, whom I took for a long time to be a musician of the salons. Once past this period, I surrendered with delight to his example. Debussy and Fauré made a very useful counterbalance, in my aesthetics and my feeling, to the classics and Wagner.[4]

The influence of Debussy and Fauré is certainly pronounced in many of the songs that figure predominantly in the list of his works (see Table 3, pages 33-35) between the 1913 string quartet 'Study' and the two pieces that he wrote in the autumn of 1917 which mark the end of his student-days with a most authoritative and powerful stamp, namely the third movement of the *String Quartet (No. 1)* and *Le chant de Nigamon.* The specific influence of Debussy is so clearly reflected in the *Prélude (pour Aglavaine et Sélysette)* (January 1917) and the *Rhapsodie* (April 1917) that the term 'pastiche' is not far from being applicable. Both works are noteworthy, nevertheless, because they feature certain formal aspects which appear in many subsequent works.

In the *Prélude*, Honegger varies a simple ABA^1 design by making the bulk of the middle section a development of material from the initial A section and merely framing it, (B), with very obviously contrasted and essentially static material. As a direct consequence of this procedure, he is able to foreshorten considerably the final A^1 section to the proportions of a cyclic coda. The *Rhapsodie* is cast in a much more regular three-part (ternary) form, with the middle section consisting of a single new theme (subtly foreshadowed near the end of the A section and referred to in the closing bars of A^1), that is developed extensively.

In both works there is a tonal design that is carefully and consistently argued and reference to Diagram 1 overleaf will reveal the predominance of moves and relationships characterized by the intervals of either a second or a third (major or minor).

In both works the establishment of the principal tonality of the initial A section is deliberately delayed; with regard to the *Rhapsodie*, the tonality of F major is not restored until half-way through the final section and this organically compensates for the fact that the A^1 section is not substantially reduced in length as was the case in the *Prélude.*

Similar parallels in formal construction can be drawn between the sonata-form design used for the second movement of the *String Quartet (No. 1)* (April 1916) and the first movement of the *Violin Sonata No. 1* (July 1916), as well as with the *Prélude* and *Rhapsodie* schemes (see Diagram 2 overleaf).

The only significant deviation from the almost textbook rigidity of Classical sonata-form is the reversed recapitulation of the bipartite first thematic group. In doing so, Honegger achieves a perspective in the recapitulation which enhances the role and structuring of the coda in terms of the pronounced cyclic feeling from which these two movements aesthetically benefit so greatly.

Diagram 1:

Prélude (pour Aglavaine et Sélysette)

(A)	(B)	(A^{1})
(Bars 1-62)	(Bars 62-129)	(Bars 129-143)
Brief sequential references to e (1-) and f (12-) lead to e♭ (20-) and E♭ (35-). A clouded reference to f (49-) leads via sequential attempts to establish e♭ (52-55) and D♭ (58-60) to	A dominant preparation (62-69) for a minor (70-) which moves via a clouded D♭ (104-) to the dom. of f (116-) and a transitional passage (123-)	After an attempt to establish G (132-34) it concludes in C despite the added dominant seventh

Rhapsodie

(A)	(B)	(A^{1})
(-4A[4])	(10B[5] - 9A[12])	(3B[13] - end)
F established from [2] after passing references to C, A♭, c♯, D and D♭ respectively	c♯ (with a brief reference to E 1-5A [9])	F re-established from 2B [16] after transition from C♯ (3B[13]-) made via F♯ ([14] -)

Diagram 2:

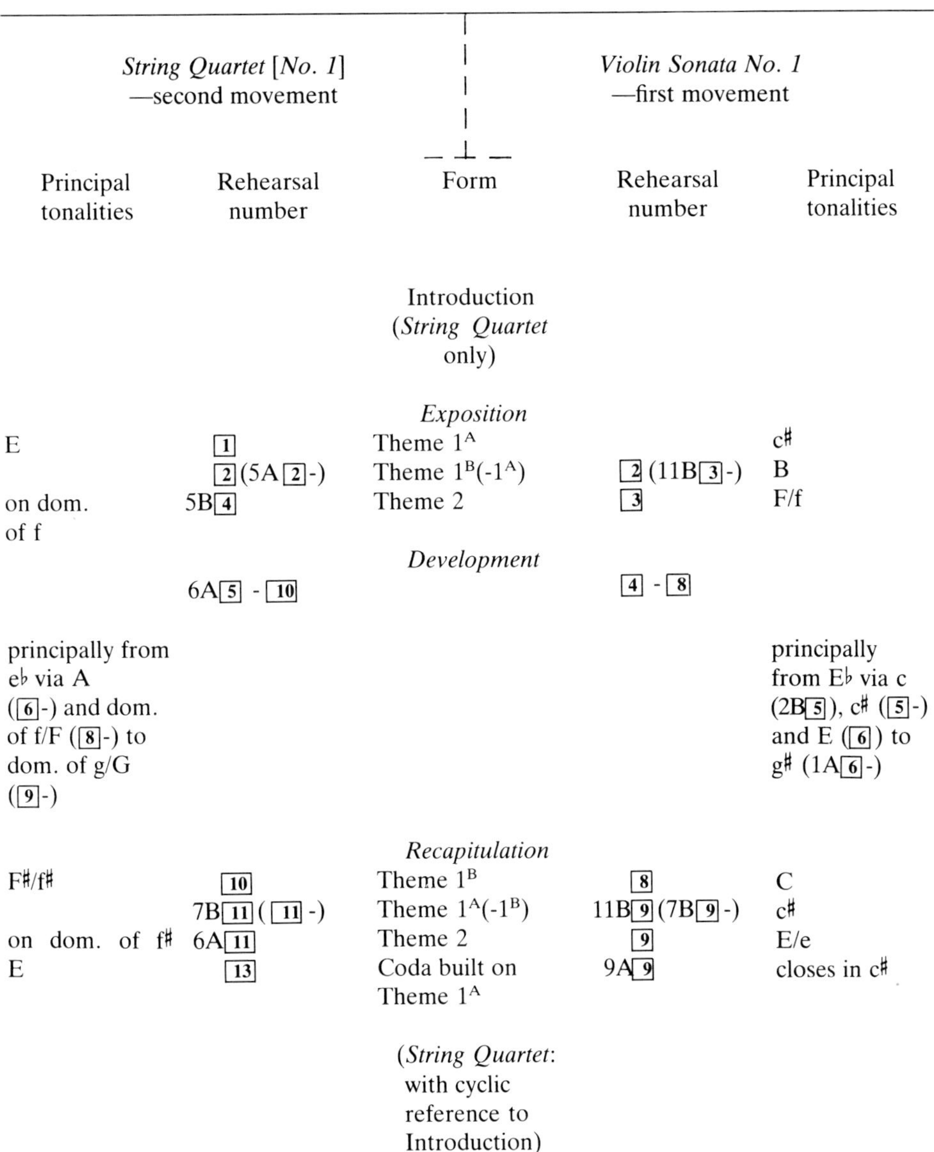

	String Quartet [*No. 1*] —second movement		*Violin Sonata No. 1* —first movement	
Principal tonalities	Rehearsal number	Form	Rehearsal number	Principal tonalities
		Introduction (*String Quartet* only)		
		Exposition		
E	[1]	Theme 1^{A}		c♯
	[2] (5A[2]-)	Theme $1^{B}(-1^{A})$	[2] (11B[3]-)	B
on dom. of f	5B[4]	Theme 2	[3]	F/f
		Development		
	6A[5] - [10]		[4] - [8]	
principally from e♭ via A ([6]-) and dom. of f/F ([8]-) to dom. of g/G ([9]-)				principally from E♭ via c (2B[5]), c♯ ([5]-) and E ([6]) to g♯ (1A[6]-)
		Recapitulation		
F♯/f♯	[10]	Theme 1^{B}	[8]	C
	7B[11] ([11]-)	Theme $1^{A}(-1^{B})$	11B[9] (7B[9]-)	c♯
on dom. of f♯	6A[11]	Theme 2	[9]	E/e
E	[13]	Coda built on Theme 1^{A}	9A[9]	closes in c♯
		(*String Quartet*: with cyclic reference to Introduction)		

As with the *Prélude (pour Aglavaine et Sélysette)* and *Rhapsodie*, the pronounced system of tonal organization involving tertiary relationships is exploited here to most effective ends. The tertiary intervals dominate the melodic construction too, so it is hardly surprising that the music exhibits extreme qualities of organic cohesion.

All the material is motivic in both conception and design and suitable not only for a typically rigorous and progressive Beethovenian development, but also to provide a web that cradles the whole with unfathomable strength. It is interesting further to note that the tertiary tonal system is extended in both these works to cover the relationship between the three separate movements (see Diagram 3 below).

Diagram 3:

		Overall Key	
	1st movt	2nd movt	3rd movt
String Quartet [*No. 1*]—	c	E	c
Violin Sonata No. 1—	c♯	F	c♯

Spanning the works discussed so far are Honegger's first song-settings of poems by Fontainas, Jammes, Tchobanian, Laforgue, Fort and Apollinaire. In all of them the formal precision and clarity — most of them are cast as ABA[1] and involve cyclic or refrain principles — clearly parallel Honegger's work in other genres and reflect his attitude to song writing which he summarized as:

> Je ne me fais pas scrupule de t'avouer que j'aime beaucoup les histoires de Souvestre et Allain. Toute 'littérature' en est bannie et c'est bien quelque chose. De ces imaginations librement déchaînées, de ce choc d'épisodes invraisemblables, jaillit une poésie extraordinaire et que j'aime. La lecture de 'Fantômas' et de 'Nez en l'air' me procure un incomparable délassement. Les textes que j'ai pris aux poètes pour les mettre en musique sont d'une autre qualité sans doute; mais, là encore, ce n'est pas la 'littérature' qui m'a séduit. Fort égoïstement, je l'avoue, je demande avant tout à un poème de me fournir le prétexte et les éléments d'une construction musicale parallèle à sa construction littéraire. Si les mots du poète font, en outre, vibrer en moi quelque corde sensible, je tiens mon affaire. 'Automne', par exemple, l'un des *Alcools* d'Apollinaire satisfait également à mon double besoin de géométrie et d'émotion: j'ai vu, que dis-je, j'ai moi-même été le 'paysan cagneux' d'Apollinaire, du temps que je faisais, sans gloire, sinon toujours sans ennui, mon service militaire en Suisse. C'est dire que je ne crois pas à la vertu des vers de mirliton, hors du style bouffe.[5]
>
> [I am not at all ashamed of confessing to you that I do enjoy the stories of Souvestre and Allain. All that is 'literature' is excluded from them, and that really is something! Out of these imaginings freely unfettered, out of this clash of unbelievable episodes, there springs forth poetry of an extraordinary nature — which I appreciate. Reading *Fantômas* and *Nez en l'air* gives me an incomparable feeling of relaxation. The texts which I

> took from the poets for setting to music are doubtless of a different quality; but even there, it is not the 'literature' which seduced me. Very selfishly, I admit, above all I require of a poem that it should provide me with the pretext and the elements of a musical construction, parallel to its literary construction. If the words of the poet, furthermore, touch one of my sensitive spots, I am happy. For example, 'Automne', one of Apollinaire's *Alcools*, satisfies my double need of geometry and emotion! At the time when, without glory, I was doing my military service in Switzerland, I saw and was even one of Apollinaire's 'knock-kneed' peasants! That is to say that I don't believe in the virtue of trashy verse except in the comic opera style.]

Technically there is also the same concentration on lines built up from thirds, contrary-motion procedures, rapid juxtapositions of tonal planes, tertiary key schemes and the derivation of the whole from a small number of minute cells of musical thought. In the *Quatre poèmes* there is a tendency for the piano textures to be overblown to an uncomfortable degree, whilst in the *Trois poèmes* (Paul Fort) the impression that the piano part is merely that of an orchestral reduction detracts from their merit in a similar way. The fact that neither of these criticisms can be levelled at the accompaniments in the *Six poèmes* (Apollinaire) is, however, not attributable to Honegger's having solved the problems, but to the very nature of the poems themselves which demand a sensitive and delicate approach. Versatility reflected in an ability always to create the appropriate musical texture in response to a visual or textual image was a talent that Honegger possessed in abundance and which was to provide the backbone of all his subsequent dramatic music, both serious (operas and dramatic 'frescoes') and commercial (incidental music, ballet, film and radio scores). In the Apollinaire settings — notably No. 4, 'Saltimbanques' — it is possible to detect the effect of his association with Satie, via Milhaud, and the *avant-garde* artistic set who were to form the background to *Les nouveaux jeunes*, and to appreciate how, through the diversification of his talent, Honegger could pen music that was to become the hallmark of *Les Six* a few years later (see Music Example 2 below).

Music Example 2: *Six poèmes* (Apollinaire), No. 4 'Saltimbanques'

Un peu plus vif
l'huis des au_berges gri _ ses Par les vil_la _ ges sans é _ gli_ses
Un peu plus vif
Tempo 1°
Et les en_fants s'en vont de _ vant Les au_tres sui _ vent en rê_vant Chaque
Tempo 1°
ar_bre frui_tier se ré_si _ gne Quand de tres loin il lui font si _ gne
gliss.
gliss.
Ils ont des poids ronds ou car_rés Des tambours des cerceaux dorés L'ours et le
sin_ge a nimaux sa_ges Quêtent des sous sur leurs pas _ sa _ ge
pp

Similarly prophetic qualities are found in the melodic lines of these songs. In embryonic stages is his ability to write *semplice* melodic lines such that through their simplicity they in fact gain qualities of grandeur and strength of immense proportions without any hint of banality, and *quasi-recitative* lines which allow the voice to deliver the text at a speed and in a manner that maximizes the listener's comprehension. There is, too, a liquidity and a feeling of organic growth in the melodic lines which have the distinction of genius — surely it is no wonder that Honegger could write much later that in the Francis Jammes setting of the *Quatre poèmes* there is 'la meilleure mélodie, la plus mélodieuse que j'ai écrite'[6] [the best and most tuneful melody that I have ever written] (see Music Example 3 below).

Music Example 3: *Quatre poèmes*, No. 3 (Jammes), bars 1-24

Mon Dieu vous m'a-vez ap-pel-é parmi les hommes me voi-ci
Je souffre et j'aime. J'ai par-
-lé a-vec la voix que vous m'a-vez don - né - e J'ai é-
-crit av-ec les mots que vous avez enseignés à ma mère et à mon pè-re qui me les ont trans-

-mis
Je pas-se sur la route comme un
p
â ne chargé dont rient les enfants et qui baisse la tê-te.
pp
très retenu
Je m'en irai où vous voudrez quand vous vou-
pp
-drez.
pp

As with the orchestral and chamber music, various influences are easily detectable. The predominance of the French influence is natural, but as late as August 1916 there is still a reminder of his German fostering in the flood of Wagnerian chromaticism and the general feeling of High German Romanticism that can be found in the first of the three settings of Paul Fort poems. The influence of Fauré is suddenly and dramatically evident in 'Clotilde' and 'L'adieu' (Nos. 2 and 5 of the Apollinaire settings), whilst his awareness of Ravel's unique musical language is reflected in a much more palatable and digested form in the 'bells' of 'Cloche du soir' (No. 2 of the Paul Fort settings) and 'Les cloches' (No. 6 of the Apollinaire settings) than it had emerged in his piano piece *Hommage à Ravel* of November 1915 (which he later used as the second of the *Trois pièces pour piano,* published in 1921). The parallels with Vaughan Williams' 'bells of Bredon' in *On Wenlock Edge* (written soon after his return from study in France), cannot be ignored. The polytonality of Milhaud (perhaps at this time better described as poly-harmonic-planes-of-activity) influenced Honegger as he was seeking to enrich his own harmonic language: in the third of the Fort settings the right-hand of the piano is in G♯ minor, whilst the left-hand centres on F♯ major/minor with an ultimate resolution of the two in B minor.

In the second and third Fort settings there are two aspects which mark the start of a pair of important traditions in Honegger's music. In the 'Chanson de fol' the melodic line has all the qualities of a folk-song, whilst in 'Cloche du soir' both the vocal line and the inner part of the piano accompaniment in bar 25 have the feeling of a chorale. Neither are borrowings; nor are any of the similar themes which appear in many of the later works, and both are quintessential in a way that an actual quotation would have failed to be.

The 'folk-song' melody is a pictorial reaction to the text, whilst the 'chorale' melody represents the ever-triumphant force of God. The most sublime example of the role of the former in Honegger's music occurs in *Jeanne d'Arc au bûcher* (see Chapter IX), whilst the latter is to be found in all the large dramatic works.

The only music Honegger wrote for the organ dates from his days as a student at the Conservatoire. The *Fugue* is exemplary of his mastery of technique — a beautiful, coherent and well-structured piece of part-writing in the Franck/d'Indy tradition — though totally unoriginal. The *Choral,* however, together with the *Toccata et variations*—the other important keyboard work from this student period — reveal a number of important features with regard to the development of his own original and fully integrated harmonic language. There is a clear move along the path of emancipation of dissonance: the prominence of the interval of a tritone and the decline of additive harmony by virtue of the increased use of contrary-motion principles, counterpoint and small, simple ostinati, both contribute to this end (see Music Example 4 opposite).

Music Example 4: *Two Pieces for Organ*, No. 2 'Choral', bars 1-24

From the *Toccata et variations* emerges clearly an overall characteristic quality of all Honegger's original and mature music. It is an aura that emanates from the immense quantities of vital energy in the music, both physical and latent; from the vastness of the proportions that appear to underline the whole and from the depth of expression which is at all times sincere, honest and humanistic. It is a quality which can embrace extremes of complexity and dissonance with simplicity and directness, without embarrassment or debasement. Nowhere else does this force reveal its omnipotence in combination with the intense lyrical romanticism that was so much part of Honegger as man and artist than in the third movement of the *String Quartet (No. 1)* and *Le chant de Nigamon.* (The quartet movement was sketched during November 1916 although it was not revised finally until October of the following year — immediately before work began on the orchestral score which he finished in late December 1917).

A consideration of the structure of the *Toccata* shows a marked influence of mosaic patterning on the formal procedure (see Diagram 4 opposite), which, whilst not being surprising in a piece of this nature, provides an interesting parallel to the internal structuring of the sonata-form third movement of the *String Quartet (No. 1)* where a multi-thematic exposition gives rise to a highly enriched and extensive development and to a recapitulation where re-ordering provides further opportunities for development as well as 're-exposition'. In combination with this mosaic sub-structuring is a considerably increased use of counterpoint and contrapuntal devices including pedal-points, canon and fugue. Together with the substantially broader tonal base and a quite liberal treatment of dissonance, the unresolved conflict between the vertical harmonic argument and linear contrapuntal procedures that stylistically ruined the first movement of the *String Quartet (No. 1)* (see pages 2-3) appears to have been solved in this piece.

Diagram 4:

Toccata (from *Toccata et variations*)

A section (Vif; 𝅗𝅥 = 76)

(1-41)

Bars :	1-5	6-7	8-9	10-13	14-19	20-23	24-26	27-33	34-41
Thematic classification :	a′-Ostinato a -Theme	b	c	a -inverted a′	d (with part of a:17-18)	a a′	b	e	a
Tonal scheme :	b♭/B♭	[B♭/E]	[b♭/E]→	b♭/B♭	C	e/E	[E/B♭]	G/g	b♭→g

B section (Lent; ♩ = 72)
(42-56)
Constructed over a G pedal which is resolved downwards to an F♯ which supports a dominant seventh of B major(*) in bars 55-56

A¹ Section (Vif; 𝅗𝅥 = 76)
(57 to end)

Bars :	57-60	61-63	64-70	71-74	75-81	82-87	88-89	90-93	(*) 94-96	97-100	101-end
Thematic classification :	a′ a	b	e	a-inv. a′	a′ a	d (with part of a: 85-86)	a a ′(var.)	b	Fragments of B section over an F♯ pedal	c	d a
Tonal scheme :	b/B	B/F	A♭/a♭	d/D	a♭/A♭	B	(A♭)	[A/E♭]		[B♭/E]	B♭

A quite logical conclusion to a study of the early songs and the *String Quartet (No. 1)* is that Honegger was a composer striving for the use of an orchestra with which to express himself. The first work in which he conducted his fellow Conservatoire students as part of the progressive d'Indy's conducting class (the *Prélude (pour Aglavaine et Sélysette),* publication of which he suppressed during his lifetime), was little more than pastiche stylistically, a criticism that is rather harder to direct at his second effort, *Le chant de Nigamon.* Ignoring the emphatic counselling of his mentor Gédalge, 'ni peinture, ni littérature'[7] [neither painting nor literature], he turned to a highly emotive episode in *Le souriquet* by Gustave Aymard, entitled 'Légende de la perte du Canada'[8], and produced a symphonic poem which reveals fully his natural sense for dramatic music and justifies completely the traditional methods by which he achieved satisfactory musical form and coherence independent of the pure inspiration of the text. The granite-like structure — a continuously expanded sonata-form — the systematic tertiary tonal relationships, the huge themes buttressed with a plethora of incisive motives all consistently used and inter-related, combine with an orchestral palette which is as roughly hewn as the subject matter and the musical language to produce a terrifyingly brutal score, the originality of which made a considerable impression. There was a directness that was appreciated by those reacting against the Impressionists, a toughness of consistency that could be tolerated after the supposed excesses of *Le sacre du printemps,* and an underlying sincerity of expression that was welcome at a time of general lack of musical confidence. The influence of R. Strauss — *Elektra* in particular — and of Dukas can be detected in the undercurrents of the piece, but the genuinely original qualities of the work as a whole impressed many distinguished musicians of the time.

During the period between the completion of his studies at the Conservatoire and the creation of *Le roi David,* his compositions clearly reflect the divisions that mark his whole creative output. The scandal surrounding the performances of *Le dit des jeux du monde* at the Théâtre du Vieux-Colombier in December 1918 fortunately did not prevent recognition of the merit of Honegger's score and an appreciation of his talent as a composer of incidental music which resulted in many highly important commissions (see Table 1 below).

TABLE 1

Incidental Music Scores

Title	Author	Date of first performance
Le dit des jeux du monde	Paul Méral	Dec. 1918
La mort de Sainte Alméenne	Max Jacob	Not performed
La danse macabre	Carlos Larronde	May 1919
Le roi David	René Morax	June 1921

Title	Author	Date of first performance
Saül	André Gide	June 1922
Antigone	Jean Cocteau (after Sophocles)	Dec. 1922
La tempête	Shakespeare trans. Guy de Pourtalès	1923
Liluli	Romain Rolland	March 1923
Judith	René Morax	June 1925
[Le roi, son vizir et son médecin	Jacques Copeau	Unfinished]
L'impératrice aux rochers (Un miracle de Notre-Dame)	Saint-Georges de Bouhélier	Feb. 1927
Phædre	Gabriel d'Annunzio trans. André Doderet	April 1926
Marche sur la Bastille (*for* 14 juillet)	Romain Rolland	1936
Prélude à la mort de Jaurès (*for* Liberté)	Jaurès trans. Edmond Rostand	1937
La construction d'une cité	J.-R. Bloch	1937
La mandragore	Machiavelli	Sept. 1941
L'ombre de la ravine	Synge trans. Maurice Bourgeois	1941
Les suppliantes	Aeschylus trans. A. Bonnard	July 1941
Huit cents mètres	André Obey	July 1941
La ligne d'horizon	Serge Roux	Oct. 1941
Sodome et Gomorrhe	Jean Giraudoux	Oct. 1943
Le soulier de satin	Paul Claudel	Nov. 1943
Charles le Téméraire	René Morax	May 1944
Prométhée	Aeschylus trans. A. Bonnard	June 1946
Hamlet	Shakespeare trans. André Gide	Oct. 1946

Continued overleaf

Title	Author	Date of first performance
Œdipe	Sophocles trans. André Obey	1947
L'état de siège	Albert Camus	Oct. 1948
On ne badine pas avec l'amour	Alfred de Musset	Dec. 1951
Œdipe-Roi	Sophocles trans. Thierry Maulnier	1952

Similarly attributable is the first commission for a ballet score, *Vérité? Mensonge?*, a genre on which he was repeatedly asked to collaborate (see Table 2 below).

TABLE 2

Ballet Scores

Title	Created by	Date of first performance
Le dit des jeux du monde	Paul Méral	Dec. 1918
Vérité? Mensonge?	André Hellé	Nov. 1920
Horace victorieux	Guy Fauconnet after Titus Livius	Dec. 1927
Marche funèbre (La noce massacrée) *for* Les mariés de la Tour Eiffel	Jean Cocteau	June 1921
Skating Rink	Canudo	Jan. 1922
Fantasio	Georges Wague	?
Sous-marine	Carina Ari	June 1925
Roses de métal	Elisabeth Grammont de Clermont-Tonnerre	?
Les noces d'Amour et Psyche (Bach arr./orch. Honegger)	Ida Rubinstein	1930
Sémiramis	Paul Valéry	May 1934

Title	Created by	Date of first performance
Les petits lits blancs (with Milhaud)	?	June 1935
Icare (composed to rhythms by Serge Lifar; with Szyfer)	?	July 1935
Un oiseau blanc s'est envolé	Sacha Guitry	1937
Le cantique des cantiques (composed to rhythms by Serge Lifar)	Gabriel Boissy	Feb. 1938
La naissance des couleurs	E. Klausz and René Morax	?
Le mangeur de rêves	H. René Lenormand	1941
L'appel de la montagne	R. Favre le Bret	July 1945
Chota Rustaveli (with Tcherepnine and Harsanyi)	Serge Lifar	1945
De la musique	R. Wild	?

In terms of purely original scores there is orchestral music (*Pastorale d'été* and *Horace victorieux*) and choral music (*Cantique de Pâques*) as well as his first attempt at writing a concerto (the *Entrée, Nocturne et Berceuse* for piano and chamber orchestra). In relation to his output after *Le roi David* there is also a surprisingly large corpus of chamber music which drew attention not only through its originality but because, at the time, it was relatively unusual for a 'French' composer to write considerable amounts of significant music for this genre.

In the two *Violin Sonatas,* the *Viola Sonata* and the *Cello Sonata* it is possible to see quite clearly Honegger consolidating his position totally by absorbing the plethora of influences that his various studies, artistic friendships and contact with the rich international musical scene of Paris brought to bear, and continuously extending his own originality. Considering formal procedures first with reference to the chamber music, it is significant to note that he uses only three-part form and sonata-form. In the second movement of the *Violin Sonata No. 1* (March 1917), the ABA^1 is marked by the violent contrast of the middle section and a complex key scheme of tertiary relationships; whilst in the second movement of the *Violin Sonata No. 2* (August 1919), the aspects of both violent contrast and complexity of tonal organization give way to those of simplicity (ABA^1 with a corresponding key scheme of D minor/F minor/D minor) where rhetorical strength and dramatic intensity are an integral part of the musical language rather than a result of a formal superimposition. It is this latter movement to which can be traced the precedents for the formal procedures in the first movement of the *Viola Sonata* (March 1920), where the cohesion and unity of an $aba^1b^1a^2b^2$ structure is enhanced by the superimposition of an overall ABA^1 design (see Diagram 5 overleaf).

Diagram 5:

Viola Sonata — first movement

(a) (b)	(a^1) (b^1)	(a^2) (b^2)
(A)	(B)	(A^1)

(N.B. The sub-structure (a) sections are the *Andantes* and the (b)'s the *Vivaces*.)

A simultaneous broadening and consolidation of the tenets of three-part form is also achieved in the second movement of the *Viola Sonata* (January 1920), where the B section is itself organized as an aba structure, both thematically and tonally; and it is significant that he returns, in the second movement of the *Cello Sonata* (June-July 1920), to a simple ABA^1 structure where the B section is conceived as a symmetrically curved arch whilst remaining a unitary element of the whole.

The sonata-form procedures in the first movement of the *Violin Sonata No. 1* and the second movement of the *String Quartet (No. 1)* — where the absence of part of the first subject group from the development is highlighted in a partially reversed recapitulation to further the attempts to create a cyclic feel at the end of the work (see page 5) — are extended in the third movement of the *Violin Sonata No. 1* (February 1918). The pronounced cyclic aspect of the movement — due to the buttressing of a terse sonata-form by a pair of similar Adagios — is not far in effect from the strict three-part procedures found in the second movement of the same work (see above). The enclosed sonata-form of this third movement is characterized by the tremendously Beethovenian qualities of its very intense development. There is no use of reversed recapitulation here or in the subsequent sonata-form movement (the first movement of the *Violin Sonata No. 2*, April-May 1919) where the rigour and strictness of the formal procedure has all the qualities of intense compression that are found in many late Beethoven sonata-form movements. The quality of conciseness for which he was so obviously striving is fully evident in the third movement of the *Violin Sonata No. 2* (November 1919), where cyclic features, a development which omits the second subject as in Beethoven's *Symphony No. 8*, and a systematic, but simple key scheme based, as usual, on tertiary relationships, work together to provide a framework of immense strength. In the third movement of the *Viola Sonata* (February 1920), this is particularly evident; not only is there a straight reversed recapitulation, but the fundamental key scheme has a parallel form of symmetry which binds the whole in a most satisfying way (see Diagram 6 opposite).

Stylistically, too, the picture is one of consolidation. The harmonic language is subjected to considerable forces of astringency; apart from an obvious move from chords based on thirds to those constructed from fourths, there is a use of parallelism and contrary motion that is entirely divorced from any Impressionistic origins and which allows for a widening not only of the harmonic vocabulary but of the interaction face of vertical harmonic argument with linear

Diagram 6:

Viola Sonata — third movement

Exposition (bars 1-52)	:	Theme 1 in C Theme 2 (bar 27-) in B moving via b♭ (bar 47-) to
Development (bars 53-90)	:	principally moving from g via A♭ (bar 67-) to f♯ (bar 83-)
Recapitulation (bars 91-130)	:	Theme 2 in d/D Theme 1 (bar 116-) in C

---

contrapuntal procedures. Such tendencies bring the possibility of a parallel to Schönberg's musical language in the works immediately preceding the First World War, notably *Pierrot Lunaire.* The comparison with the latter work is strengthened when account is taken of the extensive use of contrapuntal devices (canon, augmentation, diminution and inversion), fugal or imitative textures and ostinati (particularly in combination with pedal points). Whilst the resemblance is quite strong at many moments in the incidental music for *Le dit des jeux du monde* (see Music Example 5 below), elsewhere only the bare roots are detectable.

Music Example 5: *Le dit des jeux du monde*, No. 10 'L'homme et l'ombre'

Fl.
Tromp
1.
Viol.
2.
Alt.
Vlles
C.B
1
p
div
unis

2
Fl.
Tromp
p
p
crescendo
crescendo
1.
Viol.
2.
Alt.
Vlles
C.B
crescendo
crescendo
crescendo
crescendo
crescendo

Fl.
Tromp
f
f
1.
Viol.
2.
Alt.
Vlles
C.B

3
Fl.
diminuendo
Tromp
diminuendo
pp
3
1.
Viol.
diminuendo
2.
diminuendo
Alt.
diminuendo
Vlles
diminuendo
C.B
diminuendo
p

II

Lent
Fl.
Tromp
1.
Viol.
2.
Alt.
Vlles
pp
Lent
p

Fl.
4
1.
Viol.
2.
Alt.
Vlles

Tempo I°
(Un peu retenu)
1.
Viol.
2.
Alt.
Vlles
p
pp
div

Tempo
Tromp
p
Tempo
1.
Viol.
2.
Alt.
Vlles

Fl.
p
Tromp
1.
Viol.
2.
Alt.
Vlles

5
Fl.
mf
Tromp
diminuendo
1.
Viol.
2.
diminuendo
div
p
Alt.
diminuendo
p
Vlles
diminuendo
C.B
pizz
arco

Fl.
Tromp
mf
1.
Viol.
2.
Alt.
Vlles
C.B
pizz

Fl.
Tromp
1.
Viol.
2.
Alt
Vlles
C.B
diminuendo

A direct result of the broadening of the harmonic base is a move towards an atonalism which has similar Schönbergian origins. This tends, however, at this stage, to manifest itself as a polarity in the same way as his use of polytonality and modality; there is usually a relatively firm tonal point of reference — often provided by a device of which he was particularly fond, namely ascending or descending scalic 'binding' patterns — which is frequently thrown into aural relief by virtue of his predilection for rapid tonal juxtapositions, both on a large and a small scale.

Melodically it is possible to see the same process of consolidation and extension of original expression by virtue of his consistent use of particular melodic genres. Apart from the pseudo-folk melodic style and quasi-liturgical thematic quality already discussed (see page 11) there is a new element which is literally best described as *joie de vivre* — examples from the third movements of the *Violin Sonata No. 2*, the *Cello Sonata* and the *Viola Sonata* illustrate well this quality which is essentially Haydnesque in its undebased naïvity (see Music Example 6 below).

Music Example 6:
(i) *Violin Sonata No. 2*, third movement, violin part, bars 23-30

(Reproduit avec l'autorisation des EDITIONS SALABERT, Paris, propriétaires de l'œuvre.)

(ii) *Cello Sonata*, third movement, cello part, bars 32-49

(Reproduit avec l'autorisation des EDITIONS MAX ESCHIG, Paris, propriétaires de l'œuvre.)

(iii) *Viola Sonata*, third movement, viola part, bars 1-12

(Reproduit avec l'autorisation des EDITIONS MAX ESCHIG, Paris, propriétaires de l'œuvre.)

These stand beside the most typical of Honegger's melodic lines (see Music Example 7 overleaf): those characterized by large intervallic leaps which distort a theme basically constructed from small intervals and scalic patterns, often heavily conditioned by chromaticism. They are, above all, lines conceived on firm Classical as opposed to Romantic aesthetics. In fact, at times, it might be more accurate to classify them as Baroque-inspired in terms of their frequent dependence on systematic, if not symmetrical, use of small motives. This results in their having a poise and balance that, when combined with the controlled use of diverse rhythmic elements, produce an incredible quality of momentum and latent energy.

Music Example 7: *Viola Sonata*, first movement, piano part:
(i) bars 1-8

(Reproduit avec l'autorisation des EDITIONS MAX ESCHIG, Paris, propriétaires de l'œuvre.)

(ii) bars 29-36

(Reproduit avec l'autorisation des EDITIONS MAX ESCHIG, Paris, propriétaires de l'œuvre.)

Part II: *Les Six*

Through Darius Milhaud, Honegger, who had been nicknamed 'le petit provencial timoré'[9] [the timid little provincial], came into contact with the very heart of the Parisian artistic climate. Whilst he mixed with the most prominent representatives of all the arts, he inevitably experienced too the decadent aspects of this unique climate. He had to suffer both the perpetual air of intellectual artificiality and the music of the 'salon', epitomized by Madame Herscher and Kœchlin. He was fortunate with his friendships: when Milhaud left with Paul Claudel for Rio de Janeiro after World War One broke out, he met Jane Bathori, whom Jacques Copeau had left in charge of the Théâtre du Vieux-Colombier while absenting himself in New York for the same reason as Claudel and Milhaud. As an impressario and a talented singer Jane Bathori proved to be a valuable friend. She also had a small salon in the Latin quarter which she had turned into a meeting-place for young poets and composers, and it was here, whilst playing second violin in the resident quartet, that Honegger met Fernand Ochsé. He later wrote of Ochsé, that he was the

> man who contributed more to my career than certain masters. . . [he was a] musician, painter, literary figure, stage designer who has had the most

happy influence on my development. He was an incomparable friend to me, whose memory I cherish in profound gratitude. His disappearance during the terrible days of the Occupation remains one of the deepest sorrows of my life. Since that time, I have never heard one of my new works without wondering: 'What would Fernand have thought of it?[10]

During this period he established a filial relationship with Fauré which lasted until the latter's death and was characterized by immense mutual respect. He also won the acclaim of the venerable and influential critic Emile Vuillermoz who was consistently to defend his music for many years.

In 1916 he and a small group of friends formed the *Cercle musical et dramatique indépendant* to promote their own works in view of the difficulty of gaining performances through the other, much older, establishments — notably the *Société musicale indépendante* and *Société nationale*. At the first concert promoted by the C.M.D.I. on 13 June 1916, Rose Armandie sang the first three of his Apollinaire settings; whilst on 15 December of the same year his *Toccata et variations* were first performed in the tiny Salle Œdenkoven, which was their base, by the brilliant young pianist Andrée Vaurabourg, a fellow-student from Widor's composition class whom he was to marry on 10 May 1926.

His music received performances with a singular degree of success (see Table 3 below). The première of his *Rhapsodie* (17 November 1917) at the Université interalliée du Parthénon under the patronage of Henry Woolett attracted much critical acclaim and resulted in a considerable number of commissions. On

TABLE 3

Compositions preceding *Le roi David*
(Full details are contained in the complete *Catalogue of Works*, pages 481-586.)

Year composition completed	Title	Date and venue of first Parisian performance	Publisher and year of publication
1910	Trois pièces	?	Desforges (Le Havre)
1916	Quatre poèmes	?	Chester, 1921
1916	Toccata et variations	15 Dec. 1916, Salle Œdenkoven, C.M.D.I. concert	Mathot, 1921
1916	Trois poèmes (Fort)	?	Senart, 1922
1917	Prélude (pour Aglavaine et Sélysette)	Private: 3 April 1917, Paris Conservatoire; Public: 7 June 1920, Salle Gaveau	[Salabert, 1956]
1917	Nature morte	?	In *La Revue SIC* (January 1917), 58-59
1917	Six poèmes (Apollinaire)	15 Jan. 1918, Théâtre du Vieux-Colombier	Mathot, 1921

Continued overleaf

Year composition completed	Title	Date and venue of first Parisian performance	Publisher and year of publication
1917	Rhapsodie	17 Nov. 1917, Parthénon	Senart, 1923
1917	Two Pieces for Organ	?	Chester, 1920
1917	String Quartet [No. 1]	20 June 1919, S.M.I. concert	La Sirène, 1921
1917	Le chant de Nigamon	Private: 18 April 1918, Paris Conservatoire; Public: 3 Jan. 1920, Cirque-d'Hiver	Senart, 1927
1918	Violin Sonata No. 1	19 March 1918, Théâtre du Vieux-Colombier	Senart, 1921
1918	Pastiche de Haydn	?	Not published
1918	Cantique de Pâques	18 March 1926, l'Opéra	Rouart Lerolle, 1925
1918	Le dit des jeux du monde	2 Dec. 1918, Théâtre du Vieux-Colombier	Senart, 1928
1918	Interlude (*from* La mort de Sainte Alméenne)	30 Oct. 1920, Théâtre du Châtelet	Not published
1919	Danse de la chèvre	May 1919	Senart, 1932
1919	La danse macabre	May 1919, l'Odéon	Not published
1919	Trois pièces	?	Mathot, 1921
1919	Entrée, Nocturne, Berceuse	1919, Salle Huyghens	Not published
1919	Violin Sonata No. 2	28 Feb. 1920, Salle du Conservatoire, S.N. Concert	Senart, 1924
1920	Sept pièces brèves	4 March 1920, Salle Gaveau, S.M.I. Concert	La Sirène, 1921
1920	Sarabande (for the 'Album des Six'.)	?	Eschig, 1920/Schott
1920	Viola Sonata	2 Dec. 1920, S.M.I. Concert	La Sirène, 1921
1920	Cadence for violin (*for* 'Le bœuf sur le toit' by Milhaud)	26 May 1921	La Sirène, 1921
1920	Sonatine for 2 violins	May 1921, Studio des Champs-Elysées	La Sirène, 1922
1920	Les Pâques à New York	28 March 1924, Salle Erard	Composer's Music Corporation, 1923
1920	Pastorale d'été	17 Feb. 1921, Salle Gaveau	Senart, 1922

Year composition completed	Title	Date and venue of first Parisian performance	Publisher and year of publication
1920	Cello Sonata	23 April 1921, Salle du Conservatoire, S.N. Concert	La Sirène, 1922
1920	Hymne	17 Oct. 1921, Art et Action Concert	[Salabert, 1984]
1920	Vérité? Mensonge?	Nov. 1920, Salon d'Automne	Not published except for a 'Danse des enfants'— Salabert, 1927
1921	Horace victorieux	1 Dec. 1921, Paris	Senart, 1924
1921	Marche funèbre (La noce massacrée) *for* 'Les mariés de la Tour Eiffel')	18 June 1921, Théâtre des Champs - Elysées	[Salabert, 1965]

1 December 1917 he attended an important repeat performance of the *Rhapsodie* at the home (Salle Huyghens) of the appropriately-named painter Lejeune in Montparnasse. Those present included Apollinaire, Auric, Bertin, Braque, Cocteau, Durey, Fauconnet, Picasso, Poulenc, Tailleferre and Blaise Cendrars, who, at the instigation of Satie had earlier in the summer formed the group known as *Les nouveaux jeunes*. Various activities were promoted for the benefit of the members including, at the suggestion of Cendrars, concerts at the Théâtre du Vieux-Colombier and the Salle des Agriculteurs under the patronage of Jane Bathori and Felix Delgrange respectively. When the war ended and many artists returned to Paris from their voluntary exile or from military service the membership of the group swelled: in particular Roland-Manuel and Milhaud joined the rank of composers. The degree of personal success which Honegger enjoyed can be easily measured by noting that in January 1918, the first *Festival Honegger* was held. There were two concerts of his music, the second being an all chamber music evening culminating in the première of the *Violin Sonata No. 1*.

It is important that the influence of the general euphoria of post-war Paris is not neglected when a consideration of Honegger as a member of *Les nouveaux jeunes* and, more particularly, of *Les Six* is made. Account must be taken, too, of the fact that Paris was the musical centre of the Western World, partly because of the attention Debussy had attracted, and partly because of the many distinguished Russian émigrés — Stravinsky and Diaghilev in particular. The institutions — the Opéra and Théâtre du Champs-Elysées — were at their height, whilst Jane Bathori and Ida Rubinstein were bravely and successfully treading new ground. There were many visiting ensembles — not least the arrival of 'the new Jazz' with Harry Pilcer's Jazz Band's first Paris appearance in November 1918. The artistic air was full of change and alive with what appeared (erroneously in some cases) to be new movements. Inevitably the time was ripe for musical change too. Looking back on a concert given of music by members of *Les nouveaux jeunes* on 15 January 1918 which was introduced by René Chalput, of which the programme was:

Honegger	*Six poèmes* (Apollinaire) (Jane Bathori with Andrée Vaurabourg)
Tailleferre	*Sonatine pour instruments à cordes.*
Auric	*Gaspard et Zoé* (Marcelle Meyer, piano)
Durey	*Carillons* (Marcelle Meyer, piano)
Poulenc	*Rhapsodie nègre*
Roland-Manuel	*Sept poèmes de Perse*

H.H. Stuckenschmidt reflected that 'avec elle, l'heure de la musique française moderne a sonné'[11] [with it, the hour of modern French music has struck].

The process took a leap forward when Satie introduced Jean Cocteau to *Les nouveaux jeunes*. Already a friend of Picasso and Diaghilev and having strong links with the absent Stravinsky, he had long nurtured his ideas and visions for a new and pure 'French' music and had found many receptive ears amongst the composers of the group for the philosophies he proposed in *Le coq et l'arlequin*[12]. The reaction in Poulenc and Auric was immediate and deep-rooted; Tailleferre followed, or was pushed, with no resistance. Durey pretended to acquiesce, lacking the courage and the tenacity to counter Cocteau with his own ideals. Milhaud appeared to become a veritable pillar of the group, but then he had the facility and talent to do anything except possibly to be negative.

The bonds of friendship between Honegger and all his fellow composers in the group were strong — as Stuckenschmidt said 'Honegger est capable de grandes amitiés et peut-être d'une fidelité à toute épreuve'[13] [Honegger is capable of striking great friendships, due probably to his unfailing integrity]. Honegger was content to enjoy the artistic companionship and the stimulation with which the group abounded, whilst never associating himself with the theories that Cocteau articulated as guidelines for the group to create a new 'French' music. As he later said 'dans notre groupe, nous avons toujours été indépendants et, contrairement à ce qu'on nous a reproché souvent, nous n'avons jamais eu une esthétique de groupe'[14] [within our group, we have always been independent and, contrary to [the widely-held belief] with which we have so often been reproached, we never have had a 'group aesthetic'].

There can be no doubt that, to an extent, he benefited from the association in terms of the publicity that they attracted — particularly when, writing an article entitled 'Premier concert donné par le *Groupe des Six*', Roussy de Salles commented that 'il faut mentionner avant tout la *Sonatine pour deux violons* de Honegger, qui est, je crois, celui des Six qui a le plus indiscutablement quelque chose à dire et qui sait le dire'[15] [I must mention, above all, the *Sonatine for Two Violins* by Honegger, who is, I believe, the member of *Les Six* who undoubtedly has something positive to say and knows how to say it].

The zenith of publicity came when, in December 1919, the distinguished music critic of the leading journal *Comœdia* was prompted by Cocteau to meet some of the new young musicians that Roussel had written about in such complimentary terms in *The Chesterian* of the previous month[16]. As Honegger related 'le critique, Henri Collet, de *Comœdia* vint un jour chez Milhaud pour faire la connaissance des jeunes musiciens. Ce jour-là, il rencontra Auric, Durey, Milhaud, Poulenc, Tailleferre et moi-même. Dans un article paru quelques jours plus tard, il nous comparait aux 5 Russes, et nous appelait les *6* Français. Cet article suscita de vives polémiques. . .'[17] [the critic of *Comœdia,* H. Collet, came one day to Milhaud's house in order to get to know some young musicians. That day he met Auric, Durey, Milhaud, Poulenc, Tailleferre and myself. In an article which appeared a few days later, he compared us to the Russian *Five* and called us *Les Six*. This article aroused much controversy. . .].

So was created the specifically musical group — *Les Six* — from the now rather distended ranks of *Les nouveaux jeunes*. The fact that Pierre Menu and Roland-Manuel were unable to accept Milhaud's invitation that day, which would have otherwise meant the creation of *Les Huit,* must be remembered in order to stress the arbitrary and fortuitous origins of this now legendary association. Just as Satie had been a mentor and father-figure to *Les nouveaux jeunes,* the new group looked for a figurehead and tacitly received the eagerly proffered credentials of Jean Cocteau. (See pages 220-22 for a further discussion of Honegger's relationship with *Les Six* and with their associated 'creed'.)

Honegger's contributions to the occasions when *Les nouveaux jeunes* and then *Les Six* presented concerts of their music form a unique corpus of music within his total output and is not without its significance in terms of his later music. In the *Six poèmes d'Apollinaire* the text of No. 4 'Saltimbanques' (reproduced on pages 9-11), provided him with the ideal opportunity to reflect the current interest in *musique nègre*. This is neither a mere reflection of the *rhythme nègre* that Debussy used in 'Golliwog's Cake-Walk' (*Children's Corner,* 1908), 'Minstrels' (*Préludes,* Book I, 1910) or 'General Lavine eccentric' (*Préludes,* Book II, 1913), nor of the 'jazz' craze (which was still a year away from Paris), in its use of certain melodic, harmonic and rhythmic clichés and glissandi. The discreet colouristic use of polytonality (bar 13), the juxtaposition of melodic tonalities (bars 5-11) and the occasional chromatic obscuring of the obvious tonality of the ostinato bars are, however, purely Honeggerian felicities. Written in March 1917, this song is the earliest example of Honegger's ability to use a style in appropriate circumstances that could be construed as linking him with the stylistic tendencies of other members of *Les nouveaux jeunes*. Suffice it to say that this is the only example in all the works written prior to the very end of 1919.

With the concentration of effort in a purely musical direction surrounding the 'birth' of *Les Six,* it is interesting to note the sudden proliferation of works that Honegger produced for their 'occasions' which can be said to be tainted with the stylistic qualities that were over-exposed by most of the rest of the group. In the fourth movement from *Sept pièces brèves* for piano (see Music Example 8 overleaf), written in December 1919, there is a simplicity in the construction of the right-hand melody that is purely *Les Six* in feeling — in particular, it has the limpid pastorality that characterizes so much of Milhaud's music — but underlining this is a control of the bitonal procedures that is masterly in a way only attributable to Honegger. Within the ABA^1 structure the bitonal combination of G and B majors occurs in the outer A sections whilst there is a carefully worked-out procedure whereby the bitonal combinations are brought closer and closer together in relationship to each other as the B section progresses — a move which psychologically increases the aural impression of continuity — before the tension is released immediately prior to the return of A section material. (The same is true of the 'Cortège' (No. 5) in *Le roi David* — see Chapter II.

Music Example 8: *Sept pièces brèves,* No. 4, bars 1-12 and 15-16
(N.B. bars 13-14 = bars 1-2)

During the first half of 1920 he wrote the *Sonatine pour deux violons* for a *Les Six* concert, in which a feeling of joyfulness and a lack of anxiety are new to his music and thoroughly in keeping with the 'group spirit'. Despite the basic simplicity of thematic and tonal procedures there are many features of the work, however, which raise it above the levels both aimed at and achieved in the other works provided for the occasion, namely Poulenc's *Piano Sonata*, Milhaud's *Saudades do Brazil* and Auric's *Les joues en feu* in particular. The contrapuntal discipline that can be found in all the movements, but most notably in the fugally-structured finale, together with the rigidly controlled tonal freedom of the first movement and the expressive modality of the middle movement — the latter anticipating the 'Chant de la servante' (No. 18) and 'La chanson d'Ephraïm' (No. 22) in *Le roi David* — have an artistry about them which reveals a composer of genius working in a relaxed and lighter vein suitable to the medium rather than one setting out to create music which involves processes of negation and debasement in an attempt to realize Cocteau's radical musical creed.

An examination of the pieces which the others of the group contributed for the piano *Album des Six*, published in 1920, highlights a consistency of style involving over-regular phrasing, exaggerated dependence on tonic and dominant harmonies, deliberate wrong-note chords and ostinati, over-simplified structures, undistinguished melodic germs and a lack of developmental aspects which is generally barren and disconcertingly lacking in any form of musicality. The degree of contrast which Honegger's piece, *Sarabande*, provides is embarrassing. The convincing ABA[1] structure, integrated contrapuntal features and the thoroughly uncompromising harmonic argument combine with the tough consistency of the textures to produce a piece that is completely out of keeping with all the professed ideals of the group (see Music Example 9 below).

Music Example 9: *Sarabande* (No. 3 from *Album des Six*), bars 1-20

A similar disparity exists between the first and subsequent two settings of poems by Jean Cocteau which he made in May and June 1920, and which form the first half of the *Six poésies de Jean Cocteau* (1920-23). The use of neo-classical themes and ragtime-like contra-rhythms in 'Le nègre' (see Music Example 10 (i) below) recall vividly the mood of 'Saltimbanques' in the Apollinaire settings and is a close parallel to the Poulenc of *Bestiaire.* There is, too, the trace of irony that is pure Chabrier and the tart clarity of Ravel in *Les enfants et les sortilèges.* This piece of *Les Six* contrasts sharply with the purely Honeggerian 'Locutions' (see Music Example 10 (ii) opposite) and the Fauré/Debussy-influenced 'Souvenirs d'enfance' (see Music Example 10 (iii), pp. 42-43).

Music Example 10: *Six poésies de Jean Cocteau*:
(i) No. 1 'Le nègre', bars 1-17

-mais pleu-voir ne mouil - - le pâ-lit courbé dans la houille bleue et bru-te
du soleil dur
f
pp sub.

(ii) No. 2 'Locutions', bars 1-10

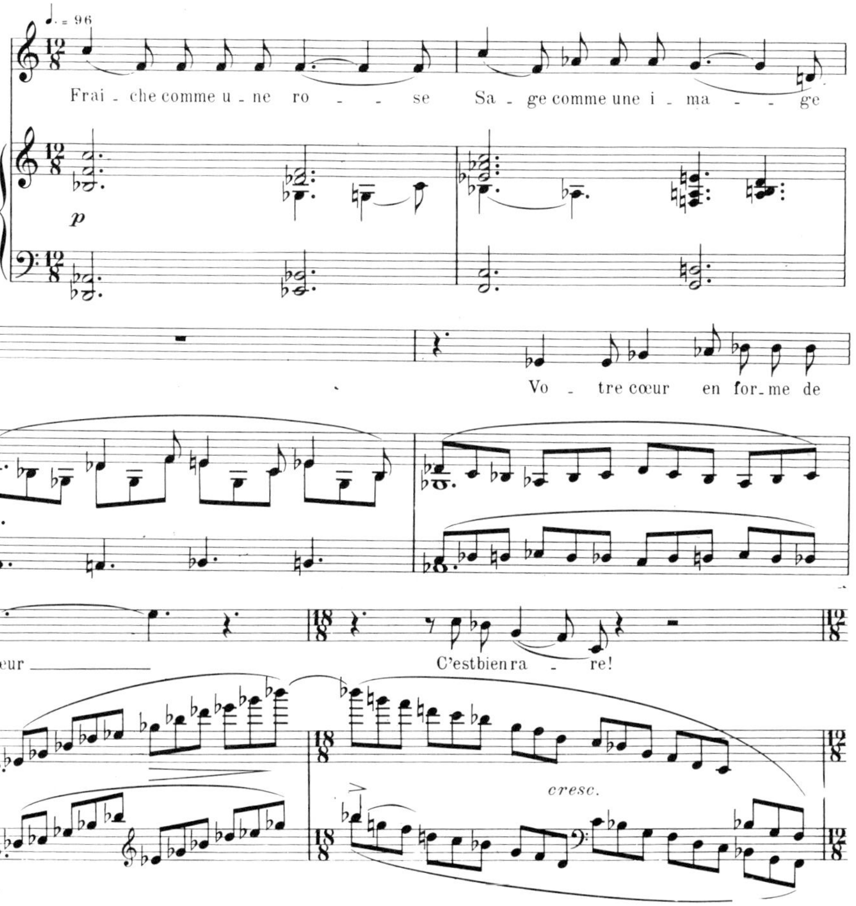

♩. = 96

Frai - che comme u - ne ro - - - se Sa - ge comme une i - ma - - ge

p

Vo - tre cœur en for-me de

cœur ______ C'est bien ra - re!

cresc.

(iii) No. 3 'Souvenirs d'enfance', bars 1-30

quel_que cho_se El_le at_ten_dra le ma_tin
Les noix ta
mè - re les do - re pour ton ar - bre de No - -
_ël
Sou_liers au bord de l'au_ro_re ils ap_pri_voi_sent le ciel
Ja - dis
pp

Nowhere in the handful of works which Honegger wrote for the occasions when he appeared as a member of *Les Six* or, previously, as an associate of *Les nouveaux jeunes*, can one find any debasement of the music, any banality or neglect of artistic responsibilities — qualities so sadly evident in much of the music of even the best of the others. Honegger was capable of being light and humorous in music when the situation or the medium demanded such treatment, but he would not allow his integrity to be undermined by a creed which urged that nothing was sacred or serious. However, the long-held belief that Honegger was no real part of *Les Six* is in fact only partially true, particularly when it is borne in mind that he continued to use techniques pioneered by others of the group in later works — in particular the *Sonatine* (for clarinet and piano), *Concertino* (for piano and orchestra) and the operettas *Les aventures du roi Pausole* and *La belle de Moudon* (see Chapters II and VI) — as well as contributing the 'Marche funèbre' to the score for *Les mariés de la tour Eiffel* in which he almost succeeds in defeating *Les Six* at their own game through his parody of the famous 'valse' from Gounod's *Faust*[18].

Honegger was certainly the most strong-minded and intellectual of the group and his involvement with its artistic infamy only strengthened his belief in the need for continuous evolution and development of artistic sincerity — a course which he pursued relentlessly in the handful of orchestral and vocal works immediately preceding his score for *Le roi David.*

The two orchestral scores from this period illustrate a dichotomy which is fundamental to Honegger as man and artist. The contrast that the tender, relaxed and lyrical *Pastorale d'été* provides with the massive, complex and powerful *Horace victorieux* has an exact parallel in the case of the *Third* and *Fourth Symphonies*. The opposing forces are, fundamentally, strong and weak whether it is as violence and tenderness, or masculinity and feminity (Judith and Osias in *Judith*), the result of differing personal states of mind or subject conditioning, or the expression of good versus evil — which is the case in all the large-scale dramatic scores. Nor is it confined to cases of differing works — the conflict is within almost every work, providing a force of immense latent power always well harnessed to the structuring of the whole.

Of the two works involving the voice, the *Cantique de Pâques* for three solo female voices, female chorus and orchestra, of July 1918, provides a fascinating preview of many aspects of *Le roi David.* Based on the very short text 'Alleluia, Christ est ressuscité. Alleluia, Il est ressuscité, le Fils de Dieu. Alleluia, Il est ressuscité, Christ, le Seigneur, le Fils de Dieu', it is the first work that survives which reflects Honegger's deep and sincere religious convictions. A devout Protestant, the Bible was to be the source of inspiration for many of his later works — indeed he had written earlier that he would be happy to spend his whole life writing biblical works, a wish that was in a way to be fulfilled. There are still elements of the struggle he was having to rid his style of overtly Impressionistic elements evident in this work: the shadows of Debussy's *Le martyre de saint Sébastien* in particular, still loom large, not least in terms of the unusual scoring. Nevertheless, there are many original elements too: the *vocalise*, the ebb and flow of the 'Alleluias' and the stylized 'antico-religious' feeling that pervades the whole are pure antecedents of those specific procedures in *Le roi David*. Indeed, the parallels to Nos. 16 and 27, in particular, of *Le roi David*, are furthered by a close similarity in large-scale mosaic formal structuring. The writing is often very busy; complex textures are created by the consistent use of counterpoint and the characteristic trait of a theme always having several counter-subjects, as opposed to merely one. The clarity and logical progression of all the diverse elements is helped considerably by the orchestration — much attention is paid to the separation of the overall texture into sub-strata with relative importance, these often being linked to a division of the orchestra into the obvious three strata of woodwind, brass and strings.

At one extreme there is a modality of disarming simplicity, at the other a tonality stretched to its limits (a dichotomy totally characteristic of Honegger in a way just as personal as the frequent use of parallel triads over extended pedal points). The tonal scheme is heavily conditioned by tertiary relationships and is a close parallel to that of the final movement of *Le roi David* in terms of the feeling of relief and fulfilment that is implicit in the attainment of the blazing C major under the 'chorale' (see Music Example 11 below).

The feeling of joyous exultation, which is both meditative and jubilant, is in a tradition that stems from Fauré's *Messe basse* and finds expression in later works of the French school such as Poulenc's *Litanies à la vierge noire,* as well as in so many of Honegger's religious frescoes and his *Une cantate de Noël.*

Music Example 11: *Cantique de Pâques,* 7 - 10

Al - le - lui - a Il est res - sus - ci - té
Al - le - lui - a Il est res - sus - ci - té
Al - le - lui - a Il est res - sus - ci - té
Il est res - sus - ci - té Al - le - lui - a
Il est res - sus - ci - té Al - le - lui - a
Il est res - sus - ci - té Al - le - lui - a
8
sempre
cresc.
Al - le-lui a Il est res - sus - ci - té Il est res -
Al - le-lui-a Il est res - sus - ci - té Il est res
Al - le-lui-a Il est res - sus - ci - té Il est res -
Il est res - sus - ci - té Il est res - sus - ci - té
Il est res - sus - ci - té Il est res - sus - ci - té
Il est res - sus - ci - té Il est res - sus - ci - té

9 Tres large
_sus _ ci_té Il est res _ _ sus _ ci_té
_sus _ ci_té Il est res _ _ sus _ ci_té
_sus _ ci_té Al _ le _ lui _ a
f de près
Il est res _ sus _ ci_té Al _ le_lui _ a
Il est res _ sus _ ci_té Al _ le _ lui _ a
Il est res _ sus _ ci _ té
f Très large
Allelui _ a Alle _ lui _ a Allelui _
Allelui _ a Alle _ lui _ a Al_le_lui_a A
Il est res sus ci té
Al _ le _ lui _ a Al _ le_lui_a Al _ le _ lui _
Al _ le _ lui _ a Al _ le _ lui _
Il est res _ sus _ ci_té

(Reproduit avec l'autorisation des EDITIONS SALABERT, Paris, propriétaires de l'œuvre.)

Providing many exact parallels to the *Cantique de Pâques,* as well as illustrating the advance and maturity of style that Honegger had achieved in the two years which separate them, is the song-cycle for solo voice and string quartet, *Les Pâques à New York,* of 1920. The three extracts from Blaise Cendrars' cycle of poems of the same name, are full of a mysticism which is beautifully paralleled in Honegger's setting. The writing for the quartet has a lightness and transparency absent from the earlier *String Quartet (No. 1)* which, together with moments of intense richness and freedom of the accompaniment generally, create a supreme atmosphere of immateriality and unreality perfectly married to the poems. The choice of the quartet medium for the accompaniment is fortuitous but not unexpected in the light of Honegger's earlier problems of containing his thought within the scope of the piano.

Transition

With his incidental music for the biblical drama *Le roi David*, by the Swiss playwright René Morax, first performed in June 1921, Arthur Honegger achieved world-wide fame and critical recognition. In doing so he was placed in a position where he appeared to be the most suitable candidate for the role of 'leader of the French School' in succession to Debussy. Despite his dual nationality he occupied this position until Messiaen, with undeniable appropriateness, assumed the mantle. The details of Honegger's elevation to this temporary but prolonged status — to be titled regent rather than monarch to avoid unfair recriminations of pretension — are an important element of this study.

Notes to Chapter I

[1]See Willy Tappolet, *Arthur Honegger* (Editions de la Baconnière, Neuchâtel, 1957), 14.

[2]Quoted by José Bruyr, *Honegger et son œuvre du Scherzo des 'Pièces pour piano' (1910) à la symphonie liturgique (1946)* (Editions Corrêa, Paris, 1947), 37.

See also the account of another conflict between d'Indy and Honegger in Frank Bonavia 'The Future of Music according to Honegger', *Musical Times,* May 1928, 413-14.

[3]See Arthur Honegger, *I am a Composer* (Faber and Faber, London, 1966), 98-99.

[4]Arthur Honegger, *I am a Composer* (Faber and Faber, London, 1966), 91.

[5]Quoted by Roland-Manuel, 'Opinions d'Arthur Honegger', *Dissonances*, No. 4 (April 1925), 84-87 (p. 85). See also pp. 7-9.

[6]Quoted by Marcel Landowski, *Honegger* (Editions du Seuil, Paris, 1957), 51.

[7]Ibid., 53.

[8]Le grand chef iroquois et ses guerriers sont faits prisonniers par l'ennemi . . . Tareah le Huron avait réservé Nigamon et les autres chefs iroquois, pour les brûler vifs. Le feu fut mis aux bûchers. Lorsque les flammes commencèrent à monter, Tareah bondit à travers et scalpa impitoyablement Nigamon et ses compagnons en les souffletant avec leur propre chevelure. Alors les Iroquois commencèrent leur chant de mort, mais lorsque Nigamon entama le sien, les autres se turent pour l'écouter . . . (p. 286) [The Big Chief of the Iroquois and his braves had been captured by the enemy . . . Tareah the Huron had reserved Nigamon and the other Iroquois chiefs to burn them alive. Fire was set to the stakes. When the flames began to climb, Tareah leapt across and scalped Nigamon and his companions mercilessly and beat them with their own scalps. The Iroquois began their death chant, but when Nigamon began his own the others stopped to listen to him . . .].

[9]See Arthur Honegger, *I am a Composer* (Faber and Faber, London, 1966) 92.

[10]Arthur Honegger, *I am a Composer* (Faber and Faber, London, 1966) 92.

[11]*Neue Musik* (Berlin, 1951), 122.

[12](Stock, Paris, 1918). English translation by Rollo H. Myers, *Cock and Harlequin* (Egoist Press, London, 1921).

[13]*Neue Musik* (Berlin, 1951), 122.

[14]Arthur Honegger, 'Les Six ont dix ans', *Candide,* no. 301 (19 December 1929), 13.

[15]*La Revue Musicale,* January 1921, 68.

[16]'Young French Composers', *Chesterian,* no. 2 (October 1919), 33-37.

[17]'Les Six ont dix ans', *Candide,* no. 301 (19 December 1929), 13.

[18]See Darius Milhaud, *Notes sans musique* (Juilliard, Paris, 1949), 126.

CHAPTER II

From *Le roi David* to 'Le roi Arthur'

Roussel, writing in 1919, noted that 'Honegger is one of those who possess the most complete knowledge of their craft'[1], whilst Milhaud, in 1921, openly admitted that 'at a time when impressionistic music is being frittered away in vain and sterile complications, encroaching on the domains of literature and painting; at a time when, on the other hand, certain young composers tend towards the popular music of the circus and the music-hall, Arthur Honegger comes to us as a champion of chamber, symphonic and dramatic music,' and that 'he is one of those on whom we may rely to keep alive the traditions of absolute music, independent of literature, of philosophy, of painting; music that needs for its full expression nothing but the guidance of his inspiration and his patiently acquired and unfailing craftsmanship'[2].

Henri Collet, in the now famous articles which appeared in his *Comœdia* column 'La musique chez soi' on 16 January and 23 January 1920, and which gave rise to the naming of *Les Six,* acknowledged Honegger to be 'le plus profond des *six'* [the most profound of *Les Six*], whilst Roland-Manuel pointed out that 'le talent de M. Honegger s'affirme de mieux en mieux, avec une étonnante maîtrise'[3] [with astonishing craftsmanship, Honegger's talent is becoming more and more obvious].

A spiritual leader for the French School, in succession to Debussy, was urgently needed at that moment because of the unstable musical situation which was further exacerbated both by Satie's abortive attempt to fulfil the role through his leadership of *Les nouveaux jeunes*, and the regrettable unsuitability of Ravel.* When the critical acclaim and respect of his fellow musicians for Honegger is considered with the performances of the already extensive list of works written before *Le roi David,* the proposed adoption of him as Debussy's successor by default is seen to be justifiable, and the catalytic role of *Le roi David,* in his securing the necessary international reputation, is thrown into dramatic relief.

*By the use of the phrase 'regrettable unsuitability' I wish to draw attention to his intense desire for personal privacy, the achievement of which resulted in his relative isolation; it is not to be seen as a reflection on the quality of his work.

The first performance of *Le roi David* — a biblical drama by René Morax with incidental music by Honegger — at the Théâtre du Jorat[4] on 11 June 1921, was followed by nine scheduled repeats and then a further two the next month, occasioned by its unexpected success. The intense popular and critical reaction in favour of the work resulted in considerable pressure being brought to bear on Honegger and Morax to produce a concert version. Because of the demands of other commitments, Honegger declined to alter the musical score apart from rescoring it in 1923 for full orchestra[5]. He obviously did not anticipate the appeal of the work in this version, otherwise he might well have mitigated the principal problematic feature — the disparate lengths of the various movements and the predominance of very brief items in Part I — which he himself later identified in *I am a Composer* (Faber and Faber, 1966, p.100). Nevertheless, with a narration provided by Morax to link the twenty-seven items, this concert version of the work (subtitled by Honegger 'Psaume symphonique') swept the world in the space of but a few years and in Paris it was performed on consecutive nights for three months! As the highly perspicacious commentator on French music, David Drew, pointed out in his annotation for the Decca complete recording in 1962[6]:

> together with Kodaly's *Psalmus Hungaricus* it was almost the only major work by a young continental composer to find favour in England during the twenties. Its first English performance — in the stage version — was given in Cambridge in 1923[7], and in 1928 it [the concert version] achieved the rare distinction of being performed at the Three Choirs Festival in Gloucester. Its success with the more conservative critics possibly encouraged Walton to try his hand at a biblical oratorio.

The inevitable question must be asked though: despite the popular and critical acclaim both then and now, together with a performance tally that is high in the realms of five figures the world over, why is it that the concert version of this work is such a success when its genesis, gestation and format would all seem to count against it? The history is well-known, but it is necessary to recount the facts.

Morax asked Honegger to write the incidental music for his drama only after others, including his regular collaborator, Gustave Doret, had refused to accept such a magnitudinous task at short notice. He was recommended by Ansermet and Stravinsky, no less, and completed the task in two months — twenty-seven numbers of much variety and differing lengths occupying ninety-three pages of vocal-score! The concert version contains no alterations apart from the rescoring: it merely consists of the items of music strung together by a narrator who uses the spoken word.

The first factor which must be examined in reply to the question posed is that of the structure of the work (see Diagram 7, pages 52-53 and the subsequent explanation of the symbols on pages 54-55). A structural analysis of this kind reveals a series of tonal and thematic correspondences which give the work a strong and cohesive dramatic viability in its own right.[8]

Le roi David

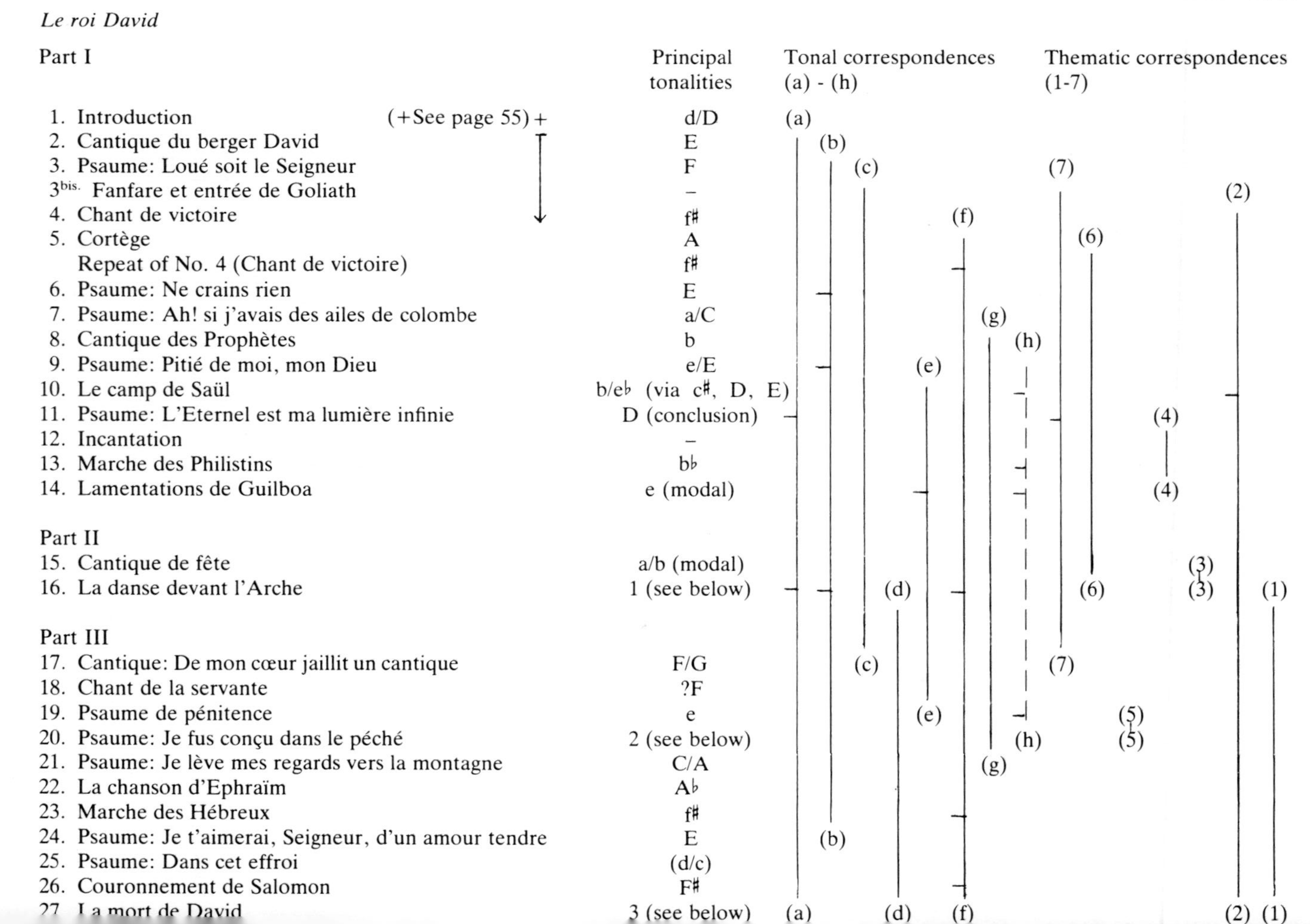

Part I	Principal tonalities	Tonal correspondences (a) - (h)	Thematic correspondences (1-7)
1. Introduction (+See page 55) +	d/D	(a)	
2. Cantique du berger David	E	(b)	
3. Psaume: Loué soit le Seigneur	F	(c)	(7)
3bis. Fanfare et entrée de Goliath	–		(2)
4. Chant de victoire	f♯	(f)	
5. Cortège	A		(6)
Repeat of No. 4 (Chant de victoire)	f♯		
6. Psaume: Ne crains rien	E		
7. Psaume: Ah! si j'avais des ailes de colombe	a/C	(g)	
8. Cantique des Prophètes	b	(h)	
9. Psaume: Pitié de moi, mon Dieu	e/E	(e)	
10. Le camp de Saül	b/e♭ (via c♯, D, E)		
11. Psaume: L'Eternel est ma lumière infinie	D (conclusion)		(4)
12. Incantation	–		
13. Marche des Philistins	b♭		
14. Lamentations de Guilboa	e (modal)		(4)
Part II			
15. Cantique de fête	a/b (modal)		(3)
16. La danse devant l'Arche	1 (see below)	(d)	(6) (3) (1)
Part III			
17. Cantique: De mon cœur jaillit un cantique	F/G	(c)	(7)
18. Chant de la servante	?F		
19. Psaume de pénitence	e	(e)	(5)
20. Psaume: Je fus conçu dans le péché	2 (see below)	(h)	(5)
21. Psaume: Je lève mes regards vers la montagne	C/A	(g)	
22. La chanson d'Ephraïm	A♭		
23. Marche des Hébreux	f♯		
24. Psaume: Je t'aimerai, Seigneur, d'un amour tendre	E	(b)	
25. Psaume: Dans cet effroi	(d/c)		
26. Couronnement de Salomon	F♯		
27. La mort de David	3 (see below)	(a) (d) (f)	(2) (1)

1.	(b)+	(d)+	(f)+			(f)+		(b)+					(d)+	(a)+	(f)+
Principal tonalities:	E	F	F♯	G	A	f♯	E♭	E	D	e♭	b♭	E♭/A♭	F	D	F♯
Rehearsal numbers:	7B[1]	4A[1] / [4]	[5]	6B[6]	[6]	4B[12]	[12]	[13]	4A[14]	3A[15]	[17]	[19]	[26]	[28]	[31]

2.		(h)+				
Principal tonalities:	g prep. for	b♭	(via e	c	e♭	) c
Rehearsal numbers :		3A[1]	5A[2]	[3]	5A[3]	9A[3]

3.	(f)+	(d)+	(a)+		(a)+
Principal tonalities:	F♯	F	D	A♭	D
Rehearsal letters :		[A]	[B]	[C]	[D] / [G]

(+ : see relevant tonal correspondence charted above)

Tonal Correspondences

(a) Parts One and Two are concerned with the defeat of evil as evident in the whole Israelite race, and Part Three with the defeat of evil as evident in the personage of King David. The key of D major is used to symbolize the righteous omnipotence of God and so it dominates Nos. 1, 16 and 27 — the three pillars of the work which support the details of the overall bipartite dramatic structure. It is also used, significantly, as the concluding tonality in No. 11 when the Israelites, realizing their fate, turn to the Lord for help.

(b) The key of E major is used to symbolize David's personal faith (cf. Nos. 2, 6, 9 and 24) and, hence, the rekindled faith of the Israelites following their defeat at the hands of David (No. 16).

(c) The two 'hymns' of praise are both set in F major (Nos. 3 and 17).

(d) F major is also the key for the two appearances of the Angel (Nos. 16 and 27) — an effective cross-reference to (c) dramatically.

(e) On the three occasions when the idea of despair resulting from defeat is to be represented, the key is E minor (Nos. 9, 14 and 19).

(f) F sharp major/minor symbolizing victory (Nos. 4, 16, 23, 26 and 27).

(g) The similarity of key-pairing involved coincides with the two occasions when David laments his inadequacy (Nos. 7 and 21).

(h) Tonal relationships involving the tritone used to highlight diametrically-opposed dramatical situations (Nos. 8 and 10; 13 and 14; 19 and 20).

Thematic Correspondences

(1) The 'Alleluias' (Nos. 16 and 27).
(2) David's motif (see Music Example 12 (ii) below):
the first significant use of it is in No. 10 (to signify his presence in Saul's camp). In terms of the intervallic delineation, it can be derived from the 'Entrée de Goliath' fanfare (No. 3bis — see Music Example 12 (i) below) thus establishing a subtle link with the Philistines on whose side he now is. In addition, a major mode version dominates No. 27 as the symbol of David (see Music Example 12 (iii) opposite).

Music Example 12: *Le roi David*:
(i) No. 3bis 'Entrée de Goliath', (trombone(s))

(ii) No. 10 'Le camp de Saül', trumpet(s), bars 1 - 7

(iii) No. 27 'La mort de David', solo soprano (Angel), [A] - [B]

(3) The main idea of No. 15 (chorus bar 8 onwards) becomes a constituent of No. 16 (chorus after [5]). As Part II consists only of these two movements, this intensifies the necessary interrelation.

(4) The main theme from No. 11 (chorus bars 2-6) returns in diminution in No. 14 (orchestra after [6]) to symbolize the same focal point of the two different areas of mourning.

(5) The return of a theme from No. 19 in No. 20 corresponds to a repeat of a portion of the text.

(6) The fanfare motives of No. 16 ([3] - [4]) are rhythmically derived from No. 5.

(7) Fragments of No. 3 recur in Nos. 11 (chorus after [2]) and 17. In terms of Nos. 3 and 17, this reinforces the significance of tonal correspondence (c).

Further to the tonal correspondences, the use of the tonal gradient (+) (see Diagram 7, page 52) aids both the dramatic progression and produces an effective platform for the first chorus entry — a technique which he had used on a larger scale to great advantage in the orchestral 'fresco', *Le chant de Nigamon*, of 1917. There is, too, an attempt in Part I to portray in the character of David's melodic lines his progress from childhood to adulthood — the full-bloodedness of his lines in No. 21, absent hitherto, reinforces this. The interaction of these two systems is finalized when the solo soprano (Angel) line in No. 27 becomes the 'chorale' sung by the chorus — the elements (a), (c), (d) and (7) work together most effectively to conclude the drama.

The varied roles of the chorus are well integrated throughout — the similarity of style employed for Nos. 3 and 17 illustrates not only this, but also supports that of tonal correspondence (c). Formal cohesion is furthered, too, by the presence of the very same quality in each individual movement — the preponderance of ABA and open-forms contributes largely to this as does the fact that the large-scale movements are either merely expansions of the ABA form or contain a use of returns (cf. No. 7 and No. 16 respectively).

> The orchestra presented a problem, since I was only allowed seventeen musicians with which to balance a large chorus. In discussing this with Stravinsky, I told him of my uncertainty and he gave me some very good advice: Imagine that you yourself wanted this arrangement of seventeen musicians. I followed his advice and scored for the following: two flutes, one oboe, two clarinets, one bassoon, two trumpets, one French horn, one trombone, piano, harmonium, celesta, timpani, double-bass and percussion (cymbals, side drum, bass drum, gong and tambourine).[9]

Underlying the whole is an excellent use of the orchestral forces available, particularly in terms of the discreet but thoroughly systematic application of tone-colour to express the geographical location. A comparison of the original chamber scoring with the later revised version for full orchestra is significant in that it reveals the woodwind and brass writing remaining essentially unaltered, whilst the strings are used for the most part to fill out only the climactic sections and not radically to alter the basic sound conceptions.

Finally there is a very tightly controlled relationship between the dramatic and musical emotive peaks — two substructures very clearly support the overall bipartite superstructure (see Diagram 8 below).

Diagram 8:

Le roi David

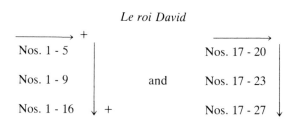

→ +		→
Nos. 1 - 5		Nos. 17 - 20
Nos. 1 - 9	and	Nos. 17 - 23
Nos. 1 - 16 ↓ +		Nos. 17 - 27 ↓

(+Thus No. 5 represents a climax in terms of the first five numbers and a similar gradation applies to Nos. 5, 9 and 16 respectively. The same is applicable to the constituent movements of Parts II and III — Nos. 17-27.)

The second factor which must be examined is that of the consistency and quality of the musical language. The most developed aspects of Honegger's original voice in this work lie in the melodic characteristics. There is a rigid dichotomy in all his mature works between the simple and the complex, which manifests itself in all the components of the language. In *Le roi David* there is a definite prominence of the former — a situation which is paralleled in only a handful of his other works: the earlier *Pastorale d'été* and *Cantique de Pâques*, and the much later *Symphony No. 4* (1946) and *Une cantate de Noël* (1941/1953). This over-riding feature of the style is clearly reflected in the melodic lines together with characteristics that Honegger was to exploit in many of the later works, notably those of the 'chorale' theme, the use of *vocalise*, the *semplice* line and melodies involving the rapid juxtaposition of tonal planes. There is an economy of thematic material and a tendency for themes to be self-developing that together support admirably his efforts to obtain formal cohesion and organic continuity. Above all, attention is paid to the shape of all the melodic lines which is purely Classical in outlook. The care with which each segment of the whole is made to contribute or to balance and the control of the tessitural peaks in relation to both the musical and textual structures are a fortuitous combination of influences from J. S. Bach and Mozart respectively. In addition, there are elements which appear in this work largely for the contribution they make to the subtle 'oriental' flavour which permeates the whole as opposed to being part of Honegger's basic idiom: the prominence of modal devices, occasional use of the whole-tone scale and a tendency to stress the chromatic notes ♭2 and ♯4.

Even though the elements of Honegger's language interact closely — and it is best not to consider harmony, counterpoint, chromaticism or tonality separately — one realizes that counterpoint is the dominant element. It is Honegger's use of counterpoint, for instance, that succeeds both in clarifying and unifying the polytonal structure of the 'Cortège' (No. 5). He uses it to articulate convincingly the atonal tissue of 'Incantation' (No. 12), and in 'Cantique du berger David' (No. 2), the simple contrapuntal device of contrary motion gives vitality to the chromaticisms with which he decorates the simple harmonic progressions.

Due to sheer variety the pedal points are prevented from being a destructive feature of Honegger's style. The single and chromatically dissonant double pedal points of the 'Introduction' (No. 1) contrast well with the Fauré-like broken-chord ostinati in 'Lamentations de Guilboa' (No. 14 — after **8**), 'Cantique de fête' (No. 15), 'La danse devant l'arche' (No. 16 — after **5**), and the 'Chant de la servante' (No. 18), whilst the chordal ostinati of the 'Psaume de pénitence' (No. 19) and 'La chanson d'Ephraïm' (No. 22) anticipate Honegger's later style with their tonal ambiguity and rich harmonic colouring.

The contrapuntal writing in the Psalm 'Loué soit le Seigneur' (No. 3), the 'Lamentations de Guilboa' (No. 14), 'La danse devant l'arche' (No. 16) and 'La mort de David' (No. 27) reveals clearly the position of J. S. Bach as Honegger's mentor both technically and spiritually. It also epitomizes the success with which he had achieved his aims, the principles being summarized so appositely by Honegger himself in a reply he made to Jean Cocteau's criticisms of his style:

> If I still participate in a state of things in their last stages, it is because it seems to me indispensable that, to progress, we must be solidly linked with what has preceded us. We must not break the tie with musical tradition. A branch separated from the trunk dies quickly. We must be the new player in the old game, because to change the rules is to destroy the game and to throw it back to its starting point. Economy of means seems to me more difficult, but also more useful, than a too headstrong audacity. There is no profit in smashing the door which you might open.[10]

To conclude the answer to the question previously posed in order that the success of *Le roi David* should be rationally appreciated, account must be taken of the nature of the critical reaction expressed at the time.

> Cette œuvre va nous permettre de nous former une opinion assez complète sur la véritable nature de son auteur. Elle est particulièrement représentative et significative. Elle est récente; elle ne fait plus partie des ballons d'essai, des esquisses ou des pochades d'étude sur lesquels un auteur ne tient pas à être jugé; . . . elle est donc spontanée sans coquetteries excessives, très sincèrement instinctive.
>
> Emile Vuillermoz, '*Le roi David,' Le Temps,* 30 December 1921.

> [This work will allow us to form a fairly complete opinion on the true nature of its author. It is particularly representative and significant. It is a recent work which no longer depends on a period of trial and error, drafts or rapid sketches on the basis of which an author does not wish to be judged . . . therefore, it is spontaneous, has no excessive frivolities and is very sincerely instinctive.]

> La probité de cet art, qui s'affirme par un égal dédain du bluff et des vaines excentricités dont tant d'autres — Darius Milhaud le tout premier — sont coutumiers . . . J'ai l'impression cependant que ce public, tout surpris qu'il ait pu être, n'est point demeuré insensible à la force expressive, à la conviction et à la sincérité, au lyrisme chaleureux qui font si vivante, si forte la partition de M. Honegger.
>
> R. Aloys Mooser, 'Après la première du *roi David, La Suisse,* 13 June 1921, 5.

> [The integrity of this art, affirmed by an equal contempt for bluff and vain eccentricities of which so many others, Milhaud above all, are in the habit of using . . . I am under the impression, however, that the public, despite being completely taken aback, has not remained indifferent to the expressive strength, the conviction and sincerity and the warm lyricism which make Honegger's score so alive and powerful.]

> Les différentes œuvres d'Honegger occupent dans le plus récent chapitre de l'histoire musicale une place à part. En un temps où l'esthétique musicale n'arrive pas à établir ses lois temporaires, à une époque où chaque artisan s'inquiète anxieusement de l'avis du voisin, écoute aux portes, craint de se laisser surprendre en délit d'opinion, l'auteur du roi David, avec une quiétude souriante, se dicte ses propres lois et ne les tient pas pour définitives, encore qu'elles viennent de lui. Il ne semble pas jaloux de prendre telle position qui lui interdise de revenir en arrière. Pourtant, il ne redoute aucune audace, étant doué de cette force persuasive qui seule devrait excuser la prétention d'écrire. Sa musique, c'est pour lui qu'il la compose, afin de répondre à l'appel impérieux de son destin, elle n'en est pas pour cela plus agressive ni plus hermétique, au contraire. De là vient son indépendance et que les parentés qu'on lui a reconnues jusqu' ici n'en excluent point d'autres plus inattendues et plus compromettantes.
>
> Maurice Bex, *'Le roi David', Revue Hebdomadaire,* 5 October 1921, 365-68 (p. 367).

[Honegger's various works occupy a unique place in the most recent chapter of musical history. At a time when a musical aestheticism cannot establish its temporary laws and when each artist is very anxious about his counterpart's opinion and listens behind doors in fear of being taken aback by adverse criticism, the composer of *Le roi David,* gently smiling, dictates his own laws which he may, if he so wishes, change as they are his own. He appears not to be anxious to take up any position which would prevent him turning back. Moreover, he fears no audacity as he is gifted with this persuasive strength which alone ought to excuse the pretension of writing. He composes his music for himself in order to reply to the pressing call of fate, and for this reason it is not more aggressive or hermetic — on the contrary. From that stems his independence, and the fact that the kinships which we have recognised in him until now do not exclude others more unexpected and more compromising.]

Je louerai ici de tout cœur la partition de M. Honegger, dont la fraîcheur, la franchise, la grâce à la fois subtile et fruste, l'intelligence et l'exquise nouveauté m'ont charmé. On est particulièrement heureux de voir toutes ces qualités, — developées dans l'atmosphère intellectuelle de Satie, — concourir aujourd'hui à une œuvre importante, chargée de sentiment de passion, pure néanmoins . . ..

Jacques Maritain, '*Le roi David* au Jorat', *Revue des Jeunes,* 10 August 1921, 332-36 (p. 333).

[Here I will whole-heartedly praise Honegger's score which has beguiled me with its freshness, openness, its subtle yet unpolished charm, intelligence and exquisite novelty. We are particularly happy to see all these qualities — developed in the intellectual atmosphere of Satie — converging today into an important work, laden with passionate though nevertheless pure feelings . . ..]

Une fois de plus, M. Honegger fit œuvre belle et grande. J'ajouterai même, n'en déplaise à l'auteur de 'Life and Habit', qui voulait que ce mot fût radicalement banni du vocabulaire des honnêtes gens, œuvre *sincère,* qualité trop rare aujourd'hui pour n'en point faire état, au risque de passer pour malhonnête aux yeux de l'illustre insulaire.

Florent Schmitt, 'A propos du *roi David* d'Arthur Honegger', *La Revue de France,* 1 November/December 1924, 152-57 (p. 157).

[Once again Honegger has written a large and beautiful work. I will even add (though I shall offend the author of *Life and Habit*† who wants 'the word completely banished from the vocabulary of honest people') that it is a *sincere* work, a quality which is too rare today not to be mentioned — this is my belief even though I run the risk of seeming impolite in the eyes of the famous Englishman.]

Au moment où les plus sincères amis de la musique invectivent contre le présent et désespèrent de l'avenir; au moment où les prophètes les mieux écoutés nous prédisent l'écroulement du temple; au moment où les plus

†Samuel Butler

illustres cliniciens tâchent à nous persuader qu'Euterpe est à toute extrémité; au moment où le plus éminent critique de ce temps élit une gazette qui s'appelle *Candide* pour y faire avec plus d'éclat ses débuts dans la sombre carrière de pessimiste; au moment où Emile Vuillermoz, puisqu'il faut l'appeler par son nom, nous dit en propres termes que la musique 'blessée, mutilée et gazée' par la guerre est décidément malade, 'très malade dans tout l'Univers', une œuvre athlétique, fraîche et jeune, franche et sereine, vient dissiper nos craintes et réduire à néant tant de sinistres rumeurs.

Car 'Le roi David' n'est pas l'exception qui confirme la règle. Son titre est un symbole, son triomphe est un signe, et réjouissant. Le seul fait qu'une œuvre comme celle-là ait pu être conçue et réalisée à une époque comme celle-ci par un musicien de vingt-neuf ans, nous prouve avec évidence que, s'il y a quelque chose de pourri dans le royaume de France, ce n'est assurément pas la musique.

Roland-Manuel, '*Le roi David* d'Arthur Honegger' *Revue Pleyel,* April 1924, 13-16 (p.13).

[At a time when the most sincere friends of music inveigh against the present and despair of the future; when the most listened-to prophets predict the collapse of the temple; when the most famous analysts try to persuade us that Euterpe* is at death's door; when the most eminent critic of our time chooses a magazine like *Candide* to create as big a stir as possible to announce the start of his most sombre career as a pessimist, and when Emile Vuillermoz (as we must call a spade a spade) tells us in realistic terms that music, which has been 'injured, mutilated and gassed' by the war, is definitely 'very ill, the whole world over', an athletic fresh, young, frank and serene work comes to dispel our fears and sweep away these many sinister rumours.

Le roi David is not the exception which makes the rule. Its title is a symbol, its triumph a sign, and it is heartening. The fact alone that such a work has been conceived and worked out at a time like now, by a twenty-nine year old musician, proves to us with conviction that, if there is something rotten in the kingdom of France, it is definitely *not* music.]

Wenn wir uns einem modernen Werk ungehemmt hingeben, so bedeutet das ein gewaltiges Ereignis. Honeggers *König David* hat, was unwahrscheinlich, ja ein Wunder scheinen musste, vollbracht: seit vielen Jahren zum ersten Male steht ein musikalisches Werk vor uns, gegen das unser Empfinden in keiner Beziehung eine Verneinung vorzubringen vermöchte.

Hans David, 'Arthur Honeggers *König David', Melos,* February 1927, 83-85 (p. 83).

[If we are able to surrender ourselves completely to a modern work, that signifies an important occasion. Honegger's *Le roi David* has achieved something which must appear unlikely, even as a miracle: for the first time in many years, a piece of music has been put before us which in no sense could produce in us a feeling of negation when listening to it.]

*The Muse of Music.

The root causes of the unstable musical situation in Paris in the years immediately following the First World War were, simultaneously, the fact that Paris had been the focal point of all the cultural arts for some years and hence the centre to a greater or lesser extent of most of the spiritual and physical revolutions that had taken place in all of them, the death of Debussy and the unnerving *fin-de-siècle* nostalgia that had been revived and prolonged by the previously unknown experience of a world war. It was this instability that fostered and nurtured *Les Six* through the personage of Jean Cocteau. Ironically though, just as Honegger was the odd-man-out of the group at its very inception and was to benefit only from the public attention accorded them by virtue of the extreme of their majority *enfant terrible* standpoint, it was precisely the instability of the social atmosphere which permitted and encouraged them that was, however, to prove insufficient and unreliable and in a swift and irrevocable counter-reaction condemn them and proclaim Honegger 'Le roi Arthur'[11] in recognition of his musical integrity, honesty and, above all else, sincerity.

When all the attacks of such bewildering variety, which came from both outside and within, are taken into account, it is surely not surprising that the cultural climate in Paris can be seen to have been so contrary in its patronage and that ultimately it would demand the quality of sincerity by way of compensation. Honegger was accorded the support and acclaim of both the public and critics and assumed the role of 'leader of the French School' in succession to Debussy, a position he had not sought to fill but one into which he threw himself and supported until it passed quite naturally and without contention to Messiaen. An assessment of Honegger's success and achievement during the years he wore this mantle lies in a consideration of his work — in particular the dramatic music that ensues from *Le roi David* in the light of Honegger's comment in 1951 that

> det mottagande som verket fick efter sitt första uppförande styrker mig i min uppfattning och i mina försök att skapa en konst som vänder sig direkt till alla, till musiker lika väl som till åhörare[12]
>
> [the reception which the work had after its first performance strengthened me in my understanding, and in my efforts to create an art which is direct in every way, both with regard to the music itself and to the listener].

Notes to Chapter II

[1]'Young French Composers', *The Chesterian*, New Series no. 2 (October 1919), 33-37 (p. 35).

[2]'Arthur Honegger', *The Chesterian*, New Series no. 19 (December 1921), 65-69 (p. 65 and p. 69).

[3]'Œuvres nouvelles d'Arthur Honegger', *La Revue Musicale*, January 1921, 65-67 (p. 66).

[4]Situated in the small village of Mézières in the Canton of Vaud, Switzerland. For an account of biographical aspects of this and the other three Morax-Honegger collaborations at this theatre see Pierre Meylan, *René Morax et Arthur Honegger au Théâtre du Jorat* (Editions du Cervin, Lausanne, 1966 and Librairie E. Ploix, Paris, 1966).

[5]The original scoring was for 2 flutes (1st doubling piccolo), oboe (doubling cor anglais), 2 clarinets (2nd doubling bass clarinet), bassoon; horn, 2 trumpets, trombone; timpani; percussion (cymbals, side drum, bass drum, gong and tambourine), celesta, harmonium, piano; double bass (and cello ad lib.).

[6]Decca LTX 5321-2 — conducted by Ernest Ansermet.

[7]In fact Mr Drew is chronologically wrong — the two performances in question took place in 1929 with Arthur Honegger conducting the second. A most interesting article by the producer and translator, Denis Arundell, detailing these performances appeared as *'King David', The Listener,* 6 January 1966, 40.

[8]See also Graham George, *Tonality and Musical Structure,* (Faber and Faber, London, 1970), particularly his theories of interlocking tonal structures in eighteenth and nineteenth century large-scale dramatic works; and also F. R. C. Clarke, 'The Structure of R. Vaughan Williams' *Sea Symphony', The Music Review,*February 1973, 58-61.

[9]'Honegger om *Konung David*', *Röster i Radio*, No. 14 (1951), 4-5 (p.4).

[10]Quoted by Bernard Gavoty in *I am a Composer* (Faber and Faber, London, 1966), 93-94.

[11]This accolade was accorded to Honegger after the first performance of *Le roi David* — see André George, *Arthur Honegger* (Claude Aveline, Paris, 1926), 107.

[12]'Honegger om *Konung David', Röster i Radio,* no. 14, 1951, 4-5 (p.5).

CHAPTER III

First interlude: consolidation

The works between *Le roi David* and *Judith*

> If I still participate in a state of things in their last stages it is because it seems to me indispensable that, to progress, we must be solidly linked with what has preceded us. We must not break the tie with musical tradition.[1]

> As far as I am concerned, symphonic works give me much trouble: they demand an effort at sustained reflection.[2]

> I experience great difficulty in determining the frame for my work. To me, a symphonic piece must be built logically without the possibility of interjecting the slightest anecdotal element between its different parts. I repeat: one must give the impression of a composition in which all is linked, the image of a predetermined structure. It has been said that architecture is frozen music. I should rather say that it is a geometry in time. Here, as elsewhere, one must be very exacting, so as to achieve an absolute equilibrium.[3]

> What gives unity to a piece of music is the totality of melodic and rhythmic relationships . . . We should concern ourselves more with the architectural proportions . . . melodic and especially rhythmic balances . . . Listeners must be able to let themselves be carried along by melodic lines or rhythmic values, without concern for other matters.[4]

Honegger's unassailable belief in the need to build upon the past rather than to reject or ignore it and his preoccupation with giving satisfactory form to his music are both features that are evident in every one of his works. In the scores of this period — between the completion of *Le roi David* and his next major work, *Judith*, another *drame-biblique* by Morax for the Théâtre du Jorat production of 1925 — there is, however, particular evidence of his conscious effort in experimenting with the renewal, adaptation and development of traditional aspects of form and tonality in conjunction with his views on melodic and rhythmic relationships and equilibria.

In 1923 he experimented in a purely original symphonic score with a 'very abstract and quite ideal concept . . . the impression of a mathematical acceleration of rhythm, while the movement itself slowed.'[5] The movement is shaped as a 'chorale prelude' of the type found in some of the late examples of J. S. Bach, where the 'chorale' is not stated in its entirety in 'cantus-firmus' fashion until near the end — the preceding musical fabric having been constructed from anticipatory fragments and versions.

The piece, *Mouvement symphonique nº 1*, is better known by its subtitle *Pacific 231*. The acceleration induced by increasing the rhythmic subdivision against the decrease in tempo is represented in Diagram 9 below.

Diagram 9:

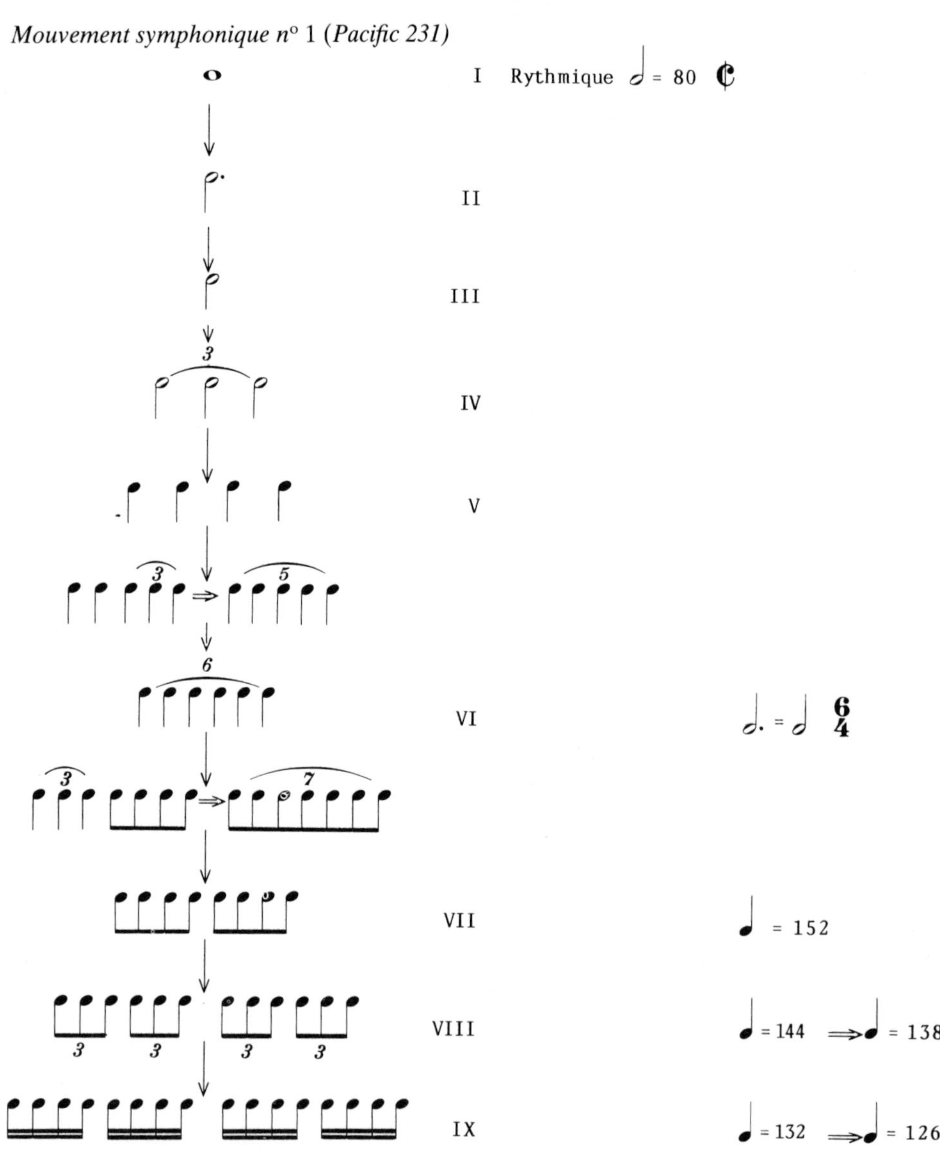

The Roman numerals in Diagram 9 can be used to link this to a summary of an analysis (see Diagram 10 below) in relation to Music Examples 13 and 14 (pages 66 - 67). (N.B.: the rehearsal numbers used in Diagram 10 below relate to the Senart/Salabert 1924 edition.)

Diagram 10:

Mouvement symphonique n°1 (Pacific 231)

- [1]	Elements of 'cantus-firmus' version β constitute harmonic fabric
[1] - [2]	Rhythmic subdivisions I-IV; Melodic shape 1
[2] - [3]	'Cantus-firmus' version β delineates harmonic fabric; Rhythmic subdivision V
[3] -7A [3]	Melodic shape 2
8B [4] -2B [4]	'Cantus-firmus' version γ hidden in harmonic fabric
[4] -8A [4]	Melodic shape 3
9A [4] - [5]	Rhythmic subdivision VI
[5] -6A [5]	Development of melodic shape 3 (Trumpets)
7A [5] - [8]	Rhythmic subdivision VII; [6] - Melodic shape 4^a anticipated rhythmically by 4^{a1}; [7]- Growth of melodic shape 4^b; Imitative use of melodic shape 4^b; Stretto treatment of melodic shape 4^a
[8] - [9]	Development by rhythmic diminution of melodic shape $2 \rightarrow 2^a$; Fragmentation of melodic shape 4^b; 5A[8]- 'Cantus-firmus' — truncated version δ
[9] - [11]	Melodic shape 5 and harmonic ostinato 5^a; Rhythmic subdivision VIII; Imitative treatment of melodic shape 5; [10]- New version of melodic shape 3 by rhythmic diminution $\rightarrow 3^a$
[11]- [12]	Development of fragment (x) from melodic shape 4^a and scale as counter-subject to melodic shape 5
[12]- [13]	Development of elements of melodic shapes 4^a and 4^b; 'Cantus-firmus' opening in version φ; Imitative use of melodic shape 4^a
[13]- [14]	Rhythmic subdivision IX using elements of 'Cantus-firmus' version ∅; Melodic shapes 2^a and 4^b
[14]- [17]	'Cantus-firmus' (version α) played by brass with elements of melodic shapes 2^a, 3^a, 4^a, 4^b and 5 used as counter-subjects
[17]- end	Rhythmic subdivisions VIII $\rightarrow$I in 12 bars

---

Music Example 13: *Pacific 231*

(* n.b. The second and third notes of each bar are played an octave lower)

Music Example 14: *Pacific 231,* Melodic shapes

3.
(Rythmique = 80)
4
Hns
marcato
etc.
4a1.
(Rythmique = 80)
Hns
f
marcato
6
4a.
(Rythmique = 80)
6
Bsns
marcato
x
7
etc.
4b.
(Rythmique = 80)
7
Vlas
marcato
pizz.
etc.
5.
(= 144)
9
Ca/cls

It is possible to interrelate much of the melodic material designated 1-5 with the 'cantus-firmus' itself by virtue of the parallel frequency of certain predominant intervals — notably that of a fifth. The consistency of approach extends, too, to relatively minor aspects of the textures — the discipline being complete in a way that is analagous to the technique used by Ravel in his *Bolero*, even if far more complex. Less clear-cut in its definition, but omnipotent in its overall contribution to the equilibrium of the whole is the force of tonality — the opening pedal G♯ acting as a dominant of the final C♯.

In conjunction with the score such a tabular analysis will suffice to show the totality of melodic and rhythmic relationships for which he was striving; this not only unifies the work in such an invincible way but also gives new life to the traditional 'chorale-prelude' form. The counterpoint is often extremely complex, but, as with his mentor J. S. Bach, always thoroughly logical and integrated. There is a strength, grandeur and passion which have been compared to the physicality of such works as *Tristan und Isolde* and *Salomé*, whilst also being used as criteria to compare the work to other 'songs of modern life'[6] by composers including Prokofiev (*Le pas d'acier*), Alkan (*Chemin de fer*) and Antheil (*Airplane Sonata*, *Ballet mécanique*, and *Mécanismes*). Honegger was undoubtedly reckless to allow what he termed a 'romantic idea' to prompt him to add the subtitle *Pacific 231* to the score.[7] The vast amount of publicity the work received on the basis of this title conveniently brought Honegger further into the public eye, but it also resulted in much adverse criticism because some refused to believe that the music was anything but purely onomatopoeic in the very worst way with which the Expressionists could be credited. After refusing to accept the work because it was unsingable and unhummable (sic), the irate Constant Lambert dismissed Honegger's comments about the genesis of the subtitle as merely an 'ingenuous disclaimer'[8].

The anonymous critic of *The Musical Mirror* mistakenly and alarmingly compared Honegger's work with that of Georges Antheil who held the view that 'one cannot continue digging up old forms of music, and after titivating about a little bit turn them into new melody. It is necessary to concentrate on something entirely new.'[9] But this is hardly surprising when Honegger was again so incautious as publicly to admit to liking trains as other men liked women.[10] Few critics were able to get past the subtitle and examine the work for what it was and how it was conceived — most were content to note in a benignant way a young man's healthy interest in the mechanical age and the power and speed of the modern life it symbolized. The all-important aspects of simplicity and classicality of the highly disciplined thought and procedure went unnoticed; only Roland-Manuel hailed it as the most rigorously ordered, powerful and original work Honegger had ever written.[11]

The *Concertino* for piano and orchestra provides many interesting parallels. The first movement contains a wonderful blend of the essential elements of ritornello form with the principle of the old Baroque concerto-grosso style, within an ABA[1] framework. The totality of melodic and rhythmic relationships in the third movement is even more remarkable than in the *Mouvement symphonique nº 1* in view of the relative proliferation of melodic material. In this work the forces of symmetry are particularly potent: the overall form of the whole as well as the individual movements, and the tonal scheme, with its customary dependence on tertiary relationships, interact with a most satisfying resultant symmetry (see Diagram 11 below).

Diagram 11:

Concertino for piano and orchestra

		Form	Rehearsal numbers	Principal tonalities
first movement	:	(A)	- [2]	E
(*Allegro molto moderato*)		Transition	[2] -3A [2]	prep. for:
		(B)	4A [2] - [7]	C/c
		(A[1])	[7] - [10]	E
second movement	:		[10] - [14]	B♭/b♭
(*Larghetto sostenuto*)				g ([13]-)
third movement	:	Introduction	[14] - [15]	prep. for:
(*Allegro*)		(A)	[15] - [19]	G
		(B)	[19] - [23]	e♭
		(A[1])	[23] -	G♭
				G([26]-)

> Les œuvres de Ravel possèdent une précision dans leur disposition générale, une clarté dans le dessin des lignes, une concision un peu sèche dans leur langage, malgré une expression lyrique à peine contenue; qualités qui distinguent l'auteur de *Daphnis et Chloë*.[12]
>
> [Ravel's works possess a precision in their general disposition, a clarity in the design of the lines and a fairly dry conciseness in their language, despite a scarcely restrained lyrical expression. These are the qualities which distinguish the composer of *Daphnis et Chloë*.]

Honegger constantly strove to attain the characteristics he saw and admired in Ravel so that his musical language would not undermine the selfsame qualities that emanated from his disciplined formal procedures. In the *Chant de joie* which he dedicated to Ravel there are shining examples of this discipleship. The clarity and concision of the highly symmetrical ABA[1] form is mirrored in the melodic lines and the harmonic tissue that support them. The strong parallels to melodic characteristics in *Le roi David* and *Pastorale d'été* reinforce this aspect.

There is still a certain heavy-handed Germanic feeling about some of the phrase structures — the shadow of Richard Strauss still looms occasionally — and there is a rather overtly Impressionistic glaze on some of the parallel chord textures, but they rarely detract to any significant degree. The polyphony is logical, organic and comprehensible at all times; the use of canon, in particular, is highly skilled and controlled. Nowhere can be found the rather effete counterpoint that plagues the *Trois contrepoints* and which provides an unfortunate link with some of the contrapuntal movements in *Le roi David.*

Qualities of clarity and concision also pervade the *Cahier romand* — five short pieces for piano, each dedicated to a particular Swiss friend. They are very similar in vein to the *Sept pièces brèves* and all the typical Honeggerian features are to be found in them, ranging from the quasi folk-song melody of No. 5, the love for contrary-motion procedures (Nos. 1 and 2) and the contrapuntally-conceived harmonic richness of No. 3, to the rhythmic excitement and almost audacious syncopations of No. 4 which hark back to the 'Psaume: 'Dans cet effroi' (No. 25) of *Le roi David.* (The latter's dedicatee, Paul Boepple, was the chorus-master at the Théâtre du Jorat.) The concentration of means on a very short time-scale was a characteristic that Satie had urged upon the composers of *Les nouveaux jeunes*, by self-example more than anything, and to which Honegger had not untypically taken in his own way in works such as these. The same combination of spontaneity and brevity characterizes the *Sonatine* for clarinet and piano. The clarity and conciseness of thought behind the first movement, together with the simplicity of the melodic material employed, give it a strong feeling of *Les Six*. The quality of the melodic line in the slow movement — Poulenc, of the late instrumental sonatas in particular — and the use of jazz-influenced rhythms and glissandi in the Finale, do little to dispel this (see Music Example 15 below).

Music Example 15: *Sonatine* for clarinet and piano:
(i) first movement, clarinet part, 3B C -7A D

(ii) second movement, clarinet part, bars 1-9

(Reproduit avec l'autorisation des EDITIONS SALABERT, Paris, propriétaires de l'œuvre.)

(iii) Finale, clarinet part, C - end

(Reproduit avec l'autorisation des EDITIONS SALABERT, Paris, propriétaires de l'œuvre.)

The jazz elements here are as integrated into the very spirit of the music as they are with Milhaud in *La création du monde*. On the other two occasions in which they appear prominently in Honegger's work (the third movement of the *Piano Concertino* and the later *Cello Concerto*) the synthesis and blend are again perfect — interestingly the mediums are essentially the same in their use of the *concertante* principle.

The other work of this period which the spirit of *Les Six* permeates is his collection of settings of poems by Jean Cocteau, entitled *Six poésies*. Of the three not already discussed, 'Une danseuse' with its grotesque mimicry comes close to paralleling the music of the so-called '*Les Six* aesthetic'. The sensuousness of 'Madame' and the fervent quality of 'Ex voto', however, act as a firm reminder that it is Honegger in question, not Auric; the position is again as it was with the first three songs (see Chapter I, pages 40-44).

Music Example 16: *Six poésies de Jean Cocteau*:
(i) No. 4 'Ex voto'

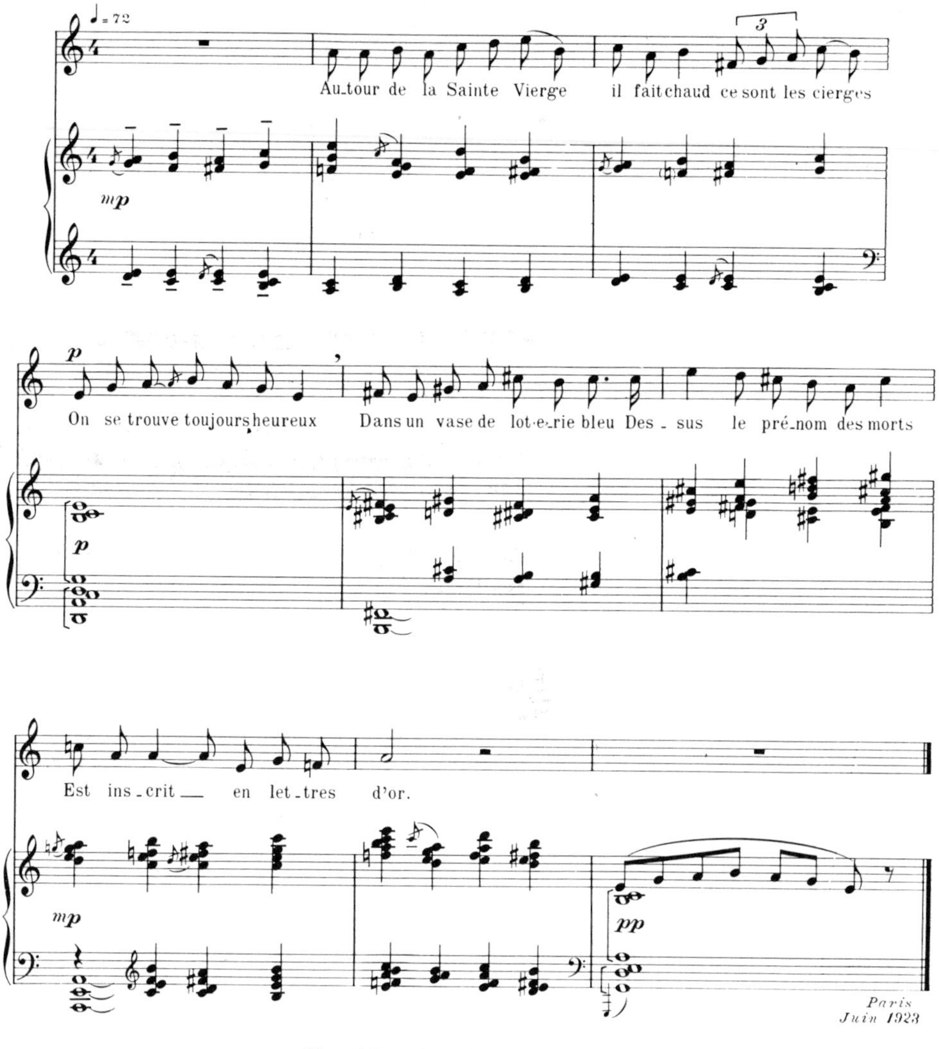

Au-tour de la Sainte Vierge il fait chaud ce sont les cierges

On se trouve toujours heureux Dans un vase de lot-e-rie bleu Des - sus le pré-nom des morts

Est ins-crit en let-tres d'or.

Paris
Juin 1923

(ii) No. 5 'Une danseuse'

poin_tes A _ vec ses bras en cor_beil _ le il sou_rit jusqu'aux o _ reil _ les

La dan _ seu _ se d'opé _ ra Au cra _ be toute pa _
p léger
_reil _ le Sort dans la coulisse pein _ te En arrondissant les bras
Paris
Juin
1923

(Reproduit avec l'autorisation des EDITIONS SALABERT, Paris, propriétaires de l'œuvre.)

(iii) No. 6 'Madame'

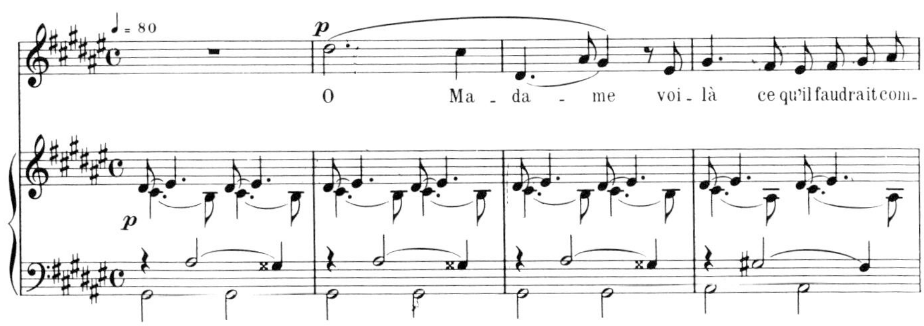
♩ = 80
p
O Ma _ da _ me voi _ là ce qu'il faudrait com_
p

-pren - dre vous me di-tes toujours que vous aimez le beau le beau qui ça ?
le beau Léan-dre
Paris
Janvier 1923

There are several important conclusions to be drawn from a consideration of a list of the works from this period (see Table 4 below).

TABLE 4

Compositions between *Le roi David* and *Judith*

1921	*Skating Rink* — Ballet Music.
1922	*Saül* — Incidental Music; *Sonatine* for Clarinet and Piano; *Trois contrepoints* — Chamber Music; *Antigone* — Incidental Music; *Fantasio* — Ballet Music.
1923	*Chant de joie* — Orchestra; *La tempête* — Incidental Music; *Liluli* — Incidental Music; *Chanson de Fagus* for Voice and Ensemble; *Six poésies* for Voice and Piano; *Le cahier romand* for Piano; *La roue* — Film Score; *Mouvement symphonique n° 1* (*Pacific 231*) for Orchestra.
1924	*Chanson* for Voice and Ensemble; *Sous-marine* — Ballet Music; *Concertino* for Piano and Orchestra; [*Fait divers*] — Film Score (unfinished)].
1925	*Prélude et Blues* — Chamber Music.

The sheer number and variety of commissions he fulfilled is both a reflection of the diversity of his talent and of the degree of respect and acclaim he had been accorded, particularly when one considers the stature of his collaborators. The most tangible result of the success of *Le roi David* in this respect is the heavy demand placed upon him to write incidental music, ballet and film scores (see Tables 1, 2 and 7 on pages 18-20, 20-21 and 242 respectively) — a pressure that persisted throughout his life to his financial benefit but not entirely to his artistic fulfilment (see Chapter VIII, 'The Crisis').

> As far as I am concerned, symphonic works give me much trouble: they demand an effort at sustained reflection. On the contrary, as soon as I can refer to a literary or visual pretext, my work becomes much easier . . . When the scenario of a ballet or a film is submitted to me . . . I very quickly imagine the appropriate music for such and such a passage . . . the subject is supplied by the picture, which immediately suggests to me a musical translation . . . the work was relatively easy, for I possess the necessary technique to write an orchestral score swiftly.[13]

Here, already, is the framework for Honegger's entire career — substantial collaboration with the aspects of the visual arts requiring music which finances his own personal creative work.

Notes to Chapter III

[1]Arthur Honegger, *I am a Composer* (Faber and Faber, London, 1966), 93.
[2]Ibid., 80-81.
[3]Ibid., 78-79.
[4]Ibid., 82-83, 70.
[5]Arthur Honegger, *I am a Composer* (Faber and Faber, London, 1966), 101.
[6]See A. Hoéreé, 'A. Honegger et les locomotives', *Revue Pleyel,* August 1927, 347-51 (p. 348).
[7]See Arthur Honegger, *I am a Composer* (Faber and Faber, London, 1966), 101.
[8]'Railway Music', *Nation,* 16 August 1930, 620-21 (p. 620).
[9]Anon., 'Machine Music', *Musical Mirror,* March 1925, 49.
[10]See André George, *Arthur Honegger* (Claude Aveline, Paris, 1926), 104.
[11]*Arthur Honegger* (Editions Senart, Paris, 1925), 23-25. An authoritative discussion of both the score and the problems concerning its subtitle is to be found in Kurt von Fischer's contribution to the *Festschrift Hans Conradin* (Verlag Paul Haupt, Bern and Stuttgart, 1983), pages 227-32, entitled 'Arthur Honeggers *Pacific 231* — Zum Problem des Realismus in der Musik'.
[12]A. Honegger, 'Ravel et le Debussysme', *Revue Musicale,* December 1938, 258-59.
[13]Arthur Honegger, *I am a Composer* (Faber and Faber, London, 1966), 80-81.

CHAPTER IV

Judith: transition

Given the triumphant success of *Le roi David* it was to be expected that it would only be a matter of time before Morax and Honegger collaborated on another biblical drama — and so it was that the Théâtre du Jorat saw the production of *Judith* in the summer of 1925. The basic concept remained unaltered —a theatrical production along lines very similar to the early English masques — but, as a detailed consideration of the score will show, there are two most important differences.

In the first instance there is the question of the number and size of the musical movements. The score for *Le roi David* is diffuse — twenty-seven numbers, all but two of which are extremely short when compared to the thirteen† movements of *Judith* where, on the contrary, only two are rather brief. In addition, movements in Parts I and III are joined together to form even larger blocks which result in the music contributing much more to the cohesion of the whole.

The techniques of thematic and tonal correspondences which were evident in embryonic form in the score for *Le roi David* are fully realized and exploited in this work. The important thematic correspondences are detailed in Nos. 1-7 below (see also Diagram 12, page 82).

(1) The 'grief motives':

the four fragments (a-d) which appear at the beginning of No. 1 are developed into thematic ideas which represent the grief of the people of Judith as they await the seemingly inevitable fate at the hands of Holopherne and his army. In addition, (e) and (f) appear in No. 2 'La trompe d'alarme', and serve the same function (see Music Example 17 opposite). Some or all of these motives are found in the movements where this grief is expressed, namely Nos. 3, 4 and 10.*

†Strictly speaking, there are sixteen — see Diagram 12, page 82.

*N.B. certain movements in the vocal score (EMS 6718) are heavily cut and others are omitted entirely—only the full score (EMS 7098) presents the complete incidental music and all references are made to this.

Music Example 17: *Judith*:
(i) No. 1 'Lamentations', bars 1-10

D

(ii) No. 2 'La trompe d'alarme', trombones, bars 4-13

(iii) No. 2 'La trompe d'alarme', horns and trombones, 1-2A 15

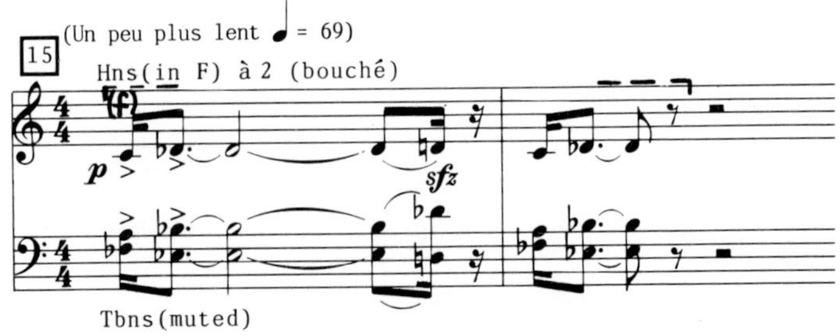

(2) The 'danger' motif:

representing the danger that Holopherne and his army present to Judith and her people. Most effective use of this (in combination with 'grief' motif (c)) is made in the 'Nocturne' which symbolizes the uneasy sleep of the people to whom the triumphant return of Judith is as yet unknown (see Music Example 18 below).

Music Example 18: *Judith*, No. 2 'La trompe d'alarme', strings, 1-4A [13]

(3) The two *vocalises*:

the first, (i), representing the initially frightened women in the besieged city; the second, (ii), forming the basis for their subsequent songs of thanksgiving (see Music Example 19 below).

Music Example 19: *Judith*:
(i) No. 2 'La trompe d'alarme', 3B [14] — 1A [14]

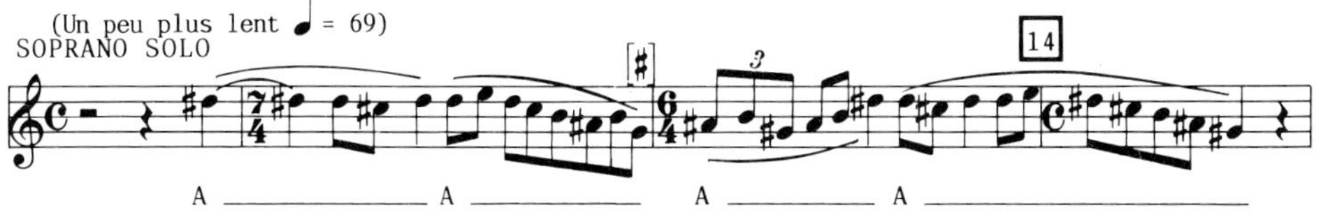

(ii) No. 11b 'Interlude', 2nd clarinet, 1-2A [21]

(4) Judith's motif/(5) Hope/faith — Jehovah motif:

the framework of Judith's opening melody (see Music Example 20 below) and of all her lines throughout the work is, characteristically, a minor seventh arpeggio.

Music Example 20: *Judith*, No. 1 'Lamentations', 3A [1] — 3A [2]

- el courbé dans la poussiè - re
cresc.

To support this there is a continuous derivation of much subsidiary material in subsequent movements from this basic characteristic of her lines to illustrate the connection of the dramatic events with the central figure of Judith:

(a) 'La trompe d'alarme':

  (i) the initial celli/bass ostinato (A);

  (ii) the trumpet call (9 -);

  (iii) the first *vocalise* (3B 14 -);

(b) 'Cantique funèbre':

  the first *vocalise* becomes the solo soprano line 5-7A 22, and this is subsequently taken up by the chorus after 24;

(c) 'Retour de Judith': opening ostinato;

(d) 'Cantique de la bataille': chorus parts.

Furthermore, in the drama good vanquishes evil. God triumphs in the person of Judith and Honegger portrays this very successfully in the music by shaping the motifs which suggest the hope of peace and salvation through the actions inspired by Judith's faith from a similar set of prominent diatonic intervals, but, in the *major* key. The ostinato (3B 12) supports the 'hope/faith' motif when it first appears (horns 2B 12) in the same way as the minor version did at the opening of the piece (No. 2, 'La trompe d'alarme'). This motif, representing hope through faith, exists side by side with Judith's opening *minore* thematic material in the 'Prière' whilst she expresses her doubts as to her ability and asks for God's guidance and strength. In Part III, as the 'Jehovah' motif, it dominates four of the last five movements whilst Judith tells her people that her personal deed was achieved with the help of God through her own faith and that, through their faith, victory over the leaderless enemy is close at hand. The simplicity of the major-minor interface is reinforced by the major arpeggio patterning of the second *vocalise* with which the women express their thanksgiving and also by the predominantly major mode tonality in Part III as a contrast to the *minore* of the first *vocalise* and the nearly consistent use of the minor mode in the first two Parts.

(6) Not only fragments, but subsequently the whole of the music of No. 6 ('Fanfare') returns in No. 8.

(7) Battle fanfares common to both movements (see [4] in both cases).

Diagram 12:

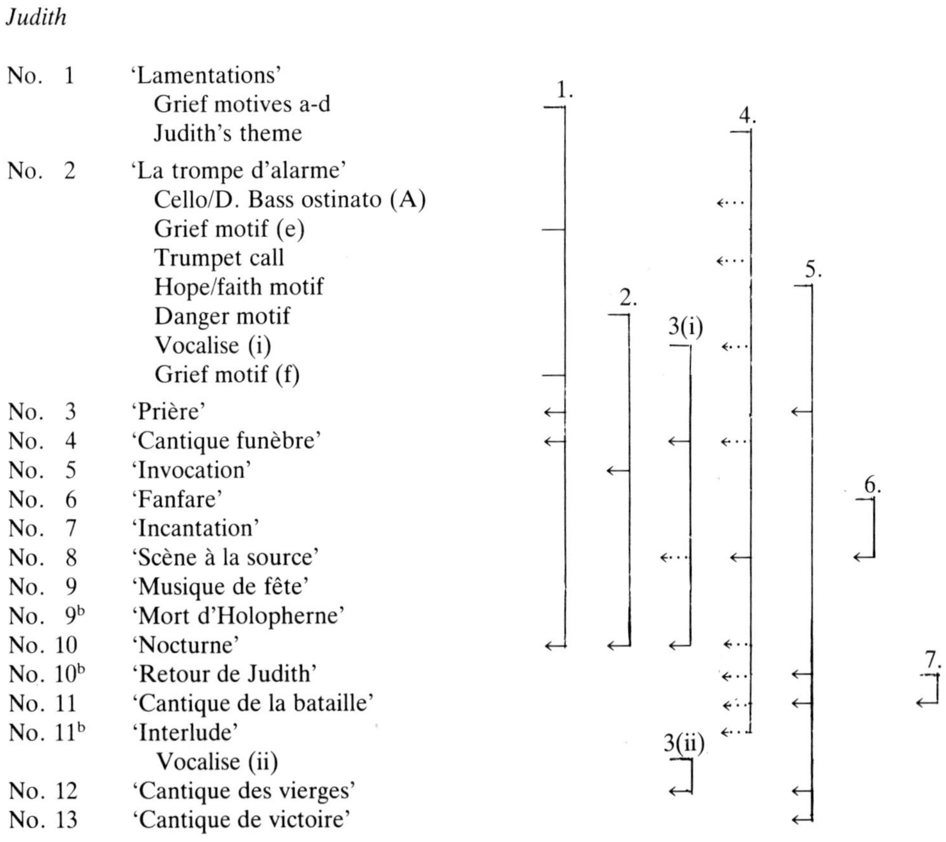

Tonally, there are several different constituent forces at work (see Diagram 13 opposite and the commentary on page 87).

Diagram 13:

Judith — a summary of the principal tonalities

PART I

No. 1 'Lamentations'

Principal tonalities :	Prep. for	e♭	g	f	e	b♭	g	e♭ (but closes on a c minor chord)
Bar references :		3A[1]	[4]	4A[4]	2B[5]	[5]	3A[5]	[6]

No. 2. 'La trompe d'alarme'

Principal tonalities : Polytonal combinations of the melodic tonalities of D♭/d-D/f and e♭
Bar references :

on dom. of D♭	e	g♯	on dom. of D♭	a	e♭	via a pedal D to No. 3 ('Prière')
3A[11] - 1B[13]	2A[13]	2B[14]	[14]	3B[15]	[15]	

No. 3 'Prière'

Principal tonalities :	Prep. for	E	f	f♯	e♭	E	via a pedal D to	e (with final *tierce de picardie*)
Bar references :		[17]	2B[18]	3A[19]	2B[20]	1A[20]		5A[21]

No. 4 'Cantique funèbre'

Principal tonalities :	b	f	b
Bar references :		[23]	1B[24]

Continued overleaf

No. 5 'Invocation'

Principal tonalities	:	e	E	f	F	f♯	G♭	A
Bar references	:	2	4	5	7	9	11	15

No. 6 'Fanfare'

Principal tonalities : G♭ pedal supporting a combination of the melodic tonalities of B♭, A♭, D♭ and E♭
Bar references :

PART II

No. 7 'Incantation'

Principal tonalities	:	e	f	e (but closing in a)
Bar references	:		[3]	[4]

No. 8 'Scene à la source'

Principal tonalities	:	Opening prep. for e also embraces foundations for an exact tonal reference to No. 6 ('Fanfare')	e	C
Bar references	:	3B[1]	[1]	1A[2]

Principal tonalities	:	e but closing in F♯	for a repeat of No. 6 ('Fanfare')		e (but closing in F♯)
Bar references	:	6A[2]	1B[3]	[3] - [4]	2A[4]

No. 9 'Musique de fête'

Principal tonality : (b)

No. 9^b 'Mort d'Holopherne'

Principal tonalities	:	over pedal a	over pedal b♭	over pedal b	over pedal d♯	close in a
Bar references	:		1B[2]	[3]	[4]	

PART III

No. 10 'Nocturne'

Principal tonalities	:	c	b	a	B	c
Bar references	:		4a[1]	[2]	[3]	6B[4]

No. 10^b 'Retour de Judith'

Principal tonalities	:	e♭	G over a dom. pedal	e♭	d	f♯	g
Bar references	:		[2]	[3]	[4]	3B[5]	[5]

No. 11 'Cantique de la bataille'

Principal tonalities	:	g	e♭	g	e♭	c♯	on dom. of D	g	e	on dom. of D♭	B♭
Bar references	:		[1]	[2]	[3]	[4]	[6]	2B[7]	[8]	3A[8]	6A[8]

Continued overleaf

No. 11^{b} 'Interlude'

Principal tonality : Prep. for No. 12 ('Cantique des vierges')

No. 12 'Cantique des vierges'

Principal tonalities	:	D♭	c♯	D♭
Bar references	:		4B[2]	5A[2]

No. 13 'Cantique de victoire'

Principal tonalities	:	Prep. for	D	D♭	on dom. of C	on dom of E	e♭	on dom. of E	c
Bar references	:		6A[2]	[3]	[5]	6B[6]	[7]	[8]	[9]

Principal tonalities	:	on dom of F	e	g	b♭	c♯	E	on dom of D	on dom of F	on dom of D	D
Bar references	:	6A[9]	10B[10]	4B[10]	[10]	5A[10]	[11]	[12]	6A[12]	[13]	[15]

In the light of the works discussed in Chapter III, the consistency of tonal relationships of a tertiary nature is not surprising. There is a symmetry in Nos. 8 and 10 which is typical in the way it acts in conjunction with the quasi-mosaic patterning of the architectural form. In the latter movement the tertiary aspect is extended in that the keys involved are all contained within a single overall interval of a third. This latter procedure is at work on a larger scale in the first half (as far as 4B **[10]**) of the 'Cantique de victoire' (No. 13), to a powerful effect.

It is surely more than coincidence that the key which Honegger chose in *Le roi David* for the movements where David expressed his personal faith (Nos. 2, 6, 9 and 24 — see Chapter II, page 54) — E major — is the same key that radiantly concludes Judith's 'Prière', where there is a similar confirmation of belief; and, furthermore, that the resounding jubilance of the final chorus expressing the rekindled faith of the peoples in both works is primarily set to a blazingly colourful D major.

However, apart from the tonal correspondence resulting from the fact that the music of No. 6 ('Fanfare') which concludes Part I reappears in Part II during No. 8 ('Scène à la source'), obvious considerations of tonal balance within individual movements, and devices to aid the linking of movements (the V — I resolution between Nos. 8 and 9 for example), large-scale tonal planning is not so intricate as was the case in *Le roi David*.

It has already been pointed out (page 76) that the larger size and smaller number of musical items constitutes the fundamental difference between *Judith* and *Le roi David*. The second important difference concerns the presence of a central character. The role of David was diffuse and although Honegger made an effort to characterize his development in the music (see Chapter II, page 55), the drama as a whole was weakened through the absence of a character who provided a single focal point. There is no such fault in *Judith* and the music does much to establish and maintain her character throughout the work and emphasize the fact that the entire drama centres around her. The aspects of a technique of thematic correspondences which Honegger used to achieve this again come as no surprise in view of the immediately preceding works.

The results of the experiments in the works that precede *Judith* (discussed in Chapter III) towards a system of melodic relationships which would be a major factor in the architectural structure of a work are evident in this piece. The achievement was a score for a theatrical production which had many of the attributes of a good opera. This was appreciated by Raoul Gunsbourg, the Director of the Monte Carlo Opera House, and he quickly persuaded Honegger to rework the score as an *opéra-sérieux*. This was done during November and December 1925 and it received its first performance in Monte Carlo on 13 February 1926. The music also attracted many further performances in a concert version — *action-musicale* — constructed in the same way as that for the music of *Le roi David*.

> C'est avant tout une action simple, serrée et dramatique. Au moment où nombre de jeunes musiciens reviennent volontiers à l'ancien opéra-bouffe, j'ai voulu reprendre le vieux cadre italien de l'opéra sérieux.[1]
>
> [It is, above all, a simple, compact and dramatic action. At a time when many young musicians willingly return to the ancient form of *opera buffa*, I wanted instead to take up the old Italian frame of *opera seria*.]

Due to the rigorous discipline of the score which he provided as incidental music, the task of transforming it into an opera was not great, and was achieved with a relatively small amount of additional material. In Act I — which includes all the music from Part I of the original except the 'Fanfare' — the only necessary move was to introduce the sung role of Ozias. This is neatly accomplished between 6[B] and 8, which correspond to the end of the former No. 1, 'Lamentations', and the beginning of No. 2, 'La trompe d'alarme'.* The music is based on the 'grief motives' and so provides a sort of recapitulatory coda by way of transition between the two formerly separate movements. Nos 2 to 5 had run concurrently in the original anyway, so there was no specific demand for any more music; but Honegger, appreciating the weakness of having introduced Ozias and not then allowing his character and function to be extended, explored and related to the other solo characters, inserted a scene for Judith and him (26 - 31) between the former 'Cantique funèbre' and 'Invocation'. There are five bars of new material before use is made of the already familiar 'danger motif' as Ozias tries to prevent Judith going away by reasoning with her. Judith's replies (27 -) are supported by a return of motives from her 'Prière' culminating in an attestation that her faith will bring God's infallible help with it: this occurs as the 'hope/faith — Jehovah' motif sounds in the orchestra (30 -). The gradual return of the new material (26 - 5A 26) after 29 provides this insertion with a most satisfying ABA[1] structure which ensures that it fits in perfectly.

A comparison of Acts I and II in relation to Parts I and II reveal that considerably more alteration was made to Part II in order that it should stand as Act II. The 'Fanfare' which closed Part I was not used in Act I but instead opens Act II. The four items that made up Part II are rearranged, and a relatively large amount of new music is added to permit the exposition of the character Holopherne — previously an entirely spoken role.

In the original, the scene was prepared for psychologically by the previous 'Fanfare' and actually opened in Holopherne's camp with the 'Incantation'. Judith's scene at the fountain just outside the city walls followed, before the 'Musique de fête' returned the action to Holopherne's camp. In the opera the 'Fanfare' fulfils the same function, but the fountain scene follows it with the return of the fanfare music which is built into it, heralding the completion of their journey to Holopherne's camp and the start of the music associated with it. The result in operatic terms is far superior because the drama progresses organically and avoids the alternating static tableau effect ('Action — Contemplation — Action') of the original stage version.

* All references are made to the vocal score of the opera. Although this bears the same plate number (EMS 6938) as the vocal score of the original incidental music, the two are clearly identifiable from the title pages. In the vocal score of the opera there are two figure 6's; for convenience I have regarded the one on page 6 as 6[A] and that on page 7 as 6[B].

The 'Musique de fête' follows on immediately from the 'Incantation' — the added two-bar modulatory link (10-11A [11]), serves as the moment when Holopherne first appears on the scene from his tent, and constitutes his principal motif. The character of Holopherne is revealed in a conversation held with Bagoas (his second-in-command), which is set to essentially new music (1A [11]^{d} - 3A [15]), with the occasional use of the main motives from the 'Incantation' fixing its relevance (see after [11]^{e} and 6B [13]-). An entire recapitulation of the 'Musique de fête' (4A [15] - 3A [19]) serves as the background for the conversation between Holopherne and Judith — the voice parts being successfully superimposed on the orchestral fabric in a way which maximizes the appreciation of the tension between the two, but does not sound in the least contrived. The meeting continues (3A [19] -) above the music that was used to introduce Holopherne (1A [11]^{d} - 3A [15]) together with a very successful series of 'flash-backs' to accompany Judith's pleas:

(a) the 'fanfare' that had heralded the celebrations in Holopherne's camp — and which Judith had heard while she was at the fountain — returns to signify the end of the jollity, the departure of the soldiers to rest and her isolation alone with Holopherne (see [22] - [23]);

(b) almost the entire texture from [19] onwards in Judith's 'Prière' returns after [26] with the exception of the principal motif (see [16] of No. 3), which is one of the three most important aspects of the music from 7A [19] - [22] ;

(c) Holopherne's motif (10-11A [11]) permeates the whole fabric from 3A [19] - [22] and the theme representing the wine (2-3A [14]) is similarly prominent (5B [21] - 6B [25]);

(d) the 'grief' motives and *vocalise* (i) appear as Judith tells him who will suffer despite their innocence (see [25] - [29]);

(e) the main elements of the 'Incantation' symbolizing the omnipresence of Holopherne's troops and the threat of battle as they talk (see 3-4A [24] and after [27]).

This leads to the unaltered use of the 'Mort d'Holopherne' music from the original as he falls asleep and Judith prepares to carry out her plan (see [30] -).

Act III consists of all the material of Part III (which was played uninterrupted in the original), with one most important and fundamental addition. The jubilance of the final D major fanfares is gradually controlled (the original concluding two bars being replaced by 1B [42] -) and soft canonic use of the 'Jehovah' motif heralds the return of the orchestral theme ([23] -) from her conversation with Holopherne in his tent (that which accompanied his words 'tu es près de moi et je t'ai toujours attendue resplendissante et redoutable, femme aux yeux mystérieux comme la mort' [you are near me and I have always waited for you, resplendent and redoutable woman whose eyes are as mysterious as death], as she expresses her regret concerning her action. Whilst she tells of her decision to devote her life to God in an effort to forget her deeds through repentance, the principal 'Prière' motif ([16]-) returns and co-exists with the 'Jehovah' motif to the end. The cadence is appropriately in A minor — the unresolved dominant of the act's D major. This is an obvious parallel to the concluding A major $^{6}_{3}$ of Act I and the open fifth of A minor which led the close of Act II into the D major which wanted to assert itself right from the very beginning of Act III. This unexpected ending is subtly prepared for in the only other alteration made to the music from Part III — the superimposition of a conversation between Judith and Ozias over the orchestral introduction to what was the 'Cantique de victoire' (see [26] - [28]), where Judith expresses her regret as Ozias asks her why she looks so miserable when in fact she has been so triumphant. This conversation serves further to relate the role of Ozias as created in Act I in a truly traditional operatic way.

The resulting structure of the opera is eminently satisfying. Act I has a sonata-form outline: - [8] constitutes an 'exposition' characterized by cohesion resulting from the concision of the thematic material already identified and the very limited amount of independent melodic material; [8] - [22] a 'development' which prepares the way for the rest of the work and a 'recapitulation', [22] to [31], which admirably sums up the first of the two dramatic situations in the plot and is capped by a 'coda' which, in its juxtaposition of danger and safety with fear and hope through faith, is an apotheosis of a fine calibre. The integration of the chorus in this Act is achieved partially from the way in which it frames the action with an ABA^1 CA^2 structure and also because it does not merely comment upon the action, but continually underlines the mood.

The structure of Act II, already discussed in detail (see pages 88-89), is tableau-esque, but does not suffer from this in any way because the different characters of Judith and Holopherne are so well drawn and the resultant tension between the two is so consistently maintained. In Act III, three separate forces work to a common end. The piety of Judith, well expressed in Act I, is carefully paralleled and provides the perfect resolution of the intensity of her confrontation with Holopherne in Act II; the domination of the whole of Act III by the chorus balances its previously supportive role; while the persuasive use of the 'Jehovah' motif binds the whole in a most convincingly symphonic way.

There are some important parallels between the music for *Le roi David* and that for *Judith* which represent fundamental aspects of his style. The genuine quality of religious fervour that emanates from the melodic line of the 'Alleluias' and the 'chorale' in the finale of *Le roi David* is exactly paralleled in the 'Jehovah' motif of *Judith*. The same is true in respect of the simple diatonic lines that are characteristic of the Angel in *Le roi David*, and those in Judith's 'Prière', whilst the atmospheric use of *vocalise* in both works transcends the barriers of time so appositely. The large-scale contrapuntal constructions in *Judith* involving the chorus, at [19] , [27] and [40] in particular, are natural extensions of the 'al fresco' style that was so powerfully effective in Nos. 16 and 27 of *Le roi David*, just as the 'Fanfare' in Act II is derived from the style used in No. 3*bis*, and the 'Cantique des vierges' from such a movement as 'La chanson d'Ephraïm' (No. 22).

The scoring of both versions of *Judith* is for 2 flutes (2nd doubling piccolo), 2 oboes (2nd doubling cor anglais), 2 clarinets (2nd doubling bass clarinet), 2 bassoons; 2 horns, 2 trumpets, 2 trombones; harmonium, 2 pianos; cymbals, bass drum, side drum, tamtam, triangle and strings. Despite the presence of the string section there is the same prominence of woodwind and brass as there was in *Le roi David* even after it had been rescored, and the same tendency to score very heavily in the already dense bass region. There is far more doubling of the chorus parts in *Judith* than was the case in *Le roi David* — the Théâtre du Jorat chorus found many difficulties in the first work so it was presumably a wise precaution in this second and much more difficult score. As with *Le roi David* though, there is little doubling of the solo vocal lines in *Judith*, and in both the thematic recurrences are always reinforced by the use of the same scoring wherever practical. The harmonium is similarly employed for sustaining purposes and the pianos are used frequently to give a percussive element to the string writing as well as appearing to serve as suitably loud harps! Appropriate colouring for the setting is obtained mainly from the prominence of the woodwind and brass, although there are some interesting string textures. The tendency that Honegger had shown towards a style of orchestration which relied heavily upon the sectional nature of the orchestra and which suited his contrapuntal methods so admirably, is here in evidence, and both the degree and nature of the brass writing, in particular, give the music a peculiarly tense strength of sound which is quite personal.

Despite the cohesive symphonism of the score, the fact that the story concentrates on an isolated incident in the history of the Israelites as opposed to the 'images from a long story' nature of *Le roi David* and the firmly objective approach — again supplanting the obviously weaker subjectivism of *Le roi David* — there are basic faults in *Judith* which prevented it from remaining for long in the operatic repertoires. The immediate popular appeal lay in the strength of the 'al fresco' qualities which derive from a cinema-type tableau style, in the powerful, highly original and extensive chorus writing and in the most evocative qualities of the music in general. To his devoted followers, there was all the strength, vitality and power of *Horace victorieux* and none of the too overtly emotional music of *Le roi David*. The fact that the music was more consistently demanding in its originality and maturity than ever before seemed to present few problems: here, more than in any other score to date, the assurance of his polyphonic technique and its complete reconciliation with a consistent linear harmonic argument results in a language that continually rewards efforts at aural comprehension.

None of these creditable features, however, can fully answer the criticisms that were levelled at it by contemporary opera critics: notably that Morax's text is monochrome in its imagery and too monotonous in its language for the operatic stage, particularly when compared, for example, with libretti of the calibre of Wilde's for *Salomé*. Yet, despite the strength of Judith's character and the integration of her dominance in the music, the *dea ex machina* nature of her role prevents any psychological conflict, development and resolution in the characterization, resulting in the absence of one of the most important fundamentals of opera — particularly that of the twentieth century. In operatic terms, too, it was claimed that there is also an excessive use of the chorus in Act III which causes the lack of an appreciable focus despite the appended closing scene with Judith.

Finally, the contemporary criticism, voiced notably by German critics, was that insufficient attention had been paid by Honegger to the question of pure beauty in the melodic lines. A consideration of the justification of all these criticisms is best made in conjunction with a study of *Antigone*, the opera he had started to compose in 1924 and which occupied him continuously until 1927. What remains to be pointed out is that the influence of the 'Dance of Kastchei' from Stravinsky's *L'oiseau de feu* in the 'Cantique de victoire' is countered in full by the reverse influence of the 'litany' and 'psalmody' aspects that first appeared in the *Cantique de Pâques*. These were extended in *Le roi David*, find full flood here in *Judith*, and are very evident in Stravinsky's *Symphony of Psalms* as well as in many of the latter's subsequent works. Arthur Hoérée's remark, quoted by Robert Godet, 'nous comprend-on quand nous disons que la musique d'Arthur Honegger n'est pas toujours 'intéressante', mais que son moindre geste est musical?'[2] [do people understand when we say that Arthur Honegger's music is not always interesting, but his slightest gesture is always musical?] probably contains the most convincing explanation of why *Judith* as an *opéra-sérieux* received productions in opera houses including those of Boston, Breslau, Brussels, Chicago, Cologne, Darmstadt and Zürich near the turn of the decade and dominated the large-scale 'Festival Honegger' held in Paris in 1928; and why the *action-musicale* version received performances in the concert halls of Charleroi, Haarlem, Leipzig, London, Rotterdam and Toulouse to name but a few.[3]

Notes to Chapter IV

[1]Arthur Honegger quoted by Georges Auric, '*Judith*', *Le Ménéstrel,* 5 March 1926, 114.

[2]*La Revue Musicale*, August 1925, 161-68 (p. 168).

[3]The work was translated into English for Chicago (1926), German (Léo Melitz) for Cologne in 1927, Flemish for Antwerp in 1931, and Italian (G. Savagnone) for Naples in 1937.

CHAPTER V

Antigone: 'Ma fin est mon commencement et mon commencement ma fin.'[1]

'My dream would have been to compose nothing but operas.'[2]

Honegger started work on the score of the opera *Antigone* in January 1924 and finished it in February 1927. Apart from the *Concertino* for piano and orchestra and *Judith,* he also composed two substantial incidental music scores during this period — *L'impératrice aux rochers* and *Phædre* — as well as the *Cantique des cantiques de Salomon* for reciter and orchestra and a set of three songs: *La petite sirène.* Despite this, the gestation period is unusually long for Honegger and, as a result, the work is characterized by a discipline and refinement of language and form that is intensely severe even for him. His first contact with Cocteau's high original adaptation of Sophocles' tragedy came in December 1922 when Charles Dullin produced it at the little pioneer Théâtre d'Atelier and commissioned him to write the incidental music. He wrote five pieces for oboe (doubling cor anglais) and harp (all but a few bars long); nothing of this music, however, is used in the opera score.

Honegger appears to have been drawn to the subject in the same way as other artists of the period were drawn to parallel episodes — notably Satie (*Socrate*), Stravinsky (*Œdipus rex,* libretto also by Cocteau), Picasso and Maritain. The prominent return to truly classical spirit and traditions which is so clearly evident in this period, together with the inherent qualities of a neo-Renaissance revival of new humanistic forces can be seen as a most important influence on many aspects of art, music and drama. It is a rebirth entirely free from the vicissitudes of the Winckelmann tradition and not seen through the fettered eyes of a nineteenth-century Romantic. In terms of opera, Richard Strauss initiated a tradition with *Elektra* (1908) which was firmly and irrevocably established by his subsequent *Ariadne auf Naxos* and *Die ägyptische Helena*, Wellesz's *Alkestis,* Milhaud's *Oresteia* and *Les euménides,* Stravinsky's *Œdipus rex* and *Die Vögel* by Braunfels.

Cocteau's version of the story of *Antigone* is unique in terms of the radicalism with which he approached the task. The two most important aspects of this are that the pace of the tragedy is completely altered — it is intensified in the extreme to suit a twentieth-century audience — and the language used is absolutely contemporary and engagingly colloquial. A comparison between this version and the two other famous early twentieth-century adaptations — those of Emile Staiger and André Bonnard — is highly revealing. The qualities of dynamism, of dramatic thrust and relentlessly intense lyricism are skilfully highlighted in Cocteau's version in such a way as to make the other two appear bland and ineffectual. Even the arch-conservative André Gide begrudgingly acknowledged the success of this version,[3] the major premise of which was penned by Cocteau in a preface to the published score as:

> In attempting to photo Greece from a plane a new aspect is revealed — it is thus that I wanted to translate *Antigone*. Like the flight of a bird some things disappear, others emerge. They form blocks, angles, shadows, unexpected reliefs. Maybe my experience is a way of giving old masterpieces a new lease of life. If you have to live there you concentrate on them without distraction. But because I am taking a bird's eye view of a famous text everyone will think that they hear it for the first time. The extreme speed of this play does not allow the actors to express much and to retrace anything. Naturally no living characters are hinted at within.[4]

The important influence on the text of contemporary cinematographic techniques, with their particular emphasis on concentration and speed, results in a libretto of great suitability for Honegger's musical style and technique. He expressed his reasons for deciding to use Cocteau's play as a libretto for an opera as follows:

> When in 1924 I undertook to set Cocteau's/Sophocles' *Antigone* the same problem of the musical theatre as is relevant today was present. On one hand Wagnerian music-drama with its enormous symphonic methods — on the other the return towards the form of ancient opera with its arias and ensembles built on traditional formulae. The actual context of the play showed me the way. This rapid dialogue passing from familiarity to violence put over a musical adaptation as true as the convention of song in a theatre can permit. I chose this subject first of all because of its place as a peak of dramatic art, then because of Cocteau's extremely concise adaptation which made a wonderful publication. Finally, I chose it because it is not the standard anecdote of love which is the base of nearly all lyric theatre.[5]

Honegger also supplied a preface to the score. In it he lists three aims in writing the music for *Antigone,* the first of which is:

> (1) To envelop the drama with a tight symphonic construction without the movement seeming heavy.[6]

An analysis in detail of at least a portion of the score is lengthy and complex, but vital in an appreciation of Honegger's method and technique. Cocteau summarized the plot as:

> Créon, King of Thebes, commands that the body of the traitor, Polynice, should not be buried in a grave but left in the open for the animals to devour. Antigone, sister of Polynice, is determined to disobey his orders. She takes the body and buries it. For having disobeyed she must die. But the soothsayer Tirésias tells Créon that terrible things will befall him if he doesn't free Antigone. Under this impression Créon decides to take heed of these warnings. But, too late! Antigone is dead. Furious, Hémon, son of Créon and Antigone's fiancée, turns his sword against his father. He fails and himself dies over the remains of Antigone. When Queen Eurydice hears of these new tragedies she dies also. Créon, finally deprived of them all and denied support, falls too.[7]

The relationships are best represented by the following (see Diagram 14 below).

Diagram 14:

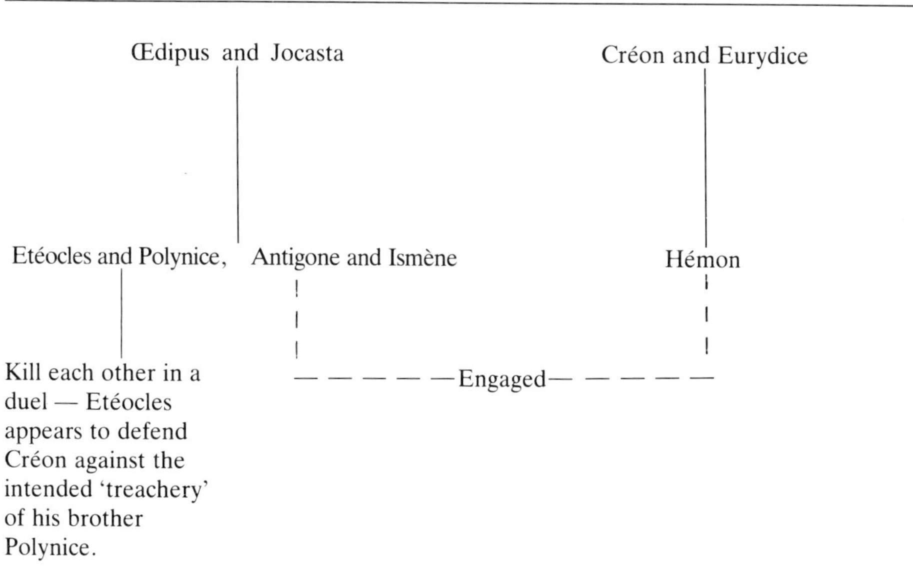

Analysis:— (The analysis of Act 1 Scene I is designed to be followed in conjunction with the annotated extracts from the published vocal score which are reproduced immediately preceding each part of the commentary.)

Act 1 Scene I depends largely, as does the whole work, on the interrelated set of five motives that represent the heritage of family tragedy and the shame that comes to Antigone and Ismène ((a), (b), (c), (d) and (e) — see Music Example 21, overleaf); on the theme (IA—see Music Example 22, pages 97-102) which accompanies specific reference to the latest incident contributing to this heritage — namely the death of their two brothers at each others' hands; and, finally, on the motif which identifies Créon, (x) — the descending interval of a minor third within the context of very strong rhythmic accentuation (see Music Example 22, pages 97-102).

Music Example 21:

In the sixteen-bar orchestral introduction the paired aspect of the 'heritage' motives ((a)/(b) and (c)/(d)) is stressed at the same time as the scalic figures in the bar before [2] (which act as the climax to the tumult of this opening) are constructed so that they can be regarded retrospectively as derivatives of (x) in illustration of the omnipresence of Créon in the heritage of tragedy and shame which the two sisters now bear.

Music Example 22:

A.
_scen - - - - do
5
p
d'Œ_di_pe que Ju_pi_ter nous é_par - gne
Eh bien je t'en an_nonce un
sf pp
au - tre
crescendo
3
de_vi - ne la
hon - te que nos en_ne_mis pré -
(c)
f
(d)
p
(a)
3
ISMÈNE
f
Je ne de_vi_ne_rai pas
3
de_puis que nos deux
_pa_rent con_tre nous
3
Theme I A
sostenuto molto
sf
f
Is.
3
frè - res se sont en_tretués
de_puis que la
trou_pe des Argiens à
3

Is.
dis_pa_ru___ je ne vois rien qui puis_se me ren_dre
Poco più lento
Un peu plus lent
plus mal_heu_reu_se ou plus heu_reu_se
ANTIGONE
f
p
E_coute Je t'ai
(x)
pp
A.
fais sor_tir du ves_ti_bu_le pour que per_sonne au mon_de ne nous en_

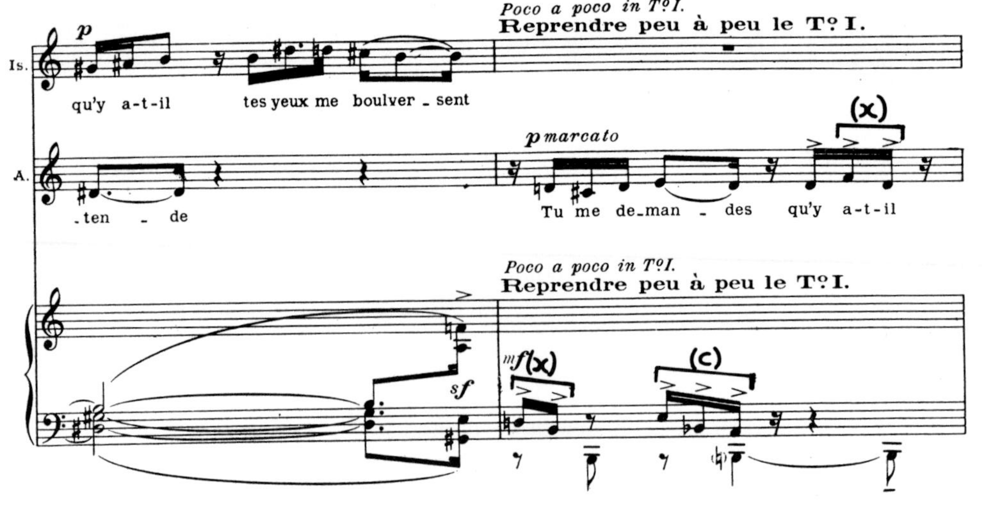
Poco a poco in T.º I.
Reprendre peu à peu le T.º I.
Is.
p
qu'y a-t-il tes yeux me boulver - sent
A.
p marcato
(x)
- ten - de
Tu me de-man - des qu'y a-t-il
Poco a poco in T.º I.
Reprendre peu à peu le T.º I.
sf
mf (x)
(c)

A.
(x)
Hé Cré-on ne donne t'il pas la sé-pul-tu - re à l'un de nos
(a)

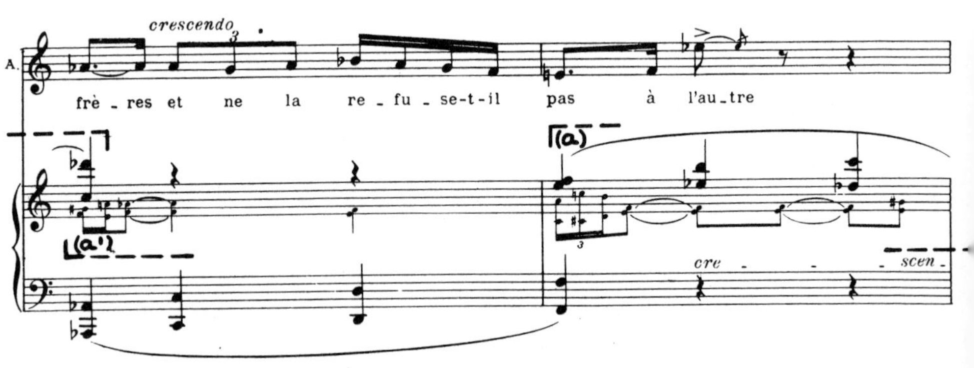
A.
crescendo
frè - res et ne la re - fu - se-t-il pas à l'au-tre
(a)
(a')
cre - - - scen -

5
E _ té _ o _ cle au _ ra l'en _ ter _ re _ ment qu'il mé _ ri _ te mais il est
- _ do
dé _ fen _ du d'en _ se _ ve _ lir Po _ ly _ ni _ ce ou de le pleu _ rer
On le lais _ se aux corbeaux
6 Tempo I.
Tels sont les
or _ _ dres que le no _ ble Cré _ on pro _ mul _ gue pour toi et pour moi Oui

(Reproduit avec l'autorisation des EDITIONS SALABERT, Paris, propriétaires de l'œuvre.)

Antigone commences by telling Ismène that further tragedy and shame are imminent (2A[2] - 1A[3]) — the accompanying orchestral fabric being constructed from some of the 'heritage' motives (3A[2] and 6A[2] : (c)/(d); 1B[3] - [3] : (a)). The theme specifying the tragic death of their two brothers (Theme IA) unfolds in the orchestra beneath Ismène's statement that she doubts whether she is capable of experiencing further distress as a result of this latest incident ([3] - [4]). (Créon's fundamental involvement in the family heritage of tragedy and shame is reflected in both this theme (IA) and the second, (b), and fifth, (e), of the 'heritage' motives, in that it is possible to detect the influence of (x) in terms of the prominence of descending minor thirds in the intervallic patterning, even though the powerful rhythmic characteristic which very specifically colours its singular use is absent.) When Antigone firmly interrupts her and begins to elaborate on the additional shame that will be inflicted upon them ([4] - [6]), the orchestral texture is dominated by gestures which highlight (x) in order to underline that Créon will be its instigator even before Antigone says as much in the sixth bar after [4]. While she vehemently relates that Créon has forbidden anyone to bury Polynice under the threat of death (6A[4] - [7]), the 'heritage' motif (a) dramatically dominates the orchestral accompaniment in both its original and two developed forms (see 2B[5] - and [6] - respectively) in anticipation of the outcome of this dictate. (In the case of both these derivatives of (a) — a′ and a″ — the 'development' is principally a rhythmic one with the essential melodic characteristic of a small interval (a semitone, or, rarely, a tone) opening out through contrary-motion procedures via an intermediary interval of a tritone to a large interval (a minor seventh or minor ninth.)

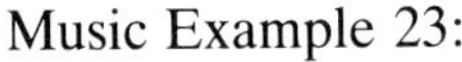

Music Example 23:

Antigone proceeds to ask Ismène if she will support her. Ismène asks her 'how'? Antigone passionately replies that she intends to bury Polynice despite Créon's orders (7 - 9). The orchestra supports this with a fabric composed of the theme specifying the tragedy of the brothers (Theme IA: 2A 7 - and

3A [8] -), an ostinato which can be regarded as a derivative of 'heritage' motif (a) in the light of the two developed forms that dominated 2B [5] - 3A [6] , and a new theme in the bass (Theme IB) which signifies the criminal aspect of the burial plans. The bass motif in the second bar after [8] , which punctuates her declaration that 'j'enterrerai mon frère et le tien' [I am going to bury *our* brother], is imbued with the same spirit of (x) as the scalic figures were in the bar before [2] — for the same reason and to the same effect!

Music Example 24:

Is.
No - tre mè - re qui é - tait sa mè - re s'est pen - du - e
Theme IC

Is.
Nos frè - res se sont entr' - é - gor - gés
(a)
f sempre

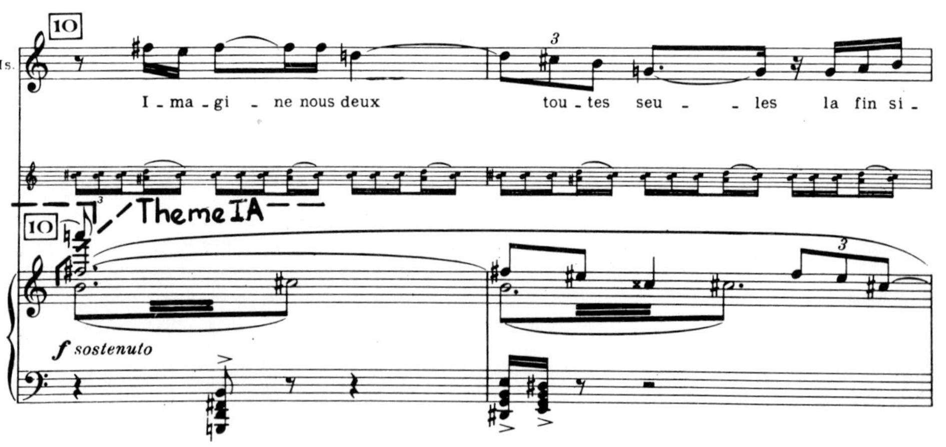
10
Is.
I - ma - gi - ne nous deux tou - tes seu - les la fin si -
Theme IA
f sostenuto

Is.
-nis - tre qui nous at-tend
si nous bra-vons nos mai - tres
Je cè - de
C'est fou d'en-tre-pren-dre des choses au des-
-sus de ses for - ces
11
ANTIGONE
A.
mf
Je ne te pous-se pas si tu
(c)
11
mf
(d)

Part of Theme IA (2B [9] - [9]) accompanies Ismène's distraught cries for her sister's attention. As she pointedly reminds Antigone of the tragic deaths of their mother and father ([9] - [10]), a new theme (IC) representing the parents is woven into a texture necessarily laced with one of the 'heritage' motives — (a). As she reminds her that they are entirely alone now their two brothers are dead, Theme IA appropriately dominates the accompaniment and continues to do so as she tells Antigone that both of them will also die if they go ahead with her plan ([10] - [11]). Antigone tells Ismène that she will not oblige her to help — she will do it alone ([11] - [12]). The 'heritage' motives (b), (c), (d) and (e) return in an almost identical way to the opening orchestral introduction — the pitch level finally being restored, too, in the bar before [12]. The cycle is complete, the position is as it was before Antigone spoke to Ismène, her resolve unaltered.

Music Example 25:

E

(Reproduit avec l'autorisation des EDITIONS SALABERT, Paris, propriétaires de l'œuvre.)

Antigone then reflects on the 'beautiful' prospect of being reunited with her brother in death by her intended actions. The theme (ID) which sings across the orchestral texture (itself containing an ostinato derivative of (a) — see after 6 and 10 respectively — to symbolize the impending 'heritage' aspect) represents this fraternal love that implicitly demands of her greater respect for the law of the gods than for the 'law' of the mere mortal Créon.

Music Example 26:

Is.
lut_ter: con_tre toute u_ne vil _ le Fol _ le
ANTIGONE
A.
Trou_ve des pré_tex _ tes
(c)
(d)
Is.
que je trem _ ble pour toi pourquoi cou_
A.
Pen - se à toi-mê_me
Is.
_rir a_près le vent
A.
Lais - se - moi
(b)
cre - scen
mf
(a)

A.
seu - le a - vec mon pro - jet S'il é -
- do
11
- chou - - - - - - - e
Je mourrai glo - rieu - se -
ff
p
Is.
f
Eh bien va donc Im - pru - den - te
- ment
(a)
crescendo
ff

Antigone chides Ismène for her attitude and suggests that further family shame will result anyway through her disrespect for the gods — this is reflected by the use of the 'heritage' motives ((c)/(d): 1A [13] and 6-8A [13]) and the brothers' 'theme' ((IA): 2-6A [13]). As the argument becomes more heated, 'heritage motives' (a) and (b) dominate the whole and lead to a climax ([14]) as Antigone asks to be left alone with her plan. It is the same climax as 1B

[2] in the orchestral introduction (the descending scalic figures based on (x) symbolizing Créon), and it occurs as Antigone says 's'il échoue' [if it fails]. She concludes that she at least will have died 'gloriously' and this gives reign to the 'heritage' motives (a)/(b) and various derivatives which sound like a death-bell in an ever-increasing frenzy as Ismène leaves after declaring the inevitable to be imminent. The texture in fact derives from that which accompanied Antigone's first passionate outburst (see 5B [5] - [6]) — its previous dramatic significance now appropriately related as it is developed to histrionic heights by way of effecting a transition to Act 1 Scene II.

The mosaic style which is so typical of Honegger has an organic strength not normally a resultant force of such an obviously patterned approach by virtue of the degree of extension, transformation and/or development to which the various motives and themes are continually subjected. The 'heritage' motif (a), in particular, was transformed into several important variants (see 2B [5] - , [6] - , [10] - , [12] - and 3A [15] -), as well as being subjected to several degrees of rhythmic diminution. The fact that it is based on the powerful principle of melodic contrary motion — a device so beloved of Honegger — means that fuller harmonic derivations are possible (bass motif 1A [3] and Theme IC [9] -) with neither a consequential weakening of motivic relationships nor an increase in complexity. The basic simplicity of the Créon motif (x) also permits a degree of permeation and cross-fertilization which is truly symphonic, but without absolute conditioning which would adversely affect the operatic prerequisites. Furthermore, the intervallic consistency between the various motives and themes creates a melodic equilibrium whose stability contributes much to the qualities of integration and balance which characterize the music as a whole. The dependence of the motif (a) solely on the intervals of a semitone (or its inversions) and a tritone, are mirrored in the other four 'heritage' motives in a way that binds their apparently disparate forces into a single convincing whole. The aspect of the interval of a third in the construction of (x) also pervades 'heritage' motives (b) and (e) so that the scalic conclusion based on (x), noted at the end of the orchestral introduction, and at [14] , rightly relates to them as an interim conclusion rather than as a mere superimposed statement (see pages 97 and 108). It also communicates the corporate identity of the 'heritage' motives, the theme intimating the specific tragedy of the brothers and Créon as far as it is necessary for the audience to understand the various forces being brought to bear upon Antigone and Ismène.

Melodic equilibria are supported admirably by the similarly happy interaction of the rhythmic elements. The extreme divergence of the rhythmic characteristics of the various motives and themes permits a series of combinations, juxtapositions and superimpositions that result in a fabric which has great rhythmical impetus. While this carries the whole along in a seemingly inevitable way towards its conclusion, it never fails to allow for melodic expansiveness whenever appropriate (cf. [7], [10] and [12] in particular).

It is significant to note the way in which Honegger carefully establishes a balance between the extensive use of the 'heritage' motif (a) and its various derivatives in the texture before 10 and the other four motives by deliberately not using it in the quasi-recapitulatory section 11 - 12, or in the early stages of the approach to the orchestral coda, before allowing it to dominate the conclusion of the scene.

In the large-scale structuring of this scene there is a clear overall ABA^1 format (see Diagram 15 below) which highlights Antigone's passionate declaration of the honour in death during the brief B section — a brevity in terms of number of bars which is countered, to a large extent, by the much slower tempo.

Furthermore, there is a sub-structure rather like a mosaic (which can be regarded as a derivative of the rondo-patterning previously much in evidence in Honegger's music) that admirably underlines the dramatic structuring (see Diagram 15 below).

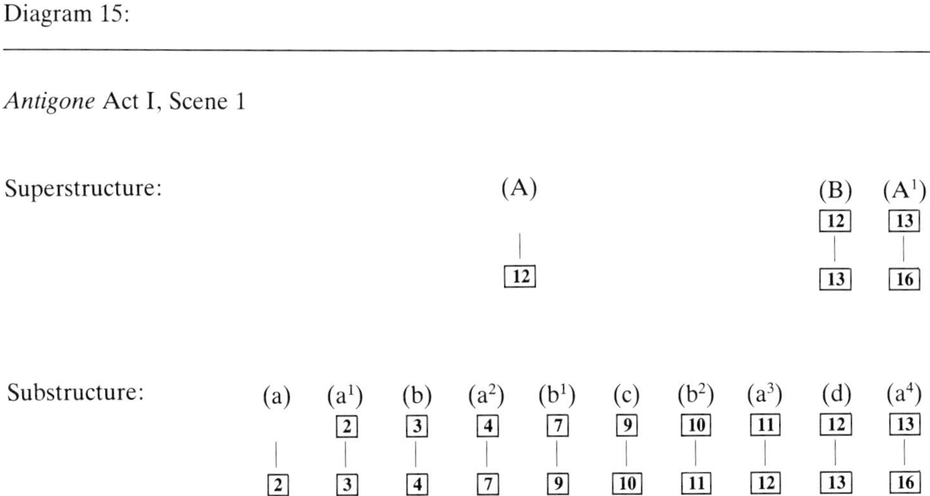

The rigour and discipline of the approach revealed by this analysis of the first scene is maintained throughout the entire opera. The attention to dramatic prerequisites in general and operatic criteria in particular is constantly maintained in harness with a desire to conceive the constituent elements, as well as the whole, in symphonic terms so that the discipline of symphonic thinking contributes significantly to solving the problems of continuity and unification peculiar to opera.

It would seem sufficient to comment on the remainder of the work in more condensed terms, pointing to the additional elements of a symphonic nature and drawing attention to the principal procedures in relation to the structure of the opera as a whole.

Act 1 Scene II: Chorus — glorification of the Thebian victory

The chorus fulfils a role here very similar to the traditional spoken chorus parts in the original Greek tragedies as they comment on the previous scene and fill in the rest of the background. Honegger's style and approach to this is very much in the 'al fresco' tradition of *Le roi David* and *Judith*. Three separate themes are introduced — the first (IIA) and third (IIC) (see Music Example 27 (i) and (iii) below) treated in an imitative fashion very typical of Honegger and the second (IIB) (see Music Example 27 (ii) below) having a strong resemblance to the simple triadic quality of the theme of Judith's 'Invocation'. After a very Honeggerian contrapuntal combination of the three themes, a fourth (IID) emerges (see Music Example 27 (iv) below).

Music Example 27: *Antigone,* Act 1 Scene II:
(i) Theme IIA, contraltos and tenors, 17 - 18

(ii) Theme IIB, sopranos 1-2A 18

(iii) Theme IIC, basses, 3A 18 - 5A 19

(iv) Theme IID, 1-3A 20

The use of a derivative of the 'heritage' motif (a) right from the beginning (bass, 16-), firmly underlines the impending tragedy which is an inevitable consequence of Antigone's decision to defy Créon, The omnipresence of the latter is secured by the use of (x) in the melodic patterning of the first three of these themes, and this also establishes the identity of the chorus as the loyal subjects of Créon. The fourth theme (IID) serves as a link to Scene III which introduces Créon for the first time in person — the aspect of the victorious people welcoming their leader is usefully stressed.

Act 1 Scene III : Créon and the Guard

This scene opens with the introduction of Créon by Theme IID (3-1B 22). The accompaniment of his speech is dominated by (x) and a large number of derivatives† in which the rhythmic character is always maintained even if the melodic interval is either expanded or contracted within an harmonic context. A spokesman thanks Créon for his leadership and as he asserts that 'il n'y a pas un homme assez fou pour chercher la mort' [no man is actually stupid enough to seek death] (3-2B 26), in response to Créon's dictate forbidding the burial of Polynice's body, part of 'heritage' motif (a) makes a brief, but telling appearance in the orchestral fabric (2B 26).

The entry of the Guard is signified by a new theme (IIIA — see Music Example 28 (i) below), which admirably illustrates his nervous and apprehensive state and dominates the whole of the first part of their conversation (- 28). But, when the Guard finally confesses to Créon that he has failed in his duty (1B 28) — someone has removed Polynice's body for burial — a new motive (IIB — see Music Example 28 (ii) overleaf), representing Créon's fury, emerges in the orchestra above the Guard's theme (IIIA) in the bass. During the subsequent conversation between Créon and the Guard, three new motives are exposed — the first symbolizes the force of the gods (IIIC); the second, destiny as shaped by the gods (IIID); and the third, the idea of a traitor (IIIE) (see Music Example 28 (iii), (iv) and (v) overleaf). After his outburst of rage, Créon and the Guard converse again (31 -) and so Themes IIIA and IIIB return. As the Guard leaves, his theme (IIIA) dominates the accompaniment (32 - 5A 32).

One further musical recurrence which serves to connect Créon with his people — the chorus — is the use of the first part of Theme IIC from Act 1 Scene II to accompany Créon's description (5A 22 -) of their victory over the evil of Polynice and the Argiens.

Music Example 28: *Antigone*, Act 1 Scene III:
(i) Theme IIIA, orchestra, 1B-4A 26

(†N.B. one particular derivative — see upper part of orchestral texture after 29 — is subsequently recapitulated (see 6B 40 -) when the essence of the text is referred to again.)

(ii) motif IIIB, orchestra, 1-3A **28**

(Reproduit avec l'autorisation des EDITIONS SALABERT, Paris, propriétaires de l'œuvre.)

(iii) motif IIIC, orchestra, 2-1B **29**

(Reproduit avec l'autorisation des EDITIONS SALABERT, Paris, propriétaires de l'œuvre.)

(iv) motif IIID, orchestra, 2-1B **30**

(Reproduit avec l'autorisation des EDITIONS SALABERT, Paris, propriétaires de l'œuvre.)

(v) motif IIIE, orchestra, 2-5A **30**

(Reproduit avec l'autorisation des EDITIONS SALABERT, Paris, propriétaires de l'œuvre.)

The scene closes with Créon standing alone at the top of the steps in the centre of the stage and, after a brief reference (3B [33] -) to the traitor's theme (IIIE) which subtly prepares us for Scene IV, there ensues a choral *Interlude* where the thematic material is heavily conditioned by (x). The outcome is not merely a strengthening of the aspect of the people's patriotic support of Créon, but an effective integration of their role in this scene by virtue of the overall structure that materializes (see Diagram 16 below).

Diagram 16:

Antigone

Act 1			
Scene I	Scene II	Scene III	Interlude
Antigone and Ismène	Chorus	Créon and Guard	Chorus
1st subject group		2nd subject group	
Antagonists		Protagonists	

The use of sonata-form terminology is not inappropriate when the essentially expository nature of all the music in Act 1 is borne in mind and when comparison is made to the music of Act 2 Scenes IV and V which is so obviously developmental in character.

Act 2 Scenes IV and V: Créon and Antigone — the first conflict

A derivative of (x) from the *Interlude* (see 2A [33] -) dominates the five-bar link between the end of the *Interlude* and the start of Scene IV (see orchestral bass [37] - 4B [38]), thus maintaining the aspect of Créon's continuing dominant presence. The Guard enters with Antigone: the combination of the *scherzo* quality of the Presto $\frac{6}{8}$ and the stumbling nature of the accompanying theme (IVA: 3B [38]-) appositely reflects his nervousness as he directs Créon's attention to Antigone whom he has caught in the act of burying Polynice. As he tells of the circumstances surrounding his discovery there is a development of material from previous scenes. Créon had threatened him with death should he fail to keep a proper watch over the body — hence his nervousness — so it is not surprising that the first thematic recall (6B [40]) should be the derivative of (x) which had supported the issue of that threat (see [29] -). The 'traitor's' theme (IIIE) reappears (2B [40] -) as the Guard's narrative gradually unfolds, and, as he slowly regains his composure, so the melodic line becomes more stable. Whilst he tells of the dust-storm which, together with the smell of the body, had prompted him temporarily to move from his post there is a rare example of Honegger indulging in quite blatant word-painting in the orchestral fabric; only the very simple nature of the figures prevent it from being an embarrassing miscalculation (see 2-5A [41]).

As the Guard continues, so the implication of his discovery looms inexorably — the accompaniment from five bars before [42] onwards not only contains a new theme (IVB: 5B [42] - 5A [42]), but also appropriately incorporates (x) — Créon — and a new derivative of the 'heritage' motif (a) — see three bars before [42] . Créon contemptuously dismisses the Guard and proceeds to question Antigone. Many of the themes and motives from Scene I are woven into the fabric (2B [45] - 3A [47]) as she resolutely defends her flagrant defiance of his orders. At the height of her defensive outburst (5A [46] -), she gloriously reaffirms the bond of fraternal love and so Theme ID returns. A representative of the chorus, in a brief interjection (1-3A [47]) which serves as a transition to Créon's reply, derides her stubbornness and dismisses it as something to be expected of the daughter of Œdipus — the orchestra appropriately supporting him with a development of the 'parental' theme (IC) from Scene I.

In an extended passage (5B [48] -), Créon points to the basic forces of evil he sees finding expression in Antigone. His bipartite thematic material (Theme IVCα and β — see Music Example 29 below), acts as a framework for an extended and complex series of developed thematic returns (6B [49] -).

Music Example 29: *Antigone,* Act 2 Scene IV, Theme IVC α/β, orchestra, 5B [48] - 3A [48]

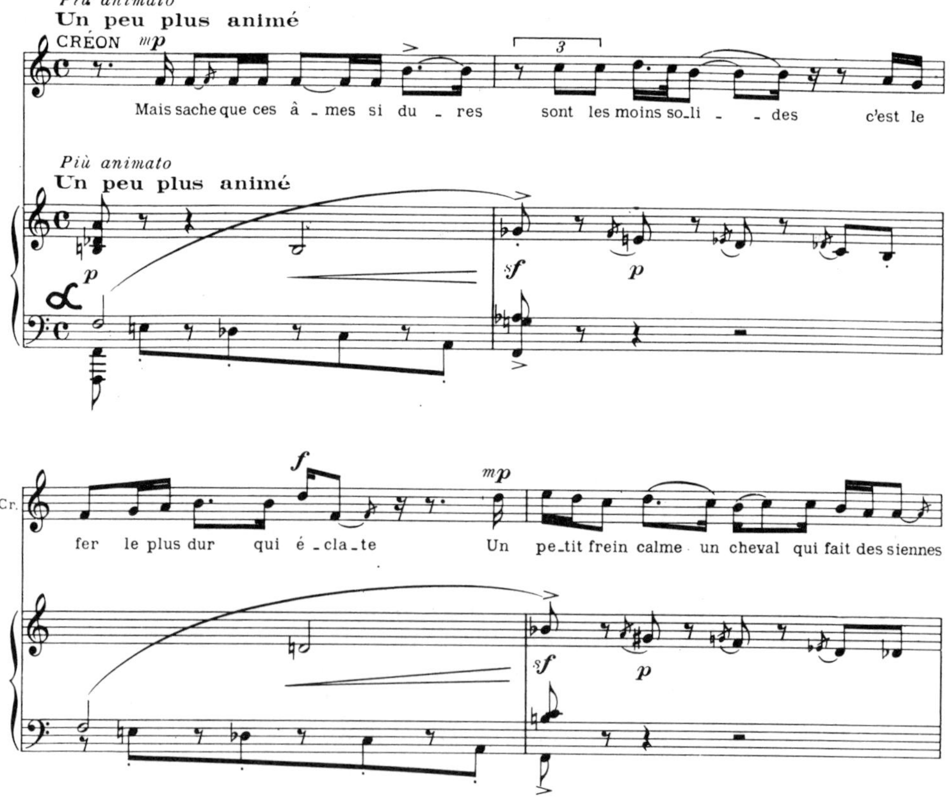

In Scene III he had stressed to his people how it was he who had saved them from Œdipus — now he wishes to assert further his authority and save them from Antigone. As he demands this absolute authority, much of the relevant material from Scene III returns and is developed, including the theme representing the force of the gods (Theme IIIC: 4B [49]). By virtue of this demand the fate of Antigone is sealed as his previously expressed 'threat' gives way to 'punishment now due', and this is appositely reflected by the use of the 'heritage' motif (a) (3A [49]-).

After an extension to the basic premises of their dispute — in effect a generalization of the principles involved ([50] -) — resulting in a partial restatement by both which allows for further material from previous scenes to be incorporated, Antigone once again attests to the all-powerful force of fraternal love (Theme ID: 2B [53] -), before the thematic material which expresses Créon's vision of evil in Antigone (Theme IVC α/β) engulfs the whole ([53] -) and effects the transition to Scene V and the entry of Ismène.

There is no obvious demarcation between Scenes IV and V — not even a double bar line; the designation of Scene V would appear to be for reasons of mere convention and certainly it does not in any way affect the progression of this first section of the 'development'. As Ismène enters there is a continuation of the conflict between the theme identifying the evil seen by Créon in Antigone (IVC α/β) and material from Scene I — notably Themes IA and IB, 'heritage' motif (a) and derivatives of the latter — within a framework heavily conditioned by (x). Ismène attempts to link herself with Antigone and the plot to bury Polynice, and the whole is in itself thus fully related to the premonitory Scene I and the omnipresence of Créon both physically and in spirit, past and present. A further reference to the theme of fraternal love (Theme ID: 5B [56] -) precipitates a restatement by Créon ([56] -) of his views, and once again the two elements (α and β) of Theme IVC dominate the whole. Even Ismène's mention of Hémon, Créon's son to whom Antigone is engaged, fails to alter Créon's resolve to execute Antigone.

The first of two new themes (VA — see Music Example 30 (i) below), which symbolizes Créon's 'sentence of death', appears when Antigone confirms that when she made her decision she was fully aware of its implications for her ultimate fate. The other new theme (VB - see Music Example 30 (ii) below), symbolizes the further, as yet unknown, tragedy that is to occur by the hands of the gods, and appears during the transition ([59] - 4A [61]) to Scene VI.

Music Example 30: *Antigone,* Act 2 Scene V:
(i) Theme VA, orchestra, 1B - 2A [55]

(ii) Theme VB, orchestra, 2-3A [59]

Act 2 Scenes VI and VII: Créon and Hémon — the second conflict

(Again there is no musical demarcation between these two scenes. From a musical as well as a dramatic point of view they form a single whole which counterbalances that created by Scenes IV and V.)

Despite a considerable amount of new thematic material in these two scenes — necessitated by the introduction of a major new character (Hémon) and an inherent set of relationships and conflicts — the all-pervading aspect of development in the musical fabric is maintained as a perfect match for the dramatic play. In view of the preceding passage which has verbally established the procedures it would seem appropriate to tabulate the material in relationship to these two scenes for the sake of concision and of continuing comprehensibility.

'Alliance?' (3B [62] — 3A [64])

Themes VIA (Hémon: see Music Example 31 (i) below) and IVCα (Créon's vision of the evil in Antigone), a derivative of 'heritage' motif (c), and motif (x) with various derivatives: Créon attempts to enlist Hémon's support for his actions.

'Change of colours' (3B [65] - 1B [67])

Theme VIB (see Music Example 31 (ii) below), together with derivatives of 'heritage' motives (a) and (c): Hémon expresses his views on the 'crime' and the present situation which are in direct conflict with those of Créon.

'Conflict' ([67] - [72])

Theme IVCα (inverted) and derivatives of 'heritage' motives (a) and (b): Créon attempts to justify his decisions in an argument with Hémon. A new theme (VIC - see Music Example 31 (iii) overleaf) emerges in the orchestra after [69]. The derivative of 'heritage' motif (b) dominates the end of the conflict ([73] -) and is used in the transition to Scene VII ([74] - [75]).

Music Example 31 : *Antigone,* Act 2 Scene VI:
(i) Theme VIA, orchestra, 3-1B [62]

(ii) Theme VIB, orchestra, 3A [65] -4A [66]

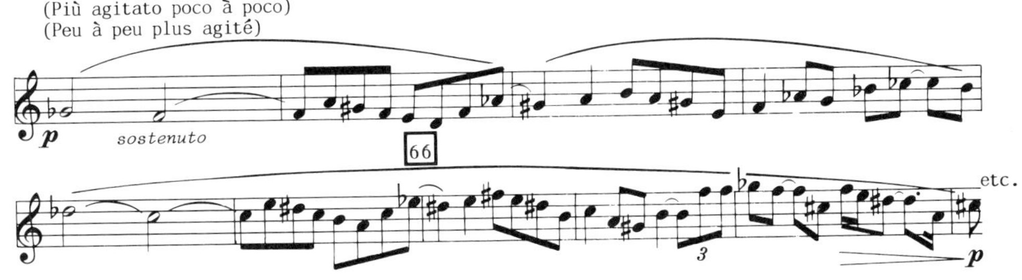

(iii) Theme VIC, orchestra, 1-4A [69]

A representative of the people urges Créon to reconsider his decision, but he pronounces the sentence of death (represented in the orchestra by Theme VIIA — see Music Example 32 (i) below), and there is an extended climactic use of the 'heritage' motif (e) which amply justifies its similar usage twice in Scene I. Over a new theme (VIIB — see Music Example 32 (ii) opposite), the 'contralto Coryphée' muses on the invisible power and quality of love, which provides a link to the next scene (VIII).

Act 2 Scene VIII : Antigone's farewell

In terms of the overall structure of the opera, this scene marks the beginning of the 'recapitulation' in respect of the sonata-form aspect. It opens with a long treble melismatic line of quite astounding expression and profundity — qualities in no small way attributable to its scoring for saxophone and musical saw. This, and all the subsequent thematic material in this scene is supported and interlaced in rondo-fashion with derivatives of 'heritage' motif (a) — an underlining of Antigone's fate — and of (x) — signifying Créon's involvement with her impending death. As Antigone reflects on her situation, various themes and motives from earlier scenes reappear in a flash-back mosaic of sound closely identifiable with contemporary cinematographic techniques — in particular the 'parental' theme (IC), as she mentions Œdipus and Theme ID ('fraternal love even unto death'): see three bars before [86] and four bars after [87] respectively. After the climax ([91] - [92]), the Coryphées attempt to chase away any memories of the scene — a task in which they succeed not least by virtue of the opposed nature of their music.

Music Example 32 : *Antigone,* Act 2 Scene VII:
(i) Theme VIIA, orchestra, 1-3A [76]

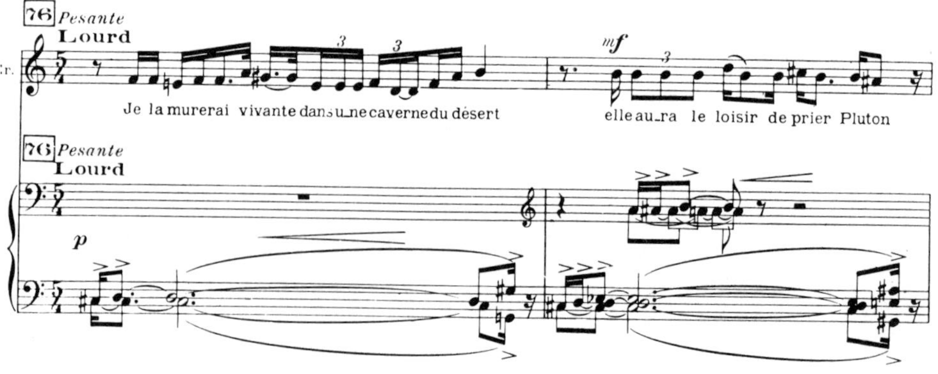

Cr.
f
el_le ver_ra si les dieux in_fer_naux la protè _ gent

(Reproduit avec l'autorisation des EDITIONS SALABERT, Paris, propriétaires de l'œuvre.)

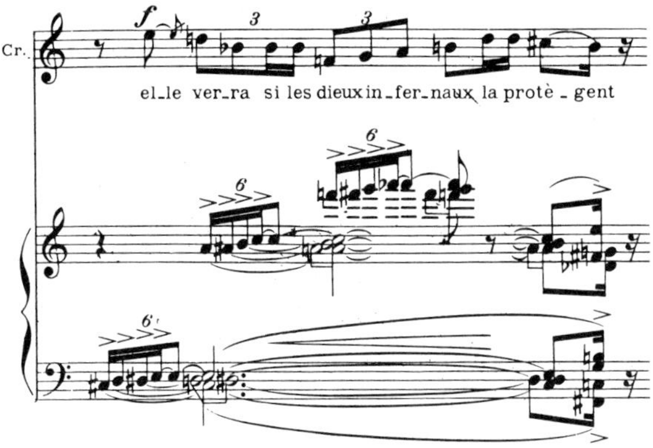

(ii) Theme VIIB, orchestra, 78 - 79

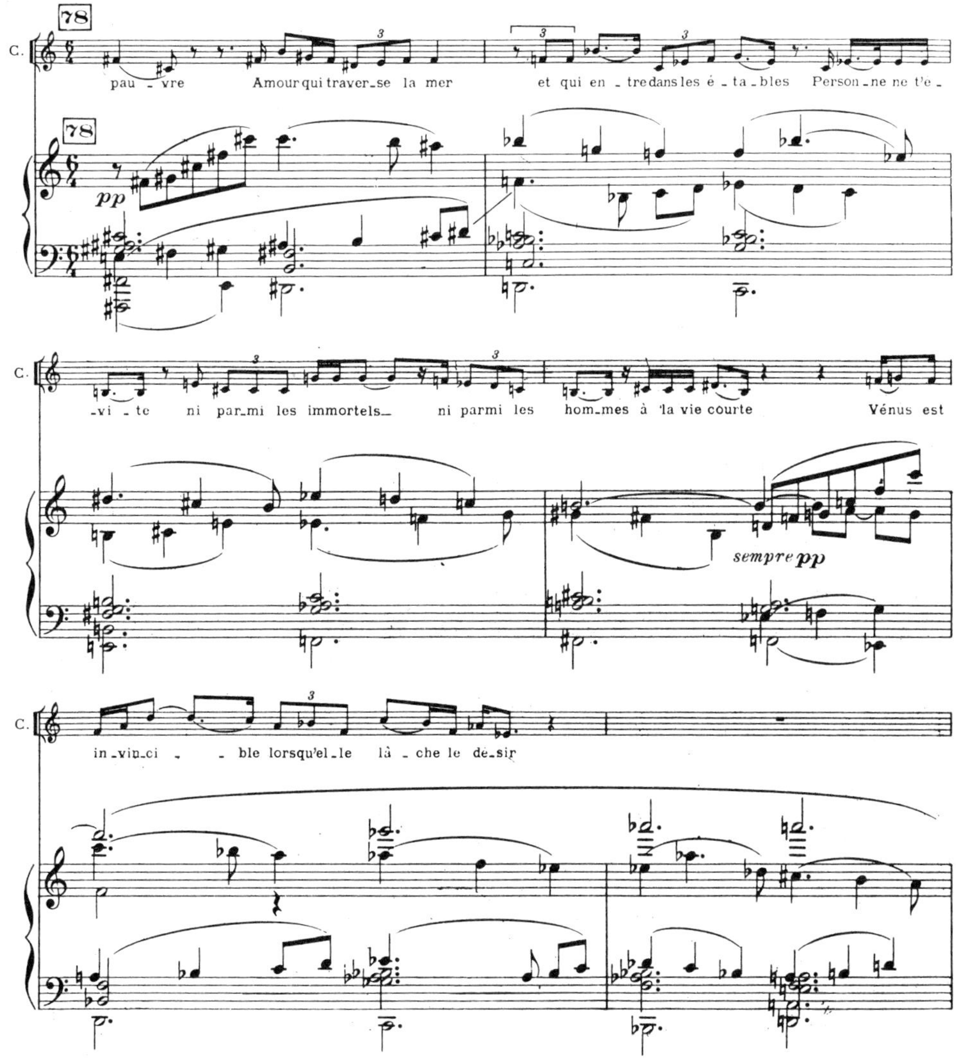

78
C.
pau _ vre Amour qui traver_se la mer et qui en _ tre dans les é _ ta_bles Person_ne ne t'é _
78
pp
_vi _ te ni par_mi les immortels_ ni parmi les hom_mes à la vie courte Vénus est
sempre pp
in_vin_ci _ _ ble lorsqu'el_le lâ _ che le dé_sir

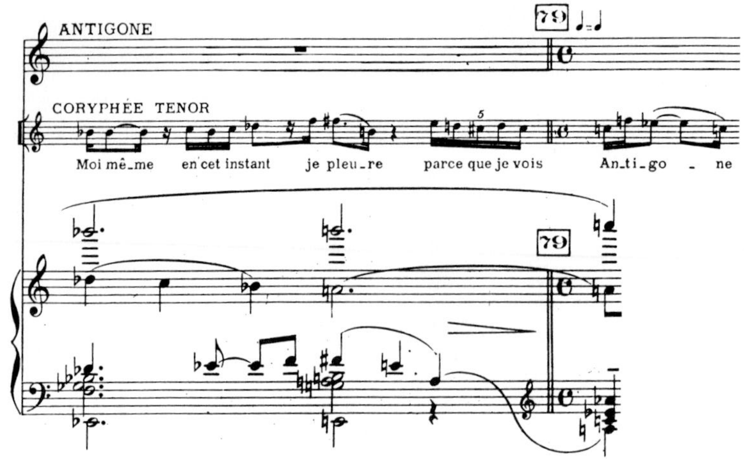

Act 2 Scene IX : Tirésias' warning to Créon

The musical fabric of this scene is built upon an almost rigid framework of the two motives (a) and (x) in numerous new versions. The theme denoting Tirésias (IXA — see Music Example 33 (i) below) occurs as he enters, each time he interrupts Créon's apparent monologue and as he makes his exit. When he warns Créon he is rebuked and called a traitor — Theme IIIE being appropriately recalled (3B 99-). As he persists, he employs the idea that all destiny is shaped by the gods (Theme IIID : 2B 100-) and that, not only will Créon's sentence of death on Antigone bring about her death, but also that of Hémon.

The new theme (IXB) which emerges in the orchestra after 104 (see Music Example 33 (ii) opposite), represents Créon's hasty departure — its similarities to the music of two bars before 62 establishes a link with the then hasty arrival of Hémon and, hence, with Hémon himself. The subsequent 'Interlude' is a close parallel to Act 1 Scene II, with its powerful choral unisoni 'Hymn to Bacchus'. Of the various thematic ideas involved, the first orchestral one is particularly influenced by motif (x). After the tremendous choral climax there is an orchestral interlude (117 - 120) of frightening power and intensity, which occurs as Créon makes his discovery of the terrible scene — Hémon and Antigone dead in each other's arms. The thematic aspects are finally superseded by two versions of 'heritage' motif (a) which toll like the veritable death-bell.

Music Example 33 : *Antigone*, Act 2 Scene IX:
(i) Theme IXA, orchestra, 2B-3A 95

(ii) Theme IXB, orchestra, 1-7A [104]

Act 3 Scene X : the entry of Eurydice

The most striking feature about the opening of this scene is that, although it is dominated by (x) — which is to be expected — this motif is contained, for the first time, in derivatives which are considerably more subdued and less arrogant in character. This results in a most suitable preparation for the wholesale repeat of the concluding orchestral interlude of the previous scene that occurs as the Messenger relates Créon's discovery. The sheer power and intensity already noted of the passage now repeated, seem concentrated and extended to even greater heights of histrionic effect as the Messenger forces himself to describe the terrible details of the scene in the cavern over the orchestral welter of sound.

The reliving in graphic detail of this terrible moment, which had previously existed only as a nightmare in instrumental sound, provides a climactic experience of completely overwhelming profundity and immensity of strength hardly creditable in view of the consistently high level of rate of action and overall intensity already established and maintained throughout the work.

Act 3 Scene XI : Créon — the final tragedy

After the pronounced recapitulatory, or, less contentiously speaking, re-expository nature of the previous four scenes, this last scene assumes the role of a coda. Four new thematic ideas are employed within the framework of a texture heavily conditioned by derivatives of the motives (x) (Créon himself) and (a) — the heritage of family tragedy and shame now added to, and perpetuated by, the death of Antigone. The first two of these new themes (XIA and XIB — see Music Example 34 (i) and (ii) overleaf) represent the two tragedies brought about by Créon. The first theme is significantly akin to 'heritage' motif (a) in terms of its dependence on contrary-motion procedures, and when the second appears it is appropriately as a counter-subject to the first — Antigone and Hémon are united in death even in Créon's eyes.

The third new theme (XIC — see Music Example 34 (iii) overleaf) symbolizes the punishment Créon is receiving at the hands of the gods, whilst the fourth (XID — see Music Example 34 (iv) overleaf) represents the last tragedy which befalls him as he learns of his wife's suicide. Créon's confession of guilt for occasioning the death of his son is followed by his mourning for his late wife which is accompanied by a tissue of orchestral sound consisting of the first of the new themes (XIA) and derivatives of (x).

Gradually the orchestral fabric is reduced to a dependence on motives (x) and (a); finally the lines, both vocal and instrumental, are constructed solely from motif (x) as the broken figure of Créon is left stranded in the quicksand of tragedy and guilt he alone has created.

Music Example 34: *Antigone*, Act 3 Scene XI:
(i) Theme XIA, orchestra, 3-4A [128]

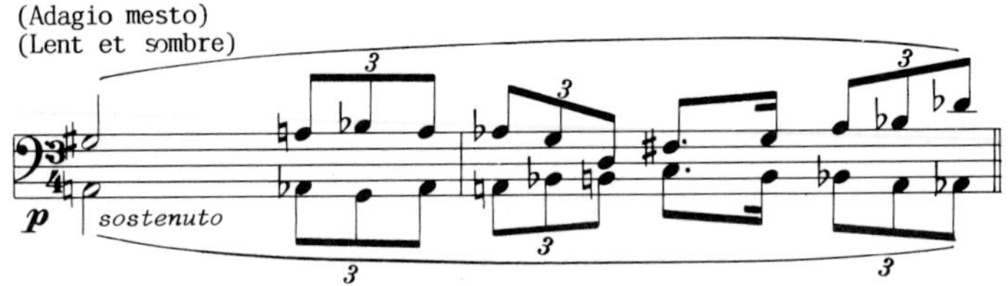

(ii) Theme XIB, orchestra, 3-1B [129]

(iii) Theme XIC, orchestra, 1B-2A [130]

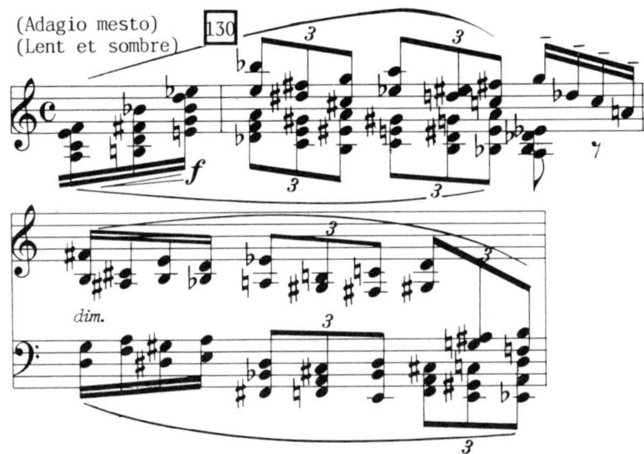

(iv) Theme XID, orchestra, 1-3A [131]

A number of interim conclusions and summations are appropriate at this point before a discussion of the problems presented by this work both as an opera and as a piece of music.

The overall structure of the work that emerges is quite clearly evident as a sonata-form outline which most admirably reflects and supports the dramatic content (see Diagram 17 below).

Diagram 17:

Antigone

Expository	Act 1 Scenes I, II and III
Developmental	Act 2 Scenes IV, V, VI and VII
Re-expository	Act 2 Scenes VIII and IX and Act 3 Scene X
Coda	Act 3 Scene XI

The role of the chorus is bipartite. The two large-scale peoples' choruses that straddle the work like buttresses (the 'Glorification of the Thebian Victory' (Act 1 Scene II) and the 'Hymn to Bacchus' which is the 'Interlude' that concludes Scene IX) are their main contribution, both of immense colour and strength with much effort made to integrate their relevance with the dramatic structuring of the work as a whole. Apart from short interjections (the 'Interlude' between Act 1 Scene III and Act 2 Scene IV and the wordless passages in Act 2 Scene IV and Act 3 Scene X), where they add a further dimension to the accompanying orchestral fabric, the burden of their second small-scale role (as the original Greek chorus constantly commentating, anticipating, linking and narrating as a back-drop to the whole in general and the important characters in particular) is borne by four solo singers from their ranks — the Coryphées. They provide essential material in the links between Scenes V and VI, VII and VIII, VIII and IX, and X and XI, as well as in the Introductions to Scenes IV, V and VII. The *Sprechstimme* role of the soprano Coryphée in Scene VIII (**81** onwards) is a remarkably effective and successful solution to the problem of promoting an apparent dialogue between Antigone and the celestial forces during her 'farewell' monologue. Similarly poignant are the small moments in Scene IX and at the close of Scene XI, when the bass Coryphée holds the stage by way of conclusion.

In his preface, Honegger expressed his two further aims as:

> (2) To replace the recitatives by a melodic vocal line which does not consist of sustained high notes — which always renders the text incomprehensible — or by purely instrumental lines; but, on the contrary, with a melodic

line created by the word itself, which, due to its clean plasticity, is designed to raise the contours and augment the relief.

(3) To look for the correct accentuation in the *'consonnes d'attaque'* as opposed to the conventional prosody which treats them as an anacrusis.[8]

The basic problems surrounding the setting of words to music in the genre of opera — notably those of accentuation and the decision to be made between recitative and aria — are those that have preoccupied all the great opera composers from Monteverdi to the present day and that have produced a myriad of similar, as well as widely divergent solutions. The basic dichotomy characterizing the debate as to whether the word or the music is more important is seen to resolve towards the end of the nineteenth century and the beginning of the twentieth. Undoubtedly inspired by the pioneering work of Schumann, in the realm of the *Lied,* towards the unity and balance of word and music, as well as of Weber in this connection, it is important to see Wagner as continuously striving towards a satisfactory equilibrium of libretto and score and of the value of the word with its musical projection, even if the final conclusion is that he failed because the sheer lyricism of the music at times rules out the possibility of such a desired balance.

For the French school, Debussy and Ravel took the *spoken* language as a basis for their prosody, and, although both must be regarded in the same way as derivative, to an extent, of Lully, their achievements are very different. As a result of intense concentration on utilizing verbal rhythmic patterns and very supple melodic lines, Debussy created a whole characterized by the feeling of continuous recitative; whilst Ravel, although using a considerable amount of recitative, obtained a much more melodious whole by virtue of the fact that absolute simplicity and uniformity of approach is always combined with a more clearly defined and potent thematic touch.

Honegger sets out here to break down completely the barriers between recitative and aria; to lose any of the dryness and perfunctoriness that are so often inherent in the former, whilst not falling into the trap of allowing melodic lyricism to exert its dangerous effect of annihilation on the aspect of projecting the text in a completely comprehensible manner. To avoid an excess of sustained high notes, lines of a purely instrumental nature and to create only lines inspired by the words themselves cannot be said to be original thought — merely the desires of an opera composer aware of the history and the implications of the genre who is filled with a desire to improve it. What is new though, is the basis from which Honegger started in order to achieve his aims. Unlike Ravel and Debussy who took the *spoken* word as their springboard, Honegger decided it was necessary for obvious practical reasons to start from the basis of 'tragic declamation' — the parallel being the closest he could see to the role assumed by the opera singer. From this vantage point he proceeded to try to extract from such a rendering of the words the appropriate melodic line to support and highlight them in the context of the opera. Consequently, the originality of the approach can be appreciated, and the method of achieving it analysed, by reference to Honegger's description of his technique, made some years later:

Of first importance in these means [by which I have achieved my aims], I should place a concept of prosody — of setting words to music and music to words — which is somewhat peculiar to me. And I should immediately add a shocking thing: French composers appear not to recognize the plastic significance of the texts which they set to music. Here I share the doubts of Richard Strauss when he was composing *Salomé,* following the text of Oscar Wilde: 'Why do the French sing differently from the way they speak? Is it atavism or tradition?' Upon which Romain Rolland advised him to study *Pelléas* carefully, which he considered to be the best example of good French words with music. Strauss bought the score, worked it over, and was astonished to discover 'that same indifference to delivery which from the beginning has so surprised me in French music'.

For me, the problem arose in the same way. At the time I was composing the music for *Antigone*, on a violent and even brutal text, I sometimes said to myself: 'If I combine words and music for this text in the customary fashion, it will lose its character, its power. *Pelléas* is an exceptional case. Maeterlinck's monochrome poem actually suggests this monotonous repetition, this impassive syllabism, by the use of which the sub-Debussyites have dragged the lyric theatre to its death. In any case Debussy's success cannot serve as a model for dramatic delivery.'

What I had to work out at all costs was the means whereby I might make others *understand* the lyric text: that, in my opinion, was the rule of the game in the realm of the lyric [theatre]. French dramatic musicians show an exclusive concern for the melodic design and a quite subordinate care for the conformity of text and music. Hence the legend that in the lyric theatre one can never understand the singers. Now, ninety-nine times out of a hundred, it is not the singers' fault, but the fault of the composers.

I had, at all costs, to dissociate myself from this careless prosody, as from the Debussyite droning. Therefore I sought for the right stress, especially on the attacking consonants, finding myself in this respect in clear-cut opposition to traditional principles. In this I had the happiness to be supported by Claudel, whose doctrine I had hitherto not known. What is important in the word is not the vowel, but the consonant: it really plays the role of a locomotive, dragging the whole word behind it. In classical singing, in the world of the *bel canto,* the vowel is queen, because one can hold the sound as long as one wishes on A,E,I,O,U. In our time, and for a dramatic delivery, the consonants project the word into the hall, they make it resound. Each word contains its potential, its melodic line. The addition of a melodic line in opposition to its own paralyses its flight, and the word collapses on the floor of the stage. My personal rule is to respect the word's plasticity as a means of giving it its full power.

Take an example from *Antigone*. At one instance, Créon violently interrupts the choir, crying out: 'Assez de sottises, vieillesse!' The conventional prosody suggests the following stress: 'Assez de sot*ti*ses, vieil*le*sse!' Try to project this phrase in anger with this rhythm: the aggressive effect is immediately blunted. Respecting the dramatic situation and Créon's anger, I made it: 'Assez de *sot*tises *vieil*lesse!' leaning on the roots of the words. The same for: 'l'homme est *i*nouï — l'homme *la*boure — l'homme *chas*se'. I placed the stress on the downbeat.

This approach has been generally disapproved [of] by composers and critics, but, to my great joy, singers, after they had raised their arms to the skies with 'Heavens, how complicated this music is!' came to me after the second rehearsal saying, 'You are right: when one has got the habit, one can no longer think of singing it otherwise.' My system helped them chiefly in sentences of rapid delivery, as well as in the high register . . ..

This prosodic system is carried to its fullest in *Antigone.* I have used it elsewhere, however. When I have a text to set to music, I have the author read it to me, or, if he is a poor reader, I imagine the way a good actor would utter it, how he would place the major stresses. If two or three key words are given their full value in a sentence, the general sense is immediately made clear. To find myself in full accord with Claudel on this point was for me a powerful satisfaction. Claudel gave me the most precious support: the theory I was advocating was no longer a whim, a musician's trick, but the studied opinion of the greatest poet of our times. I can equally invoke the testimony of Paul Valéry, who likewise agreed with me. By applying these principles, I simply wanted to restore a native simplicity and ease to French singing. Strictly speaking, I had not written a recitative, but melodies rapidly sung, so rapidly even that many thought they were not melodies. What is generally admired is the slow melody. Ask anyone to cite you a beautiful melody, and it will surely be marked *adagio*. And that is absurd. But to enumerate all the absurdities made sacred by custom would fill the shelves of a library.[9]

There can be no doubt that the text involved here is particularly suitable for Honegger to apply his theories — the notable lack of any lyrical expansion or development allows for a consistency of approach and method of unrivalled potential. It is possible to find in *Le roi David* a few examples of Honegger's theory that putting the accent on the high inflections was a new solution to the problem of textual comprehensibility — in particular his setting of the word 'Saül' (see Music Example 35 below).

Music Example 35: *Le roi David,* No. 4 'Chant de victoire', sopranos, bar 10

It is not, however, until *Judith* that sufficient examples of this vocal style occur for one to detect a systematic scheme in embryo before its fully developed, all-embracing status is encountered in *Antigone.* Nevertheless, with the exception of certain moments in the music for the confrontation between Judith and Holopherne, there is virtually no precedent for the melodic content that is uniformly characteristic of *Antigone*. The mis-accentuation characteristics in *Le roi David* and *Judith* — notably the almost total lack of up-beat treatment for anacrusic syllables — which resulted in increased clarity, is here combined with a style of melodic writing that allows for astonishingly rapid delivery of the text with absolutely no sacrifice of intelligibility. The speed of the declamation is so fast that the intensity and power of the text is liberated with even greater energy and expression of truth than before — a truly remarkable achievement bearing in mind the very nature of Cocteau's adaptation, and an apposite testament to the full, accurate and balanced alliance that he sought between the words and the music. The rapidity achieved is a model of operatic technique — never does it hold up the desirable flow of the text, not even this text with its quite unique rate of flow!

The contemporary critical reaction to this very personal and original prosody was almost unanimously favourable. André George concluded that Honegger had achieved an 'harmonious alliance, much as Debussy did in *Pelléas et Mélisande*, but with greater suppleness, with more melodic contours, less closely set intervals, [and] a more convincing rapidity and unity.'[10] Henry Prunières pointed out with disarming simplicity, but total accuracy, that 'l'effet à la lecture est assez surprenant *mais* à l'audition on s'aperçoit que cette prosodie n'a rien de choquant, qu'elle permet d'entendre tous les mots distinctement et qu'elle reproduit avec une étonnante fidélité les nuances de la déclamation'[11] [when reading it the effect is really quite surprising, *but* on hearing it one realizes that there is nothing shocking about this prosody, that, in fact, it enables one to hear all the words clearly and that it very faithfully reproduces the nuances of declamation].

Leo Mélitz used the term 'phonetic' to express just how far he felt Honegger had succeeded in finding a true musical expression for each word and was quick to point out that, although Richard Strauss, in his preface to the vocal score of *Intermezzo,* appeared to be expounding similar views, he failed where Honegger was successful because

> Strauss a été victime de son principe, qui l'a conduit à la banalité, tandis que Honegger a réussi, par l'observation fidèle de l'accent français, à créer du nouveau et, du seul point de vue de la musique, à faire une œuvre originale. Contrairement à Strauss, il incorpore déclamation des voix à tout l'ensemble: le chant n'est pas simplement enté, grâce à l'orchestre, sur un soutien musical, mais il s'en dégage naturellement et forme avec le reste des instruments, dont il est le plus expressif, un tout organique[12]
>
> [Strauss was the victim of his principle which led him to banality whilst Honegger, on the other hand, was successful in creating something new by very carefully observing the French accent, and, from the point of view of the music, was able to write an original work. Contrary to Strauss, he incorporates the declamation of the voices in the whole fabric; the voice-parts are not simply grafted on to a musical support (the orchestra), but emerge from it naturally and form with the remainder of the instruments (they being the most expressive) an organic whole].

His views on the phonetic quality of the prosody were supported by Eric

Reger,[13] whilst Emile Vuillermoz[14] also found a real and direct humanistic force behind the system — a remarkable vote of praise from a man regarded by most as the invincible keeper of all things traditional and conventional.

Two critics were unhappy: Jean Marnold[15] viewed the system as being incompatible with the idiosyncracies of the French language and, more importantly, as responsible for an indigent melodic invention; whilst Hans Müllner[16] criticized the lack of lyrical qualities, at the same time concluding that the day was saved by the distinction of the melodic cells used in the vocal lines. Keeping in focus the fact that the singers expressed simultaneously their horror at the difficult and declamatory feel of the vocal parts and their delight at the degree of communication, the plasticity, expressivity, speed, dynamic stress and intensity permitted, it is possible to see both sides quite clearly. The lack of basic melodic beauty and lyricism that can lead to a questioning of its validity as a sufficiently artistic creation in its own right can be judged by reference to passages such as the following (see Music Example 36 below).

Music Example 36: *Antigone,* Act 2 Scene VIII, **80** - **85**

crescendo
A.
dieu in_fernal va me pren _ dre vi_van _ te sans que les chants du mari _ a _ ge ré_pè _ tent mon
A.
nom. C'est la mort qui m'épou _ se
81
CORYPHÉE SOPRANO
parlé
sec et martelé
Tu mourras donc sans ê _ tre ma_la _ de sans bles_su _ res
81
très sec
A.
J'ai en_ten_du ra_conter la mort de la
S.
Libre, vierge vivan_te, cé_lè_bre seule en_tre les mortels tu entreras chez Pluton
espressivo

A.
3
fil - le de Tan-ta - le Au sommet du Si-py - le el-le sen-tit tout à coup le
82
rocher la prendre et pousser autour d'el-le comme un lier - re dur et maintenant la
82
nei-ge la recou - vre et ses lar - mes gla-cia - les cou-lent du haut en bas

83
A.
voi_la mon lit voi_la les ca_res _ ses qui m'attendent
CORYPHÉE SOPRANO
Oui_da mais nous sommes de pauvres humains et el_le é_tait
dé_es_se et fil _ le de dieu en somme c'est pour toi simple mortelle u_ne grande conso_lation que d'avoir le sort d'une
di_vi_ni_té
Moquez-vous de moi c'est bien le moment Ils n'atten_dent même pas que je dis_parais_se Ah
S.
sostenuto

Although the text benefits from being completely intelligible, the melodic projection is neither artistically entirely rewarding either to sing or listen to; this means that the success of the basic premises in the context of the whole must be questioned. A satisfactory answer surely does not proceed from treating this aspect of the work in isolation — the next section raises other such contentious issues and provides a solution to them all in the context of each other. The necessity for such a debate does not just lie in the existence of a minority group of critics who were against the favourable opinions of the majority, but is due to matters less easily definable, feelings and attitudes, undercurrents and movements, artistic credibility and audience security, all tersely hinted at by Roland Manuel:

> Prodige de franchise et de ténacité, *Antigone* apparaît comme l'œuvre la plus accomplie et la plus significative qu'ait donnée son auteur. Elle ne se contente point de mettre vivement en lumière la personalité athlétique de M. Arthur Honegger: elle le détache complètement, non sans doute de son siècle, mais de son milieu. Elle l'isole avec une sorte de cruauté et sépare curieusement sa musique du concert européen.
>
> On aime cette franchise. Elle permettra à M. Honegger de reconnaître les siens. Car *Antigone* ne peut manquer de dissiper l'espèce de malentendu qui a réuni tant de monde autour du *roi David.* Elle ne peut manquer de grossir la cohorte des fidèles d'*Horace victorieux.*
>
> *Le roi David,* qu'on le voulût ou non, situait son musicien au point de concours des tendances allemandes et françaises.
>
> Soucieux de se décider entre Richard Strauss et Fauré, M. Honegger n'avait pas attendu d'écrire *Antigone* pour choisir Honegger: *Horace* est là qui l'atteste, et *Judith,* et *Pacific 231,* sans oublier l'excellent *Concertino.* Mais *Antigone* efface jusqu'au souvenir de l'adhésion de son auteur à la Société des Nations Musicales.[17]
>
> [Marvel of frankness and tenacity, *Antigone* appears as the most accomplished and significant work of its creator. It does not merely bring to light the athletic personality of Arthur Honegger: it makes him completely stand out, if not from his century at least from his contemporaries. With a sort of cruelty, *Antigone* isolates him and curiously separates his music from mainstream European music.
>
> We like this frankness. It allows Arthur Honegger to recognize his own, because *Antigone* cannot fail to dispel the misunderstandings which united so many people against *Le roi David. Antigone* cannot fail to strengthen the numbers of the faithful supporters of *Horace victorieux. Le roi David,* whether we liked it or not, put Honegger at the point of convergence between German and French tendencies. Anxious to choose between Richard Strauss and Fauré, Honegger had not waited to write *Antigone* before choosing Honegger. *Horace victorieux* is there to bear witness to this, as are *Judith, Pacific 231* and the excellent *Concertino.* But *Antigone* goes as far as to remove the memory of its author becoming a member of the League of Musical Nations.]

> [*Antigone*] embodies my ambitions and my lyric efforts. Without shallow pride or false modesty, I believe that *Antigone* brought a little pebble to the lyric theatre. But this pebble has since fallen to the bottom of a pit and remained there.[18]

The relatively unstable position of opera being regarded by composers as a viable art-form is nowhere more clearly reflected than by the divergence of approach found in a handful of the operas that were produced in Paris in the post-First-World-War years. Ravel tried, in *L'heure espagnole,* an ingenious combination of *opera buffa* style and Wagnerian *Leitmotiv* technique; Roussel cast his eye back to the still visible remains of a once omnipresent French opera style and tradition, that of the *opéra-ballet*, in his *Padmavâtî*; whilst Stravinsky chose to cast his Cocteau tragedy, *Œdipus rex,* in a mould conditioned by the labels 'opera' and 'oratorio', with a Latin text into the bargain.

Overwhelmed by the intensity of the German and Italian nineteenth-century opera traditions, stifled, too, by the consistent pull of the French counteraction epitomized in the works of Massenet and Chabrier, it is surely little wonder that so many of the younger composers of this period either avoided opera altogether, contented themselves with what rarely rises above the quality of pastiche, or wrote mostly one-act operas in the Bizet/Offenbach tradition which would, of course, be less costly to produce. Combine this with the rigid division between the Opéra and the Opéra-Comique — the difficulty of obtaining recognition sufficient to merit attention from the former and the paucity of fare together with negative musical standards in the latter — the situation facing composers of Honegger's generation and the like-minded of others, can be seen and appreciated to be extremely difficult.

Milhaud, with a customary degree of *élan* and discerning eclecticism approaching the realms of sheer panache, took the bulls by their various horns and produced a number of large-scale operas (*Euménides* and *Orphée* in particular) which combine many of the good features of the different types, if not entirely eliminating the weaknesses of even any one of the same. Honegger, on the other hand, stands alone at this time, not only amongst his French companions, but in the Western musical tradition as a whole, as the one composer who, with *Antigone,* tried to bring the genre of *opera seria* to terms with the era without qualifications, degrees of subjectivism or techniques involving either abnegation or rejection of completely contemporary language and procedures. Bearing in mind the nature of *Le roi David,* which could have led him either to the oratorio or to a hybrid solution similar to that of Stravinsky, and the nature of his talent, which would have easily permitted him a successful career in the Opéra-Comique, the path trodden by *Judith* and numerous symphonic works is indeed a well-paved approach to the culminatory nature of *Antigone.*

In order to appreciate fully the contemporary reaction to this work and the reason why it succeeded in achieving many of its aims at the same time as it failed to remain either in the repertoire or as a consultative work for the then apprentices of opera, it is necessary to consider, in more general terms than in the previous two sections, Honegger's role in the creation of the opera as a whole. There should be no doubt that Honegger saw himself as subordinate to Cocteau in terms of the whole and that his music bore a similar relationship to the text. This deference to traditions, both old and newly revived, is paralleled by the similar way in which Cocteau himself subordinated all the other elements — he used an almost barren stage design together with white-faces for all the singers and utilized only a minimum of movement by all the characters including the chorus. However, the end-product does not bear this out — the score is so intensely symphonic that even the highly original, if contentious, prosody fails to counteract the disturbance unwittingly caused to the interrelated equilibria Cocteau was striving so hard to achieve in order that the text would be completely intelligible and dominant at all times.

Marcel Proust, at the end of *A la recherche du temps perdu,* made the assessment that Jean Cocteau would eventually exert a more profound and longer influence on the theatre than even Diaghilev by virtue of an 'action continue malaisée à définir'[19] (continuous action difficult to define). André Gide noted, with a customarily vitriolic inverted form of praise, that he approved of Cocteau's twentieth-century adaptation of Sophocles' *Antigone*, but, that it was good not *because,* but *in spite* of Cocteau![20] Bearing in mind particularly his texts for *Parade, Le bœuf sur le toit, Les mariés de la tour Eiffel, Roméo et Juliette, Le train bleu, Le pauvre matelot* and *Orphée,* Cocteau is certainly at his most original as well as *avant-garde* in *Antigone.* There is a combination of power and intensity with sincerity which is unusual for him and which finds an inevitably perfect match in Honegger's score.

The intensely powerful organic symphonism, developed and refined so wonderfully from its elemental state in works like *Pacific 231* and *Horace victorieux,* is a perfect support for the originality of the prosody but it presents two problems in its own right: (a) is the effect not more of a symphony with words which negates too many of the traditions of opera as well as challenging its basic premises too violently?; and (b) does it not also provide what really amounts only to an elaborate framework as opposed to effecting a sublime penetration of the depths of the subject?

The role of the chorus is very similar to that in Milhaud's *Euménides* — a colourful and powerful attempt at portraying the underlying forces of wisdom and good — but the question is whether or not in fact its role is consistently dramatic enough in the context of the whole? Given the uniformly high dramatic pace and degree of concentration evolved for each of the major characters the conclusion must be negative — particularly in terms of the 'Hymn to Bacchus', splendid though the music is. This criticism, however, cannot be levelled at the role of the orchestra where an independence from the vocal line is consistently maintained both to aid the declamation and to further the dramatic context by continuous provision of related material. The very personal style of orchestration, heavily characterized by the 'strata' approach which is linked simultaneously to the traditional family divisions of the orchestra and the layers of polyphonic activity, succeeds in making aurally viable many textures which appear from the piano part of the vocal score to be impossibly dissonant.

In the same way, criticisms of this nature cannot be levelled at the musical language. The style is more original and consistent than in any of his previous music. The use of atonality and an integrated role for polytonality are both aspects of his style to which he had been reconciling the public for quite some time. There is very little use of tonality throughout this work and this has the effect of defining the polytonal devices much more clearly, although never is there, at any stage, a feeling of atonality being used for its own sake, or as a means of avoiding any of the implications and inherent problems of tonal planes. The expansion of the tonal forces to the brink of atonality is always controlled such that their presence is still maintained, however distended and diversified their effect. The whole musical language is amazingly woven with the seemingly disparate forces of clarity, logicality and complexity in equal proportions.

The unbroken flow of very incisive rhythms and the sheer power and intensity of the music is all that remains to identify this score with the music of *Le roi David.* There is no Fauré or Debussy — no French elements in the *Le roi David* tradition as was the case in *Horace victorieux.* Gone, too, are the overtly Germanic heritages from Richard Strauss and Wagner — those Romantic qualities which remain in the music are lean to the point of emaciation and retrospective in a manner more akin to the Second Viennese School even if lacking that predominantly sardonic flavour which invariably tinged their lingering backward glances.

The informed musical critics of the day stood similarly divided on its merits and detractions and on its success or failure as both a piece of music and as a proffered solution to the problems of the lyric theatre. André George, Leo Mélitz, Henry Prunières, Rudolph Schülz-Dornburg, Paul le Flem, Paul Gilson, M. Denever and René Morax (*sic*)[21] all reacted very positively in its favour. All praised the prosody, the symphonic procedures, the powerful roles played by the chorus and the orchestra and the pure originality. All of them made a special point of noting derivatives which Honegger had either now omitted, continued to avoid, or improved upon. All were particularly pleased that no compromises had been permitted at any stage. Their general conclusion was that here lay the future of music-theatre; only Leo Mélitz was prepared to admit that '*Antigone* n'est [pas] un opéra pour le grand public. C'est une de ces œuvres qui devancent leur époque, bien qu'elles en résument tous les traits. Ce paradoxe est éternel'[22] [*Antigone* is not an opera for the general public. It is one of those works which is ahead of its time, although it summarizes all its features. This is an eternal paradox].

Arthur Hoérée, Roland-Manuel, Mario Pilati, Eric Reger and Emile Vuillermoz[23] — all similarly well-known for their advocacy of Honegger and, in most cases, for their close personal friendship with him — were less sure. Whilst none of them condemned it or were really willing, if actually able, to point to its weakness as an opera or as a musical score, they all expressed reservations or were notably sparing with their praise. Hoérée commented on the lack of lyricism — both in terms of lyrical expansion and lyrical development — but was happy to conclude that the text in fact had demanded a 'huge recitative approach'. Both he and Reger ventured to criticize the text. Hoérée saw it as rather too dense, whilst Reger was more positive in referring to it as a travesty. Pilati was prepared to see the work as only one of a number of possible solutions to the problems surrounding the future of the lyric theatre, but he did not see fit to commit himself in any way as regards those 'other solutions'.

Emile Vuillermoz decided that the text was simply too problematic for a composer to set to music and this is implicit, too, in Roland-Manuel's comment that the music could not portray in this case as it should, but merely outline. The isolation of this work is acknowledged by Roland-Manuel and he, like Leo Mélitz, stresses that the work is of tremendous *future* significance. None of these five 'middle of the road supporters' expressed the doubts and criticisms voiced by the majority of the general public in the way that Jean Marnold[24] and

Hans Müllner[25] did. Marnold praises all the positive features in the same way that the others had, but he also stresses the unnerving effect the prosody had on French-speakers and that the melodic invention seemed to have an unfortunately indigent quality as a direct result of it. He felt that the lack of lyrical qualities leads to a uniformly grey atmosphere which does little to alleviate the fact that the plot relentlessly and remorselessly concentrates on only one overwhelmingly pungent aspect of selective humanity. Müllner was even more worried because he saw in Honegger a talent to create such that marked him as a leader. Was this the direction Honegger was to take? If so, was it the right one for him, let alone for others, to be led along? These were his questions. In desperation almost, he quoted the words of Palestrina from Pfitzner's opera of the same name: 'restrain him — I feel he is wrong'.

When the combination of very modern words and a musical language which had a lack of charm in the Debussyian sense and little of the magnetism of the Wagnerian kind was presented to an audience in the light of Massenet, Chabrier, Chausson and d'Indy, it is surely not surprising that the public found it extremely difficult to accept. Despite an allowance for the technical difficulty of the vocal lines and the relatively restricted technique of singers of the period, the lack of sheer vocal lyricism and beauty did nothing but highlight the suffocating concentration of the whole which the audiences anyway found too personal and lacking in the basic and broad-based enough forces of all-embracing humanity which they had come to expect in operas. The fact that the audiences in general found it too relentless and uncompromising, excessively modern in its humanism, lacking in the qualities of reflection and subjectivity and too tough and personal for them to accept, cannot be attributed merely to the text because the music always *reveals* the text, continuously highlighting it and amplifying the dramatic energy of the already concentrated version — what is a near perfect musical score in response to a given text results in performance in an overall creation which was quite unacceptable at the time.

The main reason why it was so unacceptable is that it was in fact basically in the same tradition as the earlier infamous Cocteau *Les Six* contributions both to the anti-Romantic movement and the post-First-World-War reaction. The professed desire vividly to expose on the stage qualities of life and humanistic forces which were regarded as sacrosanct or too emotive to be bared in this way, combined with the approach permitting no compromise on any aspect, was still too advanced for the general public even though the shock elements of excess simplicity, vulgarity, luridness and derision of the earlier works of Cocteau and certain of *Les Six* are here all replaced by a quite natural quality of genuine sincerity. People were still not prepared to witness on the stage that stripping of the human soul that they had physically suffered and witnessed personally, and as a nation, on the battlefield; to combine it with a positive, original contribution to the progression from Romantic, anti-Romantic and post-Romantic musical styles only contributed to the problem. Leo Mélitz's conclusion, previously partially quoted, continues:

> Quiconque répugne à se laisser prendre aux faussetés d'un 'art pour le peuple' et éprouve le besoin de se regénérer dans des régions plus hautes, ne manquera pas de souscrire à l'opinion rapportée plus haut; unc chose

> est sure: ci cet opéra ne devait être qu'une apparition temporaire, il faudrait louer un temps qui produit des artistes d'un tel sérieux, d'un tel savoir et d'une telle personnalité.[26]
>
> [Whoever revolts at being caught up by the falsities of an 'art for the people' and who feels the need to be regenerated in a higher plane, will not fail to subscribe to the opinion above; one thing is certain, if this opera were only to be a temporary apparition, one would have to commend an era which produces such serious and knowledgeable artists with such personalities.]

If one reads the criticisms expressed in many German music journals and newspapers following the second performance the opera received at the Essen State Opera in 1928,[27] notably that by Martin Friedland,[28] it is possible to see how such a general public reaction can be kindled by the infiltration of political motives to inspire an anti-Honegger spirit as an advantageous part of a desired anti-French music movement. Thankfully, some — notably the critics of the *Frankfurter Zeitung, Melos, Berlin Börsenzeitung, Leipzig Neueste Nachrichten, Rheinisch Westfälische Zeitung* and the *Hamburg Nachrichten*[29] — were able to maintain their status as apolitical, independent critics and recognize the work for what it was: the most important opera in the history of musical drama in France since *Pelléas et Mélisande.* They, like Leo Mélitz, could appreciate the truth and sincerity of Honegger's fourth, and final paragraph in the preface to the score: 'as for the rest may it be the honest work of an honest workman',[30] even if they did not conclude what he and the work meant as appositely as Mélitz did by quoting Luther: 'here is my place, I can choose no other. God help me. Amen.'[31] However, not even Leo Mélitz could have realized the significance that both this opera and the public reaction to it, together with Honegger's remark and his own quotation of Luther would have a few years later as Honegger faced the first of the two crises that were, each in its own way, to alter completely his relationship with the creative side of his nature.

TABLE 5

Antigone: a bibliography

* Maurice Brilliant,	*Le Correspondant,* 25 January 1928.
* Claude Bussy,	*Le Magazine Egyptien,* 24 March 1928.
* M. Denever,	*Théâtre* (Bruxelles), 6 January 1928.
H. Denizeau,	*Appogiature,* 15 January 1931, 11-15.
Martin Friedland,	*Allgemeine Musikzeitung,* Vol. 55 (1928), 64-65.
André George,	*Chesterian,* No. 70 (April-May 1928), 190-92.
	Les Nouvelles Littéraires, 21 January 1928, 11.
* Paul Gilson,	*Midi* (Bruxelles), 31 December 1927.
Henry Hell,	*La Revue Musicale,* 1952, 5-7.
Arthur Hoérée,	*Beaux Arts,* 1 February 1928, 47-48.
	**Chantecler,* 14 January 1928.
	L'Information Musicale, 3 February 1943, 197.
	Revue Européene, March 1928, 315-20.
Jean Marnold,	*Mercure de France,* 15 June 1928, 703-05.
Leo Mélitz,	*La Revue Musicale,* October 1927, 242-48.
	**Der Scheinwerfer,* January 1928, 2-5.
René Morax,	*La Gazette de Lausanne,* 5 January 1928, 2.
Hans Müllner,	*Signale,* No. 6 (1928), 169-72.
M. Niggli,	*Neue Züricher Zeitung,* 4 January 1928, 1.
Mario Pilati,	*Bolettino Bibliografico Musicale,* February 1928, 13-20.
Henry Prunières,	*La Revue Musicale,* 1 February 1928, 59-61.
Erik Reger,	*Musikblätter des Anbruchs,* 2 February 1928, 62-65.
A. Rohlfing,	*Melos,* February 1928, 81-85.
Roland-Manuel,	*Le Ménéstrel,* 6 January 1928, 6-7.
	Musique, 15 January 1928, 165-67.
R. Schülz-Dornburg,	*Der Scheinwerfer,* January 1928, 3.
G. Systermans,	*La Libre Belgique,* 5 January 1928.
Emile Vuillermoz,	*Candide,* No. 201 (19 January 1928), 9.
	**Excelsior,* 16 January 1928.
Anon:	**Berliner Börsenzeitung,* 15 January 1928.
	**Candide,* 19 January 1928.
	**Düsseldorfer Nachrichten,* 16 January 1928.
	**Essener Allgemeine Zeitung,* 12 January 1928.
	**L'Etoile Belge,* 12 January 1928.
	**Frankfurter Zeitung,* No. 27 (15 January 1928).
	**Hamburger Nachrichten,* 14 January 1928.
	**Kölner Tageblatt,* 13 January 1928.
	**Kölnische Zeitung,* 13 January 1928.
	**Leipziger Neueste Nachrichten,* 16 January 1928.
	**Der Mittag-Düsseldorf,* 1 February 1928.
	**Die Musik,* January 1928.
	**La Revue Musicale Belge,* January 1928.
	**Rheinisch Westfälische Zeitung,* 12 January 1928.
	**Le Soir,* 30 December 1927.
	The Times, 5 January 1928.
	**Volkswacht Essen,* 12 January 1928.

*Quoted in Paul Collaer, *Etude sur 'Antigone'* (Senart, Paris, 1930).

Notes to Chapter V

[1]Title of a Rondeau by Guillaume de Machaut [My beginning is my end and my end my beginning].

[2]*I am a Composer* (Faber and Faber, London, 1966), 81.

[3]'Daybook, 16 January 1923', in *The Journals of André Gide,* translated by Justin O'Brien, Vol. II, 321.

[4]Vocal score published by Editions Senart /Salabert (EMS 7297), 1927.

[5]Full score published by Editions Senart/Salabert, 1927.

[6]Vocal score published by Editions Senart/Salabert (EMS 7297), 1927.

[7]Vocal score published by Editions Senart/Salabert (EMS 7297), 1927.

[8]Vocal score published by Editions Senart/Salabert (EMS 7297), 1927.

[9]*I am a Composer* (Faber and Faber, London, 1966), 95-98.

[10]'*Antigone* d'Arthur Honegger', *Chesterian,* No. 70 (April-May 1928), 190-92 (p. 192).

[11]'*Antigone*', *La Revue Musicale,* 1 February 1928, 59-61 (p. 60).

[12]'L'*Antigone* d'Arthur Honegger', *La Revue Musicale,* October 1927, 242-48 (p. 244).

[13]'*Antigone* von Arthur Honegger', *Musikblätter des Anbruchs,* 2 February 1928, 62-65.

[14]*Excelsior*, 16 January 1928.

[15]'*Antigone*', *Mercure de France,* No. 720 (15 June 1928), 703-05.

[16]'Honeggertage in Essen: Deutsche Uraufführung der Oper *Antigone', Signale*, No. 6 (1928), 169-72.

[17]'Bruxelles: La première d'*Antigone*', *Le Ménéstrel*, 6 January 1928, 6-7 (p. 6).

[18]*I am a Composer* (Faber and Faber, London, 1966), 99.

[19]3 vols, Nouvelle Revue Française/Gallimard, 1947, III.

[20]'Daybook, 16 January 1923', in *The Journals of André Gide,* translated by Justin O'Brien, Vol. II, 321.

[21]See Table 5, page 145, for references.

[22]'L'*Antigone* d'Arthur Honegger', *La Revue Musicale*, October 1927, 242-48 (p. 248).

[23]See Table 5, page 145, for references.

[24]'*Antigone*', *Mercure de France*, No. 720 (15 June 1928), 703-05.

[25]'Honeggertage in Essen: Deutsche Uraufführung der Oper *Antigone*', *Signale*, No. 6 (1928), 169-72.

[26]'L'*Antigone* d'Arthur Honegger', *La Revue Musicale*, October 1927, 242-48 (p. 248)).

[27]In the German translation by Leo Mélitz. The opera was revived and given in German in Zürich on 8 June 1934. An English translation was made by F. Ferguson for the first American performance given by the New York Laboratory Theatre on 24 April 1930. The work was not given in Paris until 1943, when it was staged at the Opéra, and it has yet to be produced in England.

[28]'*Antigone*', *Allgemeine Musikzeitung*, Vol. 55 (1928), 64-65.

[29]See Table 5, page 145, for references.

[30]Vocal score published by Editions Senart/Salabert (EMS 7297), 1927.

[31]'L'*Antigone* d'Arthur Honegger', *La Revue Musicale*, October 1927, 242-48 (p. 244).

CHAPTER VI

Second interlude: diversification

Part I: *Rugby*

A list of works for the two years following the completion of *Antigone* appears relatively sparse (see Table 6 below).

TABLE 6

Compositions between *Antigone* and *Amphion*

1927	*Napoléon* — Film Score.
1928	*Roses de métal* — Ballet Music;
	Mouvement symphonique n° 2 (*Rugby*) for Orchestra;
	Sur le nom d'Albert Roussel for Piano.
1929	*Vocalise — Etude* for Voice and Piano;
	Amphion — Melodrama.

The reason for this is quite simply the demands on his time that world-wide success now made. As early as 1925 the first American performance of *Le roi David* was added to over fifty European performances and led to Honegger conducting concerts in New York and Buenos-Aires during the autumn of the same year. By 1927 two monographs[1] had appeared in print to add weight to the extensive acclaim which continuously appeared in the columns of almost countless music journals in many different countries, and his collaboration was sought by many of the most distinguished practitioners of the other arts — most notably Ida Rubinstein, Gabriel d'Annunzio, Paul Valéry, Abel Gance and Jean Cocteau. As a conductor of considerable ability, he was constantly invited to direct performances of his own music: in 1927 he conducted performances in the concert halls of Athens, Boston, Brussels, Chicago, Leningrad, London, Warsaw and Zürich to name but a few. On a tour of the U.S.A. and South America during the winter of 1928-29 with his wife, Andrée Vaurabourg, as soloist in the *Concertino* for piano and orchestra, he conducted thirty concerts in twenty different towns with quite overwhelming and unanimous success.

The time-consuming nature of the preparations for the first performance of *Antigone* was doubtless exacerbated by the première of *L'impératrice aux rochers* occurring in the same year and probably accounts most for the fact that the only other score he wrote in 1927 was that for the film *Napoléon*. This was his second film score and his second collaboration with the veteran author-producer-director Abel Gance. Such was the success of his music and his stature generally that Salabert published a *Suite for Small Orchestra* consisting of eight movements from the complete score.

Although, like the film score for *Napoléon,* strictly outside the boundaries of this book, the music Honegger wrote for the ballet *Roses de métal* by Elisabeth Grammont de Clermont-Tonnerre must be noted with respect to its scoring — for piano and four dynamophones. The 'Bertrand dynamophone' was one of the forerunners of the type of instrument perfected a couple of years later by Maurice Martenot — to part of whose name it is now always referred. This experimentation is typical of Honegger; so, too, is his use of the 'musical saw' in *Antigone* and his passionate belief in the value of a saxophone section within the orchestra (both, incidentally in combination in *Antigone*!), together with his utilization of actual-pitch notation for transposing instruments in his scores and his later advocacy for the 'new and simplified' notation conceived by Nicolas Obouhow[2]. Apart from the use of the 'prepared piano' in *Jeanne d'Arc au bûcher*, his only other addition to the instrumental array is the ondes Martenot, which has a prominent part in several of the large scores from the 1930s[3].

The handful of works written in 1928 are widely different: besides the ballet score *Roses de métal*, there is the *Sur le nom d'Albert Roussel* for piano solo. The publication of a set of short pieces dedicated to a distinguished artist in celebration of an anniversary was a form of tribute much favoured by various French musical circles at this time, *La Revue Musicale* in particular; the other contributors to this one were Beck, Delage, Hoérée, Ibert, Milhaud, Poulenc and Tansman. The deep-rooted friendship, respect and admiration that was mutual between Honegger and Roussel resulted in a cameo vividly characterized by the ingenious contrapuntal interweaving of three themes — one a solmization of Albert Roussel, the other two both quotations from Roussel's own works (the first from the ballet *Festin de l'araignée,* the second from the *Piano Concerto*). Like the short didactic *Vocalise-Etude* written a few months later, early in 1929, it illustrates perfectly the firmly-original grasp Honegger had by then on the style and content of his music. Its strong broadly-based tonal planes, combined with a chromaticism kept absolutely disciplined by contrapuntal procedures and devices, support long sweeping themes where the powerful binding effect of diatonic intervallic spans together with a juxtaposition of melodic tonalities result in a colouring constantly revitalized by its kaleidoscopic nature. Perhaps the most significant factor is the organic rhythmic impulse — a very vital force that always supports the melodic, harmonic and tonal arguments and progressions in a remarkably integrated way.

The score of greatest significance from this period preceding the next major dramatic work — *Amphion* — is the orchestral *Mouvement symphonique n° 2.* Writing in *Excelsior* about the work, Honegger explained his conception of the piece, and hence the derivation of its subtitle *Rugby*, as:

> J'aime beaucoup le jeu de football, cependant le rugby me dit davantage.

Il me paraît plus spontané, plus direct, plus près de la nature que le jeu de football qui est plus scientifique. Certes, la cadence savamment préparée du football, ne m'échappe pas, mais je me sens plus spécialement attiré par le rythme sauvage, brusque, désordonné, désespéré du rugby. Il serait faux de considérer mon morceau comme de la musique à programme. Il cherche tout simplement à exprimer, dans ma langue de musicien, les attaques et les ripostes du jeu, le rythme et la couleur d'un match au stade de Colombes; par honnêteté, je me crois tenu d'indiquer mes sources. C'est la raison pour laquelle cette courte composition porte le nom de Rugby.[4]

[I very much like football, but I prefer rugby. I find it more spontaneous, more direct and closer to nature than football which is a more scientific game. I am aware of a carefully controlled rhythm in football and for me the savage, brusque, untidy and desperate rhythm of rugby is more attractive. It would be wrong to consider my piece as programme music. All it does is to try to express in my own musician's language, the attacks and ripostes of the game, and the rhythm and colour of a match at the Colombes Stadium; I honestly feel it is only right to name my sources. That is the reason why this short composition bears the title of *Rugby*.]

He was more detailed and specific about some of these matters in a conversation he had with André Obey, which was quoted by José Bruyr:

J'aime: 1° cette espèce d'euphorie, d'espoir, de joie grandiose et gratuite que donne le coup d'envoi; 2° Les phases à la fois fatales et imprévues du jeu; démarrages en dribbling des avants, descentes des trois-quarts, cafouillages mêlées, échappées, zig-zags. 3° Enfin, l'atmosphère du plein air, vibrante d'enthousiasme.[5]

[I like: (i) the euphoric atmosphere of hope, grandeur and carefree joy that surrounds the kick-off; (ii) the fateful and unexpected phases of the game; the dribbling runs by the forwards, dashes by the three-quarters, blunders, scrums, breakaways, zig-zags; (iii) finally I like the atmosphere of fresh air vibrating with enthusiasm.]

The work was the only one commissioned by the Orchestre symphonique de Paris for their inaugural concert — a fact which, more perhaps than any other, accurately reflects the tremendous standing that Honegger had in Parisian musical life. Any new work of his was seized upon by seemingly everyone for careful examination and Honegger was again distressed because, as had been the case with *Pacific 231,* most went to great lengths to identify and describe pictorial features of the work in relation to its subtitle which he himself had declared were non-existent. Nearly all of them failed to appreciate that this work is an *expression* of the various excitements characteristic of the game of rugby and not merely a *description* of any or all such features. The parallel that has often been drawn between this work and Debussy's *Jeux* is perfectly valid *if* it is appreciated that Honegger was an 'Expressionist' and Debussy an 'Impressionist' (to utilize the traditional musical categories of the period), and that the subject matters were uniquely suited to their respective approaches. The comparisons made with Louis Beydts' *Fanfares, Défilé olympique* by

Loucheur, Capdevielle's *Pérégrinos* and *Half-time* by Martinů are equally justifiable — but in all these cases final comparison based only on a consideration of artistic merit leaves *Rugby* in an elevated class of its own.

Although Honegger's aims in *Pacific 231* were very similar, the glorification of mechanical movements is occasionally subjective to a degree that makes some pictorial allegories unavoidable in comparison to this hymn to human movements that is so totally objective. To express the incredible dynamism of a game which combines sheer force with vibrancy and even lyricism of rhythmical activity, is no easy task, yet is ideally suited to Honegger's technique. The virility and organic force of the rhythmic structures in this piece are typical of his music since *Horace victorieux* and *Pacific 231,* but here they are combined with a degree of syncopation and cross-play that, whilst being Stravinskyian in origin, is peculiarly his own as it was too in *Chant de joie* and the *Concertino* for piano and orchestra. There is also a general lightness and quality of airiness about the whole fabric of *Rugby* which is the direct result of the latter two works and marks a distinct change when it is compared to the former two scores.

In *Pacific 231* he attempted to 'renew' the 'chorale-variation' form; here he sets out to give new life to the 'rondo' form, whilst imbuing it most satisfactorily with the spirit of variation technique. A summary of the overall structure of the work is presented in Diagram 18 opposite.

Several features of this opening are peculiarly Honeggerian — the subtle colouring of the leading-note start (the work is quite firmly in D major) which resolves to D and, simultaneously, by contrary motion principles, to B and A; the scalic combination of D, C and B majors together with the patterning of the quasi-arpeggiaic descending figuration in bars 3, 4 and 5 by cells of a major or minor third which are either open (i.e. with no intermediary note present, marked ∧ in Music Example 37, pages 152-53) or closed (i.e. with the intermediary note present, marked ⌒ above); and the very carefully dovetailed scoring, are all aspects of his style previously remarked upon in connection with earlier works.

The first theme is unusually diatonic for Honegger, nevertheless the broad sweep combined with a decorated triadic scheme and a sudden tonal sidestep at the end make it utterly personal (see Music Example 38 pages 152-53).

Diagram 18:

Mouvement symphonique n° 2 (*Rugby*)

- [1]		Introduction
[1] - [2]		Theme 1 (Trombones 1-6A [1]) with counterstatement (horns-trumpet 5B[2] -)
[2] - [8]		Episode 1— including ( ) figure 'x', melodic fragment E^1 (woodwind 1-3A [4]) and E^2 (upper strings 1-3A [6]), and motif 'y' (cellos 1-2A [5])
[8] - [12]		Theme 1 — developed to embrace melodic fragments E^1 and E^2 and figure 'x' together with its inverted form ( ) 'x^I'
[12] -5A [12]		Introduction (abbreviated)
6A [12] - [14]		Theme 2 and counterstatement ([13] -) involving canonic imitation
[14] - [18]		Episode 2— essentially based on 'x' and 'x^I' and leading to:
[18] -3B [19]		Theme 2 with accompaniment involving imitative fragments of Theme 2 and 'x'; 2-1B [19]: transition based on part of Episode 1 (see after [3]) to:
[19] - [25]	Episode 3: [19] -3A [22]	based on Theme 1 with various accompaniment motives derived by diminution
	6B [23] - [23]	based on motif 'y' from Episode 1 (see [5]-[8])
	[23] - [24]	Theme 2 with imitative accompaniment by diminution
	[24] - [25]	based on Episode 1 material (see [2]-[3])
[25] - [27]		Theme 1 (trombones) with part of accompaniment (flute/violin I) derived first from Theme 2 by diminution (-[26]), and then from 'x' ([26]- violins)
[27] -	Coda: [27]-[29]	Introduction — extended by development
	[29]-[30]	Reference to opening of Theme 1 (above bass based on 'x')
	[30] -	opening of Introduction and cadential gestures

Music Example 37: *Rugby,* opening - 4B[1]

à 2
à 2
à 2
à 2
3e
4e
Enlever les sourdines
div.

Arthur Honegger, Paris 1928.

Music Example 38: *Rugby,* [1] - 6A [1]

The textural aspect of pairing an ostinato-like set of figures and a simple, but rhythmically enlivened bass beneath the theme is one of his stylistic traits (cf. also [8] and 8B [13]); so, too, is the way in which the ostinato-like figures are conceived using the principle of contrary motion. A particular procedure is used twice in the 'Episode' (1) that follows: a texture is established, repeated underneath a melodic fragment (E^1 and E^2 respectively), and then stated again with an appropriate degree of transition to the next section. In the first part of Episode 1, the basic key structure is around G minor/major, whilst in the second part ([5] -), it is around B♭ minor and B major — the aspect of tertiary relationships between the two and between the latter pair and the key of the whole being a procedural device long familiar in his music.

When Theme 1 returns after the first episode ([8] -) it is followed by both E^1 and E^2 before part of it is used in a contracted version ([11] -) to achieve an appropriate climax prior to the return of the music of the Introduction. The strength of this section within the whole lies primarily in its tonal role because it is framed by the tonality of C♭ major which, as the leading-note tonality in relation to the entire work, forms a tremendous preparation for the return of the 'Introduction' at [12], in the key of D major. Typical of Honegger's fastidious attention to aesthetic balance and proportions, however, is firstly the return in between the pillars of C♯ major ([8] - and [11] -) to the tertiary related tonal centres (G major, B major and G minor) which had dominated the first episode; and, secondly, the interlocking of the material of the 'Introduction' to derive maximum tension from its return in order that the impetus generated so far should not be interrupted and dissipated.

The second theme that emerges from the truncated recapitulation of the material of the Introduction is of almost naïve simplicity and has its roots in many of the thematic procedures evident in the second and third movements of most of the earlier chamber music and some of the orchestral works, including the *Pastorale d'été* (see Music Example 39 overleaf).

Music Example 39: *Rugby*, 8B [13] - [14]

13
a 2
sostenuto
pizz

(Reproduit avec l'autorisation des EDITIONS SALABERT, Paris, propriétaires de l'œuvre.)

Its purely triadic outline and repetitive cellular rhythmic structure almost demand the imitative treatment to which it is immediately subjected when counterstated after [13]. The fact that this is understandably seen by the pictorially-minded as an expression of the relief of tension during the 'half-time' following the fray of the first half is musically insignificant; what is important is that, whatever it may be, it is prevented from being a formal gesture of quite disastrous inconsequence by virtue of the continuous integration of it into the 'play' of the 'second half' — Honegger had long since abandoned the sterile habit of an unintegrated ABA^1 structure. In both the second and third episodes that follow, there are fine examples of the 'long, slow build-up' of which Honegger was such a master. The second ([14] - [18]) takes the figuration 'x' as its starting point, and, by a technique of polyphonic juxtaposition of ever-increasing complexity, effects a long and sustained preparation for the contrapuntal web surrounding Theme 2 in which it culminates at [18]. The third proceeds likewise, but by different means: initially the culminatory Theme 1 is transformed into an urgent motif (bass line after [19]), which drives the music forward from subsection to subsection (each of which contains a fragment of Theme 1 in a different rhythmic anticipation of its full statement at [25]); subsequently (and in the pursuit of complete integration) part of Episode 1 as well as Theme 2 are involved in this tremendously long preparation for the climactic return of the Introduction at [27].

The Coda not only involves a restatement of the Introduction, but also includes a further reference to Theme 1. The tonal vagueness during most of Episode 2 gives way to a very clear F major for the return of Theme 2 at [18]. There is no comparable uncertainty about the tonality during the final episode: the D major achieved at [25] is the key of the whole by predominant patterning as well as by logical progression. The brief reference to the tonality of E♭ major at the outset of the Coda is neatly contrived to counterbalance the use of C♯ major for the final reference to Theme 1. Seven bars before the end, the C♯ major tonality conveniently reveals the note upon which the piece started, and a final D major cadence is neatly contrived by courtesy of the opening progression of the Introduction being repeated for the final time.

When considered as a whole, a questioning of the balance of musical elements must raise some doubt. The predominant force is undeniably that of rhythm — so much so that the forces of melody, harmony and tonality must be seen to be playing subsidiary roles — subsidiary, too, in the very nature of their contributions. The almost bland diatonicism of the slow melodic lines and the dry counterpoint which, combined with a very pronounced use of his 'strata' type orchestration (in itself very sober and completely lacking any percussion), result in a rather thin harmonic tissue. These features, together with the areas of obvious and rather conservative tonality, are all aspects of his style which are relatively weak in this work in comparison to the extremely inventive and consistently organic rhythmic aspect. The lack of true distinction in these fields is, however, somewhat compensated for by the strength of the formal structuring — the renewal of form is as successful here in avoiding the vissicitudes of Stravinskyian 'formal rejuvenations', as was the case with *Pacific 231*. A similar question mark must surround the next major dramatic work, too, although not all the blame lies at the feet of the composer in this instance.

Part II: *Amphion*

In 1891 Paul Valéry conceived the idea of a 'spectacle' involving the total union of words, song, orchestral music and acting, which was to be built around the story of Amphion. In an article published in the journal *Conferencia*[6] during 1932 he explained how he had been against opera as such — he saw it as chaos, particularly the Wagnerian conception of Gesamtkunstwerk. Instead, he envisaged a genuine mixture, where all the elements were well separated and the music kept to a level that would ensure a true overall balance. His innate love and concern for architectural proportions, balance and shapes is clearly reflected in this work and in the very nature of the legend on which it is based.[7]

At the time, Valéry was living in a house in Neuilly with his close friends Pierre Loüys and Claude Debussy. During the course of 1893-94 much effort on his behalf was spent in trying to persuade Debussy to collaborate with him. His refusal and a plethora of other commitments resulted in the project laying in abeyance until 1922 when, whilst delivering a lecture at the 1922 Geneva Conference entitled 'Poésie et langue', he succeeded in raising the interest of various people, including Honegger, in the broad principles behind his *Amphion* project. Seven years later, with Ida Rubinstein now the driving force behind the scheme, Honegger received the text from Valéry and a commission from her for the music for a production she was to stage at the Opéra with herself in the title-role. This was a project which, whilst utterly French in spirit and more classically based than inspired by the principles of antiquity, was motivated above all by a humanistic ideal which meant that Honegger was the perfect collaborator in spirit as well as technique. Valéry's dictum, that Amphion 'devient donc le symbole de l'artiste se sacrifiant pour son art'[8] [thus becomes the symbol of the artist who sacrifices himself for his art] could not have found a more sympathetic response than in Honegger, who recalled in *I am a Composer* that 'I launched a project which Paul Valéry had already discussed with me some years earlier. This was *Amphion* . . . a project which Valéry had previously entrusted to Debussy; a heavy responsibility, a great honour.'[9]

Valéry recognized that Honegger's task was a very difficult one and provided extensive notes of great clarity for his guidance.[10] The result was such that Valéry said 'il me fallait un grand musicien. Je l'ai eu'[11] [I needed a great musician. I got one]. He felt that 'Honegger l'a pénétrée et animée de son grand souffle'[12] [Honegger penetrated and animated the text with his great inspiration], and concluded that 'je ne vois pas beaucoup de compositeurs vivants qui eussent compris et traité le problème comme il l'a fait; et je crois d'ailleurs que cette épreuve ne sera pas sans fruit sur ses travaux ultérieurs'[13] [I cannot see many composers, alive today, who would have understood and treated the problem as he did; furthermore, I believe his experiment will bear fruit in future works].

Honegger was quick to respond with his usual modesty and warm sincerity, but when he coined Valéry's phrase 'il me fallait un grand poète'[14] [I needed a great poet] there was something particularly significant about it in view of his method of setting words and visual images to music. This probably accounts for the conclusion to which Henry Prunières came, namely that this is a great work of Honegger because the text is so good — some of his previous collaborations (not named but obviously aimed at Cocteau's *Antigone*) being somewhat dubious in this respect.[15] He drew particular attention to the mastery of the language of the text and the beauty of the poetry which he felt found perfect support in the prosody and melodic shapes of Honegger's music. Certainly the classical forces, the perfection of the structure and the delicate architectural balances that abound throughout the text are perfectly matched by a musician whose musical spirit and technique incorporate them quite naturally and spontaneously. Similarly perfect in collaboration must have been the roles of the choreographer, Massine, and the designer of the costumes and décor, Benois, if the contemporary critical and public acclaim is taken into account — the single exception apparently being Boris de Schlœzer who could find nothing to redeem the work.[16] When dealing with the musical score most discovered in it many of the desirable qualities that they had found lacking in *Antigone* — as Henri Malherbe put it, it was 'la meilleure partition qu' Honegger ait écrite: ces pages de forte structure pourraient servir de rajeunissement à toute la musique lyrique'[17] [the best score Honegger has written; these strongly structured pages could act as a rejuvenation of all lyrical music].

Honegger wrote the score in 1929 and it received its first performance when the work was staged at the Opéra in 1931. Such was the success that concert performances were arranged the very next year — the first being at the Université des Annales in conjunction with lectures on the work given by Valéry and Honegger.

The Greek myth of Amphion, son of Jupiter and Antigone, which relates his incredible achievement and the denial of his enjoyment of it, is succinctly summarized by Valéry in a preface to the vocal score[18]:

> Arrested, during his wild and primitive life, by a voice coming from the skies, Amphion receives in a dream the message of Apollo, who delivers the lyre into his hands.
>
> When he wakes, Amphion sees the magic instrument, and strikes it roughly. The lyre gives forth a dreadful sound, which disturbs nature and terrifies mankind. Filled with religious fear, Amphion touches the strings and draws from them tones, both smooth and brilliant, which charm inanimate life and living beings.
>
> By dint of trial the hero discovers the scales, and invents music and architecture. In the sight of the astonished people he brings the stones to life, and by the voice of the lyre, he builds Thebes and the Temple of Apollo, where the Muses are transformed into columns.
>
> He is applauded, and the people fain would carry him into the temple, and acclaim him as a god. But the veiled figure of a woman bars their passage, and bears him away with her, after having cast the lyre into a deep fountain.
>
> Amphion, alone of all, shall not enjoy his work of creation.
>
> Silence falls.

The work is divided into three sections: the outer two have continuous music and frame the central 'melodrama' where Amphion, having awoken and discovered the lyre and its potential powers, recalls his dream and realizes its significance.

Analysis:

Section I:

A huge gorge or crevice in the rock at the top of a mountain standing out in the sky, which is visible from the top of the theatre to the level of the stage. The lowest level of the two masses of rock right and left is planted with huge trees — oaks, beeches and chestnuts. Above, leave the rock area bare. Near the right-hand top the rock effect should be crystalline forms, like groups of prisms all mixed up, with some of the faces vaguely lit. A little bit of snow should glitter here and there on the high points.

In the middle of the scene a pool or a gentle fountain. Around it put blocks of granite or basalt. There should be general disorder amongst the blocks that can be seen and in the background, and the gap can be closed with them.

In the wood regions are to be carefully put the paths and the practical flats that are demanded by the later scenes.

The night sky is to be designed after photos of the Milky Way. Very shaded lights, with some stars of various sizes and black empty spaces here and there.

As the curtain rises little groups of nocturnal creatures are to be dancing at different points on the stage. They disappear, they are then invisible until such time as they are seen in the transparent darkness.

Men and women enter from the right looking for one another, speaking by signs, situating themselves in the trees. They prepare to sleep, going well into the shadows for cover. One listens to the calm of the Harmony of the Spheres. A high-pitched and inhuman note suggests a constant and giddy rotation. On the monotonous note the 'Song of the Streams' soon begins.[19]

(- [3]: 'Introduction')

The creation of a texture suitable in colour and mood without any trace of banality was not an easy feat, given the nature and detail of Valéry's annotations, but one which Honegger achieved admirably with his usual feel for appropriateness and immediacy (see Music Example 40 opposite).

Music Example 40: *Amphion*, - 1B [3]

(Reproduit avec l'autorisation des EDITIONS SALABERT, Paris, propriétaires de l'œuvre.)

The sheer breadth of the textural framework of superimposed fourths and fifths provides a tremendous parallel to Valéry's conception of the stage design. The deftness of the basic orchestration, together with the highly original device of percussion of indefinite pitch outlining, in basic pitch areas and augmented rhythm, the specific contour of the xylophone motives by way of an echo, succinctly reinforce the mood and atmosphere being created for the scene. The motivic procedure in the xylophone part clearly illustrates Honegger's recurrent technique of continuous expansion and development of an idea from a cell until it forms a substantial whole that is sprung with the latent energy of organic creation.

The strictly canonic interweavings of the upper strings at 2 (his inspired interpretation of Valéry's request for a 'high-pitched and inhuman note' suggesting 'a constant and giddy rotation'), emerges so naturally from the pedal chord and effects a controlled transition to the 'Chant des sources' (see Music Example 41 opposite).

Music Example 41: *Amphion*, 3 - 1B [4]

(3 - 4: 'Chant des sources'):

As with the lamenting women of *Le roi David* and *Judith*, so here too, Honegger resorts to a limpid pastorality characterized by modality (the typical ambivalence of the third and the unresolved dichotomy of tonic and dominant — A/E minors) and the use of *vocalise*, together with an appropriately free and relaxed rhythmical structuring.

(4 - 7: 'Entrée d'Amphion')

> A brief and veiled fanfare, or at least some harsh announcement of Amphion's entrance. He appears, now bending over something savage, animal, or monstrous female, or ? He ponders over it, the force knocks him off his feet and, taking a large knife, he prepares to cut its throat.

The fanfare is very typical of Honegger in its construction — the harmonic tissue controlled by contrary-motion principles of mock polyphonically-independent lines in particular highlight its parentage as those of *Le roi David* (and hence *Judith* and *Antigone*), whilst its very low tessitura and unique scoring accurately reflect the influence of the orchestral experiences of works like *Pacific 231*, *Le chant de Nigamon* and *Horace victorieux* on the formation of his own personal and original musical language and orchestral palette (see Music Example 42 below).

Music Example 42: *Amphion*, 1B 4 - 5

ENTRÉE D'AMPHION. Il s'apprête à égorger une proie.
ENTRANCE OF AMPHION. He is about to destroy a beast he has captured.
AMPHION TRITT AUF. Er geht daran, eine Beute zu töten.
4
Animé
Animé ♩= 132
C.B.
p cresc
f sourd
Timb.
Cors
Celli

The voice that interrupts the fanfare and calls to Amphion with the words 'Wherefore? do not torture the living, death is the office of immortal hands' has a melodic line that illustrates much of Honegger's art of vocal writing — the fluidity and rapidity of the delivery, together with the consistent rhythmic interpretation of the text's key words combine with the very deliberate architecture of the melodic curve to produce a musical setting of the passage which renders the essence of it in a considerably heightened manner (see Music Example 43 below).

Music Example 43: *Amphion*, [5] - 1B [7]

AMPHION lâche prise. La
AMPHION releases his hold.
AMPHION lässt von ihr ab und
vi - e. lais - se la mort aux mains des immortels!
li - ving;death is the of - fice of im mor-tal hands!
le - ben, las - se den Tod das Werk der Göt-ter sein!
mf rit.
Celli
proie s'enfuit.
The beast escapes.
das Tier entflieht.
diminuendo
M. D.
C.B.
Timb.
6 Modéré (T° du début)
Xylo.
p
Celli
AMPHION s'étend et s'endort. Des RÊVES l'environnent
AMPHION rests and falls asleep. The DREAMS surround him.
AMPHION streckt sich aus und schläft ein. TRÄUME umringen ihn.
vons
Alt.

The use of the tensile scotch-snap rhythmic cell and the powerful descending-note sequence for the setting of the initial two 'Pourquoi?' is a perfect example of Honegger's consistently unorthodox approach to the prosody of the French language, in that his belief in the value of misaccentuation having a directly proportional relationship to the degree of aural comprehensibility as well as the effective dramatic rendition of the textual emotions, here as always, bears considerable fruit.

> Amphion stands up, flings up his arm. His quarry escapes quickly. Amphion, after a moment's hesitation, moves towards a sort of grotto or a very unpretentious hole; he takes off the skins that cover his shoulders, sits and contemplates the starry sky. He stretches out and sleeps.

The appropriately restrained portrayal of the escaping beast allows the return of the music of the introduction to proceed quite naturally ([6] -) — the pedal E that had been sustained as far as the entry of the voice hardly having been negated by the modality of the A minor between [5] and [6]. The canonic distance is neatly diminished and in itself contributes in no small way to the effective dying-away which ultimately reveals the initial chord structure and the timeless monotony of the high-pitched string canons that return us to the constant void of Valéry's 'giddy rotations' achieved by Amphion himself through sleep.

([7] - [11] : 'Les rêves')

> The sky clouds over gradually obscuring the stars. On the dark ground the 'Dreams' visit the sleeper. Two warriors painted with blood attack them. A monster devours them. The people dress themselves up in ridiculous rags: 'A King of Money' etc.. Amphion talks to himself in his sleep. During the 'Dream of Rapture' the figure of a dancer, almost naked under a long cloak, appears. She is attentive over him, caresses him, plays, moving away each time the sleeping Amphion moves.

A texture with the magical qualities of purely Mendelssohnian proportions is succinctly established in six bars of $\frac{3}{4}$ measure. The three six-beat phrases, sequentially repeated across the textural spectrum of the strings, lead neatly to a descending chromatic tag, also of sequential design, which dissolves into an ostinato in the bar before [8] with a naturalness that is a monument to Honegger's art. The relationship of this 'world' to that of the preceding 'Introduction' is clearly maintained by the ever-prominent fourths and fifths in the melodic patterning. The trombone 'fanfare' that emerges beneath the ostinato at [8] is built up almost entirely from common chords — a procedure that Honegger had used consistently from the time it had first made its mark in works like *Cantique de Pâques* in a manner that, admittedly, had then not been able to disguise its origins in the late-Impressionistic roots of Debussy (*Le martyre de Saint Sébastien* in particular), but now stands as a completely personal aspect of his mature style. The antithesis of B♭ minor and D♭ major in this fanfare — the ever familiar tertiary relationship — is related and integrated in significance by its repeat, a third higher after [9]. The abundance of canonic devices in this, as in most of Honegger's scores, increases in number with the very close strict canon in the 'Songe amoureux' ('Dream of Rapture') (10 -). The sequential aspect of the superimposed triads construction and the overall patterning of falling thirds fully relates this episode to the preceding one.

(11 - 14 : 'Entrée des Muses')

> One Muse emerges from the fountain and calls. A second Muse rises from a rock and calls. A third and fourth Muse seem to detach themselves from the branches of a great oak and do the same. These calls, all *mezzo-voce* and simultaneous. They carry small wings on their heads. They alternate between the shadows and the clear light. They come together holding hands.

Against a background of various elements of the music for 'Les rêves' — used to symbolize the continuing presence of the 'Dreams' — the 'Muses' appear and their own motif (pedals which develop into chord structures) gradually assumes recognizable proportions. The various calls gradually coalesce to form a melodic line of thematic identity (4B 12 -), and, as they talk of the unpleasant task they must perform by command of the gods (12 - 13), a powerfully emotive counter-subject soars across the orchestral web of fluttering sounds — as in *Le roi David* and *Judith* it is allocated so effectively to a solo viola. To achieve their task they must first rid Amphion of the 'Dreams'. In doing so the pedal E returns, and the mood and texture change to those of the opening 'Introduction' section with the intervals of a fourth and fifth gradually assuming dominance in the melodic and harmonic structures.

> The Muses fight with the Dreams. They chase and dissipate them. The last section is a gracious struggle with the 'Dream of Rapture'. 'Liturgie'. The scene is suddenly darkened. In the darkness only one group is clear: Amphion in a silvery glimmer, the Muses in a clear bluish light.

(14 - 15 : *A*. 'Enchantement')

> The Muses charm Amphion as he sleeps, lavishing on him the gestures of charm, circling around his resting place murmuring the Psalm or 'Magic Lullaby'.

The recapitulation of the music that first introduced the Muses appropriately refocuses on them the attention that is necessary for the stage situation — the orchestral 'hymn' is purely Honeggerian in the same way as are the Angel's prayer and 'Alleluia' chorale finale to *Le roi David* and the 'Jehovah' motif in the 'Cantique de victoire' that concludes *Judith*. The move to B♭ minor is achieved in a typical manner — the pedal E resolving to A as an apparently natural consequence of much of the earlier modality centered around A minor; the A then becomes the leading-note of the new tonality.

(15 - 22 : *B*. 'Scène liturgique')

> 'Liturgie', 'Solennel'. The Muses then group themselves around Amphion in a solemn way. One at his feet, one at his head, the other two by his side facing the audience. They turn their faces towards the sky holding hands.

The tonal organization procedures seen in embryo in *Le roi David* and well-developed in *Judith,* reappear in this work after being virtually absent in *Antigone.* After the tripartite planning of the music structure so far (obviously done to coincide with the dramatic plan which is itself reinforced by the corresponding tonal organization E minor/D minor/E minor), the next large section of the music depends heavily on the tonal system of key-centres inter-related by means of tertiary patterning. The A major tonality at the opening of the 'Scène liturgique' ([15] -) first gives way to F♯ minor ([16] -); after its restoration it moves instead to C♯ major ([17] -) and, finally, the tonality of B♭ minor is established in 1A [18]. The key scheme in the course of the passage following Apollo's interjection is summarized in Diagram 19 below.

Diagram 19:

Amphion — 'Scène liturgique': principal tonalities

f♯	a	f	C♯	F♯	f♯	b
[20]	5A [20]	6A [20]	7A [20]	[21]	3A [21]	2B [22]

Apart from a single dominant-tonic move, the relationships are all of a tertiary nature, and the culminatory B♭ minor tonality 'resolves' into D♭ major at the start of Apollo's *récit* ([22] -).

Within this 'Scène liturgique' several other highly typical characteristics of Honegger's style occur. The use of the saxophone for the main orchestral thematic idea at the opening is perhaps most directly a consequence of *Antigone,* whilst the contrary motion principle governing the harmonic conception of Apollo's motif (2-3A [18]) in terms of the combination of superimposed triads (the upper one being coloured by an added note) related by the interval of a third, is a perfect example in slow motion of one of the most important components of Honegger's musical language and is in itself so obviously related to one of his principal tonal procedures (see Music Example 44 overleaf).
The individualistic setting of 'Amphion' is thoroughly in keeping with Honegger's personalized approach to prosody, whilst the choice of the intervals of a fourth and fifth in the setting of 'Apollon' and 'Amphion' subtly but firmly relates them to the aura of the 'whole' created in and sustained throughout the opening 'Introduction' in a manner that is indicative of Honegger's methodically skilful and consistent approach. The 'psalmody' harks back to *Le roi David* and *Judith,* as does the vigorous choral unisoni with its stark orchestral accompaniment. The elemental force of the gods is represented by a motif, 7B [21], that has strong parallels with the 'Jehovah' motif in *Judith* — the predominant use

Music Example 44 : *Amphion,* 18 - 4B 19

(Reproduit avec l'autorisation des EDITIONS SALABERT, Paris, propriétaires de l'œuvre.)

of intervals of a fourth or fifth fitting perfectly into the general scheme (see Music Example 45 below).

Music Example 45 : *Amphion,* 7B 21 - 2A 21

Contrapuntal devices abound in keeping with the nature of the material as well as with Honegger's style. In particular, there is the tremendously tight canonic procedure involving the countersubject at [17] and the augmentation technique at [21].

> Distant thunder. The Muses prostrate themselves — offering their praise to Apollo. The light shines on Amphion.

([22] - [41]: 'Récit d'Apollon')

With all the various motives reappearing to support the text of Apollo's narration concerning the task which he is proposing to entrust to Amphion, Honegger weaves a web of contrapuntal complexity characteristic not only for its ingenuity, but also for the clarity which results from the carefully layered scoring. A new motif representing the lyre (3A [24]) — the means Apollo gives Amphion to achieve his desire — and a theme in the bass (4A [26] -), symbolizing the building process which it will initiate, dominate this texture until [28] when Apollo thanks the Muses for their help, dismisses them and the energy of the monologue is dissipated in a passage of exquisitely beautiful polyphony held together in a truly characteristic way by means of a simple rising chromatic-scale bass. The final echoes of Apollo's motif reveal the sounds of a 'distant' chorus who poignantly predicts the outcome.

> The echoes disperse and diversify the name of god.

The brief hymn-like chorus is 'echoed' by the orchestra and the beauty of the block-chord writing, in contrary-motion, wonderfully heightened.

> The Muses rise again. They kiss his feet, head, side. Total darkness falls. One hears the Muses who call from the shadows. Day breaks gradually, and progressively the colours of dawn take hold. The Muses have gone. One sees the lyre and a plectrum at Amphion's feet. Gradually the vague vibrations of the living nature which is waking are felt. Bird calls. Sound of water. Repeat of the 'Song of the Streams'.

After the clear establishment of D♭ major at the beginning of Apollo's recitative, a series of moves results in a substantial period in A major over a pedal A (4A [23] -) before another chain of tonal shifts restores B♭ minor at the climax of his monologue (1B [28]). Amphion's dismissal of the Muses, which follows immediately, results in a return to A major (3B [30]-). This conveniently leads to E minor ([31] -) and the re-establishment of the opening scene and atmosphere by a series of 'flash-backs' (in particular to the music of the 'Entrée des Muses' from [11] and [14], and that of the 'Scène liturgique' from [15]). Simultaneously, there is a 'wind-down' which culminates in the return of the 'Chant des sources' after [33] (with a slightly different counter-subject and its extreme augmentation in the very high treble register of the orchestra). After this there is nothing left but the sounds of the opening xylophone motif and its echo ([34]-).

> One creature, half-animal, chases after another scarcely escaping. One sees men and women coming out of the woods. Some go and hunt, the others hurry off and do various jobs. A woman comes near the fountain. Another admires herself and dishevelled she makes plaits in her hair. The children play and quarrel. Amphion stirs. During this scene the different persons return gradually. The orchestra illustrate the successive motions of Amphion. He leans, looking at them, stupefied, and shows signs of awakening. He sits up briskly on the couch, dresses, takes a few steps, breathes the morning air. He comes down to the fountain and drinks for a long time. He dances to loosen his limbs. Refreshed by the activity of his dance after his sleep he sees the lyre. The lyre corresponds to all the descriptions given in all ancient writings. Amphion looks at it with astonishment. He takes hold of it in a curious way — he moves towards the audience brandishing it by one of its corners. He detaches the plectrum which was attached to it by a little thread of gold.

The interpretation of Amphion's clumsy dance ([35] - [38]) is an inspired creation. Scored for cellos and double basses *col legno*, an assortment of percussion (bass drum, castanets, cymbals, high drum, triangle) and timpani, it is a model of simplicity achieving effectiveness without banality — a factor of his art that is evident from so many pages in music of this kind. As Amphion picks up the lyre, its motif (g^{5}_{3}) with (a^{6}_{4}) superimposed) slowly unfurls itself in the orchestra and the scene is set for Amphion's discovery of its magic qualities.

I He strikes it suddenly — one string vibrates. A raucous and strong sound, which receives an answer in the form of a violent clap of thunder. A block moves backwards with a great noise. People surge in terror, others enter knocking into each other, picking a fight and exit fighting furiously. Panic exists. Stupefied and frightened Amphion looks at the lyre with a religious face. He holds it to himself. He tries again.

II A second sound. Another string is touched and a delicious sound emerges. Some rocks without force move or roll or slide towards the hero. Loved ones and lovers appear, holding hands, stiffen and withdraw slowly. Amphion puts down the lyre, considers it and reflects. He seats himself on a stone by the water and looks at his image. His dream suddenly becomes a reality to him bit by bit. He hears vaguely the 'Lullaby of the Muses' murmured with closed lips. Amphion rises and looks at the sky.

Reserve and simplicity are the key words for Honegger's interpretation of the chaos first created by Amphion's efforts. Slightly Stravinskyian in flavour, the contrast is well made between the harsh, rhythmically dominated first sound and the gentle sweetness of the relaxed melodic flute line representing the acceptability of the second. Honegger's penchant for *bouche fermée* writing (cf. *Cantique de Pâques, Le roi David* and *Judith*) here needs no justification as the music of the Muses returns for their calls to Amphion and the tonality is neatly steered towards B♭ minor ready for his recollection of the dream, which likewise had started in B♭ minor.

Section II:

([41] - [44]: 'The Melodrama')

Scene: The invisible Muses; Amphion — well stressed, a little sung. Voice of disjointed vision, gasping.

Amphion's gradual remembering of his dream is accompanied by various short and simple restatements of the principal motives concerned — two statements of Apollo's motif lead to a combination of Amphion's motif and the music symbolizing his choice from [22] - . This is followed ([42] -) by the 'lyre' music and its various components (from 3A [24] - and [26] -) before a new long-spun saxophone melody (4A [43] -) acts as an introduction to the third and final section of the work — the music comprising the 'Prélude', 'Fugue' and 'Hymne au soleil' which is played continuously as in the first section. The tonality is carefully structured in this short 'melodrama' — the B♭ minor is sequentially moved, via C major, to D major acting as the dominant of G minor, the G^{5}_{3} minor aspect of the 'lyre' motif. A pedal G links the melodrama with the start of the 'Prélude' which, after a six-bar introduction using the G♯ minor component of the 'lyre' motif as a dominant, is clearly in C major/minor.

The relative brevity of this middle section of the whole work is compensated for in no small way by the fact that a re-exposition of the principal musical elements of Amphion's dream takes on relatively larger proportions because of the very concise and thoroughly integrated nature of all the motives.

Section III:

(44 - 48 : 'Prelude')

> Amphion takes up the lyre and plectrum, raises them to the sky and starts to play, full of enthusiasm and assurance. He strikes the strings. An immense sound, prolonged and clear, rich — all the resources that the art can produce. All nature vibrates. The Echoes multiply this in reply. The scene fills with people on various levels attracted by the sound. Amphion preludizes. He creates the scales. He executes, lyre in his hands, a sort of sacred round dance. He then places it on a bit of ground at the base of the rocks on the right. He cries 'with Apollo'.

The introduction to Amphion's 'preludizing' is well contrived by the use of the 'lyre' motif both harmonically and melodically, whilst the creation of the scales is achieved in a manner remarkably free of any trace of banality — the typically Honeggerian harmonic tissue created by a polyphonic web of contrary-motion scalic patterns has again a slightly Stravinskyian flavour to it by virtue of the continuous combination of many cells of varying lengths which are basically similar in outline. Eventually the texture created is refined into an ostinato and the saxophone theme, which had linked this with the preceding 'melodrama', sings out in cantus-firmus fashion, quickly bringing to mind many similar moments in most of the major works prior to *Amphion* (see 12B 46-). A further passage of Beethovenian development of the scalic texture prefaces a second statement of the theme in a manner which is best described by terminology borrowed from the seventh art, as 'glorious technicolour' (see 47 -). This acts as a transition to the 'Fugue' which accompanies the building of the temple.

(48 - 55 : Fugue: Construction de Thèbes)

> The whole building act calls for a co-ordination as perfect as possible between the miming, the figuration and the music which is here supreme master and, in fact, commands the action of the persons and the movements of the material.
>
> A. First phase: 'March of the Stones'. The blocks raise themselves by heavy bounces, roll on the slopes; they direct themselves to the right of the onlooker, towards the left. The temple in front of which they erect themselves is on a profile of rock on the left a little above the comb; the invisible façade will supposedly turn towards the bottom at the right. The

> 'March of the Stones' is outlined in the bottom of the orchestra by very marked rhythms and accidentals which gradually untangle and order themselves.

The choice of the discipline of a fugue to interpret this scene is a stroke of genius — so too, dramatically, is the use as the subject of the very distinctive bass line that had occurred during Apollo's recitative in the first part of the work when he revealed his plan to the sleeping Amphion (see 4A [26] -). The tremendously powerful fugal texture that Honegger weaves with such ease from this tensile subject is a perfect model of his expert contrapuntal technique — the counter-subject brims with distinction and proceeds to occupy a role in the exposition of the fugue of almost equal importance to that of the subject.

> B. Invisible Choir. Second phase: the construction is there in outline. The architectural parts follow the flanks of the mountains. Walls, coping, cornices replace the irregular profile of the rock with their neat lines. The silhouette of the temple is established. A little edifice formed by some dancers dressed in tunics assemble themselves and position themselves on a ledge. Then the Muses appear dressed in gold to hide their hair. They enter solemnly and arrange themselves as columns of the Temple. If it is possible they should descend from the heights to the left. Chorus of Muses — Pillars. Clear light. Large musical development.

The involvement of the choral element gives Honegger the ideal method of separating and extending the development of the fugue without any obvious restatement involving a temporary suspension of the tension. The first choral superimposition is very typical of Honegger's approach in these 'al fresco' situations — the pairing of soprano and tenor, with a mock imitation procedure adopted for the other pairing of alto and bass, is a style he had proved to be eminently suitable and successful in many similar movements in *Le roi David*, *Judith* and *Antigone*. Characteristic too, is the sympathy that exists between the slow moving bass and the legato of the Muses' vocal line in the second choral episode, an interaction which creates a marvellous framework for the continuing fugal tissue and totally avoids the negative qualities in which such a vocal superimposition might have otherwise resulted. This is further substantiated by the instrumental incorporation of their melodic line into the final, purely orchestral 'large musical development' of the fugal texture that takes place by way of transition to the concluding 'Hymne au soleil' (see [53] -).

With reference to the tonal design of the fugue, the main tonal delineations again revolve around a system of tertiary relationships: the initial C minor gives way to a section in E♭ major ([51] -), before a period in E minor near the close (7B [55] -), and precedes a move to G♯ minor for the start of the choral finale (the G♯ minor having been psychologically prepared for by the reference to it in the fugue — see 3A [53]). The final statement of the fugue subject (4B [55] -) is contained in a texture which illustrates two important aspects of Honegger's style found in abundance in most of his scores: (a) the patterning by semitonal chromatic movement of the bass line and (b) the bipartite canonic ostinato, with the element being derived by diminution from the fugue subject (see Music Example 46 overleaf).

Music Example 46: *Amphion*, 7B [54] - 3A [55]

(Reproduit avec l'autorisation des EDITIONS SALABERT, Paris, propriétaires de l'œuvre.)

(55 - 59 : 'Hymne au soleil')

> Chorus of the People. Acclaim. They call Amphion — he designed the Temple. Chorus. They turn to Amphion — they dress him in royal trappings. During this investiture the Muses sing.

Appropriately the 'chorus of the people' is derived from the music of the invisible chorus in Section I that supported Apollo's plans (7B 21 -). The unison vocal line is doubled by four horns (the resultant texture of which Honegger was very fond) and the orchestral tissue itself is infused with elements of the preceding fugue's subject and counter-subject for the sake of continuity as well as textual relevance. As a result this 'Hymne' generates immense tension, the like of which is only paralleled by the scene in the tomb near the end of *Antigone*. By way of preparation for the final comment from the Muses, the orchestral hymn-like passage that introduced the 'Scène liturgique' in Section I returns (see 8B 15 -), and acts as a transition to the music that closes the work (61 to the end).

> The Muses disappear. At the moment when the Hero goes to rise up to the temple the form of a woman in a cloak who has entered secretly onto the scene, approaches him and bars his passage with her arms crossed. The décor is veiled progressively. The light follows suit and the sonority of the music. Amphion recoils. The cloaked figure seizes him and caresses him.

She takes his lyre on which she plays a few profound notes, and then throws it into the fountain. Amphion hides his face in the bosom of this figure who is Love or Death, and leaves, led by her while the orchestra confines itself to a very suave song, solemn and very intimate. Curtain.

In these final twenty-five bars Honegger creates a most expressive elegy — the use of the saxophone for the poignant theme that winds its way so inevitably across the slow-moving harmonies, resting on the characteristically near-chromatic descending bass-line phrases, is as emotional in its melancholy as it was for the intensely tragic farewell scene in *Antigone*.

The tonality of B♭ minor is firmly re-established, with the approach from the G♯ minor of the 'Hymne au soleil' being characterized by a series of semitonal and tertiary moves (see Diagram 20 below).

Diagram 20:

Amphion — 'Hymne au soleil': principal tonalities

g♯	a/A	c♯	b	C	E	C	b♭
2A[55]	1B[56]	[56]	4B[57]	[57]	2B[58]	6B[59]	[60]

B♭ minor emerges as the principal tonality of the work. It was first established at [8] during 'Les rêves', became the polar tonality throughout the remainder of that first section, and was then reasserted at the beginning of the 'melodrama'. The choice of E minor for the substantial areas of secondary importance is a successful dramatic move by virtue of the extremity of the tritonal relationship exhibited with the principal tonality. This return to a system of tonal relationships of the type found in embryo in *Le roi David* and in full flood in *Judith* is indicative of the overall element of retreat evident in *Amphion* from the highly experimental and extended front represented by the score for *Antigone*.

Part III: *Les aventures du roi Pausole* and the *Cello Concerto*

The degree and nature of this 'retreat' is substantial and dramatic — in fact in many ways it marks a return to strategic positions long since abandoned by works written after, and including *Judith*. The overall scale of tonal boundaries is certainly much narrower and the harmonic language correspondingly restricted and unadventurous in a way that is untypical of Honegger. Melodically, the same qualities of distinction are present, as they always seem to be in his works, but the range of emotion is curtailed — there are neither the extremes of beauty and tenderness nor the cataclysmic strength and grandeur that so dramatically polarize the majority of his scores. More negative still, is the fact that influences are detectable to an extent that contradicts much of his achievement since *Le roi David* — as has been pointed out, Stravinsky, in particular, looms large on many occasions.

If a critical look is taken at Honegger's use of 'melodrama' techniques in *Amphion* the conclusion has to be that it bears more resemblance to its primitive origins in nineteenth-century German opera than to the masterly and seemingly instinctive way in which it had been employed in *Le roi David*. Finally, there are also hints of Wagner and Honegger's early German training, both of which had given every indication of long since having been satisfactorily absorbed. The Wagnerian overtones of the opening can easily result in a quick vision of some mislaid Rhinemaidens, whilst the Germanic elements, in particular the figure of Reger, produce a heavy-handed quality that pervades the 'Fugue' in particular and a slightly less than perfect skill in the use of chromatic sequences in the first section.

Nevertheless, although all these tough criticisms can be levelled at the score as a whole, the blame for their reappearance as disfigurements of Honegger's musical style cannot be laid solely at the composer's door. The nature of Valéry's creation, leaving aside the aesthetic perfection of the language of the prose, demanded the retrospective treatment that Honegger supplied. The natural instinct with which Honegger approached the task of writing dramatic/incidental music led him to create a score which is, as has been illustrated in the preceding analysis, an exceptionally fine contribution to the conceived whole.

Valéry's project is, however, of a different era and lacks all the qualities of experimentation and progressiveness that characterize an *avant-garde* work. As a result, so many of Honegger's greatest talents — in reality the basic forces of his personal creative originality — were held in check, if not completely bypassed, by this collaboration. The basic mistake lies in Honegger actually agreeing to take part in this project. The position he had achieved meant that it could only result in a retrogression of style more dramatic than was necessary after the public failure of *Antigone*. Valéry was a very determined and persuasive old man, driven harder by the thought that it was now or never for the creation of his aged brain-child. Honegger had an over-riding respect for friendship and a seeming inability to reject a text that was a genuine artistic creation even if it was not suitable from the point of view of his personal development. The result was a side-step into a blind alley for Honegger and a perfect realization of a dream for Valéry. The public was similarly contrary from Honegger's point of view. After rejecting *Antigone* as too modern for them, they awarded *Amphion* only an ephemeral acclaim. They were not going to be lulled into any sense of false security; such illusions had been shattered for them too many times and in more ways than one, and all had changed completely since the première of *Le roi David*.

Fortunately, it would appear that, to an extent, Honegger realized his error, because the next two scores of significance are the purely instrumental *Cello Concerto* and *Symphonie [n° 1]* before the creation of the oratorio *Cris du monde*, which, based on a controversial text by René Bizet, is one of his most original works. The degree of qualification expressed is necessary because, simultaneously, he started on a course which was at a complete tangent — the composition of operettas. His first attempt at this, *Les aventures du roi Pausole*, to a libretto by Albert Willemetz from a novel by Pierre Loüys, proved to be a success of quite staggering proportions. The first production, at the Théâtre des Bouffes-Parisiens ran to five hundred (*sic*) performances[20] and it has since been restaged many times all over France, as well as translated into German and English (for American productions). This highly erotic story was originally intended by Loüys to result in a collaboration with Debussy who had said in 1916 'faîtes [-moi] donc maintenant de l'opérette'[21] [give [me] something suitable for an operetta]. The latter's untimely death resulted in the project being shelved and Honegger, for the second time, stepped into his shoes at a much later date. The score is a quite wonderful blend of all the best from the operetta styles of Chabrier, Gounod, Lecoq, Messager and Offenbach, and took both the public and the critics by surprise with its absolute suitability. They could not initially appreciate that the serious composer Honegger could exhibit such obviously genuine talent in this genre — they took time to realize just how skilled a craftsman he was and the extent of his technique.

Whilst the score is a close parallel to the genre of Chabrier, with just the right degree of Offenbach parody, there are elements of distinction that only Honegger could bring to bear. The greatest of these is the elevated quality of the melodic lines — there is incredible charm in their simplicity, the inspiration for which is contained in this statement he made about the work: 'ma partition, solide mais de genre aimable, évolue si vous voulez en un style Mozartien, gai, vif, alerte, mélodique'[22] [my score which is solid but of a likeable nature, evolves, if you like, into a Mozartian style — gay, bright, alert and melodic]. Furthermore, as he says: 'j'abandonne évidemment ici mon système de déclamation à débit rapide, avec attaque sur les temps forts. Je me rallie à la prosodie vocale conventionnelle avec ses tenues dans l'aiguë et ses syllables muettes venant au bout de huit temps quand on les attend et qu'on ne les comprend plus'[23] [obviously here I abandon my system of rapid declamatory delivery with its accents on the strong beats. I rally to a conventional vocal prosody with its very prominent sustained notes and its silent syllables coming on tail-end quavers when they are expected but not understood]. (See Music Example 47 below.)

Music Example 47: *Les aventures du roi Pausole*, n° 11 'Duo du travesti': "Etes-vous un homme? êtes-vous une femme?"

Al.
Mir.
l'un ni l'autre et je suis tous les deux
A vo_tre mine on di_rait u _ ne da _ me,
à vo_tre mise on di_rait un monsieur
Non, je suis mon pe _ tit, ce qu'on ap _
Qu'est ce que c'est qu'un traves _ ti?
_pelle un tra_ves _ ti
Vous l'ex_pli _ quer, c'est très com _
_plexe _ un tra_ves _ ti, mon Dieu, voi _ la! c'est l'as_sem_bla_ge de deux
1
p

Al.
Mir.
se_xes, c'est l'ac_cord du le et du la. En chi_mie, c'est un a_mal_
2
_ga_me, c'est un mé_lange, u_ne fu_sion, Deux corps: un homme et u_ne
ALINE
3 Un peu plus vif
Que
fem_me u_nis dans un seul pan_ta_lon, Un tra_ves_ti c'est un pro_
c'est gen_til un tra_ves_ti
_blèm'c'est un mo_yen c'est un sys_tème as_sez ma_lin et qui per_

Al.
Mir.
le fé_mi_nin d'ai_
_met à ceux qui ai_ment le fé_mi_nin d'ai_mer quand mê_
_mer quand mê_me le mas_cu_lin
4
Ah
_me le mas_cu_lin
C'est un très gen_til stra_ta_
4
que j'ai_me le tra_ves_ti que c'est gentil Ah!
_gèm' qui ré_u_nit tou_tes les sym_pa_thies Ah! sapristi que
Tempo I°
sapris_ti que c'est gen_til un tra_ves_ti
c'est gentil Ah sapris_ti un tra_ves_ti Un tra_ves_
Tempo I°

Mir.
_ti, ça sym_bo _ li _ se le mys _ tè _ re le plus ob_sé _ dant c'est comme u _ ne boite à sur _

Mir.
_pri _ se on n'sait jamais ce qu'il ya d'dans. On n'y trou_ve pas, quand on

Mir.
l'ou _ vre, ce que l'on y croyait ca _ ché mais, au contraire, on y dé _

Tempo II.
ALINE
Que c'est gen _
Mir.
cou _ vre ce que l'on n'avait pas cher _ ché. Un tra_ves _ ti, c'est un pro_blème, c'est un mo _
A Tempo II.

Al.
-til un tra-ves-ti
Mir.
-yen, c'est un sys tème as - sez ma-lin et qui per-met à ceux qui

Al.
le fé-mi-nin d'ai - mer quand
Mir.
ai - ment le fé-mi-nin d'ai-mer quand mê - - me le

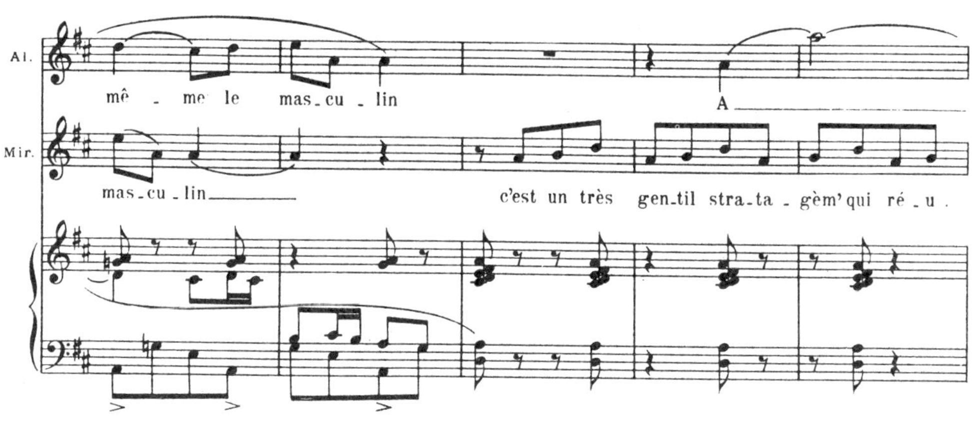
Al.
mê - me le mas-cu-lin A
Mir.
mas-cu-lin c'est un très gen-til stra-ta-gèm' qui ré-u.

(Reproduit avec l'autorisation des EDITIONS SALABERT, Paris, propriétaires de l'œuvre.)

All the standard tricks, devices, sounds and formulae of French operetta are contained in this score and handled as if in the manner born. There is no sense of accident about this score — the talent exhibited here is no less great than that shown in his serious music, the only unusual aspect being that the genius should be so evident in both fields. The interaction can occasionally be appreciated — there are some extremely judicious uses of bitonality, some oriental sounds that are highly suggestive of those in *Le roi David*, the typically assured counterpoint of the 'Ouverture' in particular and, of course, the very careful and systematic structuring involved in all the large-scale numbers. Honegger also succeeds in appropriately bringing to bear on the score some new elements — the lushness of harmony that comes straight from the pages of Debussy and Ravel is balanced by elements of the South American aspects of Milhaud's style — and it is probably true to say that what Milhaud does for the percussion instruments employed in *L'homme et son désir* Honegger does here for the xylophone, castanets and double bass played *col legno*. It is sad to think that Henry Prunières was right when he pointed out that the subject matter was not suitable for export to England,[24] the pity being that the public was deprived of an excellent operetta with music of unusual distinction.

Honegger was fundamentally embarrassed by the success of the score — for him it was so easy to write this sort of music, it demanded nothing of him and was, as such, unrewarding. He was determined not to succumb to the pressures placed upon him to write many more such works and one must at least note that such was his resolve that the only two other significant contributions he made to this genre were both done in collaboration with Ibert and thus demanded relatively little of his time and energy.[25]

Of the other three works from these two years between *Amphion* and the next major 'dramatic' work, *Cris du monde,* the *Symphonie* [*n° 1*] is discussed in Chapter X and the score *Les noces d'Amour et Psyche,* which consists of arrangements and orchestrations by Honegger of movements from the so-called English and French Suites of J.S. Bach for a ballet created by Ida Rubinstein, falls outside the scope of this book. The remaining score, the *Cello Concerto,* was the first work he wrote after *Amphion* and it is of considerable importance, not least because the first performance given by its dedicatee, Maurice Maréchal, was with the Boston Symphony Orchestra under their conductor Serge Koussevitsky. This brilliant, popular and successful work was undoubtedly responsible to a considerable extent for the commission that Honegger received, along with several other world-famous composers, including Hindemith, Ravel, Roussel and Stravinsky, to write a symphony for the twenty-fifth birthday celebrations of this famous orchestra in 1930.

Despite the time gap of five years between the *Cello Concerto* and the *Concertino* for piano and orchestra and all the unification of his personal language achieved through the seemingly contradictory aspect of diversification evident in all the works from this period, the style and approach is indeed very similar. The basic inspirational spirit is the same — the deft combination of light-hearted *joie de vivre* with a graceful and intimate lyricism, *divertissement* with expressive restraint, non-intellectuality with a clear-cut and powerful structuring and traditional aspects of development, and elements of jazz with a touch of irony. On a technical level the cello part is judiciously written, showing, as did the piano part in the *Concertino,* Honegger's depth of knowledge and expertise in handling the resources of an instrument. If anything, there is a more pronounced aspect of virtuosity in this *Cello Concerto*, but never does it show in the manner of concerto-writing much favoured by the late nineteenth and early twentieth century Romantics.

The orchestral forces he used are again very similar. From the point of view of Honegger's normal sized orchestra the choice is appropriately intimate: only double woodwind (although he does not this time require the second oboe to double cor-anglais, he still cannot resist using the bass clarinet, an instrument of which he was particularly fond, and that appears in most of his orchestral scores), two horns and two trumpets, but, instead of the single trombone he uses a tuba which has, in the last movement, what must surely be one of the most amazing parts ever written for the instrument; to these he adds timpani (making a rare appearance in one of his scores of this period) and two percussion instruments (cymbal and triangle) besides the usual complement of strings. The almost chamber orchestra proportions provide the right framework for the necessary degree of transparency which Honegger succeeds in achieving with his scoring, whilst offering a rich and varied palate of which full advantage is taken. The degree of separation achieved between the soloist and the orchestra is most admirable and provides sufficient tension in its own right to balance out the relatively undemonstrative nature of the music itself.

Formally too, this work looks back to the *Concertino* for piano and orchestra for the details of its formal construction. It also looks beyond, to the early chamber works, for its overall shape, which, like most of the various instrumental duo sonatas, is clearly patterned on the Classical format of a fairly serious and committed, moderately paced first movement, followed by a slow movement of a lyrical and expressive nature and concluding with another quick movement, faster in basic tempo than the first and definitely more lightweight, if not distinctly *giocoso* with its aspects of *bravura* and joyful conclusion. Like the *Concertino* for piano and orchestra it plays continuously with the links between 'movements' simply, but not naïvely contrived. Formally, both in terms of content and spirit it bears some resemblance to Saint-Saëns' *Cello Concerto No. 1,* itself derived from the Mendelssohn concertos which first abandoned the Classical concerto formulae and principles of Mozart and most of Beethoven. Furthermore, in terms not only of melodic, rhythmic and harmonic elements, but orchestration techniques as well, this work and the *Concertino* for piano and orchestra clearly anticipate Ravel's *Piano Concerto in G major* in respect of the jazz influence.

Honegger carefully avoids the dramatic tension which would have been inherent in utilizing the Classical ritornello-based concerto sonata-form. He reverses the late nineteenth-century tendency towards formal inflation, eschews all ideas of theatrical effect inherent in virtuoso display, and deliberately sets out to ensure that this is not a concerto for cello *against* an orchestra by having the cellist playing almost continuously as both soloist and sometimes accompanist. All these factors give credence to the remark quoted of Honegger by S.S. Dale, 'that the music of a concerto may be brilliant and entertaining, and it is not essential for it to try to be profound, nor indeed that it need be dramatic.'[26]

The formal design of the work is summarized in Diagram 21 opposite.

Diagram 21:

Cello Concerto

(first movement)

-[13]	Form		Principal tonalities
Andante	Introduction :	4½×2-part refrain: (a) Orchestra (b) Solo cello (accompanied)	C
♩ = 𝅗𝅥 Allegro	Exposition -[5] :	Theme 1 and varied restatement	C
		Theme 2A (1-4A [3]), Theme 2B (4-1B[4]) with countersubject element 2C in solo cello (2A [3]) and varied restatements of Theme 2A Closing section (4B [5]-): Theme 2B with countersubject element 2C	b
	Development [5]-7A[9] :	Introduction refrain element (b) with countersubject element 2C	F♯/f♯
		Statement of Themes 2A and 2B ([8]-) with development of latter by canonic imitation	d/D
	Recapitulation 8A [9]-[13] :	Theme 1 (8A [9]-) with varied restatement	on dom. of C
		Theme 2A ([10]-) with varied restatement	b moving to C for
𝅗𝅥 = ♩ Andante	Coda [11]-[13] :	4½×2-part refrain from Introduction: (a) Orchestra (b) Now scored for woodwind with solo cello [semiquaver figure] decoration added	C
♩ = 𝅗𝅥 Allegro		Theme 1 (7B [13]-) — transition to	
(second movement) [13] [20] Lento	Theme (solo cello 4A [13]-) Variation I ([14]-)		f♯
	[16]- Unaccompanied cadenza followed by quasi-accompanied cadenza ([17]-) leading to		[17] - e♭ 4A [17] - e
	Variation II ([18]-)		f♯ (with final *tierce de picardie*)
	(Cadenza *ad lib.* link to)		
(third movement) [20]- Allegro marcato	Exposition [20] -4A [26] :	Theme 1	C with final move (4-5A [21]) to e
		Transition (5A [21]-): primarily based on Theme 1	e [22] - c [23] - G 6B[24] - f/F
		Theme 2 (16B [25]-) and restatement involving canonic imitation	F♯
		Closing section ([26]-)	D
	Development 5A [26]-[29] :	Theme 1 with new theme 3 in solo cello ([28]-)	E♭ [27] - E [28] - E♭
	Recapitulation [29]- :	Theme 2 ([29]-)	b
		Transition ([30]-): reverses order of events but preserves importance of Theme 1 and includes reference to Theme 2 ([31]-)	E♭ [31] - D 9B[32] - e
		Theme 1 ([32]-) — leading to	C
Lento	Coda [34]- :	Material from first movement 'Introduction' (2×(a) and 1×(b)) Theme 1 from first movement (6A [34]-)	C
Presto		Theme 1 of third movement ([35]-)	

The parallels to the formal design of the *Concertino* for piano and orchestra are numerous. The most obvious is the use of a simple refrain principle for the opening of both works, although here it perhaps works more organically in view of the structure of the purely orchestral motif (a) as a chord over a rising triadic sequence, beautifully balanced by the aspect of the descending triadic sequence which constitutes the orchestral part beneath the solo cello line of motif (b) (see Music Example 48 below).

Music Example 48: *Cello Concerto,* bars 1-18

The structure is tighter and more effective now than in the *Concertino* for piano and orchestra by virtue of this refrain enclosing a regular sonata-form Allegro, rather than being a part of it. The sonata-form is tremendously concise — there is no transition from Theme 1 to Theme 2 and the development is rigorous in a truly Beethovenian manner — a mosaic held together by the ostinato-like chordal sequence that pervades the whole and vertically frames the otherwise purely linear aspect of the imitatively contrapuntal development to which the material is subjected.

Tonally, the organization is systematic as is to be expected. The middle movement, like that of the *Concertino* for piano and orchestra, is cast in the key a tritone away from the main key centre of the work, although here the whole process is that much more effective because the tritonal relationship is prepared and utilized functionally in both of the outer movements. Tertiary tonal relationships are much in evidence as, too, are such subtleties as the avoidance of the actual tonic in the recapitulation section of the first movement Allegro, so that its achievement coincides with the cyclic return of the opening Andante — the use of such a static introduction by way of a coda would have been disastrous without such a move despite the allocation of the cello theme to the woodwind and the addition of a demisemiquaver decoration in the solo part. This cyclic aspect also extends to the coda of the third movement, where a brief reference is made both to the introductory Andante and to the first subject of the Allegro before the movement concludes with a precise reference to its own first theme (typically utilizing a tertiary antithesis with A♭ major in the final four bars) which had been appropriately highlighted by the reversed recapitulation.

Stylistically, this work is personal and original; indeed, it is prophetic in that the flavour of the first theme of the third movement and some of the developmental techniques in both outer movements anticipate the style that Stravinsky was to arrive at in works like *Dumbarton Oaks* in the middle and late thirties and early forties — a rather ironic situation in the light of *Amphion*! The jazz elements are even more integrated than they were in the *Concertino* for piano and orchestra, most noticeably in the first theme of the Allegro of the first movement (see Music Example 49 below) and the second theme of the third movement (see Music Example 50, pages 198-99).

Music Example 49: *Cello Concerto*, bars 19-32

(Reproduit avec l'autorisation des EDITIONS SALABERT, Paris, propriétaires de l'œuvre.)

Much of the assured and relaxed atmosphere that pervades this work offers a direct parallel to *Pastorale d'été* in particular, and some parts of works like *Rugby* and *Chant de joie*. The effortless and completely natural way that Honegger can place one of his most familiar hallmarks — a thematic entity presented above a harmonic structure conceived upon a simple rising scale — as he does on the second theme of the first movement Allegro is equally indicative of his complete mastery of his own musical style as features such as the expert contraction of material for the recapitulation in the Allegro and the unique textures in the Lento are of his extensive technique and originality.

The structure of the slow movement is utterly simple but unusually effective in its use of first a brief unaccompanied cello cadenza followed immediately by what is, in effect, little more than an orchestrally-accompanied cadenza, as an interlude between the variations. Willy Tappolet is quoted as saying that he believed the melody of this Lento to have been inspired by an Indian melody[27] — it is probably more accurate to reflect on the suggestion that Honegger, with his respect for tradition and being faced with the task of writing his first cello concerto, would have turned to such masterpieces of the genre as that of Dvořák for study and learnt not only the necessary lessons, but would also have been inspired by the appropriateness of Dvořák's melodic language to the cello in this context. After all, the over-riding influence of the interval of a third on Honegger's melodic, harmonic and tonal thinking would be most closely paralleled by that evident in the music of Dvořák.

The nature of some of the textures in this work — particularly that enveloping the first subject of the third movement — combine with aspects of the style of the music to suggest that Shostakovitch was influenced by this work when he wrote his first *Cello Concerto* in E♭ major (1952). The rather obviously four-square phrase structuring, the feeling of controlled aggression about the rhythmic drive and the very pronounced contrast between the two themes of the third movement are further examples which support this proposition — indeed Shostakovitch is about the only other composer who could also successfully manage to conceive and utilize a theme of the ilk of Honegger's second subject in the third movement and proceed to score it for flutter-tonguing tuba in the recapitulation! (see Music Example 50 below).

Music Example 50: *Cello Concerto,* 29 - 1B 30

(Reproduit avec l'autorisation des EDITIONS SALABERT, Paris, propriétaires de l'œuvre.)

However, of the two, one suspects that it is in Honegger's hands alone that it remains capable of sounding, as it does, neither incongruous nor downright vulgar.

This work stands as the last monument to the happy and optimistic side of Honegger's character — the gentleman; ever faithful and supportive friend to so many; the lover of the excitement of sports, fast cars and locomotives; devoted husband and father. The 'last monument' because the next few years brought to Honegger not only further national and international success and acclaim, but also the awareness of the futility of so many aspects of his role both as an artist and as a member of a seemingly doomed society. As a musician and composer of the most innate kind, the problems he tackled mentally found spontaneous outlets in his music. Within a couple of years he was to experience a major artistic crisis and the spirit of the music that he wrote after it is, as a result, most significantly different in terms of basic emotional spirituality. Never again are works to be found of this nature — the basic quality of pessimism that was one of the outcomes of the crisis, pervades all his remaining works to a greater or lesser extent.

Notes to Chapter VI

[1]a) Roland-Manuel, *Arthur Honegger* (Editions Senart, Paris, 1925);
b) André George, *Arthur Honegger* (Claude Aveline, Paris, 1926).

[2]See the *Deux esquisses* for piano, 1943-44 (Durand, 1944) and Arthur Honegger, *Incantations aux fossiles* (Editions d'Ouchy, Lausanne, 1948), 143-58.

[3]See *Sémiramis* (Ballet Music) 1933
Jeanne d'Arc au bûcher (Dramatic Oratorio), 1933-35
Icare (Ballet Music), 1936
Les mille et une nuits (Cantata), 1937
Les suppliantes (Incidental Music), 1941
Le soulier de satin (Incidental Music), 1943
Hamlet (Incidental Music), 1946
Sortilèges (ondes Martenot), 1946

[4]29 November 1927.

[5]*Arthur Honegger et son œuvre* (Editions Corrêa, Paris, 1947), 128.

[6]'Histoire d'*Amphion*', No. 16 (5 August 1932), 157-62.

[7]See also Paul Valéry, *Eupalinos ou l'architecture* (Editions de la Nouvelle Revue Française, Paris, 1924).

[8]Quoted by Arthur Hoérée in '*Amphion,* Mélodrame — ce qu'en dit Paul Valéry', *Candide,* 380 (25 June 1931).

[9]pp. 108-09.

[10]Reproduced in *'Amphion', Conferencia,* No. 16 (5 August 1932), 163-78.

[11]Paul Valéry, *'Amphion', Conferencia,* No. 16 (5 August 1932), 157-62 (p. 162).

[12]Ibid., p. 157.

[13]Quoted by José Bruyr, *Arthur Honegger et son œuvre* (Editions Corrêa, Paris, 1947), 136.

[14]Quoted by Willy Tappolet, *'Amphion', Journal de Genève,* 1 December 1932.

[15]'*Amphion* d'Arthur Honegger et Paul Valéry', *Revue Musicale,* October 1931, 239-43.

[16]'*Amphion*', *Nouvelle Revue Française,* No. 215 (1931), 347-49.

[17]Quoted by José Bruyr, *Arthur Honegger et son œuvre* (Editions Corrêa, Paris, 1947), 136.

[18]Published by Rouart Lerolle in 1931 in a limited edition of 525 copies (RL 11778). The copyright is now held by Editions Salabert.

[19]I have supplemented the meagre portions of Valéry's instructions that appear in the vocal score with my own translation of the full details which were published in '*Amphion*', *Conferencia*, No. 16 (5 August 1932), 163-78.

[20]*I am a Composer* (Faber and Faber, London, 1966), 108.

[21]Quoted by José Bruyr: *Arthur Honegger et son œuvre* (Editions Corrêa, Paris, 1947), 137.

[22]Quoted by José Bruyr: *Arthur Honegger et son œuvre* (Editions Corrêa Paris, 1947), 137.

[23]Quoted by Marcel Landowski: *Arthur Honegger*, (Editions du Seuil, 1957), 95.

[24]'*Le roi Pausole*' *La Revue Musicale*, January 1931, 60-61 (p. 61).

[25]*Les petites Cardinal* (1937) and *L'aiglon* (1936). There is also *La belle de Moudon* (1931), but the extent of Honegger's contribution means that this is more accurately described as an incidental music score.

[26]'Contemporary Cello Concerti — No. XVII Arthur Honegger', *The Strad,* March 1974, 655-61 (p. 661).

[27]Jacques Feschotte, *Arthur Honegger* (Editions Seghers, Paris, 1966), 97-98.

CHAPTER VII

Cris du monde: the imminent crisis

During a holiday period at Villennes in 1930, Honegger expressed to a close friend, the poet René Bizet, his desire to initiate a project based on the outlines of Keats' *Hymn to Solitude*. The outcome was the text for *Cris du monde* which Honegger set to music mainly whilst on a concert tour of South America during the autumn of that year. The philosophy which Bizet took as his starting point was that it is fundamental and necessary that man should be driven by a desire to gain true knowledge of himself and that to achieve this he needs solitude and silence. In particular he needs relief from the myriad of pressures and demands — the 'cries' — emanating from the temporal world of man; but he is continually deprived of this state conducive to meditation by the sheer weight and volume of these 'cries'.

After an introduction, illustrating the coming of morning and the first of the pleadings by the soloists (soprano and baritone) who represent man hopefully searching the impending day for peace and tranquillity, the dawn breaks and the 'Voices of Morning' smother him with their song of the noise of factories, the cries of his brothers in distress, the calls of hard-pressed workmen and the call to arms of patriots. The picture is chaotic, seething, soulless, relentless and overtly mechanical. In the second part the sea, the mountains, foreign lands and even space, all extend invitations to man to explore their hitherto unknown terrain — each and all to whom he looks for solace prevent him from expressing that which lies in the depths of his being. This search leads him to forget the duties of his marital bond and the quiet lament of a neglected woman leads to the third and final part. Will the coming of night herald the repose for which he is searching ? The 'Voices of Night' offer only renewed noise and excitement. The workers leaving their factories; the trains, trams, cars; the noise of the wireless news programmes, the cinemas: all these recreate the chaos brought by morning and the relative happiness of the world — the whole world should dance with them is their cry. The soloists make a last impassioned cry for freedom, but it is totally lost in the mêlée.

Bizet's text, to which Honegger became immediately attached and remained so for the rest of his life, is a most powerful and quite unique creation. The lack of poetry, the original versification and the utter clarity of the imagery result in a perfect opposition of the need for solitude with the whole ethos of the modern world; a philosophical argument which is full of vivid contrasts, driven by a thrusting force of immense power and consistent energy, but totally unified through its large-scale block structure. The tripartite superstructure conceals a substructure of eight sections (see Diagram 22 below).

Diagram 22:

Cris du monde

Part I	Part II	Part III
Introduction	Voix de la mer et de la montagne	Voix de la nuit
Voix du matin	Voix des espaces	
Voix des autres	Voix des villes inconnues	
	Voix de femme	

A consideration of Honegger's approach to the formal architecture and tonal design of the work reveals not only his characteristically sympathetic and appropriate response to the task, but also just how significant, if unfortunately exaggerated, the return to the methods that he had formulated in *Le roi David* and *Judith* was in *Amphion* after their relative absence in *Antigone*.

Structural Analysis

PART I:

The basic architectural designs and principal tonal components of each of the three sections which comprise the first part of this work are represented in Diagram 23 opposite.

The main tonality of the work as a whole is C minor and the overall achievement of the tonal patterning in this 'expository' first part is to effect a move from the 'tonic' to its 'dominant' — G minor — ready for the start of the 'developmental' second part. Looking at the tonal design in more detail, it will be observed that the 'dominant' is achieved at the end of both subsections ([9] and [15]). In the case of the second of these, its pertinence is substantiated by the prior re-establishment of the 'tonic' — C minor; whilst in the third section it is restored at a midway point to prevent any dissipation of its relevance. The G minor achieved at the end of the third section corresponds to the return of the 'Voix du matin' music and becomes an enormous pedal which irrevocably establishes its role as that of the dominant of the opening. The predominance of tonal relationships of a tertiary nature throughout this first part is most significant and the subtlety of many of the shifts in tonal plane is consistently logical and artistic. In the 'Introduction' the initial move from C minor to the powerfully contrasted centre of E major is beautifully prepared for by a chord sequence which hints at E minor and occurs three times (3-1B [1], 6-1B [2] and 1- 5A [3]) before the move to E major is actually made.

Diagram 23:

Cris du monde — Part I

('Introduction') ('Invocation au matin'): -[9]

Formal design :	(a)	(b)	(a^1)	(b^1)	(a^2)	(b^2)	(c)	(b^3)	(a^3)
Bar references :	-4B[1]	3-1B[1]	1-11A[1]	6-1B[2]	[2]-[3]	1-5A[3]	6-1B[4]	[4]-[5]	[5]-[6]
Principal tonalities :	c	C/e		C/e	c	C/e	E	G D	c

Formal design :	(d)	(c^1)	(b^4)
Bar references :	[6]-[7]	[7]-12A[8]	5-1B[9]
Principal tonalities :	g (over a dominant pedal)	F♯	modulating link moving to g for the start of 'Voix du matin':

Continued overleaf

'Voix du matin' : [9]-[15]

Formal design	:	(a)	(b)	(a^1)	(b^1)	(a^2)	(b^2)	(a^3)	(b^3)
Bar references	:	1-9A[9]	10-12A[9]	7-1B[10]	1-3A[10]	4-11A[10]	3-1B[11]	1-8A[11]	3-1B[12]
Principal tonalities	:	g		b♭		c♯		e	
Formal design	:	(a^4)	(b^4)	(a^5)	(b^5)	(a^6)	(b^6)	(a^7)	
Bar references	:	1-5A[12]	3-1B[13]	1-5A[13]	6-8A[13]	4-1B[14]	1-3A[14]	8-1B[15]	
Principal tonalities	:	g♯		c		e		g	

'Voix des autres' : [15]-[24]

Formal design	:	(a)	(a^1)	(b)	(a^2)	(a^3)		Transition to start of Part II
Bar references	:	[15]-2A[16]	3A [16]-[17]	[17]-[19]	[19]-[21]	[21]-[23]		[23]-[24]
Subsidiary formal design features	:					Combined with a return of the (a) element from 'Voix du matin'		
Principal tonalities	:	b♭	g	f/F	c♯	g		

In the second subsection, 'Voix du matin', there is a clear pattern of rising thirds to the tonal scheme which results in a most satisfying sense of achievement when the C minor is reached at [13]. The support given by this device to the crescendo of 'noise' that represents dawn is perfect — particularly the temporary switch from rising minor to major thirds in order to avoid the anticlimax of too quick a return to G minor — which he turns to further advantage by bringing in the chorus for the first time on the crest of its wave. The return to steps of a minor third after the C minor is achieved serves admirably to balance the desired relaxation in tension necessary for the return to G minor and the start of the final section.

As far as the architectural design is concerned, the detailed features evident are very typical of Honegger's compositional process. The procedure used in 'Voix du matin' is a fundamental aspect of his style — two elements are presented alternately, each one 'developed' on reappearance, either, as is usual, by the addition of a counter-subject or, as happens on occasions, by lateral expansion. A basically similar mosaic approach, but combined with elements of rondo-form, is found in the 'Introduction'.

PART II:

The four sections that constitute the second part of the work represent an enormous 'development' section within the terms of reference of the sonata-form which is applicable to the whole. The fact that this 'development' is based on entirely new material does not totally alter the relevance of the proposition (Honegger had previously created 'development' sections within a sonata-form construction where the proportion of new material was relatively high without any negation of the intrinsic value of the structure) because the totality of this aspect is balanced by the fact that the music is continuously imbued with the spirit of development despite the occurence of a simultaneous process of presentation of new material. This is appropriately highlighted by the very static nature of the 'exposition' (i.e. Part I) — a technical aspect which has not been noted previously in any similar structures — and by the nature of the structuring of the individual sections, which are summarized in Diagram 24 overleaf.

Diagram 24:

Cris du monde — Part II

'Voix de la mer et de la montagne': [24]-[33]

Formal design	:	(a)	(b)	(a^1)	(c)	(b^1)			
Bar references	:	1-16A[24]	6-1B[25]	[25]-[26]	[26]-[28]	[28]-[30]			
Subsidiary formal design features	:		(x)			(x)	(y)	(x^1)	(y^1 combined with part of (a))
Bar references	:					1-3A[28]	3-6A[28]	7A [28]-5A[29]	5A [29] - [30]
Principal tonalities	:		(e)	[A tone higher relative to (a)]	Bound by c	b		b (with passing references to d and b♭] moving to:	f

Formal design	:	(a^2)	(b^2)	Transition to 'Voix des espaces'
Bar references	:	[30]-5A [31]	5A [31]-[32]	[32]-[33]
Subsidiary formal design features	:	(Combined after [31] with the (y) element from (b^1))	(Element (x) combined with part of (c))	(With part of (a) and (x))
Bar references	:			
Principal tonalities	:	After an initial reference to e, it moves via c and f to c♯ at [31] and then to:	c	Moves from c via c♯ after [32] to e/E (4B [33]-) as dom. prep. for:

'Voix des espaces': [33]-[44]

Formal design	: (a)	(b)	(a^1)	(c)			(b^1)
Bar references	: 1-5A [33]	6A [33]-4B [35]	3-1B [35]	[35]-[40]			[40]-2A [41]
Subsidiary formal design features	:			(x)	(y)	(x^1 with reference to (y) 2-1B [39])	(With reference to (x^1))
Bar references	:			[35]-[36]	[36] - [37]	[37]-[40]	6B [41]-
Principal tonalities	: A/a	A/a (with passing reference to f♯/F♯) C (13A [34]-)	B/b	B/b	F F♯ F	b moving to:	E/e

Formal design	: (d)						
Bar references	: [41]-[44]						
Subsidiary formal design features	: (s)	(t)	(s^1)	(t^1)	(s^2)	(t^2)	(s^3) leading into 'Voix des villes inconnues'
Bar references	: 3-10A [41]	4-1B [42]	1-7A [42]	8-11A [42]	8-1B [43]	1-4A [43]	12-1B [44]
Principal tonalities	: Modal a		Modal e		Modal a		Modal a

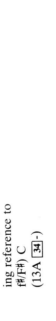

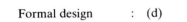

Continued overleaf

'Voix des villes inconnues': [44]-[51]

Formal design	:	(a)	Transition	(b)	(c)	(b^1)
Bar references	:	1-14A[44]	4-1B[45]	[45]-[47]	[47]-[48]	[48]-6A [49]
Subsidiary formal design features	:					
Bar references	:					
Principal tonalities	:	Modal a		Polytonal combination of a/A and f♯/F♯	D	e

Formal design	:	Transition	(a^1)	Transition to 'Voix de femme'
Bar references	:	7-9A[49]	6-1B[50]	[50]-[51]
Subsidiary formal design features	:	(Based on 4-1B[45])	(Combined with element of (b))	
Bar references	:			
Principal tonalities	:		Modal a	Moves via E♭ to:

'Voix de femme': [51]-[59]

Formal design	:	(a)								(a^1)
Bar references	:	[51]-[55]								[55]-[57]
Subsidiary formal design features	:	(x)	(m)	(x^1)	(n)	(x^2)	(o)	(x^3)	(p)	(m^1)
Bar references	:	1-5A[51]	4-1B[52]	1-5A[52]	4-1B[53]	1-4A[53]	4-1B[54]	1-5A[54]	4-1B[55]	1-4A[55]
Principal tonalities	:	a/f			e/E		c	b/B	f	c♯
Bar references	:				4B[53]			[54]	4B[55]	

Formal design	:					(b)				
Bar references	:					[57]-[59]				
Subsidiary formal design features	:	(n^1)	(o^1)	(p^1)	(x^4)	(q)	(r)	(s)	(r^1)	(s^1)
Bar references	:	4-1B[56]	1-4A[56]	6-3B[57]	2-1B[57]	1-8A[57]	6-1B[58]	1-4A[58]	6-4B[59]	3-1B[59]
Principal tonalities	:	e	c		a	a/A	b...........	moving..................	to..........	:
Bar references	:	4B[56]	[56]		2B[57]					

In the 'Voix de la mer et de la montagne', Honegger utilizes his favourite rondo-patterning to produce a tightly-knit mosaic structure, powerfully unified by the degree of cross-reference involved — particularly near the end when the tension is in danger of flagging. A similar situation occurs in 'Voix des espaces' despite the cyclic aspect of the construction of the (c) and (d) components. The relatively static nature of the final (d) element does not result in a non-organic transition to 'Voix des villes inconnues' because the final aspect (x^3) is used as the basis for the material of the new (a) component. In the third section, the unity engendered by the palindromic design is further emphasized by the fact that the final (a^1) contains elements of both the previous (b) and (c) subsections. An independent transition links it to the concluding 'Voix de femme' section where the final mosaic patterning of the (b) subsection serves as an appropriate dissemination of energy by way of introducing the 'Voix de nuit' which comprises the third and last part of the work.

The tonality of the opening of 'Voix de la mer et de la montagne' is deliberately made vague, but, despite the attempts at negation through the superimposition of so many different melodic tonalities, an element of the relationship of 'dominant of the dominant' with the preceding part exists initially to a satisfactory degree. The references to the 'tonic' (C minor) are clearly and repeatedly made in this first section, but in the subsequent three sections the tonalities of A minor and E minor assume a greater importance. Tertiary relationships still predominate, but a relatively large number of semitonal sidesteps also occur. Some dominant-tonic resolutions ensure a firm understanding of the roles of A and E minors within the section, but do not entirely obliterate the latters' separate tertiary relationships with the tonic (C minor).

PART III:

This third part consists of only one section, the large scale 'Voix de la nuit', and is truly recapitulatory in terms of the review it offers of material from the 'expository' Part I. Its structure is detailed in Diagram 25 opposite.

Diagram 25:

Cris du monde —Part III

'Voix de la nuit' : [59]-end

Formal design	: (a)				(b)	(c)		(b¹)
Bar references	: [59]-[62]				[62]-[63]	[63]-[65]		[65]-[67]
Subsidiary formal design features	:				Part of 'Voix du matin'			Part of 'Voix du matin'
Bar references	:							
Principal tonalities	: c	D♭	e	F	a♭ c	D-moving via references to b♭/B♭ and g to f/F	b♭	c♯
Bar references	:	6A[60]-	[61]-	7A[61]-	4B[63]-		2B[64]-	5B[66]-

Formal design	: (c¹)	(d)		(c²)			
Bar references	: [67]-[69]	[69]-[71]		[71]-end			
Subsidiary formal design features	:	Part of 'Voix des espaces'					
Principal tonalities	: C	c	a/A	C/c	D♭/d♭	F♯	[Pedal B which falls chromatically through a tenth to G in the penultimate bar for the final cadence in c.]
Bar references	:		6A[69]-		[72]-	[73]-	10A[73]-

The initial (a) component is a perfect example of Honegger's contrapuntal growth form — a creation which is the end-product of a gradual contrapuntal compilation of layer upon layer of musical thought. This generates an immense amount of energy which is used to focus the return of a portion from 'Voix du matin'. Similarly, the use of new material in the (c) element effects a meaningful preparation for the second different extract from the same section of Part I. The developmental aspect of components (c^1) and (c^2) ensures that the mosaic structure of the final part is imbued with a very powerful sense of growth throughout so that the end is the cataclysmic catastrophe to which the text has been building throughout the entire work.

The constant references to the tonic, C minor, provide a further rigid framework for the whole of this final section. Tertiary moves and/or semitonal shifts are predominant but the final gesture is not strictly one of tonality. The B major that appears to be a resolution of the substantial area of F♯ major is vague in outline and is followed by fifteen such similar 'patches' as Honegger allows a massive chromatically-descending set of bass pedal-notes to effect an arrival at the note G_1 for a firm cadence in C minor to conclude the work.

In order to appreciate fully other aspects of Honegger's style and technique, an examination is necessary of some of the compositional processes evident in this work, together with a consideration of his melodic and harmonic language. The predominant stylistic feature of all Honegger's music is the use of contrapuntal polyphony. Within this work it is possible to see, side by side, examples of two devices of which he was particularly fond. The first is the gradual assembly of a large-scale texture from a number of small motives in combination with a gradual *crescendo* and/or *accelerando* (see 9 - 12 and the start of 'Voix de la nuit' as far as 62). The second is that of a contrapuntally-conceived polyphonic tissue which is kaleidoscopic in the subtle variety of its constitution but utterly relaxed and lyrical — a most beautiful example being the 'Voix de femme' section. This striking dichotomy is fundamental to Honegger as man and artist, with roots evident in his very first works and a significance measurable by its prominence throughout works such as *Le roi David* and *Judith* as well as by the very existence of contrasting pairs of works like *Pastorale d'été* and *Pacific 231,* the *Concertino* for piano and orchestra and *Rugby.* The innate skill with which Honegger handles the art of contrapuntal polyphony is perhaps nowhere more evident than in this work where the effortless way in which he manages to combine two separate contrapuntal textures — with just the right degree of compression — to form a new tissue of increased intensity, yet with no inherent lack of clarity (see 19), and the almost unbelievable degree of activity achieved in the texture after 69 are both appropriate monuments to his mentor, J.S. Bach. The amount of strictly canonic counterpoint is somewhat restricted in this work compared to many of his previous pieces — the meandering canonic tissue after 7 (which is a startling harkback to those in *Le dit des jeux du monde*) and the near-canonic two-part imitative vocal writing after 16, to which he was so partial, are the only two examples; but other contrapuntal devices abound — particularly in the complexities of the polyphonic texture after 72 . As always in Honegger's music the aspect of aural clarity is consistently maintained, however complex the contrapuntal polyphony is allowed to become, by the nature of his orchestration — the lines of thought always coinciding with his strata-like scoring (cf. the texture and the scoring after 4 in particular).

A similar picture of established consistency emerges from a consideration of the nature and use of ostinati. Honegger's penchant for conceiving ostinati as the result of the interaction of two or more elements in contrary motion is frequently evident (see 24 in particular), whilst his meticulous care over not allowing ostinati to exist in an unaltered form for any length of time such that they would negate the organic flow of the music (usually resulting in an ostinato of a self-expanding nature) is likewise found abundantly in this work (cf. 26 in particular). Just as his contrapuntal technique embraces complexity and clarity, his use of complex ostinati (cf. 71) is simultaneously combined with an ability always to maintain dynamic fluidity — the nature of his scoring always ensuring that compound ostinati such as the one at 35 do not obscure the main argument in any way. Formally, too, the aspect of ostinati is as contributory as that of counterpoint. The mosaic construction of 'Voix de la mer et de la montagne' depends to a large extent for its success on the fact that the reappearance of ostinati is sufficient to maintain formal patterning and cohesion, thus permitting the degree of melodic difference that exists between recurring sections.

After the predominantly atonal nature of *Antigone* the process marking a *gradual* retreat can be seen quite clearly through the score of the *Symphonie* [*n° 1*] and this work — the very obvious and pre-emptive tonal framework of *Amphion* must only be interpreted as Honegger's appropriate reaction to a situation where the music was very much only one aspect of a creation of a very specific nature, and a slightly subservient one at that. The basic tonal framework must also be regarded as representing a midway point between that of *Judith* and the extreme reached in *Antigone.* The tonality is usually recognizable, but frequently there are periods, often quite substantial, where the boundaries of that tonality are carefully and calculatingly stretched almost to the point of negation. The fact that this line of demarcation is only occasionally touched upon, and rarely crossed, illustrates the degree and the nature of Honegger's retrenchment. Despite these aspects which mark a return to an earlier position with regard to tonal delineations as well as overall structuring, it is, however, important to realize that the situation is not a result of negation, and that the overall effect is one of further personal unification and logicality, where the originality is more happily contained and reflected by uniform absorption and dissipation. There are few moments where influences can be pinpointed with any certainty — the bitonality at 18 leads one to suspect Stravinsky still looming large on the horizon, but the more obviously polytonal construction at 45 sounds purely Honeggerian, just as does the simple combination of tonic and dominant near the beginning of the 'Voix de la nuit', now free of the qualities of pure Impressionism.

His confidence in using the enormous sequence of chromatically-descending pedal-points in the concluding pages betrays his tendency to utilize large-scale formal devices which, in lesser hands, usually heralded disaster. A similar situation is evident at [8], where he constructs a large subsection around a long rising scale — a dangerously simple technique which he quite frequently employs, although, only perhaps once before (in No. 1 of *Les Pâques à New York*) has he ever dared to use it in these proportions and with such resultant success.

The opening theme of the 'Introduction' illustrates three typical features of Honegger's melodic technique. The careful grading of the emotional and purely physical curves associated with this line is purely Classical in thought and here holds together a chromatic procedure with its ultimate symmetry (see Music Example 51 below).

Music Example 51: *Cris du monde,* bars 1-11

Simultaneously there is a controlled use of intervallic distances where, again, the grading is supportive of the melodic curve. Finally, the duality of the implied part-writing is governed such that the combination of their curves is a further contributory factor to the motion of the line. Within this work there are various examples of most of the different types of melodic styles evident in Honegger's music as a whole. The chorale-like melodic procedure that has appeared in all the large religious works so far, and whose roots were traced back to various early chamber music scores, finds appropriate points of application here, in particular before [24] and circa [34]. It also pervades much of the thematic content of the 'Voix de femme' section, its hymn-like quality giving a degree of mysticism to the simple and general lyricism and refining the pathos of the subtle chromaticisms. Here, more than anywhere else, the heritage of *Le roi David* and parts of *Judith* is quite obvious.

The *semplice* lines are also to be found quite frequently in this work — the best example being the one between 6A [3] and [4] (see Music Example 52 below).

Music Example 52: *Cris du monde,* solo baritone, 6A [3] - [4]

This characteristic quality of the line results largely from the predominant patterning using the tonic, third, fourth, fifth, sixth and final degrees of the scale, with the virtual avoidance of the seventh. The slight modal flavour of such a line is a feature that Honegger exploited in its own right and in lines such as those found at [7] (solo baritone) and [41] (cellos). It has, in isolation, more than a passing similarity to many in almost any work of Debussy, Ravel, Holst or Vaughan Williams, whilst, in context, succeeds in drawing further parallels to individualistic traits evident in works like *Cantique de Pâques, Le roi David* and *Judith*.

More generally typical of Honegger in the light of most compositions since *Judith* — particularly *Rugby* and *Antigone* — are the melodic lines where flexibility, muscularity, contrast and diversity are the predominant features. The placing side by side of the melodic line at [52] (see Music Example 53 below), and that at [3] (see Music Example 52 opposite) provides an illustration of the basic dichotomy that exists in Honegger's musical style on all levels, including that of melodic procedure.

Music Example 53: *Cris du monde,* oboe 1, [52] -4B [53]

This line is full of variety involving extensive rhythmic play and a series of different tonal planes. The melodic line at 5B [33] illustrates to what extent Honegger was frequently prepared to go in juxtaposing tonal planes to achieve the right amount of tension in a melodic line in order that it should correspond with, and complement, that which he was able to create in the spheres of harmonic and tonal thinking (see Music Example 54 below).

Music Example 54: *Cris du monde,* soli soprano/baritone, 5-2B [33]

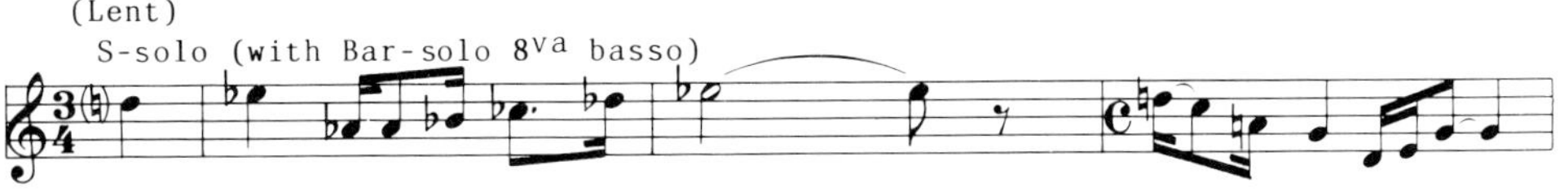

The same effect is achieved on other occasions by the sharp contrasts of diatonic and chromatic lines (cf. circa [64]) or the consistent use of relatively small intervals (cf. after [24]). The sort of line that appears so frequently in this work is a direct consequence of *Antigone* and, hence, the confrontation scene he added when he remoulded *Judith* as an opera — one that is extremely tough and sinewy, even a little neurotic (see Music Example 55 below).

Music Example 55: *Cris du monde,* solo baritone, 3-7A [57]

(Reproduit avec l'autorisation des EDITIONS SALABERT, Paris, propriétaires de l'œuvre.)

If the latter is perhaps the most characteristic type of melodic line to be found in this work, then certainly an additional factor must not be neglected — that of length. Most of Honegger's themes are extremely long, and those of a similar nature to the preceding example are even more remarkable in that the histrionic level of tension which is such a part of them is always maintained consistently throughout their entire length.

A rather isolated melodic procedure — the 'filigree' technique at *circa* [45] — is one which, whilst very typical in that examples are found in most of the works that precede this, is more prophetic in nature than any other because the purely Impressionistic origins it had, especially in the orchestral works of Debussy, are now entirely obliterated. Thus it stands on its own as an integrated feature of Honegger's personal style and as an anticipation of the considerable use to which he was to put it in many later scores — most notably the *Symphonie liturgique* [*n° 3*].

Chromaticism in Honegger's melodic lines had long since ceased to have the overtones of early Schönberg, in the same way as the chromatic aspect of his harmony had succeeded in escaping from the greasy and undisciplined clutches of the shadow of Reger. The controlled use of a melodic chromaticism which aims at a gentle and sublime colouring — as a means to an end rather than an end in itself — works so beautifully in the 'Voix de femme' to create a touchingly pathetic mood. But allow no deception: the effect is only as remarkable because the harmonic tissue which supports the melodic lines is the result of an intimate contrapuntal conception involving lines of thought identical to those used in the thematic process above. The independent originality of harmonic writing that Honegger had achieved little more than a decade earlier — by successfully integrating his natural desire to have a contrapuntal basis for his musical thought with the necessary prerequisite of a satisfactory vertical harmonic tissue — should be seen as having undergone a trial of strength in those intermediary years, surviving even the extreme rigours of *Antigone* to tell the tale of complete compatibility with the musical personality of Arthur Honegger in this work and all those that follow it.

Such is this integration that mention must be made of the interaction between traits of his tonal thinking with his melodic procedures. The chromaticism evident in the thematic material after [19] is entirely bound up with the logic of an antithesis between major and minor thirds, whilst the melodic lines at [18] want to follow the actual sequence of steps by major thirds that govern the tonal organization. The same is true of much of the harmonic thought. The triadic sequence in 6A [3], which recurs throughout as a sort of refrain, has the 'logicality' of 'falling thirds', a feature which dominates the whole of this work and so much of his previous music (see Music Example 56 below).

Music Example 56: *Cris du monde,* orchestra, 6A [3]

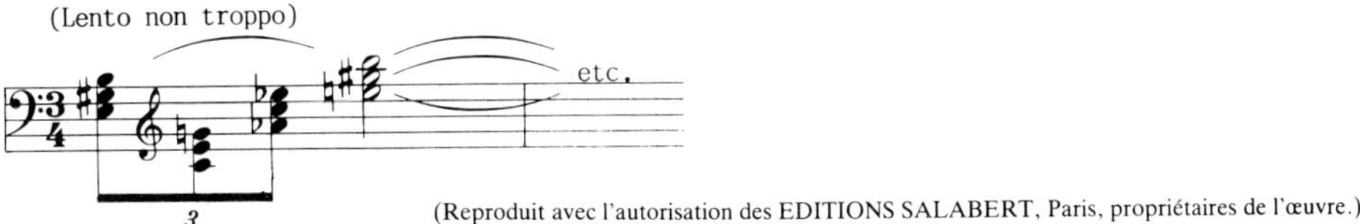

Furthermore, the interlocked series of falling and rising semitonal resolutions {G♯→G♮, G♮→A♭ and C♮→B♮ / B♭→C♭, E♮→E♭ and E♭→E♮} are unusually strong and work well in harness with the individual strengths of the rising minor sixths involved.

The dependence of the harmonic thought on the basic contrapuntal element naturally results in a great deal of patterning being detectable. The progression 3B [1] - 1B [1] relies for its unity of thought on the elliptical movement of what are essentially chords of the seventh; the tissue suggested in the counterpoint after [1] (and hence after [2] when it is repeated with the addition of a further part) is conditioned by the consistent use of the raised seventh and flattened ninth as pivot notes for the harmonic levers; and finally the aspect of contrary motion is responsible for harmonic conceptions like those at 5B [34], for the large-scale planning of the bipartite harmonic fabric at [28], and also for the way in which the chordal argument is pitted against the massive series of pedal-points near the end of the work.

Honegger's assured technique permits a free use of such devices as the string of parallel $^6_4$s at [11] and [73], and the superimposed chordal structures of [9] -, [13] - and [60] -, with no attached sense of Impressionism. The polytonality after [59] is purely constructive because the antithesis of different harmonic arguments is so very well organized and controlled, and even the simple bitonal effect at [18] is devoid of purely colouristic overtones despite being obviously a Stravinskyian derivation. His penchant for chords which are simply triads with an added second and sixth (present to counteract the tendency of any triad to act as a dominant) is seen most clearly in the 'March' ([17] - [19]) in Part I; whilst elsewhere the influence of the aspect of superimposed fourths or fifths inherent in such a chord exerts a more powerful effect — notably in the nature of the harmonic ostinato at [36] and in the chord structures *circa* [29].

The most important aspect of a consideration of the harmonic thought evident in this work is that, overall, it is unusually clean and uncluttered compared with so many previous works. It can never be said to obtrude above the surface of the whole fabric, a fact that is certainly not true of many of the scores prior to this. In comparison, it is probably less bulky — literally less thick, due to the absence of an excess of additive processes — and entirely positive in its function at all times. Maturity and assurance go hand in glove, neither pre-empting nor being divorced from the other at any stage.

Honegger's approach to the orchestration of his music is totally consistent and as dependent on the fundamental role that counterpoint plays in the fabric of his music as every other single aspect of his compositional technique. The clarity and logicality always brought by the scoring to even the most complex of harmonic-contrapuntal passages is not only remarkable but quite unique in that his approach, involving the layering of the score in correspondence with the various stratas of the 'family' structure of the orchestra, results in a very original and personal sound quality. A large orchestra was necessary not merely to do justice to the climactic moments but also to provide individual cells of sound quality, complete in themselves, in a manner totally akin to that of Wagner in conception. In general terms many of the details of *Cris du monde* correspond exactly with those of so many of the previous orchestral scores. The double basses nearly always have an independent line and are frequently left for considerable periods of time to support satisfactorily the bass of the texture in special combinations with one or more of the following:— contrabassoon, bass clarinet, piano or tuba; simultaneously, the particular colour of the cellos when used as treble melodic instruments is exploited frequently. The use of percussion is very restrained despite the number and variety of instruments employed, the piano nearly always ranking as a member of this section by virtue of its almost exclusive treatment to give a background edge to otherwise purely orchestral writing (the only exception in this work is between [67] and [68] when it has some soloistic passage work). There is no part for timpani because, as usual, he is quite content with the anonymously-pitched striking of the bass drum. His use of brass instruments is as extensive and demanding as ever — the predominantly high first horn part, the consistent and very prominent melodic use of the trumpets and the sheer variety of the trombone and tuba parts result in a sectional contribution that lacks nothing when exposed to the continuous comparisons with the other two main sections (strings and woodwind) that are an inevitable outcome of his technique of orchestration. The flutter-tonguing for the horns at 3A [63] and 6B [68] is tremendously effective; its deployment for the trombones, 3A [67], hair-raising; when the tuba joins in at 6A [69] the world disintegrates (the similar use of the tuba in the *Cello Concerto* is hardly prophetic).

The touches of pure originality are many — the three muted trumpets for the rays of dawn (see before [1] and [2]), are not Wagnerian; the simple combination of strings, flutes and piano at 6A [3] is as beautiful and sensitive as the highly original doubling of flutes, oboes, cor anglais, bassoons, trumpets and harp in the six bars before [25]. Some of the most exciting scoring occurs in the 'Voix des espaces' and involves the chorus which is, throughout, to be regarded merely as an extension of the orchestra. There are some marvellous choral effects with trills and glissandi; whilst the use of choral declamation *circa* [19] and after [60] and [65] was probably a source of inspiration to Britten (cf. the chorus in *Albert Herring* (1947) and hence the 'Sanctus' of the *War Requiem* of 1962). The choral parts are tremendously varied and often extremely difficult — the very close writing at [44], which is embraced by the cinema-like sound of all the strings spread out over a four-octave *unisoni*, is as tricky as it is effective, even if perhaps not quite so much so as the amazingly plastic vocal lines in the passage starting two bars before [74].

The 'wordless' contribution made by the chorus in the 'Voix de femme' once again restores the links with so many of the previous large dramatic scores. From moments like this which flood the memory with the similar sounds from *Pastorale d'été* and *Le roi David*, the transition is very abrupt to the very thickly scored and powerfully heavy textures that come from *Horace victorieux*, *Le chant de Nigamon* and *Pacific 231* and which are constant features of this work. Passages like those after [9], before [12] and at [73] are almost unbelievable to experience on paper, but work quite satisfactorily in performance by virtue of his skilful approach to strata-like scoring.

The first performance was given in Soleure on 3 May 1931, by the forces who had commissioned Honegger to write a work for their centenary celebrations — the Sainte-Cécile Choir, conductor Eric Schild. Tremendous interest was aroused by this work and contemporary documentation shows both the work's rapid dissemination and the extensive critical reaction and discussion that ensued. The public were divided into camps of acclaim, puzzlement and rejection. The daily press were mostly non-committal, whilst the majority of the writers in learned music journals came out in favour of the work. The Swiss reaction was almost unanimously favourable and performances followed rapidly in Anvers, Basle, Berne and Strasbourg — a translation into German was made by Gian Bundi for the performance given by Paul Sacher and his Basle Chamber Choir and Orchestra in Basle under the auspices of the thirty-second festival of the Society of Swiss Musicians on 20 January 1932. The contrast between the social conscience of the Swiss people (quite uniquely open) and that of the French (which is far more oblique and even closed), is clearly apparent from the fact that the Paris première on 3 June 1931 did not lead to another performance in France until that given under Fritz Münch in the Palais des Fêtes during 1933. There can be no doubt that the French people did not cherish their public life being so clearly portrayed in a sacred art form — they tried hard to maintain that there was now no future in Honegger's musical style by virtue of what they saw as a mistaken application. The reaction in Germany was even more forceful. To a country struggling much harder to recover from the decimation of the First World War and a people rigorously restoring their severely damaged sense of national identity and spirit, this was a work that was to be condemned as thoroughly as possible. The antagonism that had greeted *Antigone* in Essen was nothing compared to the forces of abuse unleashed at Honegger now — he was condemned as a communist and it is little wonder that, when Hitler came to power and attempted to 'purify' the musical fare with which his people were to be served, Honegger was on the list of those whose music was banned.

The music critics who supported Honegger found it easy to do so because they could confine their praise, if they wished, to the attributes of the musical score which, stylistically, is a consummate work of his mature style. Furthermore, as a vehicle for a text it is equally praiseworthy. The music and the text are always one, the music appearing to have grown out of the text such that the value of the sum of the two is always greater than that of either individually. Honegger had always shown a great respect for any text he set — the very nature of *Antigone* and *Amphion* speaks to this — but here he seems even more at one with the text and his unique technique of word-setting (which is just as rigorously applied here as it was in *Antigone*) contributes so much to a true musical expression of the text because it permits an appreciation of the sheer density of the words as well as an occasionally onomatopoeic representation.

They could point, too, at the Classical restraint with which Honegger approached his task. The score is perfectly pictorial; there is no vulgarity, no sentimentality, no reversion to facile devices, yet the emotionality of the music is utterly contagious. The uncompromising strength and hard relentlessness of the music is not merely a continuation or development of such forces found in the battle camp scene of *Judith,* the *Prélude* (from the incidental music for *La tempête*) *Pacific 231* and *Antigone,* because here it is actually only one element of the integrated fabric of the music as a whole. The entire framework of Honegger's music is wider than it had ever been — the strength is combined with lyricism and tenderness; the complexities are always completely intelligible; and continuity and logic are united. It is this broadening of the whole basis of his musical style that allows him adequately to delineate the enormity of thought and expression contained in the subject matter of the text. The sheer power of the psychological forces associated with the attempt to overthrow oppression — which is hinted at in *Le roi David,* plays an important role in *Judith* and dominates *Antigone* — is here unleashed to vent its fullest fury as the situation is made real and the oppressor is revealed to be the whole of humanity.

The outcome is that this work contains the first direct universalization of the problems and forces, external to man himself, which are a unique manifestation of the twentieth century; and, whilst being very much a product of its period, it must be seen as a catalytic force and to have continuing relevance. Honegger's musical representation of these problems and forces peculiar to our age which adversely affect man is not literal, but is achieved by the capturing of the internal excitements of visible things and thus avoids the annihilistic tendencies inherent in the methods of the earlier Italian Futurists. This work can be regarded not only as an inevitable result of his own musical development but also as a curious antithesis to a positive product of his membership of *Les Six*.

The fundamental paradox of Honegger's position in this group is illustrated quite clearly here. Jean Cocteau's thesis, on which the loyal minority of *Les Six* based their music, demanded an incorporation of the spirit of worldly sounds in the existing framework of classical music and an acceptance of this credo for the future successful development of their musical style. The concept of 'a universalization of problems and forces . . .' is applicable but not entirely accurate in its generality. Its inaccuracy lies in the degree of subjectivity that Cocteau and the few faithful members of *Les Six* both implied and employed.

The 'external problems and forces', whose spirit they chose to incorporate into their music, were, to a large extent, only those that symbolized the ethos of the Montmartre life which they so loved and would fight to maintain. They conveniently avoided all the harsh realities of life, but these were the very facets that meant most to the socially-aware young Honegger. Thus we find in this work not only a vindication of Honegger's statement that 'I am no worshipper of the fair-grounds, of the music-hall, but, on the contrary of chamber music and symphonic music, and when they are at their most serious and austere'[1], which, coming in 1920, showed immediately that he was not aesthetically a member of *Les Six*, but also a final and complete rejection of the actual foundations of Cocteau's manifesto.

In terms of Honegger's personal development, the two symphonic movements, *Pacific 231* and *Rugby,* are clear precedents for principles involved here. The parallel has already been drawn between the symbolism of the overthrowing of oppression involved in this work as well as in *Antigone, Judith* and *Le roi David.* In *Antigone* it was the principle that a person should yield to righteous conviction and always speak the truth, regardless of the fact that to do so might occasion even death. This has a direct application to Honegger in terms of his attitude to the role of the artist in society — for him the case was that artistic truth and sincerity should direct a composer even if this led to public neglect and financial doom. In this work the idea is expanded to include his view that society was gradually exterminating much genuine artistic creation by virtue of the very nature of its being which was capable even of destroying the whole of mankind. (Honegger's preoccupation with the role of the artist in twentieth-century society can be seen not only in many of his works, but also in the majority of his articles, lectures, critical notices and, in particular, throughout his two books *Je suis compositeur*[2] and *Incantations aux fossiles.*[3]) This work undoubtedly expresses the views of many of the socially-aware artists and philosophers of the period — Carl Engel in his article for the January issue of the *Music Quarterly* of 1928, entitled 'Harking Back and Looking Forward' wrote:

> The general hysteria of the moment finds vent in grotesqueness, exaggeration and caricature. The tonal material, made subservient to these ends, has yielded astonishing offshoots and unsuspected fascinations. Yet here too, surfeit will be reached sooner or later and change will be inevitable. Perhaps even after the welter of mock passion, a benign fate may lead mankind to rediscover serenity. For the noblest music, among admittedly great music, is that which fills the hearer with a serene earnestness and calm.

Honegger is clearly expressing such a warning in this work, and, in passing, it is worth noting that he articulates the concluding sentiments of Engel's viewpoint in the *Symphonie liturgique* [*n° 3*] (see Chapter XII).

Although it is possible to find a number of precedents for composers expressing their anxiety and concern for the future of 'the artist' (the most obvious being Schönberg — in Mahlerian tradition — in *Pierrot Lunaire* and *Die glückliche Hand*), they do so only in terms of images. In the same light as which the preparatory roles of *Pacific 231* and *Rugby* are seen, Hindemith's *Neues vom Tage,* Martinů's *Half-time,* Mossolov's *Iron Foundry,* Poulenc's *Promenades* and Weill's *Der Lindberghflug* must be acknowledged. However, the term 'universalization' is only applicable to Honegger's oratorio.

It is relatively easy to find equivalent parallels in literature (Mann's *Dr Faustus* and Joyce's *A Portrait of the Artist as a Young Man* for example) and to trace a subsequent direct genealogy involving a development of the theme. However, it would appear that, although *Cris du monde* acted as a catalyst, the works that are inspired by it involve a narrowing of the perspective. This is certainly the case with such works as Britten's *War Requiem,* Penderecki's *Threnody for the Victims of Hiroshima,* Schönberg's *A Survivor from Warsaw* and Tippett's *A Child of Our Time.* An interesting point to note is that the 'school' of composers headed by Cage, of whom it can be said that the opposite viewpoint is held, exhibits a tendency towards further diversification. However, despite this schism, the basic significance of the fundamental issues involved continues to be relevant. Honegger said at the time 'en réalité, j'y exprime la révolte de l'individu contre la foule qui l'écrase: sujet d'actualité'[4] [in reality I am expressing the revolt of the individual against the crowd which smothers him: an actuality], and 'où donc est l'homme qui lutte pour échapper à cette emprise, aspire à la délivrance et clame sa détresse? Il est musicalement existant'[5] [where is the man who fights to escape from this stranglehold, who seeks his deliverance and cries out his distress? — he is alive musically].

The outcome of the storm of protest with which various sections of the public greeted this work, due to their insufficient awareness and misinterpretation of its ulterior meaning, is vitally important. With regard to his position as a prominent figure in the musical scene the world over, Honegger emerged relatively unscathed, but, in terms of his personality and his creative artistry, the effect was immense upon his thinking. The scene was now set for the breaking-point of the crisis which had been developing for some time.

Notes to Chapter VII

[1]Quoted by Paul Landormy, 'Arthur Honegger', *La Victoire,* 20 September 1920. A translation by Fred Rothwell of this article appeared in *The Musical Times,* 1 September 1929, 789-91.

[2](Collection 'Mon Métier', Editions Conquistador, Paris, 1951). An English translation by Wilson O. Clough in collaboration with Allen Arthur William was published as *I am a Composer* (Faber and Faber, London, 1966).

[3](Collection 'Notre Siècle, Editions d'Ouchy, Lausanne, 1948). A German translation by Willi Reich was published as *Beschwörungen* (Scherz, Berlin, 1955), but as yet no English version has appeared.

[4]*'Cris du monde', Plans,* December 1931, 17-18 (p. 17).

[5]*'Cris du monde', Plans,* December 1931, 17-18 (p. 18).

CHAPTER VIII

The crisis

As early as 1924 Honegger had begun to express himself publicly on behalf of his fellow composers. In an article entitled 'Le métier du compositeur de musique' which appeared in *La Revue Nouvelle*[1] he dealt with two of the major problems which faced them in a disarmingly direct manner. Initially he tackled the question of the unsatisfactory nature of most first performances of large-scale works:

> Un jeune compositeur de grand talent, après une année de travail acharné contemple avec satisfaction la partition volumineuse de la symphonie qu'il vient d'achever. Six ans plus tard, ayant obtenu la faveur d'être exécuté dans un grand concert du dimanche, il passe des jours et des nuits à corriger le matériel d'orchestre que le copiste lui a livré avec un retard d'un mois. Ensuite il se précipite chez le chef d'orchestre bienveillant et lui remet la partition. Hélas, tout va s'effondrer. Le jeune auteur a eu l'imprudence d'introduire dans son orchestre un saxophone. Il a heureusement encore le temps de réparer son erreur et de transcrire la partie de l'instrument interdit. Arrivent les jours de répétition. 'Soyez là à 9 heures précises', lui dit le chef, 'je commence par vous.' Nuit blanche par crainte de ne pas être à l'heure. Dans la salle sombre, il entend d'abord l'ouverture de *Tannhäuser*, puis la *Symphonie* de Franck, suivie de la *Chevauchée des Walkyries*. Vers 11 heures, on commence la lecture de son œuvre. Malgré ses efforts, le matériel contient encore beaucoup de fautes. Les musiciens de l'orchestre le lui font remarquer sévèrement. Il s'excuse avec humilité. Le jour de l'audition est là.
>
> Pour ses amis, tous très désireux d'applaudir son œuvre, il a acheté des places, car on ne lui a donné que deux entrées au moyen desquelles il peut assister à l'exécution de son œuvre en ne payant que quelques francs de taxes diverses. Enfin, la Symphonie est jouée. Pas très bien, on n'a pas eu le temps de la répéter.

> [A very talented young composer contemplates with satisfaction the voluminous score of the symphony he has just finished after a strenuous year's work. Six years later, having obtained the privilege of a performance in a big Sunday concert, he spends days and nights correcting the orchestral

material which the copyist had returned to him a month late. He then quickly goes to the kind conductor to give him the score. Alas, all will go badly. The young composer was rash enough to introduce a saxophone into his orchestra. Luckily he still has time to correct his error and transcribe the part for the forbidden instrument. The rehearsal days arrive. 'Be there at 9 a.m. sharp; I'll begin with your piece', said the conductor. A sleepless night due to the worry of not being there on time.

In the dark hall he first hears the *Overture* to *Tannhäuser*, then Franck's *Symphonie* followed by the *Ride of the Valkyries.* At 11 a.m. they start to sight-read his work. Despite his efforts, the material still contains many errors. The instrumentalists rudely point them out to him. He humbly apologizes. The day of the performance is here.

As he had only been given two tickets so that he might be at the first performance of his work (although he himself still had to pay the various taxes due on them), he bought some seats for his friends who were all keen to applaud his work. At last, the symphony is played. Not very well because it had been insufficiently rehearsed.]

He then pointed out that this solitary performance allows for no reasoned assessment:

> Le public l'accueille avec indifférence polie. Les amis, pour montrer que l'indépendance de leur jugement n'est aucunement influencée par la sympathie qu'ils portent à l'auteur, déchirent l'ouvrage avec des sourires apitoyés. Quelques critiques bien intentionnés assurent qu'il n'est pas absolument impossible que le jeune auteur n'écrive plus tard une œuvre intéressante. La plupart n'étant pas venus au concert et ne connaissant pas le nom du compositeur, n'en parlent pas. Ses collègues plus jeunes l'envient. 'Tu en as une chance d'être joué chez X . . .'
>
> [The public welcomes it with a polite indifference. His friends, to show that the independence of their judgement is not influenced by their sympathy towards the composer, tear the work apart, smiling pitifully. Some well-meaning critics assure us that perhaps later on the young composer might write an interesting work. The majority who did not come to the concert and who do not know the composer, do not talk about it. His younger colleagues envy him: 'You were lucky to have had a performance at X . . .'].

Honegger outlined the financial implications of the concert:

> Bilan: 1,200 francs de frais de copie, 100 francs de places pour les amis, 8 francs de taxes pour son entrée personnelle, frais divers pour déplacements, perte de temps en surplus. Au bout de deux ans, le jeune compositeur se présente à la Société des Auteurs où il lui est remis la somme de 21 fr. 95. Le quatrième supplémentaire à la percussion a touché 150 francs pour le même concert.
>
> [Balance sheet: twelve hundred francs for copying, one hundred francs for tickets for his friends, eight francs in taxes for his seat alone, various transport costs and loss of time on top of it all. After two years the young

composer goes to the Composers' Society where he receives twenty-one francs and ninety-five centimes. The fourth extra percussion player received one hundred and fifty francs for the same concert.]

He also provided an illustration of the financial quicksand which is the allure of the publishing fraternity:

> Un autre compositeur de mes amis a cédé a un éditeur connu pour l'intérêt qu'il porte aux jeunes, un recueil de mélodies intitulées *Absinthes*. L'éditeur s'engage par contrat à lui verser 10% sur la vente des exemplaires. Le premier tirage étant épuisé, l'éditeur convoque l'auteur pour lui annoncer la nouvelle édition. Il lui explique que les temps sont durs, la vie chère, l'entretien des autos hors de prix, c'est pourquoi il ne peut verser à l'auteur 10% sur la première édition. Il les lui verse pour la seconde. Pas en totalité cependant. Le compositeur ne touchera que sur deux tiers de l'édition, car certains exemplaires sont donnés, d'autres s'abîment. Cependant, au reçu du chèque l'auteur s'étonne, il n'y a pas le compte. 'Mais si', explique l'éditeur. 'Vous touchez 10% sur les deux tiers de la deuxième édition au prix marqué. Le prix est de 4 francs. Je suis obligé de majorer ces prix de 150% ce qui fait que je vends vos *Absinthes* 10 francs le cahier, mais vous n'avez pas la prétention de toucher 10% sur le prix de vente?'
>
> Ainsi quand l'éditeur vendra 5,000 francs de musique du compositeur, celui-ci touchera 150 francs. Et encore nous avons affaire à un éditeur mécène.
>
> [Another of my composer friends gave a collection of songs called *Absinthes* to a publisher known for the interest he shows in the younger generation. The publisher undertakes a contract to pay him ten per cent on the sale of his copies. As the first edition has been exhausted, the publisher calls the composer to tell him of a new edition. He explains to him that times are hard, life is expensive, the cost of running a car is out of the question, and that is why he could not give him ten per cent on the first edition. He will give him ten per cent for the second. Not all of it, however. The composer will only have two-thirds of the edition because certain copies are given free, others are damaged. In the meantime, on receiving the cheque, the composer is surprised because he does not get what he was expecting. 'But yes' says the publisher, 'you will receive ten per cent of the two-thirds of the second edition at the marked price. That price is four francs. I am, however, obliged to raise the price by one hundred and fifty per cent, which means I am selling your *Absinthes* at ten francs per copy, but I hope you do not expect to get ten per cent of the sale price.'
>
> So when the publisher sells five thousand francs worth of the composer's music, the latter will receive one hundred and fifty francs. And we are dealing with a publisher who is supposedly a patron of the arts.]

Honegger was nothing if not realistic: 'voilà la situation des musiciens. Impossibilité absolue de vivre par son travail' [that is the situation for musicians — to survive on one's work is a complete impossibility]. This was qualified by: 'on me répondra que cela a toujours été ainsi et que de Bach à Fauré tous les maîtres ont fourni des exemples bien plus intéressants que ceux cités par moi.

C'est absolument vrai, mais je ne trouve tout de même pas ça juste [I will receive the answer that it has always been like this, and that from J.S. Bach to Fauré all the masters have provided much more interesting examples than the ones quoted by me. It is absolutely true, but I still don't think it at all fair].

The tragedy is that the situation has not changed significantly in the interim and shows no obvious signs of doing so in the near future.

Honegger's second campaign opened more subtly a few years later with a sizeable article entitled 'Beethoven et nous' which appeared in *Le Correspondant.*[2] Taking advantage of the centenary celebrations of Beethoven's death he attempted to draw attention to the suffocating effect on contemporary composition of the cult for music of the past. In the concluding paragraphs he allowed a discussion of Beethoven's syntax to develop and embrace two new elements of his argument: the fallacious aspects of certain trends in contemporary composition and the question of misjudged critical reaction.

> En ce qui concerne le langage proprement dit, la syntaxe, Beethoven n'a pas fait une grande révolution. Tout le monde a relevé chez lui certaines hardiesses de détail, à la vérité curieuses pour son époque, certaines 'dissonances', qui ont frappé ou scandalisé ses contemporains, gêné même des musiciens plus récents, et jusqu'à Wagner, qui s'efforçait d'atténuer l'une d'entre elles. En 1805, après la première audition de l'*Héroïque,* le critique de la *Gazette Musicale de Leipzig,* journal d'importance et qui était peut-être le *Comœdia* du temps, conseillait à Beethoven de renoncer aux symphonies, puisqu'il ne savait y entasser que des accords bizarres, et de revenir aux variations de piano. Dirai-je, timidement, que certains de nos juges actuels, quand ils découvrent, en dehors de Beethoven, des dissonances qui ne sont pas beaucoup plus avancées que celles-ci, qui même sont analogues, mais qui sont de date plus récente, se bouchent tout pareillement les oreilles? M. Pierre Lalo, qui vient de reprendre son feuilleton avec un si vif succès et dont le talent est connu, serait, je crois, ici, de mon avis. Si le mot 'polytonie' avait été inventé vers 1805, je ne doute pas qu'on l'eût employé avec prédilection en de telles rencontres, et peut-être déjà eût-on confondu de simples appogiatures avec la polytonie . . . Il suffit de dire que, par son élargissement des cadres traditionnels, Beethoven a exercé une incontestable influence sur ses successeurs et rendu possibles certaines formes souples et vastes de la période romantique. Cet élargissement était au surplus en accord avec toute son esthétique. Et on le voit bien en comparant son métier avec celui de Bach.
>
> Il est sans doute fort salutaire d'écouter, comme on le fait aujourd'hui, Jean-Sébastien Bach. Mais il faut bien l'entendre. La leçon de Beethoven a pu être dangereuse et on sait que l'imitation des quatuors — mal digérés — a causé quelques dommages. La leçon de Bach, tout de même, peut n'être pas sans péril, et je crois qu'on s'en aperçoit déjà. . . Sous prétexte, notamment, de revenir à la 'simplicité' du grand homme, il serait dommageable de renoncer à parler le langage d'aujourd'hui, d'en user comme

a fait Brahms, en quelques endroits, à l'égard de Beethoven, et de s'opposer vainement à l'évolution de la syntaxe musicale. On le tente parfois. . . il n'est pas moins vain d'imiter une mélodie de Bach, ou de la croire imiter, tout en piquant sous les lignes à l'ancienne mode quelques harmonies à la nouvelle manière — ce qui fait dire aux auditeurs de bonne volonté que Bach est ressuscité, mais avec un visage moderne. . . Cela risque de n'être ni moderne, ni ancien, ni très sincère, ni très musical. Ce qu'il faut saisir et ce qu'il faut ressusciter, c'est *l'esprit* seulement des maîtres anciens. Ainsi les modèles seront excitants, nourrissants et non point dangereux. Que chacun, au surplus, selon son caractère et sa nature musicale, aille vers le maître de ses préférences secrètes, que l'un fréquente surtout chez Bach, l'autre chez Mozart, ou encore chez Scarlatti . . . et, bien entendu, si tel est son attrait, chez Beethoven.

Car il fut très grand et, bien interrogé, mieux interrogé qu'on ne l'a fait d'ordinaire, il peut donner de hauts et profitables conseils. Seule peut-être lui a nui cette 'exclusive' qu'il n'avait point demandée, qu'on lui a, par une intempérante admiration, depuis près d'un siècle, imposée. On a fait un tyran de celui qui fut un roi, un roi parmi ceux d'autres nations. Qu'il reste donc roi, mais qu'on en souffre d'autres à ses côtés. Aussi bien, comme tous les princes du monde, n'a-t-il pas, ici et là, malgré son génie, commis quelques erreurs dans la conduite de son royaume? Citant pour finir le grand musicien que j'ai cité en commençant — un roi lui aussi, sans nul doute, — je conclurai avec Debussy: 'Je me refuse à les admirer, en bloc (les maîtres) parce qu'on m'a dit que c'étaient des maîtres . . . Je veux avoir la liberté de dire qu'une page ennuyeuse m'ennuie, quel quc soit son auteur.' Il y en a quelques-unes chez Beethoven. Mais de les avouer, ce n'est qu'admirer davantage, plus librement, plus sûrement, plus sincèrement, les pures créations de son beau génie.

[Concerning the actual language, i.e. the syntax, Beethoven was not very revolutionary. Everyone has noted of him certain bold details which are, in all honesty, curious for his time, and also certain 'dissonances' which have struck or scandalized his contemporaries and even embarrassed more recent musicians as late as Wagner who endeavoured to mitigate one of them. In 1805, after the first performance of the 'Eroica', the critic of the *Leipziger Musikzeitung*, an important newspaper of the day which was probably the equivalent of our *Comœdia*, advised Beethoven to stop composing symphonies as he only managed to amass strange chords in them, and instead to write piano variations. Dare I say that certain of our present critics likewise block their ears when they discover outside Beethoven dissonances which are hardly more advanced than his and which are even analogous, although they are of a much more recent date? Mr Pierre Lalo, a gifted person indeed, who recently resumed his articles so successfully, would, I believe, share my opinion. If the word 'polytonality' had been invented around 1805, I do not doubt that it would have been used with predilection in some circles; and perhaps one might have muddled simple *appoggiaturas* with polytonality. . . Suffice it to say that, by broadening the traditional frameworks, Beethoven exerted a great influence on his successors and made possible certain supple and vast forms of the Romantic period. This broadening was furthermore in agreement with his whole aesthetic and is clearly seen when comparing his work with that of Bach.

It is obviously beneficial to listen, as we do today, to the music of J.S. Bach. But we must listen to it carefully. Beethoven's lesson may have been dangerous and we know that poor imitation of the quartets caused some damage. Neither can Bach's lesson be without danger — I think we are already aware of that . . . Under the pretext of returning to the 'simplicity' of the great man, it really would be a shame to give up employing today's language (to make use of it like Brahms did on certain occasions with regard to Beethoven), and to oppose in vain the evolution of the musical syntax. We sometimes try to do so . . . It is no less futile to imitate a melody of Bach and actually to believe that you are imitating it just by inserting a few new-fangled harmonies underneath old style melodic lines — this causes well-disposed listeners to say that Bach has risen again, but with a modern image. This runs the risk of not being modern or ancient, neither very sincere nor very musical. One must grasp and resuscitate only the spirit of the ancient masters. Thus will the models become exciting, substantial and not dangerous. May everyone, moreover, according to his character and musical nature, consult the master of his secret preference; may one go to Bach especially, the other to Mozart, or again another to Scarlatti . . . and, of course, if such is his inclination, to Beethoven.

As he was so great and well analyzed, more so than others, he can give good sound advice. Perhaps the 'exclusiveness', for which he did not ask and which has been imposed on him for nearly a century by intemperate admirers, has been injurious to him. We made a tyrant out of a king, a king amongst royalty from other countries. May he thus remain king, but may we allow others, too, to be at his side. Like all the princes of the world, has he not, occasionally, despite his genius, committed a few mistakes in reigning over his kingdom? To end with the words of the great musician whom I quoted at the beginning — also, undoubtedly a king — I will finish with Debussy's: 'I refuse to admire them (the masters) altogether as a whole just because I was told they were masters . . . I want to be free to say that a boring page bores me, whoever its composer may be! There are indeed such pages in Beethoven. But to acknowledge them is only to admire further, more freely, more certainly and more sincerely the pure creations of its great genius.]

These views were first clarified and developed to their logical conclusion in a lecture Honegger delivered under the auspices of the Rice Institute Lectureship in Music in the Scottish Rite Cathedral, Houston, Texas on 6 March 1929.[3] He opened with what now seems a dangerous, if not actually inaccurate generalization: 'at present, there are two very marked tendencies in music, two systems which oppose each other vigorously. On one side, the school which favours "the return to the classical tradition with a vocabulary as consonant as possible". On the other side the school of "dissonance, of the free use of musical matter".' Nevertheless, he then proceeded to state the case for each against the other in such a way that it is possible to accept the tenor of his argument and hence to understand the dangers inherent in an exclusive adherence to either:

> Here we have the arguments of the former: since the war, music based on the use of dissonant chords has come to an impasse. Its creations are full of false notes without rhyme or reason and this brings about an impression of similarity and of extreme monotony in all its compositions. Its only object is the extravagant search for discordance which deadens the auditory sense and destroys the desire for clearness. Let us return, they say, to the wise laws of tonality, of modulations, of melodic sweep. Let us take for models the divine Mozart, Bach, Scarlatti. Let us pass over old deaf Beethoven; let us ignore the German romanticists and turn with horror from Wagner and his following, Richard Strauss and Schönberg, to return to the noble simplicity of Donizetti, Verdi, and Gounod. Our master, Erik Satie, is the only one who has retained a clear vision; we have one more proof of this in the fact that even Stravinsky, in his last works adheres to those principles without which there is no salvation. Music above all must please, and moreover, must be a national language; no complications, no studied elegance, only simple melodies, diatonics of harmony according to the rules, in a word compositions following the classical model!
>
> To which the other side replies: we cannot revive the past. It is impossible to ignore or to seem to ignore what has been done. Let us make use of the dissonance of modern harmonic language as of an inheritage [*sic*]. The generations which have preceded us have battled to conquer this new vocabulary. Let us keep it jealously; it is the outgrowth of a natural evolution. Let the new chords be the basis of a new harmonic system more real than the old one which is based on harmonic resonance, but cut off at its most important point (that is, at the appearance of the harmonic natural of the seventh dominant)*. You proclaim yourselves disciples of Bach and of Mozart and you take from these masters only their most superficial quality, the harmony of their days. You do not penetrate their thought and you close your eyes to their audacious innovations, which prove their efforts to widen and develop that harmonic system. Dissonance must not be an end, any more than consonance, that is certain, but it is an admirable means without which, in our era, it is impossible to create a living work. Your works in imitation of Mozart and Gounod are only so many medleys, more or less successful according to the degree of technique that you possess. At a time when even the most conservative musicians are setting forth timidly on the path of the new resonance, you are seeking by this means to pass as audacious innovators while you are really only plagiarists of authors long since fallen into disuse and, for the most part, unknown to the public.

He then examined the polarity evident in the case of objectivity versus subjectivity. As before, the outcome is an exposure of the weakness of extreme and mutually-exclusive standpoints:

> Another question, that of 'musical objectivity,' has greatly occupied young

*i.e. the seventh harmonic (or partial) of the harmonic series (e.g. B♭ in relation to C.)

composers, and is still engaging them, although the principle of it is manifestly acquired. This question has been treated in a masterly fashion by the well-known orchestra conductor, Ernest Ansermet, in a study on Stravinsky. I greatly regret not being able to quote this study in its entirety for it explains the matter much more clearly than I ever could. Objectivity consists, therefore, in the search for 'musical matter', above all, in the search for expression. A beautiful melodic line, a beautiful modulation, an interesting superposition of theme, are 'musical matter'. They have their intrinsic beauty outside of all pictorial or philosophical considerations, and this beauty is not jeopardized by time; it remains eternally young. On the contrary, subjectivity which seeks pre-eminently the expression of personality by whatever means, leads easily towards what we term 'sincerity' and which in art is an extremely dangerous objective.

How many artists do say: "Above all, I am sincere. I write what I feel. I say what I think. I give you my heart, etc. ." To which it would often be well to answer: "We don't ask for that much. Keep for yourself your heartaches and your impressions." There are crude ways of being sincere and some of them must be controlled. Roland-Manuel remarks that "sincerity may be an explanation; it is not an excuse."

This seeking for musical objectivity has little by little caused composers carefully to avoid all that which might be interpreted as music of expression or of description. They wish primarily to write 'pure music', that is to say, music which rests on nothing foreign to matter purely musical. The titles of the impressionistic works (Debussy, Ravel) tending to create in advance an atmosphere, are carefully avoided. We no longer write anything but Suites, Studies, Sonatas, etc.. That reminds me of a picture which I saw in the Salon des Indépendants by a painter who was a believer in 'pure painting' and who, afraid to choose titles, borrowed them from music. He exhibited an enormous canvas on which a winding red line intermingled with a green line. The picture was called 'Fugue in Two Colors'. The public, at first, a little bewildered, understood soon enough that the red line was one of the colors and evidently the green the other. Thus everybody was satisfied with little effort.

In music we soon came to the same point and every work not lending itself to a literary interpretation was considered 'pure music', which quality was sufficient to extract admiration. On the other hand, the musical element, however beautiful it might be, was neglected in every work expressing a certain definite sentiment, that alone condemning it *a priori*. This state of mind is the reaction of the new generation against romanticism and impressionism, and it is owing to such aesthetics that there has been a return to Bach and Mozart, 'pure' musicians. It is also the same theory which impels present composers to deny that dramatic musical art can survive. They all consider the musical theatre a dead form, incapable of regeneration.

At this point I shall take personal part in the debate and I will strongly protest against this conception. I am entirely convinced that the 'musical element' is the most important thing, the vital essence of the work, but in my opinion this 'musical element' finds itself greatly magnified if it corresponds to a general human idea. We have long admired Bach's *Choralvorspiele,* unique from the standpoint of its structure and its marvelous counterpoint, this being obviously pure music. Later, different authors, in particular Albert Schweitzer, have demonstrated that these *Choralvorspiele* are real symphonic poems drawing their subjects from the different stanzas of the chant and illustrating them by turn. Thus in the splendid chant of *Dogme en musique, Aus tiefer Not schrei ich zu dir* (the enlarged arrangement for six voices), we hear toward the end, ascending in a strongly marked rhythm, the marches which in the symbolic musical language of Bach express religious faith. In the last stanza the words of the chant express the hope of divine pardon. In the chant *Durch Adams Fall,* the bass is entirely in discordant sevenths illustrating the idea of Adam's fall. I might also mention the great choral, *An Wasserflüssen Babylon,* where the continued movement of double strokes[†] is undoubtedly the description of a river. I might continue these examples endlessly, as all those who know the works of Bach can easily understand. This symbolism of the language does not diminish the intrinsic value of the work, but, on the contrary, it makes it more human, more moving.

This naturally led him on to relating these various problems to his own situation and music, because, as he himself had said right at the beginning of the lecture:

> It is very difficult for a composer to speak of contemporary music without constantly speaking of himself, and those who attempt to avoid doing so commit a fault even more serious. In failing to name themselves they let it be understood that the qualities most lacking in their contemporaries are precisely those which they themselves possess, and seem to infer that the blindness and the prejudices of an unappreciative public cause their renown to be less great than their merits might warrant.

Honegger first dealt with the troubled waters surrounding his 'symphonic movements' by stating that:

> It is in this spirit that I am attempting to write works such as *Pacific 231* and *Rugby.* The subtitle of these pieces is *Symphonic Movement,* and that is their true title. In calling them *Pacific* or *Rugby* I am only indicating the sources of my inspiration, for reasons of honesty, and also to give to the listener a clue which will facilitate comprehension of the work. This being done, my aim is to interest my hearers not by the subject but by the music, by the 'musical matter'. My friends tell me that I have achieved my purpose. My critics tell me that I have succeeded only in imitating stupidly the noise of the locomotives and the thump of feet on the ball.

It is sufficient merely to place side by side some comments by various critics of the period:

> . . . lyricism has been overlaid by the mechanically picturesque onomatopoeics of this piece and the nostalgia of the train journey is lost in a

[†]i.e. semiquavers.

study of escaping steam and jolting points. A little more thought might have told the composer that music, which depends on varying degrees of stylized noise and speed for its expression is, on the face of it, the last medium in which to attempt an evocation of non-stylized noise and speed.[4]

As mere onomatopoeia *Pacific 231* is too well defined musically; for it starts from essentially symphonic and musical thematic material and it never reaches a synthesis of irrelevant sounds that could be taken to represent the sonorous puff of an engine.[5]

'Waves of the Ocean' has long been regarded as a properly poetic suggestion for musical composition but what would a generation ago say to 'Snorts of a Steam Engine' . . . a piece by Arthur Honegger whose title is not quite so provocative but whose content is almost as bizarre as such a title would imply.[6]

Machine music, railway locomotives . . . as inspiration for modern composers? Where will it all end? Wanted a composer who will write music suggestive of the crack of doom! Something of this kind is needed to curtail the essays of the ultra modern who are so zealously striving to outshine one another in the cult of cataclysmal clatter which they dignify by the name of music.[7]

One of Honegger's fundamental assessments was that

every work not lending itself to a literary interpretation was considered 'pure music', which quality was sufficient to extract admiration. On the other hand, the musical element, however beautiful it might be, was neglected in every work expressing a certain definite sentiment, that alone condemning it *a priori*. This state of mind is the reaction of the new generation against romanticism and impressionism, and it is owing to such aesthetics that there has been a return to Bach and Mozart, 'pure musicians'. It is also the theory which impels present composers to deny that dramatic musical art can survive. They all consider the musical theatre a dead form, incapable of regeneration. (Previously quoted in full — see pages 229-31.)

He followed this by pointing out:

I believe firmly also in the possibility of a regeneration of dramatic music. Since the days of Debussy and Strauss it must be confessed that dramatic music has fallen into a period of depression. There are several reasons for this. First, the difficulty of freeing oneself from the tutelage of Wagner, Debussy and Strauss; second, the difficulty of finding modern lyric subjects, that is, subjects of our day; third, the enchanted ring drawn around theatres by the publishing houses which hold the copyright of the current works of Gounod, Bizet, Massenet, Puccini. Last and foremost is the exclusive desire for pure music, on the part of the new school. In dramatic art, music must support and aid the drama. The desire for pure music, therefore, is in direct contradiction to its possibilities, and will cause the drama to be overwhelmed by the symphony.

A single modern composer has tried to find a balance between these extremes. Alban Berg, with his work entitled *Wozzeck,* has aroused considerable comment in Germany. The symphonic part is constructed in classical musical forms, such as *Sarabande, Variations,* etc., upon which the drama is developed. Most of the other composers, dreading it, have evaded the difficulty and have taken refuge behind an attempt to regenerate the old opera. Stravinsky with *Mavra* and *Œdipus rex,* Hindemith with *Cardillac,* Darius Milhaud with *Les malheurs d'Orphée,* Ravel with *L'enfant et les sortilèges,* Roland-Manuel with *Isabelle et Pantalon* and *Le diable amoureux,* Auric with the *Bal masqué,* and myself with *Judith,* a serious opera.

Along with these works, there are others by the same composers, in which the difficulty has been frankly faced with more or less success. For example, *La brebis égarée* by Milhaud, the three operas in one act by Hindemith, the dramas of Krenek, the *Sette Canzoni* by Malipiero, *Erwartung* and *Die glückliche Hand* by Schönberg, *Le poirier de misère* by Delannoy and my musical tragedy *Antigone.* I wish I were able to tell you of the efforts and the determination of each of these musicians, but that is impossible. There is only one work of which I may speak with a thorough knowledge. That is *Antigone.* The principal reasons for the lack of success of the great part of the work of the lyric theatre seem to me to be the following: the slowness of the action, exaggerated by the chorus and the symphony, and the impossibility of understanding the text. In this day we are accustomed to speed. The motion picture has given us the taste for a swift succession of tableaux and the public no longer has any patience. Hence the dismay of the public when confronted by works of the dimensions of those of Shakespeare and Wagner. In singing in the normal fashion or in double or triple time, one emphasizes the duration of the sounds. Everyone has already understood the end of the sentence when the singer has scarcely begun (provided that one may understand him, which is not often the case). This condition creates a very painful impression of heaviness and weariness. A further disadvantage is the drawing out of the word on the sonorous syllables, which renders it unintelligible. Each word is more or less plastic according to the place it occupies in the sentence. To draw out a part of that word to the detriment of another part destroys that plasticity. The word cannot be subordinated to the melody. It is the word, on the contrary, which ought to create the melody, for each word has a melody of its own. This melody has no more reason to be slower when sung than when spoken. "One should sing as one speaks", says Chaliapin in his *Pages de ma vie*, and he adds: "the majority of singers speak as they sing which is not a compensation."

I have sought, therefore, in *Antigone* to keep the movement of the song almost identical with the time of the spoken word. The music is none the less melodious for it, because a melody can just as well be fast as slow, a fact which is not generally taken into account. In my opinion, this constitutes the true vocal style such as Bach in his recitatives of passion* and Debussy in *Pelléas et Mélisande* have conceived it.

*i.e. the recitatives in the Passions according to St Matthew and St John.

What is the true vocal style? For me it is the manner of considering the voice as a vehicle for words. It is, therefore, a special instrument, different from all the others, which no other can ever replace. Try to play selections from the part of Pelléas on a violin or a flute. It will be absurd. But take the *airs galants* from the operas of Verdi, Puccini, Massenet, of all those who have an acknowledged reputation of writing well for the voice. These airs will lose nothing in being interpreted by an instrument. This is not then the best style for the voice since the voice can be so easily supplanted.

The recitatives of Bach are admirable from the viewpoint of expression of the word because at that time he wanted the words to be understood. When the air begins, the words, always the same, are repeated several times. Then Bach treats the voice in instrumental style, generally making it dialogue with a solo instrument which outlines the same contours. Naturally all my effort has been spent on the concentration of the symphony which supports the drama, in order that it may have a life of its own and its complete expression, without slowing the drama. When in this work the chorus intervenes, it is the lyric element, and the voices repeating the words are treated in the 'vocal-instrument and polyphonic styles'.

I have thus dwelt at some length on my own conceptions because I felt that I could do no better than to present to you altogether candidly my chief objectives and preoccupations.

When one places alongside this the hysterical criticism of *Antigone* by Guido Pannain in his chapter on Honegger in *Musicisti dei Tempi Nuovi*[8] which culminates in the wonderfully illogical final condemnation of the work because the music is so 'unmusical and particularized that it fits only the French text, rendering it impossible to translate into other tongues', one can understand the *cri de cœur,* 'ce qui est décourageant pour le musicien, c'est la certitude que son œuvre ne sera pas entendue et comprise selon ce qu'il a conçu et tenté d'exprimer'[9] [what is discouraging for a composer is the certainty that his work will not be heard or understood according to what he conceived and tried to express] that initiates the first of two outbursts representing the crisis of his long-developing fever of indignation and frustration.

POUR PRENDRE CONGE

par Arthur Honegger

Ce qui est décourageant pour le musicien, c'est la certitude que son œuvre ne sera pas entendue et comprise selon ce qu'il a conçu et tenté d'exprimer.

Tous les autres arts ont des modes de communication sans équivoque. On peut aimer ou ne pas aimer, admettre ou ne pas admettre, saisir avec plus ou moins de finesse ce qu'a voulu dire l'écrivain, l'architecte ou le peintre. Du moins, le mot, le trait, la couleur, la construction sont faits d'éléments clairs et qui parviennent aux yeux ou à l'esprit sans déformation.

La discussion porte sur une matière identique pour la totalité des lecteurs ou des spectateurs. Au contraire, la fluidité, la complexité de l'art musical ont pour effet certain de différencier l'œuvre conçue par le musicien de l'interprétation que lui donnent non seulement ses auditeurs, mais encore chacun de ceux-ci. De sorte que le musicien doit renoncer à faire entendre ce qu'il a pensé ou senti pour ne livrer au public que la matière émouvante qui sera pour celui-ci un thème individuel d'excitation. Dès lors, les jugements portés sur son œuvre pourront valoir quant aux critiques de la facture générale, des moyens techniques utilisés, de tout ce qui appartient à la forme mathématique de la composition. Elles vaudront rarement à l'égard de ce qui le touche essentiellement, de ce qui est l'essence même de son art, car alors on ne parle plus de la même chose.

Pour éliminer dans la plus grande mesure possible ce malentendu, on s'est accoutumé à aider l'auditeur avec des mots. Que ce soit le livret du drame lyrique, l'argument du programme ou seulement un titre indicatif, ces mots ont pour but de rapprocher les points de vue, de diminuer la marge des erreurs, mais ce procédé atteint mal son but. Car les mots fixeront l'attention. C'est autour d'eux qu'on stabilisera le sens vivant de la musique; c'est à leur rudesse qu'on réduira sa nuance et, ainsi, on le faussera d'une façon différente mais tout aussi parfaite, la musique étant précisément destinée à exprimer au delà de l'impuissance, de la sécheresse, de l'équivoque ou de la pauvreté des mots, ce qui ne peut se dire qu'avec des sons, des cris et des bruits.

Je me souviens qu'après la première audition de *Pacific 231,* un critique, d'ailleurs bien intentionné, me louait d'avoir puissamment exprimé la mer, croyant, sur la foi du titre, que je chantais l'océan Pacifique et non la locomotive.

Et presque tous les autres s'amusaient de cette reproduction du rythme de la machine comme ensuite un journaliste prétendait entendre dans *Rugby,* les cris de la foule et le sifflet de l'arbitre.

Je les remercie d'avoir entendu dans ces œuvres ce que je n'y ai pas mis et je voudrais seulement qu'ils l'aient entendu avec l'esprit et non avec l'oreille. Car si l'art musical devait avoir pour but une espèce de photographie des sons, il ne se justifierait pas. Cette sorte de reportage sonore, par ailleurs si émouvant et si riche en avenir, est du domaine de la T.S.F. et en partie du cinéma, plus que de celui du compositeur.

Ce que je voudrais exprimer, c'est non pas la réalité sonore d'un spectacle, d'une machine ou d'un drame humain, mais sa signification spirituelle dans le mode artistique qui est le mien.

Tout ce qui est matière artistique est susceptible d'autant d'expressions qu'il y a de modes. Au plus haut point de compréhension et de bonheur dans cette expression, la signification spirituelle aura exactement la même valeur, mais ses aspects seront naturellement différents selon qu'ils auront emprunté le mot, le son, la couleur ou la masse. Je prends, pour me faire clairement entendre, un exemple concret, et précisément celui du rugby. La géométrie, la rigueur, la jeunesse, la blancheur, la souple danse d'une partie de rugby et aussi l'atmosphère du stade, la foule, les cris, le grand ciel, l'avion qui passe, le nègre assis sur les gradins sur un journal déplié auprès du chauffeur de taxi, toute cette fête des hommes assemblés, des disciplines consenties, des mouvements ordonnés, tout cela donne une impression unique, totale, synthétique et exprimable par tous les modes. Leur description, élément par élément, avec des mots ou avec des sons, diviserait la totalité, refroidirait la vie, l'unité et comme la surimpression nécessaire. Elle trahirait la matière artistique. Ce qu'il faut, — et c'est le but même de l'art — c'est trouver le chant, le trait ou les mots qui diront, peut-être sur un autre plan et avec d'autres éléments, tout le contenu émouvant du thème, qui en seront comme le nœud, le résidu transformation, et tel qu'il contienne la force immanente de restituer logiquement tous les éléments assemblés dont il est fait, si l'esprit s'applique à le méditer ou si la sensibilité se livre à sa magie.

Le rugby, Giraudoux l'exprimera en parlant d'une jeune femme, Dufy avec quelques ombres. Le Corbusier dans un plan de ville. Ce seront des résultats apparents des aspects différents; l'essence spirituelle sera la même. Je répète ce que j'ai déjà souvent pris comme comparaison. Nous avons chacun notre cafetière et nous y mettons chacun notre café préparé. Le sujet, c'est l'eau chaude identique que chacun de nous verse dans sa cafetière. Si le contenu du filtre est de bonne qualité, cette eau chaude se transformera en quatre cafés différents mais qui seront tous quatre de bon café.

Aussi, qu'on ne cherche pas à les mélanger. Il n'y a pas de musique descriptive, la musique n'étant pas un art de description. L'expression musicale d'un fait, c'est ce que voit l'aveugle qui entend, c'est ce qu'entend le sourd qui voit. C'est l'expression dans la forme musicale de la valeur spirituelle du sujet et non de ses éléments matériels.

Pacific n'a jamais été une onomatopée de la locomotive d'un audacieux modernisme musical. On aurait pu et dû y reconnaître la forme la plus classique et la plus sévère: celle du choral d'orgue de Bach sur le modèle duquel cette œuvre a été construite. J'ai voulu, par un titre, rapprocher l'auditeur de la compréhension *vraie* de ce que j'avais voulu dire, en lui indiquant l'*origine* d'inspiration. Je n'ai réussi qu'à l'éloigner davantage en le fixant à cette origine plutôt qu'à sa transposition.

Si j'avais appelé ma symphonie *Zeppelin 42,* nul doute que d'ingénieux critiques n'eussent retrouvé les bruits d'hélices et des piétinements d'atterrissage. Faute de cet appel à la facilité, j'en ai été réduit à lire alternativement que cette œuvre était pauvre en invention mais riche en roueries techniques, et, ailleurs, qu'elle était d'une grande maladresse de facture mais d'une grande originalité de pensée; et une surprise unanime, en blâme ou en louange, à l'égard d'une fin dont nul n'a paru avoir décelé qu'elle était la dernière reprise d'un thème qui avait parcouru tout le Final selon la forme la plus usuelle. Je ne parle pas du critique éminent et membre de l'institut qui, ayant négligé de consulter le programme, confond avec la première partie de la symphonie le *Chant de joie,* ce qui lui permit de blâmer gravement le manque d'unité de l'œuvre.

Ainsi, un développement musical qui apparaît à l'auteur comme parfaitement compréhensif et clair, non susceptible d'équivoque et d'erreurs d'interprétation, est imperméable à l'auditeur, même critique professionnel. De sorte que le musicien a l'impression désespérante de ne faire qu'assembler des sons pour un vague plaisir de l'oreille plutôt que d'exprimer avec des rythmes et des notes ses émotions et ses pensées.

Et pourtant, il faut se faire entendre. L'expression artistique, c'est essentiellement le besoin de communiquer ces émotions et ces pensées et, dès lors, il vaut tout de même mieux que ce qui est entendu soit ce qui a été dit.

C'est de là qu'est venue la tentation, pour le musicien, de composer sur un cadre clair et qui limite dans la plus large mesure l'erreur d'interprétation, la mélodie, l'opéra, ou l'œuvre chorale. Malheureusement, l'opéra, en raison du mouvement dramatique qu'il suppose, de 'l'histoire précise à raconter' est trop souvent un cadre étroit pour le musicien où il trouve plus de contraintes et de devoirs pénibles que de possibilités d'expansion. Et même dans l'œuvre chorale, il risque à tout instant d'avoir ou de sembler avoir à illustrer des mots avec de la musique, ce qui est tout juste le contraire du but poursuivi. C'est ce qui explique que Wagner, lorsqu'il conçut le dessein magnifique d'exprimer l'essence même de l'esprit nordique dans ses plus vieilles légendes pour une synthèse totale de l'expression artistique, s'en fit à la fois le poète, le dramaturge et le musicien.

De telles facilités ne sont pas données à tous. Je rêve d'une collaboration qui parviendrait à être totale que, souvent, le poète pensât en musicien et le musicien en poète, pour que l'œuvre issue de cette union ne soit pas le hasardeux résultat d'une série d'approximations et de concessions, mais l'harmonieuse synthèse des deux aspects d'une même pensée.

L'opéra est fini; ses formes désuètes ne sont plus acceptables ni d'ailleurs acceptées. Le drame lyrique wagnérien est lié à son destin dans la mesure même où il en est le contrepied. Il faut définir et réaliser ce mode lyrique moderne dont les formes seront adaptées aux indications du monde nouveau et qui exprimera les nouveaux aspects de l'homme et des choses. Sera-ce le cinéma qui fournira au musicien tout au long de sa bande d'images ce moyen renouvelé? Sera-ce une nouvelle collaboration de la musique, des couleurs et des lumières? Il faudrait que l'auditeur trouvât un cadre assez précis pour permettre à celui-ci de s'exprimer entièrement. Provisoirement, je me retire du débat. Il y a tout un monde nouveau qui veut prendre conscience de lui-même, se chercher, se définir, s'exalter dans des formes esthétiques nouvelles. C'est à lui qu'est désormais limitée ma passion. Je préfère l'échec dans cette tentative à la paresse satisfaite des formes consacrées et des habitudes acquises.

[A FAREWELL by Arthur Honegger

What is discouraging for a composer is the certainty that his work will not be heard or understood according to what he conceived and tried to express.

All the other arts have methods of communication which are not ambiguous. One can like or dislike, acknowledge or not, more or less understand what the writer, architect or painter wanted to say. At least the word, the stroke of the paintbrush, the colour and the construction are all made from clear elements and all reach the onlooker's eye or mind without any distortion.

The discussion is concerned with identical material for all readers and spectators. On the contrary, the fluidity and complexity of musical art make it easy to differentiate the work conceived by the musician from the interpretation of his listeners as a group and as individuals. In other words, the musician must renounce the idea of making heard what he has thought or felt so as only to give emotive material to the public which, for them, will be an individual theme of excitement. Hereafter, judgements concerning his work will have value insofar as criticisms involving the general form, the technical means employed and all that belongs to the mathematical shape of the work. They will rarely have any value as far as concerns him essentially and the very essence of his art, because at this stage one is no longer talking about the same thing.

In order to eliminate as far as possible this misunderstanding, the custom has arisen to help the listener by means of words. Whether it be the libretto of the lyrical drama, the argument of the programme or only the descriptive title, the aim of these words is to bring closer together points of view and to reduce the margin of error, but this process rarely achieves its goal. For the words will hold attention. It is around them that the living sense of music will be stabilized; its nuance will be reduced to their coarseness and thus the music will be falsified in a way which is different but equally perfect, precisely because it is intended to express beyond the incapacity, dryness, ambiguity and poverty of words, that which can only be expressed by sounds, cries and noises.

I remember that, after the first performance of *Pacific 231,* a critic, well-intentioned nevertheless, praised me for having powerfully expressed the sea, believing on the strength of the title that I was singing the Pacific Ocean and not the engine.

And nearly all the others enjoyed the reproduction of the rhythm of the machine as, when later on, a journalist pretended he could hear the cries of the crowd and the referee's whistle in *Rugby*.

I thank them for having heard in these works things which I did not put in them and I only wish that they had listened to them with their minds and not with their ears. For if musical art were to have as its aim a sort of photography of sounds, it would not be justified. This kind of sonorous reporting, elsewhere so moving and so rich in the future, is in the domain of radio and, partly, of the cinema, more than in that of the composer.

What I would like to express instead of the sonorous reality of a spectacle, machine or human drama, is its spiritual significance in an artistic manner which is my own.

All artistic material is susceptible to as many different expressions as there are fashions. At the peak of comprehension and good fortune in this expression, the spiritual significance will be worth exactly the same, but its aspects will naturally be different according to the fact that they have borrowed the word, the sound, the colour or the whole. To make myself clearly understood, I take a concrete example — precisely that of rugby. The geometry, rigour, youth, whiteness, the supple dance of a game of rugby and also the atmosphere of the stadium; the crowd, the cries, the open sky, the aeroplane which flies over, the negro seated in the tiers on a spread-out newspaper next to a taxi-driver; this feast of men gathered, consented disciplines, ordered movements; all this gives a unique, total and synthetic impression, expressible by all means. Their description, element by element, with words or sounds, would divide the totality, make life and unity cold, like the necessary superimposition. It would betray the artistic material. What is necessary (and is indeed the very goal of art) is to find the song, stroke of paint-brush or words which will mention — perhaps on a different level and with different elements all the moving contents of the theme; these would be like the knot, the transformation residue, such that it would contain the imminent strength to restore logically all the assembled elements of which it is made, if the mind makes itself contemplate upon it or if sensitivity gives in to its magic.

Giraudoux will express rugby in terms of a young woman, Dufy in terms of several shadows and Le Corbusier in a plan of a town. The results would be noticeable and the aspects different, but the spiritual essence would be the same. I repeat what I have often already taken as a comparison. We each have our own coffee pot and we put into it our own prepared coffee. The subject is the identical hot water which each of us pours into the coffee pot. If the contents of the filter are of a good quality, this hot water will be transformed into four different coffees, but all four will be a good coffee.

Therefore let us not try to mix them up. There is no descriptive music, for music is not an art of description. The musical expression of a fact is what a blind person sees who can hear, it is what a deaf person hears who can see. It is the expression in the musical form of a spiritual value of the subject and not of its material elements.

Pacific 231 has never been an onomatopoeia of an engine by way of an audacious musical modernism. One could and ought to have recognized in it the most classic and severe form: that of a Bach organ chorale prelude on whose model this work has been constructed. I wanted, by use of a title, to bring the listener closer to the *true* understanding of what I wanted to say, by showing him the origin of my inspiration. I only succeeded in sending him further away by fixing him to this origin instead of to its transposition.

If I had called my symphonic movement *Zeppelin 42,* no doubt some ingenious critics would have found in it sounds of propellers and bumpy landings. Deprived of this facilitating device, I was reduced to read either that this work was poor in invention but rich in technical tricks, or that it was awkward in its composition but had a great originality of thought; and [to read] of a unanimous surprise as regards the end, because in blame or praise, they did not seem to have realized that it was the last return of a theme which had run across the whole piece according to the most usual form. I am not speaking of the eminent critic and member of the Institute who, having neglected to consult the programme, confuses the *Chant de joie* with the first part of the symphony, which enables him to find serious fault in the lack of unity of the work.

Thus, a musical development which seems to be completely clear and comprehensible to the composer, insusceptible to ambiguity and errors of interpretation, is impervious to the listener and even to the professional critic; the result being that the musician has the desperate impression of doing nothing but assembling sounds together for a vague pleasure of the ear rather than expressing his emotions and thoughts in rhythms and notes.

And yet, one must make oneself heard. The artistic expression is essentially the need to communicate these emotions and thoughts and, from that moment it would be much better if that which is heard is that which is said.

From this came the temptation for the musician to compose on a clear frame and which limits to a very large extent misinterpretations in song, opera or choral music. Unfortunately opera, in consideration of the dramatic movement which it supposes, of the 'precise story to tell', is all too often a narrow frame for the musician where he finds more constraints and laborious duties than possibilities of expansion. And even in a choral work, he risks all the time, to have or to seem to have to illustrate words with music, which is just the opposite of his supposed aim. It is that which explains how Wagner, when he conceived the magnificent design of expressing the very essence of the Nordic spirit in its oldest legends, for a complete synthesis of the artistic expression made of himself simultaneously poet, dramatist and musician.

Such talents are not given to everyone. I dream of a collaboration which would succeed in being total; that the poet would think of himself as a musician and the musician as a poet, in order that the work produced from this union would not be a hazardous result of a series of approximations and concessions, but the harmonious synthesis of two aspects of one and the same thought.

Opera is finished: its obsolete forms are no longer acceptable nor even accepted. The Wagnerian lyric drama is linked to its destiny in so far as it is the contrary. One must define and realize this modern lyrical method whose forms will be adapted to the indications of the new world and which will express new aspects of man and things. Will it be the cinema which will supply the musician with this renewed means through its collation of images? Will there be a new collaboration of colour, light and music? The listener must find a frame precise enough to allow the latter to express itself completely. Provisionally, I will retire from this dispute. There is a whole new world for him who wants to become aware of himself, to search himself, to define himself, to exalt himself, in new aesthetic forms. It is to that which my passion is from now on limited. I prefer the failure in this attempt to the satisfied laziness of consecrated forms and acquired habits.]

In the light of previously quoted extracts from his writings the most significant aspects are the final sentiments regarding the cinema and dramatic collaboration. His dream of 'the ideal collaboration' was to be achieved a few years later when he and Paul Claudel created *Jeanne d'Arc au bûcher* (see Chapter IX). The art of writing sound-tracks for the cinema was something which had occupied a place in his thoughts for some time and, when consideration is given to the fact that his output between *Cris du monde* and *Jeanne d'Arc au bûcher* consists only of the *Sonatine* for violin and cello, the *Mouvement symphonique n° 3,* the *Prélude, Arioso, Fughette (sur le nom de Bach)* for piano, the ballet score *Sémiramis,* the *Petite suite* and two songs[10] besides no less than ten film sound-tracks and two large scores for radio programmes,[11] the fruitful significance of this minor preoccupation is obvious.

As far back as 1923, having just composed his first film score for Abel Gance's *La roue*,[12] Honegger spoke out very strongly against the predominant practice of adapting already existing music for the purposes of film sound-tracks. In an article entitled 'Adaptations musicales', which appeared in the principal journal of the cinema world, *Gazette des sept arts*[13], he dealt with all the various arguments involved in his usual direct yet thoroughly penetrating way. He followed this up in 1931 with an article entitled 'Du cinéma sonore à la musique réelle'[14], in which he dealt most authoritatively with the aesthetic and artistic problems involved in writing film music. His understanding and perception quickly led to him assuming a leading role in this field and to writing scores for some of the immortal classics of the early French cinema as can be appreciated by the following compilation of his output in this genre (see Table 7, page 242).

Some of these sound-tracks are exceedingly large — those for both *Les misérables* and *Rapt* are reported to be over eight thousand metres long, thus being more appropriately referred to in French cinema circles as 'commentaires musicaux'.[15] A fascinating article appeared in *La Revue Musicale* of December 1934 (pages 88-91) entitled 'Particularités sonores du film *Rapt*', in which Honegger continued to theorize on the art involved and Arthur Hoérée simultaneously illustrated how they had both technically realized such theories in this particular score. Recognition of his talent came very quickly, not only in France but in other countries too — the choice of Honegger to write the score for the Asquith/Howard production of *Pygmalion* is perhaps the most obvious evidence of this.

Although he contributed this vast corpus of film music, his attention to the medium was always slightly detached. He noted in *I am a Composer* that he found

> the work was relatively easy, for I possess the necessary technique to write an orchestral score swiftly. Besides, the subject is supplied by the picture, which immediately suggests to me a musical translation . . . it suffices to see the projection and to set to work; the visual image is quite fresh before my eyes. The more recent the film is in memory, the more my work is facilitated: the important thing is to transcribe the still lively impressions without delay.[16]

This was most certainly not the case with his purely instrumental music because, as he again confessed in *I am a Composer*, 'as far as I am concerned, symphonic works give me much trouble: they demand an effort at sustained reflection.'[17] Thus 'the crisis' became a reality in his musical creativity of this period as well as in his 'literary' outpourings. The lack of any major dramatic collaboration

TABLE 7
Film Scores

1923	La roue
[1924	Faits divers—unfinished]
1927	Napoléon
1934	Les misérables Rapt (*ou* La séparation des races) L'idée Cessez le feu Crime et châtiment Le roi de la Camargue
1935	Der Dämon des Himalayas L'équipage (*ou* Celle que j'aime)
1936	Les mutinés de l'Elseneur Mayerling
1937	Nitchevo (*ou* L'agonie du sous-marin) Mademoiselle Docteur Marthe Richard au service de la France Liberté La citadelle du silence Regain Visages de la France Miarka (*ou* La fille à l'ourse) Passeurs d'hommes Les bâtisseurs
1938	Pygmalion L'or dans la montagne (*ou* Faux-monnayeurs)
1939	Le déserteur (*ou* Je t'attendrai) Cavalcade d'amour
1942	Le journal tombe à cinq heures Huit hommes dans un château
1943	Les antiquités de l'Asie occidentale La boxe en France Secrets Callisto (*ou* La petite nymphe de Diane) Le capitaine Fracasse Mermoz Un seul amour Lucrèce
1945	Un ami viendra ce soir
1946	Les démons de l'aube
1947	Un revenant
1950	Bourdelle
1951	Paul Claudel La tour de Babel

for the first time in over a decade reveals a sparse handful of works of which only one is ultimately of significance — but of a partially cruel and most ironic kind — as will be revealed shortly.

The two songs (*Le grand étang* and *Fièvre jaune*) and the *Petite suite* have little to distinguish them apart from the unfailing evidence of a craftsman's hand at work. The *Prélude, Arioso, Fughette (sur le nom de Bach)* was Honegger's contribution to the musical supplement which accompanied the December 1932 issue of *La Revue Musicale* and contained similarly inspired pieces by Casella, Malipiero, Poulenc and Roussel. Honegger achieved his ultimate aim in that the *Prélude* recreates totally the spirit of a Bach keyboard prelude without one ever being aurally aware of what would initially appear to be, from a superficial visual point of view, merely a twentieth-century harmonic titillation of the C major Prelude from Book 1 of *Das Wohltemperierte Klavier*. The handling of the B-A-C-H motif as a two-bar minim ostinato in the *Arioso* provides an ideal framework for the same wonderful melodic invention found in so many of the shorter organ chorale preludes. The *Fughette* is terse and convincingly argued — Hindemith would probably have found this a better example for didactic purposes than many of his own from *Ludus Tonalis*.

The 1932 *Sonatine* for violin and cello is a nostalgic work in many ways. The relaxed pastorality of the opening *Allegro* harks back to a style predominant in the early chamber works that had been suspended just as had his habit of creating for the medium. The AB(AB) structure of the following *Andante* is a replica of the form of such works as the *Pastorale d'été* and *Chant de joie*, but far less successful. The contrast which the rather piquantly jaunty *doppio movimento* B section presents to the A section is too sharp, particularly in view of the latter's overtly static quality, with the result that the typically Honeggerian superimposition which then occurs in the final section of this ternary movement sounds disturbingly contrived and alarmingly premature. The final *Presto* is superficially successful as regards both the Satie-like simplicity of the rondo theme and the panache of the first and fourth episodes where the capturing of the early jazz fiddler's improvisatory spirit is temporarily back in the true vein of 'Les Six'. Nevertheless, the extreme contrasts offered by the different components of this little rondo and the absence of any real attempt to move smoothly or logically from one to another ultimately militate against the movement.

The same criticisms cannot, however, be levelled at the *Mouvement symphonique n° 3* which stands as his finest achievement in the field of purely orchestral symphonic music to date. Commissioned by Furtwängler for the fiftieth birthday celebrations of his Berlin Philharmonic Orchestra, the work received its first performance in March 1933. When asked by Bernard Gavoty in *I am a Composer* why he had not given a title to this, the last of his projected triptych of symphonic movements, he replied:

> As a matter of fact, I lacked an idea for the third. But you must know that as regards *Pacific* and *Rugby,* the press turned out to be very prolix. People of great talent wrote wonderful articles describing the driving-rods, the noise of the pistons, the grinding of brakes, the oval balloon, the release of steam, the commotion of the front wheels etc., etc.. All these images

gave birth to copious studies. But my poor *Symphonic Movement No. 3* paid dearly for its barren title: it barely harvested here and there a few evasive and polite lines. Moral: but no, I have been a music critic myself, and I prefer not to speak ill of a profession which has fed me.[18]

Writing nearly two decades later, his frustration and anger had been somewhat tempered by the passage of time because his curt reaction in 1933 had been to say that it was due to their failure to recognize it as an infinitely better work than the other two. But it is not all this which upset him nearly as much as the misreading accorded to *Cris du monde* and the German public's reaction that greeted the *Mouvement symphonique nº 3.* Talking of *Cris du monde* in *I am a Composer* he pointed out that 'some saw a communist work in it, others a reactionary hymn. Actually, in it I gave expression to the revolt of the individual against the crowd that crushes him — a timely subject.'[19] As a direct result of this, when his *Mouvement symphonique nº 3* was first performed in Berlin, false word was maliciously circulated to the effect that he was a Jew. The young, but very strong and virile Nazi party inevitably seized upon this and initiated a vicious anti-Honegger campaign. It was not long before his music was ostracized from the German opera houses and concert platforms, and so an important door to musical opinions was closed to him for many years.

Late in 1933 he permitted himself one final outburst in print. Again, born of the modest manner so typically his, much of it is on behalf of young composers far less fortunate than himself; but, nevertheless, the personal anguish is evident. Had he not declared only the year before: 'take, for instance, my oratorio *Le roi David* (*King David*), which was last year played in Switzerland. My royalties amounted to fifteen francs!'[20], and was not so much of his time necessarily wasted on writing film music to enable him to buy sufficient time to do what he himself called 'serious work'? The 'crisis' remained tenaciously tormentative and took as its toll vital creative energy and, hence, an unquantifiable amount of his music. Let his article entitled 'La situation sociale du compositeur de musique'[21], stand on its own as a conclusion.

De tous temps, le musicien créateur, c'est-à-dire le compositeur, a été considéré, au point de vue social, comme un inutile, un parasite. Je soupçonne qu'on devait dire à Beethoven désirant placer sa musique: 'Pourquoi venir nous encombrer d'œuvres nouvelles? Nous avons celles de Mozart.' Et à Mozart: 'Nous nous passerons de vous: nous avons Philippe-Emmanuel Bach.'

A priori, tout contemporain était superfétatoire, le passé suffisait. On peut deviner le résultat financier de pareille situation sociale. Mozart est mort dans la misère. Sa femme étant souffrante, seuls quelques amis accompagnèrent la dépouille du divin musicien. Par malheur le temps était si détestable qu'ils n'eurent pas le courage de persévérer jusqu'au cimetière. La fosse commune termina la carrière de l'auteur des *Noces de Figaro*. On ignore aujourd'hui où il fut enterré.

Un autre exemple. Schubert dont les lieder, la *Symphonie inachevée*, ont enrichi éditeurs, chanteurs et firmes phonographiques, fut si pauvre qu'il ne put jamais acquérir un piano. Il devait demander l'hospitalité à des amis plus fortunés ou attendre qu'on lui prêtât un instrument, l'outil essentiel à son métier.

L'époque classique bénéficiait toutefois d'appréciables avantages. L'élite, la clientèle du compositeur, était musicalement cultivée, elle commandait des œuvres et payait l'artiste créateur. Les œuvres de théâtre, par exemple, étaient toujours le résultat de commandes. Et c'est Mozart, si j'ai bonne mémoire, qui se plaignait amèrement de devoir composer uniquement pour lui-même sans avoir reçu le moindre ordre.

Il faut reconnaître qu'aujourd'hui encore il reste quelques très rares mécènes qui trouvent naturel de dédommager un compositeur pour l'ouvrage qu'ils lui commandent, tout heureux de pouvoir jouer, grâce à leur fortune, le rôle d'instigateur d'une œuvre d'art.

Quelques esprits clairvoyants se sont aperçus, après un certain nombre d'années, que les créations musicales exécutées publiquement enrichissaient souvent une corporation d'intermédiares (éditeurs, exécutants) au détriment de l'auteur de l'œuvre d'art. De là est née l'idée du droit d'auteur, codifiée par Napoléon. Ce droit est encore dans l'enfance si l'on songe qu'il n'est actuellement fixé par aucune convention internationale parfaitement homogène. A la merci de sociétés alors que l'Etat devrait l'assurer, il constitue aussi une protection morale, mais combien caduque! Cinquante ans après la mort d'un compositeur en France (trente ans en Allemagne), l'héritier d'un génie musical se trouve dépossédé de son patrimoine par le jeu du 'domaine public'; tandis qu'un industriel garde son capital (l'usine) et ses bénéfices qu'il peut transmettre à sa postérité. Cette situation extravagante est identique pour le littérateur, pour le savant et en général pour tous les créateurs intellectuels. Elle rejaillit sur l'auteur de son vivant même. L'éditeur étant lui-même dépossédé dès qu'une œuvre tombe dans le domaine public, il se défend en rémunérant son auteur au minimum. Il y a quelque chose d'immoral dans le fait que la fille de Schumann est morte, durant la guerre, dans la plus grande misère. De même, malgré tout ce qui a été tenté, la volonté testamentaire de Wagner qui voulait réserver *Parsifal* exclusivement au théâtre de Bayreuth, pour assurer son existence, n'a pu être respectée. En 1913, trente ans après la mort du maître, tous les théâtres du monde entier ont monté *Parsifal.* Les innombrables représentations wagnériennes ne rapportent rien à la famille du génie qui les alimente et Bayreuth doit vivre en partie du mécénat!

Un statisticien a établi qu'un héritier actuel des droits d'auteur de Beethoven serait l'homme le plus riche du monde . . . Voilà, pour le passé, la situation du compositeur symphoniste (musique pure). Voyons ce qui lui réserve le présent. Envisageons le cas d'un musicien non célèbre, âgé de vingt à cinquante ans. Quelles sont ses possibilités de gagner sa vie? Supposons qu'il écrive une symphonie. Cela représente un an de travail. Il s'adresse à l'une des dix associations orchestrales de Paris. Neuf se récuseront, arguant de la situation difficile de leur orchestre. Il ne peut encourir les frais supplémentaires que nécessitent les répétitions d'une œuvre nouvelle aussi importante. La dixième association accepte l'œuvre, et nous envisageons qu'il s'agit d'un chef-d'œuvre, pour que le cas soit typique. Le jeune compositeur est prié d'apporter le matériel d'orchestre pour l'exécution. Il le copie lui-même: un mois de travail. S'il en a les moyens, il le fait copier: deux à trois mille francs de frais. En échange il touchera pour cette audition de cinquante à cent francs de droits d'auteur. Désire-t-il voir son œuvre éditée? Il s'entend dire par l'éditeur: 'Votre symphonie est fort belle. Si elle remporte, chez Colonne, par exemple, beaucoup de succès, elle sera jouée une seconde fois mettons dans . . . cinq ans. L'édition de cette œuvre me coûte 20,000 francs. Comment retrouver mes frais? En mettant en location mon matériel d'exécution.' Bon!. or, toutes les associations (surtout en France) diront à l'éditeur: 'Vous devriez vous estimer trop heureux que nous fassions connaître une œuvre de votre fonds. Vous pouvez bien nous prêter le matériel gratuitement.' Et l'éditeur se récuse.

Plein de courage, notre 'jeune' écrit un quatuor à cordes: dix mois de travail. Il obtient d'un quatuor ami une exécution devant un public forcément restreint, car en France la musique de chambre ne dépasse guère les cercles confidentiels. Résultat: droits d'auteur allant de 0 fr. 50 à 1 fr. 75. Il va trouver son éditeur qui lui tient ce langage: 'on ne vend pas de musique. Si j'édite votre quatuor, je pourrai l'offrir à quelques groupements — qui n'achètent jamais de la musique — à quelques critiques, aux revues spécialisées à fin de compte rendu. Jusqu'à présent je débourse et ne vois aucune rémunération.' Et l'éditeur se récuse encore.

Que reste-t-il à faire? Le 'jeune' s'immole sur le tombeau de la musique pure et condescend à suivre les voies de l'art productif. Il songe au théâtre musical.

Il y avait, en France, deux scènes qui montaient des œuvres nouvelles: l'Opéra-Comique et l'Opéra. Seul l'Opéra aujourd'hui accepte la nouveauté. Mais en dehors d'un certain nombre de spectacles du répertoire que réclament des abonnés, il doit monter les ouvrages des membres de l'Institut, des Prix de Rome, et autres officiels de la musique. Il ne reste guère de place pour notre 'jeune'.

Descendant de quelques degrés l'autel d'Euterpe, il se dirige à regret vers l'opérette. Là, il se heurte à un trust hermétiquement fermé. Directeur, éditeur, librettiste et compositeur y sont solidaires. Le directeur est éditeur ou librettiste ou les deux à la fois. Vous pouvez imaginer d'autres combinaisons; mais les membres du trust n'ont aucun intérêt à partager leurs bénéfices avec des nouveaux venus.

En désespoir de cause, le 'jeune' qui est déjà un peu moins jeune et a relégué ses illusions au fond du tiroir où dorment ses manuscrits, finit par s'agripper au film sonore, dernière manifestation musicale (?) qui nourrisse encore son homme. Là, autre trust, presque aussi inaccessible. Car, de longue date, les musiciens de troisième ordre, faute d'utilisation ailleurs, s'y sont réfugiés. Ils occupent dès le début cette citadelle et défendent jalousement son accès afin d'éliminer la concurrence de musiciens contre lesquels ils ne pourraient lutter.

Le 'jeune' devra donc attendre la Providence, s'il n'est point mort de faim. Très rarement il pourra se tailler une brèche par où il pénétrera dans ces diverses forteresses, grâce au concours de nombreuses relations, à la convergence de hasards heureux, à la ténacité de son effort.

S'il remporte avec l'une de ses œuvres un succès exceptionnel, la renommée, la célébrité peuvent l'atteindre (mais très rarement la fortune!). L'auteur a dès lors quelque chance de 'partir' et là commencent les difficultés. La jalousie des 'arrivés' s'exerce aussitôt. Ils resserrent les barrières et se demandent s'il faut admettre le nouveau candidat à la gloire. Souvent il reste en route.

Le pourcentage de ceux qui restent sur le pavé est impressionnant.

Et voici la conclusion. En 1933, plus qu'à d'autres époques, le travailleur intellectuel n'a aucun droit à l'aisance. Par contre, on trouve naturel que tout trafiquant de denrées de première nécessité spéculant sur les besoins humains, sur la *faim,* ait droit de faire fortune et de la conserver *ad vitam aeternam.*

[At all times, the creative musician, that is to say the composer, has been considered from the social point of view as useless and as a parasite. I suspect that they must have said to Beethoven as he attempted to sell his music: 'Why come and encumber us with new works? We have Mozart's.' And to Mozart: 'We can do without you: we have C.P.E. Bach.'

A priori, every contemporary was superfluous, the past was sufficient. One can guess the financial result of such a social situation. Mozart died in misery. His wife was ailing; only a few friends accompanied the remains of the divine musician. It was sheer misfortune that the weather was so bad that they did not have the courage to go as far as the graveyard. The pauper's grave finished the life of the composer of *The Marriage of Figaro.* People today do not know where he was buried.

Another example is Schubert, whose lieder and *Unfinished Symphony* have made publishers, singers and sound-recording firms rich. He was so poor that he never owned a piano. He had to ask his more wealthy friends for hospitality or wait until he was lent an instrument, the essential tool of his profession.

The Classical era enjoyed, nevertheless, appreciable advantages. The élite — the composer's clientele — were musically cultivated; they commissioned works and paid the creative artist. Theatrical works, for example, were always the result of commissions. It was Mozart, if I remember correctly, who bitterly complained of having to compose only for himself during his lifetime, not having received any commissions.

One must recognize that today a very limited number of patrons of the arts can still be found, to whom it is natural to indemnify a composer for the work that they have ordered from him. Owing to their good fortune, they are completely happy to be able to play the role of instigator for a work of art.

Several clairvoyant minds have noticed, after a certain number of years, that the musical creations publicly performed often enrich a body of intermediaries (publishers, performers) to the detriment of the author of the work of art. From there is born the idea of royalties, codified by Napoleon. This right is still in its infancy if one realizes that it is not actually fixed by any perfectly homogeneous international convention. At the mercy of societies when the State should have been making it firm, it also constitutes a moral protection, but how void. Fifty years after the death of a French composer (thirty years after that of a German), the heir of a musical genius finds himself deprived of his heritage by the lapse of copyright; whilst an industrialist keeps his capital (the factory) and his profit which he can transfer to his descendants. This extraordinary situation is identical for the literary man, the scientist and for all intellectual creators in general. It backfires on the author himself. The publisher being dispossessed as soon as the copyright of the work lapses, defends himself by paying the minimum to his author. There is something immoral in the fact that Schumann's daughter died, during the war, in the greatest poverty. Moreover, despite all that was tried, Wagner's wish expressed in his will that *Parsifal* be kept exclusively for the Bayreuth theatre to ensure its continuing existence, could not be respected. In 1913, thirty years after Wagner's death, all the theatres in the entire world produced *Parsifal*. The innumerable Wagnerian productions bring nothing to nourish his family, and Bayreuth must survive partly through patronage!

A statistician has established that an heir of the copyrights of Beethoven would, today, be the richest person in the world . . . .

So much for the past and the situation of the symphonic (pure music) composer. Let us see what the present has in store for him. Take the case of a non-famous musician, aged twenty to fifty. What are the possibilities for him earning his living? Let us suppose he writes a symphony — one year's work. He contacts one by one the ten orchestral concert organizations in Paris. Nine decline, arguing that times are hard for the orchestra. They cannot incur the supplementary costs of the necessary rehearsals for such an important new work. The tenth association accepts the work and we consider it to be a masterpiece, so that his case is a typical one. The young composer is asked to bring the parts. He copies them himself — one month's work. If he has the means, he has them copied. Two to three thousand francs worth. In exchange he will get for this performance fifty to a hundred francs of royalties. Does he want to have his work published? He hears the publisher say 'your symphony is very good. If it achieves much success at the Colonne, for example, it will be played a second time . . . say in five years. The publication of this work costs me twenty thousand francs. How will I be able to cover the costs? By hiring out my material for performance! But all the concert organizations (particularly in France) would say to me "you ought to think yourself very lucky that we get to know a work from your catalogue. You could easily lend us the material free of charge"!' And so the publisher turns down the proposal.

Full of courage, our young composer writes a string quartet — ten months' work. Thanks to a quartet player friend of his it is performed of necessity in front of a very restricted public, for in France chamber music is rarely performed outside private circles. Result: royalties from 0.50 — 1.75 francs. He seeks his publisher who tells him 'we don't sell any scores. If I publish your quartet, I will be able to offer it to a few ensembles (who never buy any scores), to a few critics and, finally, to specialized journals. Up until the present time I am spending money and seeing no returns.' The publisher again turns down the proposal.

What remains to be done? The 'young composer' sacrifices himself on the tomb of pure music and condescends to follow the paths of productive art. He thinks of the musical theatre.

There were in France two theatres which produced new works: the Opéra-Comique and the Opéra. Today, only the Opéra accepts new works. But outside a certain number of productions of the standard repertoire demanded by season-ticket holders, it must also put on the works of members of the Institute, winners of the Prix de Rome and other 'officials' of music. There is hardly any room left for the 'young composer'.

Going down a few steps from the altar of *Euterpe**, he regretfully moves towards operetta. There, he runs into an hermetically sealed clique. Director, publisher, librettist and composer are jointly responsible. The director is the publisher or the librettist or both together. You can imagine other combinations but the members of the clique have no interest in sharing their profits with newcomers.

In despair, the 'young composer', who is already a little less young and has relegated his illusions to the bottom of the drawer where lie his manuscripts, ends up by clinging on to the sound film, the last musical(?) manifestation which still gives food to its own. There, another clique, nearly as inaccessible. For it is there, through long standing, that the third-rate musicians have sought refuge because they cannot find work elsewhere. Since the beginning they have occupied this citadel and jealously defended access to it in order to eliminate the competition from musicians against whom they will not be able to stand up.

The 'young composer' will have to wait for Providence, that is if he has not died of hunger. Very occasionally, due to the assistance of numerous contacts, luck or the tenacity of his effort, he will be able to make an opening through which he will penetrate into the various fortresses.

If, with one of his works, he achieves an exceptional success, renown and fame will reach him (but very rarely money!). The author has from that time onwards some chance of 'going places', and there begin the difficulties. The jealousy of the 'successful' starts immediately. They tighten barriers and wonder if they should admit the new candidate to glory. Often he remains on his journey.

The percentage of those who remain on the streets is significant.

And here is the conclusion. In 1933, more than in other eras, the intellectual worker has no right to the easy life. On the other hand, it is considered natural that all traders in necessary foodstuffs who speculate on human needs and on hunger, should have the right to make a fortune and conserve it for evermore.]

*The muse of music.

Notes to Chapter VIII

[1]15 December 1924, 17-18.

[2]25 March 1927, 861-72.

[3]Reproduced in English in the *Rice Institute Pamphlet, Houston,* 16, No. 3 (1929), 123-31.

[4]Constant Lambert, *Music Ho! A Study of Music in Decline* revised edition (Faber and Faber, London, 1937), 243; based on 'Railway Music', *The Nation and Athenaeum,* 16 August 1930, 620-21.

[5]Guido Pannain, 'Arthur Honegger' in *Musicisti dei Tempi Nuovi* (Buratti, Turin, 1932); translation by Michael R. Bonovia, *Modern Musicians* (Dent, London, 1932), 227-28.

[6]Anon., 'Setting Locomotives to Music', *Literary Digest,* 25 October 1924, 29-30 (p. 29).

[7]Anon., 'Machine Music', *The Musical Mirror,* March 1925, 49.

[8](Buratti, Turin, 1932); translated by Michael R. Bonovia, *Modern Musicians* (Dent, London, 1932), 234.

[9]Arthur Honegger, 'Pour prendre congé', *Appogiature*, February 1932, 36-44.

[10]*Le grand étang* (Tranchant), 1932; *Fièvre jaune* (Nino), 1935.

[11]*Les douze coups de minuit*, 1933; *Radio-panoramique,* 1935.

[12]See Chapter III.

[13]25 January 1923, 4.

[14]*Appogiature,* May 1931, 105-14; also in *Plans,* 1931, 74-79.

[15]Willy Tappolet, *Arthur Honegger* translated by Claude Tappolet (Editions de la Baconnière, Neuchâtel, 1957) 229.

[16]p. 81 and p. 85.

[17]pp. 80-81.

[18]p. 101

[19]p. 108

[20]'Problems of the Professional Composer', *The Musician,* May 1932, 26.

[21]*Le Mois,* No. 32 (1933), 217-21

CHAPTER IX

Jeanne d'Arc au bûcher: the turning point

> Une des plus grandes joies de mon existence a été d'avoir pour 'librettiste' — si tant est que les merveilleux poèmes de *Jeanne d'Arc au bûcher* et de *La danse des morts* soient des 'livrets' — Paul Claudel.[1]
>
> [One of the greatest joys of my life was to have Paul Claudel as 'librettist' — that is, if one can call the marvellous poems of *Joan of Arc at the Stake* and *The Dance of the Dead* 'librettos'.]

Ida Rubinstein attended a performance of *Jeu d'Adam et Eve* given at the Sorbonne during 1933 by a student group called the 'Théophiliens'. Under the artistic direction of Professor Gustave Cohen and with the assistance of the distinguished musicologist Jacques Chailley, a fine tradition of performances of such medieval mystery plays was being established. Greatly moved by the simple reality of the genre, Rubinstein determined to produce a new and quite different version of the story of St Joan by using similar principles. In the light of the considerable success accorded to her previous collaborations with Arthur Honegger she offered the project to him, with the suggestion that they should ask Paul Claudel to provide the text. Honegger had for many years deeply admired the work of this great French Catholic man of letters and so wasted no time in approaching him through their mutual friend, Darius Milhaud. Claudel was a most obvious choice for the task — he had already created similar works with his *L'annonce faite à Marie* and *Festin de la sagesse* (set to music by Milhaud), and his creed that there had to be music in his lines made musical realizations particularly feasible and rewarding. Furthermore, he had on many occasions expressed his whole-hearted approval of Honegger's very original and highly idiosyncratic approach to prosody.

Honegger and Rubinstein were deeply disappointed by Claudel's immediate refusal even to consider the project. He maintained that Joan of Arc was an official heroine who had spoken, and thus her words were in all memories — despite a little too literal translation — and it was therefore impossible for him satisfactorily to create an historic character in a fictional story. Honegger went to Brussels to see if it were possible to persuade him otherwise, but failed. Quite soon after their meeting, however, Claudel had a personal vision which he interpreted as an indication as to how he could approach the task. He spontaneously relented and, with a quite typical single-mindedness of purpose, produced the complete libretto in the space of but fifteen days.

The vision he had was of the joining of hands which he translated as the symbolic joining of the North and South of France through Joan herself: 'toutes les mains de France en une seule main, une telle main qu'elle ne sera jamais dénouée'[2] [all the hands of France joined together in one hand, a hand which shall never be unclenched]. The qualities of spontaneity, drama, profound emotion and deeply-rooted religious conviction that fill the text he created, accurately reflect his very strong personal involvement. His strength of belief in the value of sacrifice, the eternal truth of the triumph of good over evil and the necessity of submission to the divine and to inner convictions, which are in themselves so much a part of his Catholic faith, were to find a quite unique response in the music of the Protestant Honegger who could not be prevented by barriers of creed, either artificial or real, from responding and sharing equally in a profound statement of modern humanism.

Although such librettos as *Oresteia, Prottée* and *Christophe Colomb* which Claudel created for Milhaud are all remarkably fine achievements, it is significant that students of his work were quick to point out that those he provided for Honegger — in particular *Jeanne d'Arc au bûcher* and *La danse des morts* — are on a higher level still. As far as *Jeanne d'Arc au bûcher* is concerned, certainly much of this is attributable to the success of his highly original and individualistic approach to the organization of the subject matter. Instead of adopting the traditional chronologically-governed scenic approach, Claudel constructed a suite of symbolic visions of a dream-like nature seen by Joan during the period in which she is tied to the stake prior to her ultimate sacrifice. The utilization of 'flashback' — an essentially new and uniquely cinematic device — not only results in the achievement of a culminatory effect of quite staggering proportions, but also permits the examination in minutest detail of every aspect of the curious paradox that the true message behind Joan's sacrifice — 'plus grand amour celui de donner sa vie pour ceux qu'on aime'[3] [greater love hath no man than to lay down his life for his friends] — was not appreciated until so very much later.

Although the verbal expression is of marked simplicity, the ideas conveyed are of the utmost nobility. The lack of contemporary understanding is highlighted in a particularly poignant manner by the use of animals as the principal characters to express the gross travesty of justice at her trial, and by the sardonic irony of a quasi-political card-game to decide her fate. Through an exposition of the facts by Brother Dominic, the ground is succinctly prepared for Joan's personal recollection of the more vivid events in her short life so that her fears as she waits at the stake are quite naturally revealed as a reincarnation of those experienced by Christ hanging crucified on the Cross. The stifled latent power of the divided populace is, on the one hand neatly focused on the two folk figures (Picard Heurtibeuse and La mère aux tonneaux), whilst, on the other hand, terrifyingly omnipresent in the purely popular sections 'Le roi qui va-t-à Rheims' and 'L'épée de Jeanne'.

Following the principles of the early medieval mystery plays, the scene of Joan tied to the stake in front of Rouen Cathedral is maintained throughout, with the result that an immense strain is placed on the role of Joan. Scenery was only of relatively little use, so the burden borne by the music was particularly heavy. The parallels to the early cinema are therefore further strengthened — a situation which suited Honegger only too well.

Honegger wrote the music between October 1934 and 30 August 1935 during periods in Paris and whilst visiting Rigi-Klösterli (Switzerland) and Perros-Guirec (Brittany), and completed the orchestration in Paris on 24 December 1935. The work was first performed at one of the private 'gatherings' of its dedicatee, Ida Rubinstein. Among those present were Milhaud, Jaubert, Ochsé and Ibert who were unanimous in their unqualified acclaim of the score. Claudel was delighted with the result of their collaboration and all efforts were directed towards achieving a spectacular first public performance. Many problems were encountered, however, and the planned première at the Opéra in 1936 had to be abandoned. Funds generally were very restricted and so, besides the musical difficulties in the score and the technical problems of performance, the fact that the work required exceptionally large and varied forces proved to be the largest stumbling block of all.

For a stage performance the two spoken roles of St Joan and Brother Dominic are supplemented by thirteen other parts. A minimum of six vocal soloists are needed (ideally eleven are required), and, together with a large mixed-voice chorus and a children's choir, the whole is supported by an orchestra consisting of two flutes (second doubling piccolo), two oboes, E♭ clarinet, B♭ clarinet, bass clarinet, three E♭ saxophones, three bassoons, contrabassoon; D trumpet, three B♭ trumpets, three trombones, bass trombone or tuba; two pianos, celesta; timpani, two percussion players (bass drum, cymbals, rattle, side drum, tamtam, tenor drum, triangle, woodblock); ondes Martenot; and strings.

Difficult circumstances eventually prevented a French première at all and the honour fell instead to Switzerland. Paul Sacher and the Basle Chamber Choir and Orchestra gave a concert performance on 12 May 1938 in which the principal roles of St Joan and Brother Dominic were taken by Ida Rubinstein and Jean Périer and the thirteen subsidiary spoken parts by two other speakers. The work was received with a tumultuous ovation. R.-Aloys Mooser poignantly summarized the situation when he wrote in his review of this performance: 'après *Jeanne d'Arc au bûcher*, la Suisse ne comprendra-t-elle pas enfin qu'elle possède, en Arthur Honegger, le musicien capable de renouveler et de vivifier le genre national du festspiel, enlisé aujourd'hui, par la faute de ses professionnels attirés dans la pire ornière et dans la plus accablante médiocrité?'[4] [after *Joan of Arc at the Stake,* will Switzerland not at long last realize that it possesses in Arthur Honegger the musician who is capable of renewing and rejuvenating the national genre of *festspiel* which, today, is engulfed by the fault of its professionals having been drawn into the worst of all ruts by their overwhelming mediocrity?]. Two more performances were given by Sacher in 1939 — a second one in Basle and the other in Zürich as part of the National Festival. Concert performances followed quickly in Orléans and Paris. The French première at Orléans was given on 8 May 1939 as part of the 'Joan of Arc' celebrations, despite 'political' opposition, and the first Paris performance took place on 13 June 1939 in the Palais de Chaillot with the threat of war once again looming large.

The French public seized upon the work with an enthusiasm which is hard to express adequately in retrospect and, despite the onset of war, major performances were given in Paris and Brussels in 1940 and many radio broadcasts followed. Such was the appreciation of the nature and strength of the spiritual message of humanism so powerfully expressed in this collaboration between two great exponents of the directly communicative arts of literature and music, that the work became a symbol of hope and a source of strength for the French people who were struggling against the oppression of the German occupation. Honegger and Claudel formed the 'Chantier orchestral' and the 'Commissariat aux musiciens-chômeurs' in Lyons in 1941 and, with the support of the group of composers known as 'La jeune France' which was then in its potent infancy, productions under Herbert Auriol were given in more than seventy unoccupied towns during the course of the war. There were over forty performances in 1941 alone and very much needed inspiration and courage were given to the flagging French populace.

It must be remembered that the original score published under the 1939 Editions Senart copyright did not contain the 'Prologue'. This was added to the score in 1944 (appearing in print for the first time as part of the full score published in 1947 under the Editions Salabert copyright) and is the direct result of the effect on Claudel and Honegger of the inspirational performances the work had received in unoccupied France in the preceding three years. The text is taken from that part of the Book of Genesis which deals with the creation of the world. The subtle alterations that refer it specifically to France result in it being quite simply a glorification of the Liberation.

The first stage presentation came during the war (Zürich Municipal Theatre, 3 June 1942, for which Hans Reinhart prepared a German translation), but the majority followed the ending of hostilities, including those in Montevideo, Buenos Aires, Milan and London. Paris had to wait until 1953 for the bigoted trustees of the Opéra to allow a short run under their roof, but the most profoundly emotive realization that took place in front of Rheims Cathedral itself in 1952 when the whole of France appeared to be expressing their genuine appreciation of and sincere gratitude to their elder musical statesman on his sixtieth birthday more than compensated for the degrading frustration that Honegger had suffered at their hands. The work's popularity in England stems largely from the two performances sponsored by the B.B.C. under Basil Cameron in February and April 1947 which used the English translation prepared by Denis Arundell. The latter performance was broadcast live, and popular acclaim led to a most successful London stage presentation in October 1954. Very many stage and concert performances have followed the world over despite the heavy financial investment involved and it is this that more than anything testifies to the fundamental and lasting attraction of the work.

The most important clue as to how Honegger approached the task of creating this score may be found in a remark he made about the text which Claudel had provided for him:

> Toute l'atmosphère musicale tient en pareil texte. Sa partition est établie et le compositeur n'a vraiment qu'à se laisser guider pour tourner la sauce.[5] Il suffit d'écouter Claudel lire et relire son texte. Il le fait avec une telle force plastique, si je puis dire, que tout le relief musical s'en dégage clair et précis, pour quiconque possède un peu d'imagination musicale.[6]
>
> [All the musical atmosphere stems from the text. Its score is established and the composer in fact has only to let himself be guided in order to get on with the job. It is enough just to listen to Claudel reading his text over and over again. He does it with such a plastic strength (if I may say so) that all the musical relief comes out of it clearly and precisely for whoever possesses a bit of imagination.]

Certainly the instructions Claudel gave Honegger with regard to his conception of how the music should contribute at any moment were very precise — to appreciate this one only has to note the simple clarity of his comments on the opening of Scene 1:

> Les voix du ciel: on entend un chien hurler dans la nuit. Une fois, deux fois. A la seconde fois, l'orchestre se mêle au hurlement en une espèce de sanglot ou de rire sinistre. A la troisième fois, les chœurs, puis silence. Puis les voix de la nuit sur la forêt, à quoi se mêle, peut-être, très faiblement, la chanson de Trimazo et une impression limpide de rossignol. Puis silence et quelques mesures de méditation douloureuse. Puis, de nouveau, le chœur à bouches fermées. Crescendo. Diminuendo. Puis les voix distinctes: 'Jeanne, Jeanne, Jeanne!'[7]
>
> [The voices of the sky: one hears a dog howling in the night. Once, twice. The second time the orchestra joins in with a kind of sob or sinister laugh. The third time, the choirs. Then silence. Then the voices of the night in the forest to which is added, perhaps, very feebly, Trimazo's song and a clear impression of a nightingale. Then silence and a few bars of painful meditation. Then again, the choir humming. Crescendo. Diminuendo. Then the distinct voices: 'Joan, Joan, Joan!'].

No wonder the always humble and ever modest Honegger tried to maintain that 'l'apport de Claudel a été si grand que je ne me reconnais pas comme l'auteur véritable, mais comme un simple collaborateur'[8] [Claudel's contribution has been so great that I cannot consider myself the true composer but as a simple collaborator].

Neither the musical score, nor the work as a dramatic whole, suffer from the fact that the principals do not sing, but converse in spoken dialogue — such is the rapport and achieved synthesis of all the elements. Honegger certainly had faith in Ida Rubinstein's ability to sustain the role of Joan — he described her as 'une interprète et musicienne incomparable'[9] [an incomparable interpreter and musician]. Whilst the decision could be traced back to the procedures utilized in the inspirational medieval mystery plays, his choice of the spoken voice for Joan, and hence also her interlocutor, Brother Dominic, must be seen as particularly suitable for the talents of Madame Rubinstein in the light of her successful creation of the title-role in *Amphion* (1931).

The coherence of this work on all levels is quite remarkable. The close co-operation between Honegger and Claudel makes it difficult to separate the two contributions. Claudel's essentially poetic as opposed to dramatic conception resulted in a creation full of the sense and power of continuously progressive evolution. The lack of textual aspects which would inspire a Wagnerian approach involving leitmotives or any traditional musical forms presented Honegger with a challenge in view of his development and experiences already outlined in previous chapters. In actual fact, a web of recurring motives does occur in the score, but only to reinforce a logical, dramatic and totally organic argument which exists in the music to an already wholly effective, evocative and expressive end. Thus a consideration of the analysis of thematic cross-references represented in Diagram 26 below will reveal a situation parallel to that found in *Judith* and not the highly complex and extensive format evident in the opera *Antigone*.

Diagram 26:

Jeanne d'Arc au bûcher

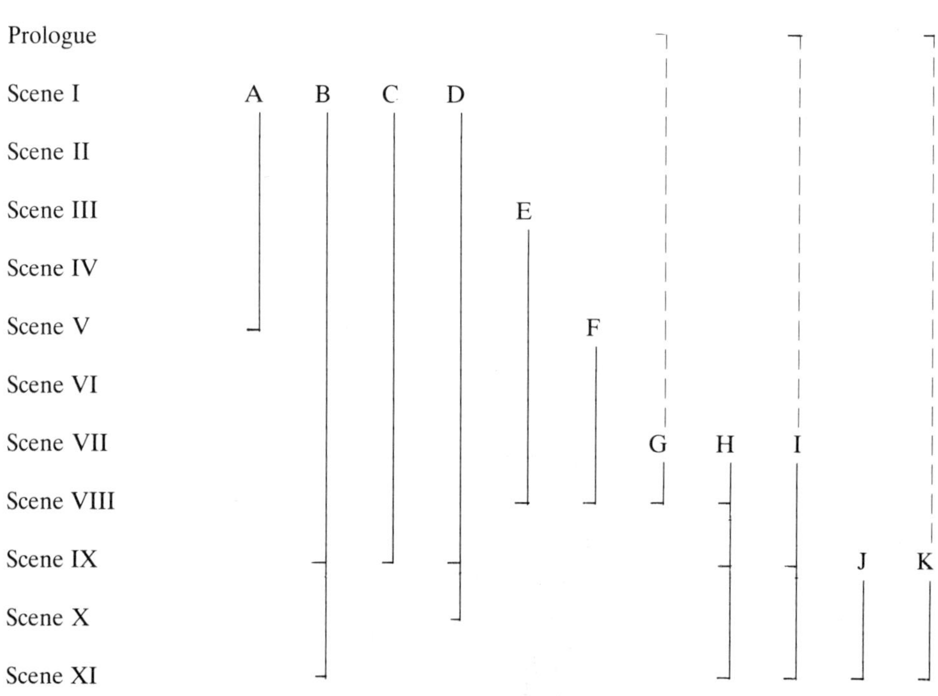

A: 'The howling dog' — opening texture of Scene I (to [1]); recapitulated 3A [33]–(opening of Scene V).

B: 'Celestial voices[a]' — flute motif 3-4A [1] and 6-8A [1] (Scene I); recapitulated in Scene IX (7-8A [66], 2-4A [67] and 3-4A [75]); transformed into one of the chorus themes after [92] in Scene XI and recapitulated in the last two bars of the work.

C: 'Celestial voices[b]' — trumpet motif 5 and 8A [1] (Scene I); recapitulated in Scene IX (9A [66] and 4-5A [67]).

D: 'Celestial voices[c]' — wordless chorus 3A [1]-1A [2] (Scene I); transformed into the solo 'voix d'enfant' theme 1B-5A [72] (Scene IX) and the song of 'Trimazo' (Jeanne: [85]-[86]) in Scene X.

E: 'Earth voices' — harmonic ostinato [5]-[8] (Scene III); recapitulated at the end of Scene V (3A [34]-[35]) and in Scene VIII ([63]-4A [64]).

F: 'Death' motif — 1-3A [33] (Scene V); recapitulated in Scene VIII (6A[65]-3B[66]).

G: 'Bell' motif[a] — harmonic ostinato after [44] (Scene VII); recapitulated in Scene VIII (8B [60]-).

H: 'Bell' motif[b] — melodic ostinato 2B[45]- (Scene VII); recapitulated in Scene VIII (after [61]), twice in Scene IX (1B[66]- and 6-8A [83]) and in Scene XI (1-3A [105]).

I: 'Flight' motif — Marguerite and Catherine 1-2A [46] (Scene VII); recapitulated in Scene IX (Catherine 2A [68]– and 5-6A[75], Marguerite 6B [69]- and 5-6A [75], Chorus 4B [70]-) and in Scene XI (La Vierge, Marguerite and Catherine 4-1B [102]).

J: 'Celestial voices[d]' — texture after [68] (Scene IX); repeated for four bars before [102] in Scene XI.

K: 'Hope-triumph' motif — 1-3A [75] (Scene IX); repeated after [102] in Scene XI.

N.B. As already noted, the 'Prologue' was added later and three of the principal ideas were appropriately incorporated:

(i) The 'hope-triumph' motif (K) — Solo soprano after [IV] and Chorus after [IX];

(ii) The 'flight' motif (I) — Chorus after [X];

and (iii) The 'bell' motif[a] (G) — the two penultimate bars.

There is again a very thorough and consistent use of tertiary patterning in the tonal scheme throughout the whole work, but its significance is now even more potent in that the interval of a minor third acts as a germinal cell which pervades every aspect of the melodic, harmonic and polyphonic conceptions in a most remarkably all-embracing manner as will be self-evident from even a cursory examination of the score.

Furthermore, there is in this oratorio none of the recourse to mere imitation of other composers' melodic and harmonic styles, rhythmic traits or formal designs for suitable effect which, for many, mars the otherwise admirable score of *Le roi David.* Honegger's style is now sufficiently original and resourceful to match the encyclopaedic textual demands for variety of colour, nuance, mood and depth of emotional content. This is not to pretend that there is no diversity of style and content — there is, and it ranges widely from the profound sentiments of the grave 'Prologue' to the bitter irony of the pastiche Couperin/Ravelesque 'Gavotte' used for the 'card-game' scene; from the innocence of the folk-song quotation for Joan's recollection of childhood May Day celebrations at Domrémy to the grossly exaggerated 'fox-trot' style used for the court scene; and from the sincere and intense religious fervour of the closing scenes containing the contribution of Catherine, Margaret and the Virgin Mary with the words of the psalms to the heartily popular portrayal of the folk heroes and the struggles for survival and independent expression of the downtrodden citizens. However, such diversity is no longer a destructive feature of his music — the variety of elements of form, style and content present are all totally integrated and synthesized into a powerfully original language with completely viable personal forces of continuity and coherence. The fact that Honegger is able to express fully the multitude of differing moods, emotions, ideas and states of activity without ever debasing his art has been justly acclaimed as a great achievement in itself.

Much praise has been directed at the blend of the spoken and sung roles with the orchestral support. In a staged oratorio where two dominant spoken roles and a host of very much less important spoken and sung subsidiary characters are found, the role of the chorus is naturally very problematic. The distinct emphasis placed on the dramatic importance of the chorus by both Claudel and Honegger is very significant in that it might have led to a sense of vying with the principal characters. This is neatly avoided by Honegger's attention to the nature of the choral writing which affords a compendium of choral techniques in terms of its range from unison writing through full-blooded part writing to carefully controlled and notated vocal declamation.

A very important role is played by the orchestra and the instrumentation is inspired and utterly personal. The saxophone section which had played an increasingly significant role in his scores now completely replaces the French Horn section. The very homogeneous sound, with its greater degree of suppleness and technical possibilities, is certainly more useful for combining with voices, and the extensive contribution they make to this score is of the utmost importance. The extension of the range of particular single instrument groups by the incorporation of such instruments as the E♭ and bass clarinets, the D trumpet and the bass trombone instead of a tuba, permits his essentially strata-based scoring technique to work so well. The use of the pianos is to be expected in the light of several scores prior to this — his consistent employment of them for melodic clarification and rhythmic definition through percussive coloration of many of his complex polyphonic textures is a hallmark of his mature scores and simultaneously marks the end of a role for the harp.

Unlike many other composers of his generation who were achieving similar results by using the glockenspiel and/or xylophone, Honegger was never overtly interested in exploring the extensive sound-world of the twentieth-century percussion section and this work is exceptional for its utilization of a large array of instruments. However, it is important to note that the various instruments are used in a very controlled fashion, contributing most positively to the overall richness and brilliant colouring of the textures, but never exploited in an obviously developmental manner in their own right. The degree of instrumental doubling is extensive but tremendously varied, with much emphasis laid upon the skilful use of timbral opposites and subtle nuances to highlight the dramatic argument. The appearance of the ondes Martenot to add an extra dimension of sonority to the writing for the string section is a quite natural outcome of his experimental use of this instrument and its forerunners in many scores prior to this.[10] In many ways a great deal of the basic emotional content of the scoring can be attributed to the successful incorporation of the ondes Martenot and saxophones.

The humanitarian sentiments expressed in the text of this work are very much those which struck a ready and sympathetic chord in Arthur Honegger. Parallels must be drawn between *Cris du monde* and the 'Prologue' specifically, as well as with the work as a whole, and between the psychological similarities of the characters of King David, Judith, Antigone and Joan. In many ways this work is in direct line of descent from *Le roi David* and *Judith,* and the nature of its conception as a 'staged' oratorio is a successful reconciliation of the differing principles behind the two versions in which both of these works exist. The mode of presentation was also directly influenced by Stravinsky's *Œdipus rex* and makes an equally important contribution to the epic 'theatre-music' genre.

In view of both the fundamental crisis from which Honegger was emerging as he wrote this work and his proposed solutions to it, his statement that 'mon goût et mon effort ont toujours été d'écrire une musique qui soit perceptible pour la grande masse des auditeurs et suffisamment exempte de banalité pour intéresser cependant les mélomanes . . . on peut, on doit parler à un grand public sans concession, mais aussi sans obscurité[11] [my taste and effort have always been to write music which is discernible to the great mass of listeners and which is sufficiently free from banality to interest even the real enthusiasts . . . one can and must talk to a general public without concession, but also without obscurity] can be regarded as having been successively achieved. It is certainly the work of greatest significance in Honegger's output to date and must surely rank as one of the most important musical works of art in modern times. Honegger spoke of it as 'une vaste fresque, populaire, s'adressant à la masse plutôt qu'à une élite . . . la musique . . . droite, simple . . .'[12] [a vast popular fresco, addressed to the general public rather than to the élite . . . the music . . . direct, simple . . .]. Vuillermoz summarized the achievement in the work with the expression 'la technique mégalithique'[13] [the megalithic technique], whilst Louis Aubert described it as a 'chef-d'œuvre tout court, qui honore l'art de notre temps et qui mérite de faire date'[14] [simply a concentrated masterpiece which honours contemporary art and which deserves to mark an epoch]. Florent Schmitt said that 'l'année 1939, celle de *Jeanne d'Arc au bûcher*'[15] [1939 is the year of *Joan of Arc at the Stake*] and the public response certainly justified the laurel: 'Arthur Honegger — un musicien de peuple'[16] [Arthur Honegger — a people's musician].

Notes to Chapter IX

[1]Arthur Honegger quoted by Willy Tappolet, *Arthur Honegger* (Editions de la *Baconnière,* Neuchâtel, 1957), 167.

[2]Quoted by Marcel Landowski, *Honegger,* (Editions du Seuil, Paris, 1957), 73.

[3]Sung by la Sainte Vierge, Sainte Marguerite and Sainte Catherine in Scene XI: 'Jeanne d'Arc en flammes' (1947 full score, pp. 257-58).

[4]*Dissonances,* No. 5 (May 1938), 129-34 (p. 134).

[5]Marcel Landowski, *Honegger* (Editions du Seuil, Paris 1957), 74.

[6]*Je suis compositeur* (Editions du Conquistador, Paris, 1951), 158.

[7]Quoted by Willy Tappolet, *Arthur Honegger* (Editions de la Baconnière, Neuchâtel, 1957), 169-70.

[8]*Je suis compositeur* (Editions du Conquistador, Paris, 1951), 140.

[9]Quoted by Willy Tappolet, *Arthur Honegger* (Editions de la Baconnière, Neuchâtel, 1957), 167.

[10]See the ballet scores *Sémiramis* and *Roses de métal* in particular.

[11]*Je suis compositeur* (Editions du Conquistador, Paris, 1951), 129-30.

[12]Quoted by A. Gabeaud, *'Jeanne d'Arc au bûcher'*, *L'Education Musicale*, No. 37, 1957, 14.

[13]*Les grandes réussites d'Arthur Honegger* (Les Publications Techniques — Galerie Charpentier, Paris, 1942), 11.

[14]Quoted by José Bruyr, *Honegger et son œuvre* (Editions Corrêa, Paris, 1947), 187.

[15]Quoted by José Bruyr, *Honegger et son œuvre* (Editions Corrêa, Paris, 1947), 187.

[16]Quoted by Willy Tappolet, *'Jeanne d'Arc au bûcher', Feuilles Musicales*, September 1952, 204-05 (p. 204).

CHAPTER X

Third interlude: rumination

The works between *Jeanne d'Arc au bûcher* and *La danse des morts*

Part I: *Symphonie [n° 1]*

Just as the symphonies of Haydn, Mozart, Beethoven, Brahms, Bruckner, Mahler, Tchaikovsky and such twentieth-century composers as Prokofiev, Shostakovitch, Nielsen, Sibelius and Vaughan Williams are considered posthumously as a generic entity, so too can the five of Honegger. Unlike those of Brahms, Honegger's symphonies are not the product of a single period of his life. Spread out over a period of twenty years, they are separated by various other comparable essays in purely instrumental thought, be they chamber music, concertos or orchestral movements. Thus they reflect various different psychological states and stages of aesthetic evolution, and their distinction as a group of symphonies lies not least in the perpetual renewal of form, style and spirit that is evident from one to another.

Honegger's symphonies played a very vital role as catalysts in the post-1930 revival and renewal of the French symphonic tradition. In the latter decades of the eighteenth century organizations including the Concert Spirituel, La Pouplinière, Concerts des Amateurs, Concert de la Loge Olympique and Concert d'Amis did much to encourage a school of French symphonists, as well as promoting the works of Haydn and Mozart and maintaining a very firm link with the Mannheim school. Symphonies flowed from the pens of Gossec, Méhul and Pleyel as well as such now forgotten figures as Bailleux, Bréval, Devienne, Jardin and Papavoine. The Société des Concerts du Conservatoire was founded in 1828 and its resident orchestra, under François Habeneck, supplied a most regular diet of Beethoven for many years. The four 'symphonies' of Berlioz had relatively slight influence on the second generation of French symphonists — Jean-Georges Kastner, André Georges Onslow, Henri Reber and Anton Reicha — who were content to dilute the acidity of Beethoven's style with a little alkaline Mendelssohn. Such works as Félicien David's *Le désert* (1844) and Ernest Raeyer's *Sélam* (1850) are a by-product both of the choral nature of Berlioz's *Roméo et Juliette* (1839) and of the contemporary cult for the Orient, and it is only possible to trace this particular genealogy as far as the eight symphonies of J. B. Weckerlin. Attempts to see the influence of the *concertante* aspect of *Harold en Italie* (1834) as extending to Lalo's *Symphonie espagnole* (1874) would be forced. Similarly, an attribution of the nature of the later nineteenth-century French school of 'poème-symphonique' composers led by Saint-Saëns and Dukas, to the programmatic qualities of both the *Symphonie fantastique* (1830) and *Harold en Italie,* would be to forget the influence of Liszt. The middle years of the nineteenth century saw only the early efforts of Saint-Saëns (No. 1, 1853, and No. 2, 1859/1878; those of 1856 and 1859 still remaining in manuscript), the D major and E minor symphonies of Gounod (1854 and 1855 respectively) and the youthful work in C major by Bizet (1855). Further stimulation was provided by the formation of the Concerts Populaires (directed by Jules Pasdeloup) in 1863 and the Société Nationale (Romain Bussine and Saint-Saëns) in 1873. Nearly all the latter's concerts included a symphony by Mozart, Haydn or Beethoven and all contained a first performance of a French symphonic work, so giving real impetus to the third generation of French symphonists, including Félicien David, Louise Farenc, Benjamin Godard, Louis Gouvey, Victorin de Joncières, Scipion Rousselot and Schneitzhœffer as well as the older Onslow and Reber. Most regional towns of any size formed a Société des Concerts and those in Bordeaux, Lille, Lyon, Marseilles, Orléans, Pau, Angers, Rennes and Toulouse, in particular, did much to foster regular performances of symphonic music.

In Paris during the latter decades the situation was almost too healthy. The Concerts du Châtelot d'Edouard Colonne were founded in 1874, the Nouveaux Concerts under Charles Lamoureux in 1880, and finally, as a result of the biased directorial policy of first Franck and then d'Indy at the Société Nationale, the Société Musicale Indépendante was formed in 1909. This latter organization continued in serious opposition to the Société Nationale until 1917, when the hatchets were buried and a 'new' Société Nationale emerged to the benefit of all the leading young French composers, including Honegger.

The 1870s saw the composition of four symphonies of distinction — Saint-Saëns's third, d'Indy's *Symphonie sur un chant montagnard français,* Lalo's in G minor and César Franck's in D minor. The contemporary French infatuation with the formal procedures and harmonic language of Wagner and Liszt is plainly evident in all these works, and the subsequent schools of symphonic composition which sprang up around Franck and d'Indy reflect this still further. Franck's influence at the Paris Conservatoire embraced the symphonies of Jacques de la Presle, Albert Dupuis, Jean Huré, Désiré Paque and Georges Antoine. D'Indy first exerted his influence via the Schola Cantorum which he helped to establish in 1896, then later through his position as director of the conducting class at the Paris Conservatoire from 1912 onwards — a class which Honegger attended for several years and under whose auspices the initial performances were given of his first orchestral pieces, the *Prélude pour Aglavaine et Sélysette* and *Chant de Nigamon.*

Simultaneously, Widor was establishing the uniquely French tradition of symphonies for solo organ in direct response to the rich, colourful and extremely varied textures of the Cavaille-Coll organs that were to be found in most Parisian churches (including Notre Dame, Saint-Sulpice and Saint-Clotilde) and many of the largest and most important provincial town churches. Between 1876 and 1900 he wrote ten such symphonies and fired the imagination of Tournemire and Vierne in the same direction. These two composers produced six organ symphonies each before the early 1920s and their pupils and disciples — including Augustin Barié, Marcel Dupré, Jacques Ermend-Bonnal, André Fleury, Jean Langlais and Julien Vaubourgin — carried the tradition right through until the early 1950s. Many of these composers also wrote symphonies for orchestra and organ in the wake of Saint-Saëns' third, often including a chorus for good measure.

In the second and third decades of this century the world-wide crisis in symphonic composition seriously affected the none-too-firmly established French school. Albert Roussel and Georges Migot both wrote a pair of symphonies between 1900 and 1930 (1905 [*Poème de la forêt*], 1921 and 1922, 1927 respectively) and in all four works can be seen the destructive conflict between the older Franco-German influences of the Schola Cantorum tradition of symphonic writing and the new 'non-symphonic' styles of Debussy, Fauré and Ravel. Only perhaps in the four symphonies of the almost isolated composer Magnard (1889, 1892, 1895 and 1913) with their Milhaud-like originality, was it possible to see any evidence of the future hope of a twentieth-century school of French symphonic composition.

Without wishing to obliterate entirely the efforts of Bloch, Casadesus, Dukas, Emmanuel, Gaillard, Gédalge, d'Indy, Magnard, Migot, Pierné, Poot, Ropartz, Siohan, Thirion, Tournemire, Vierne, Widor and Witkowsky between 1900 and 1930, it is only right to point to the premières of Honegger's *Symphonie* [*n° 1*] and Roussel's third in 1930, as heralding the renaissance in French symphonic writing; Table 8 below charts the revival and renewal which took place and draws attention to the chronological position of Honegger's symphonies in relation to it.

TABLE 8

French Symphonies 1930-55

1930	Honegger I, Roussel III, Schmitt (Concertante) Paray I
1931	Emmanuel II (Bretonne)
1932	Loucheur I Rivier I Casadesus II
1933	Kœchlin I (The Seven Stars) Delannoy I
1934	Roussel IV

Continued overleaf

1935	Paray II
1936	Aubin I (Romantique) Martinon I
1937	Rivier II Gaillard II, III (Europe) Barraine I Challan I
1938	Rivier III Poot II Barraine II
1939	Milhaud I Puig-Roget (Andorrana)
1941	Rivier IV
1942	Honegger II (Strings) Arrieu Challan II
1943	Ropartz (Petite) Kœchlin II Tomasi
1944	Loucheur II Milhaud II Aubin II Martinon II
1945	Ropartz V Paray II (Strings) Sauguet I Baudrier I
1946	Honegger III (Liturgique), IV (Deliciæ Basilienses) Milhaud III
1947	Milhaud IV Migot III, IV Mirouze (Albigeoise)
1948	Messiaen (Turangalîla) Martinon (Irlandaise)
1949	Rosenthal I Chailley I Landowski I (Jean de la Peur) Martelli (Sinfonietta)

1950	Honegger V (Di tre re) Arma Rivier V
1951	Migot V, VI Dutilleux I Bozza Brown I Sauguet (Allégorique)
1952	Bloch (Brève) Barraud I (Numance) Castérède I (Strings) Poot III
1953	Migot VII Milhaud V Capdevieille III Françaix
1954	Migot VIII Kantuser I (Chamber)
1955	Milhaud VI Désenclos Death of Arthur Honegger

Honegger and Roussel were two of the composers commissioned to write symphonies by the Boston Symphony Orchestra for its fiftieth birthday celebrations in 1931; Hindemith composed his *Konzertmusik* for brass and strings, Ravel orchestrated Mussorgsky's *Pictures at an Exhibition*, Stravinsky composed his *Symphony of Psalms* and Prokofiev his *Symphony No. 4*. The latter two were living in Paris and, like other Russian composer-*émigrés* including Glazunov, Rachmaninov and Tcherepnine, they exerted a considerable influence upon the young school of French symphonic composers in terms of prompting a spirit of emulation which gave real impetus to the movement. Many other distinguished symphonic composers of numerous nationalities — amongst them Beck, Casella, Enesco, Freitas-Branco, Hába, Harsanyi, Lajtha, Malipiero, Martinů, Mihalovici, Pizetti, Tasman and Villa-Lobos — spent some time in Paris during the thirties, forties and early fifties, and each contributed to the extent and excellence of the renewal and revival of the purely French tradition of symphonic writing.

In view of Honegger's dictum that 'I attach great importance to musical architecture',[1] it is pertinent to note some of his more detailed comments on matters of form. With regard to the ordering of the recapitulation in a sonata-form movement, he felt that

> [the] re-exposition of the order *A followed by B* is illogical, showing as it does, a defect in symmetry. In architecture you have a façade, the two left pillars of which, for instance, are arranged so that *A is followed by B*. Your object is solidly and harmoniously to rest the architrave and the pediment upon these pillars and upon those that form a pendant to them on the right. Symmetry as regards those on the right, will inevitably give you *B followed by A*, not vice versa, as the first time. Very well; in the sonata the pillars correspond to the themes; the pediment is the central development. Symmetrically, then, you must have *B followed by A* in the recapitulation since you had *A followed by B* in the exposition.[2]

His view on the defective symmetry of Classical sonata-form has a rationality which is valid to a degree, but which does not attempt to argue why late eighteenth- and nineteenth-century composers should have found so much satisfaction in such a system. He appears to have failed to appreciate that in such sonata-form movements the second subject (group) has, in the majority of cases, the character of a reply in response to the first subject (group) in that, although there is necessarily contrast, there is also a great deal of fulfilment of expectation from the tonal point of view. The two take on the character of a question and answer, and therefore, to an extent, it is meaningless to begin with the 'answer' in the recapitulation. This is further strengthened by the fact that there is usually a feeling of thematic genesis of the second subject from the first subject in some way, however distant. He moreover ignores the fact that one of Beethoven's most important contributions to the development of sonata-form was to show that a tonally well-routed transition from first subject to second subject in the recapitulation meant that the reappearance of the latter in the tonic retained some of the structural drama which it had occasioned in the exposition, and thus the logicality and continuity of the whole argument was preserved.

Paul Landormy, commenting on these two statements he had quoted, put forward his view that 'the exposition is no more than a continuous sequence of impressions bound together in an inevitable and necessary order that is *irreversible*'.[3] Irreversible in the sense that perception of time — hence music — is an irreversible fact of the universe, where as perception of space — architecture — is a reversible process, elements being visible in any direction. This is possibly a more accurate clue to the key of Honegger's subconscious views on this subject. He was not satisfied with the traditional inevitability of the recapitulation; a recapitulation had to have an organic character of its own, a satisfactory state of independence within a unified whole — literally a re-exposition. Hence his experiments with the ordering of the recapitulation, which in his sonata-form works usually takes on the character of a second development. The ordering of the themes then results from the desire for mood-balance determined from the character-structure of the development section.

Like Donald Francis Tovey, Honegger felt that

> despite the laws drawn from tradition, music contains one part miracle . . . we are wrong to think them intangible. Let us take for example the bi-thematic movement of the sonata. The treatises teach that this movement

> shows two themes confronting one another. But what no one says is that between the first and second theme there may be a multitude of others. Thus, in analysing the *String Quartet Op. 59, No. 1* of Beethoven, I find nine absolutely distinct themes. The difficulty is resolved by saying: there are the themes, the transitional episodes, the . . . (B.G.*: bridges.) These are euphemisms. Why has not a given motif — under the pretext that it is the fifth or the sixth — the right to the noble name of theme? Because the sonata is said to be bi-thematic? It is absurd.[4]

Specifically relating the question of form to his own compositional method he said:

> If I desire to compose a sonata for violin and piano, I have absolutely nothing before my eyes or in my memory. I must invent everything. (B.G.: Do not other sonatas for violin and piano furnish you with models?) One cannot be satisfied with reproducing the form. Another sonata may, indeed, serve as a model, but the important thing is the actual sound, the themes, the melodies, the rhythms. If I copy, I am a conscious imitator, but in vain . . . it is quite fruitless to imitate a sonata of another. One must invent a personal model in the abstract, and construct it ideally. But this model will have no definite form before it is realised, for according to the material employed, the model will shift its form.[5]

The primary importance of formal considerations to Honegger is clearly reflected in his statement:

> Suppose I had in mind the project of composing a symphony. First of all, I experience great difficulty in determining the frame for my work. To me, a symphonic work must be built logically, without the possibility of interjecting the slightest anecdotal element between its different parts. I repeat: one must give the impression of a composition in which all is linked, the image of a predetermined structure. It has been said that architecture is frozen music. I should rather say that it is geometry in time. Here, as elsewhere, one must be very exacting, so as to achieve an absolute equilibrium. If certain composers were the architects of their own houses, or builders of their own motorcars, they would long ago have been reduced to rubbish![6]

Speaking of himself he confessed that 'as far as I am concerned, symphonic works give me much trouble: they demand an effort at sustained reflection.'[7] He outlined the process as:

> I first seek the contour, the general aspect. Let us say, for example, that I see taking form a sort of palace in a very opaque fog. Reflection progressively dissipates this fog and permits me to see a bit more clearly into it. Sometimes a beam of sunlight appears to illuminate a wing of the palace as it grows: this fragment then becomes my model. When this phenomenon spreads, I begin to search for my materials for construction. I prospect in my note-books . . . Gédalge gave me that habit. When a motif, a rhythm, an entire

* B.G. = Bernard Gavoty.

phrase comes to me, I jot it down . . . so I check my notebooks of sketches in the hope of uncovering there some melodic design, a rhythmic plan, or some sequence of chords susceptible of being useful. Sometimes I think I have found what I am looking for, and I set to work. Often I start off on a false scent . . . I try again. I permit a melodic line to ripen, I prospect the different paths it opens to me. What disillusionment! One needs the courage to start again three, four, five times . . . Sometimes, a very secondary element will yield the key to the problem. This rhythm or this motif which seemed banal to me, I suddenly perceive in its true light, it interests me passionately, and I will not abandon it for an instant.[8]

All three movements of his *Symphonie* [*n° 1*] are in sonata-form, but only in the second movement does he follow his principles of symmetry in having an exactly reversed recapitulation. The basic structures of the three movements are represented in Diagrams 27-29 (below, opposite and page 270 respectively).

Diagram 27:

Symphonie [*n° 1*]—first movement (N.B. The relevant themes are quoted in Music Examples 57-58, pp. 273-77)

		(Principal tonalities)
Exposition:		
	Introduction +	C/c
[1]-	1st Theme and rescored restatement	C/c
[2]-	Link to +	C
[3]-	2nd Theme leading to	e — A
[4]-	3rd Theme leading to	D♭ D E♭ e♭ dom. of e
1A[5]-	4th Theme	F/f
6A[5]-	Closing section	G moving to
Development:		
[6]-	Based on Theme 4 and part of the material of the 'Link' ([2]-)	c♯ d b♭ a/A
[7]-	Exposition of 5th Theme with fragments of Introduction material +	b/B e♭/E♭
[8]-	Development continues using Themes 4 and 5 and Introduction material +	A/a
Recapitulation:		
[9]-	2nd Theme	D G
[10]-	Transition to +	B E♭ B
[12]-	3rd Theme leading to	C c (via E♭ to)
1B[13]-	1st Theme	A♭/a♭
7B[14]-	Link (based on that between [2] and [3]) to +	with final dom. prep. for
[16]-	Coda:— Themes 4 and 5 in contrapuntal combination and Introduction material +	C/c
[17]-	1st Theme and Introduction material + and (4B [18]-) the 'Link' material	C/c

Diagram 28:

Symphonie [*n° 1*] — second movement (N.B. The relevant themes are quoted in Music Example 59, pp. 278-81).

Exposition:

	1st Theme	(with two countersubject motives — 1^A and 1^B — above a rising chromatic bass. Opens in f♯ and closes in F♯)
[1]-	2nd Theme	(above a 3-part imitative texture — Violins II, Violas and 1st Cellos — and a repeat of the rising chromatic bass. Opens and closes in F♯)
[2]-	3rd Theme	(with two countersubjects — 3^A and 3^B — above a harmonic ostinato — Trombones. Opens in F♯ and closes in B♭)
4B[3]-		Closing section (melodic fragments (x) and (y))

Development:

[3]- Development of a texture consisting of a new countersubject — 1^C — over fragments of Theme 1 with the new 4th Theme superimposed 2B[4]-[5]

[5]- Climax of development: complete statement of a version of Theme 1 (some of the constituent intervals are slightly different) over rising scales of B ([5]-) and b♭ ([6]-) with countersubjects 1^A and 1^C and fragments of Theme 4

Recapitulation:

[7]-		Closing section (melodic fragments (x) and (y))
5A[7]-	3rd Theme	(with countersubjects 3^A and 3^B)
[8]-	2nd Theme	(above a 3-part imitative texture and rising chromatic bass with additional countersubject 2^A. Opens in F and closes in F♯)
[9]-	1st Theme	(with countersubjects 1^A, 1^B *and* 1^C as well as fragments of Theme 4, above a *descending* chromatic bass. (As in the Development section, some of the constituent intervals of the thematic material are altered — but not to the extent that the premises of 'recapitulation' are negated.) Opens in F♯ (1A[9]) and closes in f♯)

A most important feature of the construction of the first movement is the role played by the thematic material of the introduction. Not only are parts of it used in the section linking the presentation of Themes 1 and 2 in the exposition, but it is also the basis for the similar passages that separate the appearance of Themes 2 and 3 in the recapitulation and precede the start of

Diagram 29:

Symphonie [n° 1] — third movement (N.B. The relevant themes are quoted in Music Example 60, pp. 281-82)

		(Principal tonalities)
Exposition:		
	Introduction based on an anticipation of Theme 1 (4B[1]-)	C (with initial suggestion of e)
4A[2]-	1st Theme and counterstatements	C c
[4]-	Link to	
[5]-	2nd Theme and counterstatement	D
[7]-	3rd Theme leading to	→g
[8]-	4th Theme	E♭
[9]-	Closing section based on Theme 3	e (over dom. pedal)
Development:		
[10]-	Polyphonic texture based on Theme 1 supporting imitative treatment of Theme 4. Introduction material leads back to	e e♭ d A♭
Recapitulation:		
[13]-	1st/2nd Themes	G
[15]-	3rd Theme	→c♯
[16]-	4th Theme	D
[17]-	Link (as per [4]-[5]) to	
[18]-	Fragments of 2nd Theme	c c♯ A♭
[19]-	1st/2nd Themes	C
[22]-	Coda:— (Andante tranquillo) fragments of Themes 1 and 2	C

the coda; it is furthermore prominent throughout the development and dominates the whole of the coda (see the use of the sign + in Diagram 27, p. 268).

Unlike the first and second movements, no new theme appears in the development section of the third movement and the ordering of the recapitulation is far more orthodox (see Diagram 29 above).

In *I am a Composer,* Bernard Gavoty asked Honegger for his views on the fact that 'it appears Franck set down the tonal plan for his work at the top of his manuscript for his Symphony. It is said that he had decided upon it before having written a single note or jotted down the least theme' and that 'for Vincent d'Indy this plan played a determining role'.[9] Honegger replied that 'I have endless respect for Franck and d'Indy; their principles seem respectable to me, but not essential . . . to me such a tonal design is an abstraction . . . not that tonal music is not true to life; . . . it is a technique completely foreign to me . . . I cannot conceive of music fabricated by laws set up in advance . . . though I find it absolutely legitimate if the work benefits by it.'[10] He reinforced this personal lack of sympathy with the methods of interpreting the role of tonality in sonata-form as advocated by Franck and d'Indy when he said:

> I do not even understand what it means. I have had numerous friendly debates with d'Indy himself on this topic. I told him at the time that to me such a dogma of tonal design seemed an entirely outmoded notion. As well require a contemporary dramatist to observe the unity of place of the classical tragedy, which so many masterpieces cheerfully ignore! What gives unity to a piece of music is the totality of melodic and rhythmic relationships, elements much more powerful to affect the listener's spirit than the ties of tonality. Not everyone has 'absolute pitch' . . . It seems to me that we can no longer tolerate this fetishism of tonality, which has been a burden on entire generations of musicians. Of much greater importance than tonal equilibrium are melodic and especially rhythmic balances. We should concern ourselves more with the architectural proportions.[11]

Dr Robert Simpson, in a most penetrating attempt to define a twentieth-century symphony,[12] concluded that it is above all else a 'profoundly inclusive' entity, in that all the constituent elements become part of an activity that has an internal progression of logic which is continuous, and none of these elements are abandoned in the course of the argument. He distinguishes thus between symphonies and 'ballet music', where some elements are either abandoned, frequently left in abeyance and then later revived, or do not contribute to their full in the argument. He concludes, therefore, that the flow of the whole is necessarily neither fully fluid nor complete in itself. The logic of a prolonged argument is dependent on this and, in turn, the success of a symphony on the uninterrupted 'interpenetrative activity' of all the elements involved.

Simpson is firm in his belief that no element can be neglected — including tonality. His proposition is that the abolition of tonality and hence tonal designs leaves one of man's musical faculties unengaged, and comprehensiveness of argument is missed because a tonal design within basically tonal music is a powerful internal logical structuring force in its own right. A misinterpretation of Honegger's comments about tonal design has led commentators to criticize his symphonies from this viewpoint alone. All have argued without reference to the music that such a negation of tonal design is responsible for formal pretension. Honegger in these remarks is only expressing his personal inability to work within the framework of abstractly preconceived designs of tonal relationships, equilibria and proportions of the sort advocated by Franck and d'Indy, amongst many. There is no question of either tonality or tonal designs being absent from any of the movements in his symphonies — merely that he placed first and foremost matters of melodic and rhythmic totality and balance, with tonality, tonal relationships and equilibria being a natural outcome of the music as it was conceived and developed. Honegger used the analogy 'to write music is to raise a ladder without a wall to lean it against. There is no scaffolding: the building under construction is held in balance only by the miracle of a kind of internal logic, an innate sense of proportion'.[13] He also noted that 'fortunately, there is in music a large part of wizardry, of the inexplicable. It is not comparable to any other art. Our ancestors showed wisdom when they excluded music from the other fine arts. On one side, music. On the other, painting, sculpture, etching, architecture. Despite the laws drawn from tradition, music contains one part miracle.'[14]

A consideration of the summary of principal tonalities included for each of the three movements of the *Symphonie* [*n° 1*] in Diagrams 27-29 (pages 268, 269 and 270) will provide sufficient evidence to convince sceptics that tonal organization is present, and that various relationships and equilibria — some of a very traditional nature — can be detected. In the light of the 'tradition' of Franck and d'Indy against which Honegger was arguing, the nature of some of the designs — both within sections and movements, as well as across the symphony as a whole, is certainly unorthodox; but this will be recognized as being a fundamentally logical feature of Honegger's personal style.

Honegger's belief in the powerful effect of a totality of melodic and rhythmic relationships and a satisfactory set of balances between them all, is responsible to a large extent for the formal cohesion of each of the movements of this work and for the viability of the whole as a symphony. In the first movement the sheer wealth of both rhythmic and melodic material contained in the music of the introduction is particularly important in view of the most extensive role the various parts of this fabric have been shown to play throughout the movement (see Music Example 57 opposite).

Music Example 57: *Symphonie* [*n° 1*], first movement, bars 1-13 (Introduction)

Gdes Fl
Hautb.
C.Angl
Clar
Cl.Basse
Bassons
Ctre Bon
Cors
Flatterzunge
Trpttes
I
Trbnes
1rs Violons
IVe
2ds Violons
IVe
Altos
Vlles
Basses
arco

(Reproduit avec l'autorisation des EDITIONS SALABERT, Paris, propriétaires de l'œuvre.)

The melodic breadth of Theme 1 (see Music Example 58 (i) overleaf) is countered by the tautness of its rhythmic impulse which prevents any relaxation and literally forces the fabric to progress continuously. The tumultuous sweeps of Theme 2 (see Music Example 58 (ii) overleaf) and the rhythmic activity of the supporting texture carry the music on still further so that Theme 3 (see Music Example 58 (iii), page 277) emerges on the crest of a wave, fully in keeping with its noble character.

The achievement at this stage of a first climax in the exposition is most satisfactory because not only does it reflect the highly desirous state of continuous evolution attained prior to it, but it also permits the possibility of the construction of a viable organic approach to the start of the development in its wake. This Honegger creates by introducing a very short Theme 4 (see Music Example 58 (iv), page 277) whose rhythmic characteristics and melodic contours beg the contrapuntal treatment he initiates at the beginning of the development. In addition, the sense of continuous forward movement that was so apparent in the melodic and rhythmic characterization of Themes 1 and 2 and which was held relatively in check in the case of Theme 3, now returns to appropriate prominence with Theme 4.

The new Theme 5 (see Music Example 58 (v), page 277) which is introduced in the course of the development is extremely broad and flowing, and serves to bind together the complex and very active contrapuntal web of fragments undergoing symphonic development. Of particular significance is the fact that Themes 1, 2 and 3 do not appear in the development which concentrates solely on Theme 4 and the material of the introduction. Thus, when the recapitulation starts there is no sense of release of tension but rather of genuine climax, with the section assuming a psychological if not actually physical mantle of continuing to reflect development of material. The reordering of material in the recapitulation with respect to its appearance in the exposition may be a partial reflection of Honegger's views on architectural symmetry, but it is also most certainly an example of his belief in melodic and rhythmic balances contributing forcibly to satisfactory architectural proportions. Theme 2 had far more strength than Theme 1 in the exposition and, anyway, immediately preceded Theme 3, so for the recapitulation to proceed in this way is not without a certain logic of its own. This situation also naturally gives rise to Theme 1 being recapitulated last, thus creating a cyclic feature. Honegger, however, goes much further than this in the cause of symphonism. The presentation of Theme 3 is radically different from that in the exposition. The climactic gesture turns into a quiet and reserved appearance which, for the first time in the recapitulation, firmly establishes the principal tonality of C major. The effect of the highly energized motion, again invoked with the return of Theme 1 and the subsequent quodlibet consisting of material from the introduction, Themes 1, 4 and 5 (the new one from the development), is to highlight dramatically the fact that the end of the movement is only a temporary moment of repose within the framework of the whole symphony.

Music Example 58: *Symphonie* [*n° 1*], first movement:
(i) [1] - 8A [1], Theme 1

(Allegro marcato 𝅗𝅥 = 112)
Str
1
sempre *f*

(Reproduit avec l'autorisation des EDITIONS SALABERT, Paris, propriétaires de l'œuvre.)

(ii) [3] - [4], Theme 2

(Reproduit avec l'autorisation des EDITIONS SALABERT, Paris, propriétaires de l'œuvre.)

(iii) 4 - 7A 4, Theme 3

(iv) 2-5A 5, Theme 4

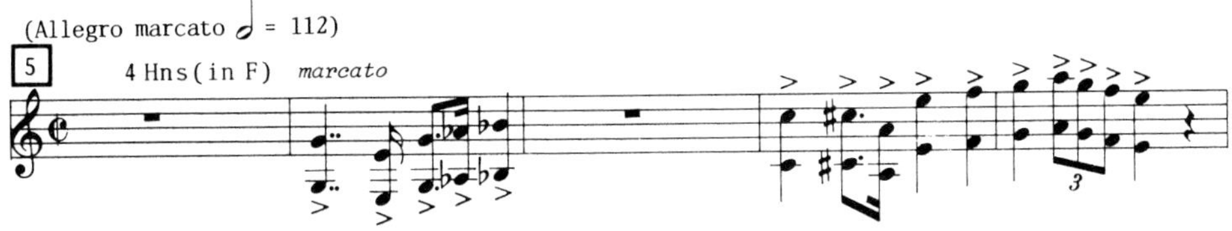

(v) 1-11A 7, Theme 5

The second movement revolves around the fact that Honegger managed to create in Themes 2 and 3 (see Music Example 59 (iv) and (v), page 279) the necessary foil to the extremely intense first theme and to achieve a sense of architectural equilibrium by the very nature of the melodic and rhythmic balances. The symmetry of this movement is further emphasized by the construction of Theme 1 (see Music Example 59 (i) overleaf) in the exposition upon a rising chromatic bass, with its appearance at the end of the recapitulation over the descending version; its domination of the development section is conceived upon a bass rising through a major and then a minor scale which contributes considerably to the overtly oppressive climax.

Music Example 59: *Symphonie* [*n° 1*], second movement:
(i) Violas/cellos, bars 1-12, Theme 1

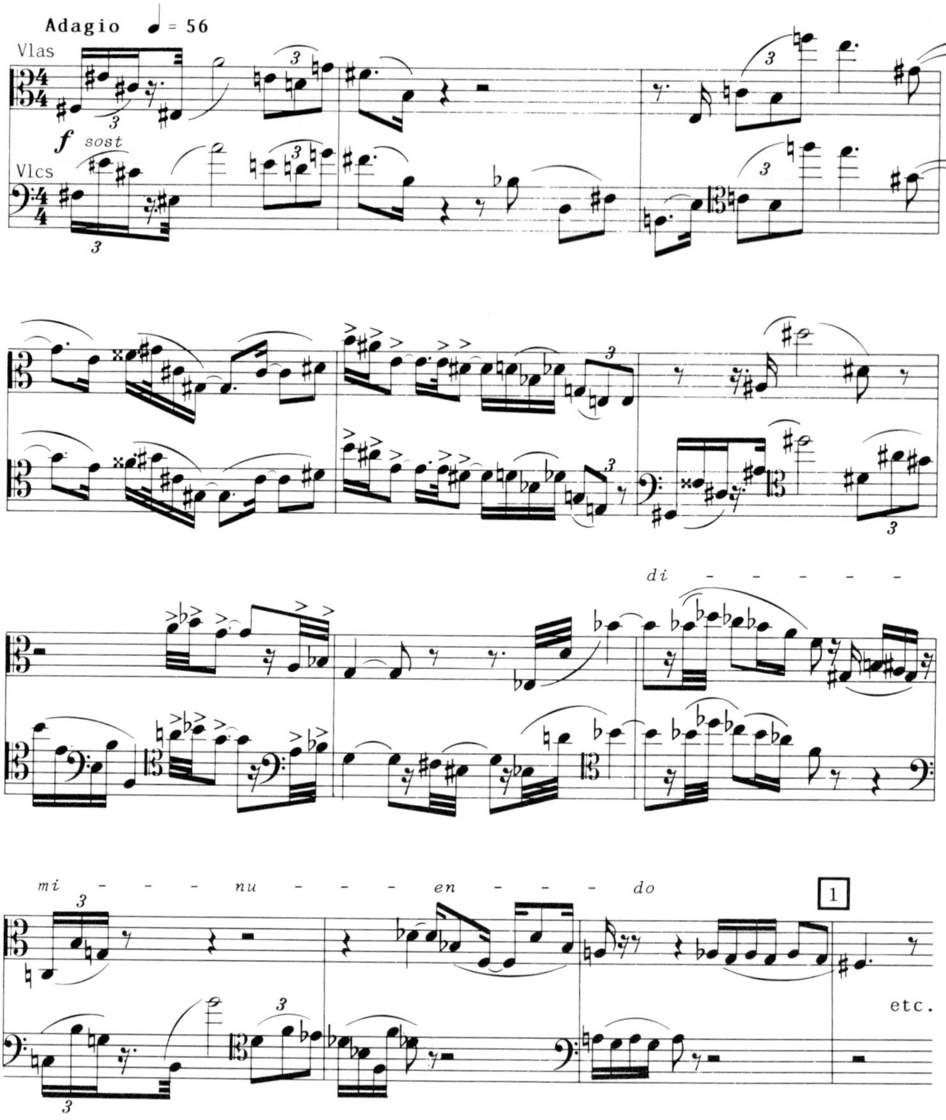

Adagio ♩ = 56
Vlas
f sost
Vlcs
di - - - - - -
mi - - - - nu - - - - en - - - - do
1
etc.

(ii) Bass clarinet, bar 2, countersubject motif 1ᴮ

(Adagio ♩ = 56)

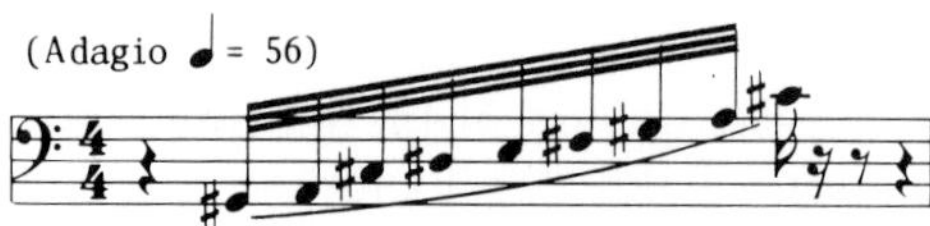

(iii) Trombone, bar 4, countersubject motif 1[A]

(iv) Violin I, 1 - 2, Theme 2

(v) Trumpet, 1-3A 2, Theme 3

(vi) Cellos, 1-7A 2, countersubject 3[A]

(vii) Bassoon, 3-7A [2], countersubject 3[B]

(viii) Violin I/cor anglais, 4-1B [3], melodic fragment 'x'

(ix) Oboe/horn, 4-3B [3], melodic fragment 'y'

(x) Violins/violas, 1-2A [3] and horns/oboes/cor anglais, 3-4A [3], countersubject 1[C]

(xi) Horns/trumpets, 2B [4] - [5], Theme 4

(Reproduit avec l'autorisation des EDITIONS SALABERT, Paris, propriétaires de l'œuvre.)

(xii) Violin I, 1B [8] - [9], countersubject 2^A

(Reproduit avec l'autorisation des EDITIONS SALABERT, Paris, propriétaires de l'œuvre.)

The extreme of the tonal relationship between the slow movement and the outer movements is sufficient to ensure that there is again only a feeling of temporary repose between this movement and the finale. The melodic material of the last movement is noticeably more diatonic than that of both the preceding movements and far less rhythmically complex despite being imbued with real impetus (see Music Example 60 below).

Music Example 60: *Symphonie* [*nº 1*], third movement:
(i) Trumpet/violin I, 4A [2] - [3], Theme 1

(Reproduit avec l'autorisation des EDITIONS SALABERT, Paris, propriétaires de l'œuvre.)

(ii) [5] - 4A [5], Theme 2

(iii) [7] - 5A [7], Theme 3

(iv) [8] - 7A [8], Theme 4

The material is obviously designed for the contrapuntal treatment to which it is continuously subjected throughout the movement, the procedure being almost always that of an initial statement followed immediately by incorporation in a fugal (if not actually canonic) texture. Sometimes the result is eminently suitable (for example the fugal episodes of the development section), but the canonic treatment of the anticipation of Theme 1 at 4B [1] is a miscalculation not only in the nature of its scoring (similar passages have been pointed out in many earlier scores), but also because the tempo marking is *Presto*, ♩. =108 (see Music Example 61 opposite).

Music Example 61: *Symphonie* [*n° 1*], third movement, 4B[1] - 9A[1]

The design of this finale is similar in many ways to that of the first movement, particularly in terms of the extremely ingenious combinations of themes that occur near the end of the recapitulation. Nevertheless, the mood is fundamentally different. This is not a 'finale symphony' in the late eighteenth- and nineteenth-century sense because the emotional emphasis is on the intense slow movement, with the first movement being a preparation for it. The finale is very much in the vein of most of those of Haydn and Mozart, but with the addition of the *Andante tranquillo* (22 - end), where the music dissolves into a spiritually reverential mood and chorale-like melodic fragments seem to give thanks to a deity for the happily concluded succession of emotional experiences. This is no trite cinematographic happy-ending, but a 'profoundly inclusive' conclusion to a symphony consisting of truly 'interpenetrative activity'.

Part II: The second and third string quartets

Speaking retrospectively of his music, Honegger noted that:

> I wrote a certain number of works 'by sheer force' — that's the way to characterize especially formidable trials. I consider them somewhat as Beethovenian by-products. You will say: the poor man's Beethoven. Agreed, but they were nevertheless those that expressed my true nature. In this category I have a secret preference for certain pieces not always warmly appreciated: the Quartets, especially the first because it exactly expressed the personality of the young man who wrote it in 1917. There are faults, slow passages, but I recognise myself in it as in a mirror. As a sample of better work I shall select my third Quartet, which marked a progress in conciseness and workmanship.[15]

The spiritual development of Honegger as a symphonist during the twelve years which separate his first two essays in this medium is vividly reflected in the two string quartets written during the middle thirties (No. 2, 1934-36 and No. 3, 1937).

In the sonata-form first movement (1935) of the *Second Quartet*, Honegger dispenses with the aspect of a wealth of thematic material which figured in all three movements of the *Symphonie [nº 1]*. With just two themes he concentrates on a most rigorous development of them both (and all the material which accompanies them) and constructs a relatively brief recapitulation in keeping with his views on architectural symmetry.

A summary analysis of the first movement of the *Third Quartet* (5 June 1937) is placed side by side with that for the same movement in the *Second Quartet* to highlight the difference in formal design involved (see Diagrams 30-31 below).

Diagram 30:

String Quartet No. 2 — first movement

Exposition:	
	Theme 1
1-4A [1]	Link (+) to
5A [1]-	Developed counter-statement of Theme 1
2-1B [2]	Repeat of part of Link (+) material
[2]-	Theme 2
7A [3]-	Closing section
Development: 6B [4]-	All material
Recapitulation:	
[8]-	Theme 2
[9]-	Closing section material (combined with Theme 2, [10] -)
[11]-	Link (+) material
[12]-	Theme 1
[13]-	Transition to second movement

Diagram 31:

String Quartet No. 3 — first movement

Exposition:	
	Theme 1 with developed counterstatement after [2] leading to
[3]-	Theme 2 leading to
[4]-	Theme 3
Development: 3B [5]-	All material
Recapitulation:	
[13]-	Theme 1 (with a fragment of Theme 3, 1B [14])
Coda: [15]-	Based on Theme 1

The development section of the first movement of the *Third Quartet* consists of a very extensive and rigorous exploitation of Theme 1 (3B [5] - [9]) and, after a brief but highly concentrated canonic treatment of Theme 3 ([9] - [10]), a substantial section ([10] - [13]) wherein Themes 2 and 3 are developed in tandem. The recapitulation is confined to thirty-two bars in length (the exposition being forty-eight bars long and the development ninety-one) and essentially presents only Theme 1. The compression of the recapitulation is heightened by the fact that the presentation of Theme 1 is in a fashion which is for the most part far more akin to further development than re-exposition.

The usage of sonata-form in the finales of both these quartets is almost identical and exhibits strong parallels both to that evident in the first movement of No. 2 with regard to symmetry and to the *Symphonie [nº 1]* in terms of the technique of introducing new thematic material in the development section which, in effect, binds together a contrapuntal web of a variety of melodic fragments (see Diagrams 32-33 below). Furthermore, there is the device utilized in the *Symphonie pour cordes* [*n° 2*] finale of concluding with the chorale-like presentation of a theme (albeit in both these quartets not in fact a new idea, but one of the movement's principal themes) triumphantly sounding above a contrapuntal mêlée of truly culminatory proportions. (It is surely a practical conjecture that the nature of Honegger's use of the trumpet for this moment in the finale of the *Symphonie pour cordes* [*n° 2*] is a direct outcome of the experience of having heard the parallels in these movements).

Diagram 32:	Diagram 33:
String Quartet No. 2 — third movement	*String Quartet No. 3* — third movement
Exposition: 1st Theme [2]- Transition [3]- 2nd Theme [4]- Closing section (based on Theme 1)	Exposition: 1st Theme and varied counterstatements [4]- 2nd Theme and counterstatement [6]- Closing section
Development: [5]- Development of all material with the inclusion of new thematic material after [5] and 4B[7]-	Development: [7]- Development of Theme 1 and closing section material with new idea first stated after [7]
Recapitulation: [11]- 2nd Theme (above Theme 1) 9A [12]- 1st Theme	Recapitulation: [14]- 2nd Theme [17]- 1st Theme [18]- 2nd Theme/Closing section material [19]- 1st Theme

As regards the anticipatory role of these quartets in the light of the *Symphonie pour cordes* [*n° 2*], the contrapuntal technique involved in the concluding page of the *Third Quartet* is one of the most significant points (see Music Example 62 below).

Music Example 62: *String Quartet No. 3*, third movement, 2B [19] - end

(Reproduit avec l'autorisation des EDITIONS SALABERT, Paris, propriétaires de l'œuvre.)

That Honegger should have written the slow movements first in both cases although they are discussed last, is not so inconsequential as it may seem, because it is in these movements that the most intense and fundamental development takes place.

The slow movement of the *Second Quartet* is cast as a simple ABA[1], with the theme of the A section being used as a counter-subject in the B section (see 3A [5] -) and the principal motivic element of B (see viola part 5A [4]) recurring throughout A[1] ([8] -). The formal procedures are very much in the tradition of his earlier chamber music and one-movement orchestral scores. The distinction of the theme upon which the A section is founded is obscured by the unchanging rhythmic design and restricted harmonic variation of the ostinato which accompanies it (see Music Example 63 overleaf).

Music Example 63: *String Quartet No. 2*, second movement, bars 1-24

(Reproduit avec l'autorisation des EDITIONS SALABERT, Paris, propriétaires de l'œuvre.)

The melodic elements of B (4 - 8) are less interesting than those in the A section and this, together with the relentless dependence on only quaver and crotchet patterning in a texture that is *à 4* with substantial amounts of double- and triple-stopping for almost its entire span, results in a particularly turgid and monotonous section with disastrous effects on the structure of the movement (see Music Example 64 below).

Music Example 64:
String Quartet No. 2, second movement, [4] - [6]

(Reproduit avec l'autorisation des EDITIONS SALABERT, Paris, propriétaires de l'œuvre.)

The problems of the A section are compounded in A¹ by the omnipresence of motif 'x' (see the viola part 5A[4]) from B which had the least melodic value and the greatest rhythmic stickiness; and because, apart from minor rescoring of the melodic line, A¹ is virtually identical to A.

The corresponding movement in the *Third Quartet* is on an infinitely higher plane in all respects. The overall ABA¹ structure is combined with the formal design of a passacaglia (see Diagram 34 below).

Diagram 34:

String Quartet No. 3 — second movement

(A)	Bars 1 - 4	Passacaglia	I		
	5 - 8	,,	II	(Transposed	up a semitone)
	9 - 12	,,	III	(,,	up a tone)
	13 - 16	,,	IV	(,,	down a tone)
	17 - 20	,,	V	(,,	up a tone)
	21 - 24	,,	VI	(,,	up a diminished 5th)
	25 - 28	,,	VII	(,,	up a semitone)
	29	Modulatory link bar			
(B)	30 - 46				
(A¹)	47 - 50	Passacaglia	VIII	(Transposed	up a tone)
	51 - 54	,,	IX	(,,	down a tone)
	55 - 58	,,	X	(,,	up a tone)
	59 - 62	,,	XI	(,,	up a diminished 5th)
	63 - 68	Recapitulation of part of B section			
	69 - 72	Passacaglia	XII	(Transposed down a semitone except for the first note)	
	73 - 74	Cadential (referring in part to both the theme of B and the Passacaglia).			

The harmonic conception of the passacaglia as initially stated is developed slightly in the second phase and it is this version which is employed for all of the remaining statements except the last, No. XII, where, in cyclic fashion, the harmonies of the initial four bars are used. The rhythmic structure of the passacaglia is varied for each return and an obvious symmetry is involved (see Diagram 35 opposite).

Diagram 35:

String Quartet No. 3 — second movement

V as III

VI as IV

VII as II except minus final 𝅘𝅥𝅯

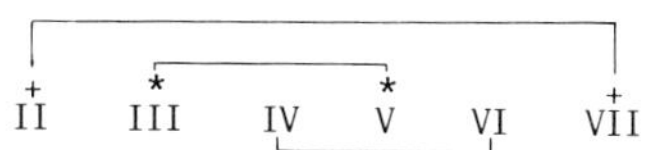

(*/+ the Passacaglia is furthermore in the same tonal position)

In the A¹ section an identical symmetry is involved between VIII and X which both occur in the same tonal position (see Diagram 36 below).

Diagram 36:

String Quartet No. 3 — second movement.

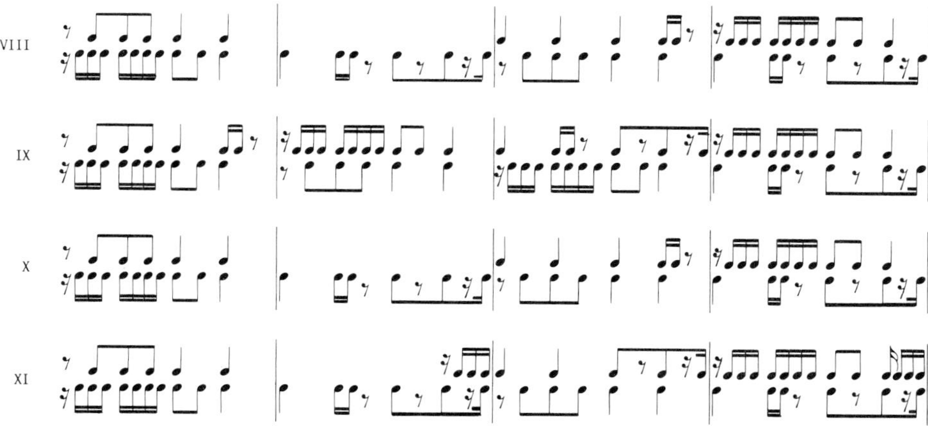

(The rhythmic structuring in the A^1 section is more complicated at times, as shown by the superimposition of patterns as they appear in the texture.)

All this is not, however, sterile formalism because it supports in the A and A^1 sections one of Honegger's very finest melodic lines in the most fundamentally organic way. 'I conceive the highest of melodic forms to be like a rainbow, which mounts and re-descends without one's being able to say at any one moment: "Here, you see, it has returned to fragment B, there to fragment A . . ."'[16] (see Music Example 65 below).

Music Example 65: *String Quartet No. 3*, second movement, bars 1-29

2
18

3
P
P
P

This is certainly a magnificent melodic line, but it is because the nature of the rhythmic structuring and the direction and degree of transposition of the passacaglia accompaniment function consistently to highlight and balance its every facet that it transcends the realms of pure craftsmanship.

A consideration of tonality as regards these two quartets is similarly revealing. The relationship of the principal tonalities of the movements in the *Second Quartet* is an exact parallel to that in the *Symphonie [n° 1]* in terms of the choice of the minor key of the raised subdominant for the slow movement with regard to that of the two outer movements. The effect of this is, however, a little more integrated by virtue of the substantial references to the basic key of the first and last movements within the B section of the middle movement (see Diagram 37 below).

Diagram 37:

String Quartet No. 2

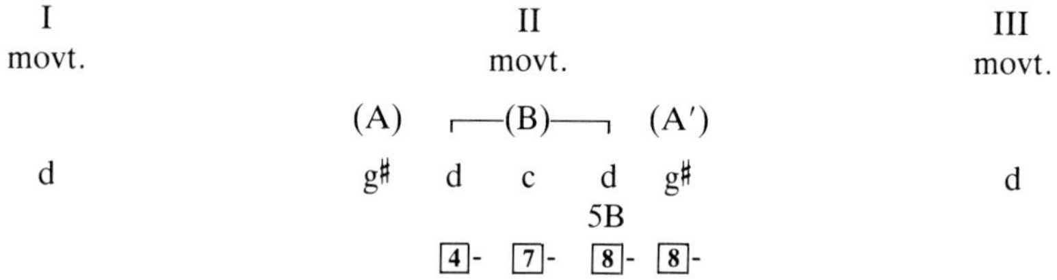

I movt.	II movt.					III movt.
	(A)	(B)			(A′)	
d	g♯	d	c	d	g♯	d
				5B		
		4-	7-	8-	8-	

In the outer movements of this *Second Quartet* Honegger's lack of belief in traditional tonal structuring is much in evidence. In neither case, for example, is there a move to a new tonal centre for the second theme — rhythmic and melodic considerations being made sufficient to effect suitable contrast and dramatic viability. Nevertheless, the key of D major is restored at the beginning of the recapitulation in both movements. In the *Third Quartet*, however, considerably more emphasis is placed on tonal structuring of the Honeggerian sort dependent on patterning by the interval of a third. The basic key of the whole quartet is E minor. In the first movement the three themes are each presented in a different tonality during the course of the exposition — the choice of key apparently relating to the psychological parallel each offers in relation to those previously used by way of complementing the theme. Thus the E minor tonality of Theme 1 is replaced by the flattened supertonic major (F) for Theme 2 with a suitably sudden increase in dramatic tension, and this in turn by the key of D major/minor for Theme 3, with the appropriate lowering of tonal temperature desired at this moment which is almost immediately prior to the commencement of the development. In the finale the E minor tonality of Theme 1 gives way to C♯ major for Theme 2 and, in the course of its presentation, the descending minor third aspect is turned into a sequential feature and the tonality falls further through B♭ major to G minor after [6]. Correspondingly in the recapitulation the tonality drops in the course of the presentation of Theme 2 from D major through B and G majors to E minor for the final recapitulation of Theme 1. Furthermore, in the first movement, the principal tonality is not restored at the outset of the recapitulation — it comes instead towards the end of the section and counterbalances the fact that only Theme 1 reappears. The recapitulation starts in the key of C minor and it is this tonality which underlines the A section of the slow movement. How infinitely more subtle and satisfying is this intimation of a link between the two movements than the transition passage which joins the same two movements in the *Second Quartet* with little short of embarrassing obviousness. (This was a structural device which Honegger had never used before and the very fact that it does not appear in any subsequent scores probably indicates his view on the nature of its success.) Although the slow movement of the *Third Quartet* begins in C minor it ends in E minor in anticipation of the finale.

In terms of the development of Honegger's musical style the significance of the second and third quartets lies in the successful degree of formal consolidation through experimentation found in each and every movement in the light of works previously discussed. As with the five symphonies, his three quartets are by no means the product of a single period in his creative life. Unlike those of Bartok, Hindemith, Maconchy, Schönberg or Shostakovich, Honegger's quartets are not usually thought of in terms of a generic entity, and it is probably more meaningful to compare them to those of Britten, Kodaly or Tippett as representing a positive contribution to a problematic genre of the era, whilst at the same time noting that it is not a medium through which the composers in question most naturally express themselves.

Like Britten, Kodaly and Tippett, Honegger was ideally equipped and suited for large choral and/or orchestral expression, but in terms of his experience in writing large-scale works in the purely abstract instrumental medium (be it symphonic or chamber music) the *Symphonie* [*n° 1*] was a landmark and the second and third quartets milestones on the obligatory path of progress through refinement and development between it and the *Symphonie pour cordes* [*n° 2*] of 1941.

None of the three quartets of Arthur Honegger has ever properly entered the repertoire of British quartets. It is only fair to acknowledge the fact that in most cases purely economic considerations in conjunction with audience conservatism are at the root of this, in that very few quartets can undertake to learn works other than those standard pieces that concert promoters and audiences will actually pay them to play regularly. Nevertheless, there is a certain quality of intimacy lacking in each of the three which does not help to endear them to quartet players. Whilst the *String Quartet* [*No. 1*] is overtly orchestral in so many ways (a factor which can be excused in what is really no more than a student's first essay in the medium), both the subsequent quartets have many moments with an over-inflated feel to them.

Notes to Chapter X

[1]Quoted by Paul Landormy, 'Arthur Honegger' (translation by Fred Rothwell), *The Musical Times*, September 1929, 789-91 (p. 789).
[2]Ibid., p. 790.
[3]Ibid.
[4]Arthur Honegger, *I am a Composer* (Faber and Faber, London, 1966), 69.
[5]Ibid., p. 68.
[6]Ibid., pp. 78-79.
[7]Ibid., pp. 80-81.
[8]Ibid., pp. 81-82.
[9]Ibid., pp. 82-83.
[10]Ibid.
[11]Ibid.
[12]*The Symphony* edited by Robert Simpson, 2 vols (Penguin, London, 1967), II, 9-14.
[13]*I am a Composer*, (Faber and Faber, London, 1966), p. 74.
[14]Ibid., p. 69.
[15]Ibid., pp. 98-99.
[16]Ibid., p. 70.

CHAPTER XI

A trilogy

Part I: *La danse des morts*

While Paul Claudel was in Basle during the spring of 1938 for the première of *Jeanne d'Arc au bûcher,* he became preoccupied with various collections of pictures on the subject of death. He was particularly drawn to the fifty-eight woodcuts preserved in the City Museum entitled *La danse des morts* by Hans Holbein the younger (1497-1543), because they attempted to celebrate the release which death brings from life's burden, rather than being content to dwell on macabre aspects.

Although baptized a Catholic, Claudel had been indifferent, even hostile to religion until he discovered, in his early twenties, the poetry of Rimbaud. He once related how, on Christmas Day 1886, he had been walking to Notre-Dame Cathedral for the main service when, like his namesake on the road to Damascus, he had been 'struck by *Grace*'. 'I had a revelation of the Supernatural . . . in one moment my heart was touched and I believed God exists, He is here . . . He is just as personal a being as I.'[1]

The Holbein woodcuts inspired in him a new dramatic poem which gave an expression of his own religious nature and enabled him to collaborate again with Arthur Honegger. Claudel took as his central ideas the powerful enjoinders:

> Remember, man, that thou art dust;
> Remember, man, that thou art spirit;
> Remember, man, that thou art a rock;

and the fundamental question:

> If a man die, shall he live again?[2]

Through a highly symbolic treatment of a wide variety of biblical texts combined in a most ingenious manner, he expressed on one level the progression of a soul from being confused by the mysteries of life to an affirmation of God's existence, and, on another, an understanding of the works of man in the sight of God and an appreciation of the saving grace of God through the Messiah.

The core of the biblical material comes from the thirty-seventh chapter of the book of the prophet Ezekiel. In these highly symbolistic writings the resurrection of the dry bones represents the revival of the dead hope of Israel and the uniting of two sticks the incorporation of Israel into Judah; and through this Christ's kingdom is promised to them. Claudel subtly adds a veneer in which the resurrection of dry bones becomes the revival of the dead Christian church; through the cross (the two united sticks), the salvation of the church and its people is assured and in Christ's kingdom there is the promise of future hope and happiness. In such a communal expression of religious faith both the convinced Protestant Honegger and the fervently Catholic Claudel could unite.

The works falls into six sections which can be summarized as:

1. An orchestral introduction leads to the 'Dialogue' between the narrator (Ezekiel 37. 1-10) and the chorus (Job 10. 9; 19. 25, 26; 14.14 and Genesis 1. 19; 1. 2) in which the drama of the raising of man from the dead as God's *re*-creation of man is realized. The words of the prophet Ezekiel are contrasted appropriately with passages from Job which stress the relevance of the question of faith and the belief in the resurrection. The passages from Genesis underline the fact that the 'dry bones' are the dead Church which is on the earth created by God himself and, therefore, the dead must be re-created to restore the Church to life.

2. 'La danse des morts': Mankind is portrayed by dancers who, with reckless abandon dance unceasingly, entirely oblivious of their impending doom. The chorus text is made up from those of three traditional songs of symbolic relevance:

   (a) 'Sur le pont d'Avignon l'on y danse' (with 'de la tombe' being substituted for 'd'Avignon');

   (b) 'Carmagnole' (sung by the crowds during the mass executions of the French Revolution);

   (c) 'Entrez dans la danse' (the chorus from the children's dance song 'Nous n'irons plus au bois').

3. 'Lamento': The solo baritone sings verses from Job (10. 9; 19. 21; 19. 20; 7. 7-19; 7. 7; 14. 12; 14. 3-6; 14. 5-6; 19. 25-26) which express humble amazement at God's grace, culminating in an assertion of personal conviction: 'I know that my Redeemer liveth . . . I shall see God who hath saved me'. There is simultaneously a self-questioning of his ability to cope with the responsibilities of the role of a believer — the fundamental weakness of mankind is reflected in his temptation to avoid and escape from his duties.

4. 'Sanglots': Cries of hollow laughter show the whole of mankind to be still unaware even in the face of their fate. The verses from Job (10. 21-22) are given by Claudel in Latin.

5. 'La réponse de Dieu': The text from Ezekiel (37. 11-14) is a continuation

of that used in Section 1 ('Dialogue'). The question 'if a man dies, shall he live again?' is reiterated and God commands Ezekiel to answer 'thus saith the Lord God — I am the Living God', and to prophesy that the land of Israel shall be restored.

6. 'Espérance dans la croix': The Christian element is introduced for the first time with the revelation of the divinity of Christ and His offering to die upon the cross for the salvation of men. The text is a freer than hitherto adaptation of verses from John (20. 20, 25 and 27; 17. 21), Matthew (11. 29), Isaiah (49. 15) and Ezekiel (37. 16, 22 and 28). The final verse of Ezekiel promises God's protection of Israel and is given by Claudel in Latin. The enjoinder 'remember, man, that thou art a rock' is repeated and extended in affirmation by 'on this rock I will build my church and the gates of hell shall not prevail against me'.[3]

The overall dramatic structure is best represented diagrammatically (see Diagram 38 below).

Diagram 38:

La danse des morts

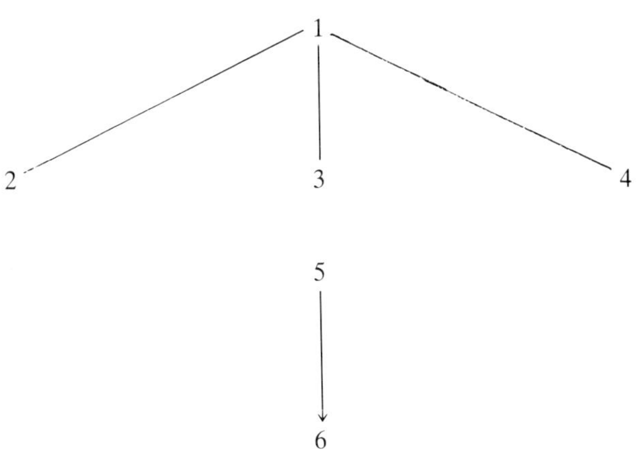

The first section is the well-head of the whole work; section three is the first point of enquiry and section five is in direct line of descent (despite containing an important development of the principles upon which the whole work is founded) and leads logically into the final section — hence the use of the arrow. The remaining two sections flank the third, their respective isolation illustrated in a basically similar fashion.

Honegger reinforces this macro-dramatic structure in several simple, but thoroughly penetrating ways. The phrase ‘I know that my Redeemer liveth . . . mine eyes shall see my God’ is set in the spirit of a Bach chorale (see Music Example 66 below).

Music Example 66: *La danse des morts*, 1B[3] - 8A[3]

(Reproduit avec l'autorisation des EDITIONS SALABERT, Paris, propriétaires de l'œuvre.)

This reappears climactically in sections three (31 -) and six (orchestra: 8A 42 - and 3A 49 -). The peal of thunder which initiates the work frames section five and appears in section six (46 - 48). A second chorale-like melodic fragment gradually emerges in the bass of the orchestra during 'La réponse de Dieu' (section five — see 5B 36) and then dominates the latter part of section six (see 43 - 46). The splendid isolation of sections two and four is achieved by their being cast as massive choral frescos where the domination by the chorus sets them apart dramatically within the framework of the work as a whole, as well as permitting them to be paired together despite the totally different musical styles involved.

On a micro-dramatic scale, an analysis of the musical structure conceived by Honegger for the first section is particularly illuminating. Claudel's request was for a rapid alternation of dialogue between the narrator and the chorus. As can be appreciated from the diagram below (Diagram 39), the potential risk of fragmentation is very great, but Honegger overcomes this with a series of masterly moves.

Diagram 39:

La danse des morts — Section I: 'Introduction/Dialogue'

Orchestral introduction	- [2]	(a)	
Narrator			
Chorus	[2]- 3A[2]	(b)	
Narrator			
Chorus	5A[2]- 9A[2]	(c)	
Narrator			
Chorus	10A[2]-11A[2]	(d)	
Narrator			
Chorus	1B[3]- 4A[3]	(e)	
Narrator			
Chorus	4A[3]- 1B[4]		
Narrator			
Chorus	[4]- [5]	(f)	
Orchestra/Chorus/Narrator	[5]- [8]	(g)	
Orchestra/Narrator	[8]- [9]	(a^1)	
Orchestra/Chorus/Narrator	[9]- [10]	(end)	(g^1)

(See also Diagram 40, p. 310.)

The orchestral introduction representing a peal of thunder returns towards the end of the section four octaves higher as 'the breath of life', producing a most satisfying cyclic framework. The initial chorus entry is the statement of the first of the fundamental propositions upon which the whole work is based:

> Think of it, man, dust thy beginning,
> and unto dust thou again returnest

and is set to a vigorous choral unison (see Music Example 67 below).

Music Example 67: *La danse des morts*, bars 1-22

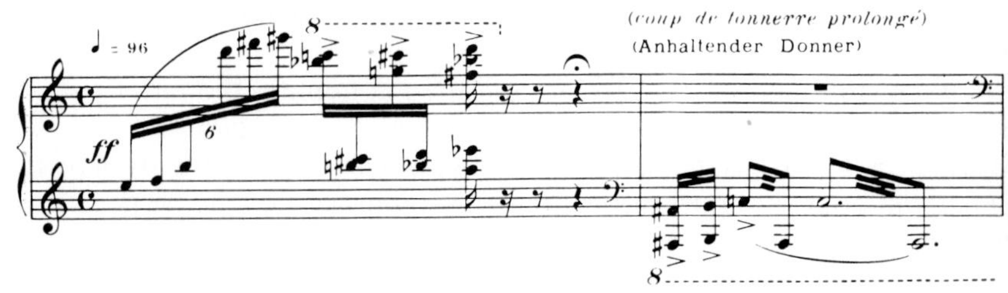

8

sempre crescendo
8

8

1
8

I. Dialogue

LE RÉCITANT: La main de Dieu s'est posée sur moi et il m'a emmené en esprit et il m'a laissé au milieu d'une vaste plaine qui était remplie d'ossements.

(Ezechiel K. 37)

DER SPRECHER: Die Hand des Herrn kam über mich, und der Herr führte mich im Geiste hinaus und liess mich nieder inmitten der Ebene, und diese war voller Gebeine.

For their second entry, with the words of God, Honegger utilizes the device of rhythmically-notated choric speech which he had previously employed to great effect in *Cris du monde* (see Music Example 68 opposite).

Music Example 68:
La danse des morts,
4A[2] - 4B[3]

(Reproduit avec l'autorisation des EDITIONS SALABERT, Paris, propriétaires de l'œuvre.)

The role of the chorus is personalized for the first time in their third entry, so Honegger allows a harmonic element to make its first appearance, thus subtly capturing the feeling of community response (see Music Example 69 below).

Music Example 69: *La danse des morts*, 4B[3] - 2B[3]

The role of the chorale which constitutes the fourth and fifth entries of the chorus with the first expression of faith has already been commented upon. The final contribution by the chorus to this rapid dialogue is one of personalized collective questioning. Honegger aptly captures the spirit of this through his use of four-part imitative polyphony, which gains real momentum both texturally and dynamically before it is left suspended at its climax — the interruption heightening the fundamental tension of the question and hence the drama as a whole (see Music Example 70 opposite).

Music Example 70: *La danse des morts*, 1B[4] - 1B[5]

(Reproduit avec l'autorisation des EDITIONS SALABERT, Paris, propriétaires de l'œuvre.)

The outcome of this gradation of effects in the chorus writing is two-fold: the pitfalls of attempting such diffuse dialogue are avoided and, from the outset, the chorus is seen and understood to be playing a multi-character role of integrated and powerful dramatic significance.

Underlining all this is the usual Honeggerian handling of tonality. The basic E minor which dominates this whole section is typically clouded by the presence of A♯s and C♮s in the opening to prevent the B♮ present having too powerful a character as a dominant such that its resolution would be a net loss of tension. The rich harmonic disguise surrounding the E at the end of the orchestral introduction completes this illusion, and the effect when the chorus enters on an E as the tonic of E minor is an apparent increase in harmonic tension. Various tertiary moves — in particular to the area of C♯ minor — occur as expected, but perhaps the most effective use Honegger makes of his fondness for tertiary patterning in tonal design comes within the chorale sections (see [3] -), where moves from E major to C♯ major and then to F major have a wonderfully appropriate and uplifting luminosity.

The continuous antithesis between the principal tonal centre of E minor and that of C♯ minor reflects the dramatic shifts and the noticeably careful disguise of any pedal B♮s (principally by the presence of D♮s and G♯s), which might otherwise take on too strong a dominant characteristic. The latter is amply justified by the side-step into E♭ minor (the D♮s revealing themselves as leading notes) which occurs as 'La danse des morts' eventually emerges in its own right at **[10]**.

A similar result is obtained from a detailed analysis of the final section of the work. The mosaic patterning which Honegger applies to his musical material to achieve a suitable representation and clarification of the textual structure is summarized in the diagram overleaf (Diagram 40), which simultaneously shows the interrelationships of much of this material with that of previous sections.

Diagram 40:

La danse des morts

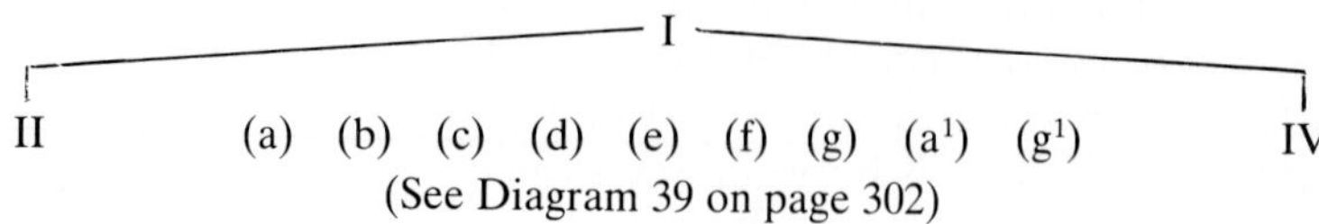

III

(h)	(i)	(h^1)	(e^1)	(h^2)
	6A			9B
26	28	29	31	32
5A			9A	
28	29	31	31	32

V

(a^2)	(j)	(a^3)
		6B
34	35	37
	17A	
35	36	37

VI

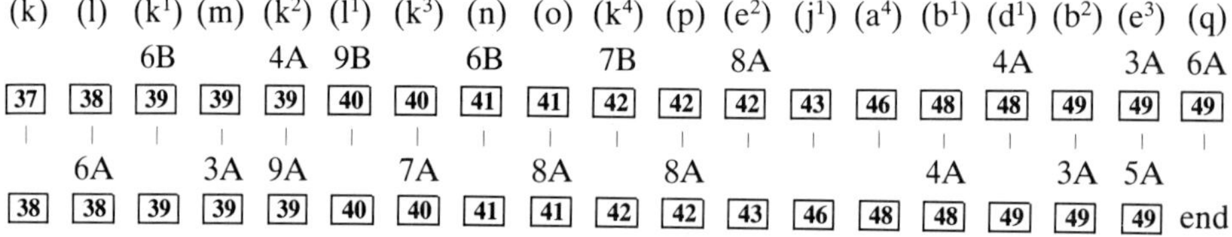

The 'Lamento' is one of Honegger's finest creations (see Music Example 71 (ii), pages 314-19). His source of inspiration is quite clearly the aria 'For love my Saviour now is dying' from Bach's *St Matthew Passion*, where the soprano lament exquisitely unfolds between the melodic arabesques of the flute and the mournful harmonic tread of two oboi da caccia. There is no question of pastiche, only the capturing in the opening of the quintessential spirit which transcends the barriers of time. The same was true of the *Arioso* in the *Prélude, Arioso, Fughetta (sur le nom de Bach)* of 1932 (see Music Example 71 (i) below) — see Chapter VIII page 243 — but here Honegger's creative powers are on a still higher plane.

Music Example 71:
(i) *Arioso* from *Prélude, Arioso, Fughetta (sur le nom de Bach)*

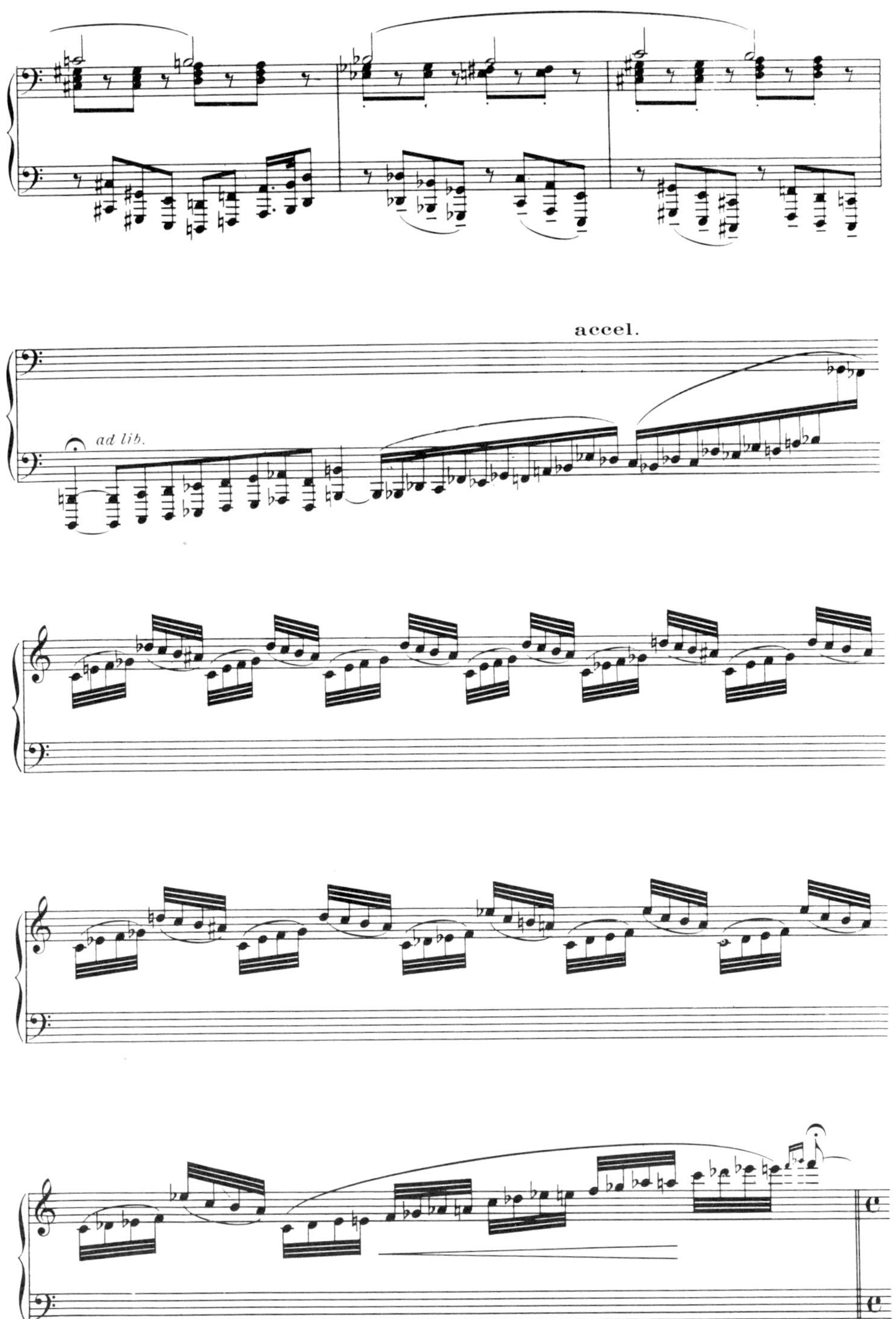
accel.
ad lib.

(ii) 'Lamento' from *La danse des morts*

28
dents autour de la bou_che
_lein grinsend noch die Zähne.
Qui __ est l'homme pour que tu le
Was ist der Mensch, dass du ihn so
28
ma_gni_fies __ et pour que Vous lui at_ta_chiez vo _ tre cœur?
hoch er_hebst und dass du, Gott, le_bend ihm dein Her _ ze schenkst?
Tu le vi_sites au point du jour et l'épreu _ ve commen_ce pour lui aus_si_tôt
Am frühen Tag suchst du ihn heim, und alsbald beginnt für ihn die Prü _ fungs _ zeit.
p
jus _ ques à quand se_ra_ce que tu ou _ blies de
Wie lang _ e Frist vergeht, dass ich ent beh re
3
m'é_pargner __ et que Tu ne me lais_ses pas le temps que j'a_va_le ma sa _ li _ ve
deine Huld und dass du mir nicht Zeit lässt, zu ver_schlin _ gen mei _ nen Spei _ chel.

Ma vie est comme le vent qui souffle — et ma substan - ce
Dem Win - de gleich vergeht mein Le - ben und mein Da - sein
devant Toi — est com - me rien
ist vor dir gleich ein - em Nichts.
L'hom - me né de la femme — et qui vit
Erd - ge-bo - ren - er Mensch du lebst nicht
29
peu Tu vois de quelles mi - sè - res, Seigneur il est rem - pli! Il s'é - lè - ve comme u - ne
lang. O Gott, du siehst, welch Elend und Lei - den ihn ganz erfüllt. Der Blume gleich wächst er
3

fleur et aus_si_tôt Il est bri_sé, il fuit comme l'ombre et
und also_gleich er ver ge_het. Er flieht wie der Schat _ ten.

ja _ mais il ne de_meu _ re dans le mème é _ tat Et
Nim _ mer ist ver_gönnt ihm, an gleicher Statt zu ruhn. Und

C'est sur un in_di_vi_du de cette es_pè_ce que tu ju _ ges di_gne de Toi d'ouvrir les
wahrlich, ein Wesen in Sünd ge_bo_ren, hältst du würdig dei _ ner Grös _ se Macht und dei_nes

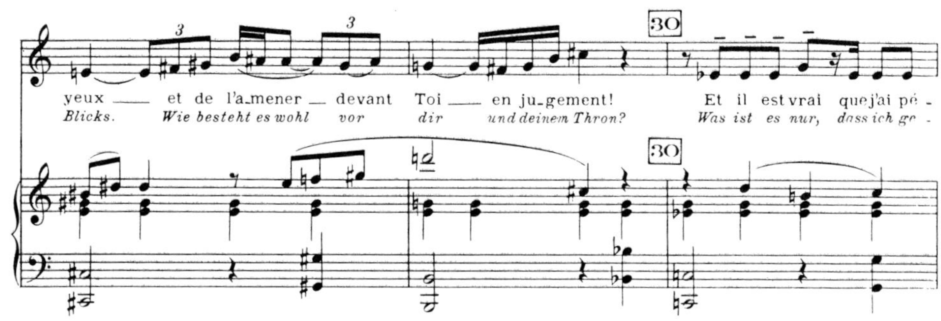
30
yeux et de l'a_mener devant Toi en ju_gement! Et il est vrai que j'ai pé _
Blicks. Wie besteht es wohl vor dir und deinem Thron? Was ist es nur, dass ich ge _
30

_ché Qui peut fai_re pur quelque cho _ se né d'u_ne se_men _ se qui ne l'est
_fehlt? Wessen Werk hat Wert, der ge _ bo _ ren von ei_ner Sä_e _ rin, die kei_ne
pas Toi seul Toi seul qui as fi _ xé le nombre de ses
ist? Du selbst, du selbst, der al _ lein du zählst seiner Monde
mois et cons_ti_tué devant lui ce ter _ me qu'il ne saurait dé_pas_ser
Zahl und fest-ge_setzt seines Le _ bens Ziel, das er nicht ü _ ber schrei ten kenn.
Re_ti_rez vous de lui un peu qu'il ait re _
Zieh dich zurück von ihm, dass Rast ihm sei ver _
_pos et que lui ar_rive en_fin comme à un mer_ce_nai _ re le
_gönnt, dass end _ lich ihm der Tag er_schei _ ne, wie dem Knecht _ e, der

31
pp
jour, le jour dé_si_ré car je sais que mon Ré_dempteur vit et
Tag, der Tag, tiefersehnt. Denn ich weiss, dass mein Er_lö_ser lebt und
au der_nier jour je me re_lè_ve_rai de la terre et de nouveau je se_rai en_ve_lop_pé de ma
dass ich aufs neu werderstehn von der Er_de und wiederum erwache, umhüllt mit einem neu_en Ge_
peau et dans ma pro_pre chair je ver_rai ce Dieu qui est mon Sau_
_wand, und dass in meinem Fleisch Gott ich wer_de schaun, der mein Retter
_veur.
ist.
enchainez

Of the two remaining sections (two and four), number two is the more interesting. Honegger's natural gift for dramatic choral writing ensures a suitably effective 'Sanglots' despite the utmost simplicity of means. The section falls into almost equal parts ([32] - [33] and [33] - [34]): the macabre soprano/contralto and orchestral 'laughter' are superimposed on the unison tenor/bass intonation in the first, with a reversal of the choral roles and a transposition of the whole fabric down a semitone serving as the second. The technique employed, however, in 'La danse des morts' is much more complex. In direct response to the unique composite nature of the text he constructs a quodlibet using the actual melodies of the three traditional songs (see page 298) together with, suitably enough, the 'Dies irae' plainchant. The result is a terrifyingly realistic *scherzo* which is superbly dramatic if not as convincing in a purely musical sense as the even larger quodlibet in *Une cantate de Noël* (see pages 358 and 360). The combination of narrator, recitative-like writing for semi-chorus, traditional four-part imitative choral music, rhythmically-notated choric speaking and a sharply defined orchestral fabric is a more assured and successful product of experimental passages in *Cris du monde* (cf. Chapter VII).

The music for *La danse des morts* was completed in October 1938 and the work was given its first performance by Paul Sacher and his Basle forces on 1 March 1940 — a performance which was broadcast live to many other European countries, including Britain. The Paris première was conducted by Charles Münch on 26 January 1941 under the auspices of the Société des Concerts — an additional performance being arranged for 2 February, such was its success. Prior to this it had been given a second performance in Zürich (in a German translation by Hans Reinhart) in the Municipal Theatre with appropriate scenery (2 June 1940). Later on it was even turned into a ballet — Margarete Wallmann being responsible for the choreography of the 1954 Salzburg Festival production. *La danse des morts* was the second major collaboration between Claudel and Honegger and as such their last, because three subsequent projects were on a much smaller scale.[4] Although many people have pointed out that Claudel cannot be credited with having created the text as he did for *Jeanne d'Arc au bûcher,* this must not be allowed to detract from the fact that he is responsible for organizing the material in an entirely new and meaningful way. The whole is characterized by qualities of compression, restriction and concentration — particularly when placed side by side with that of *Jeanne d'Arc au bûcher* or any of the myriad of texts he provided for Milhaud — and it is these very qualities which drew out of Honegger some of his most disciplined and hence uniformly finest music.

Honegger was unduly modest when he said 'si à l'exécution de cet ouvrage, il se dégage pour l'auditeur une émotion, qu'il soit bien persuadé que le mérite en revient entièrement au grand poète qui l'a créé et dont je n'ai fait que suivre les indications et tenté de réaliser de mon mieux la haute pensée'[5] [if the performance of this work frees an emotion from the listener, may he truly be persuaded that the credit falls entirely on the great poet who has created it. I have only followed his indications and tried to the best of my ability to put over his highest thought]. 'Unduly modest' because Claudel's text could not stand on its own in dramatic presentation without the music. That the text and music are completely one in the final product of the collaboration is to Honegger's sole credit.

Part II: *Nicolas de Flue*

Denis de Rougemont and Arthur Honegger were commissioned to write *Nicolas de Flue* by the committee organizing the 1939 'Journées cantonales' in celebration of the six hundred and fiftieth anniversary of the foundation of the confederated states of modern Switzerland. The first performances should have been given in the Halle de Fête on 23 and 24 September by the Neuchâtel choirs of Le Locle and La Chaux-de-Fonds under Charles Fuller as part of the National Exhibition to be held in Zürich, but problems caused by the general mobilization initiated in response to the outbreak of World War Two prevented this. The Exhibition was moved to Neuchâtel for May 1940, but the organizers were unable to manage the presentation of the whole event — the production of *Nicolas de Flue* being one of the features that was again postponed. Before it finally received its first staged production in Neuchâtel, conducted by Charles Fuller on 31 May 1941, it was given in concert performances by the same forces who had premièred *Cris du monde* — the Sainte-Cécile Choir of Soleure, conductor Eric Schild — on 26 and 27 October 1940, in Soleure, with William Aguet as narrator and the Berne Municipal Orchestra.

Rougemont's text is a very fine combination of a statement of religious faith and an expression of patriotism. Nicolas de Flue was a national Swiss hero who had been canonized in 1872 and ranks with William Tell, Davel and Pestalozzi in the annals of Swiss history. Rougemont casts the scene in Switzerland at the end of the Middle Ages. Brother Nicolas (1417-87) is aged fifty, a citizen of Flueli in the canton of Unterwald, and a widely-known and respected counsellor, judge, Diet representative and former army captain. His spiritual orientation directs him in a process of self-isolation. He first withdraws from his public life, then from his private life. Leaving a wife and ten children he retires to a wild gorge in Ranft in order to devote his remaining years to prayer and to living a severely spartan life. Soon he gains the reputation of a saint and many people make pilgrimages to him — his influence again becomes very considerable.

In the early 1470s a long period of internal and external political and armed strife for Switzerland had come to a head and its very existence was threatened. Ultimately when all else had failed Nicolas was asked to intervene. His wisdom in solving the situation has since been hailed as the spirit of support and mutual tolerance which is the seemingly invincible foundation upon which modern Switzerland still rests.

Rougemont did little except follow the story itself step by step, adding only a few very discreet poetic moments of reflection here and there. The resultant text was extremely suitable from Honegger's point of view — the vigorous national epoch flavour is a direct parallel to that in *Le roi David*, *Judith* and *Jeanne d'Arc au bûcher* which he had handled with immense popular success.

Appropriately enough an enormous role is allocated to the chorus and a magnificent vein of lyricism and powerful nobility pervades the whole. Furthermore, the humanistically religious spirit contained in the work was bound to find a rich response in Honegger's music — the work must have seemed particularly real to him in the early months of 1939. As a dramatic scenario the text is excellent — extremely clear, simple and unified. It is the capturing of the popular spirit in a spectacle situation (a *jeu populaire)* which puts it in the unique genre that had been a Swiss speciality for the best part of fifty years — a genre of which Honegger had so much successful experience as a result of his previous collaborations with René Morax.

Honegger said that above all else their aim had been 'faire une œuvre vraiment populaire; c'est-à-dire simple, claire, directe, lisible à grande distance, puisqu'elle était destinée à une très grande salle, sans pour cela tomber dans la platitude, la vulgarité ou la banalité qui ménace si souvent le genre 'Festspiel'[6] [to create a really popular work; that is to say, simple, clear, direct and intelligible at a great distance (since it was destined to be performed in an enormous hall), and which does not become platitudinous, vulgar or banal as so often happens in works for 'Festspiele']. In achieving this Honegger returns to a style and to methods of formal organization which are very close to those found in his score for *Le roi David*. The work is scored practically for an orchestra of woodwind and brass — flutes, piccolo, clarinets, saxophones, saxhorns, horns, trumpets and trombones — timpani and a large number of percussion instruments, and the wealth of sharply defined colours adds a further dimension to the 'al fresco' nature of the piece as a whole.[7] The extremely diverse twenty-seven items of *Le roi David* become thirty here, with none of them as long as either 'La danse devant l'arche' or 'La mort de David', and with probably even greater variety. The same problem naturally arises — how is the necessary prerequisite of musical coherence to be achieved in such a situation? The answer is partially provided in that Rougemont's text has several actual refrains as well as returns which automatically suggest thematic and/or whole fabric correspondences:

(A) The first of these is the strophic poem 'Il s'en va'. Rougemont uses the first two verses for Act I No. 5 — as a young man Nicolas resigns from the army because he sees it abusing its powers; in the first verse the people lament his departure, saying:

> Il s'en va, hélas, il s'en va,
> le meilleur d'entre nous s'en va.
> Qui maintiendra dans la guerre le droit?
> Qui gardera notre alliance jurée? qui la gardera?
>
> O combattant loin des armées,
> N'oublie pas ton peuple ingrat!
> Nicolas dans ton exil, souviens-toi de nos périls!

The narrator then tells how, as a middle-aged man, he was a judge — he resigns from this position too, when he witnesses a similar abuse of power; the people lament his resignation with the words of the second verse:

Il s'en va, hélas, il s'en va,
le meilleur d'entre nous s'en va,
Qui maintiendra dans la cité le droit?
Qui gardera notre alliance jurée, qui la gardera?

O justicier ta voix se tait.
N'oublie pas ton peuple ingrat!
Nicolas dans ton exil, souviens-toi de nos périls!

The third verse appears later (as Act I No. 9) when Nicolas 'resigns' his family life and leaves for the wilderness, isolation and prayer. The same music is used for this expression of grief at his final departure from them:

Il s'en va, hélas! il s'en va,
le meilleur d'entre nous s'en va.
Qui maintiendra de ta maison le droit?
Qui portera le poids du sacrifice, qui le portera?

Père, père, où sont tes fils,
Solitaire, où vont tes pas?
Nicolas, dans ton exil, souviens-toi de nos périls!

It was natural enough for Honegger to set these three verses to the same music, but the masterstroke comes when, in the last Act (III) he uses this music for the choral verse which is No. 27:

Il descend, Seigneur, Il descend!
Lui, le Saint, parmi nous, descend!
Qui sauvera, drapeau de sang, ta croix?
Qui gardera notre alliance jurée, qui la gardera?

O viens à nous dans la mêlée
N'oublie pas ton peuple ingrat!
Nicolas, reviens d'exil, Soutiens-nous dans nos périls!

The public expressions of dismay and regret at his various departures are now united with a sincere and climactic celebration of his return to help them in a moment of national crisis — an appropriate and powerfully dramatic gesture.

(B) The second musical return coincides with the displacement of the final verse of the strophic 'Solitaire' sung by the 'Chœur céleste'. In Act I No. 6 the heavenly message is delivered to Nicolas (verse 1) — that he will find eternal peace in the solitude of the wilderness; and also to Dorothy, his wife (verse 2) — through her sacrifice and subsequent loneliness will come eternal reward and the salvation of a nation. When, in Act III No. 26, Nicolas refuses to leave his isolated retreat in order to help his troubled countrymen because it was God who directed him into solitude, the message delivered to him by the celestial choir is contained in the third verse:

Solitaire! Dieu te parle par nos voix.
De ta vie le grand mystère
Au matin s'éclaircira.
Pour ton peuple, ta Patrie,
Ton salut tu sacrifies,
En Jésus livrant sa vie
Dieu lui-même est descendu!

(C) The third musical return is not in response to a textual refrain or subsequent strophe, but rather underlines two different appearances of the chorus in the same role. The weary tread accompanying the 'Chant des pèlerins' (Act II No. 11) as they travel to see Nicolas is enlivened by figures for fifes and side-drums in Act II No. 15, 'Cortèges', as they sing the same melody whilst making their way home, having received either his advice or his warning.

(D/E/F) The fourth, fifth and sixth musical returns occur between Act II Nos. 17, 18 and 19, and are battle cries shared between the three representations of strife (see Music Example 72 below).

Music Example 72: *Nicolas de Flue*:
(i) No. 17, bars 2-5 (cf. No. 19, 2A [3] - 4B [6] and 1-4A [6]) = (D)

(ii) No. 17, 1(and 3)A [1] (cf. No. 18, 1-4A [2]; No. 19, 2-1B [4]) = (E)

(iii) No. 17, 2A [1] (cf. No. 18 — used extensively throughout) = (F)

(G) The seventh and final musical refrain is similar to the first in terms both of its musical characteristics and the nature and extent of its dramatic role. In Act II No. 16 the tranquility of Nicolas's solitude is shattered by the myriad of calls from his countrymen to intervene in the political situation. Honegger once again uses the spirit of a Bach chorale to represent their appeal to him — the whole fabric is repeated in Act II No. 17 and Act III No. 24 (to parallel the repetition of similar requests for his help) and restated, finally, in Act III No. 30 as the public thank him for having acceded to their pleas for help.

Honegger is careful in view of the extreme brevity and contrast of most of the movements to make the finales of each act as substantial as possible. Although, as has been previously mentioned, not one of them is anywhere near as long as Nos. 16 and 27 in *Le roi David*, they all have a similar mosaic-like structure which effects a concentration of many of the elements already involved and each culminates in a typically Honeggerian choral outburst built up from many unisoni and/or doublings in thirds with full orchestral support. Whereas in *Le roi David* the 'Alleluias' linked Nos. 16 and 27, here brief 'Amens', derived from 10A [1^A]* in the 'Prologue', relate Nos. 7, 10, 19 and 30 (see Music Example 73 below).

Music Example 73: *Nicolas de Flue*:
(i) No. 1, 10A [1^A]

*(N.B.: There are two [1]'s in the 'Prologue' (No. 1) — for convenience I have called the first (bar 30) [1^A] and the second (bar 56) [1^B]. In No. 18, the [1] on page 50 is a misprint for [3]. (In both cases these mistakes refer to the vocal score [Fœtisch Frères, F.7050.F.].)

(ii) No. 7, 3rd bar before end

(iii) No. 10, last three bars

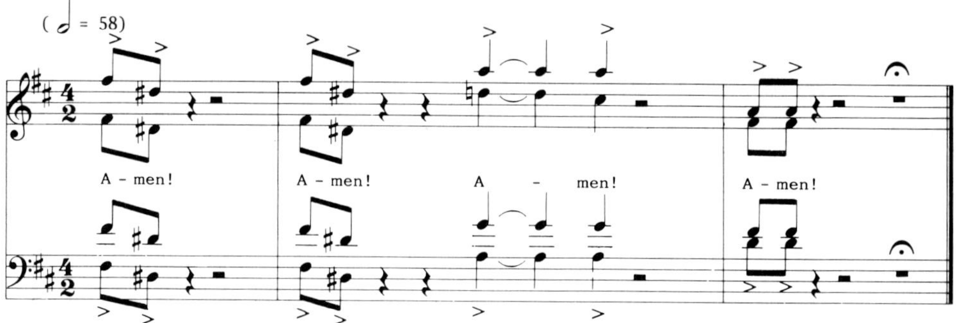

(iv) No. 19, last bar (orchestra)

(v) No. 30, see bars 3-10 (orchestra)

Of particular significance is Honegger's utilization in this score of a framework of interlocking tonalities. It is a natural extension and development of the one found in *Le roi David*. The most salient features of this scheme are represented in the three parts of the diagram (Diagram 41) overleaf. It should be read in conjunction with the explanatory notes below.

(1) The polar tonality of the whole work is E♭ major. The 'Prologue' (No. 1) is for the most part in B♭ major/minor, which acts as a suitable dominant preparation for the real 'dramatic' start of the work in E♭ major with the 'Chanson des enfants' (No. 2). (The penultimate F minor/major tonality acts as a 'dominant of the dominant' preparation, and the final side-stepping to C major does not negate the gesture in question — it merely avoids the obviousness of the dominant-tonic resolution in a characteristically colourful way.)

(2) The parts for the 'Chœur céleste' which occur briefly in the 'Prologue' (1B $\boxed{1^{A}}$ and 1B$\boxed{2}$) both start in A major. This is the key used to close their subsequent contributions in Act 1 (No. 6) and Act III (No. 26) and for one of their other major items — Act II No. 13. It should be noted that Honegger does not put Act III No. 28 into either F minor or A major (nor, for that matter, a combination of the two), but rather into B♭ major. This does not nullify the point being made — the necessity of B♭ major is obviously governed by the large-scale representation of triumph epitomized by the move from C minor to E♭ major in the course of the last four items of the final Act. The effectiveness of the dramatic unity provided by the A major reference point in the 'Chœur céleste' movements had been well established and served its purpose such that he could afford to subjugate it to the needs of another design factor at this late stage of the work.

(3) The key of C minor recurs with the music for the strophic chorale 'Il s'en va'/'Il descend' (see (A), pages 322-23). It is therefore used for Act I Nos. 5 and 9 and Act III No. 27. (Act I No. 4 is merely a very brief preface and epilogue to each verse of No. 5 and is thus understandably cast in the same key.) (See also (5) below.)

(4) The A minor tonality of Act II Nos. 11 and 15 parallels the sharing of thematic material (see (C), page 324).

(5) The tonality of E♭ major, prefaced by brief references to E♭ minor and C minor, underlines the 'chorale' music which first appears in Act II No. 16 and then recurs intact in Act II No. 17 and Act III Nos. 24 and 30. The C minor aspect also relates this 'chorale' to the first (see (3) above).

(6) The prime importance of the keys of F, E and C♯ minors in Nos. 17, 18 and 19 reinforces the thematic links between these three 'war' movements in Act II. The particular stressing of F minor and C♯ minor in No. 19 specifically in relation to No. 17, highlights the return of musical material (see (D)/(E), page 324). (It is not without significance that C♯ minor is also the key of the 'Fanfare' (Act I No. 3) that reflected Nicolas's memories of war.) The key of D minor is used to link these three Act II war movements to those in Act III (Nos. 23 and 25).

Diagram 41:

Nicolas de Flue

Act I

1. 'Prologue'

Principal tonalities :	Dom. prep. for:	B♭	b♭	A	C	b♭	A	f/F	C
Bar references :		[1A]	11A [1A]	1B [1B]	3A [1B]	5A [1B]	1B [2]	3A [2]	final bar

2. 'Chanson des enfants'

Principal tonality : E♭

3. 'Fanfare'

Principal tonality : c♯ resolution of a polytonal fabric

4. 'Chœur: "Souviens-toi!"'

Principal tonality : c

5. 'Choral: "Il s'en va" (1re et 2me strophes)'

Principal tonality : c

6. 'Chœur céleste: "Solitaire, solitaire!"'

Principal tonality : f (but closing in A)

7. 'La prière de Nicolas'

Principal tonality : C

8. 'Récitatif: "Dure est la peine"'

Principal tonality : c — A

9. 'Choral: "Il s'en va" (3e strophe)'

Principal tonality : c

10. 'La montée au Ranft'

Principal tonalities	:	d/D	e♭	b	e♭	c♯	e	on dom. of f/F	on dom. of A
Bar references	:		3A[2]	5B[3]	1B[3]	[3]	7A[4]	16B[5]	[5]

Principal tonalities	:	b	on dom. of b♭	D	G♭	D	on dom. of F♯	b♭	on dom. of F
Bar references	:	[6]	4B[7]	[7]	[8]	[9]	[10]	4A[10]	4B[11]

Principal tonalities	:	D (to end despite strong harmonic inflections)
Bar references	:	2A[11]

Continued overleaf

Act II

11. 'Chant des pélerins'

Principal tonality : a

12. 'Double chœur: "Etoile du matin"'

Principal tonality : E♭

13. 'Récitatif du Guetteur'

Principal tonality : A (but closing in F♯)

14. 'Chœur céleste: "Dieu l'a voulu"'

Principal tonality : e♭

15. 'Cortèges'

Principal tonality : a

16. 'Récitatif et Choral: "Ainsi les affaires du monde"'

Principal tonality : E♭ (After an 11 bar dom. prep. there is the suggestion of e♭ in bar 12 and a cadence into c in bar 13 before E♭ is firmly established. The e♭ — c colouring is maintained in Nos. 17, 24 and 30 (+).)

17. 'Récitatif et Choral: "Tout un peuple a prêté l'oreille"'

Principal tonalities	:	f (via sequential steps which make reference to c, A♭, c♯, d and B♭	E♭ (+)
Bar references	:	[1] -	7A[1]

18. 'Chœur des puissances'

Principal tonalities	:	d	c♯	a	d	e (but closing on its dominant)
Bar references	:		[2]	7A[2]	8B[3]	

19. 'Chœur: "Victoire et malheur!"'

Principal tonalities	:	a	F	c♯	f	c♯	f	d	f	on dom. of G♭	c♯	but closes in e
Bar references	:		3B[1]	[1]	[3]	2B[4]	[4]	2B[5]	[5]	3B[6]	5A[6]	

Act III

No. 20 'Marche des Ambassadeurs'

Principal tonalities	:	C	a	on dom. of F	D♭	f	on dom. of C	C	‖(fine)
			9B[1]	[1]	5A[1]	[2]	[4]	[5]	

Principal tonalities	:	(Trio:) F	d	F	‖(Da capo al fine)
Bar references	:		4B[6]	[6]	

Continued overleaf

No. 21 'Les compagnons de la follevie'

Principal tonality : g

No. 22 'Fanfare de la Diète'

Principal tonality : — (possibly f)

No. 23 'Récitatif: "Demain la guerre!"'

Principal tonality : d

No. 24 'Choral: "Nicolas, souviens-toi!"'

Principal tonality : E♭(+)

No. 25 'Récitatif: "Parmi nous, peuple, parmi nous"'

Principal tonality : d

No. 26 'Chœur céleste: "Solitaire, solitaire!"'

Principal tonality : f (but closing in A)

No. 27 'Choral: "Il descend"'

Principal tonality : c

No. 28 'Chœur céleste: "Terre et cieux, prêtez l'oreille!"'

Principal tonality : B♭

No. 29 'Récitatif: "Ecoute-moi, mon peuple!"'

Principal tonalities	:	Dom. prep. for:	c	C
Bar references	:		[1]	[2]

No. 30 'Récitatif des cloches et chœur final'

Principal tonalities	:	A♭	E♭ (+)	(to end despite strong harmonic inflections)
Bar reference	:		11-	

In the third and final act several longer-term tonal designs come to fruition. The basic key of the whole work, E♭ major, is irrevocably achieved in the final chorus — the opening section in A♭ major sounding like a huge plagal cadence. The role of this tonic, established so effectively at the beginning of the work, was reinforced near the start of Act II (No. 12), and its central involvement in the 'chorale' plea for help (see (5), page 327) that appeared in Act II Nos. 16 and 17 and Act III Nos. 24 and 30, ensured that its relevance would remain utterly clear. The fact that, tonally, Act I finished 'uncertainly' in the key of the leading-note (D major), and Act II finished in 'turmoil' in the key of the flattened supertonic minor (E minor), results in a perfect matching of the dramatic structure. The celestial choir's contributions all contain a reference to A major (the dominant of the D major conclusion to Act I) until Act III No. 28, when, as has already been noted (see (2), page 327), the tonality is raised to B♭ major to refocus their contribution on the final outcome.

Even without markings to aid the eye it will be obvious from the summary of principal tonalities in Diagram 41 (pages 328-33) that Honegger's fondness for tertiary patterning is yet again very much in evidence. More detailed examination of any one of the larger movements — in particular Act I No. 10, Act II No. 19 and Act III No. 20 — will reveal this fingerprint even more clearly.

To seal the formal argument of the score, Honegger uses techniques which he had previously tried in his scores for *Amphion* and *Judith* respectively: giving the name of the principal character (Nicolas) a motif which has a very specific rhythmic character ( ), and representing the omnipresence of God by a melodic cell which consists of a tonic note followed by those of the supertonic, dominant and subdominant. Both these permeate the whole fabric in motto-fashion.

When reviewing this work in *Mercure de France,* the highly perspicacious critic and music historian, René Dumesnil, asked if the success of this work was due only to 'l'équilibre des éléments assemblés dans l'œuvre' which were 'si bien joints qu'ils deviennent inséparables', or whether 'l'analyse ne peut pas révéler des réussites comme celle-ci'[8] [the equilibrium of the elements assembled in the work . . . so well joined together that it becomes impossible to separate them . . . the analysis could not reveal success like the latter]. In the light of an analysis there can be no doubt that subtleties of thematic and tonal structuring do play a very vital role in this respect, but it seems necessary either way to account for the fact that the work has not 'survived' in the same way as the score for *Le roi David* , to which it is the closest parallel amongst all his large-scale dramatic choral works.

Both in its original French and in Hans Reinhart's German translation, *Nicolas de Flue* initially enjoyed immense success and popularity in America as well as in Switzerland (the first performance in the former being given in the Carnegie Hall in 1941). The public and critics applauded the immediacy of appeal, the decisive pictorialism, the creative dexterity and the freshness of a work which yet managed to avoid the pitfalls of banality usually inherent in a score of this nature.[9]

When the work received its first French performance in the form of a radio broadcast in 1952 the general reaction was already far less spontaneously favourable and complimentary. The scores of *Le roi David* and *Jeanne d'Arc au bûcher* were set up as models and, whilst some critics spoke of the work as lacking in virtuosity, depth and richness of true invention, others tried to question the extent of the composer's personal involvement. There were even attempts by some to explain their uneasiness in retrospect by simply pointing to the Swiss flavour of the work, to its 'spectacle' qualities and to its origins as a *pièce de circonstance.* None were able or willing to admit in a simple and direct way that there had been a fundamental shift in musical tastes with the changing era and, whilst works like *Le roi David* and *Jeanne d'Arc au bûcher* would continue to maintain their popularity because of the accumulated momentum of long-term public approval, a score like *Nicolas de Flue* had come just too late to reap similar benefits.

The score for *Nicolas de Flue* contains the last example of one of the most salient features of Honegger's choral frescos — the use of the speaking-voice. In all of the major choral works discussed so far, with the exception only of *Cantique de Pâques,* the spoken word occurs either as pure narration (without a musical background) or as melodrama (narration with a background of music). Honegger uses pure narration in two ways:

(i) As a means of relating the story	—	*Le roi David, Judith, Jeanne d'Arc au bûcher, La danse des morts, Nicolas de Flue*
(ii) As the voices of specific characters in dialogue	—	*Jeanne d'Arc au bûcher* (see, for example, page 31 of the miniature score published in 1947 by Editions Salabert).

The 'story-telling' type of narrative is itself employed in two different ways, either as a preface to the sections of the work (most noticeably in *Le roi David* and *Nicolas de Flue* — see Music Example 74 overleaf), or between phrases of the chorus and/or orchestra (see Music Example 75, pages 339-40).

Music Example 74: *Le roi David* (1923 version), Nos. 3-3bis

LE RÉCITANT:

Et Samuel choisit David parmi ses frères. Et il l'oignit avec la corne d'huile. Et David était blond et de belle figure. Et dès ce jour l'Esprit de Dieu resta sur lui.

DER ERZÄHLER:

Und Isai ließ seine sieben Söhne vor dem Angesichte Samuels erscheinen. Der aber sprach zu Isai: „Der Herr hat dieser keinen auserwählt. Sind das der Knaben alle?" Und Isai antwortete: „Es ist noch einer, David, der jüngste, der die Schafe hütet auf dem Felde." Und Samuel befahl: „So sende hin und laß ihn holen!"

Also geschah. Und Gott sprach weiter: „Auf! Und salbe ihn, denn er ist's, den ich auserwählte!"

Da nahm Samuel sein Ölhorn, und er salbte David mitten unter seinen Brüdern. Und von dem Tag an kam der Geist des Ewigen über David und verblieb bei ihm.

Bas.
Trp. en ut.
Chœur.
gés. Quand les plus grands contre moi se sou - lè - vent, Au des-sus d'eux ses
Heer. Wenn die Ge - wal - ti - gen wi - der mich zie - hen, aus ih - ren stol - zen
Vcll. et Cb.
Bas.
Chœur.
for-tes mains mé - lè - vent, Des or - gueil - leux, il con - fond le des - sein Que
Reihen reißt mich seine Hand. Es trifft sein Donner den fre - velnden Feind, der
Vcll. et Cb.
Bas.
f
Cors en fa.
a 2
f sempre
f sempre
Trp. en ut.
f sempre
Chœur.
pour me perdre ils cou - vaient dans leur sein.
zum Ver - der - ben tückisch sich ver - eint.
Vcll. et Cb.
Bas.
Cors en fa.
Trp. en ut.
Vcll.
Cb.

3bis Fanfare.

LE RÉCITANT:	*DER ERZÄHLER:*
Voici, dans la vallée du térébinthe, Saül a rassemblé les soldats d'Israël contre les Philistins. Et le géant Goliath a défié l'armée.	Und da im Eichgrund sich die Männer Israels zum Kampfe gegen die Philister rüsteten, trat Goliath, der ungeschlachte, prahlerische Riese aus den Reihn, das Heer von Israel zu höhnen und zu schmähn.

Entrée de Goliath – Auftritt Goliaths.

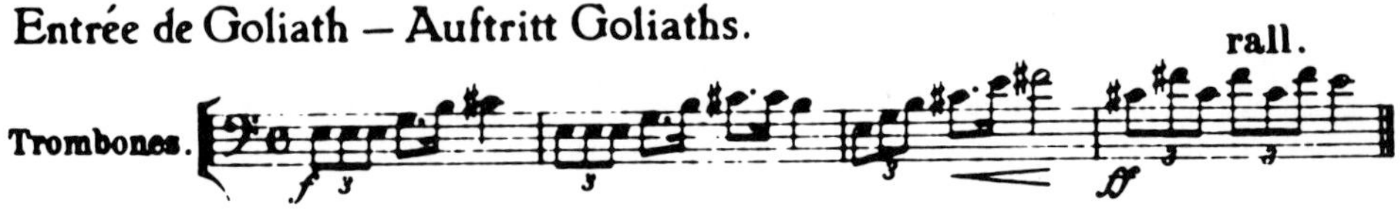

Music Example 75: *Nicolas de Flue,* No. 1, 16B [1B] — 12A [1B]

*) *Dans le texte des récitatifs, les mots en italiques sont articulés par le chœur, qui, autrement, chante a bocca chiusa pendant que le Récitant seul déclame.*

Il reste seul.
Tous crient:
Il reste
pauvre
et seul.
Tous crient:
Et lui tout
seul dit:
Paix!
De - l'or!
La
guer - re!
1
CHŒUR CÉLESTE
Paix sur la terre et dans les cieux.
CHOEUR MIXTE
Paix sur la terre et dans les cieux.
Le Récitant:
Ce soir encore,
Confédérés
Notre
héros et
notre saint
nous parle. Là-bas
tous crient:
En - sem - ble! En-sem - ble!
Prêtez l'o-reil - le!
Il reste seul.
Tous crient:
Et lui
nous dit:
Amour!
Tous crient:
Et lui, tout seul encore
Nous dit: Courage; ô peuple,
reste uni! Le matin vient!
A
mort!
La
gue - re!

It is important to note in this context that Honegger does not employ the French designation *narrateur* (the equivalent of the English word *narrator*), but chooses, instead, the term *récitant*, which has a broader meaning than would be inherent in the use of *narrateur*. The term *récitant* is related to the word *recitative* and Honegger employs it to embrace this function despite the fact that no actual recitative in the traditional sense is found in any of his works.

The passages in his music which would be labelled 'melodrama' by virtue of the definition 'spoken text with a musical background' must be subdivided into two quite distinct categories. The first of these would be headed by the twelfth number from *Le roi David* — 'Incantation' — which is truly melodramatic in view of the descriptive role of the orchestral fabric (see Music Example 76 below).

Music Example 76: *Le roi David* (1923 version), No. 12, bars 1-21

Largo, poco a poco più animato. ♩= 66

Petite Flûte et Flûte.
1 Hautbois.
Cor anglais.
1 Clarinette en la.
Clar. basse en si♭.
Basson et Contre-Basson.
4 Cors.
2 Trompettes.
3 Trombones.
Tuba.
Cymbales. Gr. Caisse.
Tambourin. Tamtam.
baguettes de timb.
Harpe.

LA PYTHONISSE: Om! Om! Par le feu et par l'eau, par la parole et par le souffle,
DIE HEXE: Om! Om! Bei dem Feuer, bei dem Wasser, bei dem Worte, bei dem

Largo, poco a poco più animato. ♩= 66

Violon I.
Violon II.
Alto.
Violoncelle.
Contre-Basse.

① ♩= 80
Pte Fl.
Fl.
Clar.
Cl.b.
Cymb.
Gr. C.
Tamb.
Tamt.
Harpe.
Cymb.
par le regard et par l'ouïe,
romps le lien de ta racine,
brise le sceau qui ferme l'urne.
Wind, beim Gesichte, beim Gehör,
brich die Schranke, brich den
Schlüssel, der die Urne schließt!
Apparais! Apparais!
C'est l'heure.
Erscheine! Erscheine!
Es ist die Stunde!
Om! Om! Je t'appelle et t'ad-
Om! Om! Aus Scheols Abgrund
① ♩= 80
Viol.I.
Pte Fl.
Fl.
Clar.
Cl.b.
Tamb.
Tamt.
Harpe.
jure: sors du gouffre noir du Schéol, rentre dans le temple
aux neuf portes.
rufe ich dich auf! Kehr' wieder in den Tempel der neun
Türen!
Apparais! Apparais!
Erscheine! Erscheine!
Viol.I.

Further examples of similar stature are found in *Amphion* (34 - 44) and *Jeanne d'Arc au bûcher* (Scene III 'Les voix de la terre', Scene IV 'Jeanne livrée aux bêtes' and Scene VII 'Catherine et Marguerite'). A case could be made for the passages of rather slighter substance in *La danse des morts* (I 'Dialogue' and V 'La réponse de Dieu') and *Nicolas de Flue* (Act I No. 10, Act II No. 15 and Act III No. 23) to be included in the same category, but the enormous bulk of examples of spoken text with musical background which remains cannot, with integrity, be categorized as melodramatic in the true sense of the word (as exhibited by the examples already cited), nor can it be described as just pure narration (i.e. with no musical background).

The second category is a hybrid of pure narration and melodrama. Frequently chords are sustained when the *récitant* is telling the story between phrases of the chorus and/or orchestra. The words are written out between bars placed above the vocal score, indicating that the line should be delivered whilst the note or chord is sustained and before the chorus sings their next phrase in the following bar. The use of this technique is to be found occasionally in *Jeanne d'Arc au bûcher,* in certain sections of *La danse des morts* and throughout *Nicolas de Flue*. In this latter score certain numbers are specifically designated as 'Récitatif et choral' (Nos. 16 and 17) or 'Récitatif des cloches et chœur final' (No. 30) — the *récitant* thus embodies the spirit of both narration and traditional recitative.

This hybrid second category can be subdivided in the same way as that for the pure narration, with a further subdivision according to whether or not some form of notation is used:

(i) Spoken narration of story with musical background	(a) Notated:	*Antigone,* *Jeanne d'Arc au bûcher*
	(b) Without notation:	*Jeanne d'Arc au bûcher* *La danse des morts* *Nicolas de Flue*
(ii) Character dialogue with musical background	(a) Notated:	*Jeanne d'Arc au bûcher*
	(b) Without notation:	*Amphion* *Jeanne d'Arc au bûcher* *Nicolas de Flue.*

Examples of all these four types are contained in the three quotations from *Jeanne d'Arc au bûcher* below (see Music Example 77 (i), (ii) and (iii) pages, 344-55).

Music Example 77: *Jeanne d'Arc au bûcher*:
(i) 10B [3] - [6]

Clar.B.
3e Trb.
JEANNE: Qui m'appelle? Qui est-ce qui m'appelle? Qui est-ce qui a dit Jeanne? Frère DOMINIQUE: Ne me reconnais-tu pas?
JOAN: Who is calling me? Who is it that is calling? Who is it that said Joan? Brother DOMINIC: And do you know me not?
JEANNE: Wer ruft mich? Wer ist's, der mich ruft? Wer rief mit Namen mich, Jeanne? Bruder DOMINIK: Erkennst du mich nicht?
Frère Dom.
Jeanne!
Joan!
Jeanne!
bocca chiusa
Altos
bocca chiusa
Bas
2ds Vns
Altos
Div
TUTTI
Celli
C.B.

JEANNE: Je reconnais l'habit de Dominique, la robe blanche et le manteau noir.

Frère DOMINIQUE: Ma robe blanche que mes frères de Paris et de Rouen ont souillée d'une telle souillure que ni la soude, ni l'herbe à foulon, ne suffiront à l'effacer.

JEANNE: Frère Dominique, la bonte de Dieu y suffira et le sang de cette fille innocente.

Frère DOMINIQUE: Jeanne, ma soeur, ainsi tu m'as reconnu?

JEANNE: Frère, frère Dominique, nous sommes des animaux de la même laine! Et moi je suis quelqu'un dans le troupeau qui reconnait la voix de son conducteur.

Frère DOMINIQUE: Puisque mes frères et mes fils m'ont trahi; puisque ceux qui devraient être la puissante voix du Vrai Se sont fait à contre-Dieu tes accusateurs et tes bourreaux, Jeanne. Puisque la parole entre ces mauvais doigts entre-mêlés est devenue grimoire. C'est moi-même, Dominique, moi Dominique, qui du ciel suis descendu vers toi avec ce livre.

JEANNE: Dominique, frere Dominique, tous ces temps, tous ces temps que voici J'ai vu beaucoup de plumes à l'œuvre autour de moi.

Frère DOMINIQUE: Tout cela a fait un livre.

JEANNE: Cette voix terrible qui me questionnait et toutes ces plumes sans relâche autour de moi. Toutes ces plumes sur le parchemin qui grincent, tout cela a fait un livre. Tout cela a fait un livre et moi, je ne sais pas lire.

Frere DOMINIQUE: Le livre que je t'apporte pour le comprendre; il n'y a pas besoin de savoir ni A ni B. Ce paquet de mots que ces Limousins sur la terre ont ficelé dans le latin de Fouarre; cette procedure qu'ils ont pétrie dans le patois de Coutances. Les Anges pour tous les temps l'ont traduit dans le ciel.

JEANNE: Lis donc, Frère, au nom de Dieu, pour moi et moi, je regarde par dessus ton épaule.

(Il s'assoit sur la premiere marche de l'escalier)

JOAN: *I know the habit all Dominicans wear, the frock of white and scapula of black.*

Brother DOMINIC: *My frock of white that all my brethren from Paris and from Rouen did defile with such defilement, Nor fuller's earth nor soda can effect its cleansing.*

JOAN: *O Brother Dominic, the Grace of God will that effect with the blood of this innocent maiden.*

Brother DOMINIC: *O Joan, my sister, so you do know me now?*

JOAN: *My brother, brother Dominic, we all are sheep that wear the same fleece! And I but one of the flock that knows the shepherd's voice.*

Brother DOMINIC: *Since by my brethren and my sons I have been betrayed, since those who should have been the mighty voice of Truth Have made themselves 'gainst God your hangmen and your prosecutors, Joan ... Since that the Word 'twixt wicked meddling hands is jargon made, 'Tis Dominic himself, I Dominic, come down from heaven before you with this book.*

JOAN: *Dominic, my brother Dominic, through all these hours _ through all these hours till now I have seen a myriad pens at work all, all around me.*

Brother DOMINIC: *All that did make a book.*

JOAN *That voice of dread with endless questioning all those unceasing pens all, all around. All of those pens upon the parchment scraping. All that did make a book. All that did make a book, and I, I cannot read.*

Brother DOMINIC: *To understant the book I bring to you there is no need to know or A or B This bundle of words these botchers of LIMOGES have knotted together in dog-latin of FOUARRE, all the proceedings they have kneaded in the lingo of COUTANCES, the Angels for all time to come have translated into heaven.*

JOAN: *Read to me, Brother, then, in the name of God; I'll follow, as you read, over your shoulder.*

(He sits on the first step of the staircase)

JEANNE: Ich erkenne das Kleid des Dominikaners, das weisse Kleid und den schwarzen Mantel.

Bruder DOMINIK: Das weisse Kleid, das meine Brüder von Paris und Rouen mit solchem Schmutz bedeckt, dass weder Messer noch Lauge es je zu reinigen vermöchten.

JEANNE: Bruder Dominik, Gottes Güte wird es vermögen und das Blut dieses unschuldigen Kindes

Bruder DOMINIK: Jeanne, meine Schwester, so hast du mich erkannt?

JEANNE: Bruder, mein Bruder Dominik, wir sind Geschöpfe aus gleichem Stoff erzeugt. Und ich, ich bin ein Schafchen aus der Herde, die da erkennt die Stimme ihres Hirten.

Bruder DOMINIK: Da meine Bruder und meine Sohne mich verrieten, da die, so der Wahrheit machtiger Mund sein wollten, sich gegen den Willen Gottes zu deinen Anklagern und Richtern gemacht haben und das Wort unter den scheinheiligen Händen zum Zerrbild schufen, bin ich es selbst, ich, Dominik, der mit diesem Buch zu dir vom Himmel herniederstieg.

JEANNE: Dominik, Bruder Dominik, allzeit sah ich so viele Schreiber rings um mich her am Werk.

Bruder DOMINIK: All dieses birgt mein Buch.

JEANNE: Diese schreckliche Stimme, die mich befrug, und all diese eifrigen Schreiber rings um mich. All diese kreischenden Federn auf dem Pergament, dies alles ward ein Buch, ein machtig Buch. Und ich, ich kann nicht lesen.

Bruder DOMINIK: Dass du das Buch verstündest, das ich dir gebracht, dazu bedarfst du keiner Schulweisheit. _ Das Bündel Worte, das diese Strassenkehrer in ihrem Küchenlatein geschrieben, dieser Prozess, den sie in ihrer derben Mundart sich zurechtgemacht, die Engel haben es auf ewige Zeiten in ihre himmliche Sprache übersetzt.

JEANNE: So lies denn, Bruder, im Nanem Gottes, dass ich es höre, derweil ich uber deine Schulter schaue.

(Er setzt sich auf die erste Treppenstufe)

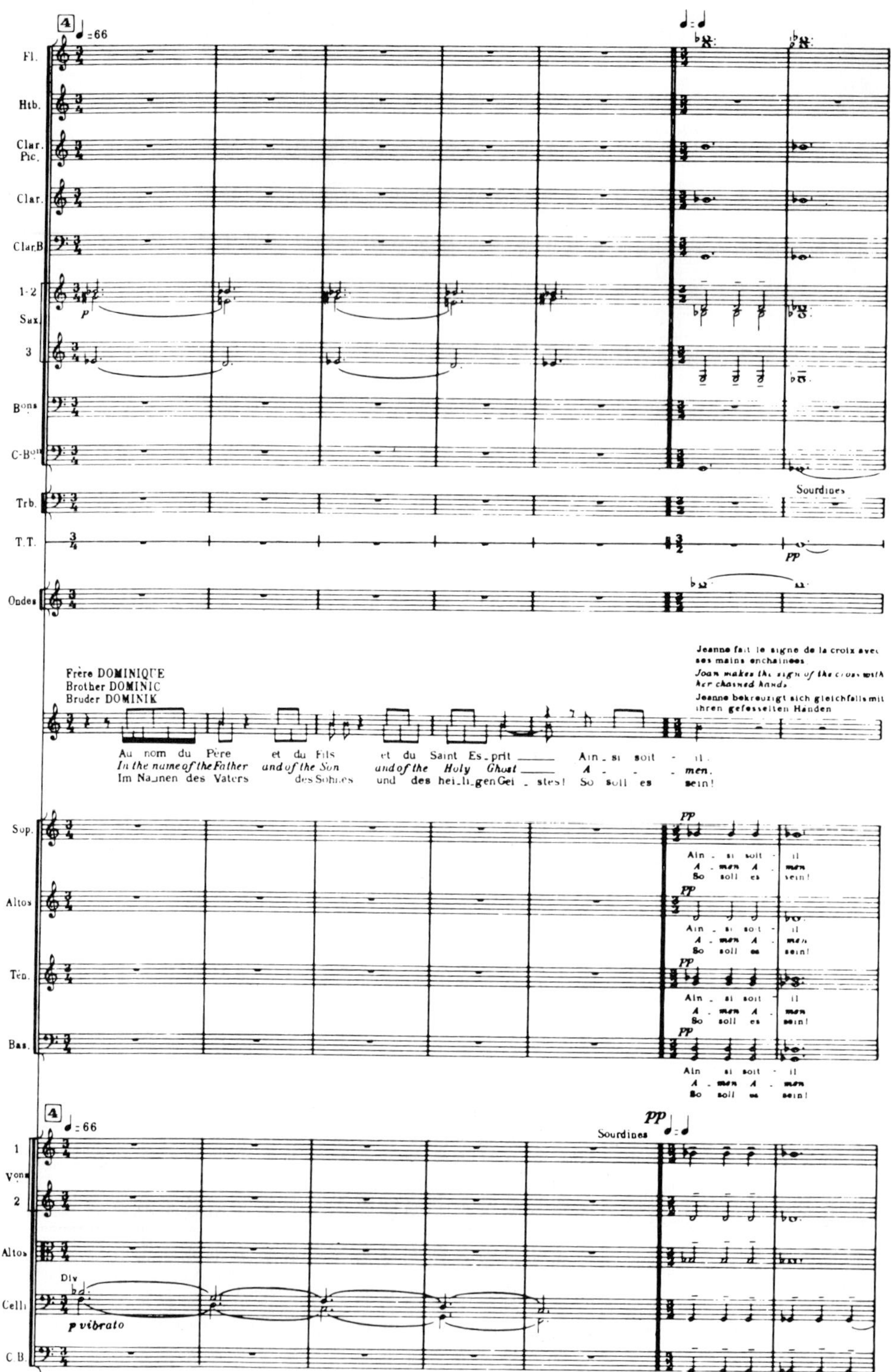

4
♩= 66
Fl.
Htb.
Clar. Pic.
Clar.
Clar.B
1-2
Sax.
3
Bons
C-Bon
Trb.
T.T.
Ondes
Sourdines
pp
Frère DOMINIQUE
Brother DOMINIC
Bruder DOMINIK
Au nom du Père et du Fils et du Saint Es_prit Ain_si soit - il.
In the name of the Father and of the Son and of the Holy Ghost A - - - men.
Im Namen des Vaters des Sohnes und des hei_ligen Gei_stes! So soll es sein!
Jeanne fait le signe de la croix avec ses mains enchainées.
Joan makes the sign of the cross with her chained hands.
Jeanne bekreuzigt sich gleichfalls mit ihren gefesselten Händen
Sop.
Altos
Tén.
Bas.
Ain_si soit - il
A_men A_men
So soll es sein!
Vons
1
2
Altos
Celli
C.B.
Div.
p vibrato

Scène III . LES VOIX DE LA TERRE
Scene III . THE VOICES OF THE EARTH
III.Szene. DIE STIMMEN DER ERDE
5
♩=62
Sax.
Bons
C-Bon
1-2 Trb.
3 & Bas.
Frere Dom.
Jeanne! Jeanne! Jeanne! Hérétique Sor _ cière Re _ lap _ se
Joan! Joan! Joan! He_re_tic Sor_ce_ress Apostate
Jeanne! Jeanne! Jeanne! Ket_ze_rin! He _ xe! Abtrünnige!
enlevez les Sourdines
1 Vons 2
Altos
Celli
C.B.
1° & 2°
2° & 3°
En_nemie de Dieu En_nemie du Roi En_ne_mie du Peuple Qu'on l'en_lève qu'on la tue qu'on la brû _ le
En_e_my of God En_e_my of King En_e_my of Country Let's prisonher let us kill let us burn her
Got_tes_fein _ din! Königs _ fein_din Feindin des Vol_kes! Fort mir ihr! Man töte, man verbrenne sie!
1.2 Vons

(Reproduit avec l'autorisation des EDITIONS SALABERT, Paris, propriétaires de l'œuvre.)

(ii) 1B 15 - 1B 17

Scène IV. JEANNE LIVRÉE AUX BÊTES
Scene IV. JOAN GIVEN UP TO THE BEASTS
IV. Szene JEANNE DEN TIEREN AUSGELIEFERT
(Entre l'Appariteur)
(The Usher enters)
(Es erscheint der Zeremonienmeister)
15
Fl
Htb.
Clar. Pic.
Clar.
Clar. B
3 Bons
C-Bon
1-2 Trp 3
1-2 Trb 3
enlevez les Sourdines
enlevez les Sourdines
Basse
Wood Bloc
G.C.
Cymb.
LE HÉRAUT (parle)
THE HERALD (speaks)
DER HEROLD
La Cour! fai-tes si-len-ce!
The Court! pray be si-lent!
Die Richter Schwei-get stil-le!
Sop.
Altos
Ten.
Bas.
1 Vons 2
Altos
Celli
C.B.

1-2
Trp.
3
1-2
Trb.
3
Wood Bloc
Tam Tam
le H.
mf
p
Le Ti - gre!
The Ti - ger!
Der Ti - ger!
L'APPARITEUR (parlé
THE USHER (speaks)
DER ZEREMONIENMEISTER
Qui se - ra le Président?
Who shall be the Pre - sident?
Wer besteigt den Richterstuhl?
Le Ti - gre se
The Ti - ger sends up -
Der Ti - ger ent -
Sop.
Altos
Ten.
Bas.
1-2
Sax.
1 2
Trb.
3
f
G.C.
Cymb.
le H.
Le Renard!
The Fox!
Der Fuchs!
Le
The
Die
l'Ap.
ré - cu - se
- o - logies
schuldigt sich
Le Renard dit qu'il est mala - de
The Fox says he is indisposed
Der Fuchs sagt, dass er krank geworden

Pte Fl.
Clar. Pic.
Cymb.
Le H.
Ser_pent!
Ser_pent!
Schlange!
Mais
But
Doch.
l'Ap.
Le Serpent s'est sif_flé lui-même au fond d'un trou.
The Serpent is hissing protests a_lone in a pit.
Die Schlange pfiff in ihrem Loch__ sich selber aus.
Sop.
Le Ser_pent!
The Ser_pent!
Die Schlange!
Altos
Le Ser_pent!
The Ser_pent!
Die Schlange!
Ten.
Le Ser_pent!
The Ser_pent!
Die Schlange!
Le Ser_pent!
The Ser_pent!
Die Schlange!
Pte Fl.
Clar. Pic.
Timb.
Wood Bloc
G.C.
Le H.
alors, il n'y a personne pour prési_der?
who then? is there then no one for pre_sident?
wie? Dann ist ja niemand der den Vorsitz führt?
Mais a_lors?
But who then?
Doch wie?
Si! si! si! si! si!
See! see! see! see! see!
Doch! doch! doch! doch! doch!
si fait il y a quelqu'un.
see there! here is some one now.
doch! doch! Es ist ei_ner da.
Altos
Mais a_lors?
But who then?
Doch wie?
Si! si! si! si! si!
See! see! see! see! see!
Doch! doch! doch! doch! doch!
si fait il y a quelqu'un.
see there! here is some one now.
doch! doch! Es ist ei_ner da.
Ten.
Mais a_lors?
But who then?
Doch wie?
Si! si! si! si!
See! see! see! see!
Doch! doch! doch! doch!
si fait il y a quel_
see there! here is some one
doch! doch! Es ist ei_ner
Bas
Si! si! si! si!
See! see! see! see!
Doch! doch! doch! doch!
si fait il y a quel_
see there! here is some one
doch! doch! Es ist ei_ner

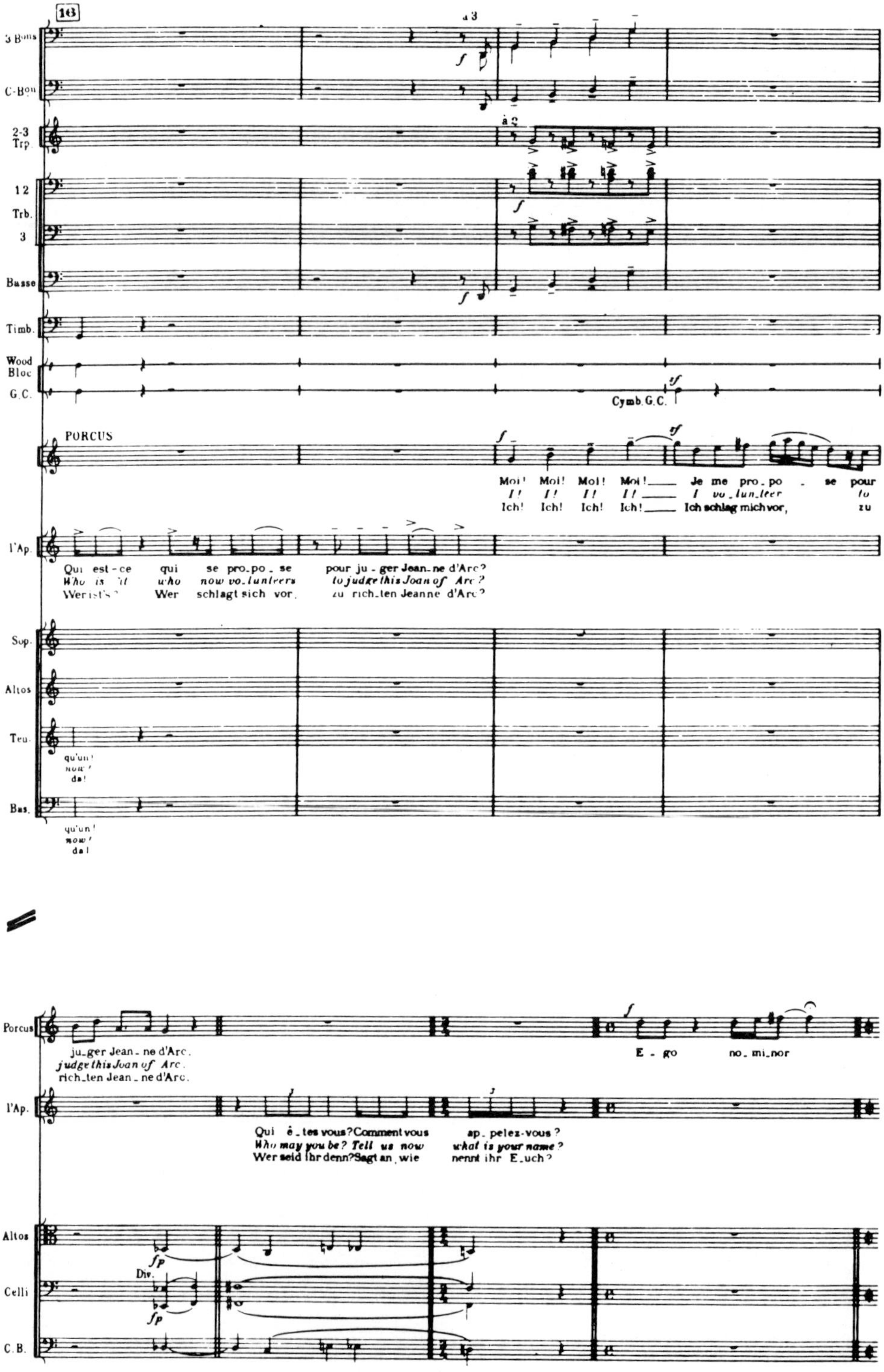

16

3 Bons
C-Bon
a 3
2-3 Trp.
à 2
1 2 Trb. 3
Basse
Timb.
Wood Bloc
G.C.
Cymb. G.C.

PORCUS

Moi! Moi! Moi! Moi! Je me pro-po-se pour
I! I! I! I! I vo-lun-teer to
Ich! Ich! Ich! Ich! Ich schlag mich vor, zu

l'Ap.

Qui est-ce qui se pro-po-se pour ju-ger Jean-ne d'Arc?
Who is it who now vo-lunteers to judge this Joan of Arc?
Wer ist's? Wer schlagt sich vor, zu rich-ten Jeanne d'Arc?

Sop.
Altos
Ten.
qu'un! now! da!
Bas.
qu'un! now! da!

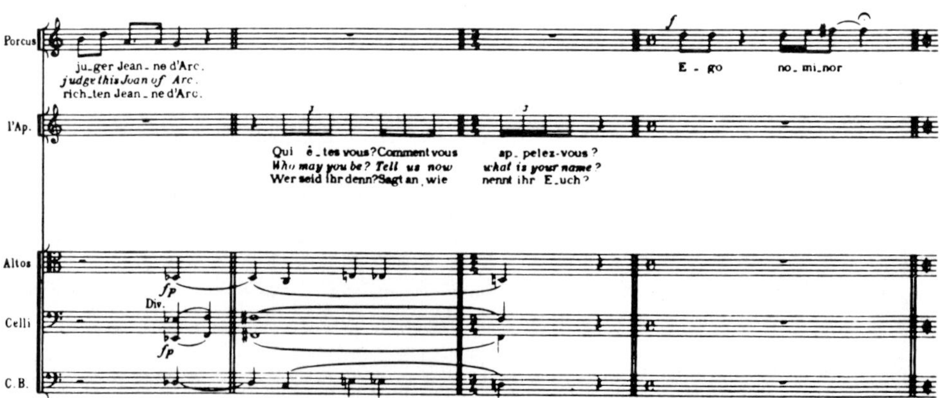

(iii) 28 - 1B 29

28
PORCUS
Faites entrer l'accusée !
Let the prisoner appear!
Führt die Angeklagte vor!
28

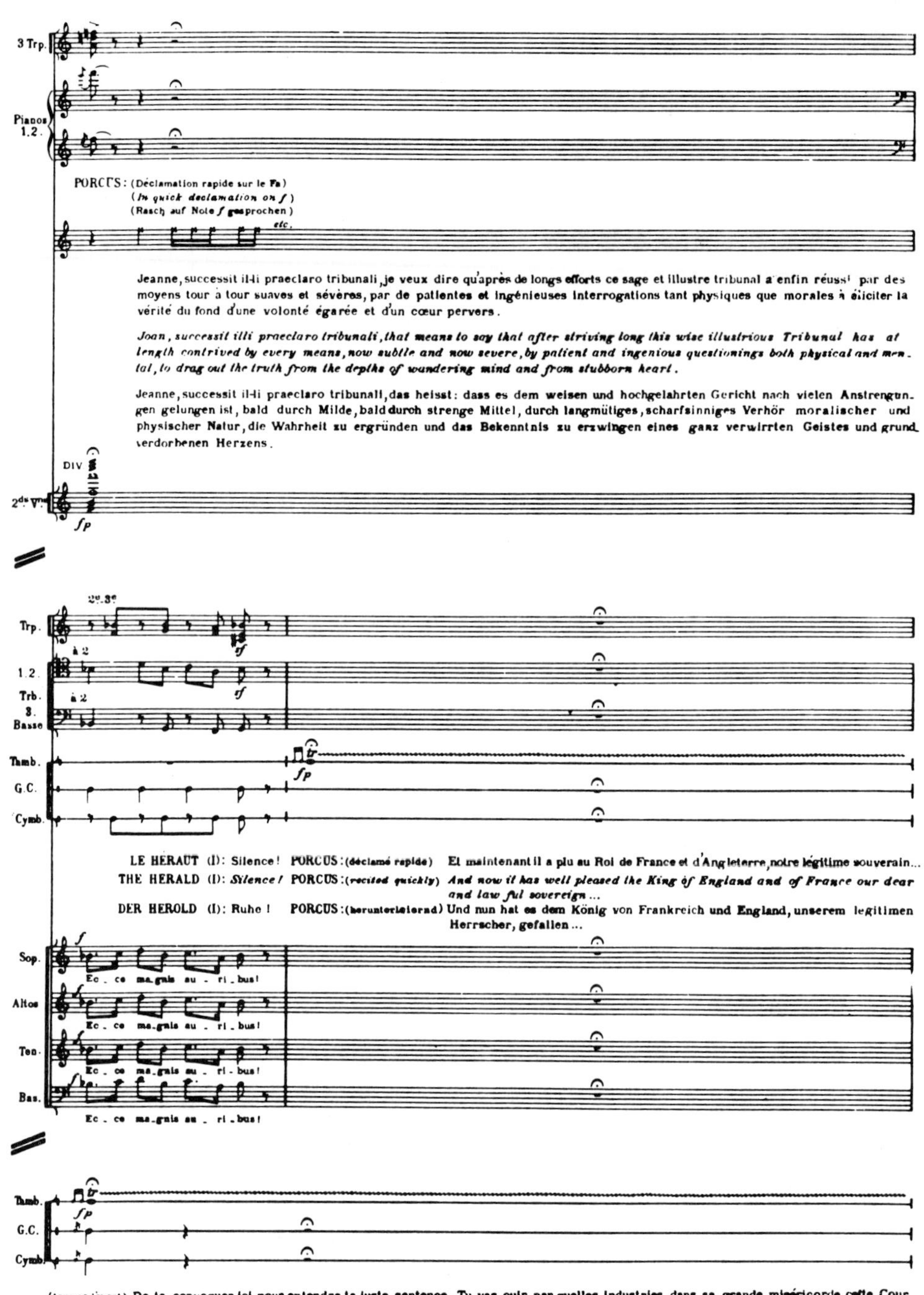
3 Trp.
Pianos 1.2.
PORCUS: (Déclamation rapide sur le Fa)
(In quick declamation on f)
(Rasch auf Note f gesprochen)
etc.
Jeanne, successit il-li praeclaro tribunali, je veux dire qu'après de longs efforts ce sage et illustre tribunal a enfin réussi par des moyens tour à tour suaves et sévères, par de patientes et ingénieuses interrogations tant physiques que morales à éliciter la vérité du fond d'une volonté égarée et d'un cœur pervers.
Joan, successit illi praeclaro tribunali, that means to say that after striving long this wise illustrious Tribunal has at length contrived by every means, now subtle and now severe, by patient and ingenious questionings both physical and mental, to drag out the truth from the depths of wandering mind and from stubborn heart.
Jeanne, successit il-li praeclaro tribunali, das heisst: dass es dem weisen und hochgelahrten Gericht nach vielen Anstrengungen gelungen ist, bald durch Milde, bald durch strenge Mittel, durch langmütiges, scharfsinniges Verhör moralischer und physischer Natur, die Wahrheit zu ergründen und das Bekenntnis zu erzwingen eines ganz verwirrten Geistes und grundverdorbenen Herzens.
DIV
2ds Vns
fp
Trp.
à 2
1.2.
Trb.
3.
Basse
Tamb.
G.C.
Cymb.
LE HERAUT (I): Silence! PORCUS: (déclamé rapide) Et maintenant il a plu au Roi de France et d'Angleterre, notre légitime souverain...
THE HERALD (I): Silence! PORCUS: (recited quickly) And now it has well pleased the King of England and of France our dear and lawful sovereign...
DER HEROLD (I): Ruhe! PORCUS: (herunterleiernd) Und nun hat es dem König von Frankreich und England, unserem legitimen Herrscher, gefallen...
Sop.
Altos
Ten.
Bas.
Ec - ce ma-gnis au - ri - bus!

(tous se lèvent) De te convoquer ici pour entendre ta juste sentence. Tu vas ouïr par quelles industries dans sa grande miséricorde, cette Cour sage et illustre que moi Cauchon je préside...

(everybody gets up) To summon you to this place to hear your lawful sentence. Now therefore, list with what great care in all its mercy, this Court, so wise, illustrious, where I, CAUCHON, do preside,

(alle erheben sich) ... dich hierher zu berufen, um ein gerechtes Urteil zu vernehmen. Du sollst nun hören, mit welch gewaltigem Eifer in seinem Mitleid dies löbliche Gericht, das ich mit Namen Cauchon präsidiere...

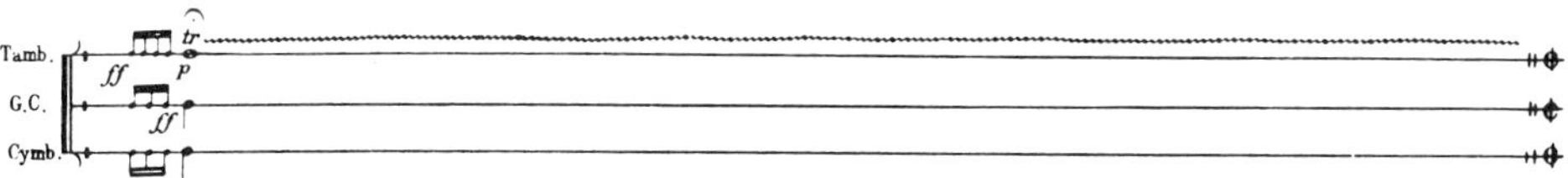

(tous se lèvent) A décidé de te débarrasser grâce à la flamme claire du feu de ce noir démon à laquelle tu t'es criminellement enchevêtrée. Mais auparavant nous voulons encore une fois de ta bouche cet aveu solennel qui est nécessaire à la securité de nos consciences ; A genoux !

(everybody gets up) Is now resolved to disencumber you with aid of the pure flame of fire, from this black demon by whom you are so criminally entangled. But, first of all, we'd hear yet once again from your own lips that most solem confession that's needful for the safety of our conscience. On your knees.

(alle erheben sich) Beschlossen hat, dich dank der hellen Flamme des Feuers von diesem Höllengeiste zu befrein, dem du, Verbrecherin, verfallen bist. Jedoch zuvor wollen wir einmal noch aus deinem Mund dein feierlich Geständnis hier vernehmen, dess' unser ruhiges Gewissen wohl bedarf. Auf die Knie !

Although there are no instances of a narrator in oratorios or cantatas composed prior to *Le roi David,* Holst's *Hymn of Jesus* (1917) is clearly a precedent for Honegger's first use of rhythmically-notated choric speech in *Cris du monde.* This device is employed extensively in each of the three subsequent scores, *Jeanne d'Arc au bûcher, La danse des morts* and *Nicolas de Flue.* Honegger, like Holst, takes the stems, flags and beams of traditional notation, but from his initial use of the technique in *Cris du monde* there are limited attempts to represent a pitch approximation. Although the alterations in position of the symbols only call for an inflection in the direction indicated, his intentions are consolidated in many cases by the use of the symbol ⨯ to indicate his desire that the voice should aim for the particular pitch notated (see Music Example 78 below).

Music Example 78: *Cris du monde,* basses, [19] - 5A [19]

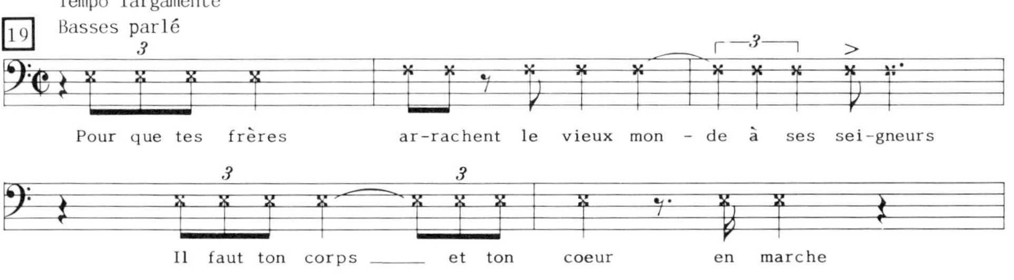

Only on a very limited scale in *Jeanne d'Arc au bûcher* does Honegger ever come near to requiring a rendition which would be a close parallel to the *Sprechstimme* in Schönberg's *Pierrot Lunaire* of 1912 (see Music Example 79 overleaf).

Music Example 79: *Jeanne d'Arc au bûcher,* 6B 26 - 1B 26

Part III: *Une cantate de Noël*

In the light of Honegger's accumulated experience in writing successful large-scale dramatic choral works, his understanding of the human voice both speaking and singing and his sincere and deeply felt religious sentiments, it is tragic that he should have embarked upon a setting of the Passion without being able to see the project realized.

In the small village of Selzach, to the west of Soleure, there was a long-established tradition of triennial performances of the Passion story each Sunday during the summer months. Despite being a much less spectacular affair than its famous counterpart in Oberammergau, the interest aroused by this uniquely Swiss *confrérie dramatique* in the neighbouring villages and towns of the Canton of Argovie was sufficient to ensure financial support and capacity audiences in the open-air wooden theatre for each of the fifteen to twenty performances. For many years the spectacle had been organized, produced and directed by three local men: a priest, H. -H. German Bobst, a musician, Erwin Widmer, and a quite famous retired man of the theatre, Albert Berchtold. However, a new committee was formed in 1939 to arrange the subsequent performances and not only was a splendid new theatre to be built under the direction of the internationally-famous Swiss architect and designer Roman Clemens, but the distinguished Bernese poet Cäsar von Arx was to be commissioned to create a *jeu de la Passion* for Honegger to set to music. The outbreak of war naturally caused many setbacks, including the cancellation of the proposed inauguration of the new Passion in 1942. Nevertheless, the building of the new theatre went ahead and von Arx began writing, scene by scene, the text for a score that would last some seven to eight hours — the idea being that each performance should take a whole day. The morning would be devoted to a substantial prelude which would set the scene by using relevant Old Testament texts. After lunch and in the evening, the New Testament story of the Passion of Our Lord Jesus Christ would unfold and culminate in the scene at Calvary.

As the war dragged on the prospect was that the creation of the work would have to be delayed until 1948 and so neither librettist nor composer worked with much haste. Honegger showed José Bruyr drafts of sections of the work right up until December 1944[10] when tragedy struck: Cäsar von Arx committed suicide and Honegger superstitiously refused to carry on with the project even though the libretto was complete and most of his music written.[11] The musical sketches and drafts were shelved and it was not until 1952 that he culled his last work from these private pages. He was prompted to do this when he was asked by Paul Sacher to provide a new choral work for the twenty-fifth anniversary of his Basle Chamber Choir. The extent of his incapacity due to the severe stroke he had suffered in 1948, combined with his desire not to disappoint Sacher — who, together with Ansermet, Koussevitsky and Münch had consistently done so much to promote his music all over the world — drove him to assemble his last work in this manner. The score of *Une cantate de Noël* is dated 'le 25 janvier 1953, d'après l'esquisse du 24 janvier 1941', and is orchestrated for the same forces he was to have had at his disposal in Selzach — mixed chorus, children's choir, orchestra, organ and solo baritone. The première was given in Zürich by Paul Sacher and his Basle forces on 16 December 1953.

The work is in three main sections — the first (1 - 15) is an expression of universal despair and pleading; the second (16 - 25) is a musical and textual quodlibet where various celebrations of belief are superimposed; and the third (28 - 36) is a unified statement of faith. The work has an instrumental prelude and coda and the three main sections are separated from each other by two accompanied interludes for solo baritone (15 - 16) and (25 - 28).

In the first section the chorus sings the Latin psalm text sentences 'De profundis clamavi ad te Domine' and 'Domine exaudi vocem meam', together with the eighteenth century hymn text:

Oh come, oh come Emmanuel!
Oh hear the prayer of Israel.
Our tears have never ceased to flow.
We weep and wait Thee here below.
O come thou star of truth so bright.
Drive out our darkness with thy light.
Out of our world of sin and strife,
O bring us back to Light and Life.

The children's choir delivers the heavenly messages:

Now rejoice, O Israel, thou soon shall see Emmanuel

and

Now rejoice, O Israel, behold he comes Emmanuel.

In the first brief interlude the solo baritone sings 'Be not afraid for I am come to bring you tidings of great joy to all mankind. Christ is born for our Salvation; born in a stable in Bethlehem, there you may see Him in a manger lying, the Holy Child.' In the second section the tunes and various verses of the popular traditional Christmas carols 'Es ist ein Reis entsprungen', 'Il est né le divin enfant', 'Vom Himmel hoch', 'Stille Nacht' and 'O du fröliche, O du selige' are combined (as far as 3A 18) with a setting of the words 'Gloria in excelsis Deo'.

In the second interlude, the solo baritone sings 'Gloria in excelsis Deo, et in terra pax hominibus bonae voluntatis' while the children's choir (and afterwards the contraltos and basses of the chorus) anticipates the incipit of the text of the final section: 'Laudate Dominum omnes gentes, laudate eum omnes populi'.

Musically, the first section of the work consists of several subsections which are interrelated and cohesively bound together in a number of technical ways familiar from Honegger's previous works (see Diagram 42 opposite).

The *Largo* opening of the work is scored for organ, harp, violas and cellos, and sees the firm establishment of the tonality of C major. The first section starts with a move to the area of the supertonic minor (d) as a means of increasing basic tension for initial impetus, and there is an orchestral statement of small-scale embryonic thematic material (A) in addition to the tenors' and

Diagram 42:

Une cantate de Noël — first section

Subsections	Rehearsal numbers:		Principal tonalities:
		Organ/orchestral Introduction	C
(A/B)	1	Orch./chorus (wordless)	d
(A)	2	Orch./chorus (wordless)	e♭
(C)	3	Orch./chorus:—De profundis clamavi	sequential semitonal moves from e♭ to b♭
(B′)	4	Orch./chorus:—Domine exaudi vocem meam	b♭
(A′)	5	Orch./chorus:— (wordless)	e
(C′ /A″)	6	Orch./chorus:—De profundis clamavi	sequential semitonal moves from c to g
(B″)	7	Orch./chorus (wordless)	After an initial reference to g it changes constantly in response to the implications of the cantus-firmus (and subsequently) before settling in A♭ at 13
(D)	10	Orch./chorus:—O come, O come Emmanuel	
(E)	13	Orch./children's choir:—Now rejoice O Israel	A♭
(D′)	4A13	Orch./chorus: — O come, O come Emmanuel	as at 10
(E′)	4B15	Orch./children's choir: — Now rejoice O Israel	A♭

basses' theme (B). The same thematic material (C) is used for both of the choral statements of 'De profundis clamavi ad te Domine'. The *vocalise* theme (B) returns between 4 and 5 and is then used in cantus-firmus fashion for the essentially orchestral transition between 7 and the climactic chorus entry at 10.

The tonal design is, as usual, heavily dependent on the colourful and dramatic use of tertiary patterning. This is particularly evident in the first brief interlude ([15] - [16]), where the tonality shifts immediately from A♭ major to F minor and there is simultaneously a strong suggestion of C♭ major by both the three-part trumpet fanfare and the solo baritone's line. The side-stepping to F♯ minor which then occurs therefore comes as no surprise because a couple of dominant-tonic moves (f♯→b[c♭]→E), neatly take the tonality to E major for the start of the middle section, and a whole series of tertiary-related key centres are thus firmly bound together.

The second section is one of the most remarkable pieces of polyphonic, polytextual and polythematic creations in all musical literature. The ease with which Honegger appears to achieve his aim is a monument to his technique and the success of this quodlibet a veritable symbol of his art. The tonality moves from E major ([16] -) to A♭ major ([18] -) — a tertiary move which relates the spirit of this section to the prophecy of its coming at the end of the previous section. From A♭ major it moves via A♭ minor (5B [20] -) back to E major (3A [20] -) and hence on to its dominant ([21] -) when a series of dominant (B) or dominant of the dominant (F♯) pedals support the climax of the quodlibet as all five carol melodies and texts are combined simultaneously.

The resolution of the dominant pedal point comes when the second interlude emerges at [25]. A series of highly chromatic harmonies shifts the tonality from E major to G♯/A♭ major for the solo child's anticipatory quotation from the final section, 'Laudate Dominum omnes gentes'. Tritone moves of A♭ major to D minor and then B♭ major to E major, colour the solo baritone and chorus statements before the modulation is quickly and finally made to C major, which reigns supreme for the whole of the last section and the concluding instrumental coda — the latter being almost as remarkable a quodlibet as the second main section of the work.

Stylistically, the work is full of Honegger's fingerprints. The trait of patterning lines by the interval of a third (major or minor) which reached its zenith in *Jeanne d'Arc au bûcher* is also obvious in many of the melodic creations of this work — the bass ostinato which starts the first section and the vocal parts after [2] are perhaps the best examples. The harmonies are still basically as diatonic as ever (moments of chromatic sliding around are few and far between compared to many of the earlier scores — the only proper examples coming in the two interludes), but the harmonic colouring effected by the utilization of added notes is consistently engaging. There are times when it is very simple, like the addition of the supertonic to avoid too obvious a tonality of the dominant minor (g) after [1]. There are more piquant examples such as after [2] (the E♭ minor is constantly coloured by the prominence of the raised fourth (A♮) and seventh (D♮) which, because of their allegiance to the tonality of the dominant, prevent the tonic tonality from 'slipping' by acting as the dominant of its own sub-dominant), and after [4] (the B♭ minor is not only coloured by the persistent raising of the fourth [E♮] but also by the harmonic ostinato consisting of the second and flattened third [C and D♭]. On some occasions the constructions are positively polyharmonic with Honegger, as usual, clarifying the principles and logic of the whole with his penchant for contrary motion (see Music Example 80 below).

Music Example 80: *Une cantate de Noël*, (10 - 4A 10)

(Reproduit avec l'autorisation des EDITIONS SALABERT, Paris, propriétaires de l'œuvre.)

As with all his previous scores many sections of this work involve a construction on or below scalic patterns. The chromatically-rising ostinato pattern between [3] and [4] is so simple yet so effective in its achievement both of a move from E♭ minor to B♭ minor and an overall *crescendo* of intensity — the same device is found between [6] and [7].

However, the use of scalic figures in contrary motion to the bassoon/horn/double bass line two bars before [10] to give final momentum to a long, sustained *crescendo* is a prime example of a questionably overworked facet of Honegger's style. The weakness of this rather facile device is compounded in its use two bars before [28] by the chromatic slithering of the harmonies employed as the tonality shifts from E major to C major. Moments of inconsistency of style such as these are very rare in this work, but are highlighted by the excellence of the passages which precede them, in particular that between [7] and [10] in which Honegger achieves a symphonic buildup beneath the choral cantus-firmus through a masterly handling of motivic development and rhythmic progression which is worthy of many of his finest purely orchestral symphonic scores.

The orchestration is, as usual, dominated by his geological strata-like approach in response to the polyphonic nature of most of the musical fabric. This can be appreciated by reference to a short and simple example such as [2] - [3], and to a more extensive and complex passage like [7] - [10]. Some of Honegger's most felicitous touches of orchestral colour occur in his scoring of ostinati or pedal points — the move from two horns and harp after [1], to clarinets and bassoons at [2], to two horns and *pizzicato* violins after [3] and, finally, to clarinets and harp ([4] -) for the respective harmonic pedal points is one such example. The organ has a very important solo part in the opening and closing instrumental sections, but also plays a fully integrated accompaniment role in the main sections. Two of the most beautiful textures in the work both involve the organ: the first being the organ, harp and violin accompaniment for the children's choir parts after [13] and before [15]; the second, the passages for organ and three trumpets in the first interlude for solo baritone ([15] -).

Many of the large-scale choruses in earlier works contain far more technical difficulties than are found in this piece — particularly in the final 'Laudate Dominum'. As a direct result the amount of orchestral doubling of the vocal lines for the purposes of support is almost negligible and the degree of translucency achieved through the almost chamber-like scoring is rather unusual for Honegger. The writing for chorus is also more restrained in comparison with previous scores, particularly as no obvious opportunities for choric speech present themselves in a work of this nature. One of the most prominent features of the choral writing in this score, as in all the previous works, is the degree of the pairing of lines. For long stretches of the first section the sopranos and contraltos are pitted together against a single line for tenors and basses, and this is countered only by the pairing of sopranos/tenors and contraltos/basses five bars before [7]. Such interlockings of voices are employed to great effect in a harmonic context too (see Music Example 81 opposite).

Music Example 81: *Une cantate de Noël*, 9B [14] - 8A [14]

14
Htb.
Clar.
Bons
à 2
1.2. Cors
3.4.
1. Trp.
2.3.
Mettez les Sourdines
1.2. Trb.
3.
S.
ton se - cours Nous er-rons tous sans but ni fin O dé - si - gne nous
-nis er - hellt Wir ir-ren hier in Trug und Wahn O führ uns auf des
with thy light Out of our world of sin and strife O bring us back to
A.
ton se - cours Nous er-rons tous sans but ni fin O dé - si - gne nous
-nis er - hellt Wir ir-ren hier in Trug und Wahn O führ uns auf des
with thy light Out of our world of sin and strife O bring us back to
T.
ton se - cours Nous er-rons tous sans but ni fin O dé - si - gne nous
-nis er - hellt Wir ir-ren hier in Trug und Wahn O führ uns auf des
with thy light Out of our world of sin and strife O bring us back to
B.
ton se - cours Nous er-rons tous sans but ni fin O dé - si - gne nous
-nis er hellt Wir ir-ren hier in Trug und Wahn O führ uns auf des
with thy light Out of our world of sin and strife O bring us back to
14
I Viol.
II
Altos
Vlc.
C.B.

(Reproduit avec l'autorisation des EDITIONS SALABERT, Paris, propriétaires de l'œuvre.)

Critical reaction to this score was uniformly favourable. R. -A. Mooser[12] noted the concentration of drama and sensible emotion in such a relatively short work. He spoke, too, of the simple dignity of this imaginative score with its cyclic moods of gravity and mysticism. The combination of texts from the Catholic liturgy and popular Christmas carols for him was done in a remarkably successful way because the result is complete as well as beautifully wrought. Willy Tappolet[13] was also impressed by the symmetry of the whole and commented on the universal expression of humanity which is the character of the entire work. Bernard Gavoty[14] referred to the C major of the opening orchestral introduction, the final section and the orchestral coda as the viewing of eternity and pointed out that, through the universal language of the orchestra, the aspirations of the whole world were united in the final pages. For him the same sense of the miraculous is achieved in this score as in *Jeanne d'Arc au bûcher.* Willi Schuh[15] saw it as Honegger's finest achievement amongst a canon of works in which the principal aim had always been to create a score understandable and acceptable to the vast majority of non-musicians, and yet sufficiently free from banality to appeal to the minority of musical intelligentsia. He, like all the others, commented on the two most prodigious polyphonic creations and noted that in them Honegger had managed to achieve clarity without sacrificing either true counterpoint or harmonic richness. Bernard Gavoty[16] succeeded in providing a single expression of all their different viewpoints on the merits of the work when he wrote 'accept my word that it is a masterpiece'.

Unlike so many of his previous works, there is no difficulty in accepting this piece for categorization as a cantata. *La danse des morts* is similarly a cantata, although not labelled as such by either librettist or composer and the *Cantique de Pâques* must also be put in this classification, despite its brevity.[17] It is a simple matter to place the version he made of his incidental music for Morax's *Judith* together with his setting of Cocteau's *Antigone* in the genre designated on their title pages, namely opera. Problems start to arise, however, when an attempt is made to categorize the remaining works. Despite the title 'psaume symphonique', it is relatively uncontroversial to class the version of *Le roi David* which Honegger and Morax made in 1923 as an oratorio, particularly in view of the sacred subject matter, the prominence of the chorus, the employment of solo voices and the utilization of an orchestral accompaniment. Similarly, it is not unreasonable to permit *Nicolas de Flue* to be called an oratorio, even though Honegger borrows the term 'légende dramatique' from Berlioz's *La damnation de Faust. Jeanne d'Arc au bûcher* is subtitled 'oratorio dramatique' and must be admitted to the annals of oratorio in the same light as *Nicolas de Flue* and *Le roi David.*

If Haydn's *Die Jahreszeiten* is to be labelled an oratorio, then it is possible also to accept *Cris du monde* as such. Certainly its size and scope make it an ungainly suitor for the title of cantata, whilst simultaneously setting the scene for many other twentieth-century 'oratorios'. Valéry and Honegger subtitled *Amphion* a 'mélodrame'. Apart from the relatively brief middle section (when Amphion discovers the lyre and its magic powers) which is truly cast as a melodrama, the work as a whole should really be called a ballet — a descriptive title which would be a more accurate reflection of the nature of the bulk of the work.

Les aventures du roi Pausole is certainly an *opérette*, but his score for Morax's *La belle de Moudon* (since withdrawn) should not be so labelled because, consisting as it does of only nine brief choruses and four short arias which are separated by substantial amounts of spoken dialogue, it is little more than incidental music.

Nevertheless, although these works can be classified as cantatas or oratorios or operas, it is important to remember that they are all, individually, quite uniquely twentieth-century manifestations of these traditional genres. Many of the adaptations, developments and extensions which Honegger brought to bear — in particular the use of the *récitant* and a developed form of choric speech — had a fundamental influence on many other twentieth-century composers of large-scale choral works.

Notes to Chapter XI

[1]'Paul Claudel' in *Twentieth Century Authors,* edited by Stanley J. Kunitz and Howard Haycroft (New York, 1942), 285.

[2]Job 14. 14.

[3]Edward Agate in his English translation effects a separation of this section as a seventh by the addition of the heading *Affirmation*. There is no indication that Claudel had this in mind; neither is it a logical outcome of an understanding of the textual structure of *Espérance dans la croix.*

[4]*Trois poèmes* (1939-40) for voice and piano; *Le soulier de satin* (1943) — incidental music; and *Tête d'or* (1948) — radio music. Honegger also wrote the music for André Gillet's 1951 documentary film, *Paul Claudel.*

[5]Quoted by Willy Tappolet, *Arthur Honegger* (Editions de la Baconnière, Neuchâtel, 1953), 179.

[6]'Arthur Honegger über *Nicolas de Flue*', *Schweizerische Musikzeitung*, May-June 1962, 155-56.

[7]Just as the later oratorio version of *Le roi David* was rescored for symphony orchestra (see Chapter II, page 51), so *Nicolas de Flue* was similarly rescored when it was recorded by the Elisabeth Brasseur Chorale, Petits Chanteurs de Versailles and Paris Conservatoire Orchestra with Jean Day (narrator), conducted by Georges Tzipine on Columbia FCX 187-88 [2 (picc) 2 (ca) 22/2331/timp perc/str.].

[8]René Dumesnil, 'Musique', *Mercure de France,* CCCXVII (January-April 1953), 517-20.

[9]See (i) R.-A. Mooser, '*Nicolas de Flue*', *Dissonances,* nos 7-8 (November-December 1940), 191-95; and (ii) Charles Faller, '*Nicolas de Flue*', *La Revue Musicale,* July 1939, 63-65.

[10]See José Bruyr, *Arthur Honegger et son œuvre* (Editions Corrêa, Paris, 1947), 249-53.

[11]Honegger similarly abandoned a project on which he had been working with Jean Giraudoux (*Alceste* — 'grand opéra de style pompeux') when the latter died suddenly in 1944.

[12]R. -A. Mooser, 'Arthur Honeggers *Une cantate de Noël*' in *Aspects de la Musique Contemporaine 1953-1957* (Labor et Fides, Geneva, 1958), 22-26.

[13]Willy Tappolet, *Arthur Honegger* (Editions de la Baconnière, Neuchâtel, 1957), 191-94.

[14]Clarendon [B. Gavoty], '*Une cantate de Noël*', *Le Figaro,* 12 January 1954, 10.

[15]Willi Schuh, 'Arthur Honeggers *Weihnachtskantate*', *Neue Züricher Zeitung,* 2 December 1953; also in *Schweizerische Musikzeitung,* February 1954, 61-63.

[16]Clarendon [B. Gavoty], '*Une cantate de Noël*', *Le Figaro*, 12 January 1954, 10.

[17]Included in the genre of cantata would be the unreleased scores of *Les mille et une nuits* and *Chant de la libération.*

CHAPTER XII

The final drama: Symphonies Nos 2-5

Part I: The programmatic aspects of Symphonies Nos 2-5

> Il ne semble pas exagéré d'affirmer que dans ses cinq symphonies, Honegger nous révèle le côté le plus substantiel et le plus humain de son inspiration, l'essence même de sa pensée et de son art.[1]
>
> [It would be no exaggeration to say that Honegger, in his five symphonies, reveals the most substantial and human side of his inspiration — the very essence of his thought and art.]

There is essentially only one basic dramatic force at work in all the large-scale choral pieces on which Honegger collaborated with various different writers: that of the humanistic spirit. The message is the same whether it is personified in the actions, trials, tribulations (and, in some cases, the ultimate sacrifice of life) of David, Judith, Antigone, Amphion, Joan and Nicolas, or collectively expressed on behalf of the whole of mankind as in *Cris du monde, La danse des morts* and *Une cantate de Noël.* The triumphs of good over evil, the omnipresence of the all-powerful aspect of faith and the ritual of salvation through martyrdom are each constituent elements present to varying degrees in the fundamental expression of the universal message of humanism.

La danse des morts was the last choral fresco Honegger was to write. Not only did the physicalities of the Second World War temporarily stop both the demand for, and the performance of, works of this nature by large choral bodies, but also when the hostilities came to an end in 1945, many of these institutions did not reassemble and those that did were severely restricted in their outlook for a considerable time. Their tradition was broken, their libraries and concert-halls destroyed; many of the experienced members were no longer alive which meant starting again as far as repertoire was concerned, and the severe financial climate meant they were no longer in a position to hire frequently a large orchestra to accompany them or offer commissions to composers of the stature of Arthur Honegger. Many of the choral societies which did survive tackled the more familiar and technically less demanding works in the repertoire and, as such, *Le roi David, Nicolas de Flue* and (to a certain extent bearing in mind the abnormal cost of production) *Jeanne d'Arc au bûcher* remained popular.

Not only did his more technically difficult works suffer neglect, but there were also no viable opportunities for him to contribute further to a genre for which he had an almost uniquely suitable talent. Nevertheless, there is a final drama but it is contained in contributions Honegger made to the medium of expression to which he turned in the 1940s and early fifties: the symphony. Both individually and collectively, the last four symphonies are characterized by the same drama of humanistic conflict that is to be found in each and every one of the choral frescos.

Writing about his *Symphonie pour cordes* [*n° 2*] Honegger said that

> Je n'ai cherché aucun programme, aucune donnée littéraire ou philosophique. Si cette œuvre exprime ou fait ressentir des émotions, c'est qu'elles sont présentées toutes naturellement, puisque je n'exprime ma pensée qu'en musique et peut-être sans en être absolument conscient.[2]
>
> [I did not look for a programme, any theme either literary or philosophical. If this work expresses or brings out emotions, it is that these emotions came of their own accord, since I express my thoughts only in music and often unconsciously.]

There can be no doubt in anyone's mind once they have heard this symphony that the picture presented is an utterly realistic portrayal of the abject misery, hidden violence and all-pervading feeling of depression that characterized Paris and her citizens during the Occupation. The elation generated by the chorale which soars out over the tumult of the closing pages of the finale engenders the same quintessential spirit of hope and faith raised so often by Bach in his sacred choral music through the use of the same device.

The programmatic nature of the *Symphonie liturgique* [*n° 3*] has been explained by Honegger himself:

> J'ai voulu, dans cet ouvrage, symboliser la réaction de l'homme moderne contre la marée de barbarie, de stupidité, de souffrance, de machinisme, de bureaucratie qui nous assiège depuis quelques années. J'ai figuré musicalement le combat qui se livre dans son cœur entre l'abandon aux forces aveugles qui l'enserrent et l'instinct du bonheur, l'amour de la paix, le sentiment du refuge divin. Ma Symphonie est un drame qui se joue, si vous voulez, entre trois personnages, réels ou symboliques: le malheur, le bonheur et l'homme. Ce sont des thèmes éternels; j'ai tâché à les renouveler.[3]
>
> [In this work I wanted to symbolize the reaction of modern man against the tide of barbarity, stupidity, suffering, mechanization and bureaucracy which have been with us for several years. I have musically represented the inner conflict between a surrender to blind forces and the instinct of happiness, the love of peace and feelings of a divine refuge. My symphony is a drama which takes place, if you like, between three characters who

are real or symbolic — misfortune, happiness and man. These are eternal themes which I have tried to renew.]

The first movement is subtitled 'Dies irae'.

> Le jour de la colère, l'explosion de la force, de la haine qui détruit tout et ne laisse rien que décombres et ruines[4]
>
> [The day of wrath, the explosion of strength and of hate which destroys everything and leaves nothing but debris and ruin].
>
> Dès les premières mesures s'exprime le tumulte indicible de l'humanité[5]
>
> [From the outset, the indescribable turmoil of humanity is expressed].

The thematic material spearheads the expression of violence and agony (see Music Example 82 below).

Music Example 82: *Symphonie liturgique* [*nº 3*], first movement:
(i) 1 - 7A 1, Theme 1

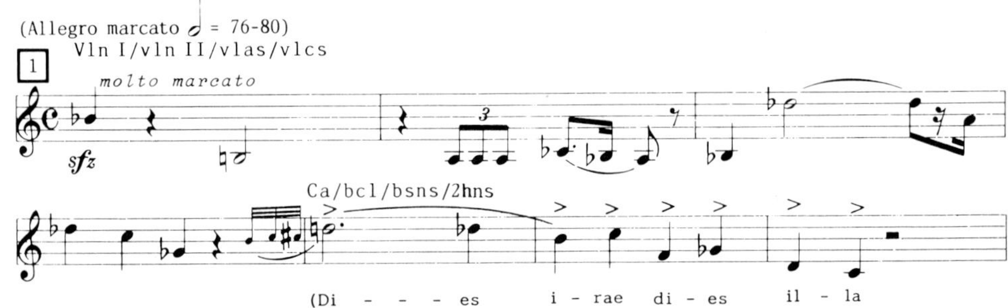

(ii) 1-3 and 9-10A 4, Theme 2 (a)/(b)/(c)

(iii) 3A 5 - 9A 5, Theme 3

(iv) 7 - 8, Theme 4

(+The underlay of the words is my own in both this and the two subsequent Music Examples.)

These qualities are inexorably multiplied by the seemingly endless rigour of the development. But,

> pas une lueur d'espoir sinon celle, encore bien faible, que symbolise un thème que j'ai appelé thème de l'oiseau et dont voici la première amorce. On dirait l'apparition lointaine et voilée de la colombe de la paix, celle qui, jadis, planait sur les eaux[6]
>
> [there is just the faintest glimmer of hope which is symbolized by a theme which I have called the bird-theme and of which this is the first appearance. One would think it to be the distant and veiled apparition of the dove of peace, who, long ago, soared above the waters].

The bird-theme emerges out of the climax to the development in the mysterious timbre of three flutes, cor anglais, three trombones and tuba unisoni spread across three octaves (see Music Example 83 below).

Music Example 83: *Symphonie liturgique* [*n° 3*], first movement, 11A 19 - 21, 'bird-theme'

But, 'l'ouragan balaie tout, aveugle, coléreux. Pour l'auditeur, pas moyen de souffler, de réfléchir . . .'[7] [the hurricane sweeps everything away, blindly and angrily. For the listener there is no time to breathe or think . . .].

The second movement is subtitled 'De profundis clamavi', and Honegger wrote:

> C'est la supplication vers une force plus haute, vers laquelle on tend les bras, à laquelle on veut offrir ce qui reste de pur, de noble, dans le fond de l'âme . . .. Que de peines ce morceau ne m'a-t-il pas coûtées! Je voulais développer une ligne mélodique en répudiant formules et procédés. Pas de tiroirs, pas de marches d'harmonie, pas de ces charnières si profitables à celui qui n'a rien à dire! J'ai repris la question au point où les classiques l'ont laissée. Aller de l'avant, marcher sans se retourner, prolonger sans redites ni arrêts la courbe initiale: ah, que c'est difficile! Et que c'est dur aussi de mettre dans des bouches humaines une prière sans espoir![8]
>
> [It is a plea to a higher force whom one asks for help and to whom one wants to offer what remains of all that is pure and noble at the depth of one's soul . . .. This piece gave me a lot of trouble! I wanted to develop a melodic line by rejecting methods and formulae. I put aside all guide-lines and harmonic progressions which are useful to those who have nothing to say! I took up the question at the point where the Classicists had left off. To advance, to go forward without looking back, to extend the initial curve without repetitions or stops: oh, how difficult it is! And how hard it is too, to put a prayer without hope into human mouths!]

The theme which constitutes the entire substance of the development and which plays such a vital role in the recapitulation in fact exists in embryonic form in the introduction and is what Honegger described as the funereal phrase 'De profundis clamavi ad te Domine' (see Music Example 84 below).

Music Example 84: *Symphonie liturgique* [*n° 3*], second movement, 3A 9 - 10

(Reproduit avec l'autorisation des EDITIONS SALABERT, Paris, propriétaires de l'œuvre.)

The bird-theme — its scoring for solo flute now justifying Honegger's description — returns at the end as '. . . l'oiseau innocent qui pépie sur les décombres'[9] [. . . the innocent bird, chirping on the debris].

The finale, 'Dona nobis pacem', represents 'l'implacable montée de l'asservissement de l'homme, de sa perte totale de liberté qui l'amène à ce cri désespéré'[10] [the relentless progress towards the slavery of man, of his complete loss of freedom which brings him to utter this desperate cry] (see Music Example 85 opposite.)

Music Example 85: *Symphonie liturgique* [*n° 3*], third movement, **15** 1B **16**

(Reproduit avec l'autorisation des EDITIONS SALABERT, Paris, propriétaires de l'œuvre.)

Initially '. . . j'ai imaginé une marche pesante pour laquelle j'ai forgé un thème, intentionnellement idiot, exposé d'abord par la clarinette basse'[11] [. . . I thought of a heavy march for which I created a deliberately idiotic theme, first heard on the bass clarinet] (see Music Example 86 (i) opposite). Themes 2^A, 2^B, 3^A, 3^B, 4^A and 4^B represent 'la marche des robots contre l'homme civilisé, titulaire d'un corps et d'une âme'[12] [the march of robots against civilized man, holder of a body and a soul] (see Music Example 86 (ii), (iii), (iv) and (v) below and overleaf).

Music Example 86: *Symphonie liturgique* [*n° 3*], third movement:
(i) bars 2-4, Theme 1

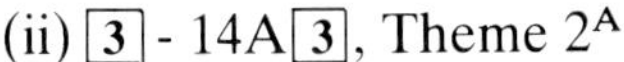
(ii) [3] - 14A[3], Theme 2^A

(iii) 1B [4] - 5A[4], Theme 2^B

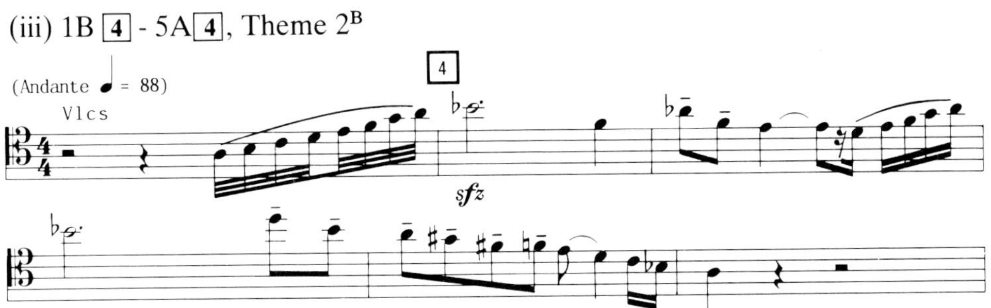

(iv) 2B [5] - 2A [5], Themes 3^A and 3^B

(v) 1-7A [6], Themes 4^A and 4^B

After the climactic plea for mercy (see Music Example 85, pages 373-74), 'j'ai voulu, par une longue phrase chantante, exprimer le vœu de l'humanité souffrante'[13] [I wanted to express the wish of suffering humanity by means of a long cantabile phrase] (see Music Example 87 below).

Music Example 87: *Symphonie liturgique* [*n° 3*], third movement, [16] - 1B [17]

Once the last echoes of the horrific march have died away 'les nuages s'entrouvrent et, dans la gloire du soleil levant, pour la dernière fois, l'oiseau vocalise'[14] [the clouds half open and, in the glory of the rising sun, the bird sings for the last time]. With the bird-theme on the piccolo, the phrase 'De profundis clamavi ad te Domine' for solo violin above the radiant C♯ major of the string texture takes on a new and purposeful meaning, and 'la *Symphonie* se termine par une — hélas! — utopique évocation de ce que pourrait être la vie dans une fraternité et un amour réciproques'[15] [the symphony ends with an — alas! — utopian evocation of what life could be like in mutual brotherhood and love] (see Music Example 88 overleaf).

Music Example 88: *Symphonie liturgique* [*n° 3*], third movement, **17** - end

18
P. Fl.
Fl.
Htb.
Cl.
Bass.
I
Trb.
II-III
Piano
Timb.
18
Viol. solo
I Viol. div. en 3
II Viol. div. en 3
Altos div.
solo
Cellos
C.B.

19
P.Fl.
sempre dolce
Fl.
Htb.
Cl.
Bass.
I
Trb.
II-III
Piano
Timb.
19
Viol. solo
Viol. div. en 3
II Viol. div. en 3
Altos div.
solo Cellos
C.B.

P.Fl.
Fl.
Htb.
Cl.
Bass.
C.Bass.
I
Trb.
II-III
sourdine
sourdine
Piano
Timb.
Viol.
solo
I Viol.
div.
en
3
II Viol.
div.
en
3
Altos
div.
Cellos
C.B.

Honegger hinted at the unique quality of the *Fourth Symphony* when he wrote:

> Dans l'année de malheur 1946, nous vivions dans une époque peu réjouissante. Les gouvernements des pays exigeaient de leurs sujets qu'ils payent les suites de la guerre. Au milieu des odieuses et stupides existences qui nous sont imposées, cette symphonie traduit l'espoir que suscite la perspective d'échapper pour un temps à cette atmosphère, en passant l'été en Suisse, entouré de l'affection d'amis chers et pour lesquels l'art musical, joue encore un rôle. Dans cet état d'âme, le premier mouvement de la symphonie fut esquissé[16]
>
> [In the year of misfortune, 1946, we were living in a scarcely jubilant era. The governments of the countries demanded that their subjects pay for the consequences of the war. In the midst of this odious and stupid existence which was imposed on us, this symphony brings hope, created by the prospect of temporarily escaping from this atmosphere, in my spending the summer in Switzerland, surrounded by the affection of dear friends for whom the art of music still has importance. In this state of mind the first movement of the symphony was sketched]

and that '. . . I value in my *Symphonie liturgique* [*n° 3*] the fact that it is very little indebted to traditional aesthetics . . . in my opinion, the following symphony, the *Deliciae Basilienses* [*n° 4*], marks a progress in craftsmanship and contrasts well with what had gone before, and this is indispensable.'[17]

The *Fourth Symphony* is certainly different from the *Symphonie liturgique* [*n° 3*], not least because it reflects an optimistic side of Honegger that, as has already been noted, is so rarely found in his mature works. The musical style of this work will be discussed later on in the chapter in conjunction with the works which are a close parallel — the *Intrada* for trumpet and piano and the *Concerto da camera*. The relaxed lyricism of the first movement is well balanced by the joyful extrovertism of the finale and they enclose a slow movement which is seriously refined but not intensely emotive. These overall qualities are abundantly evident in the melodic and rhythmic nature of the thematic material (see Music Example 89 below).

Music Example 89: *Symphony No. 4*, first movement:
(i) 7-15A [2], Theme 1 and motives (x) and (y)

Allegro ♩ = 132 à 120
Vlas
Theme 1
ClII(actual pitch)
motif x
Fls
motif y
Cls

(ii) 7A [5] - 12A [5] and 7B [7] - 5B [7], Theme 2(a)/(c)

(Reproduit avec l'autorisation des EDITIONS SALABERT, Paris, propriétaires de l'œuvre.)

(iii) [8] - 8A [8], Theme 3

(Reproduit avec l'autorisation des EDITIONS SALABERT, Paris, propriétaires de l'œuvre.)

Symphony No. 4, second movement:
(iv) bars 1-8, bass theme

(Reproduit avec l'autorisation des EDITIONS SALABERT, Paris, propriétaires de l'œuvre.)

(v) 2A [2] - [3], Theme 1

(Reproduit avec l'autorisation des EDITIONS SALABERT, Paris, propriétaires de l'œuvre.)

(vi) [3], Theme 2

(Reproduit avec l'autorisation des EDITIONS SALABERT, Paris, propriétaires de l'œuvre.)

(vii) 2-7A [6], Theme 3

(Reproduit avec l'autorisation des EDITIONS SALABERT, Paris, propriétaires de l'œuvre.)

Symphony No. 4, third movement:
(viii) 9A [3] - 12A [3], Theme 1

(Reproduit avec l'autorisation des EDITIONS SALABERT, Paris, propriétaires de l'œuvre.)

(ix) [1] - 5A [1], Theme 2

(Reproduit avec l'autorisation des EDITIONS SALABERT, Paris, propriétaires de l'œuvre.)

(x) 2 - 6A 2, Theme 3

(xi) 3 - 2A 3, Theme 4

(xii) 4 - 3A 4, Theme 5

(xiii) 8 - 11A 12, Theme 6

(xiv) 15 - 5A 15, Theme 7

Whilst in America for a lecture and concert tour during the summer of 1947, a great tragedy befell Honegger: he lost his health. After suffering a massive thrombosis followed by the almost inevitable bouts of pneumonia and phlebitis, he was left an invalid. The effect on him was shattering and only served to increase his pessimism. A series of conversations with the music critic 'Clarendon' (Bernard Gavoty) of *Le Figaro* were broadcast by French Radio in 1950; subsequently Gavoty and he had another set of conversations, the dialogue of which (in the style of Gide's *Corydon*) was published in 1951 as *Je suis compositeur (I am a Composer)* in the series called 'Mon métier' (My Profession) and subsequently translated into many languages. In both the radio talks and the book Honegger's statements are filled with a terrible sadness and frustration concerning the development of contemporary society, fundamental pessimism about the future role of the artist, and bitter implications in relation to the life and work of a composer. All of them are utterly real and true, and their reading now, a little over a third of a century later, is all the more salutary with the continuing detrimental effect of the passage of time.

His message is also contained in a number of articles directed at young musicians and composers which were published in various journals during the late forties and early fifties (see Part I of the Bibliography), but perhaps nowhere is it more cogently and persuasively expressed in words than in the paper 'The Musician in Modern Society' which he delivered to the 1954 UNESCO Conference held in Venice under the title 'L'artiste dans la société contemporaine', and which is reproduced at the end of this chapter (pages 467-79).

Musically, his final expression of these sentiments occurs in the last major work, the *Fifth Symphony*. The overwhelming intensity and profundity of dark emotions expressed in the first movement of the *Fifth Symphony* stem from the massive tutti of Theme 1 (see Music Example 90 opposite).

Music Example 90: *Symphony No. 5,* first movement, bars 1-24

1
Fl.
Hautb.
Cor A.
Clar.
Clar. B.
I
Bons
à 2
II-III
I-II
Cors
III-IV
I
Tromp.
II-III
I-II
Tromb.
III
Tuba
Timb.
f diminuendo poco a poco
1
I
Vons
II
Altos
Div.
Vlles
C.B.

Fl.
Hautb.
Cor A.
Clar.
Clar. B.
I
Bons
II-III
I-II
Cors
III-IV
I
Tromp.
II-III
I-II
Tromb.
III
Tuba
Timb.
I
Vons
II
Altos
Vlles
C.B.

When it comes in the recapitulation, rays of light fail in their attempt to shine through these omnipresent dark clouds (see Music Example 91 below).

Music Example 91: *Symphony No. 5,* first movement, 9 - 7A 10

I
Fl.
II
Hautb.
Cor A.
I
Clar.
II
Clar B.
I-II
Bons
III
I-III
Cors
II-IV
Sourd.
pp
I-II
Tromp.
III
Sourd.
Sourd.
I
Tromb.
II-III
Sourd.
pp
I Div.
Vons
II Div.
Altos
Div.
Vlles
Div.
C.B.

10
I-II
Fl.
III
Hautb.
Cor A.
I
Clar.
II
Clar.B.
I
Bons
II
espress.
I-III
Cors
II-IV
I
Tromp.
II-III
I
Tromb.
II-III
10
I Div.
Vons
II Div.
Altos
Div.
Vlles
Div.
C.B.

I-II
Fl.
III
Hautb.
Cor A.
Clar.
Clar. B.
I
B^ons
II
Cors
I
Tromp.
II-III
I-II
Tromb.
III
Tuba
I Div.
V^ons
II Div.
Altos
Div.
V^lles
Div.
C.B.

The same horrific violence and barbarity which were created in the first movement of the *Symphonie liturgique* [*n° 3*] is combined in the finale of this symphony with the feeling of relentless inevitability and expression of stupidity that had dominated the finale of the *Symphonie liturgique* [*n° 3*] — qualities that are clearly evident in the themes themselves (see Music Example 92 below).

Music Example 92: *Symphony No. 5,* third movement:
(i) 1-9A [2],Theme 1

(Reproduit avec l'autorisation des EDITIONS SALABERT, Paris, propriétaires de l'œuvre.)

(ii) [3] - 3A [3], Theme 2

(Reproduit avec l'autorisation des EDITIONS SALABERT, Paris, propriétaires de l'œuvre.)

(iii) 2A [4] - [5] Theme 3 (a) and (b)
Theme 3(a)

(Reproduit avec l'autorisation des EDITIONS SALABERT, Paris, propriétaires de l'œuvre.)

When all seems utterly lost by the middle of the development, a suggestion of salvation and hope is interjected with the new theme (4) (see Music Example 93 below).

Music Example 93: *Symphony No. 5,* third movement, 9 - 9A 9, Theme 4

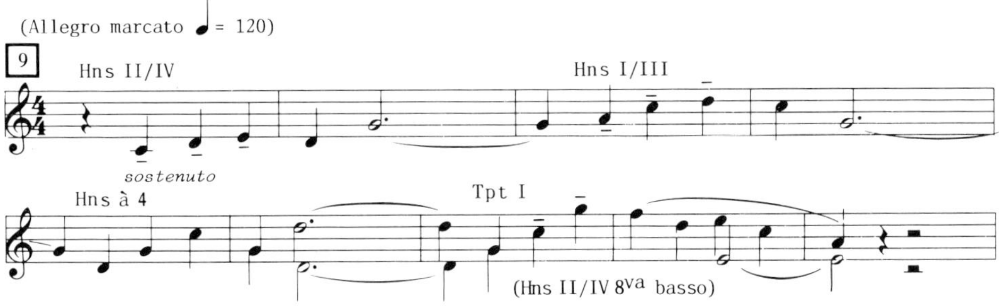

(Reproduit avec l'autorisation des EDITIONS SALABERT, Paris, propriétaires de l'œuvre.)

Like the similar chorale-inspired melodies which occur at comparable dramatic moments in each of the choral frescos and in the finale of the *Symphonie pour cordes* [*n° 2*], this melody engenders the spirit of a divine faith. But it does not survive to reign supreme in this movement. The second stage of the development pits this new theme against the others in a struggle for supremacy. The battle is lost and the symphony ends in a wilderness of uncertainty, expressing hopelessness and confusion. Honegger finally puts into musical terms his verbal expression of regret that the *Symphonie liturgique* [*n° 3*] had finished with a vision of utopia. His last drama in music closes, as *Antigone* had done some twenty years earlier, with a gesture of emptiness after so much tragedy.

Part II: *Symphonie pour cordes* [*n° 2*]

The idea of writing a second symphony occupied Honegger's mind for several years. As he subsequently explained:

> J'ai à Basle un grand ami, un chef d'orchestre qui, depuis près de trente ans, a joué partout mes œuvres et pour qui j'en ai écrit de nouvelles. C'est Paul Sacher. En 1938 il m'avait demandé une Symphonie pour le *Kammerorchester de Bâle* ou le *Collegium Musicum de Zürich,* car il dirige les deux. Pendant plus d'un an j'accumulais des tentatives qui ne me donnèrent aucune satisfaction. Enfin, pendant les tristes jours de l'occupation, je me replongeais dans les quatuors de Beethoven et l'influence de cette œuvre magnifique me stimula et me permit de me mettre au travail. Je pus faire parvenir la partition à Paul Sacher qui en donna la première audition à Zürich le 18 mai 1942[18]
>
> [I have a very good friend in Basle, the conductor Paul Sacher. For nearly thirty years he has performed my works extensively and it is for him that I have written various new works. In 1938 he asked me to write a symphony

for the *Basle Chamber Orchestra* or the *Collegium Musicum of Zürich,* both of which he conducts. For over a year I gathered together a few vague ideas; none of them satisfied me. Eventually during the sad days of the Occupation, I threw myself into the quartets of Beethoven and the influence of these magnificent pieces stimulated and enabled me to start work. I sent the score to Paul Sacher who gave it its first performance in Zürich on 18 May 1942].

In a programme note he supplied for the première he said that:

> Mes préoccupations générales concernant cette symphonie sont restées les mêmes que celles qui présidèrent à la composition de toutes mes œuvres symphoniques:
>
> 1. Rigueur de la forme, suppression de la réexposition telle qu'elle figure dans les œuvres classiques où elle donne toujours un sentiment de longueur;
> 2. Recherche de thèmes suffisamment dessinés pour attirer l'attention de l'auditeur et lui permettre de suivre le développement de toute l'histoire.[19]
>
> [My general preoccupations concerning this symphony are the same as those which dominate all my other symphonic works:
>
> 1. A rigorous form, a suppression of the recapitulation such as is found in Classical works where it always has the feeling of tedium;
> 2. A quest for themes which have sufficient character to attract the listener's attention and to enable him to follow the development of the whole story.]

He then went into specific details concerning each movement in the order he had composed them:

> La *Symphonie pour cordes* [*n° 2*] était une promesse faite depuis des années à Paul Sacher et différents départs, différentes esquisses se sont succédés sans résultat.
>
> Cependant, pendant l'hiver 1941, l'*Adagio* s'est peu à peu construit, car c'est toujours par cette partie centrale du triptyque que commence, pour moi, la composition d'une œuvre symphonique, de même qui je ne puis que par exception la concevoir autrement que sous cette forme tripartite. En l'entendant j'ai eu l'impression d'une page assez sombre et même un peu désespérée par instants. Je sens déjà que le tempo très lent ne plaira pas à tous les chefs qui l'amélioreront en le jouant un peu plus vite.[20]
>
> [The *Symphony for Strings* [*No. 2*] had been promised to Paul Sacher for several years and despite several attempts and various sketches nothing had been achieved.
>
> However, during the winter of 1941, the *Adagio* was gradually created. For a symphonic work I always start with the central part of the triptych as I am unable, apart from exceptional cases, to conceive of such a work in anything other than tripartite form. As I listened to it, I had the impression of a movement which was fairly sombre and even, at times,

desperate. I am already aware that the very slow tempo will displease some conductors who will want to improve it by taking it a little faster.]

This movement is cast in an ABA[1] format infused with both the elements of passacaglia and sonata-form (see Diagram 43 below).

Diagram 43:

Symphonie pour cordes [*n° 2*] — second movement (N.B. The whole movement is contained in Music Examples 94-96, pp. 397-405.)

(A)	-	[1]	Ground (3-part texture)
	[1]-	[2]	Theme 1 (1st Cellos) over 2nd statement of ground
	[2]-	[3]	Theme 2 (1st Violins) over repeat of Theme 1 (1st Cellos) and 3rd statement of ground
(B)	[3]-	5A[5]	New accompaniment figures emerge after [3] beneath the end of Theme 2 and these then support Theme 3 (Violas/1st Cellos 5A [3]-; 1st Violins/Violas 2A[4]-)
(A′)	6A[5]-	4A[6]	Variant of Theme 2 (over modified version of ground [6]-)
		4-1B[7]	Condensed variant of Theme 1 over modified version of ground
	[7]-	[8]	Accompaniment figures *ex* [3]- and Theme 3 (3A[7]-)
	[8]-	end	Elements of Theme 3 and outline of ground

The ground is a three-part conception whose intensity and concentration derive from the consistency of the contrary-motion principles that govern the contrapuntal nature of the harmonic structure. Theme 1 starts tentatively — the introspection and sadness which the subtle rhythmic syncopations and the narrow melodic range invoke are a strong parallel to that occasioned by Beethoven in the *Beklemmt* of the 'Cavatine' in the *String Quartet in B♭ major, Op. 130.* The second theme which emerges after [2] is in complete contrast. The hesitant and exploratory nature of Theme 1 is replaced by a theme which is utterly clear in its direction and which, with great intensity and power, carries the whole fabric through to [3] for the start of the B section. Typical of Honegger is the way in which Theme 1 is repeated as a counter-subject under the initial statement of Theme 2; together with the binding nature of the ground, the result is a particularly concentrated and integrated exposition of material which unfolds and grows with inexorable strength of logic (see Music Example 94 below).

Music Example 94: *Symphonie pour cordes* [*n° 2*], second movement, bars 1 - 24

Vns
Alt.
vles
C.B.
Div.
1
pp
p espressivo
arco

The whole B section is constructed upon the chromatic rising of the bass through the interval of a fifth. It is prevented from being an embarrassingly weak device which Honegger uses all too often by the irregularity of the periodicity. The fact that most of the accompaniment motives can be derived from material in the A section gives this B section the powerful character of a development within a sonata-form framework, despite the obviously new Theme 3 (violas/1st cellos 5A [3]). Furthermore, the material of this part of the movement is equally dominated by the interval of a third — in particular the minor form. The climax of this section ([5]) reveals a transition to the start of A^1 which contains one of the most fascinating of the many interesting string textures created by Honegger in the work (see Music Example 95 overleaf).

Music Example 95: *Symphonie pour cordes* [*n*º *2*], second movement, [3] - 1B [6]

I
Vns
II
Alt.
Vles
C. B.
4
Vns
Alt.
Vles
C. B.
f
sempre
Vns
Alt.
Vles
C. B.

crescendo
Vns
Alt.
Vles
C.B.
ff
5
simile
sff
pp
sons réels
un poco agitato
f
pp

The A[1] section commences with a re-exposition of Theme 2 — its character of constant striving is carefully replaced by one of benign resignation so that it leads quite naturally to a moment of further repose for the return of the ground. Despite this fundamental reshaping of the character of the theme it nevertheless retains enough of its melodic contour to ensure that the listener is in no doubt as to its identity and hence its origin in relation to the expository A section. The ground is modified very slightly to accommodate the restatement above it of the substantially reshaped Theme 1 (see 4B [7]). Honegger then proceeds to rework the theme (3) of the B section (complete with the rising chromatic bass and the various accompanying motives), before allowing elements from it to be combined with an appropriately truncated version of the ground after [8] in a gesture of conclusion. In the light of analyses of his handling of ABA[1] form in so many earlier works, it should come as no surprise that middle section material is thus integrated into A[1] (see Music Example 96 below.)

Music Example 96: *Symphonie pour cordes* [*n*° *2*], second movement, [6] - end

Vns
Alt.
Vles
C. B.
1 Vle solo
Div.
pizz.
arco
7
p
Vle solo
IV

Vns
Tutti
Div.
pizz.
Alt.
Vle solo
Vles
C.B.
8
pp
arco
1 solo

Formal rigour is equally achieved in the outer movements. The first movement is cast in sonata-form with very extensive evidence of Honegger's ability to handle the form having developed and improved since the *Symphonie* [*n° 1*]. The outlines of the formal shape of the movement are summarized in Diagram 44 (below).

Diagram 44:

Symphonie pour cordes [*n° 2*] — first movement (N.B. Some of the thematic material is identified in Music Examples 97-100, pp. 407-14.)

Exposition:		
opening-(Molto moderato)	:	Introduction — motif (x)
8B[2]-(Allegro)	:	Theme 1 (unisoni) and motif (y) (Violin 1 6A[2])
[3]-	:	Theme 2 (divided up between Violin 1, Violas and Cellos) and motif (z) (Violin 1 8A[3])
[4]-(Un poco meno mosso)	:	Theme 3 (Violin 1)
9A[4]-(A tempo)	:	Closing section — built up from motives (x) and (z) with the addition of the opening of Theme 1 in the bass at [6]
Development:		
9A[6]-9A[9]	:	Theme 1, motives (y) and (z)
Recapitulation:		
10B[10]-(Molto moderato)	:	Introduction
12B[11]-(Allegro)	:	Theme 2 leading via motif (x) (2-1B[11]) to
10B[12]-(Poco meno mosso)	:	Theme 3 with opening figure of Theme 1
[12]-(Tempo)	:	Theme 1, motives (x) and (z)
17A[15]-(Molto moderato)	:	Coda — Theme 3 with motif (x); (Allegro): Theme 1

Writing of this movement, Honegger said 'j'ai longuement travaillé au premier morceau afin de lui donner une forme suffisamment serrée et rigoureuse sans détruire la violence intérieure dont je me flatte de l'avoir pourvu et qui doit s'opposer à l'austerité du motif initial'[21] [I worked for a long time on the first movement in order to give it a form which was sufficiently concentrated and rigorous without destroying the interior violence which I am proud to say I have managed to create and which counteracts the austerity of the initial motif]. It opens with a slow introduction of an aba^1b^1 format. The significance of the material presented is two-fold. The melodic fragment (x), upon the multi-repetition of which are built the two (b) sub-sections, dominates the entire movement like a motto; whilst the fact that the cellular nature of the whole fabric is dependant principally on patterning by the interval of a minor third and, secondly, that of a tritone, is indicative not only of the material in this movement but of the entire symphony and results in tremendous cohesion (see Music Example 97 opposite).

Music Example 97: *Symphonie pour cordes* [*n° 2*], first movement, bars 1-29

Honegger's handling of the recapitulation section is of particular interest in the light of his comments. The development section reaches a climax at [9] which is a parallel to that achieved in the closing section (cf. [5] - [6]) in terms of its complexity of contrapuntal methods and peak of rhythmical activity (see (i) and (ii) respectively in Music Example 98 below and on page 410).

Music Example 98: *Symphonie pour cordes* [*n° 2*], first movement
(i) 1B [5] - 8A [6]

Vns
Alt.
Vles
C. B.

6
Div.
di - mi -
Vns
Div.
Div.
Alt.
Vles
C. B.

- nu - en - do
Vns
Tutti
Alt.
Vles
C. B.

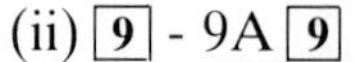

(ii) 9 - 9A 9

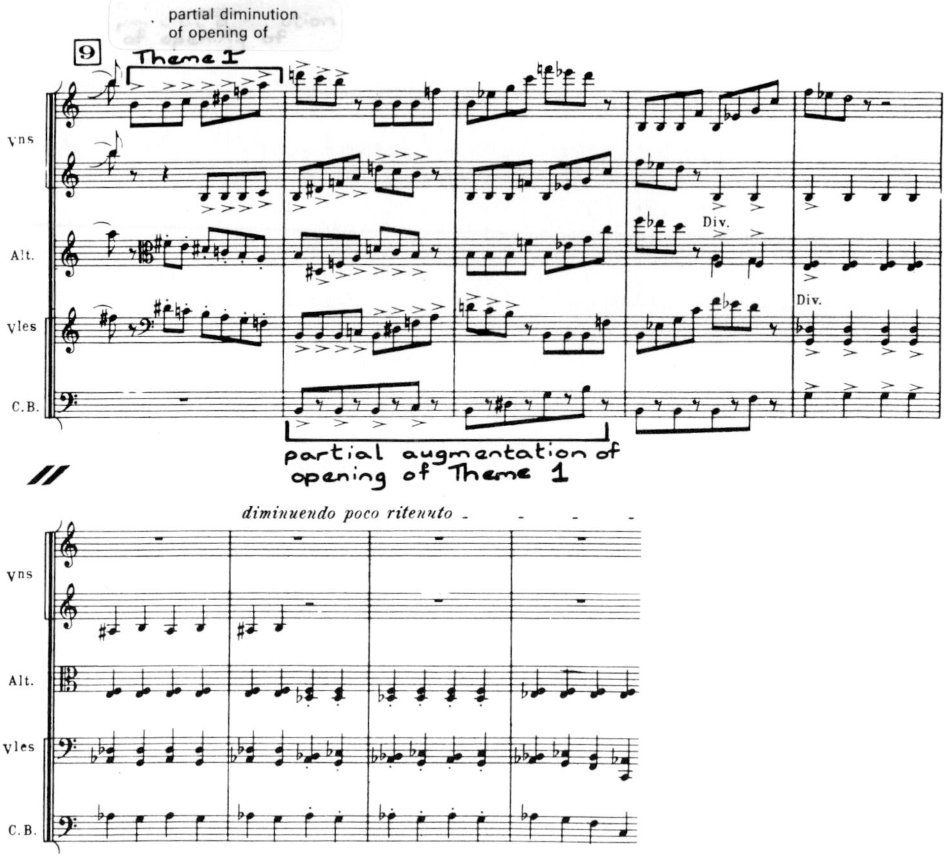

partial diminution of opening of Theme I

9

Vns

Alt.

Div.

Vles

C.B.

partial augmentation of opening of Theme 1

diminuendo poco ritenuto

Vns

Alt.

Vles

C.B.

This quickly dies away to reveal the hushed tones of the introduction at the start of the recapitulation. The aba^{1}b^1 structure of its initial presentation is coalesced here into a single whole with an enormous built-in *crescendo* (see Music Example 99 below).

Music Example 99: *Symphonie pour cordes* [*n° 2*], first movement, 10A 9 - 12A 10

Vns
Alt.
Vles
C.B.
pizz.
Div.
Div.
10
Tutti
Div.
arco
I
II
poco
a
poco
cresc.

The second and third themes were absent from the development section and so appear first. A version of Theme 2 is succeeded by a brief transition (based on motif x) to the concise and concentrated recapitulation of Theme 3. The contrapuntal complexity resulting from the immediate canonic treatment of the theme to enclose an imitative texture built on fragments of Theme 1 certainly avoids a feeling of *longueur*, just as the addition of swiftly-moving chromatic lines did for Theme 2. The recapitulation continues in a distinctly developmental fashion after 12, with a texture consisting of parts of Theme 1 and motives x and z, and is thus equivalent to a recapitulation of the development. This leads by way of the same imitative texture that constituted the closing section to a final contrapuntal mêlée (built up from various versions of motif x and Theme 1) of quite stunning complexity (see Music Example 100 below).

Music Example 100: *Symphonie pour cordes* [*n° 2*], first movement, 14 - 16A 15

Div.
vns
Div.
Div.
Alt.
vles
C.B.
15
ff Tutti
sostenuto
vns
Alt.
ff
en 3 sostenuto
vles
ff
C.B.
vns
Alt.
vles
C.B.

(Reproduit avec l'autorisation des EDITIONS SALABERT, Paris, propriétaires de l'œuvre.)

The appearance of Theme 3 (above motive x) in the coda redresses the imbalance occasioned by its non-appearance in the development and its relatively brief, if highly concentrated recapitulation. Finally, the unisoni Theme 1 effects a close in the tonic, D minor.

That this should be the first mention of tonality in connection with this movement is particularly significant. The work as a whole is in the key of D, the first two movements being in the minor mode and the finale in the major mode. In the first movement the only evidence of tonal design is the fact that the clouded D minor of the opening is clearly confirmed by Theme 1 before it effects a move to B minor/major within the framework of which appear both the second and third themes. The development concludes in B minor/major and the recapitulation begins in the same tonal area. The tonality of D minor is restored after [12] with the recapitulation of Theme 1 and the subsequent coda to the movement. Such a patterning does not relate to any traditional aesthetic, but is fully in keeping with Honegger's style as is obvious from the works which precede this; more importantly, it is a natural and inevitable outcome of the conditioning of the whole fabric by the interval of a minor third.

In relation to the second movement, the only feature of tonal design that might be said to be present is a very strong feeling of the A and B sections having a bias towards being 'on the dominant' (in Toveyian parlance), thus being, in effect, an enormous up-beat preparation for the final A¹ section. As with the first movement it is impossible to talk of a traditional tonal structure in the finale. 'I am neither polytonalist, nor atonalist, nor a dodecaphonist. It is true, our contemporary musical material is based on a ladder of twelve chromatic sounds, but used with the same freedom as are the letters of the alphabet by the poet or the prismatic colours by the painter.'[22] Nowhere else, perhaps, is this statement of Honegger's more evident than in the finale. The work contains passages which are polytonal by construction and moments when tonality is completely obscured, as well as some long stretches of a traditionally tonal character (see Music Example 101 below).

Music Example 101: *Symphonie pour cordes* [*n° 2*], third movement:
(i) bars 1-27

arco
I
Vns
II
Alt.
Vles
C.B.
2
f

(ii) 5 - 10A 6

5
Theme 4
Vns
Alt.
Vles
C. B.
dimin.
Div. en 3
Tutti
pizz.
p

Vns
Alt.
Vles
C. B.

Vns
Alt.
Vles
C. B.

6
Vns
Alt.
Vles
C. B.
Vns
Alt.
Vles
C.B.

(iii) 1B 19 - end

19
Trompette
ad libitum
Theme 5:
f sostenuto
molto sostenuto
f sempre
Vns
Alt.
Vles
Tutti
C. B.

Trp.
Vns
Alt.
Vles
C. B.
Trp.
Vns
Alt.
Vles
C. B.
20
Trp.
Vns
Alt.
Vles
C. B.

Trp.
Vns
IV
Alt.
Vles
C. B.
Trp.
Vns
Alt.
Vles
C. B.
21
Trp.
Vns
Alt.
Vles
C. B.

Trp.
Vns
Alt.
Vles
C.B.
Trp.
Vns
Alt.
Vles
C.B.
22
Trp.
Vns
Div.
ff
Alt.
Vles
C.B.

(Reproduit avec l'autorisation des EDITIONS SALABERT, Paris, propriétaires de l'œuvre.)

In this symphony where so much progress is evident in terms of Honegger's ability to handle symphonic thought, the structure of the finale is a worthy constituent (see Diagram 45 below).

Diagram 45:

Symphonie pour cordes [*n° 2*] — finale (N.B. Some of the thematic material is identified in Music Example 101, pp. 415-22.)

Exposition:

- Theme 1 (Violas/Cellos 7B[1]-)
- [2]- Theme 2 (1st Violins)
- [3]- (Theme 1 — 1st Violins; with imitation by inversion in the Cellos)
- [4]- Theme 3 (1st Violins)
- [5]- Theme 4 (1st Violins 5A[5]-)

Development:

- [7]- Theme 1
- [9]- Themes 1 and 2
- 4B[10]- Themes 1 and 3
- [11]- Theme 1

Recapitulation:

- [14]- Theme 4 (Violas 5A[14]-)
- [17]- Theme 1 (1st Violins; with imitation by inversion in the Cellos/D. Basses)
- [18]- Theme 3
- [19]- Theme 5 (1st Violins with ad. lib. Trumpet) *with* Theme 1
- [22]- Coda

There is a very happy combination of sonata-form and rondo patterning, admirably supporting and binding together the various elements which all have such excitingly extrovert characters because, as Honegger said 'pour le final, j'ai cherché un élément brillant contrastant avec les premières parties. Pour soutenir le choral qui apparaît à la fin, j'ai indiqué une trompette *ad libitum.* Cela n'est pas un effet voulu, c'est simplement un support pour la mélodie en valeurs larges des premiers violons qui risque d'être absorbée par la polyphonie des autres instruments de même timbre'[23] [I looked for a brilliant element for the finale which would be a good contrast to the first two movements. I wrote a trumpet part, marked *ad libitum*, to sustain the chorale which appears at the end. It is not a desired effect, merely a support for the melody which is in dotted minims in the first violins and which therefore runs the risk of being absorbed by the polyphony of the other instruments of the same timbre].

Part III: The structural aspects of *Symphonies Nos 3-5*

The formal designs of the movements in the subsequent *Liturgique* [*n° 3*], *Fourth (Deliciæ Basilienses)* and *Fifth (Di tre re) Symphonies* reflect an aspect of consolidation within the framework of progress through experimentation that has been illustrated in the two symphonies and two quartets discussed so far (see also Chapter X), as well as evidence of a continuing quest for re-interpreting traditional forms in a truly individual way. Of the nine movements in question, only two are not obviously cast in a mould of sonata form. The second movement of the *Fifth Symphony* is the only one in his symphonies which is not a real slow movement. The format is that of a Beethovenian double *Scherzo* and *Trio*, but its physiognomy is altered such that it represents the combination of the traditional slow and *Scherzo* movements (second and third) of a symphony. There are also implications of sonata-form in that, because the central *Allegretto* is purely developmental in character, the second *Adagio* and final *Allegretto* assume the role of a recapitulation (see Diagram 46 overleaf).

Diagram 46:

Symphony No. 5 — second movement

Allegretto:			
	Theme 1 (Violin I)	See Music Example 102 opposite	(A)
[1]-	Theme 1^{IR} (Bassoons)		
[2]-	Theme 1^{I} (Flutes)		
[3]-	Theme 1^{R} (Cor Anglais/Oboe)		
[4]-	Transition		
[5]-	Theme 2(a) : 1st Violins/1st Oboe 3A[5]- and 2(b) : Bass Clarinet/Cor Anglais 3B[6]- with varied restatement of Theme 2(a) 8B[7]-		(B)
[7]-	Theme 3(a) : 1-4A[7] and 3(b) : 5A[7]-		
[8]-	Theme 1 — extended		(A′)
[9]-	Variants of Themes 3(a) and (b)		
12A[9]-	Closing section: fragments of Theme 1		
Adagio:	([10]-[12])		
Allegretto:			
[12]-	Theme 1^{I} and Theme 1 in canon		
[13]-	Variant of Theme 3(b)		
[14]-	Theme 1^{R} and Theme 1^{IR} in canon		
8B[15]-	Variant of Theme 3(b)		
[15]-	Extensive development of Theme 1 involving imitative and canonic treatment of Theme 1^{I} and Theme 1, initially in augmentation		
Adagio:	([19]-[21]) — transposed version (down a tone) of bars 2-4 and 13-19 of the first Adagio ([10]-[12]) with various versions of Theme 1 superimposed (some appropriately reshaped)		(A)
Allegretto:			
[21]-	Theme 2(b)		(B)
[22]-	Theme 2(a) - extended		
[23]-	Theme 3(a) - extended		
[24]-	Transition (compressed version of that from [4]-[5])		
[25]-	Theme 1 in various versions to end		(A′)

Music Example 102: *Symphony No. 5,* second movement, bars 1-37

Never before have the contrapuntal procedures been so systematic or the treatment of the theme so close to a parallel of serial techniques as is the case in this movement. However, it can be appreciated from the extract quoted above (Music Example 102), that the outcome is purely Honeggerian with no sense of it all being a mere artifice.

Sonata-form is also implied in the slow movement of the *Fourth Symphony*. There is, too, a suggestion of a passacaglia in the tradition of the middle movements of the *Third Quartet* and the *Symphonie pour cordes* [*n° 2*], but, as will be appreciated from Diagram 47 below, not enough of the bass theme *in toto* is used in some of the sections for the piece actually to be labelled as a passacaglia (or, for that matter, any of its generic counterparts).

Diagram 47:

Symphony No. 4 — second movement (N.B. The thematic material is identified in Music Example 89, pp. 382-85.)

Bars		
1 - 8		Unison statement of bass theme
9 - 18	Section I	Restatement of bass theme (with the addition of a two-bar modulating extension) beneath a new countersubject
19 - 29	Section II	Extensive fragmentation, modulation and extension of period of bass theme beneath exposition of Theme 1 (1st Violins/1st Clarinet/Flute 2A[2]-) and countermotif (woodwind). Section I countersubject reappears (Oboe 4B[3]-)
30 - 37	Section III	Bass theme fragmented even further beneath exposition of Theme 2 (woodwind)
38 - 49	Section IV	Melodic transfiguration of Theme 1 over a new ostinato (brass) with Theme 2 in woodwind as countersubject. Bass theme absent
50 - 56	Section V	Developed versions of Themes 1 and 2 over a new ostinato (strings). Fragments of the bass theme return
57 - 67	Section VI	Themes 1 and 2 as countersubjects to the folksong *z' Basel an mi'm Rhy* (1st Horn 8-3B[7]) over a modified version of the string ostinato from Section V. Bass theme absent
68 - 76	Section VII	Complete statement in original form of bass theme with fragments of the countersubject from Section I and the brass ostinato from Section IV

The formal strictures of the passacaglia are treated more liberally here than they were in the *Third Quartet*, but more consistently than was the case in the *Symphonie pour cordes* [*n° 2*]. The expository nature of bars 1-37 is followed in sections IV-VI by a fabric which is developmental in style (the folk-song quotation in the final part of this section is only like the new theme Honegger so often introduced into the development sections of his earlier sonata-form movements). The brief 'recapitulation' constituted by the final section is more akin to a coda in a traditional sense, but is itself compatible with his views on the nature and size of such sections.

Of the remaining sonata-form movements the emphasis is very much on the handling of the recapitulation. In the first movement of the *Symphonie liturgique* [*n° 3*] the 'recapitulation' contains a large section which is really nothing but a second stage to the development (see † in Diagram 48 overleaf). In the development section proper (2B [11] - [15]), he deals only with the material of the introduction and Theme 1; whilst in the section of the 'recapitulation' delineated by the sign (†) he concentrates on Themes 3 and 4. As a result of the transformation which is wrought for the reappearance of Theme 1 at the beginning of the 'recapitulation' it is possible to interpret this movement as consisting only of an exposition and an enormous development section — 2B [11] - [20] — with the recapitulation being climactically replaced by the initial appearance of the bird-theme (which programmatically underlines the whole symphony) and a cyclic closing feature.

Diagram 48:

Symphonie liturgique [*n° 3*] — first movement (N.B. The thematic material is identified in Music Examples 82-83, pp. 370-71.)

Exposition:

	Introduction
[1]-	Theme 1 and developed counterstatement
[4]-	Theme 2(a), (b) and (c)
3A[5]-	Theme 3 with counterstatements including by inversion
[7]-	Theme 4
[10]-	Codetta - Theme 2(a) including augmented version

Development:

2B[11]-	Introduction material and Theme 1 with Theme 2(c) providing the link (6B[15]-) to the

'Recapitulation':

[15]-	Theme 1	
[16]-	Theme 2(c)	†
6A[16]-	Theme 3 and inversion	Second 'development'
[17]-	Theme 4 (opening)	
7A[17]-	Theme 3 and inversion	
[18]-	Theme 4 (conclusion)	
5B[19]-	Theme 3 and inversion	
[19] -	Theme 2(a) and — by diminution — 2(b) 5A[19]-	
[20]-	'Bird-theme' over version by diminution of Theme 2(b)	
[21]-	Coda — Introduction material	

The recapitulation section is absent in three subsequent sonata-form movements, although in each case there is a coda which makes reference to the first theme. In the third movement of the *Symphonie liturgique* [*n° 3*] (see Diagram 49 below), the recapitulation is replaced by a fairly substantial *Adagio* for programmatic reasons which have already been discussed (see pages 372-81).

Diagram 49:

Symphonie liturgique [*n° 3*] — finale (N.B. The thematic material is identified in Music Examples 86 (pp. 375-76), 83 (p. 371) and 84 (p. 372). The climax of the development ([15] - [16]) is presented in Music Example 85 (pp. 373-74) and the entire Adagio in Music Examples 87-88 (pp. 376-81).)

Exposition:

Theme 1 and motif (x) (c.f. Bassoons/Bass Clarinet/Cellos/D. Basses bars 7-8) with developed restatements

[3]- Theme 2 (a) and (b) with part of 2 (a) leading to

2B[5]- Theme 3 (a) and (b) with varied restatements

[6]- Theme 4 (a) and (b) — initially above part of rhythm of Theme 1 (Piano/D.Basses) — with developed restatements. Motif (x) acts as a link (4B[8]-) to the

Development:

[8]- All material

Coda:

[16]- Adagio: includes references to Theme 1 (1-4A[17]), the 'De profundis clamavi ad te Domine' theme (4B-1A [19]; 5-6A[19]) from the second movement and the 'bird-theme' (1-5A[19]) which appeared in both the first and second movements

---

The overall structure of the finale of the *Fourth Symphony* (see Diagram 50 below) was possibly a further source of inspiration for Honegger's formal design of the second movement of the *Fifth Symphony*, particularly in view of the parallel employment of prodigious contrapuntal feats (see page 426 and Diagram 46, page 424).

Diagram 50:

Symphony No. 4 — finale (N.B. The thematic material is identified in Music Example 88, pp. 378-81.)

Allegro:

	Embryo of Theme 1	'Exposition'
[1]-	Theme 2 and developed restatement	
[2]-	Theme 3 and developed restatement	
[3]-	Theme 4	
9A[3]-	Theme 1	
[4]-	Theme 5	
[5]-	Theme 4	
8A[5]-	Theme 6	
[6]-	Theme 1 with Theme 6	
[7]-	Closing section: based on parts of Themes 1 and 4; leads to	

Adagio:

[9]-[10]	Includes a fragment of Theme 1 (Trumpet/Piano)

Allegro:

[10]-	Theme 1	'Development'
[11]-	Theme 5 with Theme 1	
[12]-	Theme 6 with Themes 1 and 5	
[13]-	Theme 3 with Themes 1, 5 and 6	
[14]-	Theme 2 with Themes 1, 3, 5 and 6	
[15]-	Repeated statements of the folksong *Bäsler Morgenstreich* accompanied by a 3-part canonic treatment of Theme 1; leading to	

Coda:

8A[17]-	Adagio: transposed version of last 9 bars of the first Adagio ([9]-[10])
[18]-	Allegro: Theme 1

In the finale of the *Fifth Symphony* (see Diagram 51 below), as well as omitting the recapitulation Honegger reverts to his earlier practice of introducing a new theme in the development. This is not used, however, simply to bind together a texture made up from a myriad of fragments of thematic material from the exposition undergoing a very rigorous contrapuntal development; it has, in fact, programmatic connotations which were discussed in the light of those relating to the *Symphonie liturgique* [*n° 3*] (see page 395).

Diagram 51:

Symphony No. 5 — finale (N.B. The thematic material is identified in Music Examples 91-92, pp. 390-94.)

Exposition:

	Introduction
[2]-	Theme 1 (with varied counterstatement 8B[3]-)
[3]-	Theme 2 (with varied counterstatement 7B[4]-)
2A[4]-	Theme 3 (a) and (b) (8A[4]-)
[5]-	Closing section: Introductory material above variant of Theme 3(a) leading to part of Theme 2 (5B [6]-)

Development:

[6]-	Themes 3 (b) and 2 (5B[7]-) and Introductory material (2B[7]-)
[7]-	Theme 1 with Introductory material (-11A[7])
[8]-	Theme 2/Introductory material and Theme 1 (6A[8]-)
[9]-	Theme 4 (with fragments of Theme 1) and partial restatement 8B[11] -
[11]-	Introductory material and Theme 1
[12]-	Themes 1 and 4
[13]-	Theme 4
8B[14]-	Introductory material leading to a climax for

Coda:

[14]-	Fragments of Theme 1 and Introductory material

The remaining three movements all utilize sonata-form in a more traditional manner. In the exposition of the slow movement of the *Symphonie liturgique* [*n° 3*], Honegger presents a large number of themes in one continuous stream. The development, however, is constructed solely from the 'De profundis clamavi ad te Domine' theme (see Music Example 84, page 372) which existed in embryonic form in the introduction, and contains no reference to any of the five principal themes. Apart from transpositions (effected without any obvious patterning or reason), these five themes are recapitulated with no alterations of any consequence to their individual characteristics. Nevertheless, the whole section takes on the completely new meaning for which Honegger always strove by virtue of the fact that each theme is now embroidered and, in some cases, slightly separated from the next by a texture based on the 'De profundis clamavi ad te Domine' theme (see Diagram 52 below).

Diagram 52:

Symphonie liturgique [*n° 3*] — second movement (N.B. The 'De profundis clamavi ad te Domine' theme is given in Music Example 84, p. 372.)

Exposition:

Introduction - containing the embryo of the 'De profundis clamavi ad te Domine' theme (bars 1-3 and 8-12); an anticipation of the opening of Theme 1 (bars 4-7); an anticipation of Theme 5 (bar 3) and a brief reference to the 'bird-theme' (Flute 1B[1])

[1]- Theme 1 (Cellos-Violin I-Trumpet-Oboe)

7A[2]- Theme 2 (Violin I - Flute - Oboe - Horn - Trombone)

[4]- Theme 3 (Wind/strings) - with reference (brass 4B[5]-) to the opening of Theme 1

[5]- Theme 4 (Violin I) with countersubject 4^A (Trumpet)

2A[6]- Theme 5 (Clarinet)

[7]- Theme 4 (Oboe-Flute) with countersubject 4^B (Cellos)

5A[7]- Theme 5 (Oboe/Clarinet) beneath end of Theme 4 (Flute)

[8]- Closing section

Development:

[9]- Based on the 'De profundis clamavi ad te Domine' theme with references to the 'bird-theme' (Flute 3A[9] and 1A[10])

Recapitulation:

[13]- Theme 1 (†1B-4A[14])

4B[15]- Theme 2 (†1B-4A[15] and 1B-6A[16])

4B[17]- Theme 3 (with similar reference (brass [17]-) to the opening of Theme 1 as per [4]-(†4-1B[18])

[18]- Theme 4 with countersubject 4^A (†1B-3A[19])

2A[19]- Theme 5

5B[20]- Closing section material

[20] - Theme 1

Coda:

8A[20]- 'Bird-theme' and references to part of the 'De profundis clamavi ad te Domine' theme

(† = the 'De profundis' theme)

In the first movement of the *Fourth Symphony,* Honegger provides a slow introduction as he did for the *Symphonie pour cordes* [*n° 2*], but the degree to which the thematic material of the subsequent sonata-form *Allegro* is anticipated in embryonic form during this preface is here extended to include virtually all the themes. The development subdivides into four stages, with the first three being devoted primarily to a rigorous treatment of the three parts of Theme 2. As a direct consequence of this, the second thematic group is not recapitulated as such, although the reappearance of the slow introduction results in a satisfactory amount of reference to its essential features (see Diagram 53 below).

Diagram 53:

Symphony No. 4 — first movement (N.B. The thematic material is identified in Music Example 89, pp. 382-85.)

Introduction - including anticipations of Themes 1, 2(a), 2(c) and 3 as well as motives (x) and (y)

Exposition:

- 7A[2]- Theme 1 and countermotives (x) and (y) with developed restatements
- [5]- Transition
- 7A[5]- Theme 2(a), (b) (Tutti 1-4A[6]) and (c) with developed restatements
- [8]- Theme 3

Development:

- 4B[9]- Theme 2(b) and (c) and variants of (x)
- [11]- Theme 2(a) (5A[12]-) above ostinato treatment of Theme 1
- [14]- Theme 2(c) and (a) with Theme 3 stated 6B[15]-[15]
- [16]- Link based on variants of (x) and (y) to

Recapitulation:

- 9A[16]- Theme 1 and countermotives (x) and (y) with developed restatements
- [19]- Compressed version of Introduction

Coda:

- 5A[20]- Two statements of Theme 3 with Theme 1 used as a countersubject and with fragmentary references to Theme 2(a). Theme 1 dominates the last 12 bars

---

A similar situation is evident in the first movement of the *Fifth Symphony* which is otherwise the simplest and most Classically-inspired of his sonata-form designs. The development section primarily involves the second theme and so the latter's appearance in the recapitulation is kept to an absolute minimum — in the last sixteen bars of the movement its opening phrase merely punctuates the last echoes of Theme 1 (see Diagram 54 overleaf).

Diagram 54:

Symphony No. 5 — first movement

Exposition	:		Theme 1
		[3] -	Theme 2 (Bass Clarinet - 1st Clarinet) and developed restatement (Cor Anglais)
Development	:	[5] -	Principally around/of Theme 2 (with part of Theme 1 appearing after [8])
Recapitulation	:	[9] -	Theme 1
		6B[13] -	First two bars of Theme 2 alternating with the end of Theme 1

Part IV: The non-symphonic works 1937-1948

Apart from the two string quartets, there are a number of other pieces of chamber music from the latter half of the thirties and forties. The short piano piece *Scenic Railway,* which Honegger contributed to the volume entitled *Parc d'attractions* and which was produced by Editions Max Eschig for the 1937 *Expo* celebrations, is a rather slight piece of programme music with surprisingly little to distinguish it or to raise it above the level of two very similar pieces of 'railway music' by Martinů and Harsanyi in the same volume. A substantial *Partita* in four movements for piano duet which he wrote in 1940 was never offered for publication and his only other pieces for piano are the *Deux esquisses* (1944-45), which are musically insubstantial despite being of great interest due to their notation.[24]

Honegger wrote only two pieces of instrumental chamber music after the *Third Quartet.* The *Sonata for Solo Violin* (1941) has entered the repertoire of very few violinists, despite being premiered by Christian Ferras and advocated by Ginette Neveu, who also fingered the manuscript for publication. The formal aspects of this work are amazingly rigid for Honegger and lack a sense of organic cohesion. The music as a whole is particularly tonal, with the influence of the tuning of the violin in fifths uncomfortably strong. In addition, the dependence of the fabric on figuration and patterning is such that the work lacks spontaneity and, even if it can be said to be performer's music, it is certainly not one of Honegger's better creations.

The *Intrada* for trumpet and piano (1948) is a piece of more than relative consequence despite being written as a Paris Conservatoire examination test-piece. The style is a very close parallel to that of the *Fourth Symphony* with its canonic features, melodic diatonicism and rhythmic simplicity. The harmonic structure is equally relaxed, direct and clear, and the mood of the whole is characterized by the qualities of pastoral optimism and lyrical buoyancy that Honegger exploited in such early scores as *Pastorale d'été, Chant de joie* and *Rugby,* but which had only recently been rekindled in the *Fourth Symphony* after many years of absence.

The *Concerto da camera* of 1948 is the only other work written in the same vein. Dated October 1948, the work is scored for the unlikely combination of soli flute and cor anglais with the accompaniment of a string orchestra. The first movement has a relaxed lyricism very similar to that in the same movement of the *Fourth Symphony,* although the start anticipates those of the *Fifth Symphony,* the 'Ouverture' of the *Suite archaïque* and the *Monopartita* with its texture of two planes of harmonic activity opposed in contrary motion. There is also a profusion of thematic material which parallels that in the outer movements of the *Fourth Symphony.* The review of material offered in the recapitulation is characteristically restrictive in that Theme b^2 from the second thematic group as well as the entire third thematic group (harmonic texture C^1 and Themes c^1 and c^2) are not represented (see Diagram 55 below).

Diagram 55:

Concerto da camera — first movement

Exposition:

	1st	Thematic Group: Harmonic texture A^1 (strings) and Themes a^1 (Cor Anglais 5B[1]-) and a^2 (Flute 5A [1]-)
[2]-	2nd	Thematic Group: Themes b^1 (Cor Anglais/Flute [2]-), b^2 (strings 1B[3]) and b^3 (Flute/Cor Anglais [3]-)
3B[4]-	3rd	Thematic Group: Harmonic texture C^1 (strings) and Themes c^1 (Flute [4]-) and c^2 (Flute 3A[4]-)

Development:

[5]	a^1
[6]	b^2 and a^2
2B[7]	b^1
[7]	b^3
3B[8]	b^1
[8]	c^1
4B[9]	c^2/C^1
[9]	a^1/a^2
[10]	a^2
5A[10]	b^1

Recapitulation:

3B[11]	A^1 with b^1 ([11]-)
8B[12]	A^1 with a^1 then a^2 (6B[12]-) then b^3 (3B[12]-)
1B[12]	A^1 with a^1 ([12]-)
3A[12]	b^1 above end of A^1 then above accompaniment *ex* [2]- (5A[12]-)

The basic mood of the second movement of this concerto is a direct consequence of the slow movement of the *Symphonie liturgique* [*nº 3*]. Two themes (A and B) and a developed version of each (A[1] and B[1]) alternate in mosaic fashion:— (A ; B [8B [1] -]; A[1][[1] -]; B[1] [[2] -]; A [2A [3] -]; B[1] [2A [5] -]; B [[6] -]; A[1] [[7] -]; Coda [2B [8] -] based on A). The emphasis is on contrapuntal embroidery and the result is probably the greatest testament to Honegger's skill in this art and a worthy tribute to his mentor, J.S. Bach (see Music Example 103 below).

Music Example 103: *Concerto da camera,* second movement:

Fl.
C.A.
I
Vons
II
Alt.
Velle
C.B.
pizz.
arco
pizz.
p
3
Von II
Velle Div.

1
Fl.
C.A.
Von II
Div.
Tutti
Alt.
arco
Velle Div.
C.B.

Fl.
C.A.
Von II
Alt.
Velle Div.
Div.
C.B.

2
C.A.
I
Vons
II
Alt.
Velle
Div.
C.B.
p
pizz.
pizz.

C.A.
I
Vons
II
Alt.
Velle
3
arco

C.A.
I
Vons
II
Alt.
Velle
C.B.
3
Fl.
p espressivo tranquillo
C.A.
p
I
Vons
II
Alt.
Velle
arco
C.B.
pizz.

Fl.
C.A.
I
Vons
II
Alt.
Velle
C.B.
arco
pizz.

Fl.
C.A.
I
Vons
II
Alt.
Velle
C.B.
Fl.
C.A.
I
Vons
II
Alt.
Velle
C.B.

4
Fl.
C.A.
I
Vons
II
Alt.
Velle
C.B.
6
3
Fl.
C.A.
I
Vons
II
Alt.
Velle
C.B.
3

5
Fl.
C.A.
I
Vons
II
Alt.
Velle
C.B
Fl.
C.A.
I
Vons
II
3
Alt.
Velle
C.B.

6
Fl.
C.A.
I
Vons
II
Alt.
Velle
C.B.
pp
3
Fl.
C.A.
I
Vons
II
Alt.
Velle
C.B.
3

Fl.
C.A.
I
Vons
II
Alt.
Velle
C.B.
Div.
Div.
7
Fl.
C.A.
pp
I
Vons
II
Div
Alt.
Tutti
Velle
B.

Fl.
C.A.
I
Vons
II
Alt.
Velle
C.B.
Fl.
C.A.
I
Vons
II
Alt.
Velle
C.B.

Fl.
C.A.
I
Vons
II
Alt.
Velle
C.B.
8
p

(Reproduit avec l'autorisation des EDITIONS SALABERT, Paris, propriétaires de l'œuvre.)

This, too, is a prayer, but instead of a prayer consisting of desperate cries from the wilderness of a lost people as in the *Symphonie liturgique* [*n° 3*], it is a prayer of thanksgiving characterized by the restrained and thankful sadness of one who had miraculously not long since survived a possibly fatal illness.

Restraint is also the principal characteristic of the finale of this work as it looks both backwards to the carefree jollity of the last movement of the *Fourth Symphony,* and forwards to the tightly-reined *scherzo* qualities found in the second movement of the *Fifth Symphony* and the 'Pantomime' of the *Suite archaïque.* The controlled jauntiness in the outer sections of the ternary structure contrasts well with the broad sweep of the theme and its energetic accompaniment that constitute the B section (see (i) and (ii) respectively of Music Example 104 below).

Music Example 104: *Concerto da Camera,* third movement:
(i) bars 1-23

1
Fl.
C.A.
pp leggiero
I
Vons
II
Alt.
Velle
C.B.
Fl.
C.A.
I
Vons
II
Alt.
Velle
C.B.

crescendo
Fl.
C.A.
I
Vons
II
Tutti
Alt.
Velle
C.B.

(ii) 8B [8] - [9]

p dolce
arco
p
pizz.

Fl.
pp
C.A.
Von II
Alt.
Velle
C.B.
Fl.
C.A.
Von II
Alt.
Velle
C.B.

8
Fl.
C.A.
Vcn II
Alt.
Velle
C.B.

(Reproduit avec l'autorisation des EDITIONS SALABERT, Paris, propriétaires de l'œuvre.)

The various song settings which span this period are in many ways the most interesting because they reflect so closely the nature of Honegger's inspiration as expressed in his major achievements, the last four symphonies. Leaving aside the undistinguished strophic *Hommage au travail*, with its rather poor text by Maurice Senart which Honegger presumably set out of respect for a business friendship, the remainder of his songs can be divided into three categories. In the first of these come the *Saluste du Bartas* (*Six villanelles*) of 1941 which are settings of poems about Queen Marguerite of Navarre by Pierre Bédat de Monlaur (1544-1590), the five *Petits cours de morale* of 1941 (settings of verses from Jean Giraudoux's book *Suzanne et le Pacifique*), and the fourth song from the *Quatre chansons pour voix grave* — a poem by Ronsard (no date). In all these little miniatures Honegger returns to the carefree and happy spirit that is to be found in his song-settings of the period when he was associated with *Les Six*. They are characterized by the same sophisticated poise, unpretentious expressivity and simple emotions which, together with a liberal amount of wit and gentle mockery, had so vividly coloured his Apollinaire and Cocteau settings more than twenty years earlier. In these exquisite songs it is possible to see the side of Honegger which could prompt the remark that 'c'est à Paris que j'ai sans doute connu mes heures les plus belles, je ne vois pas pourquoi je quitterais cette ville au moment du malheur: je n'ai rien du rat qui fuit le navire en pleine tourmente!'[25] [it is in Paris that I have undoubtedly spent my happiest hours so I don't see why I should leave this city during these troubled times; I have nothing within me, unlike the rat, which makes me want to flee the ship in the midst of a howling gale!] and would want to write with such telling reserve to Paul Sacher in July 1940 that 'je voulais t'écrire depuis longtemps déjà mais je dois t'avouer que j'ai été un peu déprimé par les tristes événements que nous vivons'[26] [I have wanted to write to you for a long time now, but I must admit that I have been rather depressed by the sad events which are affecting us at present].

In the second category come the first three of the *Quatre chansons pour voix grave* (settings of poems by Tchobanian — December 1945; Aguet — undated; and Verlaine — 24 February 1944, respectively) and the *Trois poèmes de Claudel* (1939-40). Of the latter set, the second song, 'Le delphinium' is probably Honegger's finest *mélodie,* with every aspect seeming perfect in both conception and balance. The other two are more obviously stamped with unique features of Honegger's style; in the first, 'Siesta', the mosaic-structuring works with indefinable logic and cohesion, but the piano part yearns too much for orchestration; whilst in the last, 'Le rendez-vous', the concentration of the rich additive harmony in the bass and the non-functional chromaticism of certain ostinati detract from its merits. The other three poems are all marred to a greater or lesser extent by an overt simplification of harmonic language on Honegger's part. This certainly does not suit him and it is debatable, moreover, whether or not it is appropriate in the case of these particular texts.

The remaining songs, constituting the third and final category, are those in which it is possible to see an exact parallel to the programmatic content of the *Symphonie pour cordes* [*n*° *2*], *Symphonie liturgique* [*n*° *3*] and *Fifth Symphony.* The same vivid expression of profoundly felt emotions of tragic and depressing import which characterizes the *Symphonie liturgique* [*n*° *3*] is found in the last song he wrote. Written within a few months of the *Symphonie liturgique* [*n*° *3*], *Mimaamaquim* takes as its text a transliteration of the Hebrew version of Psalm 130, 'Out of the depths have I cried unto thee, O Lord'.

The same quality is dominant in the second of the *Trois psaumes* (1940-41), whose text is the first verse of Théodore de Bèze's translation of Psalm 140, 'Deliver me, O Lord, from the evil man, preserve me from the violent man'. In both songs, the nobility of the melodic line (with its soaring curve and unswerving direction) and the strength of the harmonic support (with its dependence on the powerful conditioning by contrary motion principles) produce an expression of tremendous dignity, breadth and concentration of persuasion in the same vein as was achieved in the *Symphonie pour cordes* [*n*° *2*] and *Symphonie liturgique* [*n*° *3*] (see Music Example 105 below).

Music Example 105: *Trois psaumes,* No. 2 (Psalm 140)

mf
-eux Pré-ser-ve-moi___ de la nui-san-ce de cet hom-me ma-li-ci-eux O___
___Dieu don-ne-moi dé-li-vran-ce de cet hom-me per-ni-ci-eux.
p largamente
f
O___ Dieu donne-moi dé-li-vran-ce de cet hom-me perni-ci-eux Pré-ser-ve-
moi de la nui-san-ce de cet hom-me ma-li-ci-eux O Dieu Donne-moi
pp
p

dé_li_vran _ ce
don_ne-moi dé_li_vran _ ce .

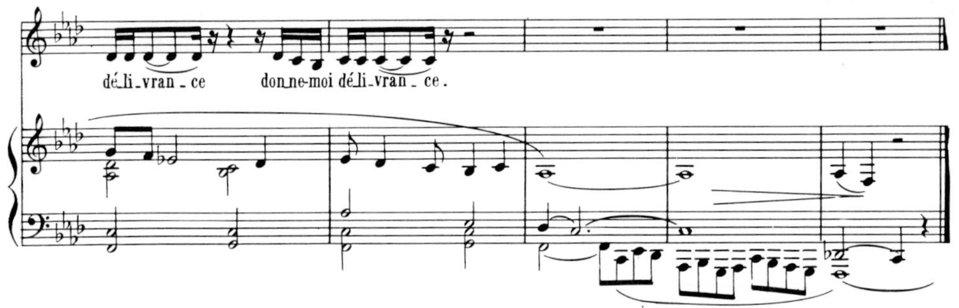

(Reproduit avec l'autorisation des EDITIONS SALABERT, Paris, propriétaires de l'œuvre.)

The outer two settings of the *Trois psaumes* are very different from the one they frame. In both it is possible to see Honegger returning to the spirit of Bach in the same extrovert way as in *Le roi David.* The derivation of the style of writing in the first, a setting of Théodore de Bèze's translation of Psalm 34 ('I will bless the Lord at all times, His praise shall continually be in my mouth') is obviously that of the later chorale-cantatas, but the way in which the piano part stops for the first four vocal statements is decidedly disconcerting (see Music Example 106 below).

Music Example 106: *Trois psaumes,* No. 1 (Psalm 34)

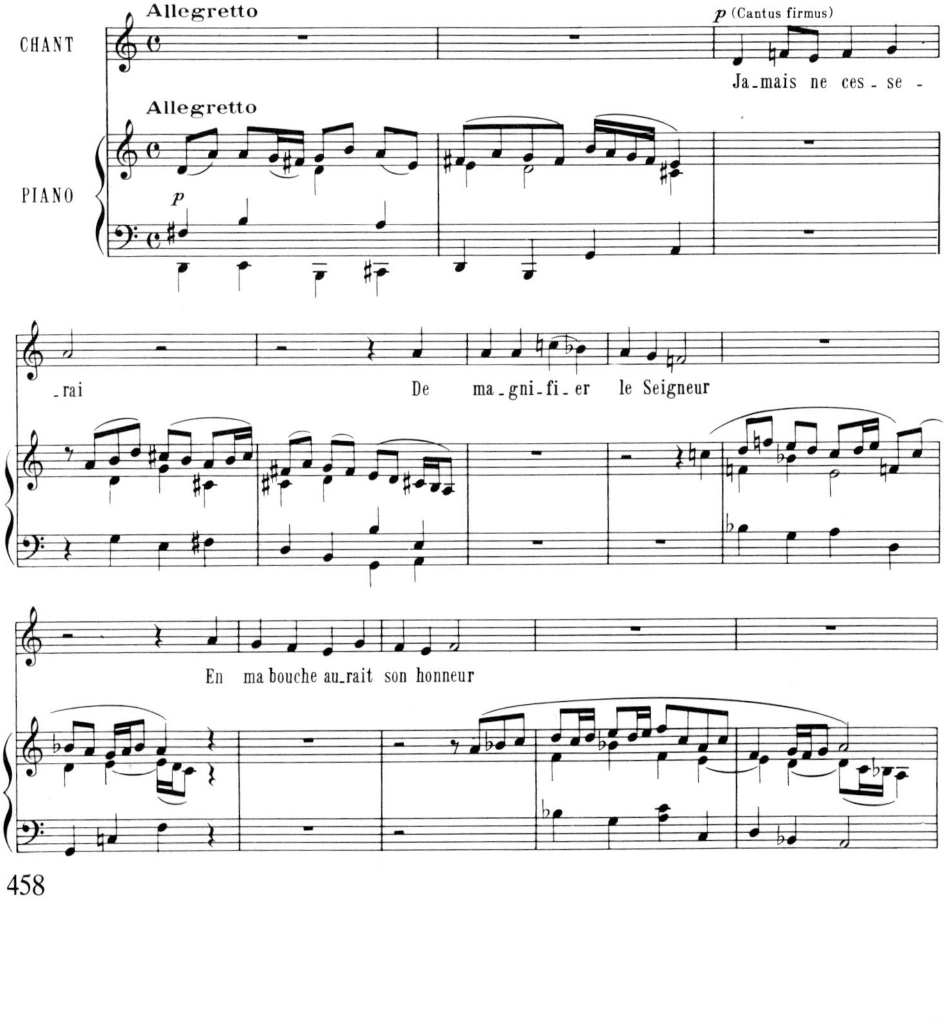

Allegretto
CHANT
p (Cantus firmus)
Ja_mais ne ces - se -
Allegretto
PIANO
p
_rai
De ma_gni_fi_er le Seigneur
En ma bouche au_rait son honneur

Tant que vi_vant se _ rai
Mon coeur plai_sir n'au _ ra
Qu'a_voir son Dieu glo_ri _ fi _ é
Dont maint bon cœur hu_mi_li _ é
L'o _ yant s'é_jou_i _
_ ra .
rall

In the last (Clement Marot's translation of Psalm 138: 'I will praise thee with my whole heart, before the gods will I sing praise unto thee') the exhilarating cantus-firmus is restricted somewhat by the discipline of the canonic treatment, and its rhythmic squareness becomes rather too exaggerated as a result (see Music Example 107 overleaf).

Music Example 107: *Trois psaumes,* No. 3 (Psalm 138)

- re - rai Cé - lè - bre - rai ta re - nom - mé - e
Pour l'a - mour de ta grand' bon - té Et fé - au -
- té tant es - ti - mé - - - - - e.
rit

(Reproduit avec l'autorisation des EDITIONS SALABERT, Paris, propriétaires de l'œuvre.)

Nevertheless, as a set of three psalm settings the effect is telling; the desire for jubilant praise is completely overshadowed by the intensity of the central expression of grief at the evils of war and, as such, the nature of Honegger's inspiration shines through clearly.

Part V: 1951 — the last symphonic works

Despite the incapacity he suffered as a result of his illness in 1947 Honegger still managed to compose. Honours and acclaim were showered upon him to an even greater extent in the last few years of his life, with hardly a month going by without a 'Festival Honegger', a production of a stage work, or major performances of one of his large-scale choral works, world-wide. Musical celebrations were extensive in 1952 to mark his sixtieth birthday and made up for the fact that World War II, and the occupation of Paris in particular, had severely restricted those of 1942. His membership of *Les Six* was acknowledged by anniversary concerts and the issue of special recordings both in 1949 and 1954. He was still too ill to undertake a major project for the 1949 celebrations, so he produced the *Prélude, Fugue et Postlude* for orchestra from his score for *Amphion,* which involved a minimum of actual work. Apart from the *Concerto da camera,* most of the music Honegger wrote after his illness in 1947 was for him relatively untaxing, being music for radio, stage, film or ballet (see Table 9 below).

TABLE 9

Compositions 1947-55

1947	*Intrada* for Trumpet and Piano; *Mimaamaquim* for Voice and Piano; *Œdipe*—Incidental Music; *Un revenant* — Film Score.
1948	*L'état de siège* — Incidental Music; *Concerto da camera* (Soli Flute and Cor Anglais with String Orchestra).
1949	*Saint François d'Assise* — Radio Music; *Marche contre la mort* — Radio Music.
1950	*Tête d'or* — Radio Music; *De la musique* — Ballet Score; *Bourdelle* — Film Score; *Panis angelicus* for Voice and Piano; *Symphony No. 5* for Orchestra.
1951	*Suite archaïque, Monopartita* and *Toccata* for Orchestra; *Paul Claudel* — Film Score; *La tour de Babel* — Film Score; *On ne badine pas avec l'amour* — Incidental Music; *La rédemption de François Villon* — Radio Music.
1952	*Œdipe-Roi*—Incidental Music.
1953	*Une cantate de Noël* — Oratorio; *Romance* for Flute and Piano.

He confided in Bernard Gavoty that '. . . one has to pass the time'[27] and that he was '. . . given to painful insomnia. To drive away my darker moods I jot them down on paper.'[28] These comments were, as Gavoty pointed out, thankfully in direct conflict with the statement made as a conclusion to the July 1950 radio interviews, namely that he had no future projects for symphonic music and therefore that he would 'doubtless never compose again, feeling no need, and seeing not the slightest necessity, for it. What is the use?'[29]

Whilst in America in 1947 he had been asked by the Koussevitsky Foundation to write a work in memory of Natalie Koussevitsky, but after his illness he had felt unable to cope with the commission. Nevertheless, as he told Gavoty, the jottings of an insomniac 'gave me some sketches. Having put some of them together, I noted that it would make a symphony; so I orchestrated it.'[30] Not only were these sketches responsible for the *Fifth Symphony,* but also for two further smaller orchestral works, the *Monopartita* and the *Suite archaïque.* Both were responses to commissions from orchestras who had done much to promote his music — the Zürich Tonhallegesellschaft Orchester and the Louisville Symphony Orchestra respectively — but in neither is there any of the compromise of style or emotional content that might have been suggested by the fact that both were intended for performance in concerts of a festive and celebratory nature. Wrongly-focussed initial reaction certainly did not help the general public to appreciate the significance of these works which, because of the nature of the *Toccata*[31] and the fact that *Une cantate de Noël* is based on material from the unfinished *Passion,* represent in a very special and unique way his last purely original and symphonic utterances. They are both characterized in a ritualisitc manner by qualities of summary retrospection and final personal confession. In the 'Ouverture' of the *Suite archaïque,* the polychoral style of the late sixteenth- and early seventeenth-century Venetian school is clearly evoked by the style of orchestration, whilst the use of the old Huguenot melody for Psalm 143 ('Hear my prayer, O Lord, give ear to my supplication') is the musical expression of the apposite confession contained in this psalm. The ghostly steps of the 'Pantomime' and the solemn dead-march of the 'Ritournelle et sérénade', with the wailing reflected in the interpolated cadenzas, are mysteriously evocative of things past, and the 'Processional' which concludes the work sees a return to the grave and noble religiosity of the opening movement as the music from the 'Ouverture' is presented in a halo of string scales.

In the *Monopartita* the Italian derivation of the word 'partita' as meaning *set,* is reflected in the joining together of six short movements to form a whole (a fact that also embraces its deployment as an alternative to the word *suite*). The seventeenth- and eighteenth-century use of the word to include the aspect of variation is reflected by the fact that the fourth movement is a variant of the second, the fifth of the third, and the last of the first. The prefix *Mono* refers to the fact that all the material used in the work evolves out of the interval of a minor third. The result is one of the most intensely rigorous structures that Honegger ever created, and one in which he successfully avoids all the pitfalls of diffuseness that had marred the *Nocturne* for orchestra (1936), conceived upon somewhat similar lines.

R.-Aloys Mooser was one of the few critics who recognized in these last two works that

> entre les trouvailles les plus significatives de son auteur, on retrouve cet accent pathétique dont on est fondé à juger qu'il est bien l'un des traits les plus reconnaissables de la figure musicale d'Arthur Honegger, et qui donne tant de prix à certains de ses ouvrages . . . Mais, ici, ce sentiment est plus profond et plus pénétrant peut-être. Les termes dans lesquels il s'exprime rendent un écho plus poignant et troublant. Comme si la pénible maladie que le musicien a traversée ces années dernières et le repliement sur soi qu'elle dut nécessairement provoquer avaient aiguisé encore sa sensibilité,

en la mettant face à face avec la misère et l'incertitude de l'existence humaine . . .'[32]

[between the most significant discoveries of its creator one finds again this pathetic accent which one is justified in believing to be amongst the most easily recognizable features of the musical figure of Arthur Honegger; it is also one which brings such value to certain works. But here, the feeling is deeper and perhaps more penetrating. The terms in which he expresses himself echo with ever-increasing poignancy and agitation. It is as if the painful illness from which the musician has suffered these last years and his withdrawing into himself which it inevitably brought about, had further increased his sensitivity by putting it face to face with the misery and uncertainty of human existence . . .].

Part VI: Coda

Throughout this book an attempt has been made to explore by analysis every aspect of Honegger's musical style. The quality of his musical ideas, the satisfying nature of his formal constructions, the originality, breadth and distinction of individual aspects of his personal musical language have all been exposed and discussed in an effort to reveal Honegger as a composer whose music, as Arthur Hoérée pointed out in a remark that has already been quoted once earlier on, may not always be of fundamental interest, but whose least gesture is always a musical one.[33] The context of each of his major works and the contemporary reaction to them has been incorporated to effect an assessment of his role and presence in the period. Despite the conscious effort made to avoid the obvious type of value judgement which would reveal far more about the author than the subject, a personal and necessarily contemporary evaluation has been interwoven with the analytical commentary on each major work.

It is sufficient to refute the words of an anonymous critic who is quoted as saying 'qu'Arthur Honegger, finalement, n'était pas un grand musicien parce que sa musique n'était que du cinéma, un peu comme un vulgaire commentaire de la vie de tous les jours'[34] [that Arthur Honegger is, after all, not a great musician because his music is nothing more than a rather vulgar cinematographic commentary on everyday life] by pointing out that even if it were possible to find such a commentary in every single work of his, it is always a message that transcends not only his own era, but will continue to transcend the barriers of time as the spirit of modern humanity does in the works of countless other contemporary composers.

Of all the eulogistic phrases that poured from the mouths and pens of so many composers, artists, musicians, friends and compatriots after his death on 27 November 1955, perhaps the most penetrating remark was made by Jean Cocteau at the cremation, and it is this which stands as the most suitable conclusion to this book:

Arthur, tu es parvenu à obtenir le respect d'une époque irrespectueuse. Tu joignais à la science d'un architecte du moyen âge la simplicité d'un humble ouvrier des cathédrales. Tes cendres sont brûlantes et ne refroidiront plus, même si notre terre cesse de vivre. Car la musique n'est pas que de ce monde et son règne n'a pas de fin[35]

[Arthur, you have managed to obtain the respect of a disrespectful era. You linked to the skill of an architect of the Middle Ages the simplicity of a humble craftsman of cathedrals. Your ashes are still burning and will never become cold, even if our earth ceases to exist, because music is not only of this world; its reign has no end].

Notes to Chapter XII

[1]Georges Favre, *Musiciens français contemporains,* 2 vols (Durand, Paris, 1956), II, 77.

[2]Jean Maillard and Jacques Nahoum, *Les symphonies d'Arthur Honegger* (Alphonse Leduc, Paris, 1974), 56.

[3]Ibid., p. 75.

[4]Ibid., p. 78.

[5]Ibid., p. 78.

[6]Ibid., pp. 80-81.

[7]Ibid., p. 81.

[8]Ibid., p. 82.

[9]Ibid., p. 84.

[10]Ibid., p. 85.

[11]Ibid., p. 85.

[12]Ibid., p. 85.

[13]Ibid., p. 87.

[14]Ibid., p. 87.

[15]Ibid., p. 78.

[16]Willy Tappolet, *Arthur Honegger* (Editions de la Baconnière, Neuchâtel, 1957), 251-52.

[17]Arthur Honegger, *I am a Composer* (Faber and Faber, London, 1966), 99.

[18]From the textual transcription provided with the record *Arthur Honegger vous parle,* Festival FLD 50, side 1.

[19]Programme note of the Basle Chamber Orchestra for 9 October 1943, reproduced in *Alte und Neue Musik: 25 ans d'orchestre de chambre sous la direction de Paul Sacher* (Atlantis, Zürich, 1952), 159-61 (in German); and in Willy Tappolet, *Arthur Honegger* (Editions de la Baconnière, Neuchâtel, 1957), 238-39 (in French).

[20]Ibid.

[21]Ibid.

[22]*I am a Composer* (Faber and Faber, London, 1966), p. 83.

[23]Programme note of the Basle Chamber Orchestra, op. cit.

[24]See Chapter VI, pages 148/200 and Chapter VIII, page 241.

[25]Jean Maillard and Jacques Nahoum, *Les symphonies d'Arthur Honegger* (Alphonse Leduc, Paris, 1974), 55.

[26]Ibid., p. 54 (from a letter to Paul Sacher).

[27]*I am a Composer* (Faber and Faber, London, 1966), p. 128.

[28]Ibid.

[29]Ibid.

[30]Ibid.

[31]See entry No. 198 in the Catalogue of Works.

[32]'*Monopartita*', *La Suisse*, 19 June 1951.

[33]See Chapter IV, page 92.

[34]Quoted by Jean Maillard and Jacques Nahoum, *Les symphonies d'Arthur Honegger* (Alphonse Leduc, Paris, 1974), 12.

[35]Quoted by Willy Tappolet, *Arthur Honegger* (Editions de la Baconnière, Neuchâtel, 1957), 276.

Appendix

U.N.E.S.C.O. INTERNATIONAL CONFERENCE,

VENICE, 22-28th September 1954.

'L'artiste dans la société contemporaine'

The Musician in Modern Society

by Arthur Honegger

I have been asked to write a report on the "status of the musician in the world today". This is a very broad subject, covering as it does the position of the performer and the composer, the singer and the music teacher alike. But in modern society, the composer is obviously in the most vulnerable position in this year of grace or, if you like, disgrace—1952; he has to contend with countless difficulties in bringing his works before the public and in having them performed and published, and his livelihood has become extremely precarious.

I should like to begin by defining what I understand by the word "composer", a title which is given to two categories — I might even say two classes — of producers of musical works, now more sharply distinguished than they used to be.

To the first belong authors writing facile, everyday music for which there is a steady demand, in other words, light music, dance music, songs and *Unterhaltungsmusik* intended for the entertainment of the public, at dinner dances, cabarets, night-clubs, music-halls, *café-concerts* and other such places. We may also include in this category most of the music accompanying films and a few lavishly produced light operas, owing little to the art of Euterpe.

Those of our colleagues who have specialized in all these forms might be called music manufacturers or producers. I assure them that I do not use the words in any derogatory sense, since great technical skill, talent and inventiveness are often needed for the creation of such music.

I shall therefore reserve the title of composer for the second type of creators — for those whose aim is not to cater for the public's taste in everyday enjoyment but, first and foremost, to create a work of art, to express some thought, some emotion, to crystallize their attitude to aesthetic or purely human problems.

They wish to earn a place in the history of music as worthy successors to the great masters of the past. A man with such an ambition is an idealist, which nowadays means a harmless type of lunatic.

As there is a regular demand for light music, it may be likened to other forms of commercial production. The man who produces an article for which there is a steady market may or may not be well paid, but he is usually guaranteed a bare livelihood at least. In the field of music, he is in close contact with the performers of his compositions, and, in fact, is frequently himself a performer or the leader of a group of instrumentalists. Thus we find the accordion-player or the conductor of a jazz-band performing his own works. In such cases, the commercial efficiency is higher: the manufacturer sets off the performer, and the performer the manufacturer. Music of this kind is brought to the public ear every day; and when the public ear is won, a handsome profit can be made. If a manufacturer's music scores greater and greater success, he prints it himself, augmenting his earnings as composer and performer by his earnings as publisher. In course of time, he finds himself obliged to open on office, organize publicity, and supervise the export of his goods to foreign countries. This leaves him no leisure to write his music himself. No matter. He hands over that task to other musicians, whose gifts have impressed him but on whom fortune has not smiled so brightly, while he himself, merely acts, in future, as director of production.

I do not wish to appear censorious of these practices — for one thing, because they have come down from the past, and it is our duty to respect our ancestors; and for another thing — and this is more important — because, having nothing to do with art, but belonging solely to the domain of trade and industry, they have often helped talented musicians in the early stages of their careers.

None of us would, for a moment, expect Mr. Packard or Mr. Citroën, with their own hands, to fit the engines into the cars that bear their names.

Such methods are in current use in the production of film music, where they operate in certain countries such as, principally, the United States, with the perfection of a conveyor-belt, smoothly, steadily, and with a satisfactory output. Just as a motor-car factory has its assemblers, electricians, fitters and testers, so a well-organized music studio has its melody-writers, harmonists and orchestrators, all specialists of undoubted skill. It is, surely, only reasonable that the abilities of all these experts should be put to the best use.

The drawback is, of course, that music manufactured in this way rarely brings fame to its author. Very few people could say who wrote the latest song hit that "everyone" is humming or whistling! Still, the royalties earned are in direct ratio to the number of hummers and whistlers.

Very different is the position of the composer — the poor lunatic who nurses the illusion that his contemporaries will be in the least interested in what he has to offer them. He is at grips with every kind of material difficulty, and finds it even harder than it was for his forerunners to overcome the obstacles that constantly arise to cut off his compositions from their potential audience. It is of him that I wish to speak now.

The distinguishing characteristic of the composer is that he is a man whose whole effort and overriding concern is to produce a commodity for which there is no demand. He may be compared to a manufacturer of old-fashioned bowler hats, button-boots or "mystery" corsets. We all know how heartily the present-day public despises these objects which, in the recent past, were the hallmark of elegance. In music, and this is where my comparison breaks down, the public wants only what was written 100 years ago. It regards the art of music as consisting in the performance of classical and romantic works, with the possible addition of a few more modern compositions which have waited an appreciable time in outer darkness. The modern composer is a kind of gate-crasher, forcing his way into a party to which he has not been invited.

We are thus faced with the fact that music must be 100 years old, or, at least, have reached a sufficiently respectable age to ensure that the majority of listeners will, I do not say "understand" it, for that word is meaningless in connexion with music, but at any rate listen to and enjoy it.

What is the reason for this state of things? The average listener is really interested only in music that he has had occasion to hear frequently. New works therefore arouse an instinctive mistrust, which the average listener expresses by keeping away from first performances. Experience has shown, however, that the more often the listener hears a good composition, the more he wants to hear it. So what keeps the public away is not only, as the critics try to make out, the "modernism" of a work, but chiefly its unfamilarity.

Here is a case in point. Ravel cannot be regarded as a "classic" in the ordinary sense of the word. He wrote *Daphnis and Chloé* in 1912. For some 30 years it was seldom performed. Then, after a particularly brilliant rendering by Charles Münch and the Société des Concerts du Conservatoire de Paris, it was suddenly "launched". Since when, this *Second Suite* has been constantly played at concerts and over the wireless (I have seen it announced nine times in a single week). It has as great a success, and draws as large audiences, as Beethoven's *Pastoral Symphony.* And quite rightly. Here is another example: a few years ago, Toscanini brought back to light *La Scala di Seta*, a charming little overture by Rossini. With Toscanini as its conductor, it was bound to have a great success, and since then it has been included in the repertory of many other conductors. Whereas *William Tell* and *Semiramis,* having been forgotten by Toscanini, are left to the male-voice choirs.

This is the tragedy of the present-day situation. People are no longer interested in listening to music, they merely come to admire its execution. The number of concerts given increases day by day, but the number of works performed diminishes year by year. This applies equally to the innumerable recitals given by pianists, who confine themselves strictly to the three "accepted" composers. The work itself is of no importance — that is a fact that cannot be too often repeated — it is merely an instrument enabling the virtuoso to show off his skill, an opportunity for the display of mechanical perfection or choreographic gesture by the executant.

There can be no doubt, therefore, that the contemporary leaders of musical life are the famous conductor and the celebrated performer.

The great conductor may come once or twice a year to give a gala performance. Naturally, his programme consists of those works which have earned him most success throughout the world. For 40 years (or more) he will conduct *Schumann's Fourth,* "in which he is unequalled by any rival". Or it may be the *Pathetic Symphony.*

If a conductor unexpectedly lapsed and tried to introduce a new work into his programme, the impresario would throw himself at his feet in tears. "You want to play X's Symphony, instead of the Brahms that everyone expects from you? There wouldn't be a soul in the house, it would be the ruin of me! Maestro, I pay you a huge fee in order to fill my hall. No eccentricities, I implore you. Why change from the works you know so well, and which you can conduct by heart?"

The same applies to the great international soloist who, every year, announces his "Third one-and-only Recital of the Season". The complete works of Chopin by the celebrated Malicutzo. There are about 50 of them who go from one town to another giving the same programme.

Let us now consider the permanent symphony orchestras. There is one in almost every major city in the world. Here again, the programmes hardly vary at all. Tchaikowski and Sibelius have gained ground with English and American audiences, while Brahms, a much later arrival, now reigns supreme in France, where he has been installed by the German conductors together with Richard Strauss — a composer whose works set off not only the conductor but the orchestra. These orchestras are run by committees, which help the conductor to draw up the programmes and prevent him from doing anything rash. The programmes are based on the most classical repertory, since that is what brings box-office success. Such contemporary works as are included owe their presence to a government subsidy, which is more than recovered by the State through the "entertainment" tax levied, in many countries, at any rate, on all performances. In any case, these subsidies are given for "first performances". The intrinsic value of the work is therefore of little importance, and even if it is well received, it will be a long time before it is heard again.

Committees, very naturally, represent the interests of the members. Everybody likes and admires Beethoven. So there has to be a Beethoven series. After that, they go back to the programme of previous years. And everyone is satisfied, except the new composers, who consider themselves meanly treated. Why?

There are no longer performing rights to be paid on a famous symphony, and the score is in the society's library. As it is constantly being played, few rehearsals are required. A new symphony needs more rehearsals, being more difficult and less familiar to the performers. In addition to this, there is the cost of hiring scores. The classic symphony fills the hall. The new symphony empties it.

In Haydn's and Mozart's day, the public clamoured for new works. That accounts for the vast output of these composers. Nowadays, I repeat, the public does not go to listen to a work, but to witness the performance of a work it knows already.

Let us turn to the opera. This is practically defunct in all countries except Germany and Italy. There the last war destroyed a considerable number of opera houses. They are not being rebuilt, for opera never pays. Garages or cinemas will be put up in their place.

In France, it must be admitted, the serious situation of the opera is attributable to the system adopted. No costly new work was ever put on unless it was unavoidable — that is, unless it bore the signature of a member of the Institute, of a man with political influence, or of someone whose position made it impossible to refuse him. No one believed in its chances of success, but, for politeness' sake, a virtue had to be made of necessity. If by any chance some work by a gifted musician found its way into the repertory, nothing was done to help it. The opera is notoriously old-fashioned; it has sunk to the level of a fancy-dress concert, whose music consists of barrel-organ tunes. "If we want the Opéra-Comique to pay its way," someone said to me once, "we should have to give *Carmen* every night". Young people leave this kind of entertainment to their elders, to whom it brings back memories.

The situation is much the same in the United States of America and Latin America. The Metropolitan in New York, as old-fashioned as the Gaîté Trianon and the Colon in Buenos Aires, performs operas from the Ricordi repertoire which are sung by a handful of surviving stars.

Towns which still have an "Opera" cling to it out of cultural vanity, so to speak; the idea is that the town would be incomplete without one. It is used for the old tried and tested repertory. The production of a new opera today costs a fortune and places a crippling burden on the management. So, as there is no public demand for new operas, they are not produced. If the public wants something new, it looks to films or the theatre — not even to the ballet, where interest is focused on the dancers instead of on the works themselves.

Light opera, too, is a thing of the past; its place has been taken by the music-hall type of entertainment. The titles are changed from time to time, but the show stays the same. It includes parades of costumes, the French cancan, a flight of pigeons or an all-in wrestling match, all of which has a far surer appeal to the crowd than an operatic performance, even if given by a popular tenor, who in any case can be heard over the wireless.

Lastly, provincial opera-houses are dying a slow death, with the steady withdrawal of subsidies, which are now not enough for the maintenance of an orchestra.

A familiar figure in novels, plays and films is the composer who becomes famous because of his natural genius; he marries the girl he loves and lives in a luxurious private mansion, far removed from all material cares. I have already protested vehemently against these incitements to launch out into the musical world, for which ignorant writers are to be blamed. One success at the opera, and there you are, rich and famous! This may, perhaps, have been possible once. About half a century ago a fortune could be made by writing operas. Massenet in France, Richard Strauss in Germany, and Puccini in Italy did so. We need only remember that, under his contract with his publisher, Massenet received 150,000 francs a year in gold, not to mention his royalties. The Khedive of Egypt paid the same amount to Verdi for *Aïda,* which was composed for the opening of the Cairo Opera-House. Tantalizing thought.

As for the royalties received for symphonies, quartets, sonatas, songs and other trifles, we know that Gabriel Fauré, the Director of the Conservatoire and a Commander of the Legion of Honour, the musician whose magic touch opened up undreamt-of vistas, was unable, for all his fame, to raise the sum needed for admission to life membership of the Society of Authors, Composers and Publishers of Music, and he died at the age of 79.

I have already spoken my mind on the subject of virtuoso concerts, where the programmes are eternally the same and only a few celebrities draw audiences and make profits. Chopin, Chopin and Liszt or Beethoven are all one ever hears from pianists; and violinists, 'cellists and singers, too, cautiously keep to the same few favourites. No other instrument has any chance of trying its luck. The flute, clarinet and horn are relegated to the full orchestra.

Chamber music ensembles, quartets, quintets and trios are likewise practically never heard these days. While the takings have to be divided between several performers, each one has to pay the same travelling and hotel expenses as the single artiste. It is, therefore, a material impossibility for such ensembles to pay their way, even when they choose the safest of programmes, since the audience for such performances has also fallen off considerably.

The Big Festivals

The last few years have seen a great increase in the number of big summer festivals. The first, such as the Salzburg Festival in 1921, were intended to bring new music to the fore, and to them we owe the establishment of the International Society for Contemporary Music. The competition soon became really formidable, much to the detriment of contemporary music, since the very latest novelty had, at all costs, to be performed. Gifted composers were overwhelmed by the spate of mediocrity and quietly disappeared. The public followed their example.

Nowadays, most of these festivals are organized as tourist attractions, always exploiting the same names — Mozart and Wagner for the opera, famous conductors and soloists for the concert hall.

It was originally excessive taxation which, by a happy turn of events, suggested the holding of these festivals. People preferred to throw away their money by giving a few really fine concerts rather than to have it taken away directly by the revenue authorities. The tax collector is none the worse off, since he ultimately recovers his dues from the artists performing at these festivals. This may be all very well but it is of no real benefit to music. Those who profit are the railway companies, hotels and restaurants.

Films

For some time, films came to the composer's rescue. The breakdown of the opera and chamber music, the miserable returns from symphonic works, and the practical impossibility of getting music published, made composers turn to the films, where, backed up by some of that industry's most enlightened representatives, they finally found a livelihood.

None the less, a few years ago, when a group of composers specializing in film music drew up a draft standard contract for the organizing committee of the film industry (which, incidentally, never received official consideration), it contained the following sentence: "The name of the composer must figure on posters in letters at least as large as those used for the humblest actor."

Which goes to show that these composers cherished no illusions about the importance of their share in the creation of great films. They had long been accustomed to being treated as poor relations and were perfectly well aware that no one goes to the cinema to hear music, and that no one hearing it really listens to it.

Thus there was a rapid reversion to the old practices — to the industrial manufacture which I have already described — and as the production situation becomes more critical, non-organized manufacturers fall out of the running.

Publishing

There is a great difference between the publication of literature and that of music. It is easy to get a book published, because there is a steady market for books, whereas fewer and fewer people buy music, which has become increasingly difficult to read. It is also very expensive. Fifty years ago, all middle-class homes had a piano and kept a collection of classical sonatas, together with the pianoforte and vocal scores of the best known operas. Things are very different now; people have so much more difficulty in sight-reading and playing music that the sale of these scores has dropped to practically nothing. This is partly because the old lovers of chamber music have become radio listeners in this field. From the publisher's point of view, it is an act of sheer philanthropy to publish a new quartet or quintet, as there are no buyers, and the few professional ensembles who are willing to make the effort of including such works in their programmes naturally receive them free of charge.

The initial outlay for a symphonic work is increasingly heavy and can only be recovered after many years, and then only if the composer is known and his works played abroad.

The hire of scores may cover part of the expenses incurred by the publisher. A table prepared by the Durand firm, showing the rate of sales of a few pieces of contemporary music, makes interesing study in this connexion.

Author and work	*Instruments*	*1st edition*		*Sold out in (*Not sold out)*
		No. of copies	*Date*	
Debussy				
Première Arabesque	Piano	400	1891	1903
Children's Corner	Piano	1,000	1908	1909
Ravel				
Histoires Naturelles	Piano-voice	500	1907	1913
Ma Mère l'Oye	Piano duet	500	1910	1912
Messiaen				
Huit Préludes	Piano	500	1930	*
Milhaud				
Onzième Suite Symphonique	Orchestral score	100	1921	*

On the other hand, a literary work by a young and unknown author has been known to sell 150,000 copies, in the year of its publication.

We come up against exactly the same set of problems with regard to records; in other words, there will be 10 editions of Beethoven's *Pastoral Symphony* with different conductors and orchestras, whilst it is impossible to secure modern works, or even classical works which are not in the regular repertory.

However, there is room for optimism; the long-playing records at 33 r.p.m. may develop the music lover's taste for collecting, so that he will build up a kind of music library comparable with that of the humanist. Unfortunately, the high price of those records limits the number of those who can afford to buy them. One very important field still remains to be discussed — broadcasting. But I think it better to hold this over until we come to the subject of remedies. I shall first say something about the responsibility incurred by the composers themselves.

There is no point in dwelling on the recurrent complaint of tunelessness, which is reiterated whenever the harmonic process changes or when composers return to a more horizontal style.

In my opinion, what has estranged the music-lover from the contemporary composer is the latter's rather childish pretentiousness in expressing himself in a deliberately complicated form. As sight-reading is already none too easy, there is no need to add to its difficulty. It is, however, far harder to find a clear than an ultra-subtle form of expression, and all too often the composer yields to the temptation of writing in a style that appals the performer. He lightly imagines he is showing transcendent skill by changes in time, torrents of notes and chords piled up like sky-scrapers. Mere childishness! Today every stage in the production of music costs a fortune. It is a foolish offence to waste time and money by such writing, which no longer impresses the simple but is a sure sign of incompetence.

There is no denying that the effort needed to bring a new work before the public is out of all proportion to the number that are of any real value. Under a kind but misguided policy, all too many mediocre works get performed once, thus giving a certain rash satisfaction to one person and doing disservice to the general interests of young composers.

Now, our aim is to discover how we may improve the lot of the composer, especially those of proved talent, as any benefit will rebound to the advantage of the whole body of composers and make the beginner's career easier.

We have seen how insignificant a place is allotted to contemporary music in the world today.

How can we remedy this situation? Some of the remedies which have been suggested to me are listed below.

1. *Education, starting in the primary school, by making music a compulsory subject like drawing*

I agree that a love of music should be instilled in children, but am not in favour of forcing them to take music analysis lessons and to learn dates for the history of music.

What is needed is to bring music to the children — either by direct performance, or through the gramophone or radio — and, *above all, to begin with contemporary composers and work gradually back towards the classics.* The living language, that of the listener's own period, should come first, then the study of the languages out of which it developed. The foremost concern should be to train listeners, "consumers" of music, eager students of the musical art, not would be professionals, such as the academies of music turn out.

It is these establishments, and those who teach in them, who are chiefly to blame for the present lack of interest in music. The students practise the technique of performance, not the "art of music".

As a test, take 20 pianists who have won first prizes. They will all show a remarkable turn of speed when called upon to play a Chopin study or the finale of a Beethoven sonata. But, faced with a score such as that of *Ariane et Barbe Bleue,* for instance, they will be unable to read eight bars without stumbling.

They have never been taught to read music. They have been forced to thump out tunes, to rattle off scales and arpeggios until their wrists ached on the keyboard.

People are more reasonable with regard to sport. There are cyclists who enjoy their Sunday run without feeling the urge to enter for the Tour de France. The virtuoso is a rare creature. Yet every young pianist is put into training as though he were expected to become a virtuoso. A good sight-reader is infinitely more valuable to the art of music than any champion in the Chopin-Liszt contest.

It would therefore seem highly desirable to restrict the flood of first-prize-winners that gushes out every year from the various academies of music, each one of whom, by virtue of his award — which has, in fact, like an inflated currency, lost much of its value — claims to give yet another Chopin recital, resulting in yet another embittered failure.

What we should do is to train sight-readers, who will spend their spare time in deciphering a Schubert sonata or a Poulenc impromptu for their own pleasure, or perhaps even in playing a sonata with a 'cellist friend.

But we should take no steps to encourage the budding virtuoso. He and his kind are only too numerous, and do more harm than good to the cause of music.

2. *Increased grants to symphony orchestras, and compulsory inclusion of one modern work in every programme except those of festivals devoted to a single composer*

I am, of course, most sympathetic towards the idea of the State's being made to pay more substantial grants. But yet I have my doubts, for while this might give temporary relief, there is always much more danger of the authorities' reducing subsidies wrested from them against their will.

Roger Fernay's most interesting report tells significantly how the budget for fine arts in France has been progressively slashed since the end of the last war, in order to aid preparations for the next.

We know that in the provinces, the theatre, and above all, the opera, is being gradually starved out of existence.

The subsidies granted by the authorities have been reduced as follows: 240 millions in 1948, 120 millions in 1949, 80 millions in 1950, and 46 millions in 1951.

State aid may act as a soporific, preventing the patient from suffering in his death-throes; but it will not cure his illness. I must repeat, because it can never be said too often, that the only possible cure is a public demand for new works.

The compulsory inclusion of a new work in any programme is no reliable remedy either. It will not mean a single Beethoven festival the less, and the new works will meet the same fate as most of the "first performances" that State-subsidized orchestras are required to give. They will be executed, sometimes in the most violent sense of the word, and that will be the end of them. The problem of quality really must not be overlooked. If a work has vitality and merits support, it requires to be brought before the public not once only, but a number of times. There must be no more string-pulling out of friendship, no more intrigue and influence; what is needed is courage to put off those composers who are no good, in favour of those who have some chance of winning the public ear. Who is to be responsible for this? The critics, the musicians, or the People's Commissars? Here again, whether we like it or not, the last word must be left to the public, after they have been given a chance to compare the different works. The Concerts Pasdeloup have tried to do this, and the public's judgment was found not to differ so very widely from that of the adjudicators.

At all events, it would be preferable to withhold all grants until the *end* of the season, and then proportion them to the efforts of the individual orchestras.

Certain orchestras are supported solely by private music-lovers, with no recourse to the public authorities; one of these is the Basle Kammer Orchester, which has just celebrated the twenty-fifth anniversary of its foundation. Not a single Beethoven symphony has been performed by the orchestra in the course of those 25 years, while they were continually included in the programmes of all other orchestras. This particular group has confined itself to the presentation of classical works disdained by others, and modern compositions. The early period was difficult, of course; but an ever-growing audience has been induced to take an interest in works with which it was unfamiliar, and to listen to the music instead of comparing the idiosyncrasies of the performers. This is an instance of artistic education.

In my view, it would be only fair that, where subsidies exist, they should be given to chamber ensembles as well as to symphony orchestras. Chamber music is one of the purest and finest types of music, and therefore appeals to a relatively small public. It is highly desirable that it should be saved from extinction, firstly, in the interests of listeners and, secondly, in the interests of composers. The performance of a new quintet involves less expense than a symphony, but we have seen above that the need for help in forming a small ensemble (quartet or quintet) is keenly felt, because of the constant rise in concert costs.

Another advantage of subsidies would be to give some security of livelihood to performers who, though not top flight soloists, could with regular practice, form first-class chamber ensembles and compete successfully with the virtuosos. This has happened (and still does, but under enormous difficulties) when ensembles like the Joachim, Capet, Calvet and Löwenguth quartets, and others like the Cortot, Thibaud and Casals Trio, played chamber music exclusively. That was really music.

3. *Commissioning of works by the State for the theatre, schools and radio; competition pieces for academies of music*

The competition system has been in operation for some years but its effect in improving the lot of composers is negligible. Otherwise, it is unusual for the State to commission musical works. Wartime slaughter is glorified by heroic statues erected above rolls of honour: not by cantatas. In any case the commissions would be given to "recognized" composers and not to young musicians.

It would be difficult to make a fair division between the twelve-tone school and even more advanced composers.

We have seen that it is rather late in the day to commission operas — a proceeding which would, incidentally, involve governments in most unaccustomed generosity. The Verdi Prize in Italy was worth 4 million lire. But the award entailed an obligation to produce the work which cost 30 million lire.

Ballet. Since the days when Diaghileff brought ballet to fame and fashion, the importance of the music has steadily declined.

We are coming back to the athletic virtuoso performance. Often the music accompanying those performances is classical: *Invitation to the Waltz,* pieces by Chopin, fragments from Tchaikowski arranged for a second-class orchestra. Nowadays only the great State-subsidized theatres can play proper scores.

In order to retain complete freedom, choreographers are more and more inclined to use music which was not written for ballet: classical symphonies, symphonic poems, or even oratorios. So the modern composer is deprived of another outlet for his talents.

Films. For the past 20 years, musicians have been interviewed on the subject of "Music and the Cinema". Their answers have always been the same; but so far no lasting improvement has followed. In a budget of millions there is never a penny for the composer. For the orchestra or conductor, yes. They come on to the salaries bill. But musical composition? That could only figure as a series of noughts, or lead to undignified haggling among the sort of business gentlemen who deal in copyright. And this, as I said at the beginning, is a very different business from composing music.

I am not so naïve as to suggest a reduction in taxation at a time when every country is making all possible efforts to extract the maximum from its citizens. Authors, composers and other unattached workers without proper "trade unions" are naturally the first to be sacrificed. I know that it is quite as vain to hope for an increase in royalties, although this is essential in some countries. Industries closely connected with the Government, or which are in fact run by the Government, do not attempt to hide what a nuisance they find the rights connected with a long-outworn conception of freedom, and especially the much-talked-of moral right whereby the author has sole power to decide what shall be done with his work. By open and underhand methods, the author's right to a livelihood from his work is challenged and attacked on every side. We must have the courage to see things as they are, instead of relying on the airy assurances of after-dinner speeches at congresses and other convivial gatherings.

It is just the same with *broadcasting* and it will be the same with *television.* Someone said to me: "All your jeremiads fall flat before the work that is being done in broadcasting. What does it matter if concert societies and opera-houses disappear, so long as there is broadcasting and it can afford — since most broadcasting stations are State-owned, and therefore are the State itself — to pay all deficits out of your pocket? But I am not at all sure that this tap which is always turned on, pouring a ceaseless stream of noise over mankind, is good for the art of music. A man left too long in too bright a light goes blind. Modern life is becoming more and more noisy. Soon we shall all go deaf because of the noise in which we have to live. Your concierge's or your neighbour's wireless pours out a flood of noise from dawn to midnight. It may be the *Mass in B minor* or the wild wailing of accordions. You will find the same noise everywhere — in streets, stores, cafés, restaurants, even taxis. It is forcibly inflicted in factories. Can you imagine a man who has perhaps heard the *C Minor Symphony* six times during the day rushing to a concert in the evening where he will have to pay a comparatively high price to hear it again? Many schoolchildren and students do their mathematics home work with the wireless on. They get used to thinking of music as a "background noise" to which they pay no more attention than they do to the colour of the walls.

Let us read over Stravinsky's very apt comments in his *Poétique musicale*: "To spread music by every means is an excellent thing, in itself; but to do so indiscriminately, offering it at random to the general public, who are not ready to hear it, is to expose them to a very grave risk of saturation. The days are past when Johann Sebastian Bach would cheerfully make a long journey on foot to hear Buxtehude. Today the wireless delivers music at home at any time of the day or night. The only effort the listener has to make is to turn a knob. But musical appreciation comes, and grows, only with practice. In music, as in everything else, the faculty atrophies unless it is used. Heard in that way, music becomes a form of drug, paralysing and deadening the mind instead of stimulating it. With the consequence that the very people who are trying to cultivate an appreciation of music by broadcasting it more and more, often end by making those whose interest and taste they wish to develop lose all interest in it."

Lastly, let us think clearly what would happen under the omnipotent dictatorship of a single organization. Naturally the ultimate object of a broadcasting station is to become the sole source of transmission, with the widest possible listening range. The result will be that provincial stations, necessarily of poorer quality, will shortly go out of business. (This will automatically mean the end of local orchestras and, still more, local opera-houses.)

For years societies of authors and composers have been fighting to raise royalties, the French rate being one of the lowest in the world. The State, as the only authority, will force them to accept unconditional surrender. We should also remember that broadcasting has its personal tastes. One composer is played very often, another less often, a third rarely, a fourth never. What will happen to the latter when all other openings have disappeared? We shall soon arrive at one of those totalitarian systems, whose blessings we have already experienced and can still see.

CONCLUSIONS

1. First of all, the young composer must be made to realize that he cannot earn his living by composing, save in exceptional circumstances and late in life. Until then he must have a second profession or a private income. Towards the end of the last century this was already the case with most poets (Verlaine, Mallarmé, Valéry, Claudel, and so on).

2. No attempt should be made to "discover" talented young composers. It would be better to discourage them. There are already too many for the market. On the other hand, all possible help should be extended to those

who have already given proof of their talent, so that they are not overwhelmed by unfair competition from the great classical composers.

3. Musical education should be directed towards creating an audience for modern music. Music should be defended against the exploitation of virtuosity in every form.

4. In this way, the public should be led to take the same interest in new aspects of music as in literature, drama, films and painting.

Catalogue of the works of Arthur Honegger

NOTES

Every entry contains all the available information organized in the following way:

Serial Number. TITLE (as on title page). Genre. Year(s) of Composition.
Subtitle (if any).
Commissioned by/created for/collaboration with or contributions by other composers.
Scoring (where applicable).
Author(s) and source(s) of text(s) with name(s) of translator(s) (in the case of vocal works).
Titles of movements/ Tempo markings.
Place and date of composition/orchestration.
Other versions.
Dedication.
Duration.
Publisher(s)/Plate Number(s)/Language(s) (in vocal scores)/Year of publication.
Details concerning (publication of) subsequent version(s).
Details of first performance: Performers; Date; Concert organization; Venue.
Details concerning first performance(s) of subsequent version(s).

In the case of film scores, information concerning the British première and British distribution has been included, but not the names of actors and actresses.

If no durations are marked in the score those supplied are enclosed in parentheses and are derived from two sources, namely the *Editions Salabert Catalogues* of 1968 and the *BBC Music Library Orchestral Catalogue*. They are presented respectively either side of a /, which permits identification of source(s) and the presentation of significantly divergent figures.

An *Alphabetical Index of Titles* and an *Index of Titles by Genre* are provided (see pp. 488 - 93 and pp. 494 - 500 respectively).

The abbreviations used in presenting the *instrumentation* of each work are in accordance with Appendix III of the *Anglo-American Cataloguing Rules*. Whilst specific reference should be made in case of doubt concerning their interpretation, by way of an example, the entry for No. 95 translates as follows:

An orchestra comprising:

2 Flutes (second doubling piccolo); 2 Oboes; 1 Clarinet (in B♭ and/or A), 1 E♭ Clarinet, 1 Bass Clarinet (total of three players); 3 E♭ Alto Saxophones; 3 Bassoons and Contra-Bassoon (total four players)/*No* Horns; 3 B♭ Trumpets and 1 D Trumpet (total four players); 3 Trombones and 1 Bass Trombone (total four players); 1 Tuba *if* no Bass Trombone available/Timpani; 2 percussion players playing the more usual instruments/Celesta; ondes Martenot; 2 Pianos/Strings. [The position is further clarified by noting that neither Harp (hp), Organ (org) nor Harmonium (hnm) are required in the keyboard section and a Cor Anglais (ca) is not employed. If only standard percussion instruments are required, the composer sometimes merely specifies the necessary number of players; otherwise the instruments are listed with or without the number of players needed being noted.];

and

15 Reciters (which may be reduced to 4); 3 Solo Sopranos; 1 Solo Contralto; 4 Solo Tenors (which may be reduced to 1); 2 Solo Basses (which may be reduced to 1); 1 Solo Child's voice; Children's Chorus; Mixed (S.A.T.B.) Chorus.

The derivation of all abbreviations used elsewhere in the catalogue is indicated in the List of Abbreviations (see pp. 483 - 87).

List of Abbreviations

Liste des abréviations

Liste von Abkürzungen

Abbreviation	*English*	*français*	*Deutsch*
A	(Solo) Contralto (voice), Alto	(voix solo de) contralto,	(Solo) Alt(singstimme)
accomp	accompaniment, accompanied by	accompagnement, accompagné par	Begleitung, begleitet von
add	additional	supplémentaire	zusätzlich
A.H.	Arthur Honegger	Arthur Honegger	Arthur Honegger
AM	Au Ménéstrel	Au Ménéstrel	Au Ménéstrel
anv	anvil	enclume	Amboss
arec	treble (alto) recorder	flûte à bec	Blockflöte
arr	arranged, arrangement	adapté, adaptation	bearbeitet, Bearbeitung
Ass	Assistant	aide	Gehilfe
asx	alto saxophone	saxophone contralto	Altsaxophon
attrib	attributed to	attribué à	zugeschrieben
Aug	August	août	August
aug	augmented	augmenté	vergrössert
B	(Solo) Bass (voice)	(voix solo de) basse	(Solo) Bass(singstimme)
Bar	(Solo) Baritone (voice)	(voix solo de) baryton	(Solo) Bariton(singstimme)
barsx	baritone saxophone	saxophone baryton	Baritonsaxophon
bary	baryton (viola de bordone)	baryton (viole di bordone)	Bariton (Bratsche di bordone)
B.B.C.	British Broadcasting Corporation	British Broadcasting Corporation	British Broadcasting Corporation
B.B.C.S.O.	B.B.C. Symphony Orchestra	Orchestre symphonique de la BBC	BBC Sinfonie Orchester
bcl	bass clarinet	clarinette basse	Bassklarinette
bdm	bass drum	grosse caisse	Grosse Trommel
bells	tubular bells	cloches tubulaires	Röhrenglocken
bjo	banjo	banjo	Banjo
Bprem	British première	première britannique	Uraufführung in Grossbritannien
br	brass	cuivres	Blechinstrumente
brdcst	broadcast	émission radiodiffusé	Rundfunk-Sendung
brec	bass recorder	flûte à bec basse	Bassblockflöte
Brit. dist	British distribution by	distribué en Grande Bretagne par	verteilt in Grossbritannien von
bsn	bassoon	basson	Fagott
bsx	bass saxophone	saxophone basse	Basssaxophon
btbn	bass trombone	trombone basse	Bassposaune

c	circa	ca:	zirka, ca
C	Choudens	Choudens	Choudens
ca	cor anglais	cor anglais	Englischhorn
cast	castanets	castagnettes	Kastagnetten
cb	double-bass (instrument)	contrebasse	Kontrabass
cbcl	contra-bass clarinet	clarinette contrebasse	Kontrabassklarinette
cbsn	contra-bassoon	contrebasson	Kontrafaggott
CC	Chamber Choir	ensemble vocal	Kammerchor
C du M	Editions Chant du Monde	Editions Chant du Monde	Editions Chant du Monde
cel	celesta	célesta	Celesta
ch-chorus	chamber mixed-voice (SATB) choir	ensemble vocal (SATB)	gemischter Kammerchor (SATB)
Ch. Mus	Chamber Music	musique de chambre	Kammermusik
ch-orch	chamber orchestra	orchestre de chambre	Kammerorchester
chorus	mixed-voice (SATB) choir	chœur mixte (SATB)	gemischter Chor (SATB)
cl	clarinet	clarinette	Klarinette
C.M.D.I.	Cercle Musical et Dramatique Indépendant	Cercle Musical et Dramatique Indépendant	Cercle Musical et Dramatique Indépendant
cnt	cornet	cornet à pistons	Kornett
CO	Chamber Orchestra	orchestre de chambre	Kammerorchester
collab	composed in collaboration with	composé en collaboration avec	komponiert gemeinsam mit
Conc	Concerto, concertante, concertino, concert(s)	concerto, concertant, concertino, concert(s)	Konzert, Konzertant, Sologruppe, Konzert(e)
cond	conductor, conducted by	chef d'orchestre, dirigé par	Dirigent, dirigiert von
Cons	Conservatoire	Conservatoire	Konservatorium
cont	continuo	basse continue	Generalbassinstrument
cv	(Solo) child's voice	voix (solo) d'enfant	(Solo) Kindstimme
cv chorus	children's choir	chœur d'enfants	Kinderchor
cym	cymbal	cymbales	Becken
D	Editions Demets	Editions Demets	Editions Demets
dbl	doubling	jouant deux rôles, doublement	eine Doppelrolle Spielen, Verdopplung
Dec	December	décembre	Dezember
Ded	Dedication	dédicace	Weihung
Dir	Directed by	dirigé par	dirigiert von
dm	drum	tambour	Trommel
drec	descant recorder	flûte à bec soprano	Sopranblockflöte
Dtrpt	trumpet in D	trompette en ré	Trompete in D
Dur	Duration	durée	Dauer
E♭cl	clarinet in E♭	clarinette en mi bémol	Klarinette in E♭
Eng	English	anglais	englisch
Eng. trans	English translation by	traduction anglaise par	Englische Übersetzung von
EOF	Editions Œuvres Françaises	Editions Œuvres Françaises	Editions Œuvres Françaises
ER	Editions Royales	Editions Royales	Editions Royales
ESI	Editions Sociales Internationales	Editions Sociales Internationales	Editions Sociales Internationales
fbp	first broadcast performance	première radiodiffusée	Rundfunk-Uraufführung
f*concert*p	first concert performance	première musicale	Konzert-Uraufführung

Feb	February	février	Februar
f*Eb*p	first English broadcast performance	première radiodiffusée anglaise	Englische Rundfunk-Uraufführung
f*E*p	first English performance	première anglaise	Englische Uraufführung
FF	Edition Fœtisch Frères (Lausanne) (now Hug Musique)	Edition Fœtisch Frères (Lausanne) (maintenant Hug Musique)	Edition Fœtisch Frères (Lausanne) (jetzt Hug Musique)
f*French*p	first French performance	première française	Französische Uraufführung
fl	flute	flûte	Flöte
f*London*p	first London performance	première à Londres	Londoner Uraufführung
fp	first performance	première	Uraufführung
f*Paris*p	first performance in Paris	première parisienne	Pariser Uraufführung
fpub	first published	première publication	erst veröffentlicht
f*public*p	first public performance	première publique	Öffentliche Uraufführung
Fr	French	français	französisch
Fr. trans	French translation by	traduction française par	Französische Übersetzung von
f*staged*p	first staged performance	première sur scène	Bühnen-Uraufführung
f*theatre*p	first theatrical performance	première théâtrale	Theater-Uraufführung
fv chorus	female voice choir	chœur de femmes	Frauenchor
Ger	German	allemand	deutsch
Ger. trans	German translation by	traduction allemande par	Deutsche Übersetzung von
glock	glockenspiel	glockenspiel	Glockenspiel
Gram	Gramophone record(ing)	disque	Schallplatte
gtr	guitar	guitare	Gitarre
H	Editions Heugel	Editions Heugel	Editions Heugel
hn	(French) horn	cor	Horn
hnm	harmonium	harmonium	Harmonium
hp	harp	harpe	Harfe
hpsd	harpsichord	clavecin	Cembalo
Inc. Mus	Incidental Music	musique de scène	Bühnenmusik, Begleitmusik, Schauspielmusik
Jan	January	Janvier	Januar
JF	Editions Josette France	Editions Josette France	Editions Josette France
LCMC	London Contemporary Music Club	London Contemporary Music Club	London Contemporary Music Club
LCS	Lithocopie Ch. Schneklüd	Lithocopie Ch. Schneklüd	Lithocopie Ch. Schneklüd
L.P.O.	London Philharmonic Orchestra	Orchestre philharmonique de Londres	Londoner Philharmonisches Orchester
LS	Editions de la Sirène (now Editions Max Eschig)	Editions de la Sirène (maintenant Editions Max Eschig)	Editions de la Sirène (jetzt Editions Max Eschig)

M	Editions Mathot (now Editions Salabert)	Editions Mathot (maintenant Editions Salabert)	Editions Mathot (jetzt Editions Salabert)
ME	Editions Max Eschig	Editions Max Eschig	Editions Max Eschig
MO	Municipal Orchestra	Orchestre municipal	Städtisches Orchester
movt(s)	movement(s)	mouvement(s)	Satz (Sätze)
mrc	maracas	maracas	Maracas
mss	manuscript(s)	manuscrit(s)	Manuskript(e)
Mus/mus	music, musical	musique, musical	Musik, musikalisch
mv chorus	male voice choir	chœur d'hommes	Männerchor
Mz	(Solo) Mezzo-Soprano (voice)	(voix solo de) mezzo-soprano	(Solo) Mezzosopran (singstimme)
Narr	Narrator	narrateur	Erzähler
No(s)	Number(s)	numéro(s), no(s)	Nummer, Nr
Nov	November	novembre	November
Npf	Not performed	pas exécuté	nicht aufgeführt
Npf/b	Not performed or broadcast	pas exécuté ni radiodiffusé	weder aufgeführt, noch gesendet
Npub	Not published	pas publié	nicht veröffentlicht
ob	oboe	hautbois	Oboe
ob-d'a	oboe d'amore	hautbois d'amour	Oboe d'amore
Oct	October	octobre	Oktober
om	ondes Martenot	ondes Martenot	ondes Martenot
opt	optional	facultatif	fakultativ
Orch/orch	orchestra, orchestral, orchestration (by)	orchestre, orchestral, orchestré par	Orchester, Orchestral, orchestriert von
Orch. de la S.R.	Orchestre de la Suisse Romande	Orchestre de la Suisse Romande	Orchestre de la Suisse Romande
l'Orch. Sym. de Paris	Orchestre Symphonique de Paris	Orchestre Symphonique de Paris	Orchestre Symphonique de Paris
org	organ	orgue	Orgel
orig	original	original	original
Paris Cons. Orch	Paris Conservatoire Orchestra	Orchestre du Conservatoire de Paris	Orchestre du Conservatoire de Paris
PC	Piano Conductor	Piano conducteur	Klavier-direktion
perc	percussion	batterie	Schlagzeug
perf	performance, performed (by)	exécution, exécuté par	Aufführung, aufgeführt von
Pf/pf	Pianoforte	piano	Klavier
picc	piccolo	petite flûte, piccolo	Kleine Flöte, Pikkoloflöte
PO	Philharmonic Orchestra	Orchestre philharmonique	Philharmonisches Orchester
prem	première	première	Uraufführung
Prod	Produced by	produit par	dirigiert von
Prom	Promenade Concert, London	concert promenade de Londres	Londoner Promenaden-Konzert
Pub/pub	Publisher, published by	Editeur, publié par	Herausgeber, herausgegeben von
rec	recorder (instrument)	flûte à bec	Blockflöte
redn	reduction	réduction	Verkürzung
retr	reciter	récitant, rôle parlé	Rezitator
RL	Editions Rouart Lerolle (now Editions Salabert)	Editions Rouart Lerolle (maintenant Editions Salabert)	Editions Rouart Lerolle (jetzt Editions Salabert)
rpm	revolutions per minute	tours à la minute	Umdrehungen pro Minute

S	Editions Salabert	Editions Salabert	Editions Salabert
S	(Solo) Soprano (voice)	(solo voix de) soprano	(Solo) Sopran(singstimme)
sbells	sleigh bells	grelots	Schellen
sdm	side (snare) drum	tambour militaire	Kleine Trommel
Sept	September	septembre	September
S(H)	Editions Salabert (*hire only*)	Editions Salabert (*seulement à louer*)	Editions Salabert (*nur zu vermieten*)
S.M.I.	Société Musicale Indépendante	Société Musicale Indépendante	Société Musicale Indépendante
S.N.	Société Nationale	Société Nationale	Société Nationale
S.O.	Symphony Orchestra	orchestre symphonique	Sinfonie-Orchester
Soc	Society	société	Gesellschaft
S-S	Editions Senart (now Editions Salabert)	Editions Senart (maintenant Editions Salabert)	Editions Senart (jetzt Editions Salabert)
ssx	soprano saxophone	saxophone soprano	Sopransaxophon
suppl	supplement	supplément	Ergänzungsband
str	strings	cordes	Streichinstrumente
sx	saxophone	saxophone	Saxophon
T	(Solo) Tenor (voice)	(solo voix de) ténor	(Solo) Tenor(singstimme)
tamb	tambourine	tambour de basque	Schellentrommel
tamtam	tam-tam	tam-tam	Tam-tam
tbn	trombone	trombone	Posaune
tdm	tenor drum	caisse roulante	Rührtrommel
timp	timpani	timbales	Pauken
tpt	trumpet	trompette	Trompete
Tr/tr	treble	aigu	Diskant
trans	translated	traduit	übersetzt
trec	tenor recorder	flûte à bec ténor	Tenorblockflöte
tri	triangle	triangle	Triangel
tsx	tenor saxophone	saxophone ténor	Tenorsaxophon
ttuba	tenor tuba	tuba ténor	Tenortuba
tuba	bass tuba	tuba basse	Basstuba
U.E.	Universal Edition	Universal Edition	Universal Edition
U.S.A.	United States of America	Etats-Unis d'Amérique	Vereinigten Staaten von Amerika
ver	version (for)	version (pour)	Version für
viol	viols	violes	Violen
vla	viola	alto	Bratsche
vla-d'a	viola d'amore	viole d'amour	Viola d'amore
vla-db	viola da braccia	viole baryton	Viola da bracchia
vla-dg	viola da gamba	viole de gambe	Viola da gamba
vlc	violoncello	violoncelle	Violoncello
vln	violin	violon	Violine, Geige
Voc. Mus	Vocal Music	musique vocale	Vokalmusik
VS	Vocal Score	partition vocale, partition piano et chant	Klavierauszug
ww	woodwind	les bois	Holzblasinstrumente
xyl	xylophone	xylophone	Xylophon
YMCA	Young Men's Christian Association	Association chrétienne de jeunes gens	Christl. Verein Junger Männer
Z.C.M.	Collegium Musicum of Zürich	Collegium Musicum de Zürich	Collegium Musicum Zürich
Ø	Full Score	partition d'orchestre	Orchesterpartitur
4tet, 5tet, etc.	quartet, quintet, etc..	quatuor, quintette, etc..	Quartett, Quintett, u.s.w.

ALPHABETICAL INDEX OF TITLES

53b Judith (Oratorio).
Légende dramatique — see *Nicolas de Flue.*
107 Liberté (Film Score).
146 La ligne d'horizon.
43 Liluli.
164 Lucrèce.
105 Mademoiselle Docteur.
140 La mandragore.
145 Le mangeur de rêves.
190 Marche contre la mort.
33 Marche funèbre (for *Les mariés de la Tour Eiffel*).
101 Marche sur la Bastille (for *14 juillet*).
(Les mariés de la Tour Eiffel — see *Marche funèbre*).
106 Marthe Richard au service de la France.
99 Mayerling.
158 Mermoz.
115 Miarka (ou *La fille à l'ourse*).
102 Les mille et une nuits.
184 Mimaamaquim.
55 Un miracle de Notre-Dame (ou *L'impératrice aux rochers*).
82 Les misérables.
197 Monopartita.
169 Morceau de concours.
16 La mort de sainte Alméenne.
Mouvement symphonique – see *Radio panoramique.*
48 Mouvement symphonique n° 1 – *Pacific 231.*
62 Mouvement symphonique n° 2 – *Rugby.*
79 Mouvement symphonique n° 3.
Les musiciens du ciel — see Appendix G.
192 De la musique.
Musique d'ameublement — see Appendix B.
98 Les mutinés de l'Elseneur.
136 La naissance des couleurs.
60 Napoléon.
6 Nature morte.
55a La neige sur Rome (from the Incidental Music *L'impératrice aux rochers*).
129 Nicolas de Flue.
104 Nitchevo (ou *L'agonie du sous-marin*).
104b Nitchevo . . . (triste est mon cœur) (from the Film Score *Nitchevo* ou *L'agonie du sous-marin*).
La noce massacrée – see *Marche funèbre.*
72 Les noces d'Amour et Psyche.
96 Nocturne.
131a O Salutaris (from the Film Score *Cavalcade d'amour*).
168 O temps suspends ton vol.
185 Œdipe.
203 Œdipe-Roi.
108 Un oiseau blanc s'est envolé.
141 L'ombre de la ravine.
201 On ne badine pas avec l'amour.
127 L'or dans la montagne (ou *Faux-monnayeurs*).
48 Pacific 231 (Mouvement symphonique n° 1).
170 Paduana.
194 Panis angelicus.
27 Les Pâques à New York.
66 Partita (piano, 4 hands).
134 Partita (two pianos).
160 Pasiphae.
117 Passeurs d'hommes.
13 Pastiche de Haydn.
28 Pastorale d'été.
199 Paul Claudel.
142 Petit cours de morale.
Petit décor musical – see *Pasiphae.*

s

INDEX OF TITLES BY GENRE

170	Paduana.
183	Intrada.
205	Romance.
	Arioso — see Appendix B.
	(? Musique d'ameublement) — see Appendix B.

Choral music (a capella)

175	Hymne à la liberté.

Choral Music (with orchestra)

14	Cantique de Pâques.
34a/34b	Le roi David.
53b	Judith.
73	Cris du monde.
95	Jeanne d'Arc au bûcher
102	Les mille et une nuits.
126	La danse des morts.
129	Nicolas de Flue.
151	Chant de la libération.
204	Une cantate de Noël.
	Selzach Passionspiel — see Appendix C.
	La femme du marin — see Appendix F.
	Les trois princesses au pommier doux — see Appendix F.

Choral Music (with piano)

114	Armistice.
	Untitled — see Appendix B.

Concertos

20	Entrée, Nocturne, Berceuse (Piano).
51	Concertino (Piano).
67	Cello Concerto.
188	Concerto da camera (Flute and Cor Anglais).

Film Scores

47	La roue.
60	Napoléon.
82	Les misérables.
83	Rapt (ou *La séparation des races*).
84	L'idée.
85	Cessez le feu.
86	Crime et châtiment.
87	Le roi de la Camargue.
91	Der Dämon des Himalayas.
92	L'équipage (ou *Celle que j'aime*).
98	Les mutinés de l'Elseneur.
99	Mayerling.
104	Nitchevo (ou *L'agonie du sous-marin*).
105	Mademoiselle Docteur.
106	Marthe Richard au service de la France.
107	Liberté.
110	La citadelle du silence.
111	Regain.
112	Visages de la France.
115	Miarka (ou *La fille à l'ourse*).
117	Passeurs d'hommes.
118	Les bâtisseurs.
125	Pygmalion.
127	L'or dans la montagne (ou *Faux-monnayeurs*).

130 Le déserteur (ou *Je t'attendrai*).

131 Cavalcade d'amour.

149 Le journal tombe à cinq heures.

150 Huit hommes dans un château.

153 Les antiquités de l'Asie Occidentale.

154 La boxe en France.

155 Secrets.

156 Callisto (ou *La petite nymphe de Diane*).

157 Le capitaine Fracasse.

158 Mermoz.

159 Un seul amour.

164 Lucrèce.

174 Un ami viendra ce soir.

177 Les démons de l'aube.

186 Un revenant.

193 Bourdelle.

199 Paul Claudel.

200 La tour de Babel.

Colloque — see Appendix B.

Faits divers — see Appendix C.

Les musiciens du ciel — see Appendix G.

Incidental Music Scores

15 Le dit des jeux du monde (see also Ballet Music).

16 La mort de Sainte Alméenne

18 La danse macabre.

34 Le roi David.

36 Saül.

39 Antigone.

42 La tempête.

43 Liluli.

53 Judith.

55 L'impératrice aux rochers (ou *Un miracle de Notre-Dame*).

56 Phædre.

101 Marche sur la Bastille (for *14 juillet*).

116 La construction d'une cité.

119 Prélude à la mort de Jaurès.

140 La mandragore.

141 L'ombre de la ravine.

143 Les suppliantes.

144 Huit cents mètres.

146 La ligne d'horizon.

162 Sodome et Gomorrhe.

163 Le soulier de satin.

166 Charles le Téméraire.

179 Prométhée.

180 Hamlet.

185 Œdipe.

187 L'état de siège.

201 On ne badine pas avec l'amour.

203 Œdipe-Roi.

Le roi, son vizir et son médicin — see Appendix C.

Melodramas

57 Cantique des cantiques de Salomon.

65 Amphion.

Operas

53a Judith.

59 Antigone.

Operettas

71	Les aventures du roi Pausole.
74	La belle de Moudon.
103	L'aiglon.
124	Les petites Cardinal.
	Choucoune — see Appendix E.

Orchestral Works

5	Prélude pour Aglavaine et Sélysette.
11	Le chant de Nigamon.
13	Pastiche de Haydn.
16	Interlude (from the Incidental Music *La mort de Sainte Alméenne*).
28	Pastorale d'été.
31a	Danse des enfants (from the Ballet Music *Verité? Mensonge?*).
32	Horace victorieux. (See also Ballet Music).
34c	Suites from the Oratorio *Le roi David.*
41	Chant de joie.
42a	Prélude pour La tempête (from the Incidental Music *La tempête*).
48	Mouvement symphonique n° 1 — Pacific 231.
55b	Suite from the Incidental Music *L'impératrice aux rochers* (ou *Un miracle de Notre-Dame*).
56a	Suite from the Incidental Music *Phædre.*
60a	Suite from the Film Score *Napoléon.*
62	Mouvement symphonique n° 2 — Rugby.
63	Fanfare pour Albert Roussel.
65a	Prélude, Fugue, Postlude (from *Amphion*).
69	J'avais un fidèle amant.
70	Symphonie [n° 1] (Symphony [No. 1]).
71b	Suite from the Operetta *Les aventures du roi Pausole.*
72a	Suite from the Ballet Music *Les noces d'Amour et Psyche.*
78a	Prélude, Arioso, Fughette (sur le nom de Bach).
79	Mouvement symphonique n° 3.
82a	Suite from the Film Score *Les misérables.*
96	Nocturne.
104c	Suite from the Film Score *Nitchevo* (ou *L'agonie du sous-marin*).
106a	Suite from the Film Score *Marthe Richard au service de la France.*
107a	Interlude (from the Film Score *Liberté*).
111a	Suite from the Film Score *Regain.*
130a	Suite from the Film Score *Le déserteur* (ou *Je t'attendrai*).
147	Symphonie pour cordes [n° 2] (Symphony [No. 2]).
152	Le grand barrage.
158a	Suites from the Film Score *Mermoz*: (i) La traversée des Andes; (ii) Le vol sur l'Atlantique.
161a	Jour de fête suisse (suite from the Ballet Music *L'appel de la montagne*).
177a	Suite from the Film Score *Les démons de l'aube.*
178	Symphonie liturgique [n° 3] (Symphony [No. 3]).
182	Symphony No. 4 (Deliciæ Basilienses).
195	Symphony No. 5 (Di tre re).
196	Suite archaïque.
197	Monopartita.
198	Toccata.
	Chevauchée — see Appendix B.
	Prélude n° 1 et fugue de J. S. Bach — see Appendix B.
	Untitled — see Appendix B.
	L'eau vive — see Appendix E.

Organ

9	Two Pieces (Fugue, Choral).

Piano (2 hands) — original and arrangements

1	Trois pièces (1910).
3	Toccata et variations.
19	Trois pièces (1915-19).
22	Sept pièces brèves.
23	Sarabande (for *Album des Six*).
46	Le cahier romand.
48	Mouvement symphonique n° 1 — Pacific 231.
55a	La neige sur Rome (from the Incidental Music *L'impératrice aux rochers*).
55b	Suite from the Incidental Music *L'impératrice aux rochers*.
62	Mouvement symphonique n° 2 — Rugby.
63	Sur le nom d'Albert Roussel.
71a	Suite from the Operetta *Les aventures du roi Pausole.*
78	Prélude, Arioso, Fughette (sur le nom de Bach).
106a	Suite from the Film Score *Marthe Richard au service de la France.*
120	Scenic Railway.
139	Petits airs sur une basse célèbre.
158	Film Score *Mermoz.*
165	Deux esquisses.
174a	Souvenir de Chopin (from the Film Score *Un ami viendra ce soir*).
177a	Suite from the Film Score *Les démons de l'aube.*
186	Film Score *Un revenant.*
	Untitled — see Appendix B.

Piano (4 hands)

66	Partita.

Piano (4 hands) — arrangements

10	String Quartet (No. 1).
11	Le chant de Nigamon.
28	Pastorale d'été.
32	Horace victorieux.
38	Trois contrepoints.
41	Chant de joie.
42a	Prélude pour La tempête (from the Incidental Music *La tempête*).
48	Mouvement symphonique n° 1 — Pacific 231.

2 Pianos (4 hands)

134	Partita.

2 Pianos (4 hands) — arrangement

51	Concertino (Piano).

2 Pianos (8 hands) — arrangement

48	Mouvement symphonique n° 1 — Pacific 231.

Radio Music

81	Les douze coups de minuit.
89	Radio panoramique.
132	Grad us — En avant.
135	Christophe Colomb.
160	Pasiphae.
167	Battements du monde.
172	Sérénade à Angélique.
189	Saint François d'Assise.
190	Marche contre la mort.
191	Tête d'or.
202	La rédemption de François Villon.

Solo Voice(s) and Instrumental Ensemble

2	Quatre poèmes (No. 4).
4	Trois poèmes (No. 1) (Paul Fort).
6	Six poèmes (Apollinaire) (Nos. 1, 3-6).
27	Les Pâques à New York.
42b	Deux chants d'Ariel (from the Incidental Music *La tempête*).
45	Six poésies (de Jean Cocteau).
49	Chanson (Ronsard).
58	(Trois chansons de) la petite sirène.
77	Le grand étang.
85a	La chanson de l'escadrille (from the Film Score *Cessez le feu*).
85b	La chanson du cul-de-jatte (from the Film Score *Cessez le feu*).
85c	Valse de Lagasse (from the Film Score *Cessez le feu*).
118a	Les gars du bâtiment (from the Film Score *Les bâtisseurs*).
121	Jeunesse.
154a	Hymne au sport (from the Film Score *La boxe en France*).
159a	Deux romances sentimentales (from the Film Score *Un seul amour*).
173	Quatre chansons pour voix grave (Nos. 2 and 3).
174	L'hymne de la délivrance (from the Film Score *Un ami viendra ce soir*).
184	Mimaamaquim.
	Untitled — see Appendix B.

Solo Voice(s) and Piano

2	Quatre poèmes.
4	Trois poèmes (Paul Fort).
6	Nature morte.
7	Six poèmes (Apollinaire).
27	Les Pâques à New York.
42b	Deux chants d'Ariel (from the Incidental Music *La tempête*).
44	Chanson de Fagus.
45	Six poésies (de Jean Cocteau).
49	Chanson (Ronsard).
58	(Trois chansons de) la petite sirène.
64	Vocalise-étude.
65c	Valse pour le roi Pausole (from the Operetta *Les aventures du roi Pausole*).
77	Le grand étang.
85a	La chanson de l'escadrille (from the Film Score *Cessez le feu*).
85b	La chanson du cul-de-jatte (from the Film Score *Cessez le feu*).
85c	Valse de Lagasse (from the Film Score *Cessez le feu*).
90	Fièvre jaune.
97	Du whisky pour Jo.
104a	De l'Atlantique au Pacifique (from the Film Score *Nitchevo* ou *L'agonie du sous-marin*).
104b	Nitchevo. . . (triste est mon cœur) from the Film Score *Nitchevo* (ou *L'agonie du sous-marin*).
113	Tuet's weh!
115a	Chanson de la route (fron the Film Score *Miarka* ou *La fille à l'ourse*).
115b	Chanson de l'eau (from the Film Score *Miarka* ou *La fille à l'ourse*).
116a	Chanson des quatre (from the Film Score *La construction d'une cité*).
116b	Chanson de l'émigrant (from the Film Score *La construction d'une cité*).
118a	Les gars du bâtiment (from the Film Score *Les bâtisseurs*).
121	Jeunesse.
122	Trois chansons (R. Kerdyk).
124a	C'est le charme de Florence (from the Operetta *Les petites Cardinal*).
124b	A plaisance (from the Operetta *Les petites Cardinal*).
128	Hommage au travail.
131a	O Salutaris (from the Film Score *Cavalcade d'amour*).
133	Trois poèmes de Claudel.
138	Trois psaumes.
142	Petit cours de morale.
148	Saluste du Bartas (Six villanelles).

154a Hymne au sport (from the Film Score *La boxe en France*).
157a Sérénade de Scapin (from the Film Score *Le capitaine Fracasse).*
159a Deux romances sentimentales (from the Film Score *Un seul amour*).
168 O temps suspends ton vol.
173 Quatre chansons pour voix grave.
174 L'hymne de la délivrance (from the Film Score *Un ami viendra ce soir*).
177a Plein air (from the Film Score *Les démons de l'aube*).
184 Mimaamaquim.
194 Panis angelicus.
Route de Mandalay — see Appendix B.

JUVENILIA:

This Catalogue of Works commences with Honegger's first published work. The only items of juvenilia which have been preserved to my knowledge at the time of writing are the following (except where noted to the contrary, the ms are to be found in the Bibliothèque Nationale, Paris):

(i) **SIX SONATES POUR PIANOFORTE ET VIOLON.** Ch. Mus. (1908)

Vln/pf.

(i) C minor.

Allegro molto (Crotchet = 138); Adagio cantabile (Crotchet = 46); Minuetto: Allegretto molto vivace (Crotchet = 132); Allegro vivace.

[Le] Havre, 8/March/1908.

(ii) F major.

Allegro con brio (Crotchet = 112); Andante con variaz[i]oni (Quaver = 69); Rondo: Allegro moderato (Quaver = 120).

[Le] Havre, 25/April/1908.

(iii) C minor.

Allegro molto ma con brio (Crotchet = 126); Adagio appassionata e cantabile (Crotchet = 50); Scherzo: Allegro vivace (Crotchet = 126); Finale: Allegro molto agitato (Crotchet = 120).

(iv) B minor.

Allegro ma non tanto (Crotchet = 96) — Allegro vivace (Crotchet = 152); Scherzo: Vivace (Quaver = 152); Andante cantabile (Quaver = 63); Fuga: Allegro moderato (Crotchet = 116).

[Le] Havre, 16/June/1908.

(v) A minor.

Allegro (Dotted crotchet = 69); Adagio molto espressivo (Quaver = 58); Allegro (Crotchet = 104).

[Le] Havre, 25/June/1908.

(vi) G major.

Andante con sentimento religioso (Crotchet = 52); Allegretto moderato (Quaver = 96); Tempo di Minuetto (Crotchet = 72); Lento (Quaver = 54) — Fuga: Allegro ma non troppo (Crotchet = 108).

[Le] Havre, 3/July/1908.

(ii) **SONATE POUR VIOLON ET PIANO EN RE MINEUR.** Ch. Mus. (1912).

Vln/pf.

(i) Largo (Crotchet = 63) — Agitato (Crotchet = 160) — Largo assai (Quaver = 66).

[Le] Havre, 12/Feb/1912.

(ii) Molto adagio (Quaver = 63).

[Le] Havre, 22/June/1912.

(iii) Sostenuto (Dotted crotchet = 46) — Allegro (Dotted minim = 80).

[Le] Havre, 23/Oct/1912.

(iii) **TRIO EN FA MINEUR.** Ch. Mus. (1914).

Vln.vlc/pf.

(i) Allegro vivace (only).

Zürich, August-October (3), 1914.

(Photocopy of ms supplied by Pascale Honegger, Geneva, Switzerland.)

(iv) **[COUNTERPOINT EXERCISES].**

(i) In 4 parts; 'Sujet de Onslow'; Grave; Unfinished;

(ii) In 6 parts above and below a cantus-firmus; Examen de contrepoint; January 1918;

(iii) In 4 parts;

(iv) In 7 parts above a cantus-firmus;

(v) One three-part and 3 four-part fugues all on the same subject.

(Mss shown to the author by Andrée Vaurabourg-Honegger at her residence — 21, rue Duperée, Paris — during the summer of 1979.)

1. **TROIS PIECES.** Pf. (1910).

(i) Scherzo. (ii) Humoresque. (iii) Adagio espressivo.

Ded: Robert Charles Martin.

Pub: Desforges (Le Havre).

2. **QUATRE POEMES.** Voc. Mus. (1914-16).

Medium voice/pf.

(i) No title; (Sur la basalte . . .).
A. Fontainas.
Calmement.
Zürich, Nov. 1914.

(ii) Petite chapelle.
J. Laforgue.
Grave.
Paris, May 1916.

(iii) De l'angelus de l'aube à l'angelus du soir.
F. Jammes.
Très lent et expressif.
Zürich, July 1915.

(iv) La mort passe.
A. Tchobanian.
Modéré.
Paris, March 1916.

Ded: Jane Bathori.

Pub: Chester (J. and W.C. 3855), 1921.

(No. iv orch. by A. Hoérée for perf. by Lina Falk, Orch. Pasdeloup, cond. A. van Raalte; 25/Jan/ 1930; Théâtre des Champs-Elysées, Paris. See also Catalogue Nos. 4 and 7).

3. **TOCCATA ET VARIATIONS.** Pf. (1916).

Vif. Grave.

Paris, Sept. 1916.

Ded: 'En mémoire de mon Oncle O.H.' [Oscar Honegger].

Pub: M-S (SECA 217), 1921.

fp: Andrée Vaurabourg; 15/Dec/1916; C.M.D.I. Concert, Salle Œdenkoven, Paris.

f*Eb*p: Jehanne Chambard; 29/April/1936.

4. **TROIS POEMES.** Voc. Mus. (1916).

Voice/pf.

Paul Fort: *Complaintes et dits.*

(i) Le chasseur perdu en forêt.
Animé.
Paris, Aug. 1916.
Ded: Madeleine Bonnard.

(ii) Cloche du soir.
Modérément.
Paris, Oct. 1916.
Ded: Rose Armandie.

(iii) Chanson de fol.
Vif et léger.
Paris, Nov. 1916.
Ded: Elisabeth Vuillermoz.

Pub: S-S (EMS 4752), 1922.

(No. i fpub. as part of the mus. supp. of *La Revue Musicale*, Jan. 1922. See also Catalogue No. 45).

(No. i orch. by A.H. for perf. by Lina Falk, Orch. Pasdeloup, cond. A. van Raalte; 25/Jan/1930; Théâtre des Champs-Elysées, Paris. See also Catalogue Nos. 2 and 7.)

f*Eb*p (No. 3): Sophie Wyss; 17/Feb/1931.

5. **PRELUDE POUR AGLAVAINE ET SELYSETTE.** Orch. (1916-17).

After Maurice Maeterlinck.

1122/2100/str (10.10.6.6.2).

Modéré.

Paris, 1/Jan/1917.

Pub: S (EAS 15939), 1956.

fp: Paris Conservatoire, orchestration class; cond. A.H.; 3/April/1917.

f*public*p: Orch. Golschmann, cond. V. Golschmann; 7/June/1920; Concerts Golschmann, Salle Gaveau, Paris.

6. **NATURE MORTE.** Voc. Mus. (1917).

Voice/pf.

(La corbeille de porcelaine contient des pêches et du raisin blanc . . .).

Vanderpyl.

($\frac{9}{8}$; 16 bars)

Paris, Feb. 1917.

Pub: in *La Revue SIC* (January 1917), 58-59.

7. **SIX POEMES.** Voc. Mus. (1916-17).

Voice/pf.

Guillaume Apollinaire: *Alcools*.

(i) A la santé
Lent.
Paris, May 1916.

(ii) Clotilde.
Souplement.
Paris, March 1916.

(iii) Automne.
Très modéré.
Zürich, Aug. 1915.

(iv) Saltimbanques.
Tranquillement.
Paris, March 1917.

(v) L'adieu.
Pas trop lent.
Paris, Jan. 1917.

(vi) Les cloches.
Animé.
Paris, March 1917.

Ded: Fernand Ochsé.

Pub: M-S (SECA 251), 1921.

fp: Jane Bathori with Andrée Vaurabourg; 15/Jan/1918; Théâtre du Vieux-Colombier, Paris.

(fp (Nos. i-iii): Rose Armandie; 11/July/1916; C.M.D.I. Concert, Salle Œdenkoven, Paris).

(Nos. i, iii-vi orch. by A. Hoérée for perf. by Lina Falk, Orch. Pasdeloup, cond. A. van Raalte; 25/Jan/1930; Théâtre des Champs-Elysées, Paris.

(i) 2000/hp/str.
Pub: M-S (SECA 68)/S(H), 1921.

(iii) 1000/2010/hp/str.
Pub: M-S (SECA 56)/S(H), 1921.

(iv) 1(picc)110/0210/cel.hp/vla.-solo.str(no vln).
Pub: M-S (SECA 55)/S(H), 1921.

(v) 1000/2000/cel.hp/3vln.2vlc.
Pub: M-S (SECA 57)/S(H), 1921.

(vi) 1010/2210/cel.hp/cym.tri.wdbl.
Pub: M-S (SECA 32)/S(H), 1921.

See also Catalogue Nos. 2 and 4).

f*Eb*p: (Nos. v and vi): Dora Stevens; 4/Jan/1927.

8. **RHAPSODIE.** Ch. Mus. (1917).

2fl. cl/pf [= 2vln.vla/pf)].

Larghetto — Allegro — Larghetto.

Paris, April 1917.

Ded: Charles M. Widor.

Pub: S-S (EMS 6131), 1923.

fp: Manouvrier, le Roy (fls), Tournier (cl), Andrée Vaurabourg (pf); 17/Nov/1917; Parthénon, Paris.

?f*E*p: 5/March/1922; Contemporary Chamber Concert, London.

f*Eb*p: Joseph Slater (fl), Jean Pougnet (vln), Rebecca Clarke (vla), Angus Morrison (pf); 26/Aug/1936.

(A recording exists of an arr. A.H. made whilst in America in 1947 for fl.ob.cl/pf — Unicorn: UNLP 1005).

9. **TWO PIECES.** Org. (1917).

(i) Fugue.
Moderato.
Ded: Robert Charles Martin.

(ii) Choral.
Lento sostenuto.
Ded: Andrée Vaurabourg.

Paris, Sept. 1917.

Pub: Chester (J. and W.C. 3026), 1920.

10. **STRING QUARTET [No. 1].** Ch. Mus. (1916-17).

(i) (Violent et tourmenté) Appassionato.
Paris, July 1917.
(After a study dated Sept. 1913).
Dur: 8′ 24-30″.

(ii) (Très lent) Adagio.
Paris - Le Havre, March - April 1916.
Dur: 16′.

(iii) (Rude et rythmique) Allegro.
Paris, Oct. 1917.
(After a study dated Nov. 1915).
Dur: 9′.

Dur: 33′ 24-30″.

Ded: Florent Schmitt.

Pub: LS-ME (ED43LS), 1921; arr. by Jacques Larmanjat for pf. duet LS-ME (SM 145), 1928.

fp: Capelle Quartet; 20/June 1919; S.M.I. Concert, Paris.

?f*E*p: Brosa Quartet; 26/Oct/1927; L.C.M.C. Concert, London.

f*Eb*p: Stratton Quartet; 23/March/1931.

11. **LE CHANT DE NIGAMON.** Orch. (1917).

2+picc2+ca22+cbsn/4231/timp.bdm.cym.tri/str.

Lent — Animé.

Paris, Dec. 1917.

Ded: Rhené-Baton.

(Dur: 10/11′).

Pub: S-S (EMS 7178 and 7646), 1927; arr. by A.H. for pf. duet (EMS 7040), 1926.

fp: Paris Conservatoire, orchestration class, cond. A.H.; 18/April/1918.

f*public*p: Orch. Pasdeloup, cond. Rhené-Baton; 3/Jan/1920; Cirque-d'Hiver, Paris.

12. **VIOLIN SONATA No. 1.** Ch. Mus. (1916-18).

Vln/pf.

(i) Andante sostenuto.
Paris, July 1916.

(ii) Presto.
Paris, March 1917.

(iii) Adagio — Allegro assai — Adagio.
Paris, Feb. 1918.

Ded: Andrée Vaurabourg.

Pub: S-S (EMS 4398), 1921.

fp: Hélène Jourdan-Morhange with Andrée Vaurabourg; 19/March/1918; Théâtre du Vieux-Colombier, Paris.

(fp. of movts. i and ii : A.H. with Andrée Vaurabourg; 19/Jan/1918; Festival Honegger Concert; Parthénon, Paris).

f*E*p: André Mangeot and Yvonne Arnaud; 30/May/1922; St. John's Institute (Tufton Street), London.

13. **PASTICHE DE HAYDN.** Orch. (1918).

Written as an entry for a Counterpoint Competition organised at the Paris Conservatoire (awarded a Certificate of Merit [2nd prize]).

14. **CANTIQUE DE PAQUES.** Cantata. (1918).

2222/2200/cel.hp/str/SMzA-soli.fv chorus.

Modéré — Très calme.

Eng. trans. by Robert Hess (1974).

Paris, July 1918.

Ded: Robert Godet.

(Dur: /9′).

Pub: RL-S(H) (RL 11547), 1925; VS with pf. redn. by A.H. (RL 11475), 1924; Chorus parts LCS (LCS 141), ?1927; VS with org. redn. by Philip Brunelle and opt. hp. part for performance with org., 1974.

fp: 27/March/1923; Toulouse.

f*Paris*p: Gabrielle Gills, Bartélémy, Debonte with l'Art Choral and Orch. cond. A.H.; 18/March/1926; l'Opéra, Paris.

15. **LE DIT DES JEUX DU MONDE.** Inc. Mus./Ballet Mus. (1918).

Subtitled: 'Dix danses, 2 Interludes, Epilogue pour orchestre de chambre pour le poème de Paul Méral'.

Fl(picc)/tpt/timp.bdm.cym.sdm.bouteillophone [=tri]/str (2.2.2.2.2).

(i) Le soleil et la fleur;
(ii) La montagne et les pierres;
(iii) L'enfant et la mer;
(iv) L'homme tournant sur le sol;
(v) L'homme fou (Interlude 1);
(vi) Les hommes et le village;
(vii) Les hommes et la terre;
(viii) L'homme et la femme;
(ix) L'homme qui lutte et conduit (Interlude 2);
(x) L'homme et l'ombre;
(xi) Le rat et la mort;
(xii) L'homme et la mer;
(xiii) Epilogue.

Paris and Etel, May-Nov. 1918.

Ded: Fernand Ochsé.

(Dur: /50′).

Pub: S-S (EMS 7541 and 7645), 1928.

fp: cond. W. Straram; 2/Dec/1918; Théâtre du Vieux-Colombier.

f*concert*p: Orch. Golschmann, cond. V. Golschmann; Jan. 1921; Concerts Golschmann, Salle Gaveau, Paris.

16. **LA MORT DE SAINTE ALMEENNE.** Inc. Mus. (1918).

Mystery by Max Jacob.

Orch. [?1111/1100/str. (ms Ø incomplete)] and four solo voices [3 female and 1 male (? SMzABar - soli)].

Ier Tableau: Un jardin fleurit dans un cloître; Scène II: Entrée la Sœur; Scène III: Entré le jeune homme; Scène IV: St. Alméenne paraît au fond; Rideau/Interlude;
II^{d} Tableau: La cellule; Scène I; Scène II: Entrée la Sœur.

Paris, Dec. 1918.

Npub.

Nperf.

(An 'Interlude' and 'Fin' were later made into a single *Interlude* which was fp: Orch. Colonne, cond. Gabriel Pierné; 30/Oct/1920; Théâtre du Châtelet, Paris.)

17. **DANSE DE LA CHEVRE.** Ch. Mus. (1919).

Fl.

Lent. Danse: Vif — Lent.

Ded: René le Roy.

Pub: S-S (EMS 8438), 1932.

fp: René le Roy; May 1919; Dance recital by Lysana.

18. **LA DANSE MACABRE.** Inc. Mus. (1919).

Play by Carlos Larronde.

Orch.

Npub.

fp: May 1919; l'Odéon, Paris.

19. **TROIS PIECES.** Pf. (1915-19).

(i) Prélude.
Lourd et grave.
Paris, May 1919.
Ded: Walter Morse Rummel.

(ii) Hommage à Ravel.
Modéré.
Paris, Nov. 1915.

(iii) Danse.
Rapide.
Paris, May 1919.
Ded: Ricardo Viñès.

Pub: M-S (Z860M), 1921.

20. **ENTREE, NOCTURNE, BERCEUSE.** Concerto. (1919).

Pf/ch-orch.

Npub.

fp: 1919; Salle Huyghens, Paris.

21. **VIOLIN SONATA No. 2.** Ch. Mus. (1919).

Vln/pf.

(i) Allegro cantabile.
Paris, April-May 1919.

(ii) Larghetto.
Engelberg, Aug. 1919.

(iii) Vivace assai.
Paris, Nov. 1919.

Ded: Fernande Capelle.

Pub: S-S (S6604), 1924.

fp: A.H. and Andrée Vaurabourg; 28/Feb/1920; S.N. Concert, Salle du Conservatoire, Paris.

22. **SEPT PIECES BREVES.** Pf. (1919-20).

(i) Souplement.
Oct. 1919.
Ded: Rose Martin-Lafon.

(ii) Vif.
Nov. 1919.
Ded: Minna Vaurabourg.

(iii) Très lent.
Jan. 1920.
Ded: Andrée Vaurabourg.

(iv) Légèrement.
Dec. 1919.
Ded: Marcelle Milhaud.

(v) Lent.
Jan. 1920.
Ded: Mytyl Fraggi.

(vi) Rythmique.
Jan. 1920.
Ded: Mme E. Alleaume.

(vii) Violent.
Jan. 1920.
Ded: Robert Casadesus.

Pub: LS-ME (ED42LS), 1921.

fp: Andrée Vaurabourg; 4/March/1920; S.M.I. Concert, Salle Gaveau, Paris.

f*Eb*p: Walter Frey; 21/Dec/1930.

23. **SARABANDE.** Pf. (1920).

Issued as No. 2. in the **ALBUM DES SIX** (1. Prélude—Auric; 3. Romance sans paroles — Durey; 4. Mazurka — Milhaud 5. Valse — Poulenc; 6. Pastorale — Tailleferre).

Pub: D-ME (E1979D; E1964D), 1920; Schott ('Das neue Klavierwerk' series). Pub. separately by D-ME (M.E. 3168), 1920 (E1979D; E1960D; E1964D; E1961D; E1959D; E1962D).

24. **VIOLA SONATA.** Ch. Mus. (1920).

Vla/pf.

(i) Andante—Vivace.
Paris, March 1920.

(ii) Allegretto moderato.
Paris, Jan. 1920.

(iii) Allegro non troppo.
Paris, Feb. 1920.

Ded: Henri Casadesus.

Pub: LS-ME (ED58LS), 1921.

fp: Henri Casadesus with Robert Casadesus; 2/Dec/1920; S.M.I. Concert, Paris.

f*Eb*p: Watson Forbes with Myers Foggin; 3/Oct/1938.

25. **CADENCE.** Ch. Mus. (1920).

Cadenza for vln. for the 'Cinéma-Fantaisie pour violon et piano d'après *Le bœuf sur le toit* par Darius Milhaud'.

Pub: LS-ME (ED68LS), 1921.

fp: M. Benedetti; 26/May/1921.

26. **SONATINE**. Ch. Mus. (1920).

2vln.

(i) Allegro non tanto.
Paris, April 1920.

(ii) Andantino.
Paris, June 1920.

(iii) Allegro moderato.
Paris, May 1920.

Ded: Darius Milhaud.

Pub: LS-ME (ED113LS), 1922.

fp: Darius Milhaud and A.H.; May 1921; Studio des Champs-Elysées, Paris.

f*E*p: André Mangeot and Kenneth Skeaping; 5/May/1922; British Music Society Concert, Y.M.C.A. (Great Russell Street), London.

f*Eb*p: A. Onnon and L. Halleux (of the Pro Arte Quartet); 7/Nov/1927.

27. **LES PAQUES A NEW YORK**. Voc. Mus. (1920).

Subtitled: Trois Fragments, extraits de "Les Pâques à New York de Blaise Cendrars, extraits de *Du monde entier*".

S-solo/str4tet [=S-solo/pf].

(i) C'est à cette heure-ci.
Grave.
Paris, March 1920.
Dur: 2′ 30″.

(ii) Faîtes, Seigneur.
Tourmenté.
Aix-en-Provence, March 1920.
Dur: 2′ 10″.

(iii) Dic nobis Maria.
Modéré.
Zürich, July 1920.
Dur: 2′ 38″.

Dur: 7′ 18″.

Pub: Composers' Music Corporation (Carl Fischer, New York, U.S.A.), 1923; VS with pf. redn. by A.H. (788-12) and set of parts (787-3).

fp: Rose Féart with the Pro Arte Quartet; 24/Jan/1924; 'Nouvelles auditions' concert, Geneva.

f*Paris*p: Gabrielle Gills and the Poulet Quartet; 28/March/1924; Salle Erard, Paris.

?f*E*p (broadcast): Claire Croiza with Victor Hely-Hutchinson; 4/Feb/1929; Arts Theatre Club, B.B.C. concert, London.

28. **PASTORALE D'ETE**. Orch. (1920).

Subtitled: Poème symphonique.

Prefaced quotation: "J'ai embrassé l'aube d'été" — J.A. Rimbaud.

1111/1000/str.

Calme — Vif et gai — Calme.

Wegen Aug. 1920.

Dur: 6½'.

Ded: Roland-Manuel.

Pub: S-S (EMS 4763 and 6617), 1922; arr. by A.H. for pf. duet (EMS 4560), 1921; Philharmonia/U.E. (W. Ph. V287), 1924.

fp: Orch. Golschmann, cond. Vladimir Golschmann; 17/Feb/1921; Concerts Golschmann, Salle Gaveau, Paris. (Awarded the 1921 *Prix Verley* by the audience).

f*E*p: Goosens Orch., cond. (Sir) Eugene Goosens; 27/Oct/1921, Queen's Hall, London, (N.B. f*E*p orig. announced for 20/April/1921, Edward Clark concert.)

f*Eb*p: Newcastle Station Orch., cond. Edward Clark; 11/Oct/1925.

29. **CELLO SONATA**. Ch. Mus. (1920).

Vlc/pf.

(i) Allegro non troppo.
Zürich, Sept. 1920.

(ii) Andante sostenuto.
Paris-Zürich, June-July 1920.

(iii) Presto.
Zürich, Sept. 1920.

Ded: René Gosselin.

Pub: LS-ME (ED114LS), 1922.

fp: Diran Alexanian with Andrée Vaurabourg; 23/April/1921. S.N. Concert, Salle du Conservatoire, Paris.

f*E*p: Beatrice Harrison with Gerald Moore: 13/May/1927; Wigmore Hall, London.

30. **HYMNE**. Ch. Mus. (1920).

Strl0tet.

Modéré et soutenu.

Zürich, 9/Oct/1920.

Version A: Scored for the ensemble of ten different sized stringed instruments of the violin family designed and made by the luthier, Léo Sir. (1. Sursoprano en fa; 2. Violon; 3. Mezzo soprano; 4. Alto; 5. Contralto; 6. Tenor; 7. Baryton; 8. Violoncelle; 9. Sousbasse en sol grave; 10. Contrebasse.)
Npub.
fp: Dixtuor Léo Sir; 17/Oct/1921; Art et Action concert, Paris.

Version B: Scored for 4 violins, 2 violas, 2 cellos and 2 double basses.
Pub: S (EAS 17853), 1984.

31. **VERITE? MENSONGE?** Ballet Mus. (1920).

Puppet ballet by André Hellé.

[? Fl.cl.bsn/str.]

[? Prologue: Lent; Refrain des appariteurs; Ier Tableau; IIème Tableau.]

Nov. 1920.

Npub.

fp: Nov. 1920; Salon d'Automne, Paris.

31a. **DANSE DES ENFANTS.** Orch. (1920).

From the Ballet Music *Vérité? Mensonge?* (see Catalogue No. 31).

Pub: S (2621), 1927.

32. **HORACE VICTORIEUX.** Orch. (1920-21).

Subtitled: Symphonie mimée (G.-P. Fauconnet after Titus Livius).

3(picc)2+ca2+bcl2+cbsn/4331/timp.bdm.cym.rattle.sdm.tamtam/hp/str.

Paris, Dec. 1920 - Feb. 1921; Orch. Zug and Zürich, Aug. 1921.

Ded: Serge Koussevitsky.

(Dur: /20′).

Pub: S-S (EMS 6527), 1924; arr. by A.H. for pf. duet (EMS 6369), 1924.

f*concert*p: Orch. de la S.R., cond. Ernest Ansermet; 31/Oct/1921; Lausanne.

f*Paris*p: cond. Koussevitsky; 1/Dec/1921.

f*staged*p: Régie-Jens Keith, cond. R. Schulz-Dornburg; 28/Dec/1927; Municipal Theatre, Essen.

f*E*p: cond. Ernest Ansermet; 16/Dec/1921; Ursula Greville Concert, Queen's Hall, London.

33. **MARCHE FUNEBRE.** Ballet Mus. (1921).

Subtitled: La noce massacrée.

Composed for Jean Cocteau's ballet *Les mariés de la Tour Eiffel* — musical score by members of 'Les Six':—

(i) Ouverture (le 14 juillet) — Auric;
(ii) Marche nuptiale — Milhaud;
(iii) Discours du général (Polka pour deux cornets à pistons) — Poulenc;
(iv) La baigneuse de Trouville (Carte postale en couleurs) — Poulenc;
(v) Fugue du massacre — Milhaud;
(vi) Valse des dépêches — Tailleferre;
(vii) Marche funèbre sur la mort du général — Honegger;
(viii) Quadrille (Pantalon—Eté—Poule—Pastourelle—Final) — Tailleferre;
(ix) Ritournelles — Auric;
(x) Sortie de la noce — Milhaud.

2221+cbsn/2231/timp.bdm.cym.sdm/str.

Paris, Feb. 1921.

(Dur: /2′ 55″).

Pub: S(H); (EAS 16.877) 1965; (EAS 16.899) 1965; (EAS 17.203) 1963; (EAS 17.202) 1963; (EAS 17.000) 1972; (EAS 17.204) 1963; (EAS 16.897) 1965; (EAS 17.205) 1963; (EAS 16.896) 1965; (EAS 16.898) 1965.

fp: Pierre Bertin and Marcel Herrand (narr), Carina Ari, Jean Borlin, Ballet Suédois de Rolf de Mare, cond. D.-E. Inghelbrecht; 18/June/1921; Théâtre des Champs-Elysées, Paris.

(N.B. Honegger utilizes the principal theme from Milhaud's *Marche nuptiale* (ii).)

34. **LE ROI DAVID.** Inc. Mus. (1921).

'Drame biblique' by René Morax.

2(picc)1(ca)2(bcl)1/1210/timp.bdm.cym.sdm.tamb.tamtam/cel.hnm.pf/[vlc]cb/SAT-soli.chorus.

(i) Introduction;
(ii) Cantique du berger David (A-solo);
(iii) Fanfare et entrée de Goliath;
(iv) Chant de victoire (chorus);
(v) Cortège;
(vi) Psaume: Ne crains rien (T-solo);
(vii) Cantique des prophètes (mv chorus);
(viii) Psaume: Ah! si j'avais des ailes de colombe (S-solo);
(ix) Psaume: Pitié de moi, mon Dieu (T-solo);
(x) Le camp de Saül;
(xi) Psaume: L'Eternel est ma lumière infinie (chorus);
(xii) Incantation;
(xiii) Marche des Philistins;
(xiv) Lamentations de Guilboa (S A-soli, fv chorus);
(xv) Cantique: De mon cœur jaillit un cantique (chorus);
(xvi) Cantique de fête (S-solo, fv chorus);
(xvii) La danse devant l'arche (S-solo, chorus);
(xviii) Chant de la servante (A-solo);
(xix) Psaume de pénitence (chorus);
(xx) Psaume: Je fus conçu dans le péché (chorus);
(xxi) Psaume: Je lève mes regards vers la montagne (T-solo);
(xxii) La chanson d'Ephraïm (S-solo, fv chorus);

(xxiii) Marche des Hébreux;
(xxiv) Psaume: Je t'aimerai, Seigneur, d'un amour tendre (chorus);
(xxv) Psaume: Dans cet effroi (chorus);
(xxvi) Psaume: Loué soit le seigneur (chorus);
(xxvii) Couronnement de Salomon;
(xxviii) La mort de David (S-solo, chorus).

Paris and Zürich, 25 February to 28 April 1921.

Pub: FF; VS(Fr.), 1921.

fp: cond. Arthur Honegger; 11/June/1921; Théâtre du Jorat, Mézières, Vaud, Switzerland.

(Nos. ii, viii and xviii were fp. by Mme Schéridan with M. Schéridan (pf); 2/June/1921; S.M.I. Concert, Salle Gaveau, Paris.)

34a. **LE ROI DAVID.** Oratorio. (1923).

Subtitled: 'Psaume symphonique en trois parties d'après le drame de René Morax'. (Ger. trans. by Hans Reinhart; Eng. trans. by Edward Agate.)

Arr. from the Inc. Music for *Le roi David* (1921) — see Catalogue No. 34. Scoring as Catalogue No. 34, with the addition of a narrator. The movt. titles remain as in No. 34, but they are re-ordered as follows:
i, ii, xxvi (=iii), iii (=iiib), iv-xiv=Part 1; xvi (=xv), xvii (=xvi) = Part 2; xv (= xvii), xviii – xxv, xxvii (= xxvi), xxviii (= xxvii) = Part 3.

Dur: c. 75′.

Ded: 'à mes parents'.

Pub: FF; Ø (F5918aF) (Fr./Ger./Eng.); VS (F5990F) (Fr./Ger./Eng.); 1924-25.

34b. **LE ROI DAVID.** Oratorio. (1923).

As Catalogue No. 34a, except rescored for: 2 (picc)2(ca)2(bcl)2(cbsn)/4231/timp. bdm.cym.sdm.tamb.tamtam.tri/cel.hp.org/str/narr.SAT-soli.chorus.

Re-orch. Summer 1923.

Pub: FF; Ø (F6198F) (Fr./Ger./Eng.); VS (Fr./Ger./Eng.), 1924-25.

fp: Clara Wirz-Wyss, Lisa Appenzeller, Carl Seidel, Chorus and Stadtorchester, cond. Ernest Wolters; 2/Dec/1923; Stadthaus, Winterthur, Switzerland (sung in Ger.).

f*Paris*p: Jacques Copeau (narr), Gabrielle Gills, Cellier, Charles Panzéra, La Chorale Française and l'Art Choral with Orch. cond. Robert Siohan; 14/March/1924; Salle Gaveau, Paris.

f*E*p:Robert Loraine (narr), Elsie Suddaby, Phyllis Archibald, Frank Titterton, National Chorus and Orch. cond. A.H.; 17/March/1927; B.B.C. National Concert, Royal Albert Hall, London.

34c. **SUITES FROM THE INCIDENTAL MUSIC FOR 'LE ROI DAVID'.** Orch. (1921).

Please see Appendix A.

35. **SKATING RINK.** Ballet Mus. (1921).

Subtitled: Symphonie chorégraphique.

Ballet by Canudo:'pour patins à roulettes'.

2(picc)2(ca).[E♭sx].2(bcl)2(cbsn)/4230/bdm.cym/hp/str.

Dec. 1921.

Pub: UE.

fp: Jean Borlin, Ballet Suédois de Rolf de Mare, cond. D.-E. Inghelbrecht; 20/Jan/1922; Théâtre des Champs-Elysées, Paris.

36. **SAUL.** Inc. Mus. (1922).

Play by André Gide.

May 1922.

Npub.

fp: 16/June/1922; Théâtre du Vieux-Colombier, Paris.

37. **SONATINE.** Ch. Mus. (1921-22).

Cl[= vlc]/pf.

(i) Modéré.
Zürich, July 1922.

(ii) Lent et soutenu.
Zürich, Oct. 1921.

(iii) Vif et rythmique.
Paris, Nov. 1921.

Ded: Werner Reinhart.

Pub: RL-S (RL 11514), 1925.

fp: Cahuzac and Jean Wiéner; 5/June/1923; Concerts Wiéner, Salle Pleyel, Paris.

f*Eb*p: Reginald Kell and Kathleen Cooper; 19/June/1937.

38. **TROIS CONTREPOINTS.** Ch. Mus. (1922).

Picc.ob(ca)/vln.vlc.

(i) Prélude à 2 voix (ob/vlc).
Allegro marcato, alla breve.
Ded: Maurice Jaubert.

(ii) Chorale à 3 voix (vln/ca/vlc).
Largo.
Ded: Jacques Brillouin.

(iii) Canon sur basse obstinée à 4 voix (picc/vln/ca/vlc).
Presto.
Ded: Marcel Delannoy.

Paris, Nov. 1922.

Pub: Hansen/Chester; set of parts (2692-4) and redn. for pf.duet by A.H. (2695).

fp: Fleury (picc), Gaudard (ob(ca)), Krettly (vln), Pierre Fournier (vlc); 6/Feb/1926; S.M.I. Concert, Salle Erard, Paris.

(f*European*p. of pf. duet ver: Pierre Maire and A.H.; 31/March/1930; École Normale de Musique, Paris).

(f*American*p. of pf. duet ver: Andrée Vaurabourg-Honegger and Arthur Honegger; summer 1929 [described by Honegger in an interview with Arthur Hoérée (*Musique*, 11-12 (15 September 1929) as one of "deux partitas"].)

39. **ANTIGONE.** Inc. Mus. (1922).

Play by Jean Cocteau after Sophocles.

5 pieces for ob(ca)/hp.

Dec. 1922.

Pub: Mus. suppl. to *Feuilles Libres*, Jan. 1923.

fp: 20/Dec/1922; Théâtre de l'Atelier, Paris.

40. **FANTASIO.** Ballet Mus. (1922).

Subtitled: Sketch en trois images.

Pantomime ballet by Georges Wague.

1(picc)111/1110/timp.bdm.cym/str.

Dec. 1922.

Npub.

CHOUCOUNE. Operetta. (?1922).

Please see Appendix E.

41. **CHANT DE JOIE.** Orch. (1923).

2+picc2+ca2+bcl 2+cbsn/4331/bdm.cym/cel.hp/str.

Vigoureux et rythmé — Calme — Tempo 1°—Largo.

Paris, Nov. 1922; Orch. Paris, Jan. 1923.

Ded: Maurice Ravel.

(Dur: 4½-5′/7′).

Pub: S-S (EMS 6551), 1924; arr. by A.H. for pf. duet (EMS 6553), 1924.

fp: Orch. de la S.R., cond. Ernest Ansermet; 7/April/1923; 24th Festival of the Association of Swiss Musicians, Geneva.

f*Paris*p: cond. Serge Koussevitsky; 3/May/1923; l'Opéra, Paris.

f*E*p: cond. Ernest Ansermet; 22/Nov/1923; Royal Philharmonic Society, London.

f*Eb*p: Newcastle Station S.O., cond. Edward Clark; 1/Nov/1926.

42. **LA TEMPETE.** Inc. Mus. (1923).

Play by Shakespeare trans. Guy de Pourtalès.

Acte I:

(i) Prélude (pendant toute la Ière scène);
(ii) avec reprise à prévoir;
(iii) Manteau magique;
(iv) Motif d'Ariel;
(v) Entrée de Caliban;
(vi) Chant d'Ariel;
(vii) Enchantement;
(viii) Reprise du $\frac{9}{8}$;

Acte II:

(ix) Le manteau;
(x) Motif d'Ariel;
(xi) Chant;
(xii) Sortie;
(xiii) Ritournelle Caliban;
(xiv) Chanson Stefano;
(xv) Chanson Caliban;
(xvi) Ritournelle Caliban;

Acte III:

(xvii) Final;
(xviii) Ritournelle Stefano;
(xix) Motif d'Ariel;
(xx) Pipeau;
(xxi) Ritournelle Stefano;
(xxii) (Calme);
(xxiii) Ariel;
(xxiv) (Calme);
(xxv) Quelques mesures;

Acte IV:

(xxvi) Grotte Prospero;
(xxvii) Motif d'Ariel;
(xxviii) Cérès (Musique d'Impératrice);
(xxix) Danse des enfants;
(xxx) Danse des enfants;
(xxxi) Ritournelle Caliban;
(xxxii) Chasse (Fanfare);
(xxxiii) Chasse (Impératrice);

Acte V:

(xxxiv) Manteau magique;
(xxxv) Chaconne de l'Impératrice;
(xxxvi) Chant d'Ariel;
(xxxvii) Final;
(xxxviii) Caliban;
(xxxix) Final.

fp: 1923; l'Odéon, Paris.

42a. **PRELUDE POUR 'LA TEMPETE'.** Orch. (1923).

From the Incidental Music for *La tempête* (see Catalogue No. 42).

1+piccl+ca1+bcl 1+cbsn/4231/bdm.cym.tamtam.tri/str.

Lourd et agité.

Paris, Feb. 1923.

Ded: Mme L. Maillot.

(Dur: 8′).

Pub: S-S (EMS 6338), 1924; arr. by A.H. for pf. duet (EMS 6477), 1924.

f*concert*p: cond. Walter Straram; 1/May/1923; Théâtre des Champs-Elysées, Paris.

f*E*p: New Queen's Hall Orch., cond. Sir Henry Wood; 8/Jan/1927; Queen's Hall, London.

42b. **DEUX CHANTS D'ARIEL.** Voc. Mus. (1923).

From the Incidental Music for *La tempête* (see Catalogue No. 42).

2122/2200/cel.hp/str/S-solo.

Shakespeare, from *The Tempest* trans. Guy de Pourtalès.

(i) Modéré—Plus lent.
Ded: Gabrielle Gills.

(ii) Un peu animé.
Ded: Joy [Demarquette-] MacArden.

Paris, April 1923.

Pub: S-S; VS with pf.redn. by A.H. (EMS 6884), 1925.

f*concert*p: Joy Demarquette-MacArden, Strasbourg MO, [cond. Arthur Honegger]; 18/Nov/1925; Palais des Fêtes, Strasbourg.

43. **LILULI.** Inc. Mus. (1923).

Play by Romain Rolland.

(i) Chœur des ouvriers: Ah Joseph dites-nous. (Ier Chœur — voix aiguës; 2^ème^Chœur — voix graves/picc/vlc/pf.)

(ii) Liluli: 'Laïra'. (Voice/pf).

Pub: S(H).

fp: 31/March/1923; Salle des fêtes de Suresnes.

44. **CHANSON DE FAGUS.** Voc. Mus. (1923).

S-solo.SATB4tet/pf.

May, 1923.

Ded: Paul Pélissier.

Pub: S (EAS 17852), 1984.

fp: Gabrielle Gills, Groupe Nivard with Andrée Vaurabourg; 24/March/1926; La Revue Musicale Concert, Salle Gaveau, Paris.

45. **SIX POESIES.** Voc. Mus. (1920-23).

Voice/pf.

Poems by Jean Cocteau.

(i) Le nègre (from 'Températures').
Paris, May 1920.

(ii) Locutions.
Paris, May 1920.

(iii) Souvenirs d'enfance.
Paris, June 1920.

(iv) Ex voto.
Paris, June 1923.

(v) Une danseuse.
Paris, June 1923.

(vi) Madame.
Paris, Jan. 1923.

Ded: Rose Féart.

Pub: S-S (EMS 6602), 1924.

fp: Rose Féart; Geneva.

f*Paris*p: Claire Croiza with A.H.; 17/Nov/1924; Salle Pleyel, Paris.

f*Eb*p (No. iii): Dora Stevens; 4/Jan/1927.

(Arr. by A. Hoérée for voice/str4tet [=str]. Pub: S(H). fp. *chamber* ver: Régine de Lormoy, Quatuor Bruxelles, cond. A. Hoérée; 12/Dec/1930; Festival Honegger, Bruxelles Conservatoire. fp. *orchestral* ver: M. Cuénod, Orch. Féminin de Paris, cond. Jane Evrard; 5/Dec/1936; Salle Gaveau, Paris.)

46. **LE CAHIER ROMAND.** Pf. (1921-23).

(i) Calme.
Zürich, Sept. 1921.
Ded: Alice Ecoffey.

(ii) Un peu animé.
Paris, July 1923.
Ded: Jacqueline Ansermet.

(iii) Calme et doux.
Zürich, July 1921.
Ded: Miquette Wagner-Rieder.

(iv) Rythmé.
Paris, June 1923.
Ded: Paul Boepple.

(v) Egal.
Paris, April 1922.
Ded: René Morax.

Pub: S-S (EMS 6250), 1925.

(No. i fpub. as part of the mus. suppl. of *La Revue Musicale*, Jan. 1922. See also Catalogue No. 4.)

fp: Andrée Vaurabourg; 30/Jan/1924; S.M.I. Concert, Salle Erard, Paris.

47. **LA ROUE.** Film Score. (1923).

Silent Film. Dir: Abel Gance (Ass: Blaise Cendrars).

Prod: Charles Pathé.

48. **MOUVEMENT SYMPHONIQUE N° 1.** Orch. (1923).

Subtitled: Pacific 231.

2+picc2+ca2+bcl2+cbsn/4331/bdm.cym.sdm.tamtam/str.

Paris — Winterthur — Zürich, 1923.

Ded: Ernest Ansermet.

(Dur: 6¼/8′).

Pub: Philharmonia/UE (W.Ph.V.151), 1924. S-S (EMS 6443 and EMS 6680), 1924; also ver. by Francis Salabert for small orch. (2(picc)121/2230/bdm.cym.sdm.tamtam/str.) (EAS 6145), 1931; arr. for pf. duet (EMS 6550), 1924; arr. for 2pf/8 hands; and arr. by Adolphe Borchard for pf. (EMS 7028), 1926. (Dur. of Salabert ver. 5′/). (Borchard ver. for pf. ded. to Andrée Vaurabourg).

fp: cond. Serge Koussevitsky; 8/May/1924; l'Opéra, Paris.

f*E*p: Hallé Orch., cond. Sir Hamilton Harty; Nov. 1924, Manchester.

f*London*p: cond. (Sir) Eugene Goosens; 29/Jan/1925; Royal Philharmonic Society, Queen's Hall, London.

f*Eb*p: Hallé Orchestra, cond. Sir Hamilton Harty; 26/March/1925.

(The following films used the score as the sound track:
(a) *Pacific 231* — Dir: Tsekhanuski; Russia, 1931. (b) *Pacific 231* — Dir: Jean Mitry; France, 1949.)

49. **CHANSON.** Voc. Mus. (1924).

Voice/fl/str[=str4tet] [Voice/pf].

Ronsard.

(Plus tu connais que je brûle pour toi . . .).

Doucement.

Paris, Feb. 1924.

Ded: Charles Panzéra.

Pub: S-S (EMS 6616 and 7841), 1929; VS with pf. redn. by A.H..

(fpub. as part (v) of the mus. suppl. of *La Revue Musicale,* May 1924, entitled 'Tombeau de Ronsard': (i) Paul Dukas: Sonnet; (ii) Albert Roussel: Rossignol, mon mignon; (iii) Louis Aubert: La fontaine d'Hélène; (iv) André Caplet: (Sonnet); (vi) Roland-Manuel: Sonnet; (vii) Maurice Delage: Ronsard à sa muse; (viii) Maurice Ravel: Ronsard à son âme.)

fp (pf. ver.): Claire Croiza; 15/May/1924; Revue Musicale Concert (Hommage à Ronsard), Théâtre du Vieux-Colombier, Paris.

fp (chamber ver.): Régine de Lormoy, Blanquart, Poulet Quartet, cond. A. Hoérée; 24/Jan/1925, Paris.

f*Eb*p (chamber ver.): Claire Croiza and instrumental ensemble; 4/Feb/1929; Arts Theatre Club, London.

50. **SOUS-MARINE.** Ballet Mus. (1924).

Ballet by Carina Ari ('Scène mimée').

21+ca1+bcl2/4000/cym/cel.hp/str.

Très calme — Un peu moins lent — En animant peu à peu.

Montfort — L'Amaury, Sept. 1924.

Ded: Carina Ari.

Pub: S(H).

fp: Carina Ari; 27 June 1925; l'Opéra-Comique, Paris.

f*concert*p: cond. Robert Siohan; 8/Dec/1929; Concerts Siohan, Théâtre de la Gaîté-Lyrique, Paris.

51. **CONCERTINO.** Concerto. (1924).

22(ca)2(bcl)2/2210/str/pf-solo.

Allegro molto moderato — Larghetto sostenuto — Allegro.

Paris, Sept. - 17/Nov/1924.

Ded: Andrée Vaurabourg.

Dur: 10-12′.

Pub: S-S (EMS 7008 and 7631), 1926; arr. by A.H. for 2pf. (EMS 6886), 1925.

fp: Andrée Vaurabourg, orch. cond. Serge Koussevitsky; 23/May/1925; l'Opéra, Paris.

f*E*p: Gordon Bryan, Bournemouth Municipal Orchestra, cond. Sir Dan Godfrey; 3/Jan/1929; Bournemouth.

f*London*p: Elsa Karen, Wood S.O., cond. Sir Henry Wood; 24/Aug/1929; Promenade Concert, Queen's Hall, London.

FAITS DIVERS. Film Score. (1924).

Please see Appendix C.

52. **PRELUDE ET BLUES.** Ch. Mus. (1925).

4hp (arr. by Jeanne Daliès).

Npub., but recorded by the Quatuor Harpes Chromatiques de M. - L. Casadesus on Gram. L. 668 (78 r.p.m.).

fp: Quatuor de harpes Casadesus; 24/March/1925; Salle des Agriculteurs, Paris.

53. **JUDITH.** Inc. Mus. (1925).

Biblical drama by René Morax. (Ger. trans. by Léo Mélitz.)

2(picc)2(ca)2(bcl)2/2220/bdm.cym.sdm.tamtam.tri/hnm.2pf/str/S(Servant)Mz(Judith)S3TBar-soli.retr.chorus.

(i) Lamentations;
(ii) La trompe d'alarme;
(iii) Prière;
(iv) Chant funèbre;
(v) Invocation;
(vi) Incantation;
(vii) Fanfare;
(viii) Scène à la fontaine;
(ix) Musique de fête;
(x) Nocturne;
(xi) Cantique de la bataille;
(xii) Cantique des vierges;
(xiii) Cantique de victoire.

Paris, April 1925.

Ded: Claire Croiza.

(Dur: /50′).

Pub: S-S; Ø (EMS 7098), 1925; VS (Fr.) (EMS 6718), 1925; VS (Fr./Ger.) (EMS 6718), 1927; No. iii pub. separately in arrs. by A.H. for voice/pf. (EMS 6903), 1925, and voice/orch. (2111/2200/cym.tamb/pf/str.) (H).

fp: Claire Croiza (Judith), Mme Andréossi (Servant), cond. A.H.; 13/June/1925; Théâtre du Jorat, Mézières, Vaud, Switzerland.

53a. **JUDITH.** Opera. (1925).

Libretto by René Morax. (Ger. trans. by Léo Mélitz.)

Created with additional music from the Incidental Music Score for *Judith* (see Catalogue No. 53).

Chorus/orch (as Catalogue No. 53) S(Servant).Mz(Judith).Bar(Holopherne).B(Ozias).T(Bagoas, un soldat, une sentinelle, voix dans la coulisse)-soli.

Paris, Nov.-Dec. 1925.

Ded: Claire Croiza.

(Dur: /65′).

Pub: S-S; Ø (Fr.) (EMS 7099), 1925; Ø (Fr./Ger.), c.1930; VS (Fr.) (EMS 6938), 1925.

fp: Mme Bonavia (Judith), Tikin Gervais (Holopherne), Orch. and Chorus of the Monte-Carlo Opera, cond. A.H.; 13/Feb/1926; Monte-Carlo Opera House.

53b. **JUDITH.** Oratorio. (1926).

Subtitled: Action-musicale.

Text by René Morax; Music as Catalogue No. 53.

Scoring as Catalogue No. 53a with the addition of a narrator.

Pub: S (See Catalogue No. 53 for relevant details).

fp: 1926, Rotterdam; (principal soloists Berthe Serven and Evert Cornelis).

54. **HOMMAGE DU TROMBONE EXPRIMANT LA TRISTESSE DE L'AUTEUR ABSENT.** Ch. Mus. (1925).

Commissioned by *Comœdia*.

Tbn/pf.

Modéré.

Mézières, June 1925.

Ded: Serge Koussewitsky.

fp: June 1925; premises of *Comœdia*.

55. **L'IMPERATRICE AUX ROCHERS (UN MIRACLE DE NOTRE-DAME).** Inc. Mus. (1925).

Drama in 5 Acts and a Prologue by Saint-Georges de Bouhélier.

2+picc2+ca2+bcl 2+cbsn/4331/timp.bdm.bells.cym.sdm.tamtam/cel.hp/str/S-solo.chorus.

(i) Prologue;
(ii) Prélude, Acte 1;
(iib) La chasse de l'empereur (fanfare);
(iii) Interlude;
(iv) La salle du conseil;
(v) Entrée du Pape;
(vi) Sortie de l'empereur (chorus);
(vii) Prélude, Acte 2 (La neige sur Rome);
(viii) Interlude;
(ix) La tour;
(x) Postlude;
(xi) Prélude, Acte 3 (Les jardins du palais);
(xii) Concert champêtre;
(xiii) Postlude;
(xiv) Le retour de l'empereur;
(xv) Cortège de l'impératrice;
(xvi) L'orage;
(xvii) Prélude, Acte 4 (L'orgie au palais);
(xviii) Musique de fête;
(xix) (Animé) (S-solo);
(xx) Le rocher;
(xxi) Apparition (chorus);
(xxii) (Calme) (chorus);
(xxiii) (Lent) (chorus);
(xxiv) Prélude, Acte 5 (Les ruines du temple);
(xxv) Le parvis de la cathédrale;
(xxvi) Chœur finale (chorus).

6 Aug.-13 Nov. 1925.

Ded: Ida Rubinstein.

Pub: S-S, 1926; VS with pf.redn. by A.H. and Andrée Vaurabourg (EMS 6888), 1926.

fp: Ida Rubinstein, Suzanne Desprès, Hervé, Grétillat, Desjardins, Orch. and Chorus of l'Opéra, cond. Philippe Gaubert; 17/Feb/1927; l'Opéra, Paris.

(No. xv, 'Cortège de l'Impératrice', was subsequently rearranged for 2pf and included as the fourth movement — Allegro moderato — of the *Partita* (1940). See Catalogue No. 134.)

55a. **LA NEIGE SUR ROME.** Pf. (1925).

Arr. by A.H. for pf.solo of No. vii — Prélude, Acte 2 (La neige sur Rome) from the Incidental Music for *L'Impératrice aux rochers* (see Catalogue No. 55).

Lent et doux.

Pub: S-S (EMS 7478), 1926.

55b. SUITE FROM THE INCIDENTAL MUSIC FOR 'L'IMPERATRICE AUX ROCHERS'. Orch. (1925).

Scoring for orch. as Catalogue No. 55.

(i) La chasse de l'empereur (iib);
(ii) La neige sur Rome (vii);
(iii) Orage (xvi);
(iv) Le jardin (xi);
(v) Orgie (xvii).

(Dur: /20′).

Pub: S-S (EMS 7537 and 7644), 1928; also pf. redn.

fp: Orch, Straram, cond. A.H.; 18/May/1928; Paris.

56. PHÆDRE. Inc.Mus. (1926).

Tragedy by Gabriel d'Annunzio. (Fr. trans. by André Doderet).

2(picc)2(ca)22/2231/timp.cym/str/8A.

Acte 1: (i) Prélude; (ii) Cortège des suppliantes;

Acte 2: (iii) Prélude; (iv) Le baiser: (v) Imprécations de Thésée;

Acte 3: (vi) Prélude; (vii) Lamentations d'Aethra; (viii) Chœur des prêtresses d'Aphrodite; (ix) Mort de Phædre.

Feb.-March, 1926.

Ded: André George.

?Npub. in full; for 6 items see Catalogue No. 56a below.

fp: Ida Rubinstein (Phædre), cond. A.H.; 19/April/1926; Teatro Costanzi; Rome.

56a. SUITE FROM THE INCIDENTAL MUSIC FOR 'PHÆDRE'. Orch. (1925).

Suite of six movements (as Catalogue No. 56 except omitting nos. iv, vii and viii) for orch. (as Catalogue No. 56).

(i) Prélude;
(ii) Cortège des suppliantes;
(iii) Prélude;
(iv) Imprécation de Thésée;
(v) Prélude;
(vi) Mort de Phædre.

(Dur: /18′).

Pub: S-S (EMS 8146 and 8224), 1930.

57. **CANTIQUE DES CANTIQUES DE SALOMON.** Melodrama. (1926).

Ch-orch./reciter.

May 1926.

Npub.

fp: Chocana (/Suzanne) Avivitt, Orch. Golschmann, cond. V. Golschmann; 16/June/1926; Concerts Golschmann, Salle Gaveau, Paris.

58. **LA PETITE SIRENE.** Voc. Mus. (1926).

Voice/pf [=fl/str4tet = str].

René Morax after Hans Anderson.

(i) Chanson des sirènes.
Lent.

(ii) Berceuse de la sirène.
Tranquille.

(iii) Chanson de la poire.
Vif.

Ded: Régine de Lormoy.

Pub: S-S; VS (EMS 7342), 1927; Score and folio of parts (EMS 7573), 1928.

fp: (chamber ver.) Régine de Lormoy, Rémon, Roth Quartet, cond. A.H.; 26/March/1927; Durand Concert, Salle Pleyel, Paris.

LE ROI, SON VIZIR ET SON MEDECIN. Inc. Mus. (1926).

Please see Appendix C.

59. **ANTIGONE.** Opera. (1924-27).

Tragedy in 3 Acts, libretto by Jean Cocteau after Sophocles. (Ger. trans. by Gian Bundi).

3(picc)2+ca2+bcl.asx.2+cbsn/432+btbnl/timp.bdm.cym.saw.sdm.tamtam/cel.hp/str/SMzAT2Bar2B-soli.SATB4tet.chorus.

Paris and St. Jacut de la mer, Jan. 1924-Feb. 1927; Orch. Paris, Dingle, Lahinch, Montfort l'Amaury and Perros-Guirec, June-Sept. 1927.

Ded: Vaura [Andrée Vaurabourg].

Pub: S-S; VS (Fr.) (EMS 7297); VS (Ger.) (EMS 7298), 1927.

fp: E. Colonne (Créon), S. Ballard (Antigone), E. Deulin (Ismène), M. Gerday (Eurydice), M. Yovanovitch (Tirésias), P. Gilson (Hémon), J. Sales (le messager), Chorus and Orch. of the Théâtre Royal de la Monnaie, Brussels, cond. Corneil de Thoran; 28/Dec/1927; Théâtre Royal de la Monnaie, Brussels.

f*concert*p: Cl. M. Elshorst (Antigone), Heinrich Gürtler (Créon), Chorus and Orch. of the Bäyerisches Rundfunks, cond. Hermann Scherchen; 19/May/1931.

60. **NAPOLEON.** Film Score. (1927).

Silent Film. Author/Dir: Abel Gance.

Editor: Adriano Baumann.

60a. **SUITE FROM THE FILM SCORE 'NAPOLEON'.** Orch. (1927).

(i) La romance de Violine.
1110/0000/hnm.pf/str.
Andantino
Dur: 2′30″.
Pub: S (EAS 4443), 1927.

(ii) Calme.
1111/2000/hnm.pf/str.
Lent.
Dur: 4′.
Pub: S (EAS 4444), 1927.

(iii) Danse des enfants.
1011/0000/hnm.pf/str(no cb).
Vif.
Dur: 1′30″.
Pub: S (EAS 4445), 1927.

(iv) Interlude et Finale.
1121/22.2cnt.20/timp/hnm.pf/str.
Andante con moto; Agitato.
Dur: 4′.
Pub: S (EAS 4446), 1927.

(v) Napoléon.
2122/2331/bdm.cym/[hnm].pf/str.
Allegro moderato.
Dur: 1′30″.
Pub: S (EAS 4643), 1927.

(vi) Chaconne de l'impératrice.
[1]1[2]1/20.[2cnt].3[2]0/timp.tri/hnm.pf/str.
Dur: 4′.
Pub: S (EAS 4502), 1927.

(vii) Les ombres.
[1][1][2][1]/[2]2[3]0/bdm.cym/pf/str.
Lent.
Dur: 2′30″.
Pub: S (EAS 4655), 1927.

(viii) Les mendiants de la gloire.
2221/2230/bdm.cym.tdm/hnm.pf/str.
Dur: 5′15″.
Pub: S (EAS 4656), 1927.

N.B. Editions Salabert has recently replaced the above with a 'version originale reconstituée par Adriano (Zürich)'. All the movements detailed above are present, but re-ordered: (ii), (i), (iii), (iv), (vi), (v), (vii), (viii). The 'overall orchestration' is given as : 2(picc)222/4331/timp.perc/str. The total duration is estimated at 'c.25 minutes'.

61. **ROSES DE METAL.** Ballet Mus. (1928).

Subtitled: Blues.

Ballet by Elisabeth Grammont de Clermont-Tonnerre.

1111/1100/str.

(Minim = 56) (57 bars).

Npub.

fp: Petite-Scène; Paris.

62. **MOUVEMENT SYMPHONIQUE N° 2.** Orch. (1928).

Subtitled: Rugby.

2+picc2+ca2+bcl 2+cbsn/4331/str.

Allegro.

Paris, Aug. 1928.

Ded: René Delange.

(Dur: 7-8′).

Pub: S-S (EMS 7818 and 7825), 1928; ver. for pf. by A.H. with lithographs by Josué Gaboriaud pub. 1929 (300 copies only of facsimile of autograph score).

fp: Inaugural Concert of l'Orch. Sym. de Paris, cond. Ernest Ansermet; 19/Oct/1928; Paris.

f*E*p: Wood S.O., cond. Sir Henry Wood; 7/Sept/1929; Promenade Concert, Queen's Hall, London.

63. **SUR LE NOM D'ALBERT ROUSSEL.** Pf. (1928).

Paris, 13/Dec/1928.

Ded: to A.R. [Albert Roussel] for his 60th birthday.

Pub: S-S (EMS 7988), 1928.

(fpub. as part of mus. suppl. to *La Revue Musicale*, April 1929, entitled 'Hommage à Roussel').

fp: Pierre Maire; 13/April/1929; Festival Roussel, Salle de l'Ancien Conservatoire, Paris.

(? Orchestrated by Honegger as *Fanfare pour Albert Roussel* and recorded by the Orchestre Radio-symphonique de Paris, cond. Tony Aubin, on 18/April/1951 — Radio France archives, no. MM29.)

64. **VOCALISE — ETUDE.** Voc.Mus. (1929).

Voix moyennes (B♭-F♯)/pf.

Written for the 1929 Paris Conservatoire Examinations.

Pub: Leduc (AL 17, 476), 1929 as No. 73 in Vol. 8 of A.L. Hettick's *Répertoire moderne de vocalises.*

65. **AMPHION.** Melodrama. (1929).

Melodrama by Paul Valéry. (Ger. trans. Walter Klein. Eng. trans. Edward Agate.)

22(ca)22/2231/timp.3perc.xyl/cel.hp/str/B-solo.4fv-soli.chorus.

Paris, 1929.

Ded: Ida Rubinstein.

(Dur: /40′).

Pub: RL-S; VS (Fr./Ger./Eng.) (RL 11778), 1931 (525 copies only). Chorus parts (RL 11778bis).

fp: Ida Rubinstein (Amphion), Charles Panzéra (Apollo), Nelle Martyl, Madeleine Mathieu, Mady Arty, Mlle Kirova (Les muses), Chorus and Orch. of l'Opéra, cond. Gustave Cloëz; 23/June/1931; l'Opéra, Paris.

f*concert*p: Ida Rubinstein and Henri Fabert, cond. Robert Siohan; 14/Jan/1932; Université des Annales, Paris.

65a. **PRELUDE, FUGUE, POSTLUDE.** Orch. (1948).

Arranged from *Amphion* (see Catalogue No. 65).

3(picc)2+ca3(bcl).E♭asx.2cbsn/4331/bdm.cym.tamtam/cel.hp/str.

Andante tranquillo, Largo, Allegro marcato — Marcato pesante — Largamente.

Dur: 13½′.

Pub: S (EAS 15085), 1948.

fp: l'Orch. de la S.R., cond. Ernest Ansermet; 3/Nov/1948; Geneva.

66. **PARTITA.** Ch. Mus. (pre-summer 1929).

Pf. duet.

Ouverture; Intermezzo; Marcia.

fp: Andrée Vaurabourg-Honegger and Arthur Honegger; Summer 1929; U.S.A.

67. **CELLO CONCERTO.** Concerto. (1929).

222(bcl)2/2201/timp.cym.tri/str/vlc-solo.

Andante — Lento — Allegro marcato.

Paris, Aug. 1929. (Ver. for vlc/pf. dated Nov. 1929.)

Ded: Maurice Maréchal.

(Dur: 17¼/15′).

Pub: S-S (EMS 8329 and 8394), 1931; ver. for vlc/pf. (S.8247), 1931; both with cadenza by M. Maréchal. (Cadenza by Maurice Gendron pub. by Edition Georges Delrieu (GD1441), 1971, in *Cadences pour violoncelle*, pp.22-23.)

fp: Maurice Maréchal, Boston S.O., cond. Serge Koussevitsky; 17/Feb/1930; Boston.

f*Paris*p: Maurice Maréchal, l'Orch. Sym. de Paris, cond. Pierre Monteux; 16/May/1930; Salle Pleyel, Paris.

f*Eb*p: Anthony Pini, B.B.C. Orch; cond. Julian Clifford; 29/July/1935.

68. **BERCEUSES.** Ch. Mus. (1929).

Fl[=vln]/tpt[=vla]/vln.vlc/pf[=hp].

Paris, December 1929.

Ded: Pour [Lo]la Bobesco".

Npub.

A fifteen bar combination of themes from Berceuses by Fauré, Godard and Chopin, and the popular melody "Fais dodo, Colin, mon p'tit frère".

69. **J'AVAIS UN FIDELE AMANT.** Orch. Mus. (1929).

Str.

Paris, Dec. 1929.

Ded: 'pour [Lo]la Bobesco'.

Npub.

70. **SYMPHONIE [N° 1].** Orch. (1929-30).

3(picc)2+ca2+bcl 2+cbsn/4331/bdm.tamtam/str.

(i) Allegro marcato; (ii) Adagio; (iii) Presto.

Paris, Dec. 1929 — April, 1930; Orch. Mougins, April-May, 1930. (i: Brussels, 10/March/1930; ii: Paris, 3/April/1930).

Ded: Boston S.O. and Serge Koussevitsky.

Dur: 21′ 25″. (i: 6′; ii: 8′15″; iii: 7′10″).

Pub: S-S (EMS 8156 and 8219), 1930.

fp: Boston S.O., cond. Serge Koussevitsky; 13/Feb/1931; Boston.

f*Paris*p: Orch. Straram, cond. A.H.; 2/June/1931; Festival Honegger, Paris.

f*Eb*p: B.B.C. Orch., cond. Ernest Ansermet; 24/Jan/1932.

71. **LES AVENTURES DU ROI PAUSOLE.** Operetta. (1929-30).

Libretto by Albert Willemetz from a novel by Pierre Louÿs (Eng. trans. Wayne Shirley and Richard Ringler. Ger. trans. Franz Schulz.)

1(picc)11.asx(+tsx).1/1110/timps.bdm.canon.cast.cym.sbells.
tamb.tamtam.bells.tri.wbl.xyl/cel/str/soloists/chorus.

Overture;

Acte 1:

(i) Chœur de la sieste (Les reines);
(ii) Sortie des reines (Les reines);
(iii) Air de Taxis: J'ai fait, pourquoi le taire, tous les métiers (Taxis);
(iv) Air de la blanche Aline: Papa veut toujours, seule, hélas! que je m'amuse (Aline);

(v) Ballet;
(vi) Entrée des bois de justice (Pausole et chœur);
(vii) Air de Giglio: J'ai l'honneur d'être votre page (Giglio);
(viii) Septuor des sept avis différents (Les reines);
(ix) Final;

Acte 2: Prélude;

(x) Chœur des fermières: Frottons, époussetons (Le métayer, les fermières);
(xi) Duo du travesti: Etes-vous un homme? êtes-vous une femme? (Aline et Mirabelle);
(xii) Ritournelle de la mule;
(xiii) Cantate: Vive le roi Pausole (Le métayer, Thierette, les fermières);
(xiv) Air de la coupe de Thulé: Descendant du roi de Thulé (Pausole);
(xv) Sortie américaine du Roi;
(xvi) Trio: Vos joues sont d'exquises pêches (Aline, Mirabelle, Giglio);
(xvii) Air d'Aline: Pardon, mon papa que j'adore (Aline);
(xviii) Air de Diane: Si vous saviez combien c'est long d'attendre (Diane);
(xix) Duetto de la révolte (Taxis, Perchuque);
(xx) Final;

Acte 3:

(xxi) Chœur des soubrettes: Chut! pas de bruit le roi sommeille (Les caméristes);
(xxii) Duo du rêve: J'ai fait un rêve merveilleux (Diane, Giglio);
(xxiii) Entrée du chocolat espagnol: Voilà le chocolat espagnol (Thierette et tous);
(xxiv) Air de Taxis: Ah! mon Dieu, qu'ai-je vu (Taxis);
(xxv) Duo du téléphone: Allô, le roi? (Aline, Pausole);
(xxvi) Air de Giglio: l'amour, c'est comme la musique (Giglio);
(xxvii) Les adieux de Pausole: Adieu, mon peuple aimé (Pausole);
(xxviii) Final.

Paris, May 1929 — Buenos Aires, 18/Nov/1930.

Ded: 'Au musicien de "Choucoune" à Fernand Ochsé'.

Pub: S; VS (EAS 6333) (Fr.), 1930; Chorus parts (EAS 6333bis), 1931; Orchestral parts (EAS 6693).

fp: Dorville (Le roi Pausole), Koval (Taxis), Jacqueline Francell (La blanche Aline), Pasquali (Giglio), Meg Lemonnier (Mirabelle), Blanche (Le fermier), Germaine Duclos (Diane à la Houppe), Claudie de Sivry (Dame Perchuque), Régine Paris (Thierette), D'Ary Brissac (Le brigadier des gardes), Mlles Cora-Lynn, Moussia Favier, Huguenin, Beryl, Naury (Les reines), Clauday (La jeune fille violée), Mlles Dubost, Mona D'Eze, Magny, Marc, Clairval, Verney (Les danseuses), Villers (Le marin catalan), Marsac (Le grand ecuyer), Michel (Le grand chancelier), Cochois (Le grand chambellan); Chorus and Orch., cond. Bervily; 12/Dec/1930; Théâtre des Bouffes-Parisiens, Paris.

71a. **SUITE FROM THE OPERETTA 'LES AVENTURES DU ROI PAUSOLE'.** Pf. (1931).

(i) Ouverture;
(ii) Ritournelle de la mule (xii);
(iii) Les adieux (de Pausole) (xxvii);
(iv) Air d'Aline (xvii);
(v) Le chocolat espagnol (xxiii).

Pub: S (EAS 6636), 1931.

71b. **SUITE FROM THE OPERETTA 'LES AVENTURES DU ROI PAUSOLE'.** Orch. (1931).

Please see Appendix A.

71c. **VALSE POUR LE ROI PAUSOLE.** Voc. Mus. (1931).

Please see Appendix A.

72. **LES NOCES D'AMOUR ET PSYCHE.** Ballet Mus. (1930).

Ballet by Ida Rubinstein.

Movements from Bach's English and French Suites for keyboard, orch. A.H.

Npub.

fp: Ida Rubinstein; 1930; l'Opéra, Paris.

72a. **SUITE FROM THE BALLET SCORE 'LES NOCES D'AMOUR ET PSYCHE'.** Orch. (1933).

22(ca)2(bcl).B♭ssx.2/4300/cel.hp/str.

(i) l'Anglaise.
Dur: 2½′.

(ii) Sarabande.
Dur: 2½′.

(iii) Gavotte.
Dur: 1½′.

(iv) Menuet.
Dur: 2′.

(v) Gigue.
Dur: 3′.

(Total Dur: 11½′).

Pub: UE (No. 10.527), 1933.

fp: Orch. Sym. de Paris, cond. Gustave Cloëz; 5/Feb/1933; Concerts Poulet, Paris.

73. **CRIS DU MONDE.** Oratorio. (1931)

Libretto by René Bizet. (Eng. trans. Edward Agate; Ger. trans. Gian Bundi.)

3(picc)2+ca2+bcl3(cbsn)/4331/bdm.cym.sdm.tamtam.tri.wdbl/pf/str/SABar-soli.chorus.

Paris, 1/March /1931; Orch. (à Briançon) 24/March/1931.

Ded: Cäcilienverein, Solothurn and their conductor Dr. Erich Schild.

(Dur: 52′/55′).

Pub: S-S: Ø (EMS 8325) (Fr./Ger./Eng.), 1931; VS (EMS 8275) (Fr./Ger.), 1931; Chorus parts (EMS 8266) (Fr.), 1931, (EMS 8266) (Fr./Ger.), 1931, (EMS 8592) (Fr./Eng.), 1933.

fp: Berthe de Vigier, Pauline Hoch, Carl Rehfuss, Cäcilienverein, Orch., cond. Erich Schild; 3/May/1933; Solothurn, Switzerland.

f*Paris*p: Berthe de Vigier, Lina Falk, Charles Panzéra, Cäcilienverein, Orch. Straram, cond. Erich Schild; 3/June/1931; Paris.

f*Eb*p: Kate Winter, Betty Bannerman, Mark Raphael, Wireless Choir and Orchestra, cond. (Sir) Adrian Boult; 22/Dec/1933 (in Eng.).

74. **LA BELLE DE MOUDON.** Operetta. (1931).

Operetta in 5 Acts, libretto by René Morax.

Br/2pf/cv chorus.chorus.SA-Soli.

(Acte I):

(i) Ouverture;
(ii) Romance (de la pâquerette) (Isabelle);
(iii) Chœur des laveuses (à l'unisson);
(iv) Chœur des laveuses (à l'unisson);
(v) Chœur de la diligence (à l'unisson);

(Acte II):

(vi) Chœur: C'est l'heure où tout repose (à l'unisson);
(vii) Valse;
(viii) Chanson de petit Jean (Gizele);

(Acte III):

(ix) Chœur (SATB): Ombre et silence;
(x) Voix de la forêt (cv chorus.chorus): Allez devant les vers luisants;

(Acte IV):

(xi) Introduction;
(xii) Air d'Isabelle: Tu fuis, ingrat, qui me juras ta foi . . .;
(xiii) Barcarolle (à la manière de . . .) (mv chorus): Viens avec moi mon ami;
(xiv) Entrée de la fanfare;
(xv) Polka;

(Acte V):

(xvi) Chœur: Un an se passe (à l'unisson);
(xvii) Couplet final (Belinda/Chorus): Je suis heureuse.

(Andrée Vaurabourg also composed a chorus for this operetta.)

Paris, March 1931.

Npub.

fp: Lucy Berthrand (Isabelle), S. André-Weith (Gizèle), Hélène Rieder, Alice Ecoffey (2pf), Moudon Brass Band, cond.Charles Pasche; 30/May/1931; Théâtre du Jorat, Mézières, Vaud, Switzerland.

75. **PRELUDE.** Ch. Mus. (1932).

Cb/pf.

Crotchet=69 (84 bars).

Paris, Feb. 1932.

Ded: André Laurent.

Npub.

76. **SONATINE.** Ch. Mus. (1932).

Vln/vlc.

(i) Allegro; (ii) Andante; (iii) Allegro.

Paris, Sept. 1932.

Ded: Albert and Anna Neuburger.

Pub: S-S (EMS 8495), 1932.

fp: Roth and van Dooeren; Dec. 1932; Concert du Triton, Ecole Normale de Musique, Paris.

77. **LE GRAND ETANG.** Voc. Mus. (1932).

Voice/pf.

Jean Tranchant.

Npub., but orch. ver. recorded by Marianne Oswald with orch. cond. Pierre Chagnon on Columbia DF 1114.

78. **PRELUDE, ARIOSO, FUGHETTE (SUR LE NOM DE BACH).** Pf. (1932).

Allegro — Grave — Allegro.

Paris, Oct. 1932.

Ded: Maurice Senart.

Pub: S-S (EMS 8522), 1933.

(fpub as No. (v) of the mus. suppl. of *La Revue Musicale*, Dec. 1932 entitled 'Hommage à Bach': (i) (-) — Albert Roussel; (ii) Ricercare sul nome BACH — Alfredo Casella; (iii) Valse – Improvisation —Francis Poulenc; (iv) Prélude à une fugue imaginaire — G. Francesco Malipiero.

fp: Andrée Vaurabourg; ?; Concert des enfants; Salle de Géographie, Paris.

f*E*p: Jehanne Chambard; 10/Oct/1935; Royal Academy of Music New Music Society, Duke's Hall, London.

f*Eb*p: Eileen Ralph; 5/Feb/1937.

78a. **PRELUDE, ARIOSO, FUGHETTE (SUR LE NOM DE BACH).** Orch. (1936).

Str.

Arr. by A.H. of the pf.original (see Catalogue No. 78).

Allegro — Grave — Allegro.

(Dur: /6′).

Pub: S-S (EMS 8727), 1937.

fp: Orch. Féminin de Paris, cond. Jane Evrard; 5/Dec/1936; Salle Gaveau, Paris.

79. **MOUVEMENT SYMPHONIQUE N° 3.** Orch. (1932-33).

2+picc2+ca2.asx.cbcl[=cbsn].2+cbsn/4331/bdm.cym.tamtam/str.

Allegro marcato — Poco più pesante — Tempo 1° — Adagio.

Paris, 20/Oct/1932; Orch; Chésières – Paris, Dec. 1932 – Jan. 1933.

Dur: 10′.

Ded: Wilhelm Furtwängler and the Berlin P.O.

Pub: S-S (EMS 8518 and 8520), 1933.

fp: Berlin P.O., cond.Furtwängler; 26/March/1933; Berlin.

f*Paris*p: Orch. Pasdeloup, cond. A.H.; 21/Oct/1933; Théâtre des Champs-Elysées, Paris.

f*E*p: ?; 16/Sept/1933, Promenade Concert, Queen's Hall, London.

80. **SEMIRAMIS.** Ballet Mus. (1933).

Ballet-Melodrama in 3 tableaux ('Le char'; 'Le lit'; 'La tour') by Paul Valéry.

Ww/br/2hp.2pf.om/4vln.6vla.6vlc.

Allegro vivace;
Scene I: Serviteurs;
Scene II: Entrée des captifs;
Scene III: Entrée de Sémiramis; Episode I; Episode II; Episode III;
Scene IV: Entrée des idoles des vaincus; Repère de nuit; Cortège; Rideau; Rideau; Rideau; Danse astrale; Rideau.

Paris, May 1933.

Pub: S.

fp: Ida Rubinstein (Sémiramis), Leister (Le beau prisonnier), Ballets Ida Rubinstein, cond. Gustave Cloëz; 11/May/1934; l'Opéra, Paris.

81. **LES DOUZE COUPS DE MINUIT.** Radio Mus. (1933).

Radio-mystère by Carlos Larronde.

Hp/org/pf-duet/timp/perc.(bdm.cym.tamtam.tdm.tri.wdbl)/chorus.

(i) Cortège;
(ii) Danse;
(iii) La pierre;
(iiia) Le bois;
(iiib) Le métal;
(iiic) Le verre;
(iv) Cascade des métaux;
(v) Cloche de fer;
(vi) Cloche d'Airain;
(vii) Chanson des ivrognes;
(viii) (Très lent);
(ix) Chorus: Avec la règle et le compas;
(ixb) Disque de jazz;
(x) Les aviateurs;
(xi) Chorus: Ouvrez les yeux.

Npub.

fp: Art et Action groupe; 27/Dec/1933; Radio-Colonial.

82. **LES MISERABLES.** Film Score. (1934).

In three parts after Victor Hugo.

Cond: Maurice Jaubert.

Dir: Raymond Bernard.

Prod: Pathé-Natan.

112(bcl).asx[=ca].1/1110/bdm.cym.tdm/hp.pf/str(no cb).

Part I:

(i) Prélude I (Générique);
(ii) Jean Valjean sur la route – Passeport – Place du village (Place de Bigne);
(iii) (Evocation des) Forçats;
(iiib) Passeport déchiré;
(iv) Jean Valjean avec la carte;
(v) Fantine — La route, nuit;
(vi) Fantine à l'infirmerie — Javert;
(vib) Chant de Fantine —Mort de Fantine;
(vii) Fuite de Jean Valjean;

Part II:

(viii) Prélude II (Cosette et Marius);
(ix) Musique de la foire lointaine (La fête à Montfermeil) — dans la forêt (Cosette dans la forêt) – Jean Valjean et Cosette;
(ixb) Transition (Le gâteau);
(x) Sortie de l'église;
(xi) (Le) Luxembourg — prévenir la police;
(xii) Le jardin de la rue Plumet;

Part III:

(xiii) Prélude III (L'Emeute);
(xiv) La tour St. Jacques;
(xv) Après la chute de Mabeuf (Emeute) (Mort de Mabeuf);
(xvi) Emeute (Mort de Gavroche);
(xvii) Emeute (Mort d'Eponine) – Eponine et Marius — Jean Valjean et Javert — Mort d'Eponine;
(xviii) Emeute (Après le parlementaire) (l'Assaut);
(xviiib) —;
(xix) Transition (Matin sur Notre Dame);
(xx) Dans les égouts;
(xxi) Musique (de fête) chez Gillenormand;
(xxii) Solitude de Jean Valjean;
(xxiii) Mort de Jean Valjean.

Brit. dist: Part 1 only, 1934.

82a. **SUITE FROM THE FILM SCORE 'LES MISERABLES'.** Orch. (1934).

Orch. (see Catalogue No. 82).

Pub: S, 1984.

fp: 19/Jan/1935; Concerts Siohan, Salle Rameau, Paris.

83. **RAPT** (ou **LA SEPARATION DES RACES).** Film Score. (1934).

After C.F. Ramuz.

Collab: A. Hoérée.

Dir: Dimitri Kirsanov.

Principal items:
(i) Procession;
(ii) Danse paysanne — au matin;
(iii) Chanson d'Eloi (words by J. Kessel): Frühlings Nacht, Märchen Nacht.

Bprem: Academy Cinema, London, 1934.

(No. ii, 'Danse paysanne', was used again by Honegger as the 'Danse des filles des cantons' — no. ii — in the Ballet Music Score *L'Appel de la montagne* (see Catalogue No. 161) and, under the same title, as no. ii in *Jour de fête suisse (Schwizerfaschttag)*, the orchestral suite based on the Ballet Music Score *L'Appel de la montagne* — see Catalogue No. 161a.)

84. **L'IDEE.** Film Score. (1934).

Music for an animated film, written, directed and photographed by Bertold Bartosch, from woodcuts by Franz Masereel.

Principal items:
(i) Générique;
(ii) Arbres et idées;
(iii) Facteur;
(iv) Tribunal;
(v) Usine;
(vi) Cortège funèbre;
(vii) Savant;
(viii) La rotation;
(ix) Cortège ouvriers-soldats;
(x) Coda.

Bprem: London Film Society.

85. **CESSEZ LE FEU.** Film Score. (1934).

After Joseph Kessel.

Collab: A. Hoérée.

Dir: Jacques Baroncelli.

Principal items:
(i) Chanson du cul-de-jatte (words by Zimmer);
(ii) Valse de Lagasse;
(iii) (La Marseillaise);
(iv) Fox-trot;
(v) Tango, major and minor;
(vi) Signal;
(vii) Chanson de l'escadrille (words by J. Kessel);
(viii) Valse musette.

85a. **LA CHANSON DE L'ESCADRILLE.** Voc. Mus. (1934).

§ March from the Film Score *Cessez le feu* (see Catalogue No. 85).

Voice/pf[=orch].

Joseph Kessel.

Orch. arr. by Paul Saegal (000.2asx.tsx.0/0210/bdm.cym.sdm/bjo/str(no vla)).

Pub: Editions Coda; Voice only (ECP 114), 1934; Voice and pf. (EC 197), 1934; Orch. arr. (ECO 127), 1934.

85b. **LA CHANSON DU CUL-DE-JATTE.** Voc. Mus. (1934).

From the film score *Cessez le feu* (see Catalogue No. 85).

85c. **VALSE DE LAGASSE.** Voc. Mus. (1934).

From the film score *Cessez le feu* (see Catalogue No. 85).

B. Zimmer.

Pub: Editions Coda.

86. **CRIME ET CHATIMENT.** Film Score. (1934).

After Dostoievsky.

Dir: Pierre Chenal.

Prod: Compagnie Générale de Productions Cinématographiques.

Brit. dist: Film Society, 1936.

87. **LE ROI DE LA CAMARGUE.** Film Score. (1934).

After Jean Aicard.

Collab: Roland-Manuel.

Dir: Jacques de Baroncelli.

Principal items:
(i) Poursuite et bataille;
(ii) L'église;
(iii) Fanfare;
(iv) Nuit devant la cabane;
(v) Final;
(vi) Deux chansons (words by G.-A. Cuel): (a) Ma plaine finit vers l'occident. (b) En Camargue, les filles sont belles.

88. **PETITE SUITE.** Ch. Mus. (1934).

2 treble instruments/pf.

The three movements have no titles or tempo marks and no designation of scoring for the two treble lines.

(i) is for one solo treble line/pf; (ii) is for two treble lines only; whilst (iii) is for two treble lines/pf.

Paris, Aug. 1934.

Ded: Yvonne and Peter Stadler.

Pub: ESI (ESI 63), 1936 ('sous la direction de la fédération musicale populaire'); ESI-CduM (ESI 63), 1970.

The work has been recorded twice with different scorings on each — see the Discography.

89. **RADIO PANORAMIQUE**. Radio Mus. (1935).

Subtitled 'Mouvement symphonique'.

111.asx.1/1110/timp.bdm.cym.sdm.tdm/org.pf/str/ST-soli.chorus [=S-solo].

Paris, Jan. 1935.

Ded: Radio Geneva for the 10th anniversary of their foundation.

Dur: 9′.

Pub: Les Œuvres Françaises—S(H).

fp/f*b*p: Violette Andréassi, Ernest Bauer, Roger Vuataz, J.-M. Pache, cond. Hermann Scherchen; 4/March/1935; Salle du Conservatoire, Geneva (10th anniversary of Radio Geneva).

f*Paris*p: Orch. Pasdeloup, cond. Albert Wolff; 19/Oct/1935; l'Opéra-Comique, Paris..

90. **FIEVRE JAUNE**. Voc. Mus. (1935).

Voice/pf.

Nino (Eng. trans. Yvonne Deneufville; Ger. trans. Hansi Gosselin).

Pub: LS-ME (SM 201) (Fr./Ger./Eng.), 1935.

91. **DER DAMON DES HIMALAYAS**. Film Score. (1935).

Collab: André Jolivet.

Dir: Andrew Marton in collab. with Gunther Oskar Dyhrenfurth.

Principal items:

(i) Générique chanté; Om mani pad me hum;
(ii) Rumba;
(iii) La lettre;
(iv) Voyage;
(v) Szynagai;
(vi) Les jardins de Moghul;
(vii) Défile de la caravane;
(viii) Danse des lamas (song);
(ix) Vision;
(x) Caravane des Kulis (chorus);
(xi) Chant nocturne des Kulis (chorus);
(xii) Récit de la femme;
(xiii) Himalaya;
(xiv) Montée de la caravane;
(xv) Tempête de neige;
(xvi) Bataille des Kulis;
(xvii) Chant de joie (song);
(xviii) Final chantée.

Feb. 1935.

(The orchestration of this score includes a part for 'trautonium'.)

92. **L'EQUIPAGE** (ou **CELLE QUE J'AIME**). Film Score. (1935).

After J. Kessel.

Collab: Maurice Thiriet, with music by Chopin, Schumann, Planquette.

Dir: Anatole Litvak.

Prod: Pathé-Natan.

Principal items: (i) Chanson du lapin (words by J. Kessel);
(ii) Premier vol.

Brit. dist: Colmore Distributors.

Bprem: Studio One, London; 29/April/1938.

93. **LES PETITS LITS BLANCS.** Ballet Mus. (1935).

'*Bal des petits lits blancs* organisé par 'Le Jour' au cercle interallié mis gracieusement à la disposition de l'œuvre'.

Music by A.H. (*Berceuse*) and Milhaud.

Paris, 1935.

Pub: Draeger, 1935. (Ms reproduced in programme for fp.)

fp: 4/June/1935.

94. **ICARE.** Ballet Mus. (1935).

Composed to rhythms by Serge Lifar in collaboration with Szyfer.

Perc/om/chorus.

Score not signed by A.H. became of his contractual obligations to the Ballets Ida Rubinstein.

Npub.

fp: 9/July/1935; l'Opéra, Paris. N.B. Under the name of Szyfer only.

95. **JEANNE D'ARC AU BUCHER.** Dramatic Oratorio. (1933-35).

Text by Paul Claudel (Ger. trans. Hans Reinhart. Eng. trans. Dennis Arundell).

2(picc)21+E♭cl+bcl.3E♭asx.3+cbsn/03+Dtpt3+btm[=1]/timp 2perc/cel.om.
2pf/str/15retr[=4].3SA4T[=1]2B[=1]–soli.cv.cv chorus.chorus.

Prologue (added in 1947);

(i) Les voix du ciel;
(ii) Le livre;
(iii) Les voix de la terre;
(iv) Jeanne livrée aux bêtes;
(v) Jeanne au poteau;
(vi) Les rois, ou l'invention du jeu de cartes;
(vii) Catherine et Marguerite;
(viii) Le roi qui va-t-à Rheims;
(ix) L'épée de Jeanne;
(x) Trimazo;
(xi) Jeanne d'Arc en flammes.

Paris, Rigi-Klösterli, Perros-Guirec, 30/Aug/1935; Orch. Paris, 24/Dec/1935.

Ded: Ida Rubinstein.

Dur: 80′.

Pub: S-S; Voice parts (Fr.), 1935; VS (EMS 8819) (Fr./Ger./Eng.), 1939; Ø (including 'Prologue') (EAS 15615), 1947.

fp: Ida Rubinstein, Jean Périer, Serge Sandos, Charles Vaucher (retr), Ginevra Vivante, Berthe de Vigier, Marianne Hirsig-Löwe (S-soli), Lina Falk (A-solo), Ernest Bauer (T-solo), Paul Sandoz (B-solo), Les Singknaben de l'église évangélique-réformée, Basle C.C. and C.O., Maurice Martenot (om), cond. Paul Sacher; 12/May/1938; Basle, Switzerland.

f*French*p: Ida Rubinstein, Solange Delmas, Turba-Rabier, Almona, Josette Barré, Jean Hervé, De Trévi, Mme de Chauveron, Chorale Felix Rangel, Orch., cond. Louis Fourestier; 6/May/1939; Orléans.

f*Paris*p: Marie-Hélène Dasté (Joan); Turba-Rabier (Marguerite), Eliette Schenneberg (Catherine), Jean-Louis Barrault, Julien Bertheau, Jean Hervé, Chorus and Orch. de la Soc. des Conc. du Cons., cond. Charles Münch; 13/June/1939; Palais de Chaillot, Paris.

f*Eb*p: Olive Groves, Nancy Evans, Gladys Ripley, Parry Jones, Bradbridge White, René Soames, Norman Walker, Choir of Mary Datchelor School, B.B.C. Chorus and S.O., cond. Basil Cameron; 16/April/1947; London.

f*E*p*(concert)*: Constance Cummings, Olive Groves, Nancy Evans, Gladys Ripley, Valentine Dyall, Parry Jones, Martin Boddey, René Soames, Norman Walker, Choir of Mary Datchelor School, B.B.C. Chorus and S.O., cond. Basil Cameron; 4/Feb/1948; London.

96. **NOCTURNE**. Orch. (1936).

2picc2ca2bcl.E♭sax.3/42Dtrpt01/cym.rattle.sdm.tamb.tri.wdbl/hp/str.

March, 1936.

Ded: Hermann Scherchen.

Dur: 9′.

Pub: UE (U.E. Ltd. 63), 1939; Boosey and Hawkes.

fp: Orch. Sym. de Bruxelles, cond. Hermann Scherchen; 30/April/1936; Brussels.

f*Paris*p: cond. Charles Münch; 9/April/1940; Deuxième concert de l'Association de Musique Contemporaine, Paris.

f*E*p: L.P.O., cond. (Sir) Malcolm Sargent; 9/Dec/1939; Courtauld-Sargent concert, Queen's Hall, London. (f*E*p orig. announced for a Prom. concert, 24/Aug/1939).

97. **DU WHISKY POUR JO**. Voc. Mus. (1936).

Voice/pf.

Nino.

Pub: LS, 1936.

98. **LES MUTINES DE L'ELSENEUR.** Film Score. (1936).

After Jack London.

Dir: Pierre Chenal.

Prod: General-Productions.

Principal item: Song — Le voilier l'Elseneur est un voilier à vaches (Robert Desnos).

Brit. dist: Associated British Picture Corporation, 1940.

99. **MAYERLING**. Film Score. (1936).

After Claude Anet.

Collab: Maurice Jaubert, with music by Gounod, Mozart, Strauss and Weber.

Dir: Anatole Litvak.

Prod: Nero-Film.

Principal items: (i) Générique; (ii) Dans le fiacre; (iii) Dans les couloirs; (iv) Jardins; (v) Scène finale.

Brit. dist: Gaumont-British (later re-issued by Exclusive Films).

Bprem: Curzon Cinema, London; 22/Oct/1936.

100. **STRING QUARTET No. 2.** Ch. Mus. (1934-36).

(i) Allegro. (Attacca subito).
Dur: 7′.

(ii) Adagio.
1934-35.
Dur: 10′30″.

(iii) Allegro marcato.
Paris, June 1936.
Dur: 6′.

Ded: Pro-Arte Quartet.

Dur: 23′ 30″.

Pub: S-S (EMS 8708), 1936 (autograph facsimile).

fp: Pro-Arte Quartet; Sept. 1936; Venice.

f*Paris*p: Calvet Quartet; 8/March/1937; Le Triton Concert, Ecole Normale, Paris.

f*Ep*/f*Eb*p: Brosa Quartet; 18/April/1937.

101. **MARCHE SUR LA BASTILLE.** Inc. Mus. (1936).

Contribution to the score for the play *14 juillet* by Romain Rolland.

Acte 1
- (i) Ouverture — Ibert;
- (ii) Palais-Royal — Auric;
- (iii) Introduction et marche funèbre de la liberté (Final de l'Acte I) — Milhaud;

Acte 2
- (iv) Prélude: La nuit du grand soir — Roussel;
- (v) Chœur : Liberté, dans ce beau jour — Kœchlin;
- (vi) Prélude: Marche sur la Bastille — Honegger;
- (vii) Final — Interlude — Fête populaire de la liberté — Lazarus.

2+piccl 1+E♭cl.asx.tsx.barsx.2+cbsn/433+btbn1+ttuba/bdm.cym.sdm.tamtam/cb/unison chorus.

Paris, June 1936.

Dur: 6′.

Pub: ESI.

?fp: Théâtre Alhambra, Paris; 1936.

f*concert*p: cond. Roger Désormière; 14/July/1936; La maison de la culture.

102. **LES MILLE ET UNE NUITS.** Cantata. (1937).

Written for the 1937 Exposition des Arts et Techniques — Fête de la lumière et de l'eau sur la Seine. Text trans. Mardrus.

2(picc)02(E♭cl).3sx[=ca].2/0330/anv.cym.rattle.sdm.tamtam.tdm.tri.wdbl/cel.hp.4om[=1].pf/str (10.0.6.6.0)/ST-soli.

Prélude: Les contes — Les nuits. Dur: 1′40″;
Tableaux
- (i) Le roi Schahrian. Dur: 1′;
- (ii) Schéhérazade. Dur: 1′10″;
- (iii) Les palais. Dur: 1′30″;
- (iv) Les jardins. Dur: 2′30″;
- (v) Schahrian et Schéhérazade. Dur: 2′;
- (vi) La lampe d'Aladin. Dur: 2′;
- (vii) Ali Baba. Dur: 2′30″;
- (viii) Sindbad le marin. Dur: 2′30″;
- (ix) Combat des génies. Dur: 3′10″;
- (x) La ville d'Airain. Dur: 2′30″;
- (xi) Schahrian et Schéhérazade — Apothéose. Dur 1′30″.

Paris, 3/Jan/1937.

Dur: 24′.

Pub:Ø(Fr.),S(H).

fp: Germaine Cernay (S), Edouard Kriff (T), cond. Gustave Cloëz; not later than 9/July/1937.

f*concert*p: cond. Robert Siohan; 4/Dec/1937; Concerts Poulet, Paris.

103. **L'AIGLON**. Operetta. (1936-37).

Music by A.H. (Acts II, III, and IV) and Ibert (Acts I and V).

Libretto by Henri Cain after Edmund Rostand.

2(picc)222/4331/timp.bdm.cym.sdm.tamtam.tdm.tri/hp/str/soloists/chorus.

Acte I Les ailes qui s'ouvrent;

Acte II Les ailes qui battent (Jan. 1936);

Acte III Les ailes meurtries (orch. Paris, Dec. 1936);

Acte IV Les ailes brisées (Jan. 1937);

Acte V Les ailes fermées.

Ded: Raoul Gunsbourg.

Pub: Au Ménéstrel/Heugel; Chorus parts (H31020), 1937; VS (H31021), 1936-37.

fp: Fanny Heldy (S: Frantz), Vanni Marcoux (Bar: Séraphin Flambeau), Mlle Schirman (Mz: Fanny Essler), Mlle Branèze (S: Thérèse de Lorget), Mlle Gadsen (Marie-Louise), Germaine Chellet (S: La comtesse Camerata), Endrèze (B: Le prince de Metternich), Marvini (B: Le maréchal Marmont), Fraikin (T: Frédéric de Gentz), Chorus and Orch. of the Monte-Carlo Opera, cond. Félix Wolfes; 10/March/1937; Opera House, Monte-Carlo.

f*Paris*p: Heldy, Marcoux, Odette Ricquier, Jacqueline Courtin, Anita Volfer, Milly Morère, Endrèze, Narçou, Nové, cond. François Ruhlmann; 1/Sept/1937; l'Opéra, Paris.

104. **NITCHEVO** (ou **L'AGONIE DU SOUS-MARIN**). Film Score. (1937).

After Jacques de Baroncelli.

Collab: Oberfeld.

Dir: J. de Baroncelli.

Prod: Méga-Film.

Principal items:
- (i) Song — De l'Atlantique au Pacifique, nous n'avons jamais de chagrin (words by J. Féline);
- (ii) Dans le sous-marin;
- (iii) Explosion;
- (iv) Tramonto;
- (v) Après l'attentat;
- (vi) Souks;
- (vii) Jardins à Bizerte;
- (viii) Canot Sarak;
- (ix) De l'Atlantique au Pacifique;
- (x) Valse-Nitchevo, triste est mon cœur.

Brit. dist: United Artists, 1937.

Bprem: Berkeley Cinema, Tottenham Court Road, London; Oct. 1937.

104a. **DE L'ATLANTIQUE AU PACIFIQUE.** Voc. Mus. (1937).

Song from the Film Score *Nitchevo* (see Catalogue No. 104).

Voice/pf.

Words by Féline.

Pub: R. Ventura (RVF 142) (Fr.), 1937.

104b. **NITCHEVO. . .(TRISTE EST MON CŒUR).** Voc.Mus. (1937).

Song from the Film Score *Nitchevo* (see Catalogue No. 104).

Voice/pf.

Words by Féline.

Pub: R. Ventura (RVF 141) (Fr.), 1937.

104c. **SUITE FROM THE FILM SCORE 'NITCHEVO'.** Orch. (1937).

1(picc)01.asx.tsx.barsx.0/0320/timp.cym.sdm.tamtam.tdm/gtr.pf/vln.cb/unison treble voices.

(i) Airel-Fox;
(ii) En mer;
(iii) Valse;
(iv) Explosion;
(v) Dans le sous-marin;
(vi) Souks;
(vii) Le jardin à Bizerte;
(viii) Après l'attentat;
(ix) Tramonto;
(x) Canot Sarak.

Pub: R. Ventura (RVF 143-152), 1937.

105. **MADEMOISELLE DOCTEUR.** Film Score. (1937).

After Georges Neveux.

Collab: Oberfeld.

Dir: G. W. Pabst.

Prod: Films Trocadero.

Principal items:

(i) Ouverture;
(ii) Hôtel à Berne;
(iii) Cáfe Turc;
(iv) Port de Salonique;
(v) Départ en auto;
(vi) Villa abandonnée;
(vii) Micro dans la nuit (Préludes Nos. 1 and 2);
(viii) Réveil;
(ix) Dans le beuglant;
(x) Bristol — Valse;
(xi) Maison de passe;
(xii) Dans la ferme;
(xiii) Blues;
(xiv) La soirée: tango;
(xv) Poursuite;
(xvi) Final.

106. **MARTHE RICHARD AU SERVICE DE LA FRANCE.** Film Score. (1937).

After Bernard Zimmer.

Dir: Raymond Bernard.

Prod: Paris — Films.

Principal items:—

(i) Générique;
(ii) Entrée des Allemands;
(iii) Village en flammes;
(iv) Chanteur espagnol;
(v) Musique de gitane (Valses I and II);
(vi) Tango de Mata-Hari;
(vii) Ludow au piano;
(viii) Marthe et Ludow;
(ix) Combat naval;
(x) Annonce du torpillage;
(xi) Tango de Charlotte;
(xii) Sur la falaise;
(xiii) Sonnerie au phono;
(xiv) Orgue dans l'église;
(xv) Banquet;
(xvi) Mobilisation américaine;
(xvii) Attaque des avions;
(xviii) Final de l'armistice.

Brit. dist: Unity Films, 1939.

106a. **SUITE FROM THE FILM SCORE 'MARTHE RICHARD AU SERVICE DE LA FRANCE'.** Orch. (1937).

(i) Entrée des Allemands;
(ii) Village en flammes;
(iii) Chanteur espagnol;
(iv) Madame Guilbert Valse I;
(v) Madame Guilbert Valse II;
(vi) Ludow au piano;
(vii) Marthe et Ludow;
(viii) Annonce du torpillage;
(ix) Tango de Charlotte;
(x) Orgue dans l'église;
(xi) Musique de banquet;
(xii) Attaque des avions;
(xiii) Sur la falaise;
(xiv) Sonnerie au phono;
(xv) Combat naval;
(xvi) Final de l'armistice.

Pub: C (AC 18354-18369), 1938; also pf. redn. 1938.

107. **LIBERTE.** Film Score. (1937).

Jean Kemm after Bartholdi.

Collab: Arthur Hoérée.

107a. **INTERLUDE FROM THE FILM SCORE 'LIBERTE'.** Orch. (1937).

f*concert*p: cond. M. Rostand; 1/May/1937; Théâtre des Champs-Elysées, Paris.

108. **UN OISEAU BLANC S'EST ENVOLE.** Ballet Mus. (1937).

Ballet by Sacha Guitry. Written for "un gala des Hautes Etudes commerciales".

1(picc)11.asx.1/01.Dtpt.10/bdm.cym.rattle/pf/str.

Paris, 26/May/1937.

Npub.

fp: ? cond. Arthur Honegger; 1937 Exposition des Arts et Techniques (24/May/1937-), Théâtre des Champs-Elysées, Paris.

109. **STRING QUARTET No. 3.** Ch. Mus. (1936-37).

(i) Allegro.
Paris, 5/June/1937.
Dur: 7′50″.
(ii) Adagio.
Paris, May 1937.
Dur: 9′.
(iii) Allegro.
Paris, Sept. 1936.
Dur: 6′20″.

Ded: Mrs. Elizabeth Sprague-Coolidge.

Dur: 23′10″.

Pub: S-S (EMS 8737), 1937 (facsimile of autograph).

fp: Pro Arte Quartet; 22/Oct/1937; Salle de la Réformation, Geneva.

f*Paris*p: Pro Arte Quartet; 25/April/1938; Triton Concert, Paris.

f*E*p: New Hungarian Quartet; 4/Oct/1938; London Contemporary Music Centre Concert, Cowdray Hall, London.

f*Eb*p: New Hungarian Quartet; 7/Oct/1938.

110. **LA CITADELLE DU SILENCE.** Film Score. (1937).

Collab: Darius Milhaud.

Cond: Manuel Rosenthal.

Dir: Marcel L'Herbier.

Prod: Impérial-Film.

July, 1937.

111. **REGAIN.** Film Score. (1937).

After Jean Giono.

Written, directed and produced by Marcel Pagnol.

Principal items:
(i) Générique;
(ii) Hiver et printemps;
(iii) Refrain de Gédémus;
(iv) Nuit dans la grange;
(v) Printemps . . . été;
(vi) Mort de Mamèche;
(vii) Nocturne;
(viii) Le soc;
(ix) Panturle;
(x) Panturle abat des arbres;
(xi) Foire à Manosque.

Sept. 1937.

Brit. dist: Connoisseur Films.

Bprem: Academy Cinema, London; 26/Oct/1956.

111a. **SUITE FROM THE FILM SCORE 'REGAIN'.** Orch. (1937).

1(picc)1(ca)1.asx.1/0220/bdm.cym.rattle.tamtam.tdm.tri/pf/str.

(i) Le Panturle. Dur: 3′20″;
(ii) Hiver. Dur: 4′25″;
(iii) Printemps. Dur: 2′10″;
(iv) Gédémus le remouleur. Dur: 55″;
(v) Regain. Dur: 5′10″.

Dur: 16′.

Pub: Ø S(H), 1937.

f*concert*p: cond. Charles Münch; 3/July/1942; Palais du Chaillot, Paris.

112. **VISAGES DE LA FRANCE.** Film Score. (1937).

Dir: A. Vigneau.

Oct. 1937.

113. **TUET'S WEH!** Voc. Mus. (1937).

Voice/pf.

Chanson de cabaret d'après W. Lesch (Beim Coiffeur, ja do ischs mir wohl . . .).

5/Oct/1937.

? Ded: 'pour mon cher Hegi' [Emil Hegetschweiler] affectueusement.

Npub.

114. **ARMISTICE.** Choral Mus. (1937).

Chorus (unison)/pf.

René Kerdyk.

(Crotchet = 63).

Paris, 1/Nov/1973.

Npub.

115. **MIARKA** (ou **LA FILLE A L'OURSE**). Film Score. (1937).

After Jean Richepin.

Collab: Tibor Harsanyi.

Dir: Jean Choux.

Prod: Henri Doru.

(i) Générique;
(ii) Chanson de la route;
(iii) Chanson de l'eau;
(iv) Après le baptême;
(v) Tétée;
(vi) Ruisseau petit jardin;
(vii) Rythme du chaudron;
(viii) Danse petite Miarka;
(ix) Scène de la prédiction et Final;
(x) Scène des œufs;
(xi) Scène des abeilles;
(xii) Scène de l'ourse;
(xiii) Scène des confitures;
(xiv) Chanson sans paroles;
(xv) Signal Radio;
(xvi) Conférence;
(xvii) Sortie de la conférence;
(xviii) Danse estrade;
(xix) Danse;
(xx) Incendie;
(xxi) Danse de Miarka (suite);
(xxii) Mort de Sarah;
(xxiii) Miarka triste;
(xxiv) Viol;
(xxv) Disque et montée à la tour;
(xxvi) Valse de l'escalier;
(xxvii) L'innocent et l'oiseau.

(Nos. (i), (ii), (iii), (viii), (xiv), (xv), (xxvi) and (xxvii) are by A.H., the remainder by Harsanyi.)

Texts by Jean Richepin.

Nov. 1937.

Pub: S (Fr.), 1938.

115a. **CHANSON DE LA ROUTE.** Voc. Mus. (1937).

Song from the Film Score *Miarka* (ou *La fille à l'ourse*) (see Catalogue No. 115).

Voice/pf.

J. Richepin.

Pub: S, 1938.

115b. **CHANSON DE L'EAU.** Voc. Mus. (1937).

Song from the Film Score *Miarka* (ou *La fille à l'ourse*) (see Catalogue No. 115).

Voice/pf.

J. Richepin.

Pub: S, 1938.

116. **LA CONSTRUCTION D'UNE CITE.** Inc. Mus. (1937).

After J.-R. Bloch.

Collab: D. Milhaud.

116a. **CHANSON DES QUATRE.** Voc. Mus. (1937).

Song from the Incidental Music for *La construction d'une cité* (see Catalogue No. 116).

Voice/pf.

J.-R. Bloch.

Pub: R. Deiss-S, 1937.

116b. **CHANSON DE L'EMIGRANT.** Voc. Mus. (1937).

Song from the Incidental Music for *La construction d'une cité* (see Catalogue No. 116).

Voice/pf.

J.-R. Bloch.

Pub: R. Deiss-S, 1937.

117. **PASSEURS D'HOMMES.** Film Score. (1937).

After Martial Lekeux.

Collab: Arthur Hoérée.

Principal items: (i) Cabarets; (ii) Piano mécanique; (iii) Ivresse; (iv) Le mat.

118. **LES BATISSEURS.** Film Score. (1937).

After R. Desnos.

Principal item: Chanson des gars du bâtiment (words by R. Desnos).

118a. **LES GARS DU BATIMENT.** Voc. Mus. (1937).

Song from the Film Score *Les bâtisseurs* (see Catalogue No. 118).

Voice/pf[=orch].

R. Desnos.

119. **PRELUDE A LA MORT DE JAURES.** Inc. Mus. (1937).

Play by Jaurès trans. Maurice Rostand.

Contribution to the Incidental Music Score for *Liberté*. The other composers who wrote music for this production were Delannoy, Hoérée, Ibert, Jaubert, Milhaud, Roland-Manuel, Souveplane and Tailleferre.

fp: 1937; Théâtre de l'Alhambra.

120. **SCENIC RAILWAY.** Pf. (1937).

Contribution to *Parc d'attractions — Expo 1937: Hommage à Marguerite Long*:—A. Tcherepnine — Autour des montagnes russes: (a) Le guichet, (b) Les 'On dit', (c) Le 'Swing', (d) Et voilà; B. Martinů — Le train hanté; F. Mompou — Souvenirs de l'Exposition: (a) Tableaux de statistiques, (b) Le planétaire, (c) Pavillon de l'élégance; V. Rieti — La danseuse aux lions; E. Halffter — l'Espagnolade; A. Tansman — Le géant; M. Mihalovici – Un danseur roumain; T. Harsanyi – Le tourbillon mécanique.

Moderato — Allegro.

Ded: Marguerite Long.

Pub: ME (5685), 1938.

fp: Nicole Henriot; 28/Nov/1938; Salle Gaveau, Paris.

121. **JEUNESSE.** Voc. Mus. (1937).

Voice/pf[= orch].

Paul Vaillant-Couturier.

Ded: 'Créé pour la fédération de la jeunesse'.

Pub: ESI (ESI 303), 1937; Voice part only: CduM, 1945; also published in *Chantons Jeunesse*, pp.10-11 (La jeune Algérie).

(An arr. by Durey for unison chorus and orch. of ww. and br. was recorded by the Chorale Populaire de Paris and Orch. cond. Roger Désormière on Chant du Monde 501 (LDY 4171) and pub. by Éditions Micro; an *a capella* version was recorded on Chant du Monde CDM LDY 4171 — cond. Gilbert Martin.)

122. **TROIS CHANSONS.** Voc. Mus. (1935-37).

Voice/pf.

R. Kerdyk.

(i) On est heureux; (ii) Chanson de la route; (iii) Le naturaliste.

Pub: EOF (Nos. i and ii only).

123. **LE CANTIQUE DES CANTIQUES.** Ballet Mus. (1937).

A 'poetic argument' by Gabriel Boissy in 2 Acts based on the 'Song of Solomon'.

Rhythms by Serge Lifar.

Orch.(Flutes, oboe, clarinets, saxophones, bass drum, cymbals, gongs, iron-cymbals, rattle, tambour de basque, tambourin provençal, tamtam, whip, woodblock, celesta, ondes Martenot, cellos and double-basses)/ATBar-soli.chorus.

Act I: 'Les vignes d'Eu Gaeldi':

(i) Les vignerons;
(ii) La Sulamite (A-solo, chorus);
(iii) Le berger (chorus);
(iv) La Sulamite et le berger (chorus);
(v) Salomon (chorus);
(vi) La Sulamite, le berger, Salomon;
(vii) Départ de la Sulamite et de Salomon (chorus);

Act II 'Le palais de Salomon':

(viii) Solitude dans le palais;
(ix) Salomon (Bar-solo);
(x) La Sulamite et Salomon (Bar-solo);
(xi) Les spectacles I/II/III (chorus);
(xii) Rêve de la Sulamite (A-solo);
(xiii) Le berger (T-solo);
(xiv) La Sulamite et le berger (A.T-soli);
(xv) Le berger et Salomon;
(xvi) Libération (chorus).

Score not dated. (Page 120 of the ms is dated 'Paris 1937'.)

Ded: Francis and Andrée Winter.

Pub: AM/H; VS (H 31029) (Fr.), 1938.

fp: Carina Ari (La Sulamite), Serge Lifar (Le berger), Paul Goube (Le roi Salomon), Antoinette Duval (A), Chastenet (T), Cotta (Bar), cond. Philippe Gaubert; 2/Feb/1938; Académie Nationale de Musique, Paris.

124. **LES PETITES CARDINAL.** Operetta. (1937).

Music by A.H. and Jacques Ibert.

Libretto by Albert Willemetz and Paul Brach from a novel by Ludovic Halévy (2 Acts).

Acte I:

(i) Introduction;
(ii) Scène du berger;
(iii) Y'a quelqu'chose à faire;
(iv) Entrée des petites Cardinal;
(v) Interlude;
(vi) Couplets de Monsieur Cardinal;
(vii) Couplets de la Tour de Nesle;
(viii) Interlude;
(ix) De la Madeleine à l'Opéra;
(x) Interlude;
(xi) Quatuor des jeunes gens;
(xii) Couplets du bon diable;
(xiii) Final;

Acte II:

(xiv) Entr'acte;
(xv) Trio de la migraine;
(xvi) Finaletto—Revue;
(xvii) C'est le charme de Florence;
(xviii) Musique de scène;
(xix) Une lionne à la gare de Lyon;
(xx) Musique de scène;
(xxi) Air de la Calomnie;
(xxii) Interlude;
(xxiii) Interlude;
(xxiv) L'utile et l'agréable;
(xxv) Si nous avions un Colonel;
(xxvi) Musique de scène;
(xxvii) Couplet final;
(xxviii) Sortie du public.

No indication as to separate authorship (ms evidence proves A.H.'s authorship of *at least* items nos. (ii), (iv), (xii), (xiii), (xiv), (xv) and (xxi)).

Paris — Rennes, Nov.-Dec. 1937.

Pub: C/ER (AC 17668) (Fr.), 1946.

fp: Saturin Fabre (Monsieur Cardinal), Marguerite Pierry (Madame Cardinal), Robert Pizani, Henri Fabert, Bertolasso, cond. Cariven; 13/Feb/1938; Théâtre des Bouffes-Parisiens, Paris.

124a. **C'EST LE CHARME DE FLORENCE.** Voc. Mus. (1937).

Song ('valse-arioso') from the Operetta *Les petites Cardinal* (see Catalogue No. 124).

Voice/pf.

Pub: C (AC 17871), 1939.

124b. **A PLAISANCE.** Voc. Mus. (1937).

Song from the Operetta *Les petites Cardinal* (see Catalogue No. 124).

Voice/pf.

Pub: C (AC 17874), 1939.

125. **PYGMALION.** Film Score. (1938).

After George Bernard Shaw.

Collab: W. Axt.

Dir: Antony Asquith.

Prod: Gabriel Pascal.

July, 1938.

126. **LA DANSE DES MORTS.** Oratorio. (1938).

Libretto by Paul Claudel (Eng. trans. by Edward Agate. Ger. trans. by Hans Reinhart).

2(picc)2(ca)24[=2]/4[=2].24[=2].0/2timp.3perc(bdm.cym.rattle.sdm.tamtam.tri.wdbl)/org.pf/str/retr. SABarsoli.chorus. (In the absence of the organ the full number of ww. and br. are required).

(i) Dialogue;
(ii) Danse des morts;
(iii) Lamento;
(iv) Sanglots;
(v) La réponse de Dieu;
(vi) Espérance dans la Croix.

Paris, 25/Oct/1938.

Ded: Paul Sacher.

Dur: 35′.

Pub: S-S; Ø (EMS 8845), 1939; VS (EMS 8844) (Fr./Ger./Eng.), 1939.

fp/f*(E)b*p: Jean Hervé (retr), Ginevra Vivante (S), Gina Falk (A), Martial Singher (Bar), Edouard Müller (org), Basle CC and CO (aug.), cond. Paul Sacher; 2/March/1940; Basle, Switzerland. (Relayed by the B.B.C.).

f*Paris*p: Jean-Louis Barrault (retr), Turba-Rabier (S), Eliette Schenneberg (A), Charles Panzéra (Bar), La Chorale Gouverné, Paris Cons. Orch., cond. Charles Münch; 26/Jan/1941; Salle de l'Ancien Conservatoire, Paris.

f*E*p: Dennis Arundell (retr), Isobel Baillie (S), Anne Wood (A), Bruce Boyce (Bar), Margaret Cobb (org), B.B.C. Chorus and B.B.C.S.O., cond. (Sir) Adrian Boult; 29/Dec/1948; B.B.C. Concert, Royal Albert Hall, London.

127. **L'OR DANS LA MONTAGNE** (ou **FAUX-MONNAYEURS).** Film Score. (1938).

After C. F. Ramuz.

Collab: Arthur Hoérée.

Dir: Max von Haufler.

Prod: Clarté-Films.

Principal items: (i) Générique; (ii) Brume du matin; (iii) La mort: final.

Oct. 1938.

Prem: 9/Feb/1939; ABC Cinema, Geneva.

128. **HOMMAGE AU TRAVAIL.** Voc. Mus. (1938).

Voice/pf.

Maurice Senart.

Modéré.

31/Dec/1938.

Pub: Editions Senart (EMS 8801) (Fr.), 1939; ME (ME 6814a), 1955.

129. **NICOLAS DE FLUE.** Dramatic Oratorio. (1939).

Subtitled: Légende dramatique.

Orchestra (flutes, piccolos, clarinets, saxophones (soprano, altos, tenors, baritone), saxhorns (bugles, altos, barytons, basses, contra-basses), 4 horns, 2 trumpets, 3 trombones, timpani, bass drum, bells, caisse claire, caisse roulante, cymbals, rattle, suspended cymbals, tamtam, tenor drum, woodblock) / retr.cv chorus.chorus.

Libretto by Denis de Rougemont (Ger. trans. Hans Reinhart).

Act I:

(i) Prologue;
(ii) Chanson des enfants;
(iii) Fanfare;
(iv) Chœur: Souviens-toi!;
(v) Choral: Il s'en va (1e et 2e strophes);
(vi) Chœur céleste: Solitaire, solitaire!;
(vii) La prière de Nicolas (Gebetlein);
(viii) Récitatif: Dure est la peine;
(ix) Choral: Il s'en va (3e strophe);
(x) La montée au Ranft;

Act II:

(xi) Chant des Pélerins;
(xii) Double chœur: Étoile du matin;
(xiii) Chœur céleste: Dieu l'a voulu;
(xiv) Récitatif du guetteur;
(xv) Cortège;
(xvi) Récitatif et Choral: Ainsi les affaires du monde;
(xvii) Récitatif et Choral: Tout un peuple a prêté l'oreille;
(xviii) Chœur des puissances;
(xix) Chœur: Victoire et malheur!;

Act III:

(xx) Marche des ambassadeurs;
(xxi) Les compagnons de la follevie;
(xxii) Fanfare de la Diète;
(xxiii) Récitatif: Demain la guerre!;
(xxiv) Choral: Nicolas, souviens-toi!;
(xxv) Récitatif: Parmi nous, peuple, parmi nous;
(xxvi) Chœur céleste: Solitaire, solitaire!;
(xxvii) Choral: Il descend;
(xxviii) Chœur céleste: Terre et cieux, prêtez l'oreille!;
(xxix) Récitatif: Ecoute-moi, mon peuple!;
(xxx) Récitatif des cloches et chœur final.

5/Feb/1939.

Ded: 'Aux cinq cents Neuchâtelois qui, sur l'initiative de l'Institut Neuchâtelois et de son président Monsieur Claude du Pasquier, ont collaboré à la réalisation de ce 'Nicolas de Flue' lors de l'Exposition Nationale Suisse de 1939, à Zürich.'

(Dur: /60′).

Pub: FF - S; VS (F7050F) (Fr.), 1939.

f*concert*p: St. Cecilia Choir (cond. Eric Schild), William Aguet (retr), Berne M.O., cond. Eric Schild; 26/Oct/1940; Soleure, Switzerland.

f*staged*p: Choirs of Locle and La Chaux-de-Fonds (Neuchâtel), cond. Charles Faller; 31/May/1941; Neuchâtel, Switzerland.

(The work was rescored for the recording made by the Elizabeth Brasseur Chorale, Petits Chanteurs de Versailles, Paris Cons. Orch., Jean Davy (retr), cond. Georges Tzipine on Columbia FCX 187-8 (PLM 17 064), for 2(picc)2(ca)22/2331/timp.bdm.bells (A♭ and E♭). caisse claire.caisse roulante.cym.schnarre. sdm.tamb.tamtam.tri.wdbl/str.)

130. **LE DESERTEUR** (ou **JE T'ATTENDRAI**) Film Score. (1939).

After Michel Deligne and Jacques Companeez.

Collab: H. Verdun, H. Christiné and others.

Dir: Léonide Moguy.

Prod: Eclair—Journal.

March, 1939.

Brit. dist: G.C.T. Distributors, 1947.

130a. **SUITE FROM THE FILM SCORE 'LE DESERTEUR** (ou **JE T'ATTENDRAI)'.** Orch. (1939).

Subtitled: 'Fragments symphoniques' (see Catalogue No. 130).

Pub: S, 1939.

131. **CAVALCADE D'AMOUR.** Film Score. (1939).

After Jean Anouilh and Jean Aurenche.

Collab: Darius Milhaud.

Dir: Raymond Bernard.

Prod: Arnold Pressburger/CIPRA.

Principal items:

(i) Projet;
(ii) Rencontre;
(iii) Marche nuptiale;
(iv) Messe de mariage: Kyrie, O Salutaris;
(v) Final.

July, 1939.

Music orch. and cond. by Roger Désormière.

131a. **O SALUTARIS.** Voc. Mus. (1939).

Song from the Film Score *Cavalcade d'amour* (see Catalogue No. 131).

S-solo/pf[= hp].org.

Larghetto.

Ded: Ginette Guillamat.

Pub: H (PCH 461), 1943.

f*concert*p: Noémie Pérugia; 3/Oct/1943; Eglise Saint-Séverin.

132. **GRAD US – EN AVANT.** Radio Mus. (1939).

Military march commissioned by Basle Radio.

Military Band.

Pub: Hug (GH 8725), Zürich.

fp/f*b*p: Basle Radio.

LES MUSICIENS DU CIEL. Film Score. (1939).

See Appendix G.

133. **TROIS POEMES DE CLAUDEL.** Voc. Mus. (1939-40).

Paul Claudel.

(i) Siesta.
Calme.
Paris, 31/March/1939.

(ii) Le delphinium.
Animé.
Zürich, 18/Jan/1940.

(iii) Le rendez-vous.
Large.
Zürich, 16/Jan/1940.

Ded: Pierre Bernac.

Pub: S (No. 13716), 1942.

fp: Pierre Bernac with Francis Poulenc; 15/Nov/1941; Salle Gaveau, Paris.

134. **PARTITA.** Ch. Mus. (1940).

2pf.

(i) Largo.
Dur: 3′20″;

(ii) Vivace — Allegretto.
Dur: 4′30″;

(iii) Largo.
Dur: 1′30″;

(iv) Allegro moderato.
Dur: 4′35″.
(This is an arrangement of no. xv, 'Cortège de l'Impératrice', from the Incidental Music Score for *L'Impératrice aux rochers (Un miracle de Notre-Dame)* — see Catalogue No. 55.)

Zürich, 31/Jan/1940.

Ded: Franz-Josef Hirt.

Dur: 13′55″.

Pub: S (EAS 17617), 1984.

fp: Franz-Josef Hirt and A.H.; 31/Jan/1940; Zürich, Switzerland.

f*Paris*p: Monique Haas and Ina Marika; 26/March/1940; Paris.

135. **CHRISTOPHE COLOMB.** Radio Mus. (1940).

'Jeu radiophonique' by William Aguet, commissioned by Radio Lausanne Studio.

1121/2320/timp.2perc(bdm.bells.cym.rattle.sdm.tamtam.wdbl)/pf/str/2T-soli.chorus.

Zürich, 21/Feb/1940.

(i) Prologue;
(ii) Evocation;
(iii) Sacre burlesque;
(iv) Sortie du roi;
(v) Fin de la messe;
(vi) Procession (Chœur des marins);
(vii) Lamentations des femmes de Palos;
(viii) Départ de Christophe Colomb;
(ix) La traversée;
(x) Prière des mousses;
(xi) Miracle du vent;
(xii) Mélopée;
(xiii) Prière de Christophe Colomb;
(xiv) Te Deum;
(xv) Prière des morts;
(xvi) (Lent);
(xvii) Final.

(Dur: /55′).

Pub: S.

fp/fbp: Chorus (F. Porchet), Orch. de la S.R., cond. Ernest Ansermet; 16/April/1940; Studio of Radio Lausanne, brdcst. by Emetteur National de Sottens.

(No. x, 'Prière des mousses', was used subsequently by Honegger as the second of the *Quatre chansons pour voix grave* — Derrière Murcie en fleurs . . . (William Aguet) — see Catalogue No. 173.)

136. **LA NAISSANCE DES COULEURS.** Ballet Mus. (1940).

Ballet by E. Klausz and René Morax.

2(picc)2(ca)22/4331/timp.anv.bdm.cym.sdm.tamtam.tdm.tri.wdbl[=cast].whip/S-solo.chorus.

Paris, 12/May/1940; Orch. Bagnoles de l'Orne 15/May/1948.

Dur: 32′45″.

137. **SONATA.** Ch. Mus. (1940).

Solo vln.

(i) Allegro; (ii) Largo; (iii) Allegretto grazioso; (iv) Presto.

Totenberg, New York, 1940.

Fingered by Ginette Neveu.

Pub: S(EAS 14696), 1948.

fp: Christian Ferras; Paris.

138. **TROIS PSAUMES.** Voc. Mus. (1940-41).

Voice/pf.

(i) Psalm XXXIV (trans. Théodore de Bèze).
Allegretto.
Paris, 20/Jan/1941.

(ii) Psalm CXL (trans. de Bèze).
Andante.
Paris, 28/Dec/1940.

(iii) Psalm CXXXVIII (trans. Clément Marot).
Allegramente.
Paris, 8/Jan/1941.

Ded: Eliette Schenneberg.

Pub: S (EAS 13889), 1943.

fp: Pierre Bernac with Francis Poulenc.

139. **PETITS AIRS SUR UNE BASSE CELEBRE.** Pf. (1941).

Pf.

(i) Andantino;
(ii) Allegretto;
(iii) Andante;
(iv) Vivace;
(v) Allegretto;
(vi) T[emp]o di Marcia;
(vii) Allegro;
(viii) Quasi Siciliana;
(ix) Mains croisées;
(x) Larghetto;
(xi) Espressivo;
(xii) Presto.

February 1941. (No. vii dated Paris, January 1941.)

Ded: 'pour Tartouillonniomet de son papa'.

Npub.

(Photocopy of ms suppplied by Pascale Honegger, Geneva, Switzerland.)

140. **LA MANDRAGORE**. Inc. Mus. (1941).

Play by Machiavelli.

100.asx.0/0000/tamb/hp.pf/str.

(i) Prologue — 1bis Cloches — Ritournelle I — Ritournelle II;
(ii) Reprise des cloches et ritournelle I;
(iii) Ritournelle III. Dur: 25-35″;
(iv) (Andante). Dur: 2′30″;
(v) Reprise de (iv) à la lettre **A** puisqu'à la fin enchaîner coda. Dur: 55″;
(vi) (Allegro). Dur: 50″;
(vii) (Moderato);
(viii) Nocturne. Dur: 2′30″;
(ix) Ritournelle IV enchaîner les cloches.

Paris, 11/March/1941.

fp: 18/Sept/1941; Théâtre Fontaine, Paris.

141. **L'OMBRE DE LA RAVINE.** Inc. Mus. (1941).

Play by Synge, trans. by Maurice Bourgeois.

Fl/hp/str.

(i) Prélude pour 'L'ombre de la ravine'
Paris, 18/March/1941.
Dur: 3′5″;

(ii) Postlude;
Paris, 19/March/1941.
Dur: 1′40″.

fp: 1941; Théâtre Fontaine, Paris.

142. **PETIT COURS DE MORALE.** Voc. Mus. (1941).

Jean Giraudoux from 'Suzanne et le Pacifique'.

(i) Jeanne.
17/April/1941.

(ii) Adèle.
18/April/1941.

(iii) Cécile.
16/April/1941.

(iv) Irène.
15/April/1941.

(v) Rosemonde.

Paris, 12-18 April, 1941.

Ded: Elsa Scherz-Meister.

Pub: S (EAS 14854), 1947.

(fpub. as a mus. suppl. in *Arthur Honegger*, by Claudel, Hoérée, Roland-Manuel, Vuillermoz (Les Publications Techniques/Galerie Charpentier, Paris, 1942.)

fp: Pierre Bernac with Francis Poulenc; 1/July/1942; Festival Honegger, Salle Gaveau, Paris.

143. **LES SUPPLIANTES.** Inc. Mus. (1941).

Play by Aeschylus, trans, by A. Bonnard.

0022/033.btmb.0/timp.bdm.cym.rattle.sdm.tamb.tamtam.tri/om/chorus.

(i) Prélude;
(ii) Mélodrame I;
(iii) Chœur I: 'Mais, d'abord';
(iv) Salutation aux Dieux;
(v) Chœur II: 'O fils de Palaichton';
(vi) Chœur III: 'Seigneur des Seigneurs';
(vii) Mélodrame II;
(viii) Chœur IV: 'Voici l'heure pour les Dieux';
(ix) Entrée des Egyptiens;
(x) Chœur V;
(xi) Mélodrame III (Sortie du roi);
(xii) Chœur VI: 'Que la cité prospère';
also a 'Fanfare pour les suppliantes'.

VS of Choruses and Mélodrame II dated Paris, 27/May/1941; Ø dated Paris, 7/June/1941.
fp: Chorale Yvonne Gouverné, Paris Cons. Orch., cond. Charles Münch; 5/July/1941; Stade Roland-Garros, Paris.

144. **HUIT CENTS METRES.** Inc. Mus. (1941).

'Drame sportif' by André Obey.

fp: Chorale Yvonne Gouverné, Paris Cons. Orch., cond. Charles Münch; 5/July/1941; Stade Roland-Garros, Paris.

145. **LE MANGEUR DE REVES.** Ballet Mus. (1941).

Ballet by H. René Lenormand.

Npub.

fp: 1941, Salle Pleyel.

146. **LA LIGNE D'HORIZON.** Inc. Mus. (1941).

Play by Serge Roux.

111.asx.1/1220/cym.tamtam.tdm.tri.wdbl/gtr.pf/str/T-solo.chorus.

(i) —. Dur: 2′20″;
(ii) —. Dur: 2′-2′18″;
(iii) —. Dur: 2′40″;
(iv) (Modéré). Dur: 2′20″;
(v) —. Dur: 2′10″;
(vi) (Modérément animé);
(vii) ([Modéré] sans lenteur). Dur: 2′16″;
(viii) (Modéré). Dur: 1′35″;
(ix) (Lent). Dur: 2′10″.

fp: Oct. 1941; Théâtre des Bouffes-Parisiens, Paris.

147. **SYMPHONIE POUR CORDES [NO. 2].** Orch. (1941).

[Tpt]/str.

(i) Molto moderato — Allegro.
Paris, 8/May/1941.
Dur: 11′30″.

(ii) Adagio mesto.
Paris, 15/March/1941.
Dur: 8′.

(iii) Vivace, non troppo.
Paris, 13/Oct/1941.
Dur: 5′45″.

Ded: Paul Sacher.

Dur: 25′15″.

Pub: S (EAS 14303), 1942.

fp: Z.C.M., cond. Paul Sacher; 18/May/1942;

f*E*p: Boyd Neel Orch., cond. Boyd Neel; 26/April/1944; Wigmore Hall, London.

f*Eb*p: B.B.C.S.O., cond. Ernest Ansermet; 27/Feb/1946.

148. **SALUSTE DU BARTAS**. Voc. Mus. (1941).

Subtitled: Six Villanelles.

Voice/pf.

Words by Pierre Bédat de Monlaur.

(i) Le château du Bartas.
Rythmé, sans lenteur.

(ii) Tout le long de la Baïse.
Calme.

(iii) Le départ.
Animé.

(iv) La promenade.
Modéré.

(v) Nérac en fête.
Vif et léger.

(vi) Duo. Lent.

Paris, Sept. 1941.

Ded: Noémie Pérugia.

Pub: Henry Lemoine (23224[b] HL), 1942.

fp: Noémie Pérugia with I. Aïtoff; 21/March/1942; Salle Gaveau, Paris.

149. **LE JOURNAL TOMBE A CINQ HEURES.** Film Score. (1942).

After O.-P. Gilbert.

Dir: George Lacombe.

Prod: SNEG-Gaumont.

Principal items:

(i) Machines;
(ii) Blues;
(iii) Tango;
(iv) Sandetti;
(v) Villa Rabaud;
(vi) En perdition;
(vii) Expédition;
(viii) Le bâteau-phare;
(ix) Final.

Prem: 21/May/1942; Colisée.

Pub: pf. redn. Choudens (AC 20705-13), 1942.

150. **HUIT HOMMES DANS UN CHATEAU**. Film Score. (1942).

After Jean Kéry.

Collab: Arthur Hoérée.

Dir: Richard Pottier.

Prod: Sirius Films.

Principal items: (i) Aurore; (ii) Hallucination; (iii) Fantôme; (iv) Enigme; (v) Victoire.

151. **CHANT DE LA LIBERATION**. Cantata. (1942).

Orchestra/Bar-solo.chorus.

Text by Bernard Zimmer.

Npub.

fp: Jacques Rousseau (Bar), Paris Cons. Orch., cond. Charles Münch; 22/Oct/1944; Concerts du Conservatoire, Paris.

152. **LE GRAND BARRAGE.** Orch. (1942).

Subtitled: 'Image musicale pour orchestre'.

32+ca32+cbsn/4330/bdm.cym.tamtam.tri/cel[=bells].hp/str.

Dotted crotchet=60 — Poco più tranquillo (Dotted crotchet=56).

(Dur: /6′).

Pub: S, 1966.

153. **LES ANTIQUITES DE L'ASIE OCCIDENTALE.** Film Score. (1943).

Documentary film produced by the 'Office français des films d'art et d'histoire'.

Dir: Henri Membrin.

Principal items:

(i) Générique;
(ii) Vase Our Nina;
(iii) Tête de taureau;
(iv) Gudea-Apis;
(v) Code Hamourabi;
(vi) Grande salle;
(vii) Transport et tributaires;
(viii) Cheval et char de guerre;
(ix) Cylindres;
(x) Frise des archers;
(xi) Chapiteaux aux taureaux;
(xii) Bas-relief hittite;
(xiii) La dame d'Elcké.

154. **LA BOXE EN FRANCE.** Film Score. (1943).

Collab: André Jolivet.

Dir: Lucien Gasnier-Reymond.

Prod: Hermina-Film.

(i) Hymne au sport ('Soyons unis! Amples poitrines'). Words by José Bruyr;
(ii) Générique boxe en France;
(iii) Gravures sur boxe de l'antiquité;
(iv) La foire;
(v) Arrivée des boxeurs.

Nos. ii-v are by Jolivet and published by Choudens (AC 21030-3).

No. v is based on No. i with additions to the accompaniment.

No. i is by Honegger and published separately — see Catalogue No. 154a.

154a. **HYMNE AU SPORT.** Voc. Mus. (1943).

Extract from the Film Score *La boxe en France* (see Catalogue No. 154).

Voice/orch [=pf].

Words by José Bruyr.

Pub: Choudens, 1943; Voice/pf (AC 17987); Voice part only (AC 17988).

155. **SECRETS.** Film Score. (1943).

Bernard Zimmer after Tourguenieff.

Dir: Pierre Blanchar.

Prod: Pathé-Cinéma.

Principal items:
(i) Générique;
(ii) Claire;
(iii) René et Michel;
(iv) Au pigeonnier;
(v) Amadou;
(vi) Réveil;
(vii) Michel et Marie-Thérèse;
(viii) Le bassin;
(ix) Jalousie;
(x) Amour;
(xi) Song — Le ciel a caché ses nuages (words by Jean Solar);
(xii) Colère;
(xiii) Réconciliation;
(xiv) Adieu de Michel.

Prem: 17/March/1943; l'Ermitage et Helder.

156. **CALLISTO** (ou **LA PETITE NYMPHE DE DIANE**). Film Score. (1943).

Animation: André Marty.

Collab: Roland-Manuel.

Le Récitant (?S).Mz-soli/pf.

Pub: Pierre Noel, 1944.

157. **LE CAPITAINE FRACASSE.** Film Score. (1943).

After Théophile Gautier.

Cond: Arthur Honegger (Chorale Yvonné Gouverné and Orch. de la Soc. des Conc. du Cons.).

Dir: Abel Gance.

Prod: Lux-Film.

Principal items:

(i) Générique;
(ii) Orage;
(iii) Sigognac;
(iv) Guitare;
(v) Les comédiens;
(vi) Banquet des comédiens;
(vii) (iv);
(viii) Attaque des comédiens;
(ix) Recherches des comédiens;
(x) Requiem;
(xi) (Le) Capitaine Fracasse;
(xii) Duel dans le cimetière;
(xiii) Musique de théâtre;
(xiv) Scène d'amour;
(xv) Faux enterrement;
(xvi) Bataille (de) brigands;
(xvii) Poursuite du carosse;
(xviii) Duel chez les Valombreuses;
(xix) Sigognac mourant;
(xx) Ariette: 'Si mon cœur parlait, Lysandre' (Text by A. de Badet);
(xxi) Chanson du chariot de Thespis: 'Portant le rire et le drame' (Text by A. de Badet);
(xxii) Chanson pour Isabelle: 'Avant que la journée de notre âge qui fuit . . .' (N.B. arr. by A.H.).

Pub: Editions Josette France; pf. redn. of Nos. i-xix (JF 44), 1945; No. xx (J1F); No. xxi; No. xxii. Editions Josette France also publish a pf. redn. of: (a) Matamore, (b) Isabelle and (c) Danse de Scapin (J44F). Apart from a transposed version of No. x which is included in (a), none of the music is contained in Nos. i-xxii.

157a. **SERENADE DE SCAPIN.** Voc. Mus. (1943).

Song from the Film Score *Le capitaine Fracasse* (see Catalogue No. 157).

Voice/pf.

J. Giot.

Pub: Frèrebeau.

158. **MERMOZ.** Film Score. (1943).

Dir: Louis Cuny.

Prod: Françaises Cinématographiques.

Principal items:

(i) Mermoz;
(ii) Misère;
(iii) L'officine;
(iv) Départ du courrier;
(v) Le poème d'Icare;
(vi) La ligne;
(vii) Amérique du sud;
(viii) Nocturne à Rio;
(ix) L'envol;
(x) Sur les Andes;
(xi) Le vent se lève;
(xii) Lever du jour;
(xiii) Réparation de l'avion;
(xiv) Traversée de l'Atlantique;
(xv) Montmartre;
(xvi) Conseil d'administration/Ricanement;
(xvii) Attente;
(xviii) Evocation des morts;
(xix) Final.

Prem: 3/Nov/1943; Triomphe et Scala.

Pub: pf. redn. Choudens (AC 21135-53), 1944.

158a. **SUITES FROM THE FILM SCORE 'MERMOZ'.** Orch. (1943).

(i) La traversée des Andes (1ère suite d'orchestre)

111.asx.1/0220/bdm.cym/pf/str.

Pub: Choudens (AC 16803), 1945.

(This Suite contains most of i and parts of x and xi from Catalogue No. 158.)

(ii) Le vol sur l'Atlantique (2ème suite d'orchestre)

1(picc)11.asx.1/0220/bdm.cym.tamtam.tri./pf.str.

Pub: Choudens (AC 16804), 1945.

(This Suite is based on No. xiv from Catalogue No. 158.)

159. **UN SEUL AMOUR.** Film Score. (1943).

Bernard Zimmer after H. de Balzac.

Dir: Pierre Blanchar.

Principal items:

(i) Générique;
(ii) La sylphide;
(iii) En voyage;
(iv) Couloirs de l'Opéra;
(v) Dans la loge;
(vi) Mort de Clara;
(vii) Le château;
(viii) Petit déjeuner;
(ix) Les lettres;
(x) Songs:
 (a) Quand tu verras les hirondelles (words by Zimmer);
 (b) Si le mal d'amour (ibid.);
(xi) Appréhension;
(xii) L'inquiétude;
(xiii) Le serment;
(xiv) Vengeance de Clergue;
(xv) Adieu;
(xvi) Mort de Clergue;
(xvii) Tombeau;
(xviii) L'espérance.

159a. **DEUX ROMANCES SENTIMENTALES.** Voc. Mus. (1943).

Two songs from the Film Score *Un seul amour* (see Catalogue No. 159).

Voice/pf.[=orch]

Bernard Zimmer.

(i) Quand tu verras les hirondelles; (ii) Si le mal d'amour.

Pub: S (EAS 14052), 1946.

160. **PASIPHAE.** Radio Mus. (1943).

Subtitled: Petit décor musical.

Commissioned by the Studio d'Essai, Paris.

2ob/2cl/asx/2bsn.

Words by Henry de Montherlant.

(i) Crotchet = 52 (28 bars). Dur: 1′50″; (ii) Crotchet = 60 (14 bars). (iii) Crotchet = 56 (22 bars).

Paris, 24/Jan/1943.

Npf/b.

Pub: S (EAS 18057), 1984.

161. **L'APPEL DE LA MONTAGNE.** Ballet Mus. (1943).

Ballet by R. Favre le Bret.

3(2picc)2+ca23/4331/timp.bdm.cym.dm.sdm.tamtam.tdm.tri.wdbl/cel.pf/str.

Grosrouvres — Paris, 20/Oct/1943.

Ier Tableau

(i) Introduction et ensemble;
(ii) Danse des filles des cantons;
(iii) Entrée de MacGuire;
(iv) Entrée d'Haecky et des bergers;
(v) Danse générale;
(vi) Danse de MacGuire;
(vii) Danse de la Suissesse;
(viii) Appel aux jeux;
(ix) Lancement des pierres;
(x) Luttes;
(xi) Distribution des prix;
(xii) Alpenglühn;

II^d Tableau

(xiii) L'ascension;

IIIème Tableau

(xiv) Apparition des déesses;
(xv) Ronde des déesses;
(xvi) Entrée des dieux maléfiques
(Enchaîner en reprenant au (xi) et continuer);
(xvii) Apparition de la Jungfrau;
(xviii) (Tuba sur la scène).

fp: cond. Louis Fourestier; 9/July/1945; l'Opéra, Paris.

(No. ii, 'Danse des filles des cantons', is the 'Danse paysanne' — no. ii — from the Film Score for *Rapt* — see Catalogue No. 83.)

161a. **JOUR DE FETE SUISSE (SCHWIZERFASCHTTAG).** Orch. (1943).

Suite from the Ballet Score *L'appel de la montagne* (see Catalogue No. 161).

3(picc)2+ca23/4331/timp.cym.sdm.tdm.tri.wdbl/cel.pf/str.

(i) La place de fête (Am Fäschtplatz);
(ii) Danse paysanne (Puretanz);
(iii) Entrée des bergers (d'Sänne chömmed);
(iv) Valse suisse (Ländler);
(v) Lancement des pierres (Schteischtosse);
(vi) Lutte au caleçon (Hoselupf);
(vii) Fin de la fête et 'Alpenglühn' (Fäschtabschluss und Alpeglüe).

(These are movements i, ii, iv, v, viii, x and xi/xii respectively from Catalogue No. 161.)

(Dur: /23′)

Pub: S(H) (EAS 14108), 1947.

fp: cond. Ernest Ansermet; 14/Nov/1945; Winterthur, Switzerland.

(No. ii, 'Danse paysanne (Puretanz)' is the 'Danse paysanne' — no. ii — from the Film Score *Rapt* — see Catalogue No. 83.)

162. **SODOME ET GOMORRHE.** Inc. Mus. (1943).

Play by Jean Giraudoux.

Ensemble of trombones.

fp: 11/Oct/1943; Théâtre Herbertot, Paris.

163. **LE SOULIER DE SATIN.** Inc. Mus. (1943).

Play by Paul Claudel.

0010/0100/bdm.cym.mrc.sdm.tamtam.tri/om.pf/str/SBar-soli.

(i) Mouvement de Rumba;
(ii) La mer – Plénitude de la mer;
(iii) La vierge;
(iv) –;
(v) Rumba de Jobarbara;
(vi) L'ange gardien;
(vii) Scene XIV Ière journée: melodic fragments (a) Don Balthazar, (b) Don Balthazar, (c) Les Chinois, (c^bis^) La négresse, (d) Don Balthazar and (e) Voix de musique;
(viii) (Lent);
(ix) Prélude pour la 2de journée;
(x) (a), (b) and (c);
(xi) Saint Jacques (Interlude);
(xii) Thème de Dona Musique – Forêt vierge – Ruisseaux;
(xiii) La mer – Sonate au clair de lune;
(xiv) Sicile (Interlude) – Cors siciliens;
(xv) L'ombre double;
(xvi) La lune;
(xvii) Dona Musique à Prague;
(xviii) –;
(xix) Petit orchestre sur scène: melodic fragments (a)-(g) Dona Isabel;
(xx) Rythme;
(xxi) Mort de Prouhèse;
(xxii) Marche funèbre;
(xxiii) Scène finale: (a)-(g).

Pub: S(H).

fp: cond. Pierre Boulez; 27/Nov/1943; Théâtre Comédie-Française, Paris.

164. **LUCRECE.** Film Score. (1943).

Léo Joannon.

Collab: Roland-Manuel.

165. **DEUX ESQUISSES.** Pf. (1943-44).

Written in Nicolas Obouhow's simplified notation.

(i) Large et rapsodique.
Paris, 9/Oct/1943.
Ded: Mme. Aussenac de Broglie.

(ii) Allegretto malinconico.
2/July/1944.
Ded: Yvette Grimaud.

In fact ii was first published in *Paris 1943. Arts et lettres* (Presses universitaires de France, Paris, 1943) as "Une pièce inédite pour piano de Arthur Honegger: Esquisse" (pp. 119-21) after an article "Musique: Arthur Honegger" (p. 118). It is dated 'Paris 15 avril 42', and not printed in Obouhow's 'simplified notation'.

Pub: Durand; No. 1 (DF 13198), Jan. 1944; No. 2 (DF 13199), July 1944.

166. **CHARLES LE TEMERAIRE.** Inc. Mus. (1944).

Play by René Morax in 4 acts (6 tableaux) with a Prologue.

0000/021.btbn.0/timp.bdm.bells.tamtam.tdm/fifes/chorus.

Prologue: Fanfare n° 1; Chœur n° 1 (3 couplets: "Victoire au duc . . .", "Il tient en main l'épée . . ." and "Il n'y a plus ni pays . . .";

Acte I: tacet;

Acte II: Chœur n° 2 (2 couplets: "L'Eternel est une fortresse . . ." and "La nation que Dieu protège..."); Chœur n° 3 (mv chorus) (3 couplets: "Les taons ont réveillé . . .", "Nous avons délié . . .", and "Ses pieds dans le sentier . . .");

Acte III: Chœur n° 4 ("Amour que tu es grande peine . . .") with solo (3 couplets: "Chante captif . . .", "Chante, mon cœur . . .", and "La cloche sonne . . ."); Chœur n° 5 (1st couplet: "Charlot le Téméraire va partir pour la guerre . . ."); Fanfare n° 2;

Acte IV: Chœur n° 6 (fv chorus): "Salva nos Domine . . .", Chœur n° 7 (4 couplets: "Il est venu . . ."; "Il a brisé . . .", "Comme le blé . . ." and "Ils sont tombés . . ."); Prière ("O Seigneur Dieu . . ."); Chœur n° 5 (2nd and 3rd couplets: "Charlot le Téméraire est parti pour la guerre . . ." and "Charlot le Téméraire est revenu de la guerre . . ."); Chœur n° 8 (4 couplets: "La pauvre âme . . .", "Comme la feuille . . .", "Cette porte . . .", and "Entre ma tourterelle . . ."); Chœur final ("Requiem aeternam . . .").

Pub: S(H). (N.B.: 'Cette version n'étant pas reconnue authentique, son exécution est interdite. Seule l'exécution des parties chorales avec lecture du teste intercalé, est autorisée' (Extract from Salabert's *Catalogue A*, Paris, Nov. 1967).

(Dur: /12').

fp: Chœur de femmes et Union Chorale de Vevey, cond. Carlo Hemmering; 27/May/1944; Théâtre du Jorat, Mézières, Vaud, Switzerland.

167. **BATTEMENTS DU MONDE.** Radio Mus. (1944).

'Jeu radiophonique' by William Aguet.

Commissioned by Radio Lausanne.

2(picc)222/2220/timp.bdm.cym.sdm.tamb.tri/hp.pf/str/Scv-soli.cv chorus.fv chorus.

In 50 mostly very short sections.

VS dated Paris, Jan. 1944; Ø dated Paris, March 1944;

fp/*fb*p: Orch. de la S.R., cond. Ernest Ansermet; 18/May/1944; Lausanne Radio.

SELZACHER PASSIONSSPIEL. Passion. (1940-44).

Please see Appendix C.

168. **O TEMPS SUSPENDS TON VOL.** Voc. Mus. (1945).

Voice/pf.

(Venir un jour de Pâques . . .)

Henri Martin.

(C; 30 bars).

Paris, Jan. 1945.

Npub.

169. **MORCEAU DE CONCOURS.** Ch. Mus. (1945).

Vln/pf.

Molto moderato un poco rubato.

Paris, 21/June/1945.

Pub: S (EAS 17851), 1984.

170. **PADUANA.** Ch. Mus. (1945).

Vcl.

Paris, July 1945.

Dur: 3′

Npub.

171. CHOTA RUSTAVELI. Ballet Mus. (1945).

Ballet by Serge Lifar.

Music by A. H. (Tableaux 1 and 4), Tcherepnine and Harsanyi.

1er Tableau:
Prélude. Dur: 2′;
(i) Oiseaux. Dur: 1′;
(ii) Entrée du léopard. Dur: 2′55″;
(iii) (i);
(iv) Entrée et danse Chota. Dur: 4′30″;
(v) (i);
(vi) Combat avec le léopard. Dur: 4′55″;
(vii) Apparition et danse de Tsetskhli. Dur: 3′10″;
(viii) (Poème récité). Dur: 2′;
(ix) Apparition de Thamar. Dúr: 3′55″.

4ème Tableau:
(i) Chota et Tsetskhli. Dur: 5′45″;
(ii) (i) from Ier Tableau;
(iii) Danse guerrière de Chota. Dur: 2′05″;
(iv) Danse de Tsetskhli. Dur: 2′20″;
(v) Chota – Tsetskhli – Thamar. Dur: 9′15″;
(vi) Final. Dur: 3′10″.

Dur: 1er Tableau 26′25″; 4ème Tableau 23′35″.

Pub: S.

fp: New Monte Carlo Ballet; 1945; Théâtre de Monte Carlo.

f*E*p: New Monte Carlo Ballet; July 1946; London.

172. SERENADE A ANGELIQUE. Radio Mus. (1945).

111.E♭asx[=ca].1/2110/cym.sdm/hp/str.

Allegretto comodo — Larghetto — Molto vivace — Tempo 1° (Allegretto comodo).

Paris, 15/Oct/1945.

Ded: Beromünster.

(Dur: 8′)

Pub: S (EAS 14663), 1947.

fp/f*b*p: Zürich Radio Orch., cond. Hermann Scherchen; 19/Nov/1945; Radio Zürich.

f*Paris*p/f*Frenchb*p: Paris Radio Orch., cond. Tibor Harsanyi; 11/Dec/1947; Paris Radio.

173. QUATRE CHANSONS POUR VOIX GRAVE. Voc. Mus. (1944-45).

Voice/pf.

No titles.

(i) (La douceur de tes yeux . . .).
A. Tchobanian.
Allegretto.
Paris, Dec. 1945.
Ded: Elsa Cavelti.

(ii) (Derrière Murcie en fleurs . . .).
William Aguet.
Poco largamente.
Ded: Madeleine Martinetti.
(This song is taken from the Radio Music, *Christophe Colomb* — no. x, 'Prière des mousses' — see Catalogue No. 135.)

(iii) (Un grand sommeil noir . . .).
Paul Verlaine.
Adagio.
Paris, 14/Feb/1944.
Ded: Eliette Schenneberg.

(iv) (La terre les eaux va buvant . . .).
Pierre de Ronsard.
Giocoso.
Paris, 17/March/1944.
Ded: André Gensac.

Pub: S (EAS 14853), 1947. (No. iv fpub. as a mus. suppl. to the *Spectateur*, 24/Dec/1946.)

fp: Ginette Guillamat with Pierre Sancan; 21/May/1944; Salle du Conservatoire, Paris.

?f*Eb*p: Nancy Evans with Ernest Lush; 19/March/1951.

(Nos. ii and iii in an orch. arr. by A. H. have been recorded by Madeleine Martinetti with an orch. cond. by A. H. on Columbia LFX 741. S(H) pub. No. iii — 3333/4431/timp.perc/hp/str.)

174. **UN AMI VIENDRA CE SOIR.** Film Score. (1945).

After Jacques Companez.

Dir: Raymond Bernard.

Prod: Compagnie Générale Cinématographique.

Principal items:
(i) Générique;
(ii) Berceuse de Mme Bexlin;
(iii) Jacques au piano;
(iv) Rumeur;
(v) Valse viennoise;
(vi) Dans le parc au clair de lune;
(vii) Prélude à la mort;
(viii) Postlude;
(ix) Retour d'Hélène;
(x) Chant de la délivrance: 'Nous sommes cent, nous sommes mille . . .'.

Dec. 1945.

Prem: 19/Feb/1946; Paris.

Brit. dist: Cameo-Polytechnic Distributors.

Bprem: Feb. 1950; Cameo-Poly Cinema.

Pub: Choudens (AC 21.888-897), 1946. No. (x) was published under the title 'Hymne de la délivrance'. The words are by José Bruyr and it is scored for voice/orch [=pf].

174a. **SOUVENIR DE CHOPIN.** Pf. (1945).

From the music for the Film Score *Un ami viendra ce soir* (see Catalogue No. 174).

Andante.

Ded: Jacqueline Potier-Landowski.

Pub: Choudens (AC 16857), 1947.

NB: According to Andrée Vaurabourg 'of the 99 bars, only the first 83 are by A.H. – the remainder are by Choudens'.

175. **HYMNE A LA LIBERTE.** Choral Mus. (?1945).

SATB.

Jean Anouich.

176. **L'EAU VIVE.** [?Orch. Mus.] (?1945).

Please see Appendix E.

177. **LES DEMONS DE L'AUBE.** Film Score. (1946).

Collab: Arthur Hoérée. The score also included 'En avant la musique' (words and music by Jacques Besse).

Dir: Yves Allégret.

Prod: Gaumont.

Principal items:

(i) Générique;
(ii) Les démons de l'aube;
(iii) Plein air;
(iv) Attaque nocturne;
(v) Escalade;
(vi) Les démons de l 'aube.

Jan. 1946.

Prem: 9/April/1946; Madeleine-Cinéma.

(Jacques Besse's 'En avant la musique' was pub. by Choudens (AC 21.988) in 1947. Other items by Arthur Honegger and Arthur Hoérée were published by Choudens as a suite for orchestra — see Catalogue No. 177a.)

177a. **SUITE FROM THE FILM SCORE 'LES DEMONS DE L'AUBE'.** Orch. (1946).

Movements i-iv by A. H., movts. v-ix by A. Hoérée.

(i) Les démons de l'aube générique;
(ii) Attaque nocturne;
(iii) Escalade;
(iv) Plein air (unisson chant sans paroles).;
[(v) Souvenirs;
(vi) Héroïsme;
(vii) Sur le bateau;
(viii) Mort de Michel;
(ix) Finale].

Pub: pf. redn. Choudens (AC 21. 898-906), 1946.

178. **SYMPHONIE LITURGIQUE [N°3].** Orch. (1945-46).

Subtitled: Symphonie liturgique.

Written "à l'instigation de la communauté de Travail 'Pro Helvetia' ".

3(picc)2+ca2+bcl 2+cbsn/4331/timp.bdm.cym.sdm.tamtam/pf/str.

(i) Dies irae.
Allegro marcato.
Paris, 5/Dec/1945.
Dur: 6'30".

(ii) De profundis clamavi.
Adagio.
Paris — Sils-Maria — Pratteln. Jan.-Oct. 1945.
Dur: 11'30".

(iii) Dona nobis pacem.
Andante.
Paris, 21/April/1946.
Dur: 10'55".

Dur: 28'55".

Ded: Charles Münch.

Pub: S(EAS 14695), 1946.

fp: Orch. de la Tonhalle et du Théâtre, cond. Charles Münch; 17/Aug/1946; Zürich, Switzerland.

f*Paris*p: cond. Charles Münch; 14/Nov/1946, Paris.

f*E*p/f*Eb*p: B.B.C.S.O., cond. Charles Münch; 7/Dec/1946.

179. **PROMETHEE.** Inc. Mus. (1946).

Play by Aeschylus trans. André Bonnard.

0033/0330/perc/fvchorus.

(i) Prélude (orch). Paris, March 1946;
(ii) —(orch);
[(iii) ? = (vii)]
(iv) —(orch);
(v) Chœur des Océanides (Larmes et pitié sur ton sort de maudit . . .);
(vi) Chœur des Océanides (Terrible puissance des dieux! . . .);
(vii) —(orch);
(viii) Chœur des Océanides (Pitié, Io, sur ton destin! . . .);
(ix) —(orch);
(x) Chœur des Océanides (Funeste (?) est la haine des dieux . . .);
(xi) Final (orch); Morges, 19 May 1946.

Npub.

fp: 5/June/1946: Open-air theatre, Avenches, Vaud, Switzerland.

f*concert*p: Orch. de la S.R., fv chorus, cond. Pierre Colombo; 25/April1965; Maison de la radio, Geneva, Switzerland.

180. **HAMLET.** Inc. Mus. (1946).

Play by Shakespeare trans. André Gide.

0001/0330/timp.3perc(bdm.cym.sdm.tri.wdbl)/om.

In the score the items appear in the following order:

Fanfares pour Hamlet:

(i) Introduction;
(ii) Fanfares du réveil;
(iii) Entrée et sortie du roi;
(iii[b]) Fanfare du banquet;
(iv) Trompettes de Fortimbras;
(v) Fanfares du duel;
(vi) Arrivée de Fortimbras;
(vii) Cortège funèbre;

Hamlet:

(a) Monologue;
(b) Interlude;
(c) Pantomime;
(d) Mélodrame;
(e) Entrée de Lucianus;
(e[bis]) Sommeil du roi;
(f) Entre la fanfare (vi) et la fanfare (vii);

Chant (Ophélie):

(a) 'Comment puis-je entre tant d'amours reconnaître le seul fidèle?';
(b) 'Chantons tire lire';
(c) 'S'il n'est pas déjà de retour';

Chanson de route des comédiens;

Chanson du Fossoyeur.

Pub: S(H).

fp: 17/Oct/1946; Théâtre Marigny, Paris.

181. **SORTILEGES.** Ballet Mus. (1946).

4 ondes Martenot.

Ded: Lelia Bederkhan.

fp: Lelia Bederkhan and her dance company (8); summer 1946; la Comédie des Champs-Elysées.

182. **SYMPHONY NO. 4.** Orch. (1946).

Subtitled: Deliciæ Basilienses.

2(picc)121/2100/cym.glock.tambour-bâlois[=sdm]tamtam.tri/pf/str.

(i) Lento e misterioso – Allegro; (ii) Larghetto; (iii) Allegro.

Ded: Paul Sacher and the Basle C.O. for their 20th anniversary.

Dur: $31\frac{3}{4}'$.

Pub: S(EAS 14760), 1947.

fp: Basle C.O., cond. Paul Sacher; 21/Jan/1947; Basle, Switzerland.

f*Paris*p: 25/Feb/1950.

?f*E*p: S.O., cond. Foster Clark; 24/March/1958; Chelsea Town Hall, London.

183. **INTRADA.** Ch. Mus. (1947).

Composed for the 'Concours international d'éxécution musicale, Geneva, 1947'.

Tpt/pf.

Maestoso — Allegro — Maestoso.

Paris, April 1947.

Pub: S(EAS 14920), 1947 (facsimile).

184. **MIMAAMAQUIM.** Voc. Mus. (1947).

Low voice/pf[=orch].

Words: transliteration of Hebrew ver. of Psalm CXXX ('Des profondeurs de l'abîme').

Grave.

Paris, 8/June/1947.

Ded: Madeleine Martinetti.

(Dur: /3′).

Orchestral acomp. for 1111/1000/hp/str.

Pub: pf. ver., S (EAS 14855), 1947; orch. ver., S (H).

185. **ŒDIPE.** Inc.Mus. (1947).

Play by Sophocles trans. André Obey.

Pub: S.

fp: 1947; Théâtre des Champs-Elysées.

186. **UN REVENANT.** Film Score (1947).

Dir: Christian-Jaque.

Prod: Compagnie Franco-Coloniale Cinématographique.

Principal items: (i) Un revenant; (ii) Ballet romantique; (iii) Andromède et Persée.

Brit. dist: Film Traders (Academy Cinema), 1948.

Pub: Choudens (AC 21967-9), 1947 (facsimile of pf. score).

(Honegger appeared in this film playing himself.)

PRELUDE, FUGUE, POSTLUDE. Orch. (1948).

See Catalogue No. 65a.

187. **L'ETAT DE SIEGE.** Inc. Mus. (1948).

Play by Albert Camus.

Pub: S(H).

fp: 27/Oct/1948; Théâtre Marigny, Paris.

188. **CONCERTO DA CAMERA.** Concerto. (1948).

Commissioned by Mrs Elizabeth Sprague-Coolidge.

Fl/ca/str.

(i) Allegretto amabile.
Paris, Aug. 1948.

(ii) Andante.
Paris, Sept. 1948.

(iii) Vivace.
Paris, 28/Oct/1948.

Ded: Mrs Elizabeth Sprague-Coolidge.

Dur: $16\frac{1}{2}'$.

Pub: S(EAS 15143), 1949; also ver. for fl/ca/pf (EAS 15144), 1949.

fp: André Jaunet (fl), Marcel Saillet (ca), Z.C.M., cond. Paul Sacher; 6/May/1949; Zürich, Switzerland.

f*E*p/f*Eb*p: Gareth Morris (fl), Terence MacDonagh (ca), Philharmonia Orch., cond. Ernest Ansermet; 10/April/1950.

189. **SAINT FRANCOIS D'ASSISE.** Radio Mus. (1949).

'Jeu radiophonique' by William Aguet.

2(picc).2rec.2(ca)22/0330/timp.bdm.bells.cym.tamtam.tdm/pf.spinet[=hp]/TrAviols.vla-d'a.bary[=vlc].vla-dg/str/chorus.

Commissioned by Radio Lausanne.

(i) (Allegretto);
(ii) Le bateleur;
(iii) -;
(iv) Musique du banquet (Ménestrandie);
(v) Chanson de troubadour (Ménestrandie);
(vi) -;
(vii) -;
(viii) -;
(viii^{b}) -;
(ix) -;
(x) -;
(xi) -;
(xii) -;
(xiii) Plain chant;

(xiv) (Magnificat . . .);
(xv) -;
(xvi) Les oiseaux;
(xvii) -;
(xviii) -;
(xviii[b]) -;
(xix) -;
(xx) Le feu;
(xxi) -;
(xxii) -;
(xxiii) -;
(xxiv) Le cantique du soleil;
(xxv) -.

Pub: S.

fp/*f*bp: William Aguet (retr), Hugues Cuénod (Bar), Chœur de La Tour de Peilz (cond. Carlo Boller), Orch. de la S.R., cond. Ernest Ansermet; 3/Dec/1949; Studio de la Sallaz sur Lausanne, Radio Lausanne. (Awarded the 'Prix de la Radiodiffusion Suisse'.)

190. **MARCHE CONTRE LA MORT.** Radio Mus. (1949).

Text by Antoine Saint-Exupéry in memory of Henri Guillaumet.

Commissioned by the Studio d'Essai de la Radiodiffusion française.

Npub.

?Nperf.

191. **TETE D'OR.** Radio Mus. (1950).

Text by Paul Claudel.

11(ca)11/0330/timp.bdm.cym.rattle.sdm.tdm/str.

The following details were taken from the ms:

(i) (Largamente);
(ii) 'Les champs à la fin de l'hiver'. Modéré;
(iii) 'Ils marchent . . .'. Lent;
(iv) 'Deux arbres et toute la nuit dernière'. Assez lent;

Tête d'or II[de] partie:

(v) La nuit dans le palais. Lent;
(vi) Mesure du temps (Crotchet=60);
(vii) Le rossignol A and B;
(viii) Entrée et pantomime de la princesse. Très lent mais rythmé;
(ix) Le rêve éveillé. Très lent comme distendu; Entrée rapide du messager; Récit. de la bataille;

Tête d'or Suite II[de]: Entrée de Tête d'or

(a) Je ne le précède que de peu;
(b) . . . la voix de la trompette; Marche de Cérès; Mort du roi; Final II[de] partie;

Tête d'or IIIème partie:

Le Caucase;
Crucifixion. Violent. 'O mains . . .';
Fond sonore de la déroute. Modérément animé;
Tête d'or blessé. Lent et lugubre.

Zürich, Jan. 1950.

Pub: S(H) (a photographic reproduction of the ms).

192. **DE LA MUSIQUE.** Ballet Mus. (1950).

Ballet by R. Wild.

Pub: S.

193. **BOURDELLE.** Film Score. (1950).

Documentary film directed by René Lucot.

Prod: DOC.

The ms appears incomplete, but contains the following items: Générique; Large (12 bars); '1ère séquence. Poco lento' (14 bars); — (Allegro molto — 35 bars; ? incomplete); 'Séquence des bustes de Beethoven' (?60 bars of unorchestrated music).

194. **PANIS ANGELICUS.** Voc. Mus. (1950).

Voice/pf.

Andantino.

Pub: Mus. supp. to *La Revue de l'Opéra de Paris*, 2 (Oct/Nov. 1950).

195. **SYMPHONY NO. 5.** Orch. (1950).

Subtitled: Di tre re.

3(picc)2+ca2+bcl3/4331/[timp]/str.

(i) Grave.
Paris, 5/Sept/1950; Orch. 28/Oct/1950.
Dur: 8′.

(ii) Allegretto.
Paris, 1/Oct/1950; Orch. 23/Nov/1950.
Dur: 12′ 20″.

(iii) Allegro marcato.
Paris, 10/Nov/1950; Orch. 3/Dec/1950.
Dur: 6′ 20″.

Ded: 'For the Koussewitsky Music Foundation. Dedicated to the memory of Natalia Koussewitsky'.

Dur: 26′ 40″.

Pub: S(EAS 15386), 1951.

fp: Boston S.O., cond. Charles Münch; 9/March/1951; Boston.

f*E*p/f*Eb*p: Boston S.O., cond. Charles Münch; 26/May/1952; Royal Festival Hall, B.B.C. broadcast.

196. **SUITE ARCHAIQUE.** Orch. (1950-51).

Commissioned by R. Whitney.

2222/0220/str.

(i) Ouverture.
Largamente.
Paris, 17/Dec/1950.
Dur: 4′25″;

(ii) Pantomime.
Presto.
Dur: 5′;

(iii) Ritournelle et sérénade.
Andantino.
Dur: 5′5″.

(iv) Processional.
Largo.
Paris, 15/Jan/1951.
Dur: 4′.

Ded: Louisville Philharmonic Society.

Dur: 18′30″.

Pub: S(EAS 15399), 1951.

fp: Louisville S.O., cond. R. Whitney; 28/Feb/1951; Louisville, U.S.A.

f*Ep*/f*Eb*p: Leighton Lucas Orch./cond.; 7/Aug/1952.

197. **MONOPARTITA.** Orch. (1951).

Commissioned by the Tonhalle - Gesellschaft, Zürich.

22+ca2+bcl2/4330/timp/str.

Largo — Vivace marcato —Adagio — Vivace — Adagio — Largo.

26/March/1951.

Ded: Tonhalle — Gesellschaft, Zürich.

(Dur: /15′).

Pub: S(EAS 15408), 1951.

fp: Orch. de la Tonhalle, Zürich, cond. Hans Rosbaud; 12/June/1951; Tonhalle, Zürich, Switzerland.

198. **TOCCATA.** Orch. (1951).

Subtitled: Sur un thème de Campra.

Contribution to 'Guirlande de Campra':— D. Lesur — Sarabande et farandole; R.-Manuel — Canarie; G. Tailleferre — Sarabande Campra; F. Poulenc — Matelote provençale; H. Sauguet — Variation; G. Auric — Ecossaise.

2222/2200/str.

Allegro moderato.

Paris, Nov. 1951.

Pub: S, 1954 (facsimile, 250 copies only).

fp: Orch. de la Soc. des Conc. du Cons., cond. Hans Rosbaud; 31/July/1952; Aix-en-Provence Festival.

199. **PAUL CLAUDEL.** Film Score. (1951).

Documentary film directed by André Gillet.

Prod: Atlantic-Film.

200. **LA TOUR DE BABEL.** Film Score. (1951).

Collab: Arthur Hoérée; Tibor Harsanyi (Nos. 2, 9, 13, 15, 19, 23, 27, 31, 34 and 37).

Documentary film directed by George Rony.

Prod: Films-Rony.

Prem: 26/Dec/1951; Studio de l'Etoile.

201. **ON NE BADINE PAS AVEC L'AMOUR.** Inc. Mus. (1951).

Play by Alfred de Musset.

Pub: S.

fp: 13/Dec/1951; Théâtre Marigny, Paris.

202. **LA REDEMPTION DE FRANCOIS VILLON.** Radio Mus. (1951).

Text by José Bruyr.

1111/1200/cym/str/chorus.

(i) Neige. Dur: 3′;
(ii) Pluie et vent. Dur: 1′;
(iii) Ier Tableau : Chanson de la grosse Margot;
(iv) II[d] Tableau : Trompe;
(v) ('En me quittant Robin Robinet').

Pub: S.

203. **ŒDIPE-ROI.** Inc.Mus. (1952).

Play by Sophocles trans. Thierry Maulnier.

1111/0110/bdm.bouteillophone.high dm.low dm. tamtam/om.

(i) Ouverture et scène I;
(ii) Entrée de Créon;
(iii) Sortie d'Œdipe;
(iv) Entrée du peuple et Ritournelle pendant le chœur I;
(v) Entrée de Tirésias Scène III;
(vi) Ritournelle pendant le chœur II;
(vii) Ritournelle pendant le chœur III;
(viii) Entrée de Jocaste;
(viii[b]) Cri de Jocaste;
(ix) Ritournelle pendant le chœur IV;
(x) Ritournelle pendant le chœur V;
(xi) Mélodrame: Œdipe et le chœur;
(xii) Final.

Valmont, 3/April/1952.

Pub: S.

fp: 1952; Théâtre Comédie-Française, Paris.

204. **UNE CANTATE DE NOEL.** Oratorio. (1953).

Liturgical and popular texts (Eng. trans. Rollo H. Myers; Ger. trans. Fred. Golbeck).

2(picc) 222/4330/hp.org/str/Bar-solo.cv chorus.chorus.

N.B.: Based on parts of the sketches for an unfinished work, *Selzacher Passionsspiel* (libretto by Cäsar von Arx), made between Dec. 1940 and 25/Dec/1944.

Paris, 25/Jan/1953.

Ded: Basle C.O. on its 25th anniversary and its founder Paul Sacher.

Dur: 27′.

Pub: S; VS (EAS 15630) (Fr./Ger./Eng.), 1953; Ø (EAS 15650), 1953.

fp: Derrick Olsen (Bar), Basle C.C. and C.O., cond. Paul Sacher; 16/Dec/1953; Zürich.

f*London*p/f*Eb*p: John Noble (Bar), B.B.C. Chorus, boys from Emmanuel School Choir, B.B.C.S.O., cond. Ernest Ansermet; 7/Oct/1959; B.B.C. Concert, London.

205. **ROMANCE.** Ch. Mus. (1953).

Fl/pf.

Andantino.

Pub: Pierre Noël/Editions Billaudot (6180), 1953 — *Les contemporains écrivent pour les instruments à vent, collection Fernand Oubradous, La Flûte, Vol. 1, No. v* ((i) Gagnebin — Marche des gais lurons; (ii) L. Aubert — Lied; (iii) Arma — Deux croquis; (iv) Beydts — Tendre regret).

Appendix A

The following items are arrangements whose performance is now not encouraged. Their mention in this Catalogue is for the purposes of scholarly/historical accuracy and completeness only.

34c. **SUITES FROM THE INCIDENTAL MUSIC FOR 'LE ROI DAVID'.** Orch. (1928).

Two orch. suites from the oratorio *Le roi David* transcribed and arranged by Francis Salabert for: 2(picc)121/2230/timp.cym.tamb.tamtam/cel.hp/str.

Suite 1:

(i) (a) Introduction. Dur: $1\frac{1}{2}'$; (b) Cortège. Dur: $1\frac{1}{4}'$;
(ii) Psaume (Ah! si j'avais des ailes de colombe). Dur. $3'$;
(iii) (a) La chanson d'Ephraïm. Dur: $1\frac{1}{2}'$; (b) Chant de la servante. Dur: $2'$;
(iv) La danse devant l'arche. Dur: $12'$, (Total Dur: $21\frac{1}{4}'$).

Suite 2:

(i) (a) Le camp de Saül. Dur: $1\frac{1}{4}'$; (b) Couronnement de Salomon. Dur: $1\frac{1}{2}'$;
(ii) (a) Psaume (ix) Dur: $2'$; (b) Incantation. Dur: $2\frac{1}{2}'$;
(iii) Lamentations de Guilboa. Dur: $3\frac{1}{4}'$;
(iv) La mort de David. Dur: $5'$. (Total Dur: $15\frac{1}{2}'$).

Pub: S; [Suite 1 (EAS 4675-8); Suite 2 (EAS 4699-700, 702-3)].

71b. **SUITE FROM THE OPERETTA 'LES AVENTURES DU ROI PAUSOLE'.** Orch. (1931).

Arranged and transcribed by Francis Salabert for: 1(picc)121/2230/bdm.cym.cast.sbells.sdm/cel/str.

(i) Animé (= Ouverture). Dur: $4'$;
(ii) Modéré (= Act 2, Prélude). Dur: $1'$;
(iii) Lent (= xxvii). Dur: $2\frac{1}{2}'$;
(iv) Très doux, pas trop lent (=xvii). Dur: $3\frac{1}{4}'$;
(v) Mouvement vif de Boléro (=xxiii). Dur: $2\frac{1}{2}'$.

(Total Dur: $13\frac{1}{4}'$).

Pub: S; PC(EAS 6724), 1931.

71c. **VALSE POUR LE ROI PAUSOLE.** Voc. Mus. (1931).

Song from the operetta *Les aventures du roi Pausole* (see Catalogue No. 71).

Voice/pf.

Appendix B

The following items exist only in ms, and it has not been possible to ascertain vital pieces of information in order to be able to integrate them into the Catalogue of Works. (Except where noted to the contrary, the mss were shown to the author by Andrée Vaurabourg-Honegger at her residence — 21 rue Duprée, Paris — during the summer of 1979.)

ARIOSO. Ch. Mus. (?).

Vln/pf.

Lento (21 bars).

Ded: 'à Lipnitzki en très amical souvenir et avec mes remerciements pour les belles photos'.

Npub. (Ms in the Rubin Academy of Music, Jerusalem, Israel.)

(? MUSIQUE D'AMEUBLEMENT) Ch. Mus. (1922).

Fl.cl/tpt/S4tet/pf.

(i) Fl.cl/tpt/pf.
Vif. (10 bars.)

(ii) Fl.cl/S4tet/pf.
Lent. (8 bars.)

(iii) Fl/tpt/vln.vlc/pf.
Modéré. (17 bars).

(Photocopy of ms supplied by Pascale Honegger, Geneva, Switzerland.)

—. Choral Mus. (1939).

Chorus (unison)/pf [hnm].

(Possèdes-tu pauvre pêcheur . . .). (17 bars.)

Paris, 14/July/1939.

(Photocopy of ms supplied by Pascale Honegger, Geneva, Switzerland.)

COLLOQUE. (?Film Score). (?).

Fl/cel/vln. vla.

Générique — Fondu; Poco largo (Dur: 15″); Silence (Dur: 15″); Adagio — Andantino (Dur: 18″); Galop: Allegro (Dur: 12″). Total Dur: 1′.

PRELUDE N° 1 ET FUGUE DE J. S. BACH. Orch. (?).

222.ssx.asx.3/4331/perc/str.

Dur: 6′.

Pub: U.E.

CHEVAUCHEE. (? Orch. Mus.).

111.sax.1/0220/bdm.tdm/pf/str.

(46 bars)

Dur: "sans reprise 1′ 50″; avec [reprise] 3′ 20″".

(Photocopy of ms supplied by Pascale Honegger, Geneva, Switzerland.)

—. Orch. Mus. (?).

Str.

Largo (Crotchet = 56). 56 bars.

—. Pf. (?).

Pf.

Très modéré (Crotchet = 60).

Npub.

—. Voc. Mus. (?).

2222/str/S-solo.

(La nuit est si profonde qu'elle entre dans mes yeux . . .)

(52 bars.)

(Photocopy of ms supplied by Pascale Honegger, Geneva, Switzerland.)

ROUTE DE MANDALAY. Voc. Mus. (?).

Voice/pf.

—. ? (?).

(i) La nativité;
(ii) —;
(iii) —;
(iv) —;
(v) Gloria;
(vi) —;
(vii) —.

Appendix C

Honegger left the following unfinished:

(i) **FAITS DIVERS.** Film Score. (1924).

Claude Autant-Lara.

(ii) **LE ROI, SON VIZIR ET SON MEDECIN.** Inc. Mus. (1926).

Play by Jacques Copeau.

(iii) **SELZACHER PASSIONSSPIEL.** Passion. (1940-44).

Libretto by Cäsar von Arx.

For performance in two 'demi-journées' [half-days]:

Morning: A survey of the Old and New Testaments up to the birth of Christ;

Afternoon: The Passion story — from the journey to Calvary to Christ's burial.

Soloists, children's choir, mixed-voice choir, orchestra and organ.

The fragments of ms contain the following in order of composition:

'Lobet den Herren . . .' (Dec/1940);

'Laudate Dominum . . .' (Jan/1941);

'Am Anfang schuf Gott . . . (début)' (9/Feb/1941);

'O Haupt voll Blut . . .' (16/Nov/1942);

'Scène du Paradis terestre' (Dec/1944).

Appendix D

André Vaurabourg-Honegger presented four volumes of sketchbooks to the Bibliothèque Nationale, Paris. They are labelled:

(i) Cahier pour brouillons 1932-1936;

(ii) Cahier pour brouillons [Sept.] 1936 - [Feb.] 1939;

(iii) Cahier pour brouillons Feb. 1939 - May 1943;

(iv) Cahier pour brouillons 22/May/1943 - Dec. 1948.

Appendix E

Honegger orchestrated the following works by other composers:

(i) **CHOUCOUNE.** Operetta. (?1922).

An operetta by Fernard Ochsé.

?Npub.

(ii) **L'EAU VIVE.** [?Orch. Mus.] (?1945).

A piece by Maurice Jaubert.

?Npub.

Appendix F

Honegger arranged the following for solo(ists), (chorus) and orchestra, which were recorded in 1936 or 1937 (please see Discography for further details):

(i) 'La femme du marin' (Aunis);

(ii) 'Les trois princesses au pommier doux' (Franche - Comté).

Appendix G

Although Honegger's name appears in the credits of this film (*Les musiciens du ciel*), he did not, in fact, compose any of the music.

Bibliography

NOTES

(i) For practical convenience I have divided my bibliography into four parts as follows:

PART I The writings of Arthur Honegger — Section A: Books and Prefaces; Section B: Articles in Music Journals; Section C: Collections of his writings;

PART II Books and dissertations devoted entirely to the life and works of Arthur Honegger;

PART III Articles in Journals etc., relating to the life and works of Arthur Honegger — Section A: Unsigned; Section B: Signed;

PART IV Books, dissertations and encyclopedia entries relating to the period.

(ii) The contents of Part I, Section B and Part III, Section A are listed chronologically.

(iii) In Part III a limited number of articles are listed which are in fact contained in certain of the more important English, French, German and Swiss daily newspapers (and their supplements). For the most part their inclusion was prompted by the stature of the authors in question as musicologists as well as critics.

(iv) Additional reference should be made to Table 5 (Chapter V), pp. 000-000: *Antigone* — a bibliography.

(v) The derivation of abbreviations employed in this bibliography is indicated in the *List of Abbreviations* below.

(vi) Arthur Honegger's name has been abbreviated to A.H.

ABBREVIATIONS OF MUSIC JOURNALS IN BIBLIOGRAPHY

Anbruch	=	Musikblätter des Anbruchs
FMS	=	Feuilles Musicales Suisses (Revue Suisse)
HR	=	Hudebni Rozhledy
IM	=	L'Information musicale
JMF	=	Revue des Jeunesses Musicales de France
LM	=	Le Ménestrel
MA	=	Musical America
MC	=	Musical Courrier
MeM	=	Mens en Mélodie
MF	=	Mercure de France
ML	=	Music and Letters
MM	=	Music and Musicians
MO	=	Musical Opinion
MQ	=	Music Quarterly
MT	=	Musical Times
Musica	=	Musica of Cassel
NRF	=	Nouvelle Revue Française
NYT	=	New York Times
NZM	=	Neue Zeitschrift für Musik
NZZ	=	Neue Züricher Zeitung
OM	=	Österreichische Musikzeitschrift
RIM	=	Revue internationale de musique
RM	=	La Revue Musicale
RMSR	=	Revue Musicale de Suisse Romande
RP	=	Revue Pleyel

RPL	=	Revue politique et littéraire (Revue bleue)
SKM	=	Sovetskaja Muzyka
SM	=	Schweizerische Musikzeitung
SMB	=	Schweizerische Musikpädagogische Blätter (Feuillets suisses de pédagogie musicales)
SR	=	Saturday Review

PART I

The Writings of Arthur Honegger

Section A: Books and Prefaces

Incantations aux fossiles (d'Ouchy, Lausanne, 1948).
Beschwörungen (German translation by Willi Reich) (Scherz, Bern, 1955).
(with Bernard Gavoty) *Je suis compositeur* (Conquistador, Paris, 1951).
(with Bernard Gavoty) *Ich bin Komponist* (German translation by Suzanne Oswald) (Atlantis, Zürich, 1952).
(with Bernard Gavoty) *Zeneszerzö vagyok* (Hungarian translation by Oltványi Imre) (Zeneműkiadó, Budapest, 1960).
(with Bernard Gavoty) *I am a Composer* (English translation by Wilson O. Clough in collaboration with Allan Arthur Willman) (Faber and Faber, London, 1966).
Preface to R. Aloys Mooser's *Regards sur la musique contemporaine* (Lausanne, 1946).
Preface to Nicolas Obouhow's *Traité d'harmonie, tonale, atonale et totale* revised by José David and Lucien Garban (Paris, 1946) — reproduced in *RM*, November-December 1946, 15-16.
Preface to Serge Moreaux's *Béla Bartók* (Masse, Paris, 1949).
Preface to Edouard Lindenberg's *Comment lire une partition d'orchestre* (Heugel, Paris, 1952).
Preface to Marcel Delannoy's *A.H.* (Horay, Paris, 1953).

Section B: Articles in Music Journals

'Adaptations musicales', *Gazette des Sept Arts,* 25 January 1923, 4.
'Le métier du compositeur de musique', *La Revue Nouvelle*, 15 December 1924, 17-18.
'*L'enfant et les sortilèges', Musique et Théâtre,* 15 April 1925, 5.
'Beethoven et nous', *Le Correspondant,* 25 March 1927, 861-72.
'Modern Music', *The Rice Institute (Houston) Pamphlet,* 16, No. 3 (1929), 123-31.
'*Les Six* ont dix ans', *Candide,* 301 (19 December 1929), 13.
'Du cinéma sonore à la musique réelle', *Appogiature*, May 1931, 105-114.
'*Cris du monde*', *Plans*, December 1931, 17-18.
'Pour prendre congé', *Appogiature*, February 1932, 36-44.
'Problems of the professional composer', *The Musician*, May 1932, 26.

'La situation sociale du compositeur de musique', *Le Mois*, 32 (1933), 217-21.
(with Arthur Hoérée), 'Particularités sonores du film *Rapt*', *RM*, December 1934, 88-91.
'Ravel et le Debussysme', *RM*, December 1938, 258-59.
'Stravinsky: homme de métier', *RM*, May-June 1939, 261-63.
'Petit prélude et le festival Claude Debussy', *Comœdia*, 21 June 1941, 1 and 3.
'Franck et Stravinsky', *IM*, 19 (26 September 1941), 39-41, 63-64.
'A propos de la *symphonie pour orchestre à cordes*', *SM*, 1944, 131.
'La musique à Paris après la libération', *Dissonances*, 1-2 (January-February 1945), 11-14.
'Musique et libération', *Labyrinthe*, 5 (15 February 1945), 3.
'Uber die Musikkritiker', *OM*, June 1946, 154-56.
'Vad kan balleten göra för unga Komponister', *Prisma*, 6 (1946), 76-77.
'Souvenirs sur Othmar Schœck', *SM*, 8-9 (1946), 321-24.
'Préface au *traité d'harmonie tonale, atonale et totale* de Nicolas Obouhow', *RM*, November-December 1946, 15-16.
'La musique symphonique à Paris', *Soleils*, 1 (1947), 22-27.
'Uber die Musikkritiker', *Melos*, April 1948, 97-99.
'*Die Geschichte der Fossile*', *Melos*, January 1950, 1-3.
'Mozart', *OM*, 10 (1951), 404-5.
'Souvenirs sur la classe de Vincent d'Indy au Conservatoire', *RIM*, 10 (1951), 345.
'A.H. om *Konung David*', *Röster i Radio*, 14 (1951), 4-5.
'An die jungen Musiker', *Melos*, February 1952, 35-36.
'A.H. warnt seine Schüler: Haben Sie überlegt, was Sie erwartet?, *Das Musikleben*, February 1952, 12.
'Der Lohn des Komponisten', *Musica*, February 1953, 47-50.
'The Musician in Modern Society', *Revue Vista Musical Chilena*, January 1954, 6-22.
'The Musician in Modern Society', *National Music Council Bulletin, New York,* September 1954, 6-11.
'The Musician in Modern Society', *U.N.E.S.C.O. 1954: Conference, Venice 1952, L'Artiste dans la Société contemporaine*, 1954, 55-68.
'Collaboration avec Claudel', *NRF*, 33 (1955), 556-59.
'*Ich bin ein Komponist*', *OM*, December 1955, 270-72.
'W.A. Mozart', *NZM*, January 1956, 36-37.
'Komponisten als Filmhelden', *Melos*, 1956, 115. Also in *Musica*, February 1956, 115.
'Note sur *Antigone*', *Melos*, October 1956, 282-83.
'A.H. über *Nicolas de Flue', SM*, May-June 1962, 155-56.
'Die akustische Pest', *Musica*, 2 (1970), 165.

SECTION C: Collections of his writings

A.H. Nachklang, Schriften, Photos, Dokumente, ed. by Willi Reich (Die Arche, Zürich, 1957).
Zenéröl-zenészekröl-zeneéletröl (Hungarian translation by Várnai Péter) (Zenemükiadó, Budapest, 1965).
O muzykal'nom iskusstve, with a commentary by Vera Aleksandrova (Muzyka, Leningrad, 1979).
Beruf und Handwerk des Komponisten: Illusionslose Gespräche, Kritiken, Aufsätze, ed. by Eberhardt Klemm (trans. from Fr. by Suzanne Oswald and Willi Reich), (Reclam, Leipzig, 1980).

PART II

Books and dissertations devoted entirely to the life and works of Arthur Honegger

—. *A.H.* (Salabert Informations, Paris, 1956).

Bruyr, José, *A.H. et son œuvre* (Corrêa, Paris, 1947).

Claudel, Paul, *Sur la musique* in *A.H.* by Claudel, Vuillermoz, Manuel and Hoérée (Collection Comœdia-Charpentier Numéro spécial, Les Publications techniques, Paris, 1942).

Collaer, Paul, *A.H.: Antigone 1928 (Etude)* (Senart, Paris, 1928).

Delannoy, Marcel, *A.H.* (Horay, Paris, 1953)

A.H. Nouvelle edition augmentée du catalogue des œuvres de A.H. par G. K. Spratt (Editions Slatkine, Geneva and Paris, 1986).

Feschotte, Jacques, *A.H.* (Seghers, Paris, 1966).

Fischer, Kurt von, *A.H.* (Neujahrsblatt der Allgemeinen Musikgesellschaft, Hug, Zurich, 1978).

Gauthier, André, *A.H.* (EISE, Lyon, 1957).

George, André, *A.H.* (Aveline, Paris, 1926).

Gérard, Claude, *A.H.* (Nouvelle Revue de Belgique, Bruxelles, 1945).

Guilbert, Yves, *A.H.* (Apostolat de la Presse, Paris, 1959).

Headley, H. E., *The Choral Works of A.H.* (unpublished doctoral thesis, North Texas State University, 1959).

Hoérée, Arthur, *A.H. - La vie, l'œuvre, l'homme,* in *A.H.* by Claudel, Vuillermoz, Manuel and Hoérée (Collection Comœdia — Charpentier Numéro spécial, Les Publications techniques, Paris, 1942).

Landowski, Marcel, *A.H.* (du Seuil, Paris, 1957).

Maillard, Jean and Jacques Nahoum, *Les symphonies d'A.H.* (Leduc, Paris, 1974).

Matter, Jean, *A.H. ou la quête de joie* (Foetisch, Lausanne — Paris, 1956).

Meylan, Pierre, *René Morax et A.H. au Théâtre du Jorat* (Cervin, Lausanne, 1966; Ploix, Paris, 1966).

A.H. Humanitäre Botschaft der Musik (Huber, Frauenfeld and Stuttgart, 1970).

Nahoum, Jacques, See Jean Maillard.

Pavčinskij, Sergej, *The symphonies of A.H.* (Sovetskij Kompozitor, Moscow, 1972).

Rappoport, Lidija, *Arthur Onegger* (Muzyka, Leningrad, 1967).

Reich, Willi, ed., *A.H. Nachklang, Schriften, Photos, Dokumente* (Arche, Zurich, 1957).

Roland-Manuel, *A.H.* (Senart, Paris, 1925).

Les cinquante ans in *A.H.* by Claudel, Vuillermoz, Manuel and Hoérée (Collection Comœdia-Charpentier Numéro spécial, Les Publications techniques, Paris, 1942).

Schaeffner, André, *Le roi David, notice bibliographique* (Foetisch, Lausanne, 1925).

Sistrunk, George W., *A comparison of the two orchestrations of 'King David' by A.H.* (DMA diss., Choral Conducting; University of Miami, 1972).

Spratt, Geoffrey K., *A critical study of the complete works of A.H. with particular reference to his dramatic works* (Ph.D. diss., University of Bristol, 1979).

Catalogue des œuvres d'A.H.(Editions Slatkine, Geneva and Paris, 1986).

See Marcel Delannoy.

Szöllösy, A., *A.H.,* (Gondolat, Budapest, 1961; 2nd ed., 1980).

Tappolet, Willy, *A.H.* (Hug, Zurich, 1933).

A.H. (translated into French by Hélène Breuleux), (La Baconnière, Neuchâtel, 1938).

A.H. (Atlantis, Zurich, 1954).

A.H. (translated into French by Claude Tappolet), (La Baconnière, Neuchâtel, 1957).

Sysoeva, Elena *Simfonii A. Honeggera* (Muzyka, Moscow, 1975).

Voss, Hans Dieter, *A.H.: "Le roi David"* (Katzbichler, Munich and Salzburg, 1983).

Vuillermoz, Emile, *Les grandes réussites d'A.H.* in *A.H.* by Claudel, Vuillermoz, Manuel and Hoérée (Collection Comœdia-Charpentier Numéro-spécial, Les Publications techniques, Paris, 1942).

PART III

Articles in Journals etc., relating to the life and works of Arthur Honegger

SECTION A: Unsigned.

—. 'Setting locomotives to music, *Literary Digest*, 25 October 1924, 29-30.
—. 'Machine Music', *Musical Mirror*, March 1925, 49.
—. '*Judith* d'A.H.', *Dissonances*, 6-7 (Summer 1925), 127-28.
—. '*Antigone* — new musical tragedy by A.H.', *The Times*, 5 January 1928, 10.
—. 'A.H.', *Bolletino bibliografico musicale*, January 1929, 1-8.
—. 'A.H.' *British Musician and Musical News*, June 1930, 154-57.
—. 'Football in Music — A.H.'s *Rugby*', *British Musician and Musical News*, February 1931, 39-40.
—. 'Cinéma [*Rapt*]', *Le Mois*, September 1934, 235-36.
—. '*Christophe Colomb* d'Aguet — A.H.', *Dissonances*, 4 (April 1940) 98-102.
—. 'Münch offers American première of A.H's *4th Symphony*', *MA*, 15 January 1949, 10.
—. '*Jour de fête suisse* had its American première', *MA*, 15 January 1949, 33.
—. 'American Première [*La danse des morts*]', *MA*, 15 April 1949, 36.
—. 'A.H.'s *Fourth* [*Symphony*] by Philharmonic', *MC*, 15 January 1949, 18.
—. '*Concerto da camera*', *Notes*, September 1949, 635-36.
—. 'Varied season ends at Hollywood Bowl [*Jeanne d'Arc au bûcher*]', *MA*, September 1949, 8.
—. 'Paris Opera offers A.H.'s *Jeanne d'Arc au bûcher*', *MC*, 15 January 1951, 28.
—. 'Switzerland: three works of A.H.', *Opera*, March 1951, 198-200.
—. 'A.H.'s *5th Symphony* given New York première', *MA*, 1 April 1951, 27.
—. 'Who likes it modern?', *Time*, 24 September 1951, 83-84.
—. 'Lettre ouverte à A.H.', *Contrepoints*, 1951, 129-31.
—. 'Les Six', *Cercle musicale et dramatique independante bulletin*, 3 (January 1952), 9-15.
—. 'Review of *Ich bin Komponist*', *Das Musikleben*, February 1952, 33-35.
—. Review of *Jeg er komponist* by A. H., *Dansk Musiktidsskrift*, 3 (1952), 97-98.
—. '*Monopartita, Suite Archaïque, 5th Symphony'*, *MA*, March 1952, 40.
—. 'A.H.'s birthday', *Tempo*, Spring 1952, 1.
—. 'A.H.'s *King David*', *International Musican*, May 1952, 37.
—. 'On the Cover', *Musical News*, June 1952, 3.
—. 'Les œuvres majeures d'A.H. enregistrées en 33 tours', *Disques*, Summer—Autumn 1952, 570-72.
—. 'A.H.', *Rösteri Radio*, 11 (1952), 14.
—. 'Notes of the day: Music is in a bad way because of a lazy minded public', *MMR*, December 1952, 253-55.
—. Philadelphia Orchestra marks 50th year in New York [*Jeanne d'Arc au bûcher*]', *MA*, 15 December 1952, 8.
—. 'Speech Music [*Jeanne d'Arc au bûcher*]', *International Musician*, January 1953, 35.
—. 'H's Surrealism [*Jeanne d'Arc au bûcher*]', *American Record Guide,* May 1953, 280.
—. 'Honegger to Harpsichord [*Jeanne d'Arc au bûcher*]', *SR*, 30 May 1953, 280.
—. '*Jeanne d'Arc au bûcher*', *Disques*, Summer 1953, 444-45.
—. 'A.H. in lighter vein [*Les aventures du roi Pausole*]', *MO*, February 1954, 269.
—. 'Words from a music lover' *Time*, 17 May 1954, 62.
—. '*Jeanne d'Arc au bûcher*', *London Music*, October 1954, 22-24.
—. 'Opera [*Jeanne d'Arc au bûcher*]', *MT*, December 1954, 666-67.
—. '*Jeanne d'Arc au bûcher*', *Opera*, December 1954, 765-68. Also in *London Music*, October 1954, 23-24.
—. 'Oratorios, symphonies et œuvres diverses', *Disques*, January 1955, 61-66.

—. 'Boston hears Stravinsky work in memory of Dylan Thomas [*Une cantate de Noël*]', MA, 1 February 1955, 8.
—. '*Jeanne d'Arc au bûcher*', *Disques*, May-June 1955, 507.
—. 'Essai de discographie générale d'A.H.', *Disques*, December 1955, 898-99.
—. '*4ème Symphonie* et *3ème Mouvement symphonique*', *Disques*, December 1955, 890-91.
—. Obituary, *MA*, 1 December 1955, 32.
—. Obituary, *MC*, 10 December 1955, 58.
—. Obituary, *Billboard*, 15 December 1955, 32.
—. 'Opera has lost', *Opera News*, 19 December 1955, 14.
—. 'Weitere Todesnachrichten', *Musica*, January 1956, 61-62.
—. Obituary, *MT*, January 1956, 42-43.
—. Obituary, *Strad*, January 1956, 323 +.
—. '*Quatuors — Pacific — Symphonie — Cantate*', *Disques*, January-February 1956, 86-89.
—. 'World of Music', *Etude*, February 1956, 9.
—. 'Closing Chord', *International Musician*, February 1956, 39.
—. 'Recitals and Concerts — *King David*', *American Organist*, April 1956, 126.
—. 'La dernière interview d'A.H.', *L'Opéra de Paris*, 12 (1956), 19-20.
—. 'Seefried sings with Boston S.O. [*Symphony No. 2*]', *MA*, 1 January 1957, 16.
—. 'Ernest Ansermet dirige la nouvelle version intégrale du *roi David* d'A.H.', *Disques*, September 1957, 708-9.
—. 'Review of A. Szöllösy's *A.H.*, *Revue de Musique*, 124 (1961), 221-23.
—. 'Hovori A.H. [review of Czech translation of *Je suis compositeur*]', *HR*, 4 (1962), 148-50.
—. 'Basle A.H. Festival', *S.M.*, 4 (1962), 245-46.
—. 'Review of *Erinnerungen an R. Strauss, C. Spitteler, A. Schweitzer, M. Huber, C. Amiet and A.H.*', *Strauss*, 34 (September 1962), 22-23.
—. 'Concert Performance [*Jeanne d'Arc au bûcher*]', *Opera*, August 1966, 678 +.
—. 'Utrecht — *Jeanne d'Arc au bûcher*', *MeM*, January 1967, 26-28.
—. 'A.H. Zum 75', *Musik und Gesellschaft*, April 1967, 283-84.
—. 'A.H. and *King David*', *Amor Artis Bulletin*, 7 (January 1968), 1-2, 10-12.
—. 'Quartets by Hindemith and A.H.', *Hi Fi/Musical America*, September 1968, 78.
—. 'Tipuri de cadente finale i muzica contemporana Rumania', *Lucrari de Muzicologie*, 1968, 121-36.
—. 'Poulenc and A.H. at Julliard [*Antigone*]', *Hi Fi/Musical America*, July 1969, 21-22.
—. 'Brno — *Jeanne d'Arc au bûcher*', *Slovenska Hudba*, 8 (1969), 320 +.
—. 'Ansermet's own valedictory', *SR*, 27 December 1969, 50.
—. 'Brno — *Jeanne d'Arc au bûcher*', *HR*, 2 (1970), 49-50.
—. 'Review of L. Rappaport's *Artur Onegger*', *Ruch Muzyczny*, 13 (1970), 13.
—. '*Nicolas de Flue* (Geneva)', *SM*, 4 (1971), 234.

SECTION B: Signed.

Abendroth, Walter, 'Die Kraft der Aussage', *Die Zeit*, 13 March 1952.
Abonyi-Arany, M., 'Rozsa Miklos emlekezese Honeggerre', *Muzsika*, April 1967, 44-45.
Abrashev, B., 'A.O.i negovati kniga *Az sum Kompozitor*', *Bulgarska Muzika*, 7 (1967), 45-47.
Abravanel, Claude, 'Un manuscrit d'A.H. à Jérusalem [*Six poésies de Jean Cocteau*]', *SM*, CXI, 5 Sept.-Oct. (1971), 267-71.
Ackere, Jules E. van., 'Muziek, menselijk document', *Vlaanderen* XXVIII/168 (January-February 1979), 1-40.
Allorto. R., 'Cantania [*Jeanne d'Arc au bûcher*]', *Musici Oggi*, March 1960, 137.

Andreae, Volkmar, Contribution to 'Hommage à A.H.', *SM*, March 1952, 87.
Ansermet, Ernest, 'Hommage à A.H.', *NZZ*, 18 December 1955, 3.
Aprahamian, Felix, 'A.H.'s *Joan*', *MM*, February 1971, 20-21.
Ardoin, J., '*Judith* sung by Dessoff Choirs', *MA*, January 1961, 55 +.
Arundell, Denis, '*King David*', *Listener*, 6 January 1966, 40.
Aubin, Tony, 'Théâtre des Bouffes-Parisiens:— *Les aventures du roi Pausole*', *LM*, 26 December 1930, 551-52.
Auric, Georges, '*Judith*', *LM*, 5 March 1926, 114.
Obituary in 'Hommage à A. H.', *Combat*, 29 November 1955, 2.
Obituary in 'Hommage à A.H.', *Melos*, January 1956, 1-11.
Austin, William 'Neue Musik' (Ger. trans. by T.M. Höpfner) *Epochen der Musikgeschichte in Einzeldarstellungen* (1974), 386-461.

Bachler, Karl, 'An Honeggers Grab', *NZM*, November 1956, 617-18.
Bachmann, C.H., 'Die Operette ist doch nicht tot [*Les aventures du roi Pausole*]', *NZM*, April 1955, 246.
'*Antigone* gegen *Œdipus*', *Musica*, March 1961, 129-30.
Baker, Helen A., 'Arthur Honegger and *King David*', *Amor Artis Bulletin* VII/1 (January 1968), 1-2; 10-12.
Bárdos, Lajos, 'A "négy betü" történetéből', *Parlando XXI/9 (September 1979), 7-14.*
Barraque, Jean, 'A.H.: *Symphonie pour cordes* (1941)', *Guide du concert*, 13 May 1955.
Bathori, Jane, 'Les musiciens que j'ai connus', *Journal of the British Institute of Recorded Sound*, 15 (July 1964), 240-43.
Baud-Bovy, Samuel, 'A.H. et la musique religieuse', *FMS*, 7 (September 1952), 200.
Beck, Conrad, Contribution to 'Hommage à A.H.', *SM*, March 1952, 87.
Obituary in 'Hommage à A.H.', *Melos*, January 1956, 1-11.
Bedat de Monlaur, P., 'En témoignage de la reconnaissance gasconne à A.H.', *Bulletin de la Société archéologique, historique, littéraire et scientifique du Gers*, 1 (1956), 76-77.
Béha, Paul-Emile, 'Essai d'explication de la *Symphonie n° 5* dite *Di tre re*', *FMS*, 7 (September 1952), 210.
Bellas, Jacqueline, 'Apollinaire devant la musique et les musiciens', *Revue des lettres modernes*, 217-22 (1969), 114-40.
Belvianes, Marcel, '*L'Aiglon* à l'Opéra', *LM*, 10 September 1937, 241-42.
Benoit, F., 'A respeito de material moderno de linguagem do compositor', *Arte Musical*, 13-14 (1961), 444-46.
Béraud, Henri, 'Théâtre: *Les mariés de la Tour Eiffel*, musique des Six', *MF*, 15 July 1921, 449-51.
Berger, A., '*King David* and Reforestation', *SR*, 29 March 1952, 48.
'A.H.: *Symphony No. 5*', *MQ*, July 1954, 463-65.
Bernard, Robert, '*L'Aiglon*', *RM*, April 1937, 218-22.
'Une lettre ouverte à A.H.', *IM*, 2 October 1942, 46-47.
Berten, Waltern, 'Der Musikdramatiker A.H.', *Neue Musik Zeitung*, 11 (1928), 348-55.
Berthelot, R., 'Une lettre ouverte à A.H.', *IM*, 10 October 1941, 133-34.
Berthoin, Jean, See 'various'.
Bertrand, Paul, '*Judith*', *LM*, 21 August 1925, 355-57.
'*Le cantique des cantiques*, *LM*, 11 February 1938, 34-35.
'*Les petites Cardinal*', *LM*, 18 February 1938, 46-47.
Bex, Maurice, '*Le roi David*', *Revue hebdomadaire*, 5 October 1921, 365-68.
'*Skating Rink*', *Revue hebdomadaire*, 25 February 1922, 500-2.
'A.H.' *Revue Rhénane*, October 1922, 40-41.
Bianconi, Lorenzo, 'Review of Leo Schrade's *De Scientia musicae studia atque orationes*', *Nouva Revista Musica Italiana*, 4 (July-August 1968), 775-77.
Binet, Jean, Contribution to 'Hommage à A.H.', *SM*, March 1952, 87.

Boepple, Paul, 'Mézières memories', *NYT* , 30 April 1961, Section 2, 11.
Boll, A., Obituary, *Revue d'histoire du théâtre*, 1 (1956).
Bonavia, F., 'The future of music according to A.H.', *MT*, May 1928, 413-14.
Boulez, Pierre, Obituary in 'Hommage à A.H.', *Melos*, January 1956, 1-11.
'A.H.', *Cahiers de la Compagnie Madeleine Renauld-Jean Louis Barrault*, 15 (1956).
Bourgeois, Pierre, Obituary in 'Hommage à A.H.', *Combat*, 29 November 1955, 2.
Braneo, L. de Freitas, 'Os Seis', *Revista do Conservatorio Nacional de Musica*, October 1921, 1-5.
Bright, R., 'New Mexico — the 6th Season [*Jeanne d'Arc au bûcher*]', *MA*, October 1962, 19.
Brilliant, Maurice, 'Cinq minutes au café après *Le roi David*', *La Vie catholique*, 30 January 1925.
Bronnenmeyer, W., 'Auswege der Oper [*Judith*]', *Opern Welt*, November 1967, 44.
Browne, A.G., 'A Study of A.H.', *ML*, October 1929, 372-77.
Bruyr, José, 'De *Saint-Philippe de Néri* à *Sainte Jeanne au bûcher*', *JMF*, May 1948, 47-51.
'A.H. tel que je le connais', *FMS*, 7 (September 1952), 206.
'L'Enregistrement intégral du *roi David* d'A.H.', *Disques*, May-June 1953, 352-53.
Obituary, *Disques*, December 1955, 896-97.
'Dans le souvenir d'A.H. du *roi David* à *Jeanne d'Arc au bûcher*', RMSR, 1 June 1964, 7-8.
'A.H. mon ami', *Musica (Chaix)*, November 1965, 7-11.
Bundi, Gian, '*König-David*', *Der Bund*, 15 December 1925.
'Festliche Musiktage in Solothurn — A.H.', *Der Bund*, 4 May 1931.
Burkat, L., 'Current Chronicle — Boston: A.H.'s 60th anniversary', *MQ*, January 1952, 118-23.
'A.H.: *Symphony no. 2*', *MQ*, January 1955, 122-25.
Burkhard, Willy, Contribution to 'Hommage à A.H.', *SM*, March 1952, 87.

Chailley, Jacques, Obituary in 'Hommage à A.H.', *Combat*, 29 November 1955, 2.
'A.H. et le théâtre', *Revue d'histoire du théâtre*, 1 (1956), 7-14.
Chalupt, René, 'A.H.', *RM*, January 1922, 42-52.
Chamfray, Claude, 'Pour le 60ᵉ Anniversaire de Darius Milhaud et A.H. [*La danse des morts*)', *RM*, 212 (1952), 53-54.
Chamlee, R.M., 'Of Opera [*Jeanne d'Arc au bûcher*]', *Music of the West*, February 1955, 5 +.
Chapallaz, Gilbert, 'A.H. et la musique de cinéma', *FMS*, 7 (September 1952), 208.
Chosy, F., '*Judith*', *Le courrier musical*, 1 July 1925.
Cizik, V., '*Kral David* v Bratislave', *HR*, 4 (1968), 103.
Cocteau, Jean, 'Die Gruppe der Sechs', *Melos*, January 1954, 1-3.
Obituary in 'Hommage à A.H.', *Combat*, 29 November 1955, 2.
See 'various'.
Obituary in 'Hommage à A.H.', *Melos*, January 1956, 1-11.
Coeuroy, André, 'Un musicien moderne: A.H.', *Revue hebdomadaire*, 4 (1928), 66-72.
'*Pacific 231*: Projection musicale', *Art et Décoration*, November 1932, 341-43.
'La musique: Arthur's', *Gringoire*, 5 October 1934.
'Le tandem Honegger — Ibert', *Dissonances*, 2 (February 1938), 42-44.
Collaer, Paul 'Een kunstenaarshuis langs de Auwegemvaart', *Studia Mechliniensia. Bijdragen aangeboden aan Dr Henry Joosen ter gelegenheid van zijn 65ste verjaardag LXXIX* (1976), 471-75.
Collet, Henri, 'Un livre de Rimsky et un livre de Cocteau — Les Cinq Russes, Les Six Français et Erik Satie, *Comœdia*, 16 January 1920, 2.
'Les Six Français', *Comœdia*, 23 January 1920, 2.
Comuzio, Ermanno, 'A.H. e il cinema', *Cinema*, 1955, 1039-40.
Copland, Aaron, Obituary in 'Hommage à A.H.', *Melos*, January 1956, 1-11.

Coty, René, (Le Président de la République), Obituary in 'Hommage à A.H.', *Combat*, 29 November 1955, 2.
Cvetko, Dragotin, 'Iz korespondence Slavku Ostercu', *Muzikol Zbornik* XI (1975), 82-92.

Dale, S.S., 'Contemporary Cello Concerti — No. 17 Arthur Honegger', *Strad*, March 1974, 655-61.
Dallapiccola, Luigi, Obituary in 'Hommage à A.H.', *Melos*, January 1956, 1-11.
Dami, Aldo, 'A.H. et la réaction anti-impressioniste', *Neue Schweizer Rundschau*, 20, No. 1 (1927), 49-54.
Daniel, O., 'Louisville special-recording of *Suite archaïque*', *SR*, 14 April 1962, 31.
David, Hans, 'A.H.,'s *König David*', *Melos*, February 1927, 83-85.
'Umschau. Berliner Konzerte 1927 [*Concertino* for piano and orchestra], *Melos*, July 1927, 276-77.
'Review of Willy Tappolet's *A.H.*', *SM*, 15 December 1933, 785-86.
Davies, M.E., 'A review of the Paris Season', *MO*, September 1961, 737.
Delange, R., 'Paris fête Milhaud et A.H.', *Vie musicale*, March 1952, 15.
'A.H. le constructeur', *France Illustration*, 15 March 1952, 258.
Delannoy, Marcel, 'Bach et les musiciens d'aujourd'hui', *RIM*, 8 (1950), 181-83.
Demarquez, S., '*Sémiramis* d'A.H.', *RM*, June 1934, 45-46.
'Aux Bouffes Parisiens — *Les petites Cardinal*', *RM*, March 1938, 215-16.
'Paris revives d'Indy's stage works on centenary [*Suite archaïque*]', *MC*, 1 February 1952, 8.
'Paris honours Milhaud and A.H. at 60', *MC*, 1 May 1952, 5.
Demuth, Norman, Obituary, *MO*, February 1956, 275 and 277.
Denizeau, H., 'Création en France de l'*Antigone* de Cocteau et Honegger', *Appogiature*, 15 January, 1931, 11-15.
'La création des *Cris du monde* d'A.H.', *Appogiature*, May 1931, 114-27.
Douël, J., 'Une lettre ouverte à A.H.', *IM*, 28 August 1942, 2.
Douël, M., 'A.H.', *Chesterian*, 58 (November 1926)), 37-40.
Dumesnil, René, '*Jeanne au bûcher*', *MF*, 1 July — 1 August 1939, 194-99.
'Musique' [*Nicolas de Flue* d'A.H.], *MF*, CCCXVII (January-April 1953), 517-20.
See 'various'.
'Adieu à A.H.', *Musica* (Paris), January 1956.
Durey, Louis, 'Les Six', *Créer*, June 1922.
Durgin, C., 'A.H. *Symphony* première given by Boston S.O. [*5th*]', *MA*, 1 April 1951, 19.

Egk, Werner, Obituary in 'Hommage à A.H.', *Melos*, January 1956, 1-11.
Egli, Ernst, 'A.H.'s männliche Ahnen', *SM*, May-June 1962, 173-74.
Ehinger, Hans, 'Basel. A.H.'s *La danse des morts*', *NZZ*, 1 April 1940, 100. Also in *SM*, 80 (1940), 100.
'A.H.', *NZM*, February 1956, 74-76.
'Basle A.H. Festival', *NZM*, July-August 1962, 363-64.
'A.H. als Musikdramatiker', *NZM*, November 1962, 485-92.
Einem, Gottfried von, Obituary in 'Hommage à A.H.', *Melos*, January 1956, 1-11.
Elvin, René, 'The Music of A.H.', *MM*, December 1952, 7.
Epstein, Peter, 'A.H.'s *Judith*', *Melos*, November 1929, 497-500.
Evans, Edwin, 'The life story of *King David*', *Radio Times*, 8 February 1935, 12.
Ewen, David, 'The Futuristic music of A.H. and Korngold', *Jewish Tribune*, 2 December 1927, 18-19.

Fähnrich, Hermann, 'Music in the letters of Paul Valéry', *ML* LV/1 (January 1974), 48-60.
Faller, Charles, 'Suisse: *Nicolas de Flue*,' *RM*, July 1939, 63-65.
'Les oratorios d'A.H.', *FMS*, 7 (September 1952), 202.
Fauchois, René, See 'various'.

Favart, R., 'Du nouveau sur les scènes lyriques [*Le roi David*]', *Musica (Chaix)*, January 1961, 22-23.
Favre, Max, 'A. H.'s *Sinfonien*', *Der Bund*, 10 March 1952.
Feschotte, Jacques, 'A.H. et les explorateurs du ciel', *SM*, March-April 1966, 89-91.
Fiechtner, H.A., 'Die Uberwindung des Impressionismus', *OM*, April 1962, 165-74.
Fierz-Bantli, G., 'Helvetische Diskothek', *Musica Schallplatte*, 4 (1959), 73-77.
Fischer, Kurt von, 'A.H. erstes veröffentlichtes Lied aus dem Jahre 1914', *Vetter Festschrift*, 383-88.
'A.H.' in 'Die Ernte', Schweizer Jahrbuch 1966, 158-79.
'A.H.'s *Pacific 231* — Zum Problem des Realismus in der Musik', in *Festschrift Hans Conradin* (Bern, 1983), 227-32.
Fischer, M.M., 'A.H. work in stage première [*Jeanne d'Arc au bûcher*]', *MA*, 15 November 1954, 12.
Fortner, Wolfgang, Obituary in 'Hommage à A.H.', *Melos*, January 1956, 1-11.
Frankenstein, A., 'Mr. Honegger comes to America', *Review of Reviews*, January 1929, 158.
Friedland, Martin, 'A.H.: *Antigone*, *Der siegreiche Horatier*', *Allgemeine Musikzeitung*, 55 (1928), 64-65.
Frissard, Claude, 'Les dix meilleurs disques d'A.H.', *Musica* (*Paris*), September 1957, 18-22.

Gabeaud, A., '*Jeanne d'Arc au bûcher*', *L'Education musicale*, 37-39 (1957), 14-17, 10-11, 6-7.
Gagnebin, H., '*Judith* au Théâtre de Mézières', *Le Monde musical*, August 1925, 278.
Gaillard, P.-André, '*La danse des morts* d'A.H.', *FMS*, 7 (September 1952), 225.
Gauthier, André, 'La *V^{e} symphonie* d'A.H.', *RIM*, 11 (1951), 501-3.
Gavoty, Bernard, 'Les opinions d'A.H.', *Formes et couleurs*, 2 (February 1948).
'*La symphonie liturgique*', *JMF*, February 1948, 2-10.
'Du *roi David* à *Nicolas de Flue*', *Le Journal musical français*, 23 October 1952, 1 and 8.
'*Une cantate de Noël* d'A.H.', *Le Figaro*, 12 January 1954, 10.
'Dans l'intimité d'A.H.', *Le Figaro Littéraire*, 10 December 1955, 7.
George, André, 'Les Concerts. *Le roi David* d'A.H.', *RM*, 1 April 1924, 70-72.
'*Pacific 231* d'A.H.', *RM*, May 1924, 246-47.
'*Pâques à New York* par A.H.', *RM*, 1 May 1924, 250.
'A.H.', *Bibliothèque universelle et La Revue de Genève*, December 1924, 663-74.
'A.H.', *Le Monde musical*, February 1926, 9-10.
'A.H. — *Antigone*', *Les Nouvelles littéraires*, 21 January 1928, 11.
'A.H.'s *Antigone*', *Chesterian*, 70 (April-May 1928), 190-92.
'A.H.', *Pro Musica*, 7 (June 1928), 4-12.
Gerbacht, Wolfram, 'A.H.'s *zweite Sinfonie*', *Melos*, May-June 1947, 221.
Ghéon, Henri, 'Au théâtre du Jorat: *Le roi David*', NRF, July-December 1921, 362-66.
Giegling, Frank, 'Der Begriff *Konzert* in der Barokmusik', *SM*, 1 November 1944, 381-88.
Godet, Robert, 'Suisse: La *Judith* d'A.H.', *RM*, 1 August 1925, 161-69.
Goldbeck, Fred, 'La *Symphonie* [*n° 1*] d'A.H.', *RM*, October 1931, 243-45.
'Honegger oder der Triumph der Nativität', *Die Musik*, November 1932, 116-20.
'A.H.: *Sonatine pour violon et violoncelle*', *RM*, January 1933, 53-54.
'A.H. *IIe quatuor*', *RM*, April 1937, 197-98.
Goldman, R.F., '*Jeanne d'Arc au bûcher*', *MQ*, October 1953, 656-57.
Goléa, Antoine, 'H. ou le pouvoir de synthèse', *FMS*, 7 (September 1952), 195.
'Musikalischer Herbst [*Le roi David*]', *NZM*, January 1961, 31.
'Une belle reprise à l'Opéra — *Antigone* d'A.H.', *Le Journal musical français*, 157 (19 May 1967).
'Vu et entendu [*Jeanne d'Arc au bûcher*], *Le Journal musical français*, 191 (April 1970), 19-20.

Haeusler, R., 'Basle [*Horace Victorieux*]', SM, 2 (1969), 91.
Hanna, James, 'Review of *I am a Composer*', *Journal of Research in Music Education*, XV, No. 1 (Spring 1967), 95-96.
Harrison, J.S., 'The New York Music Scene [*Jeanne d'Arc au bûcher*], *MA*, November 1963, 25.
Hartmann, Karl Amadeus, Obituary in 'Hommage à A.H.', *Melos*, January 1956, 1-11.
Hell, H., 'Trois étapes du théâtre lyrique [*Antigone*]', *RM*, February 1952, 3-9.
Helm, E., 'A.H. 1892-1955', *SR*, 31 December 1955, 39.
'Donaneschingen Festival pays tribute to A.H.', *MA*, 15 December 1956, 11.
Helman, H., 'From an organist's notebook', *MO*, January 1956, 239.
Henahan, D.J., 'Choral Performances [*Jeanne d'Arc au bûcher*], *American Choral Review*, 4 (1967), 51-52.
Henze, Hans Werner, Obituary in 'Hommage à A.H.', *Melos*, January 1956, 1-11.
Herold, F., 'Mel Honegger pravdu? *C durova* notace a persperktivy', *HR*, 6 (1965), 246.
Hill, E.B., 'Musical Boston in the Gay 90's', *Etude*, April 1949, 229 +.
Hillen, C.W., 'Groupe des Six vijftig jaar', *MeM*, February 1970, 40-43.
Hirsch, Nicole, 'A.H., un romantique contemporain', *Toute la Danse*, January 1956, 24.
Hoérée, Arthur, '*Le roi David*, psaume dramatique de René Morax, musique d'A.H.', *Beaux-Arts*, 1 May 1924, 140-41.
'A.H.', *Eolus*, January 1926, 5-13.
'Opéra: Festival Honegger', *Beaux-Arts*, 15 April 1926, 126.
'A.H. et les locomotives', *RP*, August 1927, 347-51.
'*Antigone*', *Chantecler*, 14 January 1928.
'*Antigone*', *Beaux-Arts*, 1 February 1928, 47-48.
'*Antigone* à la Monnaie de Bruxelles', *La Revue européene*, March 1928, 315-20.
'Les Concerts: *Judith*', *RM*, 1 May 1928, 197-99.
'Salle Pleyel — Première de *Judith* au Festival Honegger', *Beaux-Arts*, 15 July 1928, 220-21.
'*Judith*', *La Revue européene*, 1, No. 9 (1928), 968-71.
'*Rugby - Mouvement symphonique* par A.H.', *Beaux - Arts*, 1 December 1928, 316-17.
'A.H., musicien populaire', *RM*, January 1929, 189-99.
'Une visite à A.H.. Impressions d'Amérique et Projets', *Musique*, 11-12 (15 September 1929), 1029-36. Also in *SM*, 1 September 1929, 581-87.
'A.H., folk musician (translated by Felix Goodwin)', *Sackbut*, 10 (November 1929), 90-96.
'*Le roi David* et la révolution', *SM*, June 1931, 459-61.
'*Amphion*, mélodrame — ce qu'en dit Paul Valéry', *Candide*, 308 (25 June 1931).
'Honegger, l'optimiste', *Candide*, 437 (28 July 1932), 10.
(with A.H.) 'Particularités sonores du film *Rapt*', *RM*, December 1934, 88-91.
'*Les misérables*, suite par A.H.', *RM*, February 1935, 131-32.
'*Prélude, Arioso, Fughetta* par A.H.', *RM*, December 1936, 446-47.
'*Troisième quatuor à cordes* par A.H.', *RM*, July-August 1938, 50-52.
'*La danse des morts*', *IM*, 7 February 1941, 304.
'A.H.', *IM*, 1 July 1942, 1009-10.
'*Antigone*', *IM*, 3 February 1943, 197.
Obituary in 'Hommage à A.H.', *Combat*, 29 November 1955, 2.
Hudec, V., 'Orlik v Olomouci [*L'Aiglon*]', *HR*, 7 (1968), 198.
Hughes, A., 'Les Six a generation later — their spirit endures', *MA*, 15 February 1954, 12 and 128.
'A.H., death was often his theme', *MA*, 1 January 1956, 7.
Hughes Jones, L., 'New Records [*Une cantate de Noël*]', *MM*, December 1962.
Hugli, P., 'Mézières: *Le roi David*', *SM*, 4 (1971), 238.

Ibert, Jacques, Obituary in 'Hommage à A.H.', *Combat*, 29 November 1955, 2.
See 'various'.
Obituary in 'Hommage à A.H.', *Melos*, January 1956, 1-11.

Inghelbrecht, D-E., '*Nitchevo*', *RM*, November-December 1946, 11-14.

Jacobson, B., 'Festival Orchestra: Dunn, *Le dit des jeux du monde*', *Hi Fi/Musical America*, May 1967, 16-17.
Jasińska, Danuta, '*Król David* Arthura Honeggera', *Muzyka* XXIV/2 (1979), 79-94.
Jaton, Henri, 'Deux instants dans la production d'A.H.', *FMS*, 7 (September 1952), 213.
Jaubert, Maurice, '*Judith*', *RP*, March 1926, 15-16.
Jirko, I., 'A.H.', *HR*, 22 (1960), 928-29.
Joachim, H., 'Französische Operette und biblisches Festspiel in Hamburg [*Les aventures du roi Pausole*]', *Melos*, May 1955, 141-42.
Jural, A., Obituary, *Canon*, September 1956, 46-47.
Jurik, M., '*Jana z Arcu* v Bratislave', *HR*, 6 (1965), 246.

Kalošina, Galina, 'The primacy of the sonata principle in respect to the symphonic music of A.H.' in *Čerty sonatnogo formoobrazovanija, XXXVI,* (Gosudarstvennyj muzykal'no-pedagogičeskij institut imeni Gnesinyh, Moscow, 1978).
'Principles of symphonism in the large vocal works of A.H.' in *Teoretičeskie voprosy vokal'noj muzyki*, compiled by Nikolaj Tiftikidi (Gosudarstvennyj muzykal'noj-pedagogičeskij institut imeni Gnesinyh, Moscow, 1979).
Kammerer, R., 'Henryk Szeryng soloist with the Boston S.O. [*Symphonie* [*n° 1*]]', *MA*, May 1961, 40.
Kanski, J., 'Rebuilding the Warsaw Opera [*Judith*]', *Opera*, July 1962, 456-57.
Kerman, Joseph, 'San Francisco 1954 [*Jeanne d'Arc au bûcher*]', *Opera News*, 11 November 1954, 6.
Klimovitsky, A., 'Prem'era *Tret'ey sinfonii* Oneggera [*Symphonie liturgique* [*n° 3*] première], *SKM*, January 1962, 104.
Koch, G.R., 'A.H.-Ibert: *Junger Adler* [*L'Aiglon*]', *Musica*, 3 (1968), 217-18.
Kocknitzky, Leo, '*Le quatorze juillet*', *RM*, July-August 1936, 42.
Kolodin, I., '*King David*', *SR*, 3 May 1952, 33.
Koopman, John, 'Honegger as a song composer', *National Association of Teachers of Singing Bulletin*, (USA), XXXII/2 (December 1975) 12-14.
Koster, E., '*Johanna auf dem Scheiterhaufen* (Fernsehen, Köln)', *Musica*, May 1960, 300-1.
Kulz, Werner, '*Judith*', *Signale*, 39 (1928), 1108-9.

Lacloche, M., '*Le roi David*', *RPL*, 7 February 1925, 102-3.
Laloy, Louis, '*L'Aiglon*', *Revue des deux mondes*, 15 April 1937, 944-46.
Lambert, Constant, 'Railway Music', *Nation*, 16 August 1930, 620-21.
Landormy, Paul, 'Le Groupe des Six', *Bibliothèque universelle et La Revue de Genève*, September 1921, 393-409.
'A.H.', *La Victoire*, 20 September 1920.
'A.H. (translated by Fred Rothwell)', *MT*, 1 September 1929, 789-91.
Lapommerage, P. de, 'Théâtre des Champs-Elysées. [Ballets Suédois-*Skating Rink*]', *LM*, 27 January 1922, 35-36.
Latzko, Ernst, 'A.H.: *Judith*', *Melos*, April 1928, 201-2.
Ledesma, O.W., 'Association Wagneriana [*Jeanne d'Arc au bûcher*]', *Buenos Aires Musical*, 434 (1971), 2.
Lewinski, W.E. von, 'Darmstadt Pathetisches Pasticcio {*L'Aiglon*]', *Opern Welt*, May 1968, 42.
'Ein Pasticcio am Napoleons Sohn in Darmstadt', *Melos*, June 1968, 254-55.
Lichtenhahn, Ernst, 'Aus Paul Sachers Briefwechsel mit Arthur Honegger', *ÖM*, XXXI/4-5 (April-May 1976), 208-15.
Lindberger, Örjan, '*Dödsdansen*. Ett oratorium om köttets uppståndelse', *Nutida Musik*, 3, No. 5 (1959-60), 4-6.

Lindlar, Heinrich, 'A.H. zwischen *Pacific* und *Monopartita*', *Melos*, June 1954, 165-68.
'Universalist und Humanist', *Melos*, 1956, 113-15. Also in *Musica*, February 1956, 113-15.
Lockspeiser, E., 'A.H.', *Chesterian*, 185 (Winter 1956), 61-65.
'A composer's memoirs', *MT*, 869-70.
Lonchampt, Jacques, '*La quatrième symphonie* d'A.H.', *Images Musicales*, 29 October 1948, 4.
'*La 5ᵉ symphonie di tre re* d'A.H.', *JMF*, June 1951.
Lubin, E., 'A.H.'s *Antigone*', *NYT*, 9 March 1952, Section 2, 7.
Luttwitz, H., 'Düsseldorf: Oratorien auf der Szene von Dallapiccola und A.H.', *NZM*, July-August 1966, 284-86.
'Dallapiccola's *Hiob* und A.H.'s *Judith* in Düsseldorf', *Das Orchester*, September 1966, 346-48.

Machabey, A., 'A.H. et la musique française', *IM*, 3 October 1941. 98-99.
Macudzinski, R., 'Honegger ma pravdu! (Graficka klavirna Skola)', *Slovenska Hudba*, 4 (1965), 170-71.
Maire, Simone, 'La musique moderne au studio. Avec les auteurs du film *Rapt*', *Les Beaux Arts*, 8 June 1934, 5-6.
Malipiero, Francesco, Obituary in 'Hommage à A.H.', *Melos*, January 1956, 1-11.
Maritain, Jacques, '*Le roi David* au Jorat', *Revue des Jeunes*, 10 August 1921, 332-36.
Marnold, Jean, 'Concerts Koussevitsky: A.H. *Pacific 231*; A.H. *Le roi David*', *MF*, 625 (1 July 1924), 235-40.
'*Antigone*', *MF*, 720 (15 June 1928), 703-5.
Marot, André, 'Le groupe des six: 1918-1922', *Le Carnet critique*, June 1922, 70-75.
Martin, Frank, Contribution to 'Hommage à A.H.', *SM*, March 1952, 87.
Obituary in 'Hommage à A.H.', *Melos*, January 1956, 1-11.
Mason E., 'Music in Concert: Holst and Honegger [*Le roi David*]', *Choir*, February 1962, 29.
Mauriac, F., 'En marge de la *Symphonie liturgique* [*n° 3*]', *Le Figaro*, 21 August 1948, 1.
Maw, Nicolas, 'Review of *I am a Composer*', *Tempo*, 79 (Winter 1966-67), 24-25.
McCabe, N., 'Bournemouth [*Symphonie liturgique* [*n° 3*]]', *MT*, May 1967, 442.
Mélitz, Leo, 'A.H.', *Die Musik*, January 1927, 249-53.
'A.H.', *SMB*, 1 February 1927, 40-45.
'L'*Antigone* d'A.H.', *RM*, October 1927, 242-48.
'A.H.', *Der Scheinwerfer*, January 1928, 2-5.
Mersmann, Hans, 'Neue Werke von A.H.', *Melos*, May 1928, 242-45.
Messiaen, Olivier, Obituary in 'Hommage à A.H.', *Melos*, January 1956, 1-11.
Meyer, Alfred H., 'A.H.'s new symphony given Boston première', *MA*, 25 February 1931, 1 and 26.
Meyer, Louis, 'Holland: *Le roi David* à Rotterdam', *RM*, 1 July 1925, 81-82.
Meylan, Pierre, 'Listes des œuvres d'A.H., arrêtés au 1ᵉʳ septembre 1952', *FMS*, 7 (September 1952), 219.
'Renaissance de l'opéra *Judith* d'A.H.', *RMSR*, 5 (1968), 7-8 +.
'Une partition peu connue d'A.H. — *Charles le Téméraire* (1944)', *RMSR*, 5 (1969), 2-5.
Mieg, Peter, 'Zum Tod von A.H.', *SMB*, January 1956, 1-4.
Milhaud, Darius, 'A.H.', *Chesterian*, 19 (December 1921), 65-69.
'Einige kleine Aufklärungen', *Anbruchs*, May 1922, 150-52.
Obituary in 'Hommage à A.H.', *Combat*, 29 November 1955, 2.
'Honegger, mon ami', *Le Figaro Littéraire*, 3 December 1955, 1.
Obituary in 'Hommage à A.H.', *Melos*, January 1956, 1-11.
'Min ven Honegger', *Dansk Musiktidsskrift*, February 1956, 2.
Mitchell, D., 'London Music [*Symphonie liturgique* [*n° 3*]]', *MT*, April 1955, 209-10.
Monnikendam, Marius, 'A.H.', *Musikale Ommegang*, 1943, 525-28.

Mooser, R. Aloys, 'Après la première du *roi David*, *La Suisse*, 13 June 1921, 5.
'La création de *La belle de Moudon*', *La Suisse*, 1 June 1931.
'*Le mouvement symphonique n° 3* d'A.H.', *Dissonances*, November 1933, 310-15.
'Musique et musiciens suisses à l'étranger', *Dissonances*, May 1936, 147-48.
'*Jeanne d'Arc au bûcher*', *Dissonances*, 5 (May 1938), 129-34.
'*Nicolas de Flue*', *Dissonances*, 7-8 (November-December 1940), 191-95.
'*La deuxième symphonie* de A.H.', *Dissonances*, 11-12 (November-December 1942), 161-66.
'*Monopartita*', *La Suisse*, 19 June 1951.
Morax, René, 'La première d'*Antigone*', *La Gazette de Lausanne*, 5 January 1928.
'Souvenirs de la première du *Roi David*, *RMSR*, 2 (1968), 2-4.
Moreaux, Serge, '*Jeanne d'Arc au bûcher*', *RM*, July 1939, 28-34.
Morris, Léon, 'Le Vieux-Colombier:— *Saül*, drame en cinq actes d'André Gide', *LM*, 23 June 1922, 274-75.
Müller, Hans-Peter, 'Review of *2nd Symphony* (Eterna 820 570)', *Musik und Gesellschaft*, 17, No. 1 (January 1967), 59.
Müllner, Hans, 'Honeggertage in Essen: Deutsche Uraufführung der Oper *Antigone*', *Signale*, 6 (1928), 169-72.
Münch, Fritz, Funeral Oration, *Positions Lutheriennes*, 1 (1956), 3-9.
See 'various'.
Müry, A., 'Musikschaffen in der deutschen Schweiz', *Musica*, January-April 1959, 442.
Myszowski, Eurgeniusz, 'Problems of rendering symphonic vocal-instrumental form in the compositions of A.H., using as an example his *Antigone*' in Ogólnopolska Sesja Naukowa (VII) na temat: muzyka oratoryjna i kantatowa w aspekcie praktyki wykonawczej (2-5 września 1980 roku) (Wroclaw, Państwowa Wyższa Szkoła, Muzycznzyczna we Wrocławiu, 1981).

Navratil, M., '*Jana na Hranici* v Ostrava', *HR*, 7 (1968), 236.
Nestiev, Izrail V., 'In contact with contemporaries', *SKM* XXXI/4 (April 1967), 77-85.
'Sergei Prokofiev and his contemporaries (translated by Erzsébet Fonó)', *Magyarzene*, (VIII/5 November 1967), 487-500.
Niggli, M., 'A.H.'s *Antigone*', *NZZ*, 4 January 1928, 1.
Nollier, Jean, Obituary in 'Hommage à A.H.', *Combat*, 29 November 1955, 2.
Nölter, W., 'Germany: Hamburg [*Les aventures du roi Pausole*]', Opera, August 1955, 521.
Nystroem, Gösta, 'A.H.', *Göteborgs Handels Och Sjöfarts — Tidning*, 4 December 1933, 7.

Œsech. H., 'Basel ehrt A.H. [Basle A.H. Festival]', *Melos*, September 1962, 300-1.
Onnen, F., 'Musiek in Parijs: A.H.'s *Chant de Nigamon*', *MeM*, February 1954, 56-58.
Oswald, Contribution to 'Hommage à A.H.', *SM*, March 1952, 87.
Otto, Eberhadt, 'A.H. — Mensch unter Menschen zu seinem 60', *NZM*, March 1952, 155-56.

Paap, W., '*La danse des morts*', *MeM*, March 1951, 88-90.
Obituary, *MeM*, January 1956, 2-5.
Palmer, C., 'Religious music of A.H.', *Church Music*, 33 (1969), 8-9.
Pannain, Guideo, 'A.H.', *La Rassegna Musicale*, 1928, 467-78.
Parente, Alfredo, '*Giovanna*', *La Scala*, 53 (April 1954), 47-51.
Pauli, H., 'Bara Staden är Verklig; Schweiziska tonsättare i vaart aarhundrade', *Musikrevy*, 2-3 (1963), 62-63.
Payne, Anthony, 'A.H. and problems of communication', *Listener*, 15 June 1967, 800.
Pendelton, E., '*Jeanne d'Arc au bûcher*', *MA*, February 1921, 120.
'Paris plays A.H. to mark him as 60', *MA*, June 1952, 7 +.
'New A.H. Choral Composition [*Une cantate de Noël*]', *MA*, 1 February 1954, 23.

Pestalozza, Luigi, 'Honegger si incontra con Gance in una locomotiva del 1922', *Cinema*, 1951, 133-34.
Petrassi, Goffredo, Obituary in 'Hommage à A.H.', *Melos*, January 1956, 1-11.
Petrov, Stojan, 'Ljubomir Pipkov i revoljucionnaja bor'ba', *SKM* 9 (September 1975), 134-37.
Philips, H.E., 'New York [*Antigone*]', *Opera News*, 14 June 1969, 23.
Piel, Emma, 'A.H. en Belgique', *FMS*, 7 (September 1952), 216.
Pilati, Mario, '*Antigone* di A.H.', *Bolletino bibliografico musicale*, February 1928, 13-20.
Porter, Andrew, '*L'Aiglon*', *London Music*, March 1953, 28-30.
Poulenc, Francis, Obituary in 'Hommage à A.H.', *Melos*, January 1956, 1-11.
'A propos d'une lettre d'A.H.', *SM*, May-June 1962, 160-61.
Prieberg, Fred, K., 'A.H.'s elektronisches Experiment', *Melos*, January 1956, 20-22.
Prunières, Henry, 'A.H.', *Melos*, November 1924, 211-16.
'A.H.', *Il Pianoforte*, April 1925, 118-21.
'*Judith* d'A.H. à Monte Carlo', *RM*, 1 March 1926, 260-64.
'A.H's *Judith*', *Modern Music*, 3, No. 4 (May-June 1926), 30-33.
'*Antigone*, tragédie musicale d'A.H. et Jean Cocteau', *RM*, 1 February 1928, 59-61.
'*Rugby* d'A.H.', *R.M*, 1 November 1928, 53-54.
'A.H.', *Anbruchs*, April-May 1930, 155-57.
'*Le roi Pausole* opéretta de Willemetz et A.H.', *RM*, January 1931, 60-61.
'*Amphion* d'A.H. et Paul Valéry', *RM*, October 1931, 239-43.
'*Radio-panoramique* d'A.H.', *RM*, November 1935, 276.
'*Le cantique des cantiques*', *RM*, February 1938, 137-38.

Rageot, G., '*L'Impératrice aux rochers*', *RPL*, 5 March 1927, 152-54.
Rappoport, L., 'O muzykal'nom yazyke Artur Onegger', *SKM*, August 1962, 52-56.
Rasin, V., 'Les Six and Jean Cocteau', *ML*, April 1957, 164-69.
Reger, Erik, '*Antigone* von A.H. zur Essener Première', *Anbruchs*, 2 February 1928, 62-65.
Reich, Willi, 'A.H. — Claudel: *Joan of Arc* acclaimed', *MA*, July 1938, 18.
'A.H.'s Bildnis im eigenen Wort', *Melos*, February 1952, 41-43.
'Werke von A.H. [*Une cantate de Noël*]', *Das Musikleben*, February 1954, 64.
'A.H.'s *König Pausole* in Zürich', *Melos*, March 1954, 90.
'A.H. and Sacher [Basle A.H. Festival]', *MA*, September 1962, 92 +.
Reimers, Lennart, 'Honeggers *Dödsdansmusik*', *Nutida Musik*, 3, No. 5 (1959-60), 7-11.
Reinhardt, M., 'Romain Rolland conseille A.H.', *SM*, 3 (1969), 144-46.
Riesenfeld, Paul, 'A.H.'s *Judith* im Breslau Stadttheater', *Signale*, 44 (1929), 1329-31.
Riisager, K., 'A.H.', *Dansk Musiktidsskrift*, 4 (1927), 70-75.
'A.H. à Copenhagen', *RM*, 1 December 1927.
Rivette, M., 'Honegger — from one to six', *Opera*, January 1950, 12-13 +.
Rochat, Jean, 'La prosodie dans la musique d'A.H.', *FMS*, January 1957.
Rognoni, Luigi, 'Due colloqui con A.H.', *L'Approdo Musicale*, 19-20 (1965), 131-140.
Rohlfing, A., 'Umschau. A.H.: *Antigone*', *Melos*, February 1928, 81-85.
Roland-Manuel, 'Œuvres nouvelles d'A.H.', *RM*, January 1921, 65-67.
'*Le roi David* d'A.H.', *RP*, April 1924, 13-16.
'Douze heures avec A.H.', *RP*, January 1925, 21-23.
'Opinions d'A.H.', *Dissonances*, 4 (April 1925) 84-87.
'Belgique: *Judith* à la Monnaie de Bruxelles', *RM*, 1 April 1927, 208-9.
'Bruxelles: La première d'*Antigone*', *LM*, 6 January 1928, 6-7.
'L'*Antigone* d'A.H.', *Musique*, 15 January 1928, 165-67.
'*Le soulier de satin* à la Comédie Française', *IM*, 18 February 1944, 197-98.
Rootźen, Kajsa, 'A.H. — Som biblisk tondiktare', *Credo*, 1952, 148-53.
Rosbaud, Hans, 'Zwei neue Orchesterwerke von A.H.: *Monopartita* und *5. Symphonie*', *Melos*, February 1952, 43-45.

Rosenwald H., 'Contemporary Music', *Musical News and Herald,* October 1950, 10-11.
'Hindemith — Honegger — Harris: return to a sense of values', *International Musical News*, November 1952, 9-10.
Rostand, Claude, 'A.H. — ein beispielhafter Humanist', *Melos*, February 1952, 36-40.
Roussel, Albert, 'Young French Composers', *Chesterian*, 2 (October 1919), 33-37.
Rubbra, Edmund, 'An Oratorio of the modern city', *Radio Times*, 15 December 1933, 805.
Rudén, Jan Olof, 'Sinfonia del mare av Gösta Nystroem. En otidsenlig (?) analys', *Kungl. Musikaliska akademien. Årsskrift* (1978), 25-51.
Rufer, Joseph, 'A.H.: *Cellosonate*', *Anbruchs*, August-September 1925, 429.
Ruppel, K.H., 'A.H. und das musikalische Theater', *Melos*, January 1956, 16-19.

Sabin, R., 'New York [*Jeanne d'Arc au bûcher*]', *Opera*, December 1963, 812.
Sacarrière, Obituary in 'Hommage à A.H.', *Combat*, 29 November 1955, 2.
Sacher, Paul, Contribution to 'Hommage à A.H.', *SM*, March 1952, 87.
'Hommage de l'interprète', *FMS*, 7 (September 1952), 194.
Saegel, P., '*L'Impératrice aux rochers*', *LM*, 25 February 1927, 85-86.
Salles, Roussy de, 'Premier concert donné par le 'Groupe des Six', *RM*, January 1921, 68.
de Salis, See 'various'.
Saltuper, Julija, 'Notes on Max Reger [Influence on Hindemith, Prokofiev, Szymanovski and Honegger]', *SKM*, 12 (December 1973), 94-101.
Samazeuilh, Gustave, 'Théâtre des Champs - Elysées (Spectacle — Concert: *Le bœuf sur le toit* — cadence par A.H.), *LM*, 12 March 1920, 107.
'*Jeanne d'Arc au bûcher*', *Les annales politiques et littéraires*, 25 June 1939, 633-34.
'Concerts de l'U.N.E.S.C.O. *Symphonie liturgique* [*n° 3*], *RM*, November-December 1946, 43-45.
'Hommage à A.H.', *FMS*, 7 (September 1952), 198.
Samson J., 'La musique en Provence: *Le roi David* et la musique religieuse', *RM*, 1 October 1925, 246-48.
Sargeant, W., 'Musical Events [*Jeanne d'Arc au bûcher*]', *New Yorker*, 12 October 1963, 121-22.
Sarnette, E., 'Basle A.H. Festival', *Musici e Radio*, May 1962, 147-48.
Satie, Erik, 'Les Six', *Les Feuilles Libres*, February 1922, 42-45.
Scherer, Marguerite, 'A.H.'s *Judith* at the Théâtre du Jorat', *Chesterian*, 48 (July 1925), 263-66.
Schild-Muntzinger, M., 'Visite au Maître Honegger', *Der Caecilienbote*, May, June, July 1930.
Schlœzer, Boris de, '*Amphion*', *NRF*, 215 (1931), 347-49.
'*Jeanne d'Arc au bûcher*', *NRF*, 310 (1939), 153-55.
'A.H.', *NRF*, 37 (1956), 164-65.
Schmitt, Florent, 'A propos du *roi David* d'A.H.', *La Revue de France*, 1 November 1924, 152-57.
Schmitt-Garra, H., 'Zeitloses Märchen und zeitnahe Tendenzoper im Prinzregententheater [*Les aventures du roi Pausole*]', *Melos*, October 1955, 296-97.
'Als die Opersächlich wurde', *NZM*, September 1961, 340-44.
Schneider, E., '*Le roi David* d'A.H.', *Le Monde Musical*, March 1924, 102.
Schneider, Max F., 'Von Nägeli bis A.H.', *Melos*, 1952, 233-36.
Schœck, Othmar, Contribution to 'Hommage à A.H.', *SM*, March 1952, 87.
Schuh, Willi 'Schweizer Komponisten: Konzert des Collegium Musicum Zürcher — A.H.'s *Concerto da camera*', *NZZ*, 9 May 1949.
'A.H.'s *Monopartita*', *SM*, 1 July 1951, 308.
'Contribution to 'Hommage à A.H.', *SM*, March 1952, 87.
'A.H.'s *Weihnachtskantate*', *NZZ*, 2 December 1953.

'A.H.'s *Weihnachtskantate*', *SM*, February 1954, 61-63.
'A.H.'s Universalität', *NZZ*, 18 December 1955, 3.
Sénéchaud, Marcel, 'Discographie complète des œuvres d'A.H.', *FMS*, 7 (September 1952), 227-28.
Silver, Hector, 'A.H.'s *Liturgische Sinfonie*', *Melos*, November 1947, 383-86.
Simmons, D., 'Arrau's greatness beyond argument [*Jeanne d'Arc au bûcher*]', *Music and Dance*, August 1962, 7.
'London Music [*Joan of Arc*]', *MO*, March 1971, 281.
Sordet, Dominique, 'La Musique: *Cris du monde*', *Revue Universelle*, 1 July 1931, 126-27.
Spratt, Geoffrey K., 'A catalogue of the music of Arthur Honegger, I', *Brio* XIV/2 (1977), 29-39.
'Honegger's *Le roi David* — a reassessment' *MR*, XXXIX/1 (February 1978), 54-60.
'A catalogue of the music of Arthur Honegger, II' *Brio*, XV/1 (Spring 1978), 3-21.
'Some reflections on Honegger's first oratorio', *MO*, CI/1210 (August 1978), 459-61; 478.
'A Claudel-Honegger collaboration: *Jeanne d'Arc au bûcher*', MO, CII/1235 (September 1980), 470-74.
Staiger, Emile, 'A.H.', *SM*, May-June 1962, 150-55.
Stefan, Paul, 'A.H.', *Living Age*, March 1929, 49-50.
Stein, E., 'Paris [*Le roi David*]', *Opera*, January 1961, 33.
Stepanek, V., 'Setkani Fok's Honeggrem [*Symphonie liturgique* [*n° 3*]]' *HR*, 6 (1964), 240.
Stierlin-Vallon, H., 'A.H., gloire de la musique suisse et internationale', *FMS*, 7 (September 1952), 192-94.
Strobel, Heinrich, 'A.H.'s *Totentanz*', *Melos*, May-June 1947, 209-12.
'Gruss an A.H.', *Melos*, February 1952, 33-34.
'Abschied von A.H.', *Melos*, January 1956, 12-16.
Stuckenschmidt, H.H., 'A.H.', *Anbruchs*, October 1932, 166-69.
'Die Klassiker der modernen Musik sind West Berlin erfolgreich [*Concerto da camera*]', *Melos*, May 1971, 207.
Sysoeva, E. 'Moskovskie prem'ery: *Zhanna d'Ark na Kostre*', *SKM*, September 1966, 105-6.
Szantruczek, T., 'Poznanska *Joanna na Stosie*', *Ruch Muzyczny*, 7 (1966), 8-9.

Tailleferre, Germaine, Obituary in 'Hommage à A.H.', *Combat*, 29 November 1955, 2.
Tappolet, Willy '*König David* von A.H.', *NZZ*, 18 February 1925.
'*Judith* in Mézières', *NZZ*, 23 June 1925.
'*Judith* in Mézières', *Die Musik*, August 1925, 863.
'A.H.', *Annalen Ettorgen*, 4 (1928), 561-70.
'*König David*', *Der Caecilienbote*, 6 (October 1929), 4-11.
'Unsere Zeit und A.H.'s *König David*', *Solothurner Zeitung*, 22 October 1929.
'*La belle de Moudon* à Mézières', *SM*, 1 August 1931, 557-60.
'*Amphion*', *Journal de Genève*, 1 December 1932.
'Les récentes œuvres d'A.H.', *SM*, 1 November 1945, 417-21.
'A.H. and his recent works (translated by Natalia Galitzine)', *MMR*, May 1946, 75-81.
'Quelques récentes œuvres d'A.H.', *SM*, 1 May 1950, 248-52.
'Wie komponiert A.H.', *Le Journal de la Radio Suisse*, 38 (23-29 September 1951), 19.
'A.H. — *Je suis compositeur*', *SM*, December 1951, 499-501.
'A.H.', *SM*, March 1952, 85-87.
'*Jeanne d'Arc au bûcher*', *FMS*, 7 (September 1952), 204-5.
'Der religiöse Gehalt im Werk A.H.', *NZZ*, 18 December 1955, 3.
'A.H. La synthèse du génie français et du génie allemand', *SM*, January 1956, 1-3.
'A.H. et l'oratorio', *SM*, May-June 1962, 156-59.
Taubman, H, 'A.H., Man of our Time', *NYT*, 4 December 1955, Section 2, 9.
'Give it a hearing; public should be allowed to see film version of Claudel - A.H. work [*Jeanne d'Arc au bûcher*]', *NYT*, 22 May 1955, Section 2, 7.

Terpander, 'Fantasia on an objective theme', *Gramophone*, August 1933, 95-96.
'A.H.'s *Judith* (1925): Six Excerpts', *Gramophone*, November 1934, 211-12.
Thoresby, C. 'Music in France [*Jeanne d'Arc au bûcher*]', *MA*, August 1954, 11.
Trumpff, G.A., '*Johanna* in Grossaufnahme', *NZM*, April 1960, 139-40.
'Musikdrama von A.H. et Ibert — Der junge Adler [*L'Aiglon*]', *NZM*, May 1968, 199-200.
Tzipine, Georges, Obituary in 'Hommage à A.H.', *Combat*, 29 November 1955, 2.

Valéry, Paul, 'Histoire d'*Amphion*', *Conferencia*, 16 (5 August 1932), 157-62.
Various, 'Hommage à A.H.', Inter-Auteurs (Revue trimestrielle; Confédération Internationale des Sociétés d'Auteurs et Compositeurs, Paris), n° 121, 4e trimestre, 1955, 187-218. Discours de MM. Albert Willemetz, 188; Jean Cocteau, 190; Jacques Ibert, 191; René Fauchois, 192; de Salis 193; Jean Berthoin, 195; Allocution de M. le Pasteur Fritz Münch, 196; Hommages des organisations internationales, 200; Hommages des sociétés confédérées, 202; 'Arthur Honegger' par René Dumesnil, 218.
Viamant, René, 'Musique synthétique: Si Richard Wagner revenait parmi nous il donnerait sa préférence au cinéma [*Rapt*]', *L'Avant-Scène*, 3 October 1934.
Vicuna, M., 'La vida musical en Suiza', *Revue Vista Musical Chilena*, October-November 1957, 51-52 +.
Vinton, John, 'Review of *I am a Composer*', *Notes*, XXII (March 1967), 528.
Volek, J., 'Na zaver filharmonicke sezony [*Le roi David*]', *HR*, 10 (1964), 415-16.
Vredenberg, V., 'Over A.H.'s film er varingen', *MeM*, January 1956, 5-6.
Vuillermoz, E., 'A.H., *Le roi David*', *Le Temps*, 30 December 1921.
'A.H. and his time', *Modern Music*, 3, No. 1 (November-December 1925), 3-8.
['*Antigone*'], *Excelsior*, 16 January 1928.
'*Antigone, Horace Victorieux*', *Candide*, 19 January 1928, 9.
'Le cinéma. Chronique. *Rapt', Le Temps*, 22 September 1934, 6.
'A.H,', *Hommes et mondes*, January 1956, 240-45.

Wagner, K., 'A.H. auf Offenbachs Spuren [*Les aventures du roi Pausole*], *Musica*, April 1954, 163-64.
'A.H. als Operetten Komponist [*Les aventures du roi Pausole*]', *Das Musikleben*, June 1955, 221.
'Thomas Mann auf der Tanzbühne [*Horace Victorieux*], *Musica*, January-April 1957.
Wallez-Walewski, M., 'W stone plonacego stosu [*Jeanne d'Arc au bûcher*]', Ruch Muzyczny, 20 (1965), 5-6.
Wallner, Bo, 'Oratoriet hos A.H. och Rosenberg', *Prisma*, 5-6 (1950), 83-90.
'A.H. och Les Six', *Fransk Musik*, 1957, 138-87.
Walther, Paul, 'A.H. dirigierte', *Melos*, November 1949, 197-99.
Warrack, John, 'London's first stage performance of A.H.'s *Joan of Arc at the Stake*', *MM*, October 1954, 11.
Watt, D., 'A thing of beauty [*Jeanne d'Arc au bûcher*]', *New Yorker*, 29 November 1952, 159-61.
Weber, H., 'Frankfurt [*Jeanne d'Arc au bûcher*]', *Il Opera*, March 1961, 234.
Weeda, Robert, 'Een Zwitsers componist: Norbert Moret', *Gregoriusblad.* CIII (1979), 271-74.
Weissmann, J.S., 'A.H. and Seiber [*Le roi David*]', *Musical Events*, June 1961, 29.
Westphal, Kurt, '*Jeanne d'Arc auf dem Scheiterhaufen.* A.H. — Erstaufführung in Berlin', *Melos*, January 1948, 20-21.
Westrup, Jack, 'Review of Leo Schrade's *De scientia musicae studia atque orationes*', *ML*, 44, No. 4 (October 1968), 390.
Weterings, J., 'Honegger, musicien sportif', *Cahiers de Belgique*, December 1928, 385-87.
Whitwell, D., 'Les Six — their music for winds', *Instrumentalist*, October 1968, 54-55.
Wiener, Jean, Obituary in 'Hommage à A.H.', *Combat*, 29 November 1955, 2.

Willemetz, Albert, See 'various'.
Willm, Ch., '*Cris du monde* d'A.H. à Strasbourg', *RM*, July-August 1933, 137-39.
Winter, Hans, 'A.H.', *OM*, June 1949, 150-53.
Wise, Stanley, 'Letter from Switzerland. René Morax's [*Le*] *roi David*', *Musical News and Herald*, 14 May 1921, 620.
Wolfensberger, R., 'Winterthur [*Symphony no. 4*]', *SM*. 4 (1969), 229-30.
Wolffers, J., 'Bostonians celebrate Paris bi-millenium [*5th Symphony*]', *MC*, 15 April 1951, 17. 'Boston [*Une cantate de Noël*]', *MC*, 15 January 1955, 25-26.

Yarustovsky, B., 'Voennye simfonii Oneggera [*Symphonies Nos 2 and 3*]', *SKM*, January 1964, 112-21 and March 1964, 116-25.

Zavgorodnjaja, Galina, 'Nekotorye osobennosti Baktury v proizvedenijah A. Oneggera', *SKM* 6 (June 1975), 87-90.
Zijlstra, M., 'Bij twee jeugdliederen van A.H. [*Six poèmes* (Apollinaire)]', *MeM*, January 1964, 17-19.

PART IV

Books, dissertations and encyclopedia entries relating to the period

—. *Les concerts de chambre du Collegium Musicum, 1941-51* (Atlantis, Zurich, 1951).
—. *Dictionnaire des musiciens français* (Seghers, Paris, 1961).
Abraham, Gerald, *This modern music* (London, 1955).
Alain, *Système des Beaux-Arts* (Bibliothèque de la Pléiade, N.R.F., Paris, 1961).
Apel, Willi, *Harvard Dictionary of Music* (Harvard University Press, Cambridge Mass., 1956).
Aranovskij, Mihail (comp.), *Rasskazy o muzyke i muzykantah* (Sovetskij Kompositor, Leningrad, 1977).
Audel, Stéphane, *Le théâtre du Jorat et René Morax* (Ed. Rencontre, Lausanne, 1963).
Austin, R., ed., *Twentieth–century music* (Dent, London, 1966).

Babbitt, R.B., *The harmonic idiom in the works of Les Six* (unpublished doctoral dissertation, Boston University, 1963).
Bahle, Julius, *Eingebung und Tat im Musikalischen Schaffen* (Hirzel, Leipzig, 1939).
Baker, Theodore, *Baker's Biographical Dictionary of Musicians*, 5th edition revised by Nicolas Slonimsky (Schirmer, New York, 1958).
Bauer, Marian, *Twentieth-century music* (New York, 1933).
Blom, Eric, A.H. in *Grove's Dictionary of Music and Musicians* (5th ed.), ed. Eric Blom (Macmillan, London, 1954).
Blume, Friedrich, ed., *Die Musik in Geschichte und Gegenwart: Allgemeine Enzyklopädie der Musik* (Bärenreiter-Kassel, 1949 —).
Brelet, Gisèle, *Situation de la musique contemporaine* (Bibliothèque de la Pléiade, N.R.F., Paris, 1953).
A.H. in *Histoire de la musique*, II (N.R.F., Paris, 1953).
Brown, Frederick, *An Impersonation of Angels — a biography of Jean Cocteau* (Longmans, London, 1968).
Bruyr, José, *L'écran des musiciens* (Les Cahiers de France, Paris, 1931).
Buchet, Edmond, *Connaissance de la musique* (Corrêa, Paris, 1940).

Calvocoressi, M.D., *Musicians' Gallery* (Faber and Faber, London, 1933).

Cendrars, Blaise, *Blaise Cendrars vous parle* (Denoël, Paris, 1965).
Ferragus (Denoël, Paris, 1965).
Trop, c'est trop (Denoël, Paris, 1965).
Chailley, Jacques, *Traîté historique d'analyse musicale* (Leduc, Paris, 1947).
Charters, James, *This must be the place* (Lee Furman, New York, 1927).
Chanel, Pierre, *Album Cocteau* (Tchon, Paris, 1970).
Cocteau, Jean, *Le coq et l'arlequin* (Stock, Paris, 1918).
Cock and Harlequin (translated by Rollo Myers) (Egoist Press, London, 1921).
Rappel à l'ordre (Stock, Paris, 1926).
A call to order (translated Rollo Myers), (London, 1926).
Portraits-Souvenir (Paris, 1935).
Cœuroy, André, *La musique française moderne* (Delagrave, Paris, 1922).
Panorama de la musique contemporaine (Kra, Paris, 1928).
Collaer, Paul, *Die junge Musik in Frankreich* (Marcan, Cologne, 1925).
La musique moderne (Elsevier, Paris, 1955).
A History of Modern Music (Cleveland, 1961).
Combarieu, Jules, *Histoire de la musique des origines au début du XXème siècle* (Armand Colin, Paris, 1928).
Combe, Edouard, A.H. in *Schweizer Tonkunstler* (Geneva, 1931).
Cooper, Martin, *French music from the death of Berlioz to the death of Fauré* (O.U.P., London, 1951).
ed., *The Modern Age, 1890 — 1960, Vol. 10 of the New Oxford History of Music* (London, 1974).
Cortot, Alfred, *La musique française de piano*, III (3 vols., Presses Universitaires de France, Paris, 1948; 1 vol. PUF, Paris, 1981).
Cuetco, Dragotin, ed., *Report of the 10th Congress of the International Musicological Society (1967).* (Bärenreiter-Kassel, London, 1968).

Davies, Lawrence, *The Gallic Music* (Barnes, New York, 1967).
Deane, Basil, *Albert Roussel and his place in musical tradition* (unpublished doctoral thesis, Glasgow, 1958-59).
Albert Roussel, (London, 1961).
Demuth, Norman, *Musical trends in the twentieth–century* (Rockliff, London, 1952).
Dettelbach, Hans von, *Breviarium musicae* (Stiasny, Graz, 1967).
Drew, David, *Modern French music* in *European music in the twentieth–century* ed. Howard Hartog (Routledge, Kegan Paul, London, 1957 and Penguin Books, 3rd Edition, London 1965).
Drumeva, Kipriana, *Problems concerning contemporary vocal music* (*materials from French cantatas and oratorios in the 1930s through the 1950s*) (unpublished master's dissertation, Moscow Conservatoire, 1971).
Dufourcq, Norbert ed., *Larousse de la musique* (2 Vols., Librairie Larousse, Paris, 1957).
Dukas, Paul, *Ecrits sur la musique* (Paris, 1948).
Dumesnil, René, *La musique contemporaine en France* (2 Vols., Colin, Paris, 1930).
La musique en France entre les deux guerres, 1919-39 (Milieu du Monde, Geneva, 1946).
Histoire de la musique des origines à nos jours, IV and V (Librairie Armand Colin, Paris, 1958-).

Eeckhout, Antoon, *Musikale exploraties. Tweede Reeks: Ouverturen en symfonïsche gedichteg* (Uitgeverij de Monte, Mechelen-Leuven, 1970).
Einstein, Alfred, *Die Romantik in der Musik* edited by Liechtenstein (Vaduz, 1950).

Favre, Georges, *Musiciens français contemporains* (2 Vols., Durand, Paris, 1956).

Fellerer, Karl Gustav, 'Oratorium und geistliche Musik in Frankreich' in *Religiöse Musik in nicht-liturgischen Werken von Beethoven bis Reger*, ed. by Walter Wiora, Günther Massenkeil, Klaus Wolfgang Niemöller, Studien zur Musikgeschichte des 19. Jahrhunderts 51 (Bosse, Regensburg, 1978), 221-31.

Fischer, K. von., *Critical years in European musical history 1915-25* (Report of the 10th Congress of the International Musicological Society, 1967) ed. Dragotin Cuetco (Bärenreiter-Kassel, London, 1968).

'Précis de l'histoire musicale suisse', *RMSR*, CXVII/4-6 (1978), 211-13; 276-80; 338-42.

Fumet, Stanislas, *La poésie à travers les arts* (Paris, 1954).

Gard, Maurice Martin du, *Soirée de Paris — le théâtre et la vie 1930 – 1* (Flammarion, Paris, 1932).

Gavoty, Bernard, and Daniel Lesur, *Pour ou contre la musique moderne* (Flammarion, Paris, 1957).

See Arthur Honegger, *Je suis compositeur* (Conquistador, Paris, 1951).

Godet, Robert, A.H. in Cobbett, *Cyclopedia of Chamber Music* (3 Vols., London, 2nd Edition 1963).

Gordina, Elena, *Some problems with regard to A.H.'s symphonic writing* in *From the music history of foreign countries*, ed. Sof'ja Pitina (Muzyka, Leningrad, 1971).

Goléa, Antoine, *Esthétique de la musique contemporaine* (P.U.F., Paris, 1954).

Gowers, W.P., *Erik Satie, Les Six and French musical taste at the time of the First World War* (unpublished doctoral thesis, Clare College, Cambridge University, 1965).

Gray, Cecil, *A Survey of Contemporary Music* (London, 1924).

Guinle, Jean-Pierre, A.H. in *Encyclopédie Fasquelle* (Paris, 1959).

Hahn, R., *Journal d'un musicien* (Paris, 1933).

Hansen, Peter S., *An introduction to twentieth–century music*, second edition [Allyn and Bacon, Boston, 1967).

Harding, James, *The Ox on the Roof* (MacDonald, London, 1972).

Hartog, Howard, ed., *European music in the twentieth-century* (Routledge, Kegan Paul, London, 1957 and Penguin Books, 3rd edition, London, 1965).

Hill, E.B., *Modern French Music* (Boston and New York, 1924 and Da Capo reprint O 306 71497 3).

Hodeir, André, Since Debussy: *A view of contemporary music* (translated by Noel Burch), (New York, 1961 and Da Capo reprint 0 306 70662 8).

Hoérée, Arthur, A.H. in *Encyclopédie Bordas* (Paris, 1970).

Jans, Hans Jörg, ed., *Kunstmuseum Luzern. Ausstellung Musikerhandschriften* (Stiftung Int. Musikfestwochen, Lucerne, 1973).

Jarociński, Stefan, *Orfeusz na rozdrożu. Eseje o muzyce i muzykach XX wieku* (2nd ed.) (Wyd. Muz., Kraków, 1974).

Jean-Aubry, G., *La musique française d'aujourd'hui* (Perrin, Paris, 1916).

Juzak, Moskva, ed., *The problem of model* (Muzyka, Moscow, 1972).

Kremlev, Ju. A., ed., *Problems of music theory and aesthetics* (Muzyka, Leningrad, 1967).

Laloy, Louis, *La musique retrouvée, 1902-27* (Paris, 1928).

Lambert, Constant, *Music Ho!* (Faber, London, 1934; revised edition 1937).

Landormy, Paul, *La musique française,* III (3 Vols, Gallimard, Paris, 1943).

Lebedeva, Elena. *Kontrast kak mjzykal'naja* (*v aspekte muzyki pervoj poloving XX veka*) (MA diss., Music Theory: Inst. Iskusstvovedenija, Fol'klora: Étnografii imeni M.F. Ryl'skogo Akademii Nauk, Kiev, 1980).

Lesur, Daniel, See Bernard Gavoty.

Lesure, François, *Exposiçao Darius Milhaud* (Fundaçao Calouste Gulbenkian, Lisbon, 1968).
Liechtenstein, ed., See Alfred Einstein.
Lubbock, M., *The complete book of light opera* (London, 1962).

Machabey, A., *Introduction to contemporary music* (Dent, London, 1961).
Machlis, Joseph, *Introduction to contemporary music* (Dent, London, 1961).
Marliave, J. de., *Etudes Musicales* (Paris, 1917).
Mauclair, C., *La religion de la musique* (Paris, 1919).
Mauriac, C.J., *Cocteau — ou la vérité du mensonge* (Paris, 1945).
Mayer-Rosa, Eugen, *Musik und Technik. Vom Futurismus bis zur Elektronik*, Beiträge zur Schulmusik 27 (Möseler, Wolfenbüttel, Zürich, 1974).
Mellers, Wilfred, *Studies in contemporary music* (Dobson, London, 1948).
Meylan, Pierre ed., *Dictionnaire des musiciens suisses* (Atlantis, Zurich, 1964).
Michel, François, ed., *Encyclopédie de la musique* (3 vols., Fasquelle, Paris, 1958-61).
Milhaud, Darius, *Notes sans musique* (Julliard, Paris, 1949).
Mooser, R. Aloys, *Regards sur la musique contemporaine* (Rouge, Lausanne, 1946).
Aspects de la musique contemporaine (Labor, Geneva, 1958).
Morhange, Hélène-Jourdan, *Mes amis musiciens* (Les Editeurs Français Réunis, Paris, 1955).
Moser, Hans-Joachim, *Die Epochen der Musikgeschichte* (Cotta, Stuttgart-Berlin, 1930).
Myers, Rollo H., *Modern Music* (London, 1923).
Music in the Modern World (London, 1939).
ed., *Twentieth-century music* (Calder and Boyars, London, 1968).

Nest'ev, Izrail', comp. and ed., *Zarubežnaja muzyka XX veka. Materialy i dokumenty* (Muzyka, Moscow, 1975).

Omnen, Frank, *Excursies door le franse musick* (Spectrum, Amsterdam, 1951).

Pannain, Guido, *Modern Composers* (translated by M.R. Bonavia), (Dent, London, 1932).
Pavčinskij, Sergej, *The Symphonies of A.H.* (Sovetskij Kompozitor, Moscow, 1972).
Pitina, Sof'ja ed., *From the music history of foreign countries* (Muzyka, Moscow, 1971).
Poulenc, Francis, *Moi et mes amis (confidences recueillies par Stéphane Audel)* (La Palatine, Geneva — Paris, 1963).

Rappoport, Lidija, *Specific features of the harmony of A.H.* in *The Problem of Model* ed. Moskva Juzak (Muzyka, Moscow, 1972).
Reeks, Tweede, *Musikale exploraties : Ouverturen en symfonïsche gedichteg* (Antoon Eeckhout - Mechelen - Leuven, Uitgeverij de Monte, 1970).
Rohozinski, L., ed., *50 ans de musique française, de 1974-1925* (2 Vols., Paris 1925).
Roland-Manuel, ed., *Histoire de la musique* (2 Vols., N.R.F., Paris, 1953).
Rostand, Claude, *La musique française contemporaine* (P.U.F., Paris, 1952).
French Music Today (New York, 1955 and Da Capo reprint 0 306 70578 8).
A.H. in *Encyclopédie Larousse* (Paris, 1957).
Roy, Jean, *Musique française, Présences contemporaines* (Nouvelles Editions Debresse, Paris, 1962).

Sabin, R., *The International Cyclopedia of Music and Musicians*, 9th edition (Dodd, Mead and Co., New York, 1964).
Salazar, Adolfo, *Music in our Time* (New York, 1946).
Samazeuilh, Gustave, *Musiciens de mon temps* (Marcel Daubin, Paris, 1947).
Schrade, Leo, *De scientia musicae studia atque orationes* [*Essays and lectures on musicology*] *ed., Ernest Lichtenhahn* (Haupt, Bern, 1967).
Schuh, Willi, ed., *Schweizer Tonkunstler* (Geneva, 1931).
Zeitgenössische Musik (Atlantis, Zurich, 1947).

Schweizer Musik der Gegenwart (Atlantis, Zurich, 1948).
Almanach de la musique (Flore, Paris, 1950).
Kompositionsaufträge in *Alte and Neue Musik* by Willy Tappolet (Atlantis, Zurich, 1952).
Séré, O., *Musiciens français* (Paris, 1921).
Shattuck, Roger, *The banquet years* (New York, 1958).
Shead, Richard, *Music in the 1920s* (Duckworth, London, 1976).
Slonimsky, Nicolas, *Music since 1900* (New York, 1949).
Staiger, Emil, A.H. in *Musik und Dichtung* (Atlantis, Zurich, 1947).
Stuckenschmidt, Hans Heinz, *Neue Musik* (Berlin, 1951).
Twentieth-century music (translated by Richard Deveson), (World University Library, London, 1969).
Deutschland und Mitteleuropa : Die grossen Komponisten unseres Jahrhunderts, I (Piper, Munich, 1971).
Twentieth–century composers. II : Germany and Central Europe (Holt Rinehart Winston, New York, 1971).
Suhami, Evelyne, *Paul Valéry et la musique* (Université de Dakar, Publication de la Faculté des Lettres et Sciences Humaines, Langues et Littératures, No. 13, Dakar, 1966).
Surchamp, Dom Angelico, *Albert Roussel* (Paris, 1967).
Swiss Composers' League, *40 Contemporary Swiss Composers* (Bodensee, Amriswil, 1956).
Syssoeva, Elena, *Jeanne d'Arc au bûcher* in *From the music history of foreign countries*, ed. Sof'ja Pitina (Muzyka, Leningrad, 1971).

Tappolet, Willy, A.H. in *Musik in Geschichte und Gegenwart : Allgemeine Enzyklopädie der Musik* (Bärenreiter - Kassel, 1949-).
ed., *Alte und Neue musik ; 25 ans d'orchestre de chambre sous la direction de Paul Sacher, 1926-51* (Atlantis, Zurich, 1952).
A.H. in *Encyclopédie Bordas* (Paris, 1970).
Tiersot, Julien, *Un demi-siècle de musique française* (Paris, 1924).
Thomson, Virgil, *The State of Music* (Knopf, New York, 1939, and Da Capo reprint 0 8371 7258 6).
The Musical Scene (Knopf, New York, 1945, and Da Capo reprint 0 8371 0684 2).
The Art of Judging Music (Knopf, New York, 1948, and Da Capo reprint 0 8371 0683 4).
Music, Right and Left (Holt, New York, 1951, and Da Capo reprint 0 8371 0685 9).
Tjulin, Jurij N., ed., *Questions of theory and aesthetics of music*, V (Muzyka, Leningrad, 1967).
Tolstyh, Nonna. *Francuzskaja fortepiannaja muzyka 1920h godov* (*aniliz stilističeskih i žanrovyh osobennostej; problemy ispolnenija i ispol'zovanija v fortepiannoj pedagogike*) (MA diss., Performance: Muzykal'no - pedagogiceskij Inst. imeni Gnesinyh, Moskva, 1981).
Trojan, Jan., *K problematice oratoria dvaćátého století* [*Problems of the oratorio in the twentieth-century*], (unpublished doctoral thesis, Filosofická fakulta, U.J.E.P., Brno, 1968).

Vuillermoz, Emile, *Musique d'aujourd'hui* (Crès, Paris, 1923).
Cinquante ans de musique française, 1874-1925, IV (Librairie de France, Paris, 1925).
Histoire de la musique (Fayard, Paris, 1949).

Woerner, Karl H., *Neue Musik in der Entscheidung* (Mainz, 1954).
Worbs, Hans Christoph, *Welterfolge der modernen Oper* (Rembrandt, Berlin, 1967).

Zurlinden, H., *Erinnerungen an R. Strauss, C. Spitteler, A. Schweitzer, M. Huber, Cuno Amiet und A.H.* (Tschudy, St. Gallen, 1962).

Discography

ABBREVIATIONS OF ARTISTS

(Column 1)

C.B.S.O.	=	City of Birmingham Symphony Orchestra
C.H.S.O.	=	Concert Hall Symphony Orchestra (= Netherlands Symphony Orchestra)
C.O.	=	Chamber Orchestra
cond.	=	conducted by
E.C.O.	=	English Chamber Orchestra
Ens.	=	Ensemble
incl.	=	including
M.G.M.	=	Metro-Goldwyn-Mayer
Nat.	=	National
O.P.P.	=	Orchestre Philharmonique de Paris
Orch.	=	Orchestra
Orch. de la S.R.	=	Orchestre de la Suisse Romande
Orch. de la Soc. des Conc. du Cons.	=	Orchestre de la Société des Concerts du Conservatoire
orig.	=	original
O.R.T.F.	=	Orchestre de la Radio-Télévision Française
perf.	=	performance
pf.	=	piano
P.O.	=	Philharmonic Orchestra

P.S.O.L.	=	Philharmonic Symphony Orchestra of London (= Royal Philharmonic Orchestra)
R.(S).O.	=	Radio (Symphony) Orchestra
S.O.	=	Symphony Orchestra
str.	=	string(s)
vcl.	=	violoncello
ver.	=	version
vla	=	viola
vln(s)	=	violin(s)
Z.C.M.	=	Collegium Musicum Zürich

(For the key to other abbreviations used in this Discography, please consult the List of Abbreviations which precedes the Catalogue of Works, pp. 483–87.)

ABBREVIATIONS OF RECORD COMPANIES

(with country of origin)

(Prefixes to catalogue numbers in columns 2 and 3)

A.	=	Angel (U.S.A.)
ADD.	=	Decca Ace of Diamonds (G.B.)
Adès	=	Adès (France)
AmC.	=	American Columbia (U.S.A.)
AmD.	=	American Decca (U.S.A.)
AmPhi.	=	American Philips (U.S.A.)
Am. Soc. of CAP	=	American Society of Composers, Authors and Performers (U.S.A.)
Argo	=	Argo/Decca [PolyGram] (G.B.)
Arm.	=	Armida (Switzerland)
AS.	=	Anthologie Sonore (France)
Aud.	=	Audio (U.S.A.)

BàM.	=	Boîte à musique (France)
BIS	=	BIS [Conifer]
Bour.	=	Bourg [D sharp]
Brol.	=	Brolga (Australia)
C.	=	Columbia (G.B.)
Cal.	=	Calliope
Cap.	=	Capitol (G.B. and U.S.A. — only P prefixes available in G.B.)
Cass.	=	Cassiopée (France)
CBS	=	CBS Records (U.S.A.)
CdM.	=	Chant du monde [Harmonia Mundi] (France)
CEd.	=	Classics Edition (U.S.A.)
Chan.	=	Chandos [Harmonia Mundi]
CHS.	=	Concert Hall Society (U.S.A.)
Cla.	=	Classic (France)
Clav.	=	Claves [Gamut] (Switzerland)
CND.	=	Club nationale de disques (France)
CNR	=	CNR (Holland)
Con.	=	Conifer
Coro.	=	Coronet (U.S.A.)
Cr.	=	Crossroads (U.S.A.)
C(S).	=	Columbia (Switzerland)
Duc.	=	Ducretet-Thomson (France)
D.	=	Decca [PolyGram] (Europe)
DCap.	=	Capitol (G.B.; pressed by Decca)
Des.	=	Desmar
DG.	=	Deutsche Gramophon (Germany)

E.	=	Everest (U.S.A.)
Eli.	=	Elite (Switzerland; with a limited no. available in the U.S.A.)
EMI	=	EMI Records (G.B.)
EMI-PM.	=	EMI-Pathé Marconi [Conifer]
Ep.	=	Epic (U.S.A.)
(EP)	=	Extended play
EPhi.	=	Philips (G.B.)
Er.	=	Erato [Conifer]
ES.	=	Encyclopédie sonore (France)
Esq.	=	Esquire (France)
Ev.	=	Evasion (Switzerland)
F.	=	Fontana (G.B.)
Fest.	=	Festival (LP's: U.S.A.) (78's: France)
FY.	=	FY/Studio Import and Export
G.	=	H.M.V. Gramophone Co. (Europe, etc.)
GS.	=	Gramophonic Society (U.S.A.)
H.	=	Transatlantic/Nonesuch (U.S.A.)
Har.	=	Harlequin
HMV.	=	H.M.V. Gramphone Co.
Hun.	=	Hungaroton
In.	=	Barcaly Inédits (France)
It.V.	=	Italian Victor (Italy)
JpPol.	=	Japanese Polydor (Japan)
Lan.	=	Lanier (U.S.A.)
Lon.	=	London (U.S.A. issues of Eng. Decca)
LS.	=	Louisville Society (U.S.A)

Lut.	=	Lutin (France)
LyD.	=	Lyra Dei (France)
Mel.	=	Melodia (U.S.S.R.)
Mer.	=	Mercury [PolyGram Classics] (G.B. and U.S.A.)
MGM.	=	Metro-Goldwyn-Mayer (U.S.A. and G.B.)
MHS	=	Musical Heritage Society (U.S.A.)
Mir.	=	Mirrosonic (U.S.A.)
Mj.	=	Montjoie (France)
ML.	=	Music Library (U.S.A.)
Mon.	=	Monitor (U.S.A.)
MPS.	=	B.A.S.F. (Germany)
MS.	=	Musica Sacra (Germany)
Mtr.	=	Metronome (Denmark)
Muz.	=	Muza (Poland)
N.	=	Nonesuch
Nim.	=	Nimbus
Nix.	=	Nixa (G.B.)
Od.	=	Odéon (Europe)
Ody.	=	Odyssey (U.S.A.)
Or.	=	Orion (U.S.A.)
P.	=	Parlophone (Europe)
Pat.	=	Pathé (France)
Pauta	=	Pauta (South America — Brazil or Argentina)
Phi.	=	Philips [PolyGram Classics] (Italy, Austria, Germany, etc..)
PLM.	=	Plaisirs de la musique (French H.M.V.) (France)
PM-EMI	=	Pathé Marconi-EMI [Conifer] (France and G.B.)

Pol.	=	Polydor (Europe)
Pre.	=	Prelude
PVan.	=	Philips Vanguard
Q.	=	Quadrophonic
RCA	=	RCA (Records) Ltd. (U.S.A)
Redw.	=	Redwood (U.S.A.)
RMC.	=	Recorded Music Circle (G.B.)
Roc.	=	Rococo (Canada)
Ron.	=	Rondo (U.S.A.)
(S)	=	Stereo
S.	=	Supraphon [Counterpoint] (Czechoslovakia)
SCA.	=	Swiss Composers' Association (Switzerland)
Sel.	=	Selmer or Ducretet-Selmer (France)
SOT.	=	Sounds of our Time (U.S.A.)
T.	=	Telefunken (Europe)
TV.	=	Turnabout (U.S.A.)
Un.	=	Unicorn (U.S.A.)
Ura.	=	Urania (U.S.A.)
USSR.	=	State Music Trust (Russia)
Van.	=	Vanguard (U.S.A.)
Véga	=	Véga (France)
Vers.	=	Versailles (France)
Vic.	=	Victor (U.S.A.)
VoA.	=	Voice of America (U.S.A.)
Vox	=	Vox (Europe)
Vog.	=	Vogue
West.	=	Westminster (U.S.A.)

WRC.	=	World Record Club (G.B.)
*	=	Part of a recording of the complete piano music

Work/Artists	Identification of record make and main serial number	Identification of subsidiary record make(s) and or serial number(s)
Aglavaine et Sélysette — see *Prélude (pour Aglavaine et Sélysette).*		
L'agonie du sous-marin (ou *Nitchevo*) — see *De l'Atlantique au Pacifique.*		
L'Aiglon Cond. Dervaux	Bour. BG 3004/5	
Un ami viendra ce soir — see *Souvenir de Chopin.*		
Antigone Geneviève Serrés, Claudine Verneuil, Janine Collard, André Vessières, Jean Giraudeau, Bernard Plantey, Bernard Demigny, Michel Roux, French Nat. Radio Chorus and Orch., cond. Maurice Le Roux	Bour. BG 3015	
De l'Atlantique au Pacifique (Song from *Nitchevo* ou *L'agonie du sous-marin*) Damia (A) with chorus and orchestra cond. Walberg	C. DF 2287	C. LFX 690
Les aventures du roi Pausole 1. Extracts ('Deux airs d'Aline': No. 4, "Papa veut toujours, seule, hélas, que je m'amuse" and No. 17, "Pardon, mon Papa que j'adore"); Jacqueline Francell, cond. Pierre Chagnon	C. DF 521	
2. Extracts ('Deux airs d'Aline': No. 4, "Papa veut toujours, seule, hélas, que je m'amuse" and No. 17, "Pardon, mon Papa que j'adore"); Gabrielle Gills, Orch. Odéon d'Opérettes, cond. Arthur Honegger	Od. 238. 298	
3. Extracts (No. 14, 'Air de la coupe du roi de Thulé: "Descendant du roi de Thule")	CND. 1051	

Work/Artists	Identification of record make and main serial number	Identification of subsidiary record make(s) and or serial number(s)
4. Extracts (No. 14, 'Air de la coupe de Thulé' and No. 27, 'Les adieux de Pausole'); Dorville, Orch. Odéon d'Opérettes, cond. Arthur Honegger	Od. 166. 390	
5. Extracts ('Ouverture' and No. 5, 'Ballet'); Orch. Odéon d'Opérettes, cond. Arthur Honegger	Od. 238. 297	
6. Complete; Lowel House Musical Society (sung in Eng.)	Aud. R 95	
Cadence for Milhaud's *Le bœuf sur le toit*). René Benedetti (vln) and Jean Wiener (pf)	C. 15075	
Le cahier romand		
1. Lucette Descaves	Vers. MEDX 12004*	
2. Jürg von Vintschger	TV. TV 34377(S)*	
3. Franz-Joseph Hirt	Pol. 90026	JpPol. 30028
Une cantate de Noël		
1. Pierre Mollet, Orch. de la Soc. des Conc. du Cons., cond. Georges Tzipine (with *Symphonie liturgique* [*n° 3*])	C. FCX 336	
2. Michel Roux, Lamoureux Orch., cond. Paul Sacher	Phi. AOO. 749R	Ep. LC 5153 EPhi. NBR 6026
3. Jindřich Jindřak, Prague S.O., cond. Serge Baudo	S. SUAST 50757	Cr. 22 16 0154
4. Pierre Mollet, Chorus and Orch. de la S.R., cond. Ernest Ansermet (with *Symphonie pour cordes* [*n° 2*])	D. LXT 6003	Lon. 5686 ADD. SDD 189 (S)
Cantique de Pâques		
Cond. Jacques Jouineau	Pat. DTX 247	
Cello Concerto		
1. Maurice Maréchal, Orch. de la Soc. des Conc. du Cons., cond. Arthur Honegger	C. LFX 671/2	
2. Paul Tortelier, O.R.T.F., cond. Georges Tzipine (with *Concertino* for piano and orchestra and *Concerto da camera*)	C. FCX 665	
3. Miloš Sádlo, Czech P.O., cond. Václav Neumann	S. 1 10 0604 (S)	

Work/Artists	Identification of record make and main serial number	Identification of subsidiary record make(s) and or serial number(s)
Cello Sonata		
1. Guy and Monique Fallot	Véga C. 30 A 310	Véga C. 30 ST 20010 Duc. 300 C 054 (with *Violin Sonata No. 1*)
2. Robert Bex and Noël Lee (with *Sonatine* for violin and cello and *Sonatine* for clarinet (or cello) and piano)	BàM. LD 059	BàM. BAM LD5059 LyD. 509 5059
3. A. Lambert and G. Lecoq	Mj. MC1	
4. Janos Starker and G. Sebök	Mer. MG 50320 (SA 90320)	
5. Suzanne Besler and Annette Weisbrod (with *Sonatine* for violin and cello and *Violin Sonata No. 2*)	MHS. MHS 1869	RBM 3001
Cessez le feu (see *La chanson de l'escadrille* and *La chanson du cul-de-jatte*)		
Chanson (Ronsard)		
Irène Joachim, cond. Maurice Franck (with *Six poésies de Jean Cocteau*)	CdM. LDA 8079	CdM. LDX 78416
La chanson de l'escadrille (from *Cessez le feu*)	C. DF 1563	AmC. 4103M
Lys Gauty (with *La chanson du cul-de-jatte*)		
La chanson du cul-de-jatte (from *Cessez le feu*)	C. DF 1563	AmC. 4103M
Lys Gauty (with *La chanson de l'escadrille)*		
Chant de joie		
1. Orch. de la Soc. des Conc. du Cons., cond. Robert F. Denzler (with *Symphonie liturgique* [*n° 3*])	D. LXT 5118	
2. P.S.O.L., cond. Hermann Scherchen (with *Pastorale d'été, Prélude pour 'La tempête', Mouvement symphonique n° 2* (*Rugby*), *Mouvement symphonique n°1* (*Pacific 231*) and *Mouvement symphonique n° 3*)	Véga C 35 A158	Véga C 30 A75 West. XWN 18486 West. W 9730 West. LAB 7010 West. WG 8302 West. WG W18027 RMC. CM 61 WRC. CM 61 Lon. 21062

Work/Artists	Identification of record make and main serial number	Identification of subsidiary record make(s) and or serial number(s)
3. Czech P.O., cond. Serge Baudo (with *Pastorale d'été, Mouvement symphonique n° 1* (*Pacific 231*) and *Symphony No. 5*)	S. SUA 10516	Cr. 22 16 0077/8 (S) S. SUAST 50516
4. Südwestfunk Orch. (Baden-Baden), cond. Ernest Bour	Duc. 225 C 095	Duc. 255 C 093 (with *Symphonie pour cordes* [*n*° *2*])
5. Czech P.O., cond. Serge Baudo (with *Symphonies Nos 1-5, Mouvement symphonique n° 1* (*Pacific 231*) and *Pastorale d'été*)	S. 110 1741/3	
Le chant de Nigamon		
Orch. Pasdeloup, cond. Rhené Baton	D. K 553	AmD. 25638
Christophe Colomb — see *Murcie en fleurs*		
Concertino for pf. and orch.		
1. Monique Bérard, O.R.T.F., cond. Georges Tzipine (with *Cello Concerto* and *Concerto da camera*)	C. FCX. 665	
2. Walter Klein, Vienna Pro Musica Orch., cond. Heinrich Hollreiser	Vox PL 10840 (STLPL 510840	TV. TV 34130 (S) Vox ST
3. Eunice Norton, Minneapolis S.O., cond. Eugene Ormandy	Vic. 8765	G. DB 2686
4. Margrit Weber, Berlin P.O., cond. Ferenc Fricsay	D. DL 9900	Pol. 18338 DG. 89869 DG. DGM 18338
5. A. Lokheler, Moscow R.O., cond. Gennadi Rozdestvensky	USSR. D. 011199/200	
6. Oscar Levant, Columbia S.O., cond. Fritz Reiner	C. ML 2156	
7. Fabienne Jacquinot, Philharmonia, cond. Fistoulari	MGM. E 122	MGM. E 3041 (with *Symphonie pour cordes* [*n*° *2*]) MGM. Set K122
8. Boris Krajný, Prague C.O., cond. Stanislav Macura	S. 1410 2705	
Concerto da camera		
1. Kraft Thorwald Dilloo, Martin Lindler, Südwestfunk Orch. (Baden-Baden), cond. Ernest Bour (with *Symphonie pour cordes* [*n*° *2*])	Duc. 320 C142	

Work/Artists	Identification of record make and main serial number	Identification of subsidiary record make(s) and or serial number(s)
2. F. Dufrène, P. Taillefer, O.R.T.F., cond. Georges Tzipine (with *Concertino* for pf. and orch. and *Cello Concerto*)	C. FCX 665	
3. A. Gleghorn, W. Kosinski, Los Angeles C.O., cond. Harold Byrns	DCap. CTL 7007	Cap. P 8115
4. Jean-Pierre Rampal, Pierre Pierlot, Paris C.O., cond. Fernand Oubradous	Pat. DT 1019	
5. André Jaunet, André Raoult, Z.C.M., cond. Paul Sacher	AS. G64-11	
6. Beda, Krylov, Leningrad C.O., cond. Gennadi Rozhdestvensky	USSR. D. 15326 (SM 02689/90)	
7. John Solum, Anthony Camden, English Sinfonia Orch., cond. Neville Dilkes	EMI. SQ EMD5526 (OC 061. 06025Q)	
8. Aurèle Nicolet, Parolari, Orch. de Wintherthur, cond. V. Desarzens	CHS. CHS E 17 (EP)	
9. Maurice Sharp, Harvey McGuire, Cleveland Orch., cond. Louis Lane	C. 33X 1682 (SCX 3539)	
10. David Shostac, Allan Vogel, Los Angeles C.O., cond. Gerard Schwarz	N. D 79018	
Cris du monde		
Cond. Georges Tzipine	C. FCX 649	
Danse de la chèvre		
1. Severino Gazzelloni	Véga C 37 S 173	
2. Aurèle Nicolet (with *Romance*)	D. LXT 2849	Lon. LL 893
3. Jean-Pierre Rampal	Esq. TW 3-005	Clc. C 2094 Clc. C 6032
4. M. Lassien	Cass. 470118 (369185)	
5. Peter Lucas Graf	C(S). SEGZ 2073	Clav. LP 30-235(S) Disco 30235
6. Christian Larde	CND. 29	Van. HM 30590 MHS. MHS 1618
7. C. de Laney	Lan. 5238	
8. P. Thomas (with *Romance*)	Brol. BZM 21	
9. Roger Bourdin	Vog. CLVLX 293	
10. M. Duxheng	Or. 6911(S)	
11. René le Roy	GS. 136	
12. Werner Zumsteg	Nim. 2134	
13. Willoughby	Coro. 3005	

x

Work/Artists	Identification of record make and main serial number	Identification of subsidiary record make(s) and or serial number(s)
La danse des morts		
1. Jean-Louis Barrault (Narr), Odette Turba-Rabier (S), Eliette Schenneberg (A), Charles Panzéra (Bar), Yvette Gouverné Chorale, Orch. de la Soc. des Conc. du Cons., cond. Charles Münch (with *Symphonie pour cordes* [*n° 2*])	G. FJLP 5026	G. FALP 453 G. DB 1600-2 G. W 1600-2 G. DB 5135-7 A. 536585(S) EMI/HMV. ASD 2487(S) G. CVHS 2281 G. C 061-10.901M PM-EMI CO61-10901 Cal. 1955 EMI-PM. 1109011
2. Claudine Collart (S), Anne Seghers (A), Michael Piquemal (Bar), Jean Davy (Narr), Roland de Lassus Ens., Douai Youth S.O., cond. H. Vachey	Cal. 1855	
Deux Esquisses		
1. Lucette Descaves	Ver. MEDX 12004*	
2. Jürg von Vintschger	TV. TV 34377(S)*	
Le dit des jeux du monde		
C.O. of the Leningrad State P.O., cond. J. Dalgat	USSR. Melodia DO. 26489/90	
Folk Song Arrangements:		
(i) *'La femme du marin'* M.-T. Holley, J. Peyron, Chorale Yvonne Gouverné, choirs and orch., cond. Roger Désormière	CdM. 513	
(ii) *'Les trois princesses aux pommiers doux'* Madeleine Grey, orch., cond. Roger Désormière	CdM. 520	
Grad us — En avant		
Military band, cond. Richard	G. HE 141	
Le grand étang		
Marianne Oswald, cond. Pierre Chagnon	C. DF 1114	

Work/Artists	Identification of record make and main serial number	Identification of subsidiary record make(s) and or serial number(s)
Horace victorieux		
O.R.T.F., cond. Michel Tabachnik (with *Symphonie* [*n° 1*] and *Mouvement symphonique n° 3*)	In. 995 042(S)	
Intrada		
1. M. Stith	Redw. ES 1	
2. J. Hyatt	Coro. 1246	
3. V. Malkov with O. Krylora	USSR. D. 027155/6	
4. G. Schwarz with K. W. Piak	Har.	
5. Maurice André with Jean Hubeau	S. STU 70730	
6. Håkan Hardenberger with Roland Pöntinen	BIS/Con. LP 287 CD 287	
Jeanne d'Arc au bûcher		
1. Marthe Dugard (Jeanne), R. Gérome (Frère Dominique), F. Anspach (T: Porcus), R. Lenssens (La Vierge), Cureghem cv chorus, Antwerp Cecilia mv chourus, Belgian National Orch., cond. Louis de Voght	G. FALP 213-4	G. W 1546-54 G. FALP 35028-9 Argo LPC 11807/8
2. Vera Zorina, Philadelphia S.O., cond. Eugene Ormandy	AmPhi. AO1128-9L	AmPhi. SL 178 ML. 4669-4670 EPhi. ABL 3033/4
3. Heather Harper, London S.O., cond. Seiji Ozawa	CBS Masterworks 32 11 00 3-6	CBS SBRG 77216 BRG 72631-2 SBRG 72631-2
4. Cond. Charles Münch	VoA. DS 719-724	
5. Chateau, Rodde, Brachet, Borgeaud, Favory, Kuhn cv chorus, Czech P.O. and Chorus, cond. Serge Baudo	S. 112 1651/2	
Jeunesse		
1. Ver. for choir/orch.: Chorale populaire de Paris and orch., cond. Roger Désormière	CdM. 501	
2. Ver. for choir *a capella:* cond. Gilbert Martin	CdM. LDY 4171	
Judith		
1. Cond. Maurice Abravanel	Van. VRS 1139 (VRS 71139)	AmPhi. 04326L

Work/Artists	Identification of record make and main serial number	Identification of subsidiary record make(s) and or serial number(s)
2. Extracts ('Cantique des vierges' and 'Cantique de victoire'); J. van Hertbruggen, I. van Dyck, Claire Croiza, Antwerp Cecilia mv chorus, cond. Louis de Vocht	C. D 15240/1	AmC. 68996/7 D (See 3 below)
3. Extracts ('Cantique funèbre', 'Invocation', 'Incantation' and 'Fanfare'); I. van Dyck, J. van Hertbruggen, Claire Croiza, Antwerp Cecilia mv chorus, cond. Louis de Vocht	C. D 15240	AmC. 68996/7 D (See 2 above)
Marche funèbre		
1. O.R.T.F., cond. Darius Milhaud	Adès 15501 (17008)	
1. Philharmonia, cond. Geoffrey Simon		
Marche sur la Bastille (see *Quatorze juillet*)		
Les mariés de la Tour Eiffel — see *Marche funèbre*		
Mermoz (see '*La traversée des Andes*' and '*Le vol sur l'Atlantique*')		
Mimaamaquim		
1. Madeleine Martinetti with orch., cond. Arthur Honegger (with *Quatre chansons pour voix grave, nos 2 and 3*)	C. LFX 741	
2. As 1., but with spoken commentary by Arthur Honegger	Fest. FLD 30	
Monopartita		
Orch. Radio Nationale, cond. Paul Sacher (with *Suite archaïque)*	Pat. DT 1009	
Mouvement symphonique n° 1 (*Pacific 231*)		
1. Orch. de la Soc. des Conc. du Cons., cond. Ernest Ansermet	D. LW 5155	D. LXT 5004 Lon. LL 1156 Lon. CM 9119 E. SDBR 3283
2. Cond. Arthur Honegger (with *Mouvement symphonique n° 2* (*Rugby*))	Od. 7AOE-1005	Od. 170.111/2 Od. 177.179 AmD. 25206 Roc. 2038 P. R 20108

Work/Artists	Identification of record make and main serial number	Identification of subsidiary record make(s) and or serial number(s)
3. Orch. de la S.R., cond. Ernest Ansermet	D. LXT 6065	C(S). 6367 Lon. 6367 D. SXL 6065 D. Eclipse ECS. 756 D. Jubilee JB 36 KJBC 36 VIV 34 KVIC 34
4. Orch. de la Soc. des Conc. du Cons., cond. Georges Tzipine (with *Mouvement symphonique n° 2* (*Rugby*) and *Nicolas de Flue*)	C. FCX 187-8	
5. Orch. de la Soc. des Conc. du Cons., cond. Georges Tzipine (with *Mouvement symphonique n° 2* (*Rugby*))	C. FC 1038	PLM. 17 064 C. ESBF 207
6. Cond. Piero Coppola	G. W 870	G. D 2030 Vic. 9276 Vic. 59011
7. Czech. P.O., cond. Serge Baudo (with *Pastorale d'été, Chant de joie and Symphony No. 5*)	S. SUA 10516	Cr. 22 16 0077/8(S) S. SUAST 50516
8. C.B.S.O., cond. Louis Frémaux	EMI/HMV. ASD 2989(S)	Ara. 8035
9. Boston S.O., cond. Willis Page	Ron. 502(S)	Nix. EP 651 SOT. 1068 (SOT. 10683)
10 P.S.O.L., cond. Hermann Scherchen (with *Chant de joie, Pastorale d'été, Prélude pour 'La tempête', Mouvement symphonique n° 2* (*Rugby*) and *Mouvement symphonique n° 3*)	Véga C35 A158	West. XWN 14486 West. W9730 West. LAB 7010 West. WG 8302 RMC. CM 61 WRC. CM 61 Lon. 21062 SPA. 570
11. Utah S.O., cond. Maurice Abravanel	Van. SRV 2742D	PVan. VSL 11048 Van. VRS 1156 Van. S-274
12. New York P.O., cond. Leonard Bernstein (with *Mouvement symphonique n° 2* (*Rugby*) and *Pastorale d'été*)	C. ML 6059 (HMS 6059)	CBS. BRG 72453 (SBRG 72453) Col. MS-6659 60341 40-60341

Work/Artists	Identification of record make and main serial number	Identification of subsidiary record make(s) and or serial number(s)
13. Hamburg P.O., cond. Hans-Jürgen Walther	MGM. E 3144	MS. B 78156
14. Toulouse Capitole Orch., cond. Michel Plasson (with *Symphonies Nos 1-5*)	EMI-PM. 2C. 167 16327-9	
15. Hamburg S.O., cond. Weinberg	CMS/Sum. 1061	
16. Bavarian R.S.O., cond. Charles Dutoit (with *Symphonie [n° 1]*, *Mouvement symphonique n° 2* (*Rugby*), *Mouvement symphonique n° 3* and *Pastorale d'été*)	Er./Con. NUM 75254 MCE 75254 ECD 88171	
17. Czech P.O., cond. Serge Baudo (with *Symphonies Nos 1-5*, *Chant de joie* and *Pastorale d'été*)	S. 110 1741/3	
Mouvement symphonique n° 2 (*Rugby*)		
1. ?, cond. Piero Coppola	G. W 1015	Od. 170.111/2 Od. 177.179 Od. DSEQ 435
2. ?, cond. Arthur Honegger (with *Mouvement symphonique n° 1* (*Pacific 231*))	Od. 7AOE-1105	AmD. 25206 AmD. 25389 Roc. 2038 P. R 2018
3. Orch. de la Soc. des Conc. du Cons., cond. Georges Tzipine (with *Mouvement symphonique n° 1* (*Pacific 231*) and *Nicolas de Flue*)	C. FCX 187-8	
4. Orch. des Soc. des Conc. du Cons., cond. Georges Tzipine (with *Mouvement symphonique n° 1* (*Pacific 231*))	C. FC 1038	PLM. 17 064 C. ESBF 207
5. P.S.O.L., cond. Hermann Scherchen (with *Mouvement symphonique n° 1* (*Pacific 231*), *Chant de joie*, *Pastorale d'été*, *Mouvement symphonique n° 3* and *Prélude pour 'La tempête'*)	Véga C35 A158	West. XWN 18486 West. W 9730 West. LAB 7010 West. WG 8302 West. WG 18027 RMC. CM 61 WRC. CM 61 Lon. 21062 SPA 570
6. New York P.O., cond. Leonard Bernstein (with *Mouvement symphonique n° 1* (*Pacific 231*) and *Pastorale d'été*)	C. ML 6059 (HMS 6059)	CBS BRG 72453 (SBRG 72453) Col. MS - 6659 60341 40 - 60341
7. O.R.T.F., cond. Jean Martinon	G. CO69-11633	

Work/Artists	Identification of record make and main serial number	Identification of subsidiary record make(s) and or serial number(s)
8. Bavarian R.S.O., cond. Charles Dutoit (with *Symphonie* [*n° 1*], *Mouvement symphonique n° 1* (*Pacific 231*), *Mouvement symphonique n° 3* and *Pastorale d'été*)	Er./Con. NUM 75254 MCE 75254 ECD 88171	
Mouvement symphonique n° 3		
1. O.R.T.F., cond. Georges Tzipine (with *Symphony No. 4*)	C. FCX 337	
2. P.S.O.L., cond. Hermann Scherchen (with *Pastorale d'été, Prélude pour 'La tempête', Mouvement symphonique n° 1* (*Pacific 231*), *Mouvement symphonique n° 2* (*Rugby*), *Chant de joie*)	Véga C.35 A158	West. XWN 18486 West. W 9730 West. LAB 7010 West. WG 8302 West. WG 18027 RMC. CM 61 WRC. CM 61 Lon. 21062 SPA 570
3. O.R.T.F., cond. Michel Tabachnik (with *Horace victorieux* and *Symphonie* [*n° 1*])	In. 9950 42(S)	
4. Bavarian R.S.O., cond. Charles Dutoit (with *Symphonie* [*n° 1*], *Mouvement symphonique n° 1 (Pacific 231), Mouvement symphonique n° 2 (Rugby)* and *Pastorale d'été*)	Er./Con. NUM 75254 MCE 75254 ECD 88171	
Murcie en fleurs (from *Christophe Colomb*)		
Charles Panzéra with Magdeleine Panzéra	Mer. MG 10098	Cla. 6260
Nicolas de Flue		
Cond. Georges Tzipine (with *Mouvement symphonique n° 1* (*Pacific 231*) and *Mouvement symphonique n° 2* (*Rugby*))	C. FCX 187-8	
Nitchevo (ou *L'agonie du sous-marin*) — see *De l'Atlantique au Pacifique*)		
Pacific 231 — see *Mouvement symphonique n° 1*		
Les Pâques à New York		
1. Hélène Bouvier with Quatuor Lespine (with *String Quartet* [*No. 1*])	Fest. FLD 61	
2. Arlette Chédel with Quatuor Geneva	SCA. CTS 41(S)	

Work/Artists	Identification of record make and main serial number	Identification of subsidiary record make(s) and or serial number(s)
Pastorale d'été		
1. Concerts Arts Orch., cond. Vladimir Golschmann	Cap. P 8244	DCap. CTL 7055 Cap. FAP 8252
2. Czech P.O., cond. Serge Baudo (with *Mouvement symphonique n° 1* (*Pacific 231*), *Chant de joie* and *Symphony No. 5*)	S. SUA 10516	Cr. 22 16 00778(S) S. SUAST 50516
3. ?, cond. Arthur Honegger	Od. 170. 143	Roc. 2038 P. E 11296 AmD. 25199 Od. 177. 224
4. Orch. de la S.R., cond. Ernest Ansermet	Od. 0-8788	
5. New York P.O., cond. Leonard Bernstein (with *Mouvement symphonique n° 1* (*Pacific 231*) and *Mouvement symphonique n° 2 (Rugby)*)	C. ML 6059	CBS. BRG 72453 (SBRG. 72453) Col. MS-6659 60341 40 - 60341
6. P.S.O.L., cond. Hermann Scherchen (with *Mouvement symphonique n° 1* (*Pacific 231*), *Mouvement symphonique n° 2* (*Rugby*), *Chant de joie*, *Prélude pour 'La tempête' and Mouvement symphonique n° 3*)	Véga C35 A158	West. XWN 18486 West. W 9730 West. WG 8302 West. LAB 7010 West. WG W 18027 RMC. CM. 61 WRC. CM 61 Lon. 21062 SPA 570
7. O.R.T.F., cond. Jean Martinon	EMI/HMV. ASD 2953 (S)	
8. Lamoureux Orch., cond. Jean Martinon	APhi. 00175L	Ep. LC 3058
9. C.H.S.O., cond. Walter Goehr	CHS. H 12	CHS. H 17
10. Philharmonia Orch., cond. William Jackson	Pre. PRS 2512	
11. Bavarian R.S.O., cond. Charles Dutoit (with *Symphonie* [*n° 1*], *Mouvement symphonique n° 1* (*Pacific 231*), *Mouvement symphonique n° 2* (*Rugby*) and *Mouvement symphonique n° 3*)	Er./Con. NUM 75254 MCE 75254 ECD 88171	
12. Czech P.O., cond Serge Baudo (with *Symphonies Nos 1-5*, *Mouvement symphonique n° 1* (*Pacific 231*) and *Chant de joie*)	S. 110 1741/3	

Work/Artists	Identification of record make and main serial number	Identification of subsidiary record make(s) and or serial number(s)
Petite suite		
1. Fernand L'homme (sax), Marcel Moyse and L. Moyse (fls), Albert Locatelli (vln), Gaston Hamelin (clar) and Jean Manuel (pf)	CdM. 519	
2. Ver. for fl (Aurèle Nicolet), vln (Hansheinz Schneeberger) and pf (Pierre Souverain)	D. LXT 2849	Lon. LL 893 D. LK 40224
Petit cours de morale		
1. Jeanne Héricard with André Collard (pf) (with *Six poésies de Jean Cocteau* and *Six poèmes* (Apollinaire).	Véga C35 A114	
2. S. Nimsgen with C. Klein	MPS. 20208230(S)	
(Trois chansons de) La petite sirène		
Nos. 2 and 3 only; Claire Croiza with Arthur Honegger (pf) (with No. 3 of *Six poèmes* (Apollinaire)	C. D 13082	
Prélude, Arioso et Fughette (*sur le nom de Bach*) (orig. ver. for pf.)		
1. Lucette Descaves	Vers. MEDX 12004*	
2. Jürg von Vintschger	TV. TV 34377(S)*	
3. Trenker	Or. 79342	
4. Marie-Catherine Girod	FY 113	
Prélude, Arioso et Fughette (*sur le nom de Bach*) (ver. for str. orch.)		
1. Z.C.M., cond. Paul Sacher	C. LZX 10	
2. Musici Pragensis	S. SUA 10609 (SUA.ST 50609)	
Prélude (pour Aglavaine et Sélysette)		
Louisville Orch., cond. Jorge Mester	LS. LO (S 693) 693	
Prélude et blues (arr. Daliès)		
Quatuor Harpes Chromatiques de M.-L. Casadesus	G. L 668	
Prélude, Fugue, Postlude (from *Amphion*)		
Orch. de la Soc. des Conc. du Cons., cond. Georges Tzipine	C. FCX 264-5	C. ESBF 17064 ? ON 207 C. CX 1252 A. 35117 in Set 3515 CdM. set 594

Work/Artists	Identification of record make and main serial number	Identification of subsidiary record make(s) and or serial number(s)
Prélude pour 'La tempête'		
1. ?, cond. Arthur Honegger	Od. 238. 261	P. RO 20184 AmD. 20072
2. P.S.O.L., cond. Hermann Scherchen (with *Chant de joie*, *Pastorale d'été*, *Mouvement symphonique n° 1* (*Pacific 231*), *Mouvement symphonique n° 2* (*Rugby*) and *Mouvement symphonique n° 3*)	Véga C35 A158	West. WN 18486 West. W 9730 West. WG 8302 West. LAB 7010 West. WG W18027 RMC. CM 61 WRC. CM 61 Lon. 21062 SPA 570
Quatorze juillet (incl. *Marche sur la Bastille* by Arthur Honegger)		
1. Paris Police Band, cond. Désiré Dondeyne	CdM. LDXM 8197	
2. Goldman Band	AmD. OL 8931 (DL. 78931)	
Quatre chansons pour voix grave		
1. Nos 2 and 3 only; Madeleine Martinetti with orch. cond. Arthur Honegger (with *Mimaamaquim*)	C. LFX 741	
2. Nos 3 and 4 only; Eliette Schenneberg with Arthur Honegger (pf) (with *Trois psaumes*)	C. LFX 690	
Quatre poèmes		
Yolanda Marcoulescou (S) and Katja Phillabaum (pf)	Or. ORS 76240	CCC/Orion 630
Rhapsodie		
1. Members of the New Art Wind Quintet	CEd. Set 2006	
2. Arr. by Arthur Honegger for fl/ob/cl/pf; Berkshire Woodwind Ensemble (J. Pappoutsakis - fl; L. Speyer - ob; P. Cardillo - cl; B. Zighera - pf.)	Un. UNLP 1005	
Le roi David		
1. Orig. ver. cond. Arthur Honegger	Duc. LPG 8342-3	L. DTL. 9004/5 T. LE. 6533/4 West. Set WAL. 204
2. 1923 ver. cond. Gitton (recorded in Arthur Honegger's presence)	CND. Set 46	

Work/Artists	Identification of record make and main serial number	Identification of subsidiary record make(s) and or serial number(s)
3. 1923 ver., Suzanne Danco (S), Montmollin (A), Hamel (T), Stéphan Andel (Narr), Choir of the National Church of Vaud and Orch. de la S.R., cond. Ernest Ansermet	D. LTX 5321/2	Lon. STS 15155/6 Lon. XLL 1651/2 AmD. GOS 602/3 D. DPA 593/4 D. SXL 6098
4. Extracts from 1923 ver., Mlle Lutz (S), Choir and Orch. de la S.R., cond. Ernest Ansermet (No. 5 'Cortège', No. 7 'Ah, si j'avais des ailes', No. 23 'Marche des Hébreux', No. 24 'Je t'aimerai, Seigneur', No. 3(26) 'Loué soit le Seigneur')	C. C 8865	AmC. 68937D
5. Extracts from 1923 ver., St Guillaume Choir and Strasbourg M.O., cond. Fritz Münch (No. 17 'De mon cœur', No. 19 'Miséricorde', No. 20 'Je fus conçu dans le péché', No. 27 'La mort de David')	Od. 123.592/3	AmD. 25517/8
6. Transcriptions for Band, Fanfare de la Garde républicaine, cond. Guillaume Balay (No. 5 'Cortège', No. 10 'Le camp de Saül', No. 23 'Marche des Hébreux', No. 27 'La mort de David')	G. L 749	
7. 1923 ver. cond. Charles Dutoit	MHS. MHS 1392-3	RCA/Er. STU 70617/8
8. 1923 ver., Singher, Davrath, Utah S.O., cond. Maurice Abravanel	Van. VRS. 1090-1091	Van. VSD 2117-8 Van. AVRS 5014-5
9. 'Alleluia', cond. Arthur Honegger	ES. 320 E. 817	
Romance		
1. Jean-Pierre Rampal with Françoise Gobet (pf)	Pat. G 1056	Pat. ATX 112
2. P. Thomas and L. Sitsky (with *Danse de la chèvre*)	Brol. BZM 21	
3. Aurèle Nicolet (with *Danse de la chèvre*)	D. LXT 2849	Lon. LL 893
Rugby — see *Mouvement symphonique n° 2*		
Saluste du Bartas (*Six Villanelles*)		
1. Elsa Scherz-Meister with Kurt Rothenbühler	G. DB 10086	
2. Hugues Cuenod with Geoffrey Parsons	N. 2112	

Work/Artists	Identification of record make and main serial number	Identification of subsidiary record make(s) and or serial number(s)
Sarabande (from *Album des Six*)		
1. Lucette Descaves	Vers. MEDX 12004*	
2. Jürg von Vintschger	TV. TV 34377(S)*	
Sept pièces brèves		
1. Lucette Descaves	Vers. MEDX 12004*	
2. Jürg von Vintschger	TV. TV 34377(S)*	
Six poèmes (*Apollinaire*)		
1. Complete; Jeanne Héricard with André Collard (with *Six poésies de Jean Cocteau* and *Petits cours de morale*)	Véga C35 A114	
2. No. 3 only; Claire Croiza (with Nos 2 and 3 of *Trois chansons de la petite sirène*)	C. D 13082	
3. Nos 1, 4, 5 and 6; Dolorès de Silvera with Arthur Honegger	C. D 12.060	
Six poésies de Jean Cocteau		
1. Irène Joachim with Maurice Franck (with *Chanson de Ronsard*)	CdM. LDA 8079	CduM. LDX 78416
2. Jeanne Héricard with André Collard (with *Six poèmes* (Apollinaire) and *Petits cours de morale*)	Véga C35 A114	
Six Villanelles — see *Saluste du Bartas*		
Sonata for Solo Violin		
1. Christian Ferras	D. BAT 133071	D. LXT 2827
2. Henry Merckel	Pat. ED 25	
3. Henry Merckel (1st and 2nd movts only with a spoken commentary)	Fest. FLD 30	
4. R. Gonzalez	Pauta SL PP 1005(S)	
Sonatine for Clarinet (or Cello) and Piano		
1. Louis Cahuzac with Folmer Jensen	C. LDX 3	
2. Ulysse Delecluse with J. Delecluse	D. LX 3139	Lon. LS 1097
3. Thomas Janson with S. Ehrling	Mtr. MCLP 85043	
4. T. Friedl with Rose-Marie Buri	Ev. JDM 7021	
5. Stanley Drucker with L. Hambro	Ody. 730492(S)	Ody. Y-30492
6. Kálmán Berkes with Zoltán Kocsis	Hun. SLPX 11748	
7. Solow with Vallecillo	Des. 1006	

Work/Artists	Identification of record make and main serial number	Identification of subsidiary record make(s) and or serial number(s)
8. Stolzman with Vallecillo	Des. 1014G	
9. Claude Faucomprez with Alain Raes	HMB 5121	
10. Robert Bex with Noël Lee (with *Cello Sonata* and *Sonatine* for Violin and Cello)	BàM. BAM LD 059	BàM BAM LD 5059 LyD. 509 5059
Sonatine for Two Violins		
1. David and Igor Oistrakh	CdM. LDX A8280 (LSX A8280)	Mon. MCS 2058 (MCS 52058)
2. Gerland and Wilfred Beal	Mon. MC. 2008	
Sonatine for Violin and Cello		
1. Robert Gendre and Robert Bex (with *Cello Sonata* and *Sonatine* for clarinet (or cello and piano)	BàM. BAM LD 059	BàM BAM LD 5059 LyD. 509 5059
2. Réné Bas and Robert Krabansky	Eli. ERT 6009/10	Eli. ERT 7062/3
3. Schoenfeld Duo	E. SDBR. 3243(S)	
4. Josef Suk and André Navarra	S. SUA 10634 (SUA ST 50634)	
5. Prismoz Novsak and Suzanne Besler (with *Cello Sonata* and *Violin Sonata No. 2*)	MHS. MHS 1869	RBM 3001
6. Eleonora Turovsky and Yuli Turovsky	Ch. ABRD 1121 ABTD 1121 CHAN 8358	
Souvenir de Chopin (from *Un ami viendra ce soir*)		
1. Lucette Descaves	Vers MEDX 12004*	
2. Jürg von Vintschger	TV. TV 34377*	
String Quartet [*No. 1*]		
1. Quatuor Jean Lespine (with *Les Pâques à New York*)	Fest. FLD 61	
2. Quatuor Krettly	C. D 13.049/52	
3. Geneva Quartet (Régis Plantevin, Mireille Mercanton — vlns; André Vauquet — vla; Maurice Senn — vlc.) (with *String Quartets Nos 2 and 3*)	Er./Con. NUM 75101	
String Quartet No. 2		
1. Quatuor Jean Lespine (with *String Quartet No. 3*)	Fest. FLD 60	
2. Quatuor Dvořák (Stanislav Srp, Jiří Kolář — vlns; Jaroslav Ruis — vla; František Pišinger — vcl.)	S. SUA 10449	Cr. 22 16 0210

Work/Artists	Identification of record make and main serial number	Identification of subsidiary record make(s) and or serial number(s)
3. Geneva Quartet (Régis Plantevin, Mireille Mercanton — vlns; André Vauquet — vla; Maurice Senn — vlc.) (with *String Quartet* [*No. 1*] and *String Quartet No. 3)*	Er./Con. NUM 75101	
4. Reist Quartet	BàM 1942	
String Quartet No. 3		
1. Quatuor Jean Lespine (with *String Quartet No. 2*)	Fest. FLD 60	
2. Taneyev Quartet	Mel. 01893-4	USSR. DO23807/8 (SD 1893/4)
3. Leningrad Philharmonic Quartet	USSR. D021253/4 (SO1613/4)	
4. Berne Radio Quartet	BM. BM 305L1942	
5. Bulgarian Quartet (Dimo Dimov, Aleksandre Thomov — vlns; Dimitr Tchilikov — vla; Dimitr Kozev — vcl.)	Van. HM 30785	
6. Geneva Quartet (Régis Plantevin, Mireille Mercanton — vlns; André Vanquet — vla; Maurice Senn — vlc.) (with *String Quartet* [*No. 1*] and *String Quartet No. 2*)	Er./Con. NUM 75101	
Suite archaïque		
1. Orch. Radio Nationale, cond. Paul Sacher (with *Monopartita*)	Pat. DT 1009	
2. Louisville Orch., cond. Robert Whitney	LS. LOU 615	
Sur le nom d'Albert Roussel		
1. Lucette Descaves	Vers. MEDX 12004*	
2. Jürg von Vintschger	TV. TV 34377(S)*	
Symphonie [*n° 1*]		
1. Czech P.O., cond. Serge Baudo (with *Symphony No. 4*)	S. 110 1536(S)	
2. O.R.T.F., cond. Michel Tabachnik (with *Horace victorieux* and *Mouvement symphonique n° 3*)	In. 995 042(S)	
3. Toulouse Capitole Orch., cond. Michel Plasson (with *Symphonies Nos 2-5* and *Mouvement symphonique n° 1* (*Pacific 231*))	EMI-PM. 2C 167 16327/9	

Work/Artists	Identification of record make and main serial number	Identification of subsidiary record make(s) and or serial number(s)
4. Bavarian R.S.O., cond. Charles Dutoit (with *Pastorale d'été*, *Mouvement symphonique n° 1* (*Pacific 231*), *Mouvement symphonique n° 2* (*Rugby*) and *Mouvement symphonique n° 3*)	Er./Con. NUM 75254 MCE 75254 ECD 88171	
5. Czech P.O., cond. Serge Baudo (with *Symphonies Nos 2-5*, *Pastorale d'été*, *Chant de joie* and *Mouvement symphonique n° 1* (*Pacific 231*)	S. 110 1741/3	
Symphonie liturgique [*n° 3*]		
1. Orch. de la Soc. des Conc. du Cons., cond. Georges Tzipine (with *Une cantate de Noël*)	C. FCX 336	G. CO43-12171
2. Orch. de la Soc. des Conc. du Cons., cond. Robert F. Denzler (with *Chant de joie*)	D. LXT 5118	Lon. LL 1296 ECL. ECS 640
3. Czech P.O., cond. Serge Baudo (with *Symphonie pour cordes* [*n° 2*])	S. SUA. 10143 (SUAST 50143)	Cr. 22 16 009/10 S. SUAST 50027
4. Berlin P.O., cond. Herbert von Karajan (with *Symphonie pour cordes* [*n° 2*])	DG. 2530 068; later reissued as DG. 2543 805	
5. Orch. de la S.R., cond. Ernest Ansermet (with *Symphony No. 4*)	D. SXL 6394(S)	D. 7042 Lon. CS 6619(S) Phi. 414 435-4LE 14 435-1LE
6. Leningrad P.O., cond. Yevgeny Mravinsky (public perf)	USSR. SM 02857/8	EMI/HMV. Melodyia ASD 2964
7. S.O., cond. Arthur Honegger	D. GAB 15004/7 (1949 'Grand prix du disque')	D. FO 1792/5
8. Dresden P.O., cond. Stoschek	Ura. 7090	
9. Bucharest P.O., cond. Bonanb	Muz. XL 0021	
10. Toulouse Capitole Orch., cond. Michel Plasson (with Symphonies Nos 1, 2, 4, 5 and *Mouvement symphonique n° 1* (*Pacific 231*))	EMI-PM. ZC. 167 16327/9	
11. O.R.F. Sym. Orch., cond. Melles	CE. 11059	
12. Czech. P.O., cond. Serge Baudo (with *Symphonies Nos 1, 3-5*, *Mouvement symphonique n° 1 (Pacific 231)*, *Chant de joie* and *Pastorale d'été*)	S. 110. 1741/3	

Work/Artists	Identification of record make and main serial number	Identification of subsidiary record make(s) and or serial number(s)
Symphonie pour cordes [*n*° *2*]		
1. Boston S.O., cond. Charles Münch	RCA. A 630. 275	Vic. LM 1868 ItV. A 12R0115
2. Orch. de la Soc. des Conc. du Cons., cond. Charles Münch (with *La danse des morts*)	G. GFJLP 5026	G. FALP 453 G. DB 1600-2 G. W 1600-2 G. DB 5135-7 A. 536585(S) EMI/HMV. ASD 2487(S) G. CVHS 2281 Cal. 1955 EMI-PM. 1109011 G. C 061-10.901M
3. MGM. Str. Orch., cond. Izler Solomon	MGM. F6-MGM-102	MGM. E 3041 (with *Concertino* for pf. and orch.)
4. Südwestfunk Orch. (Baden-Baden), cond. Ernest Bour (with *Concerto da camera*)	Duc. 320 C 142	
5. Südwestfunk Orch. (Baden-Baden), cond. Ernest Bour (with *Chant de joie*)	Duc. 255 C 093	
6. Czech P.O., cond. Serge Baudo (with *Symphonie liturgique* [*n*° *3*])	S. SUA 10143 (SUAST 50143)	Cr. 22 16 009/10 S. SUAST 50027
7. Berlin P.O., cond. Herbert von Karajan (with *Symphonie liturgique* [*n*° *3*])	DG. 2530 068; later reissued as DG. 2543 805	
8. Orch. de la S.R., cond. Ernest Ansermet (with *Une cantate de Noël*)	D. LXT 6003 (SXL 6003) (HSXL 6003)	Lon. 5686 ADD. SDD 189(S)
9. Jean-François Paillard Orch./cond.	MHS. MHS 805	WRC. ST 945 Er. STU 70.280
10. E.C.O., cond. Paul Sacher (Public perf. with commentary by Bernard Keefe)	B.B.C. Transcription 129138-9	
11. Rochester C.O., cond. Hull	CHS. CHS 1189	
12. Brno P.O., cond. Bakala	Muz. L0166	
13. Leningrad P.O., cond. Katz	USSR. D 12779/80 (S. 739/40)	
14. O.P.P., cond Charles Münch	G. CVB 2281 (2 discs)	EMI VSM D2 CO51-12 592(S) ('Baccalauréat 1974')

Work/Artists	Identification of record make and main serial number	Identification of subsidiary record make(s) and or serial number(s)
15. Toulouse Capitole Orch., cond. Michel Plasson (with *Symphonies Nos 1, 3-5* and *Mouvement symphonique n° 1* (*Pacific 231*))	EMI-PM. 2C 167 16327/9	
16. Orchestre de Paris, cond. Charles Münch	HMV. ASD 2467	
17. Bavarian R.S.O., cond. Charles Dutoit (with *Symphony No. 4* (*Deliciæ Basilienses*))	Er./Con. NUM 75259 MCE 75259 ECD 88178	
18. Czech P.O., cond. Serge Baudo (with *Symphonies Nos 1, 3-5, Mouvement symphonique n° 1* (*Pacific 231*), *Chant de joie* and *Pastorale d'été*)	S. 110 1741/3	
Symphony No. 4 (*Deliciæ Basilienses*)		
1. O.R.T.F., cond. Georges Tzipine (with *Mouvement symphonique n° 3*)	C. FCX 337	
2. Orch. de la S.R., cond. Ernest Ansermet (with *Symphonie liturgique* [*n° 3*])	D. SXL 6394(S)	D. 7042 Lon CS 6619(S) Phi. 414 435-4LE 14 435-1LE
3. Orch. de la Soc. des Conc. du Cons., cond. Charles Münch	MHS. MHS 981(S)	Er. STU 70400(S) G. 068 28228(S)
4. Czech P.O., cond. Serge Baudo (with *Symphonie* [*n° 1*])	S. 1101536(S)	
5. Toulouse Capitole Orch., cond. Michel Plasson (with *Symphonies Nos 1-3, 5* and *Mouvement symphonique n° 1* (*Pacific 231*)	EMI-PM. 2C 167 16327/9	
6. Bavarian R.S.O., cond. Charles Dutoit (with *Symphonie pour cordes* [*n° 2*])	Er./Con. NUM 75259 MCE 75259 ESD 88178	
7. Czech P.O., cond. Serge Baudo (with *Symphonies Nos 1-3, 5, Mouvement symphonique n° 1* (*Pacific 231*), *Chant de joie* and *Pastorale d'été*)	S. 110 1741/3	
Symphony No. 5 (*Di tre re*)		
1. Boston S.O., cond. Charles Münch	RCA FV A630.315	It.V. A12R0110 Vic. LM 1741 WDM. 1741 G. FALP 169
2. Lamoureux Concert Orch., cond. Igor Markevitch	DG. DGM 18.385	AmD. DL 9956

Work/Artists	Identification of record make and main serial number	Identification of subsidiary record make(s) and or serial number(s)
3. Czech P.O., cond. Sergo Baudo (with *Mouvement symphonique n° 1* (*Pacific 231*), *Pastorale d'été* and *Chant de joie*)	S. SUA 10516 (SUAST 50516)	Cr. 22 16 0077/8(S)
4. Pittsburgh S.O., cond. William Steinberg	Am. Soc. of CAP CB 178	
5. Leningrad P.O., cond. Kurt Sanderling	USSR. D026043/4	
6. Czech P.O., cond. Serge Baudo (with *Symphonies Nos 1-4, Mouvement symphonique n° 1* (*Pacific 231*), *Chant de joie* and *Pastorale d'été*)	S. 110 1741/3	
7. Toulouse Capitole Orch., cond. Michel Plasson (with *Symphonies Nos 1-4* and *Mouvement symphonique n° 1* (*Pacific 231*))	EMI-PM. 2C. 167 16327/9	
La tempête — see *Prélude pour 'La tempête'*		
Tête d'Or		
Orch. cond. André Girard	Véga T31 SP8001	
Toccata et variations		
1. Lucette Descaves	Vers. MEDX 12004*	
2. Jacqueline Potier	Pat. PD 52/3	
3. Jürg von Vintschger	TV. TV 34377(S)*	
La traversée des Andes (from *Mermoz*)		
Orch. de la Soc. des Conc. du Cons., cond. Georges Tzipine (with *'Le vol sur l'Atlantique'*)	C. FC 1059	
Trois pièces		
1. Lucette Descaves	Vers. MEDX 12004*	
2. Jürg von Vintschger	TV. TV 34377(S)*	
Trois poèmes de Claudel		
Elsa Scherz-Meister with Kurt Rothenbühler	G. DB 10085	
Trois psaumes		
1. Eliette Schenneberg with Arthur Honegger (with *Quatre chansons pour voix grave*, nos 3 and 4)	C. FLX 690	
2. Hélène Ludolph with Albert de Klerk (org) (with 'Fugue' from *Two Pieces for Organ*)	CNR. LC 4000	
3. Ove Meyer-Leegrand with Garannar Ahlmank	G. 7EPS4	

Work/Artists	Identification of record make and main serial number	Identification of subsidiary record make(s) and or serial number(s)
Two Pieces for Organ		
1. Marshall Bidwell	Am. Soc. for CAP CB 188	
2. L. Roizman	USSR. D021695/6	
3. 'Fugue' only; Albert de Klerk (with *Trois psaumes*)	CNR. LC 4000	
4. 'Chorale' only; C. H. Trevor (The First International Congress of Organists, St Sepulchre's Church, London, 1952, Vol. 2)	Mir. DRE 1004	
5. Fono Schp. Münster	63701	
Viola Sonata		
1. M. T. Challey and Jean Hubeau	Er. EFM 42067	
2. Ladíslav Černy and Josef Páleníček	S. SUF 20036	
3. K. Boon and C. de Groot	APhi. 00613 R	
4. Michael Mann and Dika Newlin	PV. 72249	DG. 32207 LP. EM. 19126
5. F. Molnar and J. Vry [?T. Ura]	Argo ARL 1007	
6. Druzhinin and Yudina	USSR. D 8575	
7. E. and L. Wallfisch	F. LP 2007	
8. Kramarov and Voskresenshaya	USSR. SM 02729/30(S)	
Violin Sonata No. 1		
1. M. Crut and G. Terrasse (with *Cello Sonata*)	Duc. 300 C054	Véga C.30 ST 20010
2. Szigeti	Mer. MG 50442 (SR 90442)	
3. M. Crut and J. C. Englebert	Sel. LPG 8241	
4. Ladíslav Černy and Josef Páleníček	S. F 20026	
5. M. Rusin and I. Chemyshov	USSR. D 18501/2	
6. Golstein and Selkina	USSR. DO 19429/30	
7. Irène Nussbauer and Grazia Weudling	Arm. JK 107	
Violin Sonata No. 2		
1. Weiner and Shorr	ML. MLR 7094	
2. André Gertler and Alfred Holaček	S. LPM 361	
3. Primosz Novsak and Annette Weisbrod (with *Cello Sonata* and *Sonatine* for violin and cello)	MHS. MHS 1869	RBM 3001
Le vol sur l'Atlantique (from *Mermoz*) Orch. de la Soc. des Conc. du Cons., cond. Georges Tzipine (with *'La traversée des Andes'*)	C. FC 1059	

Work/Artists	Identification of record make and main serial number	Identification of subsidiary record make(s) and or serial number(s)
'Arthur Honegger vous parle'	Fest. FLD 50	
Honegger speaking with extracts from the following records:		
Les aventures du roi Pausole	Od. 166 390	('Air de la coupe du roi de Thulé)
Jeanne d'Arc au bûcher	G. FALP 213-4	(Finale)
La danse des morts	G. FJLP 5026	('Lamento')
Sonata for Solo Violin	Fest. FLD 30	
Mimaamaquim	Fest. FLD 30	
Symphonie liturgique [*n° 3*]	C. FCX 336	(1st movt. — 'Dies Irae')
Symphonie pour cordes [*n°* 2]	G. GFJLP 5026	(3rd movt.)
Nicolas de Flue	C. FCX 187-8	
(The spoken texts are included in the accompanying booklet.)		

Index

C.

D.

I.

J.

K.

N.

O.

P.

Q.

R.

U.

V.

W.

Z.